ABRAHAM LINCOLN

SPEECHES AND WRITINGS
1859–1865

Speeches, Letters, and Miscellaneous Writings
Presidential Messages and Proclamations

THE LIBRARY OF AMERICA

The texts in this volume are from THE COLLECTED WORKS OF
ABRAHAM LINCOLN, edited by Roy P. Basler, copyright © 1953
by the Abraham Lincoln Association, and THE COLLECTED WORKS
OF ABRAHAM LINCOLN SUPPLEMENT 1832–1865, copyright © 1974
by Roy P Basler. Reprinted by permission of
Rutgers University Press.

The paper used in this publication meets the
minimum requirements of the American National Standard for
Information Sciences—Permanence of Paper for Printed
Library Materials, ANSI z39.48–1984.

Distributed to the trade in the United States
by Penguin Putnam Inc. and
in Canada by Penguin Books Canada Ltd.

Library of Congress Catalog Number: 89–2362
For cataloging information, see end of Index.
ISBN 978–0–940450–63–9
ISBN 0–940450–63–1

Twelfth Printing
The Library of America—46

Manufactured in the United States of America

DON E. FEHRENBACHER
WROTE THE NOTES AND SELECTED
THE CONTENTS FOR THIS VOLUME

Abraham Lincoln's
Speeches and Writings 1859–1865
is kept in print by a gift from

JOHN LOGAN

to the Guardians of American Letters Fund,
established by The Library of America
to ensure that every volume in the series
will be permanently available.

The publishers wish to thank the Illinois State Historical Library,
the Lincoln Legals Project of the Illinois Historic Preservation
Agency, and the Illinois State Historical Society for
the use of Abraham Lincoln materials.

Contents

To W. H. Wells

W. H. Wells, Esq.   Springfield, Ills.
My dear Sir: Jany. 8, 1859.

Yours of the 3rd. Inst. is just received. I regret to say that the joint discussions between Judge Douglas and myself have been published in no shape except in the first newspaper reports; and that I have no copy of them, or even of the single one at Freeport, which I could send you. By dint of great labor since the election, I have got together a nearly, (not quite) complete single set to preserve myself. I shall preserve your address, and if I can, in a reasonable time, lay my hand on an old paper containing the Freeport discussion, I will send it to you.

All dallying with Douglas by Republicans, who are such at heart, is, at the very least, time, and labor lost; and all such, who so dally with him, will yet bite their lips in vexation for their own folly. His policy, which rigourously excludes all idea of there being any *wrong* in slavery, does lead inevitably to the nationalization of the Institution; and all who deprecate that consummation, and yet are seduced into his support, do but cut their own throats. True, Douglas *has* opposed the administration on one measure, and yet *may* on some other; but while he upholds the Dred Scott decision, declares that he cares not whether slavery be voted down or voted up; that it is simply a question of dollars and cents, and that the Almighty has drawn a line on one side of which labor *must* be performed by slaves; to support him or Buchanan, is simply to reach the same goal by only slightly different roads. Very Respectfully

To Elihu B. Washburne

Hon. E. B. Washburne.   Springfield
My dear Sir   Jany. 29. 1859

I have just received your brother's speech sent me by yourself. I had read it before; and you will oblige me by presenting him with my respects, and telling him I doubly thank him for making it — first, because the points are so just and well put; and next, because it is so well timed. We needed, from some one who can get the public attention, just such a speech just at this time. His objection to the Oregon constitution because it excludes free negroes, is the only thing I wish he had omitted. Your friend as ever

To Lyman Trumbull

Hon: L. Trumbull   Springfield, Feb. 3. 1859
   My dear Sir   Yours of the 29th. is received. The article mentioned by you, prepared for the Chicago Journal, I have not seen; nor do I wish to see it, though I heard of it a month, or more, ago. Any effort to put enmity between you and me, is as idle as the wind. I do not for a moment doubt that you, Judd, Cook, Palmer, and the republicans generally, coming from the old democratic ranks, were as sincerely anxious for my success in the late contest, as I myself, and the old whig republicans were. And I beg to assure you, beyond all possible cavil, that you can scarcely be more anxious to be sustained two years hence than I am that you shall be so sustained. I can not conceive it possible for me to be a rival of yours, or to take sides against you in favor of any rival. Nor do I think there is much danger of the old democratic and whig elements of our party breaking into opposing factions. They certainly shall not, if I can prevent it.
   I do not perceive that there is any feeling here about Cuba; and so I think, you can safely venture to act upon your own judgment upon any phase of it which may be presented.
   The H.R. passed an apportionment bill yesterday — slightly better for us than the present in the Senate districts; but perfectly outrageous in the H.R. districts. It can be defeated without any revolutionary movement, unless the session be prolonged. Yours as ever

Lecture on Discoveries and Inventions, Jacksonville, Illinois

We have all heard of Young America. He is the most *current* youth of the age. Some think him conceited, and arrogant; but has he not reason to entertain a rather extensive opinion of himself? Is he not the inventor and owner of the *present*, and sole hope of the *future*? Men, and things, everywhere, are ministering unto him. Look at his apparel, and you shall see cotten fabrics from Manchester and Lowell; flax-linen from Ireland; wool-cloth from Spain; silk from France; furs from the Arctic regions, with a buffalo-robe from the Rocky Mountains, as a general out-sider. At his table, besides plain bread and meat made at home, are sugar from Louisiana; coffee and fruits from the tropics; salt from Turk's Island; fish from New-foundland; tea from China, and spices from the Indies. The whale of the Pacific furnishes his candle-light; he has a diamond-ring from Brazil; a gold-watch from California, and a spanish cigar from Havanna. He not only has a present supply of all these, and much more; but thousands of hands are engaged in producing fresh supplies, and other thousands, in bringing them to him. The iron horse is panting, and impatient, to carry him everywhere, in no time; and the lightening stands ready harnessed to take and bring his tidings in a trifle less than no time. He owns a large part of the world, by right of possessing it; and all the rest by right of *wanting* it, and *intending* to have it. As Plato had for the immortality of the soul, so Young America has "a pleasing hope—a fond desire—a longing after" territory. He has a great passion—a perfect rage—for the *"new"*; particularly new men for office, and the new earth mentioned in the revelations, in which, being no more sea, there must be about three times as much land as in the present. He is a great friend of humanity; and his desire for land is not selfish, but merely an impulse to extend the area of freedom. He is very anxious to fight for the liberation of enslaved nations and colonies, provided, always, they *have* land, and have *not* any liking for his interference. As to those who have no land, and would be glad of help from any quarter, he considers *they* can afford to wait a few hundred years longer. In knowledge he is particularly rich. He knows all that can possibly be known; inclines to believe in spiritual rappings, and is the unquestioned inventor of *"Manifest Destiny."* His horror is for all that is old, particularly "Old Fogy"; and if there be any thing old which he can endure, it is only old whiskey and old tobacco.

If the said Young America really is, as he claims to be, the owner of all present, it must be admitted that he has considerable advantage of Old Fogy. Take, for instance, the first of all fogies, father Adam. There he stood, a very perfect physical man, as poets and painters inform us; but he must have been very ignorant, and simple in his habits. He had had no sufficient time to learn much by observation; and he had no near neighbors to teach him anything. No part of his breakfast had been brought from the other side of the world; and it is quite probable, he had no conception of the world having any other side. In all of these things, it is very plain, he was no equal of Young America; the most that can be said is, that *according to his chance* he may have been quite as much of a man as his very self-complaisant descendant. Little as was what he knew, let the Youngster discard all he has learned from others, and then show, if he can, any advantage on his side. In the way of *land*, and *live stock*, Adam was quite in the ascendant. He had dominion over all the earth, and all the living things upon, and round about it. The land has been sadly divided out since; but never fret, Young America will *re-annex* it.

The great difference between Young America and Old Fogy, is the result of *Discoveries*, *Inventions*, and *Improvements*. These, in turn, are the result of *observation*, *reflection* and *experiment*. For instance, it is quite certain that ever since water has been boiled in covered vessels, men have seen the lids of the vessels rise and fall a little, with a sort of fluttering motion, by force of the steam; but so long as this was not specially observed, and reflected and experimented upon, it came to nothing. At length however, after many thousand years, some man observes this long-known effect of hot water lifting a pot-lid, and begins a train of reflection upon it. He says "Why, to be sure, the force that lifts the pot-lid, will lift any thing else, which is no heavier than the pot-lid." "And, as man has much hard lifting to do, can not this hot-water power be made to help him?" He has become a little excited on the subject, and he fancies he hears a voice answering "Try me" He does try it; and the *observation*, *reflection*, and *trial* gives to the world the control of that tremendous, and now well known agent, called steam-power. This is not the actual history in detail, but the general principle.

But was this first inventor of the application of steam, wiser or more ingenious than those who had gone before him? Not at all. Had he not learned much of them, he never would have succeeded—probably, never would have thought of making the attempt. To be fruitful in invention, it is indispensable to have a *habit* of observation and reflection; and this *habit*, our steam friend acquired, no doubt, from those who, to him, were old fogies. But for the difference in *habit* of observation, why did yankees, almost instantly, discover gold in California, which had been trodden upon, and overlooked by indians and Mexican greasers, for centuries? Gold-mines are not the only mines overlooked in the same way. There are more mines above the Earth's surface than below it. All nature—the whole world, material, moral, and intellectual,—is a mine; and, in Adam's day, it was a wholly unexplored mine. Now, it was the destined work of Adam's race to develope, by discoveries, inventions, and improvements, the hidden treasures of this mine. But Adam had nothing to turn his attention to the work. If he should do anything in the way of invention, he had first to invent the art of invention—the *instance* at least, if not the *habit* of observation and reflection. As might be expected he seems not to have been a very observing man at first; for it appears he went about naked a considerable length of time, before he even noticed that obvious fact. But when he did observe it, the observation was not lost upon him; for it immediately led to the first of all inventions, of which we have any direct account—*the fig-leaf apron*.

The inclination to exchange thoughts with one another is probably an original impulse of our nature. If I be in pain I wish to let you know it, and to ask your sympathy and assistance; and my pleasurable emotions also, I wish to communicate to, and share with you. But to carry on such communication, some *instrumentality* is indispensable. Accordingly speech—articulate sounds rattled off from the tongue—was used by our first parents, and even by Adam, before the creation of Eve. He gave names to the animals while she was still a bone in his side; and he broke out quite volubly when she first stood before him, the best present of his maker. From this it would appear that speech was not an invention of man, but rather the direct gift of his Creator. But whether Divine gift, or invention, it is still plain that if a mode of communication had been left to invention, *speech* must have been the first, from the superior adaptation to the end, of the organs of speech, over every other means within the whole range of nature. Of the organs of speech the tongue is the principal; and if we shall test it, we shall find the capacities of the tongue, in the utterance of articulate sounds, absolutely wonderful. You can count from one to one hundred, quite distinctly in about forty seconds. In doing this two hundred and eighty three distinct sounds or syllables are uttered, being seven to each second; and yet there shall be enough difference between every two, to be easily recognized by the ear of the hearer. What other *signs* to represent *things* could possibly be produced so rapidly? or, even, if ready made, could be *arranged* so rapidly to express the sense? *Motions* with the hands, are no adequate substitute. *Marks* for the recognition of the eye—*writing*—although a wonderful auxiliary for speech, is no worthy substitute for it. In addition to the more slow and laborious process of getting up a communication in writing, the materials—pen, ink, and paper—are not always at hand. But one always has his tongue with him, and the breath of his life is the ever-ready material with which it works. Speech, then, by enabling different individuals to interchange thoughts, and thereby to combine their powers of observation and reflection, greatly facilitates useful discoveries and inventions. What one observes, and would himself infer nothing from, he tells to another, and that other at once sees a valuable hint in it. A result is thus reached which neither *alone* would have arrived at.

And this reminds me of what I passed unnoticed before, that the very first invention was a joint operation, Eve having shared with Adam in the getting up of the apron. And, indeed, judging from the fact that sewing has come down to our times as "woman's work" it is very probable she took the leading part; he, perhaps, doing no more than to stand by and thread the needle. That proceeding may be reckoned as the mother of all "Sewing societies"; and the first and most perfect "world's fair" all inventions and all inventors then in the world, being on the spot.

But speech alone, valuable as it ever has been, and is, has not advanced the condition of the world much. This is abundantly evident when we look at the degraded condition of all those tribes of human creatures who have no considerable additional means of communicating thoughts. *Writing*—the art of communicating thoughts to the mind, through the eye—is the great invention of the world. Great in the astonishing range of analysis and combination which necessarily underlies the most crude and general conception of it—great, very great in enabling us to converse with the dead, the absent, and the unborn, at all distances of time and of space; and great, not only in its direct benefits, but greatest help, to all other inventions. Suppose the art, with all conception of it, were this day lost to the world, how long, think you, would it be, before even Young America could get up the letter A. with any adequate notion of using it to advantage? The precise period at which writing was invented, is not known; but it certainly was as early as the time of Moses; from which we may safely infer that it's inventors were very old fogies.

Webster, at the time of writing his Dictionary, speaks of the English Language as then consisting of seventy or eighty thousand words. If so, the language in which the five books of Moses were written must, at that time, now thirtythree or four hundred years ago, have consisted of at least one quarter as many, or, twenty thousand. When we remember that words are *sounds* merely, we shall conclude that the idea of representing those sounds by *marks*, so that whoever should at any time after see the marks, would understand what sounds they meant, was a bold and ingenius conception, not likely to occur to one man of a million, in the run of a thousand years. And, when it did occur, a distinct mark for each word, giving twenty thousand different marks first to be learned, and afterwards remembered, would follow as the second thought, and would present such a difficulty as would lead to the conclusion that the whole thing was impracticable. But the *necessity* still would exist; and we may readily suppose that the idea was conceived, and lost, and reproduced, and dropped, and taken up again and again, until at last, the thought of dividing sounds into parts, and making a mark, not to represent a whole sound, but only a part of one, and then of combining these marks, not very many in number, upon the principles of permutation, so as to represent any and all of the whole twenty thousand words, and even any additional number was somehow conceived and pushed into practice. This was the invention of *phoenetic* writing, as distinguished from the clumsy picture writing of some of the nations. That it was difficult of conception and execution, is apparant, as well by the foregoing reflections, as by the fact that so many tribes of men have come down from Adam's time to ours without ever having possessed it. It's utility may be conceived, by the reflection that, to *it* we owe everything which distinguishes us from savages. Take it from us, and the Bible, all history, all science, all government, all commerce, and nearly all social intercourse go with it.

The great activity of the tongue, in articulating sounds, has already been mentioned; and it may be of some passing interest to notice the wonderful powers of the *eye*, in conveying ideas to the mind from writing. Take the same example of the numbers from *one* to *one hundred*, written down, and you can run your eye over the list, and be assured that every number is in it, in about one half the time it would require to pronounce the words with the voice; and not only so, but you can, in the same short time, determine whether every word is spelled correctly, by which it is evident that every separate letter, amounting to eight hundred and sixty four, has been recognized, and reported to the mind, within the incredibly short space of twenty seconds, or one third of a minute.

I have already intimated my opinion that in the world's history, certain inventions and discoveries occurred, of peculiar value, on account of their great efficiency in facilitating all other inventions and discoveries. Of these were the arts of writing and of printing—the discovery of America, and the introduction of Patent-laws. The date of the first, as already stated, is unknown; but it certainly was as much as fifteen hundred years before the Christian era; the second—printing—came in 1436, or nearly three thousand years after the first. The others followed more rapidly—the discovery of America in 1492, and the first patent laws in 1624. Though not apposite to my present purpose, it is but justice to the fruitfulness of that period, to mention two other important events—the Lutheran Reformation in 1517, and, still earlier, the invention of negroes, or, of the present mode of using them, in 1434. But, to return to the consideration of printing, it is plain that it is but the *other* half—and in real utility, the *better* half—of writing; and that both together are but the assistants of speech in the communication of thoughts between man and man. When man was possessed of speech alone, the chances of invention, discovery, and improvement, were very limited; but by the introduction of each of these, they were greatly multiplied. When writing was invented, any important observation, likely to lead to a discovery, had at least a chance of being written down, and consequently, a better chance of never being forgotten; and of being seen, and reflected upon, by a much greater number of persons; and thereby the chances of a valuable hint being caught, proportionably augmented. By this means the observation of a single individual might lead to an important invention, years, and even centuries after he was dead. In one word, by means of writing, the seeds of invention were more permanently preserved, and more widely sown. And yet, for the three thousand years during which printing remained undiscovered after writing was in use, it was only a small portion of the people who could write, or read writing; and consequently the field of invention, though much extended, still continued very limited. At length printing came. It gave ten thousand copies of any written matter, quite as cheaply as ten were given before; and consequently a thousand minds were brought into the field where there was but one before. This was a great *gain*; and history shows a great *change* corresponding to it, in point of time. I will venture to consider *it*, the true termination of that period called "the dark ages." Discoveries, inventions, and improvements followed rapidly, and have been increasing their rapidity ever since. The effects could not come, all at once. It required time to bring them out; and they are still coming. The *capacity* to read, could not be multiplied as fast as the *means* of reading. Spelling-books just began to go into the hands of the children; but the teachers were not very numerous, or very competent; so that it is safe to infer they did not advance so speedily as they do now-a-days. It is very probable—almost certain—that the great mass of men, at that time, were utterly unconscious, that their *conditions*, or their *minds* were capable of improvement. They not only looked upon the educated few as superior beings; but they supposed themselves to be naturally incapable of rising to equality. To immancipate the mind from this false and under estimate of itself, is the great task which printing came into the world to perform. It is difficult for us, *now* and *here*, to conceive how strong this slavery of the mind was; and how long it did, of necessity, take, to break it's shackles, and to get a habit of freedom of thought, established. It is, in this connection, a curious fact that a new country is most favorable— almost necessary—to the immancipation of thought, and the consequent advancement of civilization and the arts. The human family originated as is thought, somewhere in Asia, and have worked their way principally Westward. Just now, in civilization, and the arts, the people of Asia are entirely behind those of Europe; those of the East of Europe behind those of the West of it; while we, here in America, *think* we discover, and invent, and improve, faster than any of them. *They* may think this is arrogance; but they can not deny that Russia has called on us to show her how to build steam-boats and railroads—while in the older parts of Asia, they scarcely know that such things as S.Bs & RR.s. exist. In anciently inhabited countries, the dust of ages—a real downright old-fogyism— seems to settle upon, and smother the intellects and energies of man. It is in this view that I have mentioned the discovery of America as an event greatly favoring and facilitating useful discoveries and inventions.

Next came the Patent laws. These began in England in 1624; and, in this country, with the adoption of our constitution. Before then, any man might instantly use what another had invented; so that the inventor had no special advantage from his own invention. The patent system changed this; secured to the inventor, for a limited time, the exclusive use of his invention; and thereby added the fuel of *interest* to the *fire* of genius, in the discovery and production of new and useful things.

February 11, 1859

Speech at Chicago, Illinois

I understand that you have to-day rallied around your principles and they have again triumphed in the city of Chicago. I am exceedingly happy to meet you under such cheering auspices on this occasion—the first on which I have appeared before an audience since the campaign of last year. It is unsuitable to enter into a lengthy discourse, as is quite apparent, at a moment like this. I shall therefore detain you only a very short while.

It gives me peculiar pleasure to find an opportunity under such favorable circumstances to return my thanks for the gallant support that you of the city of Chicago and of Cook County gave to the cause in which we were all engaged in the late momentous struggle in Illinois. And while I am at it, I will through you thank all the Republicans of the State for the earnest devotion and glorious support they gave to the cause.

I am resolved not to deprive myself of the pleasure of believing, now, and so long as I live, that all those who, while we were in that contest, professed to be the friends of the cause, were really and truly so—that we are all really brothers in the work, with no false hearts among us.

For myself I am also gratified that during that canvass and since, however disappointing its termination, there was among my party friends so little fault found in me as to the manner in which I bore my part. I hardly dared hope to give as high a degree of satisfaction as it has since been my pleasure to believe I did in the part I bore in the contest.

I remember in that canvass but one instance of dissatisfaction with my course, and I allude to that, not for the purpose of reviving any matter of dispute or producing any unpleasant feeling, but in order to help get rid of the point upon which that matter of disagreement or dissatisfaction arose. I understand that in some speeches I made I said something, or was supposed to have said something, that some very good people, as I really believe them to be, commented upon unfavorably, and said that rather than support one holding such sentiments as I had expressed, the real friends of liberty could afford to wait awhile. I don't want to say anything that shall excite unkind feeling, and I mention this simply to suggest that I am afraid of the effect of that sort of argument. I do not doubt that it comes from good men, but I am afraid of the result upon organized action where great results are in view, if any of us allow ourselves to seek out minor or separate points on which there may be difference of views as to policy and right, and let them keep us from uniting in action upon a great principle in a cause on which we all agree; or are deluded into the belief that all can be brought to consider alike and agree upon every minor point before we unite and press forward in organization, asking the coöperation of all good men in that resistance to the extension of slavery upon which we all agree. I am afraid that such methods would result in keeping the friends of liberty waiting longer than we ought to. I say this for the purpose of suggesting that we consider whether it would not be better and wiser, so long as we all agree that this matter of slavery is a moral, political and social wrong, and ought to be treated as a wrong, not to let anything minor or subsidiary to that main principle and purpose make us fail to coöperate.

One other thing, and that again I say in no spirit of unkindness. There was a question amongst Republicans all the time of the canvass of last year, and it has not quite ceased yet, whether it was not the true and better policy for the Republicans to make it their chief object to reëlect Judge Douglas to the Senate of the United States. Now, I differed with those who thought that the true policy, but I have never said an unkind word of any one entertaining that opinion. I believe most of them were as sincerely the friends of our cause as I claim to be myself; yet I thought they were mistaken, and I speak of this now for the purpose of justifying the course that I took and the course of those who supported me. In what I say now there is no unkindness even towards Judge Douglas. I have believed, that in the Republican situation in Illinois, if we, the Republicans of this State, had made Judge Douglas our candidate for the Senate of the United States last year and had elected him, there would to-day be no Republican party in this Union. I believed that the principles around which we have rallied and organized that party would live;

they will live under all circumstances, while we will die. They would reproduce another party in the future. But in the meantime all the labor that has been done to build up the present Republican party would be entirely lost, and perhaps twenty years of time, before we would again have formed around that principle as solid, extensive, and formidable an organization as we have, standing shoulder to shoulder to-night in harmony and strength around the Republican banner.

It militates not at all against this view to tell us that the Republicans could make something in the State of New York by electing to Congress John B. Haskin, who occupied a position similar to Judge Douglas, or that they could make something by electing Hickman, of Pennsylvania, or Davis, of Indiana. I think it likely that they could and do make something by it; but it is false logic to assume that for that reason anything could be gained by us in electing Judge Douglas in Illinois. And for this reason: It is no disparagement to these men, Hickman and Davis, to say that individually they were comparatively small men, and the Republican party could take hold of them, use them, elect them, absorb them, expel them, or do whatever it pleased with them, and the Republican organization be in no wise shaken. But it is not so with Judge Douglas. Let the Republican party of Illinois dally with Judge Douglas; let them fall in behind him and make him their candidate, and they do not absorb him; he absorbs them. They would come out at the end all Douglas men, all claimed by him as having indorsed every one of his doctrines upon the great subject with which the whole nation is engaged at this hour—that the question of negro slavery is simply a question of dollars and cents; that the Almighty has drawn a line across the continent, on one side of which labor—the cultivation of the soil—must always be performed by slaves. It would be claimed that we, like him, do not care whether slavery is voted up or voted down. Had we made him our candidate and given him a great majority, we should have never heard an end of declarations by him that we had indorsed all these dogmas. Try it by an example.

You all remember that at the last session of Congress there was a measure introduced in the Senate by Mr. Crittenden, which proposed that the pro-slavery Lecompton constitution should be left to a vote to be taken in Kansas, and if it and slavery were adopted Kansas should be at once admitted as a slave State. That same measure was introduced into the House by Mr. Montgomery, and therefore got the name of the Crittenden-Montgomery bill; and in the House of Representatives the Republicans all voted for it under the peculiar circumstances in which they found themselves placed. You may remember also that the New York *Tribune*, which was so much in favor of our electing Judge Douglas to the Senate of the United States, has not yet got through the task of defending the Republican party, after that one vote in the House of Representatives, from the charge of having gone over to the doctrine of popular sovereignty. Now, just how long would the New York *Tribune* have been in getting rid of the charge that the Republicans had abandoned their principles, if we had taken up Judge Douglas, adopted all his doctrines and elected him to the Senate, when the single vote upon that one point so confused and embarrassed the position of the Republicans that it has kept the *Tribune* one entire year arguing against the effect of it?

This much being said on that point, I wish now to add a word that has a bearing on the future. The Republican principle, the profound central truth that slavery is wrong and ought to be dealt with as a wrong, though we are always to remember the fact of its actual existence amongst us and faithfully observe all the constitutional guarantees—the unalterable principle never for a moment to be lost sight of that it is a wrong and ought to be dealt with as such, cannot advance at all upon Judge Douglas' ground—that there is a portion of the country in which slavery must always exist; that he does not care whether it is voted up or voted down, as it is simply a question of dollars and cents. Whenever, in any compromise or arrangement or combination that may promise some temporary advantage, we are led upon that ground, then and there the great living principle upon which we have organized as a party is surrendered. The proposition now in our minds that this thing is wrong being once driven out and surrendered, then the institution of slavery necessarily becomes national.

One or two words more of what I did not think of when I

arose. Suppose it is true that the Almighty has drawn a line across this continent, on the south side of which part of the people will hold the rest as slaves; that the Almighty ordered this; that it is right, unchangeably right, that men ought there to be held as slaves, and that their fellow men will always have the right to hold them as slaves. I ask you, this once admitted, how can you believe that it is not right for us, or for them coming here, to hold slaves on this other side of the line? Once we come to acknowledge that it is right, that it is the law of the Eternal Being, for slavery to exist on one side of that line, have we any sure ground to object to slaves being held on the other side? Once admit the position that a man rightfully holds another man as property on one side of the line, and you must, when it suits his convenience to come to the other side, admit that he has the same right to hold his property there. Once admit Judge Douglas's proposition and we must all finally give way. Although we may not bring ourselves to the idea that it is to our interest to have slaves in this Northern country, we shall soon bring ourselves to admit that, while we may not want them, if any one else does he has the moral right to have them. Step by step—south of the Judge's moral climate line in the States, then in the Territories everywhere, and then in all the States—it is thus that Judge Douglas would lead us inevitably to the nationalization of slavery. Whether by his doctrine of squatter sovereignty, or by the ground taken by him in his recent speeches in Memphis and through the South,—that wherever the climate makes it the interest of the inhabitants to encourage slave property, they will pass a slave code—whether it is covertly nationalized, by Congressional legislation, or by the Dred Scott decision, or by the sophistical and misleading doctrine he has last advanced, the same goal is inevitably reached by the one or the other device. It is only travelling to the same place by different roads.

In this direction lies all the danger that now exists to the Republican cause. I take it that so far as concerns forcibly establishing slavery in the Territories by Congressional legislation, or by virtue of the Dred Scott decision, that day has passed. Our only serious danger is that we shall be led upon this ground of Judge Douglas, on the delusive assumption that it is a good way of whipping our opponents, when in fact, it is a way that leads straight to final surrender. The Republican party should not dally with Judge Douglas when it knows where his proposition and his leadership would take us, nor be disposed to listen to it because it was best somewhere else to support somebody occupying his ground. That is no just reason why we ought to go over to Judge Douglas, as we were called upon to do last year. Never forget that we have before us this whole matter of the right or wrong of slavery in this Union, though the immediate question is as to its spreading out into new Territories and States.

I do not wish to be misunderstood upon this subject of slavery in this country. I suppose it may long exist, and perhaps the best way for it to come to an end peaceably is for it to exist for a length of time. But I say that the spread and strengthening and perpetuation of it is an entirely different proposition. There we should in every way resist it as a wrong, treating it as a wrong, with the fixed idea that it must and will come to an end. If we do not allow ourselves to be allured from the strict path of our duty by such a device as shifting our ground and throwing ourselves into the rear of a leader who denies our first principle, denies that there is an absolute wrong in the institution of slavery, then the future of the Republican cause is safe and victory is assured. You Republicans of Illinois have deliberately taken your ground; you have heard the whole subject discussed again and again; you have stated your faith, in platforms laid down in a State Convention, and in a National Convention; you have heard and talked over and considered it until you are now all of opinion that you are on a ground of unquestionable right. All you have to do is to keep the faith, to remain steadfast to the right, to stand by your banner. Nothing should lead you to leave your guns. Stand together, ready, with match in hand. Allow nothing to turn you to the right or to the left. Remember how long you have been in setting out on the true course; how long you have been in getting your neighbors to understand and believe as you now do. Stand by your principles; stand by your guns; and victory complete and permanent is sure at the last.

March 1, 1859

To Henry L. Pierce and Others

Messrs. Henry L. Pierce, & others.   Springfield, Ills.
Gentlemen   April 6. 1859

Your kind note inviting me to attend a Festival in Boston, on the 13th. Inst. in honor of the birth-day of Thomas Jefferson, was duly received. My engagements are such that I can not attend.

Bearing in mind that about seventy years ago, two great political parties were first formed in this country, that Thomas Jefferson was the head of one of them, and Boston the headquarters of the other, it is both curious and interesting that those supposed to descend politically from the party opposed to Jefferson, should now be celebrating his birth-day in their own original seat of empire, while those claiming political descent from him have nearly ceased to breathe his name everywhere.

Remembering too, that the Jefferson party were formed upon their supposed superior devotion to the *personal* rights of men, holding the rights of *property* to be secondary only, and greatly inferior, and then assuming that the so-called democracy of to-day, are the Jefferson, and their opponents, the anti-Jefferson parties, it will be equally interesting to note how completely the two have changed hands as to the principle upon which they were originally supposed to be divided.

The democracy of to-day hold the *liberty* of one man to be absolutely nothing, when in conflict with another man's right of *property*. Republicans, on the contrary, are for both the *man* and the *dollar*; but in cases of conflict, the man *before* the dollar.

I remember once being much amused at seeing two partially intoxicated men engage in a fight with their great-coats on, which fight, after a long, and rather harmless contest, ended in each having fought himself *out* of his own coat, and *into* that of the other. If the two leading parties of this day are really identical with the two in the days of Jefferson and Adams, they have performed about the same feat as the two drunken men.

But soberly, it is now no child's play to save the principles of Jefferson from total overthrow in this nation.

One would start with great confidence that he could convince any sane child that the simpler propositions of Euclid are true; but, nevertheless, he would fail, utterly, with one who should deny the definitions and axioms. The principles of Jefferson are the definitions and axioms of free society. And yet they are denied, and evaded, with no small show of success. One dashingly calls them "glittering generalities"; another bluntly calls them "self evident lies"; and still others insidiously argue that they apply only to "superior races."

These expressions, differing in form, are identical in object and effect—the supplanting the principles of free government, and restoring those of classification, caste, and legitimacy. They would delight a convocation of crowned heads, plotting against the people. They are the van-guard—the miners, and sappers—of returning despotism. We must repulse them, or they will subjugate us.

This is a world of compensations; and he who would *be* no slave, must consent to *have* no slave. Those who deny freedom to others, deserve it not for themselves; and, under a just God, can not long retain it.

All honor to Jefferson—to the man who, in the concrete pressure of a struggle for national independence by a single people, had the coolness, forecast, and capacity to introduce into a merely revolutionary document, an abstract truth, applicable to all men and all times, and so to embalm it there, that to-day, and in all coming days, it shall be a rebuke and a stumbling-block to the very harbingers of re-appearing tyranny and oppression. Your obedient Servant

To Thomas J. Pickett

T. J. Pickett, Esq   Springfield,
My dear Sir.   April 16. 1859.

Yours of the 13th. is just received. My engagements are such that I can not, at any very early day, visit Rock-Island, to deliver a lecture, or for any other object.

As to the other matter you kindly mention, I must, in candor, say I do not think myself fit for the Presidency. I certainly am flattered, and gratified, that some partial friends think of me in that connection; but I really think it best for our cause that no concerted effort, such as you suggest, should be made.

Let this be considered confidential. Yours very truly

To Salmon P. Chase

Hon: S. P. Chase   Springfield, Ills. April 30. 1859.

Dear Sir   Reaching home yesterday I found your kind note of the 14th. informing me that you have given Mr. Whitney the appointment he desired; and also mentioning the present encouraging aspects of the Republican cause—and our Illinois canvass of last year. I thank you for the appointment. Allow me also to thank you as being one of the very few distinguished men, whose sympathy we in Illinois did receive last year, of all those whose sympathy we thought we had reason to expect.

Of course I would have preferred success; but failing in that, I have no regrets for having rejected all advice to the contrary, and resolutely made the struggle. Had we thrown ourselves into the arms of Douglas, as re-electing him by our votes would have done, the Republican cause would have been anihilated in Illinois, and, as I think, demoralized, and prostrated everywhere for years, if not forever. As it is, in the language of Benton "we are clean" and the Republican star gradually rises higher everywhere. Yours truly.

To Mark W. Delahay

M. W. Delahay, Esq   Springfield Ills
My Dear Sir   May 14 1859

I find it impossible for me to attend your Republican convention at Ossawatan on the 18th. It would have afforded me much personal gratification to see your fine new country, and to meet the good people who have cast their lot there; and still more, if I could thereby contribute any thing to the Republican cause. You probably will adopt resolutions in the nature of a platform; and, as I think, the only danger will be the temptation to lower the Republican Standard in order to gather recruits. In my judgement such a step would be a serious mistake—would open a gap through which more would pass *out* than pass *in*. And this would be the same, whether the letting down should be in deference to Douglasism, or to the southern opposition element. Either would surrender the *object* of the Republican organization—the preventing the *spread* and *nationalization* of Slavery. This object surrendered, the organization would go to pieces. I do not mean by this, that no southern man must be placed upon our Republican National ticket for 1860. There are many men in the slave states for any one of whom I would cheerfully vote to be either President or Vice President provided he would enable me to do so with *safety* to the Republican cause—without lowering the Republican Standard. This is the indispensable condition of a union with us. It is idle to think of any other. Any other would be as fruitless to the South, as distasteful to the North, the whole ending in common defeat. Let a union be attempted on the basis of ignoring the Slavery question, and magnifying other questions which the people just now are really caring nothing about, and it will result in gaining no single electorial vote in the *South* and losing every one in the North. Yours very truly

To Theodore Canisius

Dr. Theodore Canisius   Springfield, May 17, 1859

Dear Sir: Your note asking, in behalf of yourself and other german citizens, whether I am for or against the constitutional provision in regard to naturalized citizens, lately adopted by Massachusetts; and whether I am for or against a fusion of the republicans, and other opposition elements, for the canvass of 1860, is received.

Massachusetts is a sovereign and independent state; and it is no privilege of mine to scold her for what she does. Still, if from what she *has done*, an inference is sought to be drawn as to what I *would do*, I may, without impropriety, speak out. I say then, that, as I understand the Massachusetts provision, I am against it's adoption in Illinois, or in any other place, where I have a right to oppose it. Understanding the spirit of our institutions to aim at the *elevation* of men, I am opposed to whatever tends to *degrade* them. I have some little notoriety for commiserating the oppressed condition of the negro; and I should be strangely inconsistent if I could favor any project for curtailing the existing rights of *white men*, even though born in different lands, and speaking different languages from myself.

As to the matter of fusion, I am for it, if it can be had on republican grounds; and I am not for it on any other terms. A fusion on any other terms, would be as foolish as unprincipled. It would lose the whole North, while the common enemy would still carry the whole South. The question of *men* is a different one. There are good patriotic men, and able statesmen, in the South whom I would cheerfully support, if they would now place themselves on republican ground. But I am against letting down the republican standard a hair's breadth.

I have written this hastily, but I believe it answers your questions substantially. Yours truly

To Salmon P. Chase

Hon: S. P. Chase: Springfield, Ills.
Dear Sir   June 9. 1859
Please pardon the liberty I take in addressing you, as I now do. It appears by the papers that the late Republican State convention of Ohio adopted a Platform, of which the following is one plank, "A repeal of the atrocious Fugitive Slave Law."

This is already damaging us here. I have no doubt that if that plank be even *introduced* into the next Republican National convention, it will explode it. Once introduced, its supporters and it's opponents will quarrel irreconcilably. The latter believe the U.S. constitution declares that a fugitive slave *"shall be delivered up"*; and they look upon the above plank as dictated by the spirit which declares a fugitive slave *"shall not be delivered up"*

I enter upon no argument one way or the other; but I assure you the cause of Republicanism is hopeless in Illinois, if it be in any way made responsible for that plank. I hope you can, and will, contribute something to relieve us from it. Your Obt. Servt.

To Salmon P. Chase

Hon. S. P. Chase   Springfield, Ills.
My dear Sir   June 20. 1859

Yours of the 13th. Inst. is received. You say you would be glad to have my views. Although I think congress has constitutional authority to enact a Fugitive Slave law, I have never elaborated an opinion upon the subject. My view has been, and is, simply this: The U.S. constitution says the fugitive slave *"shall be delivered up"* but it does not expressly say *who* shall deliver him up. Whatever the constitution says *"shall be done"* and has omitted saying who shall do it, the government established by that constitution, *ex vi termini*, is vested with the power of doing; and congress is, by the constitution, expressly empowered to make all laws which shall be necessary and proper for carrying into execution all powers vested by the constitution in the government of the United States. This would be my view, on a simple reading of the constitution; and it is greatly strengthened by the historical fact that the constitution was adopted, in great part, in order to get a government which could execute it's own behests, in contradistinction to that under the Articles of confederation, which depended, in many respects, upon the States, for its' execution; and the other fact that one of the earliest congresses, under the constitution, did enact a Fugitive Slave law.

But I did not write you on this subject, with any view of discussing the constitutional question. My only object was to impress you with what I believe is true, that the introduction of a proposition for repeal of the Fugitive Slave law, into the next Republican National convention, will explode the convention and the party. Having turned your attention to the point, I wish to do no more. Yours very truly

To Nathan Sargent

Hon. Nathan Sargent.   Springfield, Ills.
My dear Sir   June 23, 1859

Your very acceptable letter of the 13th. was duly received. Of course I would be pleased to see all the elements of opposition united for the approaching contest of 1860; but I confess I have not much hope of seeing it. You state a platform for such union in these words *"Opposition to the opening of the Slave-trade; & eternal hostility to the rotten democracy."* You add, by way of comment "I say, if the republicans would be content with this, there will be no obstacle to a union of the *opposition.* But this should be distinctly understood, before Southern men are asked to join them in a National convention" Well, I say such a platform, unanamously adopted by a National convention, with two of the best men living placed upon it as candidates, would probably carry Maryland, and would certainly not carry a single other state. It would gain nothing in the South, and lose every thing in the North. Mr. Goggin has just been beaten in Virginia on just such a platform. Last year the Republicans of Illinois cast 125-000 votes; on such a platform as yours they can not cast as many by 50.000. You could not help perceiving this, if you would but reflect that the republican party is utterly powerless everywhere, if it will, by any means, drive from it all those who came to it from the democracy for the sole object of preventing the spread, and nationalization of slavery. Whenever this object is waived by the organization, they will drop the organization; and the organization itself will dissolve into thin air. Your platform proposes to allow the spread, and nationalization of slavery to proceed without let or hindrance, save only that it shall not receive supplies directly from Africa. Surely you do not seriously believe the Republicans can come to any such terms.

From the passage of the Nebraska-bill up to date, the

Southern opposition have constantly sought to gain an advantage over the rotten democcracy, by running ahead of them in extreme opposition to, and vilifacation and misrepresentation of black republicans. It will be a good deal, if we fail to remember this in malice, (as I hope we shall fail to remember it;) but it is altogether too much to ask us to try to stand with them on the platform which has proved altogether insufficient to sustain them alone.

If the rotten democracy shall be beaten in 1860, it has to be done by the North; no human invention can deprive them of the South. I do not deny that there are as good men in the South as the North; and I guess we will elect one of them if he will allow us to do so on Republican ground. I think there can be no other ground of Union. For my single self I would be willing to risk some Southern men without a platform; but I am satisfied that is not the case with the Republican party generally. Yours very truly

To Schuyler Colfax

Hon: Schuyler Colfax: Springfield, Ills, July 6, 1859.

My dear Sir: I much regret not seeing you while you were here among us. Before learning that you were to be at Jacksonville on the 4th. I had given my word to be at another place. Besides a strong desire to make your personal acquaintance, I was anxious to speak with you on politics, a little more fully than I can well do in a letter. My main object in such conversation would be to hedge against divisions in the Republican ranks generally, and particularly for the contest of 1860. The point of danger is the temptation in different localities to *"platform"* for something which will be popular just there, but which, nevertheless, will be a firebrand elsewhere, and especially in a National convention. As instances, the movement against foreigners in Massachusetts; in New-Hampshire, to make obedience to the Fugitive Slave law, punishable as a crime; in Ohio, to repeal the Fugitive Slave law; and squatter sovereignty in Kansas. In these things there is explosive matter enough to blow up half a dozen national conventions, if it gets into them; and what gets very rife out-side of conventions is very likely to find it's way into them. What is desirable, if possible, is that in every local convoca-tion of Republicans, a point should be made to avoid every-thing which will distract republicans elsewhere. Massachusetts republicans should have looked beyond their noses; and then they could not have failed to see that tilting against foreigners would ruin us in the whole North-West. New-Hampshire and Ohio should forbear tilting against the Fugitive Slave law in such way as utterly overwhelm us in Illinois with the charge of enmity to the constitution itself. Kansas, in her confidence that she can be saved to freedom on "squatter sovereignty"— ought not to forget that to prevent the spread and national-ization of slavery is a national concern, and must be attended to by the nation. In a word, in every locality we should look beyond our noses; and at least say *nothing* on points where it is probable we shall disagree.

I write this for your eye only; hoping however that if you see danger as I think I do, you will do what you can to avert it. Could not suggestions be made to the leading men in the State and congressional conventions; and so avoid, to some extent at least, these apples of discord? Yours very truly

To Samuel Galloway

Hon. Samuel Galloway   Springfield, Ills.
My dear Sir: July 28. 1859
    Your very complimentary, not to say flattering letter of the 23rd. Inst. is received. Dr. Reynolds had induced me to expect you here; and I was disappointed, not a little, by your failure to come. And yet I fear you have formed an estimate of me which can scarcely be sustained on a personal acquaintance.

Two things done by the Ohio Republican convention— the repudiation of Judge Swan, and the "plank" for a repeal of the Fugitive Slave law—I very much regretted. These two things are of a piece; and they are viewed by many good men, sincerely opposed to slavery, as a struggle against, and in dis-regard of, the constitution itself. And it is the very thing that will greatly endanger our cause, if it not be kept out of our national convention. There is another thing our friends are doing which gives me some uneasiness. It is their leaning towards *"popular sovereignty."* There are three substantial objections to this. First, no party can command respect which sustains this year, what it opposed last. Secondly, Douglas, (who is the most dangerous enemy of liberty, because the most insidious one) would have little support in the North, and by consequence, no capital to trade on in the South, if it were not for our friends thus magnifying him and his humbug. But lastly, and chiefly, Douglas' popular sovereignty, accepted by the public mind, as a just principle, nationalizes slavery, and revives the African Slave-trade, inevitably. Taking slaves into new teritories, and buying slaves in Africa, are identical things—identical *rights* or identical *wrongs*—and the argument which establishes one will establish the other. Try a thousand years for a sound reason why congress shall not hinder the people of Kansas from having slaves, and when you have found it, it will be an equally good one why congress should not hinder the people of Georgia from importing slaves from Africa.

As to Gov. Chase, I have a kind side for him. He was one of the few distinguished men of the nation who gave us, in Illinois, their sympathy last year. I never saw him, suppose him to be able, and right-minded; but still he may not be the most suitable as a candidate for the Presidency.

I must say I do not think myself fit for the Presidency. As you propose a correspondence with me, I shall look for your letters anxiously.

I have not met Dr. Reynolds since receiving your letter; but when I shall, I will present your respects, as requested. Yours very truly

Notes for Speeches

What will Douglas do now? He does not quite know himself. Like a skilful gambler he will play for all the chances. His first wish is to be the nominee of the Charleston convention, without any new test. The democratic party proper do not wish to let it go just that way. They are thinking of getting up a Slave code test for him. They better not. Their true policy is to let him into the convention, beat him then, and give him no plausable excuse to bolt the nomination. But if they press the Slave code test upon him, he will not take it; but, as in the case of Lecompton, will appeal to the North on his bravery in opposing it. True the logic of his position, as an indorser of the Dred Scott decision imperatively requires him to go the Slave code. Honestly believing in that decision, he can not, without perjury, refuse to go the Slave code. But he will refuse. He never lets the logic of principle, displace the logic of success. And then, when he thus turns again to the North, we shall have the Lecompton phase of politics reproduced on a larger scale. It will then be a question whether the Republican party of the Nation shall make him President, in magnanamous gratitude for having opposed a Slave code, just as it was, last year, a question whether the Illinois Republicans should re-elect him Senator, in magnanamous gratitude for having opposed Lecompton. Some larger gentlemen will then have a chance of swallowing the same pill which they somewhat persistently prescribed for us little fellows last year. I hope they will not swallow it. For the sake of the *cause*, rather than the *men*, I hope they will not swallow it. The Republican cause can not live by Douglas' position. His position, whether for or against a slave code, for or against Lecompton, leads inevitably to the nationalizing and perpetuity of slavery, and the Republican cause can not live by it. Dallying with Douglas is, at best, for Republicans, only loss of labor, and loss of time. Wander with him however long, at last they must turn back and strike for a policy, which shall deal with slavery as a wrong, restrain it's enlargement, and look to its termination.

———

The effort to prove that our fathers who framed the government under which we live, understood that a proper division of local from federal authority, and some provision of the constitution, both forbid the federal government to control slavery in the federal teritories, is as if, when a man stands before you, so that you see him, and lay your hand upon him, you should go about examining his tracks, and insisting therefrom, that he is not present, but somewhere else. They *did*, through the federal government, control slavery in the federal teritories. They did the identical thing, which D. insists they understood they ought not to do.

———

Negro equality! Fudge!! How long, in the government of a God, great enough to make and maintain this Universe, shall there continue knaves to vend, and fools to gulp, so low a piece of demagougeism as this.

c. September 1859

Notes for Speech at Columbus, Ohio

For Columbus
Introduction.

What it is.
Danger to.
What it is *not*.
What it *is*.
D. P. S.
What is genuine P. S.
What is D. P. S.
Copy right essay.
Minor points of
"Fatal heresy."
States *in* & States out.
Congress to say when.
Main points
Men of Revolution
History, as given
Waive inaccuracies
Admit as to real P. S.
Show they were vs. D. P. S.
Would any man but D.
Murder—
Dred Scott.
At Freeport *"exclude"*
Since then *"control"* &c

If &c. "protect"
If &c. "goes into states"
I told him so.
"Negative—not affirmative"
How D. P. S. is dangerous
    Re-open Slave trade
    Deludes & debaches—
Conclusion
    Must treat as a *"wrong."*
    Not to, yields all
    U. S. not redeem all wrongs; but
    S. impairs & endangers general welfare.
    Thou who do not think &c
    We must think for selves—
    S. where it is
    Forgotten law
    But must *prevent*—
    Have to employ *Means*.
    Must be true to purpose.
    If not, what.
    Our principles will triumph.

September 16, 1859

Speech at Columbus, Ohio

Fellow-citizens of the State of Ohio:

I cannot fail to remember that I appear for the first time before an audience in this now great State—an audience that is accustomed to hear such speakers as Corwin, and Chase, and Wade, and many other renowned men; and, remembering this, I feel that it will be well for you, as for me, that you should not raise your expectations to that standard to which you would have been justified in raising them had one of these distinguished men appeared before you. You would perhaps be only preparing a disappointment for yourselves, and, as a consequence of your disappointment, mortification to me. I hope, therefore, you will commence with very moderate expectations; and perhaps, if you will give me your attention, I shall be able to interest you to a moderate degree.

Appearing here for the first time in my life, I have been somewhat embarrassed for a topic by way of introduction to my speech; but I have been relieved from that embarrassment by an introduction which the Ohio *Statesman* newspaper gave me this morning. In this paper I have read an article, in which, among other statements, I find the following:

> In debating with Senator Douglas during the memorable contest of last fall, Mr. Lincoln declared in favor of negro suffrage, and attempted to defend that vile conception against the Little Giant.

I mention this now, at the opening of my remarks, for the purpose of making three comments upon it. The first I have already announced—it furnishes me an introductory topic; the second is to show that the gentleman is mistaken; thirdly, to give him an opportunity to correct it. (A voice—"That he won't do.")

In the first place, in regard to this matter being a mistake. I have found that it is not entirely safe, when one is misrepresented under his very nose, to allow the misrepresentation to go uncontradicted. I therefore purpose, here at the outset, not only to say that this is a misrepresentation, but to show conclusively that it is so; and you will bear with me while I read a couple of extracts from that very "memorable" debate with Judge Douglas, last year, to which this newspaper refers. In the first pitched battle which Senator Douglas and myself had, at the town of Ottawa, I used the language which I will now read. Having been previously reading an extract, I continued as follows:

Now gentlemen, I don't want to read at any greater length, but this is the true complexion of all I have ever said in regard to the institution of slavery and the black race. This is the whole of it, and anything that argues me into his idea of perfect social and political equality with the negro, is but a specious and fantastic arrangement of words, by which a man can prove a horse chestnut to be a chestnut horse. I will say here, while upon this subject, that I have no purpose directly or indirectly to interfere with the institution of slavery in the States where it exists. I believe I have no lawful right to do so and I have no inclination to do so. I have no purpose to introduce political and social equality between the white and the black races. There is a physical difference between the two which in my judgment will probably forever forbid their living together upon the footing of perfect equality, and inasmuch as it becomes a necessity that there must be a difference, I, as well as Judge Douglas, am in favor of the race to which I belong, having the superior position. I have never said anything to the contrary, but I hold that notwithstanding all this, there is no reason in the world why the negro is not entitled to all the natural rights enumerated in the Declaration of Independence, the right to life, liberty, and the pursuit of happiness. I hold that he is as much entitled to these as the white man. I agree with Judge Douglas, he is not my equal in many respects—certainly not in color, perhaps not in moral or intellectual endowments. But in the right to eat the bread, without leave of anybody else, which his own hand earns, *he is my equal and the equal of Judge Douglas and the equal of every living man.*

Upon a subsequent occasion, when the reason for making a statement like this recurred, I said:

While I was at the hotel to-day an elderly gentleman called upon me to know whether I was really in favor of producing perfect equality between the negroes and white people. While I had not proposed to myself on this occasion to say much on that subject, yet as the question was asked me I thought I would occupy perhaps five minutes in saying something in regard to it. I will say then that I am not, nor ever have been in favor of bringing about in any way the social and political equality of the white and black races—that I am not, nor ever have been in favor of making voters or jurors of negroes, nor of qualifying them to hold office, or intermarry with white people; and I will say in addition to this that there is a physical difference between the white and black races which I believe will forever forbid the two races living together on terms of social and political equality. And inasmuch as they cannot so live, while they do remain together there must be the position of superior and inferior, and I as much as any other man am in favor of having the superior position assigned to the white race. I say upon this occasion I do not perceive that because the white man is to have the superior position, the negro should be denied everything. I do not understand that because I do not want a negro woman for a slave, I must necessarily want her for a wife. My understanding is that I can just let her alone. I am now in my fiftieth year, and I certainly never have had a black woman for either a slave or a wife. So it seems to me quite possible for us to get along without making either slaves or wives of negroes. I will add to this that I have never seen to my knowledge a man, woman or child, who was in favor of producing a perfect equality, social and political, between negroes and white men. I recollect of but one distinguished instance that I ever heard of so frequently as to be satisfied of its correctness—and that is the case of Judge Douglas' old friend Col. Richard M. Johnson. I will also add to the remarks I have made, (for I am not going to enter at large upon this subject,) that I have never had the least apprehension that I or my friends would marry negroes, if there was no law to keep them from it; but as Judge Douglas and his friends seem to be in great apprehension that they might, if there were no law to keep them from it, I give him the most solemn pledge that I will to the very last stand by the law of the State, which forbids the marrying of white people with negroes.

There, my friends, you have briefly what I have, upon former occasions, said upon the subject to which this newspaper, to the extent of its ability, [laughter] has drawn the public attention. In it you not only perceive as a probability that in that contest I did not at any time say I was in favor of negro suffrage; but the absolute proof that twice—once substantially and once expressly—I declared against it. Having shown you this, there remains but a word of comment on that newspaper article. It is this: that I presume the editor of that paper is an honest and truth-loving man, [a voice— "that's a great mistake,"] and that he will be very greatly obliged to me for furnishing him thus early an opportunity to correct the misrepresentation he has made, before it has run so long that malicious people can call him a liar. [Laughter and applause.]

The Giant himself has been here recently. [Laughter.] I have seen a brief report of his speech. If it were otherwise unpleasant to me to introduce the subject of the negro as a topic for discussion, I might be somewhat relieved by the fact that he dealt exclusively in that subject while he was here. I shall, therefore, without much hesitation or diffidence, enter upon this subject.

The American people, on the first day of January, 1854, found the African slave trade prohibited by a law of Congress. In a majority of the States of this Union, they found African slavery, or any other sort of slavery, prohibited by State constitutions. They also found a law existing, supposed to be valid, by which slavery was excluded from almost all the territory the United States then owned. This was the condition of the country, with reference to the institution of slavery, on the 1st of January, 1854. A few days after that, a bill was introduced into Congress, which ran through its regular course in the two branches of the National Legislature, and finally passed into a law in the month of May, by which the act of Congress prohibiting slavery from going into the territories of the United States was repealed. In connection with the law itself, and, in fact, in the terms of the law, the then existing prohibition was not only repealed, but there was a declaration of a purpose on the part of Congress never thereafter to exercise any power that they might have, real or supposed, to prohibit the extension or spread of slavery. This was a very great change; for the law thus repealed was of more than thirty years' standing. Following rapidly upon the heels of this action of Congress, a decision of the Supreme Court is made, by which it is declared that Congress, if it desires to prohibit the spread of slavery into the territories, has no constitutional power to do so. Not only so, but that decision lays down principles, which, if pushed to their logical conclusion—I say pushed to their logical conclusion—would decide that the constitutions of the Free States, forbidding slavery, are themselves unconstitutional. Mark me, I do not say the judge said this, and let no man say that I affirm the judge used these words; but I only say it is my opinion that what they did say, if pressed to its logical conclusion, will inevitably result thus. [Cries of "Good! good!"]

Looking at these things, the Republican party, as I understand its principles and policy, believe that there is great danger of the institution of slavery being spread out and extended, until it is ultimately made alike lawful in all the

States of this Union; so believing, to prevent that incidental and ultimate consummation, is the original and chief purpose of the Republican organization. I say "chief purpose" of the Republican organization; for it is certainly true that if the national House shall fall into the hands of the Republicans, they will have to attend to all the other matters of national house-keeping, as well as this. This chief and real purpose of the Republican party is eminently conservative. It proposes nothing save and except to restore this government to its original tone in regard to this element of slavery, and there to maintain it, looking for no further change, in reference to it, than that which the original framers of the government themselves expected and looked forward to.

The chief danger to this purpose of the Republican party is not just now the revival of the African slave trade, or the passage of a Congressional slave code, or the declaring of a second Dred Scott decision, making slavery lawful in all the States. These are not pressing us just now. They are not quite ready yet. The authors of these measures know that we are too strong for them; but they will be upon us in due time, and we will be grappling with them hand to hand, if they are not now headed off. They are not now the chief danger to the purpose of the Republican organization; but the most imminent danger that now threatens that purpose is that insidious Douglas Popular Sovereignty. This is the miner and sapper. While it does not propose to revive the African slave trade, nor to pass a slave code, nor to make a second Dred Scott decision, it is preparing us for the onslaught and charge of these ultimate enemies when they shall be ready to come on and the word of command for them to advance shall be given. I say this Douglas Popular Sovereignty—for there is a broad distinction, as I now understand it, between that article and a genuine popular sovereignty.

I believe there is a genuine popular sovereignty. I think a definition of genuine popular sovereignty, in the abstract, would be about this: That each man shall do precisely as he pleases with himself, and with all those things which exclusively concern him. Applied to government, this principle would be, that a general government shall do all those things which pertain to it, and all the local governments shall do precisely as they please in respect to those matters which exclusively concern them. I understand that this government of the United States, under which we live, is based upon this principle; and I am misunderstood if it is supposed that I have any war to make upon that principle.

Now, what is Judge Douglas' Popular Sovereignty? It is, as a principle, no other than that, if one man chooses to make a slave of another man, neither that other man nor anybody else has a right to object. [Cheers and laughter.] Applied in government, as he seeks to apply it, it is this: If, in a new territory into which a few people are beginning to enter for the purpose of making their homes, they choose to either exclude slavery from their limits, or to establish it there, however one or the other may affect the persons to be enslaved, or the infinitely greater number of persons who are afterward to inhabit that territory, or the other members of the families of communities, of which they are but an incipient member, or the general head of the family of States as parent of all—however their action may affect one or the other of these, there is no power or right to interfere. That is Douglas' popular sovereignty applied.

He has a good deal of trouble with his popular sovereignty. His explanations explanatory of explanations explained are interminable. [Laughter.] The most lengthy, and, as I suppose, the most maturely considered of his long series of explanations, is his great essay in Harper's Magazine. [Laughter.] I will not attempt to enter upon any very thorough investigation of his argument, as there made and presented. I will nevertheless occupy a good portion of your time here in drawing your attention to certain points in it. Such of you as may have read this document will have perceived that the Judge, early in the document, quotes from two persons as belonging to the Republican party, without naming them, but who can readily be recognized as being Gov. Seward of New York and myself. It is true, that exactly fifteen months ago this day, I believe, I for the first time expressed a sentiment upon this subject, and in such a manner that it should get into print, that the public might see it beyond the circle of my hearers; and my expression of it at that time is the quotation that Judge Douglas makes. He has not made the quotation with accuracy, but

justice to him requires me to say that it is sufficiently accurate
not to change its sense.

The sense of that quotation condensed is this—that this
slavery element is a durable element of discord among us, and
that we shall probably not have perfect peace in this country
with it until it either masters the free principle in our government, or is so far mastered by the free principle as for the
public mind to rest in the belief that it is going to its end.
This sentiment, which I now express in this way, was, at no
great distance of time, perhaps in different language, and in
connection with some collateral ideas, expressed by Gov.
Seward. Judge Douglas has been so much annoyed by the
expression of that sentiment that he has constantly, I believe,
in almost all his speeches since it was uttered, been referring
to it. I find he alluded to it in his speech here, as well as in the
copy-right essay. [Laughter.] I do not now enter upon this
for the purpose of making an elaborate argument to show
that we were right in the expression of that sentiment. In
other words, I shall not stop to say all that might properly be
said upon this point; but I only ask your attention to it for
the purpose of making one or two points upon it.

If you will read the copy-right essay, you will discover that
Judge Douglas himself says a controversy between the American Colonies and the government of Great Britain began on
the slavery question in 1699, and continued from that time
until the Revolution; and, while he did not say so, we all
know that it has continued with more or less violence ever
since the Revolution.

Then we need not appeal to history, to the declarations of
the framers of the government, but we know from Judge
Douglas himself that slavery began to be an element of discord among the white people of this country as far back as
1699, or one hundred and sixty years ago, or five generations
of men—counting thirty years to a generation. Now it would
seem to me that it might have occurred to Judge Douglas, or
anybody who had turned his attention to these facts, that
there was something in the nature of that thing, Slavery,
somewhat durable for mischief and discord. [Laughter.]

There is another point I desire to make in regard to this
matter, before I leave it. From the adoption of the consti-

tution down to 1820 is the precise period of our history when we had comparative peace upon this question—the precise period of time when we came nearer to having peace about it than any other time of that entire one hundred and sixty years, in which he says it began, or of the eighty years of our own constitution. Then it would be worth our while to stop and examine into the probable reason of our coming nearer to having peace then than at any other time. This was the precise period of time in which our fathers adopted, and during which they followed a policy restricting the spread of slavery, and the whole Union was acquiescing in it. The whole country looked forward to the ultimate extinction of the institution. It was when a policy had been adopted and was prevailing, which led all just and right-minded men to suppose that slavery was gradually coming to an end, and that they might be quiet about it, watching it as it expired. I think Judge Douglas might have perceived that too, and whether he did or not, it is worth the attention of fair-minded men, here and else where, to consider whether that is not the truth of the case. If he had looked at these two facts, that this matter has been an element of discord for one hundred and sixty years among this people, and that the only comparative peace we have had about it was when that policy prevailed in this government, which he now wars upon, he might then, perhaps, have been brought to a more just appreciation of what I said fifteen months ago—that "a house divided against itself cannot stand. I believe that this government cannot endure permanently half slave and half free. I do not expect the house to fall. I do not expect the Union to dissolve; but I do expect it will cease to be divided. It will become all one thing or all the other. Either the opponents of slavery will arrest the further spread of it, and place it where the public mind will rest in the belief that it is in the course of ultimate extinction; or its advocates will push it forward, until it shall become alike lawful in all the States, old as well as new, north as well as south." That was my sentiment at that time. In connection with it, I said, "we are now, far into the fifth year since a policy was inaugurated with the avowed object and confident promise of putting an end to slavery agitation. Under the operation of the policy, that agitation has not only not ceased, but has constantly augmented." I now say to you here that we are advanced still farther into the sixth year since that policy of Judge Douglas—that Popular Sovereignty of his, for quieting the Slavery question—was made the national policy. Fifteen months more have been added since I uttered that sentiment, and I call upon you, and all other right-minded men to say whether that fifteen months have belied or corroborated my words. ["Good, good! that's the truth!"]

While I am here upon this subject, I cannot but express gratitude that this true view of this element of discord among us—as I believe it is—is attracting more and more attention. I do not believe that Gov. Seward uttered that sentiment because I had done so before, but because he reflected upon this subject and saw the truth of it. Nor do I believe, because Gov. Seward or I uttered it, that Mr. Hickman of Pennsylvania, in different language, since that time, has declared his belief in the utter antagonism which exists between the principles of liberty and slavery. You see we are multiplying. [Applause and laughter.] Now, while I am speaking of Hickman, let me say, I know but little about him. I have never seen him, and know scarcely anything about the man; but I will say this much of him: Of all the Anti-Lecompton Democracy that have been brought to my notice, he alone has the true, genuine ring of the metal. And now, without endorsing anything else he has said, I will ask this audience to give three cheers for Hickman. [The audience responded with three rousing cheers for Hickman.]

Another point in the copy-right essay to which I would ask your attention, is rather a feature to be extracted from the whole thing, than from any express declaration of it at any point. It is a general feature of that document, and, indeed, of all of Judge Douglas' discussions of this question, that the territories of the United States and the States of this Union are exactly alike—that there is no difference between them at all—that the constitution applies to the territories precisely as it does to the States—and that the United States Government, under the constitution, may not do in a State what it may not do in a territory, and what it must do in a State, it must do in a territory. Gentlemen, is that a true view of the case? It is necessary for this squatter sovereignty; but is it true?

Let us consider. What does it depend upon? It depends altogether upon the proposition that the States must, without the interference of the general government, do all those things that pertain *exclusively* to themselves—that are local in their nature, that have no connection with the general government. After Judge Douglas has established this proposition, which nobody disputes or ever has disputed, he proceeds to assume, without proving it, that slavery is one of those little, unimportant, trivial matters which are of just about as much consequence as the question would be to me, whether my neighbor should raise horned cattle or plant tobacco (laughter); that there is no moral question about it, but that it is altogether a matter of dollars and cents; that when a new territory is opened for settlement, the first man who goes into it may plant there a thing which, like the Canada thistle, or some other of those pests of the soil, cannot be dug out by the millions of men who will come thereafter; that it is one of those little things that is so trivial in its nature that it has no effect upon anybody save the few men who first plant upon the soil; that it is not a thing which in any way affects the family of communities composing these States, nor any way endangers the general government. Judge Douglas ignores altogether the very well known fact, that we have never had a serious menace to our political existence, except it sprang from this thing which he chooses to regard as only upon a par with onions and potatoes. [Laughter.]

Turn it, and contemplate it in another view. He says, that according to his Popular Sovereignty, the general government may give to the territories governors, judges, marshals, secretaries, and all the other chief men to govern them, but they must not touch upon this other question. Why? The question of who shall be governor of a territory for a year or two, and pass away, without his track being left upon the soil, or an act which he did for good or for evil being left behind, is a question of vast national magnitude. It is so much opposed in its nature to locality, that the nation itself must decide it; while this other matter of planting slavery upon a soil—a thing which once planted cannot be eradicated by the succeeding millions who have as much right there as the first comers or if eradicated, not without infinite difficulty and a long struggle—he considers the power to prohibit it, as one of these little, local, trivial things that the nation ought not to say a word about; that it affects nobody save the few men who are there.

Take these two things and consider them together, present the question of planting a State with the Institution of slavery by the side of a question of who shall be Governor of Kansas for a year or two, and is there a man here,—is there a man on earth, who would not say that the Governor question is the little one, and the slavery question is the great one? I ask any honest Democrat if the small, the local, and the trivial and temporary question is not, who shall be Governor? While the durable, the important and the mischievous one is, shall this soil be planted with slavery?

This is an idea, I suppose, which has arisen in Judge Douglas' mind from his peculiar structure. I suppose the institution of slavery really looks small to him. He is so put up by nature that a lash upon his back would hurt him, but a lash upon anybody else's back does not hurt him. [Laughter.] That is the build of the man, and consequently he looks upon the matter of slavery in this unimportant light.

Judge Douglas ought to remember when he is endeavoring to force this policy upon the American people that while he is put up in that way a good many are not. He ought to remember that there was once in this country a man by the name of Thomas Jefferson, supposed to be a Democrat—a man whose principles and policy are not very prevalent amongst Democrats to-day, it is true; but that man did not take exactly this view of the insignificance of the element of slavery which our friend Judge Douglas does. In contemplation of this thing, we all know he was led to exclaim, "I tremble for my country when I remember that God is just!" We know how he looked upon it when he thus expressed himself. There was danger to this country—danger of the avenging justice of God in that little unimportant popular sovereignty question of Judge Douglas. He supposed there was a question of God's eternal justice wrapped up in the enslaving of any race of men, or any man, and that those who did so braved the arm of Jehovah—

that when a nation thus dared the Almighty every friend of that nation had cause to dread His wrath. Choose ye between Jefferson and Douglas as to what is the true view of this element among us. [Applause.]

There is another little difficulty about this matter of treating the Territories and States alike in all things, to which I ask your attention, and I shall leave this branch of the case. If there is no difference between them, why not make the Territories States at once? What is the reason that Kansas was not fit to come into the Union when it was organized into a Territory, in Judge Douglas' view? Can any of you tell any reason why it should not have come into the Union at once? They are fit, as he thinks, to decide upon the slavery question—the largest and most important with which they could possibly deal—what could they do by coming into the Union that they are not fit to do, according to his view, by staying out of it? Oh, they are not fit to sit in Congress and decide upon the rates of postage, or questions of *ad valorem* or specific duties on foreign goods, or live oak timber contracts (laughter); they are not fit to decide these vastly important matters, which are national in their import, but they are fit, "from the jump," to decide this little negro question. But, gentlemen, the case is too plain; I occupy too much time on this head, and I pass on.

Near the close of the copyright essay, the Judge, I think, comes very near kicking his own fat into the fire (laughter). I did not think, when I commenced these remarks, that I would read from that article, but I now believe I will:

This exposition of the history of these measures, shows conclusively that the authors of the Compromise Measures of 1850 and of the Kansas-Nebraska act of 1854, as well as the members of the Continental Congress of 1774, and the founders of our system of government subsequent to the Revolution, regarded the people of the Territories and Colonies as political communities which were entitled to a free and exclusive power of legislation in their Provincial legislatures, where their representation could alone be preserved, in all cases of taxation and internal polity.

When the Judge saw that putting in the word "slavery" would contradict his own history, he put in what he knew would pass as synonymous with it: "internal polity." Whenever we find *that* in one of his speeches, the substitute is used in this manner; and I can tell you the reason. It would be too bald a contradiction to say slavery, but "internal polity" is a general phrase, which would pass in some quarters, and which he hopes will pass with the reading community for the same thing.

This right pertains to the people collectively, as a law-abiding and peaceful community, and not in the isolated individuals who may wander upon the public domain in violation of the law. It can only be exercised where there are inhabitants sufficient to constitute a government, and capable of performing its various functions and duties, a fact to be ascertained and determined by—

Who do you think? Judge Douglas says "By Congress!" [Laughter.]

Whether the number shall be fixed at ten, fifteen or twenty thousand inhabitants does not affect the principle.

Now I have only a few comments to make. Popular Sovereignty, by his own words, does not pertain to the few persons who wander upon the public domain in violation of law. We have his words for that. When it does pertain to them, is when they are sufficient to be formed into an organized political community, and he fixes the minimum for that at 10,000, and the maximum at 20,000. Now I would like to know what is to be done with the 9,000? Are they all to be treated, until they are large enough to be organized into a political community, as wanderers upon the public land in violation of law? And if so treated and driven out at what point of time would there ever be ten thousand? (Great laughter.) If they were not driven out, but remained there as trespassers upon the public land in violation of the law, can they establish slavery there? No,—the Judge says Popular Sovereignty don't pertain to them then. Can they exclude it then? No, Popular Sovereignty don't pertain to them then. I would like to know, in the case covered by the Essay, what condition the people of the Territory are in before they reach the number of ten thousand?

But the main point I wish to ask attention to is, that the question as to when they shall have reached a sufficient number to be formed into a regular organized community, is to be decided "by Congress." Judge Douglas says so. Well, gentlemen, that is about all we want. [Here some one in the crowd made a remark inaudible to the reporter, whereupon Mr. Lincoln continued.] No, that is all the Southerners want. That is what all those who are for slavery want. They do not want Congress to prohibit slavery from coming into the new territories, and they do not want Popular Sovereignty to hinder it; and as Congress is to say when they are ready to be organized, all that the south has to do is to get Congress to hold off. Let Congress hold off until they are ready to be admitted as a State, and the south has all it wants in taking slavery into and planting it in all the territories that we now have, or hereafter may have. In a word, the whole thing, at a dash of the pen, is at last put in the power of Congress; for if they do not have this Popular Sovereignty until Congress organizes them, I ask if it at last does not come from Congress? If, at last, it amounts to anything at all, Congress gives it to them. I submit this rather for your reflection than for comment. After all that is said, at last by a dash of the pen, everything that has gone before is undone, and he puts the whole question under the control of Congress. After fighting through more than three hours, if you undertake to read it, he at last places the whole matter under the control of that power which he had been contending against, and arrives at a result directly contrary to what he had been laboring to do. He at last leaves the whole matter to the control of Congress.

There are two main objects, as I understand it, of this Harper's Magazine essay. One was to show, if possible, that the men of our revolutionary times were in favor of his popular sovereignty; and the other was to show that the Dred Scott Decision had not entirely squelched out this popular sovereignty. I do not propose, in regard to this argument drawn from the history of former times, to enter into a detailed examination of the historical statements he has made. I have the impression that they are inaccurate in a great many instances. Sometimes in positive statement but very much more inaccurate by the suppression of statements that really belong to the history. But I do not propose to affirm that this is so to any very great extent; or to enter into a very minute examination of his historical statements. I avoid doing so upon this principle—that if it were important for me to pass out of this lot in the least period of time possible and I came

to that fence and saw by a calculation of my known strength
and agility that I could clear it at a bound, it would be folly
for me to stop and consider whether I could or not crawl
through a crack. [Laughter.] So I say of the whole history,
contained in his essay, where he endeavored to link the men
of the revolution to popular sovereignty. It only requires an
effort to leap out of it—a single bound to be entirely successful. If you read it over you will find that he quotes here and
there from documents of the revolutionary times, tending to
show that the people of the colonies were desirous of regulat-
ing their own concerns in their own way, that the British
Government should not interfere; that at one time they struggled with the British Government to be permitted to exclude
the African slave trade; if not directly, to be permitted to
exclude it indirectly by taxation sufficient to discourage and
destroy it. From these and many things of this sort, Judge
Douglas argues that they were in favor of the people of our
own territories excluding slavery if they wanted to, or planting it there if they wanted to, doing just as they pleased from
the time they settled upon the territory. Now, however his
history may apply, and whatever of his argument there may
be that is sound and accurate or unsound and inaccurate, if
we can find out what these men did themselves do upon this
very question of slavery in the territories, does it not end the
whole thing? If, after all this labor and effort to show that the
men of the revolution were in favor of his popular sovereignty and his mode of dealing with slavery in the territories,
we can show that these very men took hold of that subject,
and dealt with it, we can see for ourselves *how* they dealt with
it. It is not a matter of argument or inference, but we know
what they thought about it.

It is precisely upon that part of the history of the country,
that one important omission is made by Judge Douglas. He
selects parts of the history of the United States upon the subject of slavery, and treats it as the whole; omitting from his
historical sketch the legislation of Congress in regard to the
admission of Missouri, by which the Missouri Compromise
was established, and slavery excluded from a country half
as large as the present United States. All this is left out of
his history, and in no wise alluded to by him, so far as I re-

member, save once, when he makes a remark, that upon his principle the Supreme Court were authorized to pronounce a decision that the act called the Missouri Compromise was unconstitutional. All that history has been left out. But this part of the history of the country was not made by the men of the Revolution.

There was another part of our political history made by the very men who were the actors in the Revolution, which has taken the name of the ordinance of '87. Let me bring that history to your attention. In 1784, I believe, this same Mr. Jefferson drew up an ordinance for the government of the country upon which we now stand; or rather a frame or draft of an ordinance for the government of this country, here in Ohio; our neighbors in Indiana; us who live in Illinois; our neighbors in Wisconsin and Michigan. In that ordinance, drawn up not only for the government of that territory, but for the territories south of the Ohio River, Mr. Jefferson expressly provided for the prohibition of slavery. Judge Douglas says, and perhaps is right, that that provision was lost from that ordinance. I believe that is true. When the vote was taken upon it, a majority of all present in the Congress of the Confederation voted for it; but there were so many absentees that those voting for it did not make the clear majority necessary, and it was lost. But three years after that the Congress of the Confederation were together again, and they adopted a new ordinance for the government of this north-west territory, not contemplating territory south of the river, for the States owning that territory had hitherto refrained from giving it to the general Government; hence they made the ordinance to apply only to what the Government owned. In that, the provision excluding slavery *was inserted and passed unanimously*, or at any rate it passed and became a part of the law of the land. Under that ordinance we live. First here in Ohio you were a territory, then an enabling act was passed authorizing you to form a constitution and State government, provided it was republican and not in conflict with the ordinance of '87. When you framed your constitution and presented it for admission, I think you will find the legislation upon the subject, it will show that, "whereas you had formed a constitution that was republican and not in conflict with the ordinance of '87," therefore you were admitted upon equal footing with the original States. The same process in a few years was gone through with in Indiana, and so with Illinois, and the same substantially with Michigan and Wisconsin.

Not only did that ordinance prevail, but it was constantly looked to whenever a step was taken by a new Territory to become a State. Congress always turned their attention to it, and in all their movements upon this subject, they traced their course by that ordinance of '87. When they admitted new States they advertised them of this ordinance as a part of the legislation of the country. They did so because they had traced the ordinance of '87 throughout the history of this country. Begin with the men of the Revolution, and go down for sixty entire years, and until the last scrap of that territory comes into the Union in the form of the State of Wisconsin—everything was made to conform with the ordinance of '87 excluding slavery from that vast extent of country.

I omitted to mention in the right place that the Constitution of the United States was in process of being framed when that ordinance was made by the Congress of the Confederation; and one of the first acts of Congress itself under the new Constitution itself was to give force to that ordinance by putting power to carry it out into the hands of the new officers under the Constitution, in place of the old ones who had been legislated out of existence by the change in the government from the Confederation to the Constitution. Not only so, but I believe Indiana once or twice, if not Ohio, petitioned the general government for the privilege of suspending that provision and allowing them to have slaves. A report made by Mr. Randolph of Virginia, himself a slaveholder, was directly against it, and the action was to refuse them the privilege of violating the ordinance of '87.

This period of history which I have run over briefly is, I presume, as familiar to most of this assembly as any other part of the history of our country. I suppose that few of my hearers are not as familiar with that part of history as I am, and I only mention it to recall your attention to it at this time. And hence I ask how extraordinary a thing it is that a man who has occupied a position upon the floor of the Senate of the United States, who is now in his third term, and who looks to see the government of this whole country fall into his own hands, pretending to give a truthful and accurate history of the slavery question in this country, should so entirely ignore the whole of that portion of our history—the most important of all. Is it not a most extraordinary spectacle that a man should stand up and ask for any confidence in his statements, who sets out as he does with portions of history calling upon the people to believe that it is a true and fair representation, when the leading part, and controlling feature of the whole history, is carefully suppressed.

But the mere leaving out is not the most remarkable feature of this most remarkable essay. His proposition is to establish that the leading men of the revolution were for his great principle of non-intervention by the government in the question of slavery in the territories; while history shows that they decided in the cases actually brought before them, in exactly the contrary way, and he knows it. Not only did they so decide at that time, but they stuck to it during sixty years, through thick and thin, as long as there was one of the revolutionary heroes upon the stage of political action. Through their whole course, from first to last, they clung to freedom. And now he asks the community to believe that the men of the revolution were in favor of his great principle, when we have the naked history that they themselves dealt with this very subject matter of his principle, and utterly repudiated his principle, acting upon a precisely contrary ground. It is as impudent and absurd as if a prosecuting attorney should stand up before a jury, and ask them to convict A as the murderer of B, while B was walking alive before them. [Cheers and laughter.]

I say again, if Judge Douglas asserts that the men of the Revolution acted upon principles by which, to be consistent with themselves, they ought to have adopted his popular sovereignty, then, upon a consideration of his own argument, he had a right to make you believe that they understood the principles of government, but misapplied them—that he has arisen to enlighten the world as to the just application of this principle. He has a right to try to persuade you that he understands their principles better than they did, and therefore he will apply them now, not as they did, but as they ought to have done. He has a right to go before the community, and try to convince them of this; but he has no right to attempt to impose upon any one the belief that these men themselves approved of his great principle. There are two ways of establishing a proposition. One is by trying to demonstrate it upon reason; and the other is, to show that great men in former times have thought so and so, and thus to pass it by the weight of pure authority. Now, if Judge Douglas will demonstrate somehow that this is popular sovereignty—the right of one man to make a slave of another, without any right in that other, or any one else, to object—demonstrate it as Euclid demonstrated propositions—there is no objection. But when he comes forward, seeking to carry a principle by bringing to it the authority of men who themselves utterly repudiate that principle, I ask that he shall not be permitted to do it. [Applause.]

I see, in the Judge's speech here, a short sentence in these words, "Our fathers, when they formed this government under which we live, understood this question just as well and even better than we do now." That is true; I stick to that. (Great cheers and laughter.) I will stand by Judge Douglas in that to the bitter end. (Renewed laughter.) And now, Judge Douglas, come and stand by me, and truthfully show how they acted, understanding it better than we do. All I ask of you, Judge Douglas, is to stick to the proposition that the men of the revolution understood this proposition, that the men of the revolution understood this subject better than we do now, *and with that better understanding they acted better than you are trying to act now.* [Applause and laughter.]

I wish to say something now in regard to the Dred Scott decision, as dealt with by Judge Douglas. In that "memorable debate," between Judge Douglas and myself last year, the Judge thought fit to commence a process of catechising me, and at Freeport I answered his questions, and propounded some to him. Among others propounded to him was one that I have here now. The substance, as I remember it, is, "Can the people of a United States territory, under the Dred Scott decision, in any lawful way, against the wish of any citizen of the United States, exclude slavery from its limits, prior to the formation of a State Constitution?" He answered that they could lawfully exclude slavery from the United States territories, notwithstanding the Dred Scott decision. There was something about that answer that has probably been a trouble to the Judge ever since. [Laughter.]

The Dred Scott decision expressly gives every citizen of the United States a right to carry his slaves into the United States' Territories. And now there was some inconsistency in saying that the decision was right, and saying too, that the people of the Territory could lawfully drive slavery out again. When all the trash, the words, the collateral matter was cleared away from it; all the chaff was fanned out of it, it was a bare absurdity—*no less than a thing may be lawfully driven away from where it has a lawful right to be.* [Cheers and laughter.] Clear it of all the verbiage, and that is the naked truth of his proposition—that a thing may be lawfully driven from the place where it has a lawful right to stay. Well, it was because the Judge couldn't help seeing this, that he has had so much trouble with it; and what I want to ask your especial attention to, just now, is to remind you, if you have not noticed the fact, that the Judge does not any longer say that the people can exclude slavery. He does not say so in the copyright essay; he did not say so in the speech that he made here, and so far as I know, since his re-election to the Senate, he has never said as he did at Freeport, that the people of the Territories can exclude slavery. He desires that you, who wish the Territories to remain free, should believe that he stands by that position, but he does not say it himself. He escapes to some extent the absurd position I have stated by changing his language entirely. What he says now is something different in language, and we will consider whether it is not different in sense too. It is now that the Dred Scott decision, or rather the Constitution under that decision, does not carry slavery into the Territories beyond the power of the people of the Territories *to control it as other property.* He does not say the people can drive it out, but they can control it as other property. The language is different, we should consider whether the sense is different. Driving a horse out of this lot, is too plain a proposition to be mistaken about; it is putting him on the other side of the fence. [Laughter.] Or it might be a sort of exclusion of him from the lot if you were to kill him and let the worms devour him; but neither of these things is the same as "controlling him as other property." That would be to feed him, to pamper him, to ride him, to use and abuse him, to make the most money out of him "as other property"; but, please you, what do the men who are in favor of slavery want more than this? [Laughter and applause.] What do they really want, other than that slavery being in the Territories, shall be controlled as other property. [Renewed applause.]

If they want anything else, I do not comprehend it. I ask your attention to this, first for the purpose of pointing out the change of ground the Judge has made; and, in the second place, the importance of the change—that that change is not such as to give you gentlemen who want his popular sovereignty the power to exclude the institution or drive it out at all. I know the Judge sometimes squints at the argument that in controlling it as other property by unfriendly legislation they may control it to death, as you might in the case of a horse, perhaps, feed him so lightly and ride him so much that he would die. [Cheers and laughter.] But when you come to legislative control, there is something more to be attended to. I have no doubt, myself, that if the people of the territories should undertake to control slave property as other property—that is, control it in such a way that it would be the most valuable as property, and make it bear its just proportion in the way of burdens as property—really deal with it as property—the Supreme Court of the United States will say, "God speed you and amen." But I undertake to give the opinion, at least, that if the territories attempt by any direct legislation to drive the man with his slave out of the territory, or to decide that his slave is free because of his being taken in there, or to tax him to such an extent that he cannot keep him there, the Supreme Court will unhesitatingly decide all such legislation unconstitutional, as long as that Supreme Court is constructed as the Dred Scott Supreme Court is. The first two things they have already decided, except that there is a little quibble among lawyers between the words *dicta* and decision. They have already decided a negro cannot be made free by territorial legislation.

What is that Dred Scott decision? Judge Douglas labors to show that it is one thing, while I think it is altogether different. It is a long opinion, but it is all embodied in this short statement: "The Constitution of the United States forbids Congress to deprive a man of his property, without due process of law; the right of property in slaves is distinctly and expressly affirmed in that Constitution; therefore, if Congress shall undertake to say that a man's slave is no longer his slave, when he crosses a certain line into a territory, that is depriving him of his property without due process of law, and is unconstitutional." There is the whole Dred Scott decision. They add that if Congress cannot do so itself, Congress cannot confer any power to do so, and hence any effort by the Territorial Legislature to do either of these things is absolutely decided against. It is a foregone conclusion by that court.

Now, as to this indirect mode by "unfriendly legislation," all lawyers here will readily understand that such a proposition cannot be tolerated for a moment, because a legislature cannot indirectly do that which it cannot accomplish directly. Then I say any legislation to control this property, as property, for its benefit as property, would be hailed by this Dred Scott Supreme Court, and fully sustained; but any legislation driving slave property out, or destroying it as property, directly or indirectly, will most assuredly, by that court, be held unconstitutional.

Judge Douglas says if the Constitution carries slavery into the territories, beyond the power of the people of the territories to control it as other property, then it follows logically that every one who swears to support the Constitution of the United States, must give that support to that property which it needs. And if the Constitution carries slavery into the territories, beyond the power of the people to control it as other property, then it also carries it into the States, because the Constitution is the supreme law of the land. Now, gentlemen, if it were not for my excessive modesty, I would say that I told that very thing to Judge Douglas quite a year ago. This argument is here in print, and if it were not for my modesty, as I said, I might call your attention to it. If you read it, you will find that I not only made that argument, but made it better than he has made it since. [Laughter.]

There is, however, this difference. I say now, and said then, there is no sort of question that the Supreme Court *has* decided that it is the right of the slaveholder to take his slave and hold him in the territory; and saying this, Judge Douglas himself admits the conclusion. He says if that is so, this consequence will follow; and because this consequence would follow, his argument is, the decision cannot, therefore, be that way—"that would spoil my popular sovereignty, and it cannot be possible that this great principle has been squelched out in this extraordinary way. It might be, if it were not for the extraordinary consequence of spoiling my humbug." [Cheers and laughter.]

Another feature of the Judge's argument about the Dred Scott case is, an effort to show that that decision deals altogether in declarations of negatives; that the constitution does not affirm anything as expounded by the Dred Scott decision, but it only declares a want of power—a total absence of power, in reference to the territories. It seems to be his purpose to make the whole of that decision to result in a mere negative declaration of a want of power in Congress to do anything in relation to this matter in the territories. I know the opinion of the Judges states that there is a total absence of power; but that is, unfortunately, not all it states; for the Judges add that the right of property in a slave is distinctly and expressly affirmed in the constitution. It does not stop at saying that the right of property in a slave is recognized in the constitution, is declared to exist somewhere in the constitution, but says it is *affirmed* in the constitution. Its language is equivalent to saying that it is embodied and so woven into that instrument that it cannot be detached without breaking the constitution itself. In a word, it is part of the constitution.

Douglas is singularly unfortunate in his effort to make out that decision to be altogether negative, when the express language at the vital part is that this is distinctly affirmed in the Constitution. I think myself, and I repeat it here, that this decision does not merely carry slavery into the Territories, but by its logical conclusion it carries it into the States in which we live. One provision of that Constitution is, that it shall be the supreme law of the land—I do not quote the language— any Constitution or law of any State to the contrary notwithstanding. This Dred Scott decision says that the right of property in a slave is affirmed in that Constitution, which is the supreme law of the land, any State Constitution or law notwithstanding. Then I say that to destroy a thing which is distinctly affirmed and supported by the supreme law of the land, even by a State Constitution or law, is a violation of that supreme law and there is no escape from it. In my judgment there is no avoiding that result, save that the American people shall see that Constitutions are better construed than our Constitution is construed in that decision. They must take care that it is more faithfully and truly carried out than it is there expounded.

I must hasten to a conclusion. Near the beginning of my remarks, I said that this insidious Douglas popular sovereignty is the measure that now threatens the purpose of the Republican party, to prevent slavery from being nationalized in the United States. I propose to ask your attention for a little while to some propositions in affirmance of that statement. Take it just as it stands, and apply it as a principle; extend and apply that principle elsewhere and consider where it will lead you. I now put this proposition that Judge Douglas' popular sovereignty applied will re-open the African slave trade; and I will demonstrate it by any variety of ways in which you can turn the subject or look at it.

The Judge says that the people of the territories have the right, by his principle, to have slaves, if they want them. Then I say that the people of Georgia have the right to buy slaves in Africa, if they want them, and I defy any man on earth to show any distinction between the two things—to show that the one is either more wicked or more unlawful; to show, on original principles, that one is better or worse than the other; or to show by the constitution, that one differs a whit from the other. He will tell me, doubtless, that there is no constitutional provision against people taking slaves into the new territories, and I tell him that there is equally no constitutional provision against buying slaves in Africa. He will tell you that a people, in the exercise of popular sovereignty, ought to do as they please about that thing, and have slaves if they want them; and I tell you that the people of Georgia are as much entitled to popular sovereignty and to buy slaves in Africa, if they want them, as the people of the territory are to have slaves if they want them. I ask any man, dealing honestly with himself, to point out a distinction.

I have recently seen a letter of Judge Douglas', in which without stating that to be the object, he doubtless endeavors, to make a distinction between the two. He says he is unalterably opposed to the repeal of the laws against the African Slave trade. And why? He then seeks to give a reason that would not apply to his popular sovereignty in the territories. What is that reason? "The abolition of the African slave trade is a compromise of the constitution." I deny it. There is no truth in the proposition that the abolition of the African slave trade is a compromise of the constitution. No man can put his finger on anything in the constitution, or on the line of history which shows it. It is a mere barren assertion, made simply for the purpose of getting up a distinction between the revival of the African slave trade and his "great principle."

At the time the constitution of the United States was adopted it was expected that the slave trade would be abolished. I should assert, and insist upon that, if Judge Douglas denied it. But I know that it was equally expected that slavery would be excluded from the territories and I can show by history, that in regard to these two things, public opinion was exactly alike, while in regard to positive action, there was more done in the Ordinance of '87, to resist the spread of slavery than was ever done to abolish the foreign slave trade. Lest I be misunderstood, I say again that at the time of the formation of the constitution, public expectation was that the slave trade would be abolished, but no more so than the spread of slavery in the territories should be restrained. They stand alike, except that in the Ordinance of '87 there was a mark left by public opinion showing that it was more committed against the spread of slavery in the territories than against the foreign slave trade.

Compromise! What word of compromise was there about it. Why the public sense was then in favor of the abolition of the slave trade; but there was at the time a very great commercial interest involved in it and extensive capital in that branch of trade. There were doubtless the incipient stages of improvement in the South in the way of farming, dependent on the slave trade, and they made a proposition to the Congress to abolish the trade after allowing it twenty years, a sufficient time for the capital and commerce engaged in it to be transferred to other channels. They made no provision that it should be abolished in twenty years; I do not doubt that they expected it would be; but they made no bargain about it. The public sentiment left no doubt in the minds of any that it would be done away. I repeat there is nothing in the history of those times, in favor of that matter being a *compromise* of the Constitution. It was the public expectation at the time, manifested in a thousand ways, that the spread of slavery should also be restricted.

Then I say if this principle is established, that there is no wrong in slavery, and whoever wants it has a right to have it, is a matter of dollars and cents, a sort of question as to how they shall deal with brutes, that between us and the negro here there is no sort of question, but that at the South the question is between the negro and the crocodile. That is all. It is a mere matter of policy; there is a perfect right according to interest to do just as you please—when this is done, where this doctrine prevails, the miners and sappers will have formed public opinion for the slave trade. They will be ready for Jeff. Davis and Stephens and other leaders of that company, to sound the bugle for the revival of the slave trade, for the second Dred Scott decision, for the flood of slavery to be poured over the free States, while we shall be here tied down and helpless and run over like sheep.

It is to be a part and parcel of this same idea, to say to men who want to adhere to the Democratic party, who have always belonged to that party, and are only looking about for some excuse to stick to it, but nevertheless hate slavery, that Douglas' Popular Sovereignty is as good a way as any to oppose slavery. They allow themselves to be persuaded easily in accordance with their previous dispositions, into this belief, that it is about as good a way of opposing slavery as any, and we can do that without straining our old party ties or breaking up old political associations. We can do so without being called negro worshippers. We can do that without being subjected to the jibes and sneers that are so readily thrown out in place of argument where no argument can be found; so let us stick to this Popular Sovereignty—this insidious Popular Sovereignty. Now let me call your attention to one thing that has really happened, which shows this gradual and steady debauching of public opinion, this course of preparation for the revival of the slave trade, for the territorial slave code, and the new Dred Scott decision that is to carry slavery into the free States. Did you ever five years ago, hear of anybody in the world saying that the negro had no share in the Declaration of National Independence; that it did not mean negroes at all; and when "all men" were spoken of negroes were not included?

I am satisfied that five years ago that proposition was not put upon paper by any living being anywhere. I have been unable at any time to find a man in an audience who would declare that he had ever known any body saying so five years ago. But last year there was not a Douglas popular sovereign in Illinois who did not say it. Is there one in Ohio but declares his firm belief that the Declaration of Independence did not mean negroes at all? I do not know how this is; I have not been here much; but I presume you are very much alike everywhere. Then I suppose that all now express the belief that the Declaration of Independence never did mean negroes. I call upon one of them to say that he said it five years ago.

If you think that now, and did not think it then, the next thing that strikes me is to remark that there has been a *change* wrought in you (laughter and applause), and a very significant change it is, being no less than changing the negro, in your estimation, from the rank of a man to that of a brute. They are taking him down, and placing him, when spoken of, among reptiles and crocodiles, as Judge Douglas himself expresses it.

Is not this change wrought in your minds a very important change? Public opinion in this country is everything. In a nation like ours this popular sovereignty and squatter sovereignty have already wrought a change in the public mind to the extent I have stated. There is no man in this crowd who can contradict it.

Now, if you are opposed to slavery honestly, as much as anybody I ask you to note that fact, and the like of which is to follow, to be plastered on, layer after layer, until very soon you are prepared to deal with the negro everywhere as with the brute. If public sentiment has not been debauched already to this point, a new turn of the screw in that direction is all that is wanting; and this is constantly being done by the teachers of this insidious popular sovereignty. You need but one or two turns further until your minds, now ripening under these teachings will be ready for all these things, and you will receive and support, or submit to, the slave trade; revived with all its horrors; a slave code enforced in our territories, and a new Dred Scott decision to bring slavery up into the very heart of the free North. This, I must say, is but carrying out those words prophetically spoken by Mr. Clay, many, many years ago. I believe more than thirty years when he told an audience that if they would repress all tendencies to liberty and ultimate emancipation, they must go back to the era of our independence and muzzle the cannon which thundered its annual joyous return on the Fourth of July; they must blow out the moral lights around us; they must penetrate the human soul and eradicate the love of liberty; but until they did these things, and others eloquently enumerated by him, they could not repress all tendencies to ultimate emancipation.

I ask attention to the fact that in a pre-eminent degree these popular sovereigns are at this work; blowing out the moral lights around us; teaching that the negro is no longer a man but a brute; that the Declaration has nothing to do with him; that he ranks with the crocodile and the reptile; that man, with body and soul, is a matter of dollars and cents. I suggest to this portion of the Ohio Republicans, or Democrats if there be any present, the serious consideration of this fact, that there is now going on among you a steady process of debauching public opinion on this subject. With this my friends, I bid you adieu.

September 16, 1859

Speech at Cincinnati, Ohio

My fellow-citizens of the State of Ohio: This is the first time in my life that I have appeared before an audience in so great a city as this. I therefore—though I am no longer a young man—make this appearance under some degree of embarrassment. But, I have found that when one is embarrassed, usually the shortest way to get through with it is to quit talking or thinking about it, and go at something else. (Applause.)

WHAT DID DOUGLAS SAY?

I understand that you have had recently with you, my very distinguished friend, Judge Douglas, of Illinois, (laughter) and I understand, without having had an opportunity, (not greatly sought to be sure,) of seeing a report of the speech, that he made here, that he did me the honor to mention my humble name. I suppose that he did so for the purpose of making some objection to some sentiment at some time expressed by me. I should expect, it is true, that Judge Douglas had reminded you, or informed you, if you had never before heard it, that I had once in my life declared it as my opinion that this government cannot "endure permanently half slave and half free; that a house divided against itself cannot stand," and, as I had expressed it, I did not expect the house to fall; that I did not expect the Union to be dissolved; but, that I did expect that it would cease to be divided; that it would become all one thing or all the other, that either the opponents of Slavery would arrest the further spread of it, and place it where the public mind would rest in the belief that it was in the course of ultimate extinction; or the friends of Slavery will push it forward until it becomes alike lawful in all the States, old or new, Free as well as Slave. I did, fifteen months ago, express that opinion, and upon many occasions Judge Douglas has denounced it, and has greatly, intentionally or unintentionally, misrepresented my purpose in the expression of that opinion.

I presume, without having seen a report of his speech, that he did so here. I presume that he alluded also to that opinion in different language, having been expressed at a subsequent time by Governor Seward of New York, and that he took the two in a lump and denounced them; that he tried to point out that there was something couched in this opinion which led to the making of an entire uniformity of the local institutions of the various States of the Union, in utter disregard of the different States, which in their nature would seem to require a variety of institutions, and a variety of laws, conforming to the differences in the nature of the different States.

Not only so; I presume he insisted that this was a declaration of war between the Free and Slave States—that it was the sounding to the onset of continual war between the different States, the Slave and Free States.

This charge, in this form, was made by Judge Douglas on, I believe, the 9th of July, 1858, in Chicago, in my hearing. On the next evening, I made some reply to it. I informed him that many of the inferences he drew from that expression of mine were altogether foreign to any purpose entertained by me, and in so far as he should ascribe those inferences to me, as my purpose, he was entirely mistaken; and in so far as he might argue that whatever might be my purpose, actions, conforming to my views, would lead to these results, he might argue and establish if he could; but, so far as purposes were concerned, he was totally mistaken as to me.

When I made that reply to him—when I told him, on the question of declaring war between the different States of the Union, that I had not said I did not expect any peace upon this question until Slavery was exterminated; that I had only said I expected peace when that institution was put where the public mind should rest in the belief that it was in course of ultimate extinction; that I believed from the organization of our government, until a very recent period of time, the institution had been placed and continued upon such a basis; that we had had comparative peace upon that question through a portion of that period of time, only because the public mind rested in that belief in regard to it, and that when we returned to that position in relation to that matter, I supposed we should again have peace as we previously had. I assured him, as I now assure you, that I neither then had, nor have, or ever had, any purpose in any way of interfering with the institution of Slavery, where it exists. [Long continued applause.] I believe we have no power, under the Constitution of the United States; or rather under the form of government under which we live, to interfere with the institution of Slavery, or any other of the institutions of our sister States, be they Free or Slave States. [Cries of "Good," and applause.] I declared then and I now re-declare, that I have as little inclination to so interfere with the institution of Slavery where it now exists, through the instrumentality of the general Government, or any other instrumentality, as I believe we have no power to do so. [A voice—"You're right."] I accidentally used this expression: I had no purpose of entering into the Slave States to disturb the institution of Slavery! So, upon the first occasion that Judge Douglas got an opportunity to reply to me, he passed by the whole body of what I had said upon that subject, and seized upon the particular expression of mine, that I had no purpose of entering into the Slave States to disturb the institution of Slavery! "Oh, no," said he, "he (Lincoln) won't enter into the Slave States to disturb the institution of Slavery; he is too prudent a man to do such a thing as that; he only means that he will go on to the line between the Free and Slave States, and shoot over at them. [Laughter.] This is all he means to do. He means to do them all the harm he can, to disturb them all he can, in such a way as to keep his own hide in perfect safety." [Laughter.]

OPPORTUNITY TO SHOOT ACROSS THE LINE.

Well, now, I did not think, at that time, that that was either a very dignified or very logical argument; but so it was, I had to get along with it as well as I could.

It has occurred to me here to-night, that if I ever do shoot over the line at the people on the other side of the line into a Slave State, and purpose to do so, keeping my skin safe, that I have now about the best chance I shall ever have. [Laughter and applause.] I should not wonder that there are some Kentuckians about this audience; we are close to Kentucky; and whether that be so or not, we are on elevated ground, and by speaking distinctly, I should not wonder if some of the Kentuckians would hear me on the other side of the river.

[Laughter.] For that reason I propose to address a portion of what I have to say to the Kentuckians.

INTRODUCING HIMSELF TO KENTUCKIANS.

I say, then, in the first place, to the Kentuckians, that I am what they call, as I understand it, a "Black Republican." (Applause and laughter.) I think Slavery is wrong, morally, and politically. I desire that it should be no further spread in these United States, and I should not object if it should gradually terminate in the whole Union. (Applause.) While I say this for myself, I say to you, Kentuckians, that I understand you differ radically with me upon this proposition; that you believe Slavery is a good thing; that Slavery is right; that it ought to be extended and perpetuated in this Union. Now, there being this broad difference between us, I do not pretend in addressing myself to you, Kentuckians, to attempt prose-lyting you; that would be a vain effort. I do not enter upon it. I only propose to try to show you that you ought to nominate for the next Presidency, at Charleston, my distin-guished friend Judge Douglas. [Applause.] In all that there is a difference between you and him, I understand he is as sincerely for you, and more wisely for you, than you are for yourselves. [Applause.] I will try to demonstrate that proposition. Understand now, I say that I believe he is as sin-cerely for you, and more wisely for you, than you are for yourselves.

ADVOCATES THE "GIANT'S CLAIMS."

What do you want more than anything else to make suc-cessful your views of Slavery,—to advance the outspread of it, and to secure and perpetuate the nationality of it? What do you want more than anything else? What is needed abso-lutely? What is indispensable to you? Why! if I may be al-lowed to answer the question, it is to retain a hold upon the North—it is to retain support and strength from the Free States. If you can get this support and strength from the Free States, you can succeed. If you do not get this support and this strength from the Free States, you are in the minority, and you are beaten at once.

If that proposition be admitted,—and it is undeniable,

then the next thing I say to you, is that Douglas of all the men in this nation is the only man that affords you any hold upon the Free States; that no other man can give you any strength in the Free States. This being so, if you doubt the other branch of the proposition, whether he is for you—whether he is really for you as I have expressed it, I propose asking your attention for awhile to a few facts.

The issue between you and me, understand, is that I think Slavery is wrong, and ought not to be outspread, and you think it is right and ought to be extended and perpetuated. (A voice, "oh, Lord.") That is my Kentuckian I am talking to now. (Applause.)

I now proceed to try to show you that Douglas is as sincerely for you and more wisely for you than you are for yourselves.

DOUGLAS AT THE WORK OF THE SOUTH.

In the first place we know that in a Government like this, in a Government of the people, where the voice of all the men of the country, substantially enter into the execution,—or administration rather—of the Government—in such a Government, what lies at the bottom of all of it, is public opinion. I lay down the proposition, that Douglas is not only the man that promises you in advance a hold upon the North, and support in the North, but that he constantly moulds public opinion to your ends; that in every possible way he can, he constantly moulds the public opinion of the North to your ends; and if there are a few things in which he seems to be against you—a few things which he says that appear to be against you, and a few that he forbears to say which you would like to have him say—you ought to remember that the saying of the one, or the forbearing to say the other, would loose his hold upon the North, and, by consequence, would lose his capacity to serve you. (A Voice, "That is so.")

Upon this subject of moulding public opinion, I call your attention to the fact—for a well-established fact it is—that the Judge never says your institution of Slavery is wrong; he never says it is right, to be sure, but he never says it is wrong. [Laughter.] There is not a public man in the United States, I believe, with the exception of Senator Douglas, who has not, at some time in his life, declared his opinion whether the thing is right or wrong; but, Senator Douglas never declares it is wrong. He leaves himself at perfect liberty to do all in your favor which he would be hindered from doing if he were to declare the thing to be wrong. On the contrary, he takes all the chances that he has for inveigling the sentiment of the North, opposed to Slavery, into your support, by never saying it is right. [Laughter.] This you ought to set down to his credit. [Laughter.] You ought to give him full credit for this much, little though it be, in comparison to the whole which he does for you.

SEE-SAW.

Some other things I will ask your attention to. He said upon the floor of the United States Senate, and he has repeated it as I understand, a great many times, that he does not care whether Slavery is "voted up or voted down." This again shows you, or ought to show you, if you would reason upon it, that he does not believe it to be wrong, for a man may say, when he sees nothing wrong in a thing, that he does not care whether it be voted up or voted down, but no man can logically say that he cares not whether a thing goes up or goes down, which to him appears to be wrong. You therefore have a demonstration in this, that to Douglas' mind your favorite institution which you would have spread out, and made perpetual, is no wrong.

THE ALMIGHTY'S DIVIDING LINE.

Another thing he tells you, in a speech made at Memphis in Tennessee, shortly after the canvass in Illinois, last year. He there distinctly told the people, that there was a "line drawn by the Almighty across this continent, on the one side of which the soil must always be cultivated by slaves," that he did not pretend to know exactly where that line was, [laughter and applause,] but that there was such a line. I want to ask your attention to that proposition again; that there is one portion of this continent where the Almighty has designed the soil shall always be cultivated by slaves; that its being cultivated by slaves at that place is right; that it has the direct sympathy and authority of the Almighty. Whenever you can get these Northern audiences to adopt the opinion that Slavery is right on the other side of the Ohio; whenever you can get them, in pursuance of Douglas' views, to adopt that sentiment, they will very readily make the other argument, which is perfectly logical, that that which is right on that side of the Ohio, cannot be wrong on this, [laughter;] and that if you have that property on that side of the Ohio, under the seal and stamp of the Almighty, when by any means it escapes over here, it is wrong to have constitutions and laws, "to devil" you about it. So Douglas is moulding the public opinion of the North, first to say that the thing is right in your State over the Ohio river, and hence to say that that which is right there is not wrong here, [at this moment the cannon was fired; to the great injury of sundry panes of glass in the vicinity,] and that all laws and constitutions here, recognizing it as being wrong, are themselves wrong, and ought to be repealed and abrogated. He will tell you, men of Ohio, that if you choose here to have laws against Slavery it is in conformity to the idea that your climate is not suited to it, that your climate is not suited to slave labor, and therefore you have constitutions and laws against it.

Let us attend to that argument for a little while and see if it be sound. You do not raise sugar cane—[except the new fashioned sugar cane, and you won't raise that long] but they do raise it in Louisiana. You don't raise it in Ohio because you can't raise it profitably, because the climate don't suit it. [Here again the cannon interrupted. Its report was followed by another fall of window glass.] They do raise it in Louisiana because there it is profitable. Now, Douglas will tell you that is precisely the Slavery question. That they do have slaves there because they are profitable, and you don't have them here because they are not profitable. If that is so, then it leads to dealing with the one precisely as with the other. Is there then anything in the Constitution or laws of Ohio against raising sugar cane? Have you found it necessary to put any such provision in your law? Surely not! No man desires to raise sugar cane in Ohio; but, if any man did desire to do so, you would say it was a tyrannical law that forbid his doing so, and whenever you shall agree with Douglas, whenever your minds are brought to adopt his argument, as surely you will have reached the conclusion, that although Slavery is not profitable in Ohio, if any man wants it, it is wrong to him not to let him have it.

In this matter Judge Douglas is preparing the public mind for you of Kentucky, to make perpetual that good thing in your estimation, about which you and I differ.

THE CHANGES IN FIVE YEARS.

In this connection let me ask your attention to another thing. I believe it is safe to assert that five years ago, no living man had expressed the opinion that the negro had no share in the Declaration of Independence. Let me state that again: five years ago no living man had expressed the opinion that the negro had no share in the Declaration of Independence. If there is in this large audience any man who ever knew of that opinion being put upon paper as much as five years ago, I will be obliged to him now or at a subsequent time to show it.

If that be true I wish you then to note the next fact; that within the space of five years Senator Douglas, in the argument of this question, has got his entire party, so far as I know, without exception, to join in saying that the negro has no share in the Declaration of Independence. If there be now in all these United States, one Douglas man that does not say this, I have been unable upon any occasion to scare him up. Now if none of you said this five years ago, and all of you say it now, that is a matter that you Kentuckians ought to note. That is a vast change in the Northern public sentiment upon that question.

Of what tendency is that change? The tendency of that change is to bring the public mind to the conclusion that when men are spoken of, the negro is not meant; that when negroes are spoken of, brutes alone are contemplated. That change in public sentiment has already degraded the black man in the estimation of Douglas and his followers from the condition of a man of some sort, and assigned him to the condition of a brute. Now, you Kentuckians ought to give Douglas credit for this. That is the largest possible stride that can be made in regard to the perpetuation of your thing of Slavery.

A Voice—"Speak to Ohio men, and not to Kentuckians!"
Mr. Lincoln—I beg permission to speak as I please.
(Laughter.)

THE BIBLE THEORY.

In Kentucky, perhaps, in many of the Slave States certainly, you are trying to establish the rightfulness of Slavery by reference to the Bible. You are trying to show that slavery existed in the Bible times by Divine ordinance. Now Douglas is wiser than you, for your own benefit, upon that subject. Douglas knows that whenever you establish that Slavery was right by the Bible, it will occur that that Slavery was the Slavery of the *white* man—of men without reference to color—and he knows very well that you may entertain that idea in Kentucky as much as you please, but you will never win any Northern support upon it. He makes a wiser argument for you; he makes the argument that the slavery of the *black* man, the slavery of the man who has a skin of a different color from your own, is right. He thereby brings to your support Northern voters who could not for a moment be brought by your own argument of the Bible-right of slavery. Will you not give him credit for that? Will you not say that in this matter he is more wisely for you than you are for yourselves.

Now having established with his entire party this doctrine—having been entirely successful in that branch of his efforts in your behalf; he is ready for another.

A SUM IN THE RULE OF THREE.

At this same meeting at Memphis, he declared that while in all contests between the negro and the white man, he was for the white man, but that in all questions between the negro and the crocodile he was for the negro. (Laughter.) He did not make that declaration accidentally at Memphis. He made it a great many times in the canvass in Illinois last year, (though I don't know that it was reported in any of his speeches there,) but he frequently made it. I believe he repeated it at Columbus, and I should not wonder if he repeated it here. It is, then, a deliberate way of expressing himself upon that subject. It is a matter of mature deliberation with him thus to express himself upon that point of his case. It therefore requires some deliberate attention.

The first inference seems to be that if you do not enslave the negro you are wronging the white man in some way or other, and that whoever is opposed to the negro being enslaved is in some way or other against the white man. Is not that a falsehood? If there was a necessary conflict between the white man and the negro, I should be for the white man as much as Judge Douglas; but I say there is no such necessary conflict. I say that there is room enough for us all to be free, (loud manifestations of applause,) and that it not only does not wrong the white man that the negro should be free, but it positively wrongs the mass of the white men that the negro should be enslaved; that the mass of white men are really injured by the effect of slave labor in the vicinity of the fields of their own labor. (Applause.)

But I do not desire to dwell upon this branch of the question more than to say that this assumption of his is false, and I do hope that that fallacy will not long prevail in the minds of intelligent white men. At all events, you Kentuckians ought to thank Judge Douglas for it. It is for your benefit it is made.

The other branch of it is, that in a struggle between the negro and the crocodile, he is for the negro. Well, I don't know that there is any struggle between the negro and the crocodile, either. (Laughter.) I suppose that if a crocodile (or as we old Ohio river boatmen used to call them, alligators) should come across a white man, he would kill him if he could, and so he would a negro. But what, at last, is this proposition? I believe it is a sort of proposition in proportion, which may be stated thus: As the negro is to the white man, so is the crocodile to the negro, and as the negro may rightfully treat the crocodile as a beast or reptile, so the white man may rightfully treat the negro as a beast or a reptile. (Applause.) That is really the "knip" of all that argument of his.

Now, my brother Kentuckians, who believe in this, you ought to thank Judge Douglas for having put that in a much more taking way than any of yourselves have done. (Applause.)

THE "GREAT PRINCIPLE."

Again, Douglas' *great principle*, "Popular Sovereignty," as he calls it, gives you, by natural consequence, the revival of the Slave-trade whenever you want it. If you question this, listen a while, consider a while, what I shall advance in support of that proposition.

He says that it is the sacred right of the man who goes into the Territories, to have Slavery if he wants it. Grant that for argument's sake. Is it not the sacred right of the man that don't go there equally to buy slaves in Africa, if he wants them? Can you point out the difference? The man who goes into the Territories of Kansas and Nebraska, or any other new Territory, with the sacred right of taking a slave there which belongs to him, would certainly have no more right to take one there than I would who own no slave, but who would desire to buy one and take him there. You will not say—you, the friends of Douglas—but that the man who does not own a slave, has an equal right to buy one and take him to the Territory, as the other does?

A VOICE. "I want to ask a question. Don't foreign nations interfere with the Slave-trade?"

MR. LINCOLN. Well! I understand it to be a principle of Democracy to whip foreign nations whenever they interfere with us. (Laughter and applause.)

VOICE. "I only asked for information. I am a Republican myself."

MR. LINCOLN. You and I will be on the best terms in the world, but I do not wish to be diverted from the point I was trying to press.

I say that Douglas' Popular Sovereignty, establishing a sacred right in the people, if you please, if carried to its logical conclusion, gives equally the sacred right to the people of the States or the Territories themselves to buy slaves, wherever they can buy them cheapest; and if any man can show a distinction, I should like to hear him try it. If any man can show how the people of Kansas have a better right to slaves because they want them, than the people of Georgia have to buy them in Africa, I want him to do it. I think it cannot be done. If it is "Popular Sovereignty" for the people to have slaves because they want them, it is Popular

Sovereignty for them to buy them in Africa, because they desire to do so.

A CHAPTER ON COMPROMISES.

I know that Douglas has recently made a little effort—not seeming to notice that he had a different theory—has made an effort to get rid of that. He has written a letter addressed to somebody, I believe, who resides in Iowa, declaring his opposition to the repeal of the laws that prohibit the African Slave Trade. He bases his opposition to such repeal upon the ground that these laws are themselves one of the compromises of the Constitution of the United States. Now it would be very interesting to see Judge Douglas or any of his friends turn to the Constitution of the United States and point out that compromise, to show where there is any compromise in the Constitution or provision in the Constitution, express or implied, by which the Administrators of that Constitution are under any obligation to repeal the African Slave-trade. I know, or at least I think I know, that the framers of that Constitution did expect that the African Slave-trade would be abolished at the end of twenty years, to which time their prohibition against its being abolished extended. I think there is abundant contemporaneous history to show that the framers of the Constitution expected it to be abolished. But while they so expected, they gave nothing for that expectation, and they put no provision in the Constitution requiring it should be so abolished. The migration or importation of such persons as the States shall see fit to admit shall not be prohibited, but a certain tax might be levied upon such importation. But what was to be done after that time? The Constitution is as silent about that, as it is silent personally about myself. There is absolutely nothing in it about that subject—there is only the expectation of the framers of the Constitution that the Slave-trade would be abolished at the end of that time and they expected it would be abolished, owing to public sentiment, before that time, and they put that provision in, in order that it should not be abolished before that time, for reasons which I suppose they thought to be sound ones, but which I will not now try to enumerate before you.

But while they expected the Slave-trade would be abolished

at that time, they expected that the spread of Slavery into the new Territories should also be restricted. It is as easy to prove that the framers of the Constitution of the United States, expected that Slavery should be prohibited from extending into the new Territories, as it is to prove that it was expected that the Slave-trade should be abolished. Both these things were expected. One was no more expected than the other, and one was no more a compromise of the Constitution than the other. There was nothing said in the Constitution in regard to the spread of Slavery into the Territory. I grant that, but there was something very important said about it by the same generation of men in the adoption of the old Ordinance of '87, through the influence of which you here in Ohio, our neighbors in Indiana, we in Illinois, our neighbors in Michigan and Wisconsin are happy, prosperous, teeming millions of free men. (Continued applause.) That generation of men, though not to the full extent members of the Convention that framed the Constitution, were to some extent members of that Convention, holding seats, at the same time in one body and the other, so that if there was any compromise on either of these subjects, the strong evidence is that that compromise was in favor of the restriction of Slavery from the new territories.

But Douglas says that he is unalterably opposed to the repeal of those laws; because, in his view, it is a compromise of the Constitution. You Kentuckians, no doubt, are somewhat offended with that! You ought not to be! You ought to be patient! You ought to know that if he said less than that, he would lose the power of "lugging" the Northern States to your support. Really, what you would push him to do would take from him his entire power to serve you. And you ought to remember how long, by precedent, Judge Douglas holds himself obliged to stick by compromises. You ought to remember that by the time you yourselves think you are ready to inaugurate measures for the revival of the African Slave-trade that sufficient time will have arrived by precedent, for Judge Douglas to break through that compromise. He says now nothing more strong than he said in 1849 when he declared in favor of the Missouri Compromise—that precisely four years and a quarter after he declared that compromise to be a sacred thing, which "no ruthless hand would ever dare to touch," he, himself, brought forward the measure, ruthlessly to destroy it. (A voice—"hit him again!" Applause.) By a mere calculation of time it will only be four years more until he is ready to take back his profession about the sacredness of the Compromise abolishing the slave trade. Precisely as soon as you are ready to have his services in that direction, by fair calculation you may be sure of having them. (Applause and laughter.)

UNFRIENDLY LEGISLATION.

But you remember and set down to Judge Douglas' debit, or discredit, that he, last year, said the people of the Territories can, in spite of the Dred Scott decision, exclude your slaves from those territories; that he declared by "unfriendly legislation," the extension of your property into the new Territories may be cut off in the teeth of the decision of the Supreme Court of the United States.

He assumed that position at Freeport on the 27th of August, 1858. He said that the people of the Territories can exclude Slavery in so many words. You ought, however, to bear in mind that he has never said it since. (Laughter.) You may hunt in every speech that he has since made, and he has never used that expression once. He has never seemed to notice that he is stating his views differently from what he did then; but, by some sort of accident, he has always really stated it differently. He has always since then declared that "the Constitution does not carry Slavery into the Territories of the United States beyond the power of the people legally to control it, as other property." Now, there is a difference in the language used upon that former occasion and in this latter day. There may or may not be a difference in the meaning, but it is worth while considering whether there is not also a difference in meaning.

What is it to exclude? Why, it is to drive it out. It is in some way to put it out of the Territory. It is to force it across the line, or change its character, so that as property it is out of existence. But what is the controlling of it "as other property?" Is controlling it as other property the same thing as destroying it, or driving it away? I should think not. I should think the controlling of it as other property would be just about what you in Kentucky should want. I understand the controlling of property means the controlling of it for the benefit of the owner of it. While I have no doubt the Supreme Court of the United States would say "God speed" to any of the Territorial legislatures that should thus control slave property, they would sing quite a different tune if by the pretense of controlling it they were to undertake to pass laws which virtually excluded it, and that upon a very well known principle to all lawyers, that what a legislature cannot directly do, it cannot do by indirection; that as, the legislature has not the power to drive slaves out, they have no power by indirection, by tax or by imposing burdens in any way on that property, to effect the same end, and that any attempt to do so would be held by the Dred Scott Court unconstitutional.

Douglas is not willing to stand by his first proposition that they can exclude it, because we have seen that that proposition amounts to nothing more nor less than the naked absurdity, that you may lawfully drive out that which has a lawful right to remain. He admitted at first that the slave might be lawfully taken into the Territories under the Constitution of the United States, and yet asserted that he might be lawfully driven out. That being the proposition, it is the absurdity I have stated. He is not willing to stand in the face of that direct, naked and impudent absurdity; he has, therefore, modified his language into that of being *controlled as other property.*

SWEARING BY THE COURTS.

The Kentuckians don't like this in Douglas! I will tell you where it will go. He now swears by the Court. He was once a leading man in Illinois to break down a Court, because it had made a decision he did not like. But he now not only swears by the Court, the courts having got to working for you, but he denounces all men that do not swear by the Courts, as unpatriotic, as bad citizens. When one of these acts of unfriendly legislation shall impose such heavy burdens as to, in effect, destroy property in slaves in a Territory and show plainly enough that there can be no mistake in the purpose of the Legislature to make them so burdensome, this same

Supreme Court will decide that law to be unconstitutional, and he will be ready to say for your benefit, "I swear by the Court; I give it up;" and while that is going on he has been getting all his men to swear by the Courts, and to give it up with him. In this again he serves you faithfully, and as I say, more wisely than you serve yourselves.

A WORD ABOUT PATRIOTIC SPEECHES.

Again! I have alluded in the beginning of these remarks to the fact, that Judge Douglas has made great complaint of my having expressed the opinion that this Government "cannot endure permanently half slave and half free." He has complained of Seward for using different language, and declaring that there is an "irrepressible conflict" between the principles of free and slave labor.

(A voice—"He says it is not original with Seward. That is original with Lincoln.")

I will attend to that immediately, sir. Since that time, Hickman, of Pennsylvania expressed the same sentiment. He has never denounced Mr. Hickman: why? There is a little chance, notwithstanding that opinion in the mouth of Hickman, that he may yet be a Douglas man. That is the difference! It is not unpatriotic to hold that opinion, if a man is a Douglas man.

But neither I nor Seward, nor Hickman, is entitled to the enviable or unenviable distinction of having first expressed that idea. That same idea was expressed by the Richmond *Enquirer* in Virginia, in 1856; quite two years before it was expressed by the first of us. And while Douglas was pluming himself, that in his conflict with my humble self, last year, he had "squelched out" that fatal heresy, as he delighted to call it, and had suggested that if he only had had a chance to be in New York and meet Seward he would have "squelched" it there also, it never occurred to him to breathe a word against Pryor. I don't think that you can discover that Douglas ever talked of going to Virginia to "squelch" out that idea there. No. More than that. That same Roger A. Pryor was brought to Washington City and made the editor of the *par excellence* Douglas paper, after making use of that expression, which, in us, is so unpatriotic and heretical. From all this, my Kentucky friends may see that this opinion is heretical in his view only when it is expressed by men suspected of a desire that the country shall all become free and not when expressed by those fairly known to entertain the desire that the whole country shall become slave. When expressed by that class of men, it is in no wise offensive to him. In this again, my friends of Kentucky, you have Judge Douglas with you.

ON GIGANTIC CAPACITY.

There is another reason why you Southern people ought to nominate Douglas at your convention at Charleston. That reason is the wonderful capacity of the man; [laughter] the power he has of doing what would seem to be impossible. Let me call your attention to one of these apparently impossible things.

Douglas had three or four very distinguished men of the most extreme anti-slavery views of any men in the Republican party, expressing their desire for his re-election to the Senate last year. That would, of itself, have seemed to be a little wonderful, but that wonder is heightened when we see that Wise of Virginia, a man exactly opposed to them, a man who believes in the Divine right of slavery, was also expressing his desire that Douglas should be re-elected, that another man that may be said to be kindred to Wise, Mr. Breckinridge, the Vice President, and of your own State, was also agreeing with the anti-slavery men in the North; that Douglas ought to be re-elected. Still, to heighten the wonder, a Senator from Kentucky, whom I have always loved with an affection as tender and endearing as I have ever loved any man; who was opposed to the anti-slavery men for reasons which seemed sufficient to him, and equally opposed to Wise and Breckinridge, was writing letters into Illinois to secure the re-election of Douglas. Now that all these conflicting elements should be brought, while at dagger's points, with one another, to support him, is a feat that is worthy for you to note and consider. It is quite probable, that each of these classes of men thought by the re-election of Douglas, their peculiar views would gain something, it is probable that the antislavery men thought their views would gain something that Wise and Breckinridge thought so too, as regards their opinions, that Mr. Crittenden thought that his views would gain something, although he was opposed to both these other men. It is probable that each and all of them thought that they were using Douglas, and it is yet an unsolved problem whether he was not using them all. If he was, then it is for you to consider whether that power to perform wonders, is one for you lightly to throw away.

AN ALTERNATIVE PROPOSED.

There is one other thing that I will say to you in this relation. It is but my opinion, I give it to you without a fee. It is my opinion that it is for you to take him or be defeated; and that if you do take him you may be beaten. You will surely be beaten if you do not take him. We, the Republicans and others forming the Opposition of the country, intend to "stand by our guns," to be patient and firm, and in the long run to beat you whether you take him or not. [Applause.] We know that before we fairly beat you, we have to beat you both together. We know that you are "all of a feather," [loud applause,] and that we have to beat you altogether, and we expect to do it. [Applause] We don't intend to be very impatient about it. We mean to be as deliberate and calm about it as it is possible to be, but as firm and resolved, as it is possible for men to be. When we do as we say, beat you, you perhaps want to know what we will do with you. [Laughter]

I will tell you, so far as I am authorized to speak for the Opposition, what we mean to do with you. We mean to treat you as near as we possibly can, like Washington, Jefferson and Madison treated you. [Cheers] We mean to leave you alone, and in no way to interfere with your institution; to abide by all and every compromise of the constitution, and, in a word, coming back to the original proposition, to treat you, so far as degenerated men (if we have degenerated) may, according to the examples of those noble fathers—Washington, Jefferson and Madison. [Applause] We mean to remember that you are as good as we; that there is no difference between us other than the difference of circumstances. We mean to recognise and bear in mind always that you have as good hearts in your bosoms as other people, or as we claim to have, and treat you accordingly. We mean to marry your girls when we have a chance—the white ones I mean—[laughter] and I have the honor to inform you that I once did have a chance in that way. [A voice, "Good for you," and applause]

I have told you what we mean to do. I want to know, now, when that thing takes place, what you mean to do. I often hear it intimated that you mean to divide the Union whenever a Republican, or anything like it, is elected President of the United States. [A voice, "That is so."] "That is so," one of them says. I wonder if he is a Kentuckian? [A voice, "He is a Douglas man."] Well, then, I want to know what you are going to do with your half of it? [Applause and laughter] Are you going to split the Ohio down through, and push your half off a piece? Or are you going to keep it right alongside of us outrageous fellows? Or are you going to build up a wall some way between your country and ours, by which that moveable property of yours can't come over here any more, to the danger of your losing it? Do you think you can better yourselves on that subject, by leaving us here under no obligation whatever to return those specimens of your moveable property that come hither? You have divided the Union because we would not do right with you as you think, upon that subject; when we cease to be under obligations to do anything for you, how much better off do you think you will be? Will you make war upon us and kill us all? Why, gentlemen, I think you are as gallant and as brave men as live; that you can fight as bravely in a good cause, man for man, as any other people living; that you have shown yourselves capable of this upon various occasions; but, man for man, you are not better than we are, and there are not so many of you as there are of us. [Loud cheering.] You will never make much of a hand at whipping us. If we were fewer in numbers than you, I think that you could whip us; if we were equal it would likely be a drawn battle; but being inferior in numbers, you will make nothing by attempting to master us.

THE ORDINANCE OF '87.

But perhaps I have addressed myself as long, or longer, to the Kentuckians than I ought to have done inasmuch as I have said that whatever course you take we intend in the end to beat you. I propose to address a few remarks to our friends by way of discussing with them the best means of keeping that promise, that I have in good faith made. [Long continued applause.]

It may appear a little episodical for me to mention the topic of which I shall speak now. It is a favorite proposition of Douglas' that the interference of the General Government, through the Ordinance of '87, or through any other act of the General Government, never has made or ever can make a Free State; that the Ordinance of '87 did not make Free States of Ohio, Indiana or Illinois. That these States are free upon his "great principle" of Popular Sovereignty, because the people of those several States have chosen to make them so. At Columbus, and probably here, he undertook to compliment the people that they themselves have made the State of Ohio free and that the Ordinance of '87 was not entitled in any degree to divide the honor with them. I have no doubt that the people of the State of Ohio did make her free according to their own will and judgment, but let the facts be remembered.

In 1802, I believe, it was you who made your first constitution, with the clause prohibiting slavery, and you did it I suppose very nearly unanimously, but you should bear in mind that you—speaking of you as one people—that you did so unembarrassed by the actual presence of the institution amongst you; that you made it a Free State, not with the embarrassment upon you of already having among you many slaves, which if they had been here, and you had sought to make a Free State, you would not know what to do with. If they had been among you, embarrassing difficulties, most probably, would have induced you to tolerate a slave constitution instead of a free one, as indeed these very difficulties have constrained every people on this continent who have adopted slavery.

Pray what was it that made you free? What kept you free? Did you not find your country free when you came to decide that Ohio should be a Free State? It is important to enquire by what reason you found it so? Let us take an illustration between the States of Ohio and Kentucky. Kentucky is separated by this river Ohio, not a mile wide. A portion of Kentucky, by reason of the course of the Ohio, is further north than this portion of Ohio in which we now stand. Kentucky is entirely covered with slavery—Ohio is entirely free from it.

What made that difference? Was it climate? No! A portion of Kentucky was further north than this portion of Ohio. Was it soil? No! There is nothing in the soil of the one more favorable to slave labor than the other. It was not climate or soil that caused one side of the line to be entirely covered with slavery and the other side free of it. What was it? Study over it. Tell us, if you can, in all the range of conjecture, if there be anything you can conceive of that made that difference, other than that there was no law of any sort keeping it out of Kentucky? while the Ordinance of '87 kept it out of Ohio. If there is any other reason than this, I confess that it is wholly beyond my power to conceive of it. This, then, I offer to combat the idea that that ordinance has never made any State free.

I don't stop at this illustration. I come to the State of Indiana; and what I have said as between Kentucky and Ohio I repeat as between Indiana and Kentucky; it is equally applicable. One additional argument is applicable also to Indiana. In her Territorial condition she more than once petitioned Congress to abrogate the ordinance entirely, or at least so far as to suspend its operation for a time, in order that they should exercise the "Popular Sovereignty" of having slaves if they wanted them. The men then controlling the General Government, imitating the men of the Revolution, refused Indiana that privilege. And so we have the evidence that Indiana supposed she could have slaves, if it were not for that ordinance that she besought Congress to put that barrier out of the way; that Congress refused to do so, and it all ended at last in Indiana being a Free State. Tell me not, then, that the Ordinance of '87 had nothing to do with making Indiana a free state, when we find some men chafing against and only restrained by that barrier.

Come down again to our State of Illinois. The great Northwest Territory including Ohio, Indiana, Illinois, Michigan and Wisconsin, was acquired, first I believe by the British Government, in part at least, from the French. Before the establishment of our independence, it became a part of Virginia, enabling Virginia afterwards to transfer it to the general government. There were French settlements in what is now Illinois, and at the same time there were French settlements in what is now Missouri—in the tract of country that was not purchased till about 1803. In these French settlements negro slavery had existed for many years—perhaps more than a hundred, if not as much as two hundred years—at Kaskaskia in Illinois, and at St. Genevieve, or Cape Girardeau, perhaps, in Missouri. The number of slaves was not very great, but there was about the same number in each place. They were there when we acquired the Territory. There was no effort made to break up the relation of master and slave and even the Ordinance of 1787 was not so enforced as to destroy that slavery in Illinois; nor did the Ordinance apply to Missouri at all.

What I want to ask your attention to, at this point, is that Illinois and Missouri came into the Union about the same time, Illinois in the latter part of 1818, and Missouri, after a struggle, I believe some time in 1820. They had been filling up with American people about the same period of time; their progress enabling them to come into the Union at about the same time. At the end of that ten years, in which they had been so preparing, (for it was about that period of time) the number of slaves in Illinois had actually decreased; while in Missouri, beginning with very few, at the end of that ten years, there were about ten thousand. This being so, and it being remembered that Missouri and Illinois are, to a certain extent, in the same parallel of latitude—that the Northern half of Missouri and the Southern half of Illinois are in the same parallel of latitude—so that climate would have the same effect upon one as upon the other, and that in the soil there is no material difference so far as bears upon the question of slavery being settled upon one or the other—there being none of those natural causes to produce a difference in filling them, and yet there being a broad difference in their filling up, we are led again to inquire what was the cause of that difference.

It is most natural to say that in Missouri there was no law to keep that country from filling up with slaves, while in Illinois there was the Ordinance of '87. The Ordinance being there, slavery decreased during that ten years—the Ordinance not being in the other, it increased from a few to ten thousand. Can anybody doubt the reason of the difference?

I think all these facts most abundantly prove that my friend Judge Douglas' proposition, that the Ordinance of '87 or the national restriction of slavery, never had a tendency to make a Free State, is a fallacy—a proposition without the shadow or substance of truth about it.

POPULAR SOVEREIGNTY CAUSING FREEDOM.

Douglas sometimes says that all the States (and it is part of this same proposition I have been discussing) that have become free, have become so upon his "great principle"—that the State of Illinois itself came into the Union as a slave State, and that the people upon the "great principle" of Popular Sovereignty have since made it a Free State. Allow me but a little while to state to you what facts there are to justify him in saying that Illinois came into the Union as a Slave State.

I have mentioned to you that there were a few old French slaves there. They numbered, I think, one or two hundred. Besides that there had been a Territorial law for indenturing black persons. Under that law, in violation of the Ordinance of '87, but without any enforcement of the Ordinance to overthrow the system, there had been a small number of slaves introduced as indentured persons. Owing to this the clause for the prohibition of slavery, was slightly modified. Instead of running like yours, that neither slavery nor involuntary servitude, except for crime of which the party shall have been duly convicted, should exist in the State, they said that neither slavery nor involuntary servitude should thereafter be introduced, and that the children of indentured servants should be born free; and nothing was said about the few old French slaves. Out of this fact, that the clause for prohibiting slavery was modified because of the actual presence of it, Douglas asserts again and again that Illinois came into the Union as a Slave State. How far the facts sustain the conclusion that he draws, it is for intelligent and impartial men to decide. I leave it with you with these remarks, worthy of being remembered, that that little thing, those few indentured servants being there, was of itself sufficient to modify a Constitution made by a people ardently desiring to have a free Constitution; showing the power of the actual presence of the institution of slavery to prevent any people, however anxious to make a Free State, from making it perfectly so.

I have been detaining you longer perhaps than I ought to do. [Long and repeated cries of "go on."]

COMPARISONS.

I am in some doubt whether to introduce another topic upon which I could talk awhile. [Cries of "Go on," and "Give us it."] It is this then. Douglas' Popular Sovereignty as a principle, is simply this: If one man chooses to make a slave of another man, neither that other man or anybody else has a right to object. [Cheers and laughter.] Apply it to government, as he seeks to apply it and it is this—if, in a new Territory, into which a few people are beginning to enter for the purpose of making their homes, they choose to either exclude slavery from their limits, or to establish it there, however one or the other may affect the persons to be enslaved, or the infinitely greater number of persons who are afterwards to inhabit that Territory, or the other members of the family of communities, of which they are but an incipient member, or the general head of the family of states as parent of all—however their action may affect one or the other of these, there is no power or right to interfere. That is Douglas' Popular sovereignty applied. Now I think that there is a real popular sovereignty in the world. I think a definition of popular sovereignty, in the abstract, would be about this—that each man shall do precisely as he pleases with himself, and with all those things which exclusively concern him. Applied in government, this principle would be, that a general government shall do all those things which pertain to it, and all the local governments shall do precisely as they please in respect to those matters which exclusively concern them.

Douglas looks upon slavery as so insignificant that the people must decide that question for themselves, and yet they are not fit to decide who shall be their Governor, Judge or secretary, or who shall be any of their officers. These are vast national matters in his estimation but the little matter in his estimation, is that of planting slavery there. That is purely of local interest, which nobody should be allowed to say a word about. [Applause.]

Labor is the great source from which nearly all, if not all, human comforts and necessities are drawn. There is a difference in opinion about the elements of labor in society. Some men assume that there is a necessary connection between capital and labor, and that connection draws within it the whole of the labor of the community. They assume that nobody works unless capital excites them to work. They begin next to consider what is the best way. They say that there are but two ways; one is to hire men and to allure them to labor by their consent; the other is to buy the men and drive them to it, and that is slavery. Having assumed that, they proceed to discuss the question of whether the laborers themselves are better off in the condition of slaves or of hired laborers, and they usually decide that they are better off in the condition of slaves.

In the first place, I say, that the whole thing is a mistake. That there is a certain relation between capital and labor, I admit. That it does exist, and rightfully exists, I think is true. That men who are industrious, and sober, and honest in the pursuit of their own interests should after a while accumulate capital, and after that should be allowed to enjoy it in peace, and also if they should choose when they have accumulated it to use it to save themselves from actual labor and hire other people to labor for them is right. In doing so they do not wrong the man they employ, for they find men who have not of their own land to work upon, or shops to work in, and who are benefited by working for others, hired laborers, receiving their capital for it. Thus a few men that own capital, hire a few others, and these establish the relation of capital and labor rightfully. A relation of which I make no complaint. But I insist that that relation after all does not embrace more than one-eighth of the labor of the country. At least seven-eighths of the labor is done without relation to it.

Take the State of Ohio. Out of eight bushels of wheat, seven are raised by those men who labor for themselves, aided by their boys growing to manhood, neither being hired nor hiring, but literally laboring upon their own hook, asking no favor of capital, of hired laborer, or of the slave. That is the true condition of the larger portion of all the labor done in this community, or that should be the condition of labor in well-regulated communities of agriculturists. Thus much for that part of the subject.

Again: the assumption that the slave is in a better condition than the hired laborer, includes the further assumption that he who is once a hired laborer always remains a hired laborer; that there is a certain class of men who remain through life in a dependent condition. Then they endeavor to point out that when they get old they have no kind masters to take care of them, and that they fall dead in the traces, with the harness of actual labor upon their feeble backs. In point of fact that is a false assumption. There is no such thing as a man who is a hired laborer, of a necessity, always remaining in his early condition. The general rule is otherwise. I know it is so, and I will tell you why. When at an early age, I was myself a hired laborer, at twelve dollars per month; and therefore I do know that there is not always the necessity for actual labor because once there was propriety in being so. My understanding of the hired laborer is this: A young man finds himself of an age to be dismissed from parental control; he has for his capital nothing save two strong hands that God has given him, a heart willing to labor, and a freedom to choose the mode of his work and the manner of his employer; he has got no soil nor shop, and he avails himself of the opportunity of hiring himself to some man who has capital to pay him a fair day's wages for a fair day's work. He is benefited by availing himself of that privilege. He works industriously, he behaves soberly, and the result of a year or two's labor is a surplus capital. Now he buys land on his own hook; he settles, marries, begets sons and daughters, and in course of time he too has enough capital to hire some new beginner.

In this same way every member of the whole community benefits and improves his condition. That is the true condition of labor in the world, and it breaks up the saying of these men that there is a class of men chained down throughout life to labor for another. There is no such case unless he be of that confiding and leaning disposition that makes it preferable for him to choose that course, or unless he be a vicious man, who, by reason of his vice, is, in some way prevented from improving his condition, or else he be a singularly unfortunate man. There is no such thing as a man being bound down in a free country through his life as a laborer. This progress by which the poor, honest, industrious, and resolute man raises himself, that he may work on his own account, and hire somebody else, is that progress that human nature is entitled to, is that improvement in condition that is intended to be secured by those institutions under which we live, is the great principle for which this government was really formed. Our government was not established that one man might do with himself as he pleases, and with another man too.

I hold that if there is any one thing that can be proved to be the will of God by external nature around us, without reference to revelation, it is the proposition that whatever any one man earns with his hands and by the sweat of his brow, he shall enjoy in peace. I say that whereas God Almighty has given every man one mouth to be fed, and one pair of hands adapted to furnish food for that mouth, if anything can be proved to be the will of Heaven, it is proved by this fact, that that mouth is to be fed by those hands, without being interfered with by any other man who has also his mouth to feed and his hands to labor with. I hold if the Almighty had ever made a set of men that should do all the eating and none of the work, he would have made them with mouths only and no hands, and if he had ever made another class that he had intended should do all the work and none of the eating, he would have made them without mouths and with all hands. But inasmuch as he has not chosen to make man in that way, if anything is proved, it is that those hands and mouths are to be co-operative through life and not to be interfered with. That they are to go forth and improve their condition as I have been trying to illustrate, is the inherent right given to mankind directly by the Maker.

In the exercise of this right you must have room. In the filling up of countries, it turns out after a while that we get so thick that we have not quite room enough for the exercise of that right, and we desire to go somewhere else. Where shall we go to? Where shall you go to escape from over-population and competition? To those new territories which belong to us, which are God-given for that purpose. If, then, you will go to those territories that you may improve your condition, you have a right to keep them in the best condition for those going into them, and can they make that natural advance in their condition if they find the institution of slavery planted there?

My good friends, let me ask you a question—you who have come from Virginia or Kentucky, to get rid of this thing of slavery—let me ask you what headway would you have made in getting rid of it, if by popular sovereignty you find slavery on that soil which you looked for to be free when you get there? You would not have made much headway if you had found slavery already here, if you had to sit down to your labor by the side of the unpaid workman.

I say, then, that it is due to yourselves as voters, as owners of the new territories, that you shall keep those territories free, in the best condition for all such of your gallant sons as may choose to go there.

I do not desire to elaborate this branch of the general subject of political discussion at this time further. I did not think I would get upon this topic at all, and I have detained you already too long in its discussion.

HOW TO WIN THE FIGHT.

I have taken upon myself in the name of some of you to say, that we expect upon these principles to ultimately beat them. In order to do so, I think we want and must have a national policy in regard to the institution of slavery, that acknowledges and deals with that institution as being wrong. (Loud cheering) Whoever desires the prevention of the spread of slavery and the nationalization of that institution, yields all, when he yields to any policy that either recognizes slavery as being right, or as being an indifferent thing. Nothing will make you successful but setting up a policy which shall treat the thing as being wrong. When I say this, I do not mean to say that this general government is charged with the duty of redressing or preventing all the wrongs in the world; but I do think that it is charged with the duty of preventing and redressing all wrongs which are wrongs to itself. This government is expressly charged with the duty of providing for the general welfare. We believe that the spreading out and perpetuity of the institution of slavery impairs the general welfare. We believe—nay, we know, that that is the only thing that has ever threatened the perpetuity of the Union itself. The only thing which has ever menaced the destruction of the government under which we live, is this very thing. To repress this thing, we think is providing for the general welfare. Our friends in Kentucky differ from us. We need not make our argument for them, but we who think it is wrong in all its relations, or in some of them at least, must decide as to our own actions, and our own course, upon our own judgment.

I say that we must not interfere with the institution of slavery in the states where it exists, because the constitution forbids it, and the general welfare does not require us to do so. We must not withhold an efficient fugitive slave law because the constitution requires us, as I understand it, not to withhold such a law. But we must prevent the outspreading of the institution, because neither the constitution nor general welfare requires us to extend it. We must prevent the revival of the African slave trade and the enacting by Congress of a territorial slave code. We must prevent each of these things being done by either Congresses or courts. The people of these United States are the rightful masters of both Congresses and courts (Applause) not to overthrow the constitution, but to overthrow the men who pervert that constitution. (Applause.)

To do these things we must employ instrumentalities. We must hold conventions; we must adopt platforms if we conform to ordinary custom; we must nominate candidates, and we must carry elections. In all these things, I think that we ought to keep in view our real purpose, and in none do anything that stands adverse to our purpose. If we shall adopt a platform that fails to recognize or express our purpose, or elect a man that declares himself inimical to our purpose, we not only take nothing by our success, but we tacitly admit that we act upon no other principle than a desire to have "the loaves and fishes," by which, in the end our apparent success is really an injury to us.

I know that it is very desirable with me, as with everybody else, that all the elements of the Opposition shall unite in the next Presidential election and in all future time. I am anxious that that should be, but there are things seriously to be considered in relation to that matter. If the terms can be arranged, I am in favor of the Union. But suppose we shall take up some man and put him upon one end or the other of the ticket, who declares himself against us in regard to the prevention of the spread of slavery—who turns up his nose and says he is tired of hearing anything about it, who is more against us than against the enemy, what will be the issue? Why he will get no slave states after all—he has tried that already until being beat is the rule for him. If we nominate him upon that ground, he will not carry a slave state; and not only so, but that portion of our men who are high strung upon the principle we really fight for, will not go for him, and he won't get a single electoral vote anywhere, except, perhaps, in the state of Maryland. There is no use in saying to us that we are stubborn and obstinate, because we won't do some such thing as this. We cannot do it. We cannot get our men to vote it. I speak by the card, that we cannot give the state of Illinois in such case by fifty thousand. We would be flatter down than the "Negro Democracy" themselves have the heart to wish to see us.

After saying this much, let me say a little on the other side. There are plenty of men in the slave states that are altogether good enough for me to be either President or Vice President, provided they will profess their sympathy with our purpose, and will place themselves on the ground that our men, upon principle, can vote for them. There are scores of them, good men in their character for intelligence and talent and integrity. If such a one will place himself upon the right ground I am for his occupying one place upon the next Republican or Opposition ticket. [Applause] I will heartily go for him. But, unless he does so place himself, I think it a matter of perfect nonsense to attempt to bring about a union upon any other basis; that if a union be made, the elements will scatter so that there can be no success for such a ticket, nor anything like success. The good old maxims of the Bible are applicable, and truly applicable to human affairs, and in this as in other things, we may say here that he who is not for us is against us; he who gathereth not with us scattereth. [Applause] I should be glad to have some of the many good, and able, and noble men of the south to place themselves where we can confer upon them the high honor of an election upon one or the other end of our ticket. It would do my soul good to do that thing. It would enable us to teach them that inasmuch as we select one of their own number to carry out our principles, we are free from the charge that we mean more than we say.

But, my friends I have detained you much longer than I expected to do. I believe I may do myself the compliment to say that you have stayed and heard me with great patience, for which I return you my most sincere thanks.

September 17, 1859

Address to the Wisconsin State
Agricultural Society, Milwaukee, Wisconsin

Members of the Agricultural Society and Citizens of Wisconsin:

Agricultural Fairs are becoming an institution of the country; they are useful in more ways than one; they bring us together, and thereby make us better acquainted, and better friends than we otherwise would be. From the first appearance of man upon the earth, down to very recent times, the words *"stranger"* and *"enemy"* were *quite* or *almost*, synonymous. Long after civilized nations had defined robbery and murder as high crimes, and had affixed severe punishments to them, when practiced among and upon their own people respectively, it was deemed no offence, but even meritorious, to rob, and murder, and enslave *strangers*, whether as nations or as individuals. Even yet, this has not totally disappeared. The man of the highest moral cultivation, in spite of all which abstract principle can do, likes him whom he *does* know, much better than him whom he does *not* know. To correct the evils, great and small, which spring from want of sympathy, and from positive enmity, among *strangers*, as nations, or as individuals, is one of the highest functions of civilization. To this end our Agricultural Fairs contribute in no small degree. They make more pleasant, and more strong, and more durable, the bond of social and political union among us. Again, if, as Pope declares, "happiness is our being's end and aim," our Fairs contribute much to that end and aim, as occasions of recreation—as holidays. Constituted as man is, he has positive need of occasional recreation; and whatever can give him this, associated with virtue and advantage, and free from vice and disadvantage, is a positive good. Such recreation our Fairs afford. They are a present pleasure, to be followed by no pain, as a consequence; they are a present pleasure, making the future more pleasant.

But the chief use of agricultural fairs is to aid in improving the great calling of *agriculture*, in all it's departments, and minute divisions—to make mutual exchange of agricultural discovery, information, and knowledge; so that, at the end, *all* may know every thing, which may have been known to but *one*, or to but a *few*, at the beginning—to bring together especially all which is supposed to not be generally known, because of recent discovery, or invention.

And not only to bring together, and to impart all which has been *accidentally* discovered or invented upon ordinary motive; but, by exciting emulation, for premiums, and for the pride and honor of success—of triumph, in some sort—to stimulate that discovery and invention into extraordinary activity. In this, these Fairs are kindred to the patent clause in the Constitution of the United States; and to the department, and practical system, based upon that clause.

One feature, I believe, of every fair, is a regular *address*. The Agricultural Society of the young, prosperous, and soon to be, great State of Wisconsin, has done me the high honor of selecting me to make that address upon this occasion—an honor for which I make my profound, and grateful acknowledgement.

I presume I am not expected to employ the time assigned me, in the mere flattery of the farmers, as a class. My opinion of them is that, in proportion to numbers, they are neither better nor worse than other people. In the nature of things they are more numerous than any other class; and I believe there really are more attempts at flattering them than any other; the reason of which I cannot perceive, unless it be that they can cast more votes than any other. On reflection, I am not quite sure that there is not cause of suspicion against you, in selecting me, in some sort a politician, and in no sort a farmer, to address you.

But farmers, being the most numerous class, it follows that their interest is the largest interest. It also follows that that interest is most worthy of all to be cherished and cultivated— that if there be inevitable conflict between that interest and any other, that other should yield.

Again, I suppose it is not expected of me to impart to you much specific information on Agriculture. You have no reason to believe, and do not believe, that I possess it—if that were what you seek in this address, any one of your own number, or class, would be more able to furnish it.

You, perhaps, do expect me to give some general interest to the occasion; and to make some general suggestions, on practical matters. I shall attempt nothing more. And in such suggestions by me, quite likely very little will be new to you, and a large part of the rest possibly already known to be erroneous.

My first suggestion is an inquiry as to the effect of greater *thoroughness* in all the departments of Agriculture than now prevails in the North-West—perhaps I might say in America. To speak entirely within bounds, it is known that fifty bushels of wheat, or one hundred bushels of Indian corn can be produced from an acre. Less than a year ago I saw it stated that a man, by extraordinary care and labor, had produced of wheat, what was equal to two hundred bushels from an acre. But take fifty of wheat, and one hundred of corn, to be the *possibility*, and compare with it the actual crops of the country. Many years ago I saw it stated in a Patent Office Report that eighteen bushels was the average crop throughout the wheat growing region of the United States; and this year an intelligent farmer of Illinois, assured me that he did not believe the land harvested in that State this season, had yielded more than an average of eight bushels to the acre. The brag crop I heard of in our vicinity was two thousand bushels from ninety acres. Many crops were thrashed, producing no more than three bushels to the acre; much was cut, and then abandoned as not worth threshing; and much was abandoned as not worth cutting. As to Indian corn, and, indeed, most other crops, the case has not been much better. For the last four years I do not believe the ground planted with corn in Illinois, has produced an average of twenty bushels to the acre. It is true, that heretofore we have had better crops, with no better cultivators; but I believe it is also true that the soil has never been pushed up to one-half of its capacity.

What would be the effect upon the farming interest, to push the soil up to something near its full capacity? Unquestionably it will take more labor to produce *fifty* bushels from an acre, than it will to produce *ten* bushels from the same acre. But will it take more labor to produce fifty bushels from *one* acre, than from *five*? Unquestionably, thorough cultivation will require more labor to the *acre*; but will it require more to the *bushel*? If it should require just as *much* to the bushel, there are some *probable*, and several *certain*, advantages in favor of the thorough practice. It is probable it would develope those unknown causes, or develope unknown cures for those causes, which of late years have cut down our crops below their former average. It is almost certain, I think, that in the deeper plowing, analysis of soils, experiments with manures, and varieties of seeds, observance of seasons, and the like, these cases would be found. It is certain that thorough cultivation would spare half or more than half, the cost of land, simply because the same product would be got from half, or from less than half the quantity of land. This proposition is self-evident, and can be made no plainer by repetitions or illustrations. The cost of land is a great item, even in new countries; and constantly grows greater and greater, in comparison with other items, as the country grows older.

It also would spare a large proportion of the making and maintaining of inclosures—the same, whether these inclosures should be hedges, ditches, or fences. This again, is a heavy item—heavy at first, and heavy in its continual demand for repairs. I remember once being greatly astonished by an apparently authentic exhibition of the proportion the cost of inclosures bears to all the other expenses of the farmer; though I can not remember exactly what that proportion was. Any farmer, if he will, can ascertain it in his own case, for himself.

Again, a great amount of "locomotion" is spared by thorough cultivation. Take fifty bushels of wheat, ready for the harvest, standing upon a *single* acre, and it can be harvested in any of the known ways, with less than half the labor which would be required if it were spread over *five* acres. This would be true, if cut by the old hand sickle; true, to a greater extent if by the scythe and cradle; and to a still greater extent, if by the machines now in use. These machines are chiefly valuable, as a means of substituting animal power for the power of men in this branch of farm work. In the highest degree of perfection yet reached in applying the horse power to harvesting, fully nine-tenths of the power is expended by the animal in carrying himself and dragging the machine over the field, leaving certainly not more than one-tenth to be applied directly to the only end of the whole operation—the gathering in the grain, and clipping of the straw. When grain is very thin on the ground, it is always more or less intermingled with weeds, chess and the like, and a large part of the power is expended in cutting these. It is plain that when the crop is very thick upon the ground, the larger proportion of the power is directly applied to gathering in and cutting it; and the smaller, to that which is totally useless as an end. And what I have said of harvesting is true, in a greater or less degree of mowing, plowing, gathering in of crops generally, and, indeed, of almost all farm work.

The effect of thorough cultivation upon the farmer's own mind, and, in reaction through his mind, back upon his business, is perhaps quite equal to any other of its effects. Every man is proud of what he does *well*; and no man is proud of what he does *not* do well. With the former, his heart is in his work; and he will do twice as much of it with less fatigue. The latter performs a little imperfectly, looks at it in disgust, turns from it, and imagines himself exceedingly tired. The little he has done, comes to nothing, for want of finishing.

The man who produces a good full crop will scarcely ever let any part of it go to waste. He will keep up the enclosure about it, and allow neither man nor beast to trespass upon it. He will gather it in due season and store it in perfect security. Thus he labors with satisfaction, and saves himself the whole fruit of his labor. The other, starting with no purpose for a full crop, labors less, and with less satisfaction; allows his fences to fall, and cattle to trespass; gathers not in due season, or not at all. Thus the labor he has performed, is wasted away, little by little, till in the end, he derives scarcely anything from it.

The ambition for broad acres leads to poor farming, even with men of energy. I scarcely ever knew a mammoth farm to sustain itself; much less to return a profit upon the outlay. I have more than once known a man to spend a respectable fortune upon one; fail and leave it; and then some man of more modest aims, get a small fraction of the ground, and make a good living upon it. Mammoth farms are like tools or weapons, which are too heavy to be handled. Ere long they are thrown aside, at a great loss.

The successful application of *steam power*, to farm work is a *desideratum*—especially a Steam Plow. It is not enough, that

a machine operated by steam, will really plow. To be successful, it must, all things considered, plow *better* than can be
done with animal power. It must do all the work as well, and
cheaper; or more *rapidly*, so as to get through more perfectly
in season; or in some way afford an advantage over plowing
with animals, else it is no success. I have never seen a machine
intended for a Steam Plow. Much praise, and admiration, are
bestowed upon some of them; and they may be, for aught I
know, already successful; but I have not perceived the demonstration of it. I have thought a good deal, in an abstract way,
about a Steam Plow. That one which shall be so contrived as
to apply the larger proportion of its power to the cutting and
turning the soil, and the smallest, to the moving itself over
the field, will be the best one. A very small stationary engine
would draw a large gang of plows through the ground from a
short distance to itself; but when it is not stationary, but has
to move along like a horse, dragging the plows after it, it
must have additional power to carry itself; and the difficulty
grows by what is intended to overcome it; for what adds
power also adds size, and weight to the machine, thus increasing again, the demand for power. Suppose you should construct the machine so as to cut a succession of short furrows,
say a rod in length, transversely to the course the machine is
locomoting, something like the shuttle in weaving. In such
case the whole machine would move North only the width of
a furrow, while in length, the furrow would be a rod from
East to West. In such case, a very large proportion of the
power, would be applied to the actual plowing. But in this,
too, there would be a difficulty, which would be the getting
of the plow *into*, and *out of*, the ground, at the ends of all
these short furrows.

I believe, however, ingenious men will, if they have not
already, overcome the difficulty I have suggested. But there is
still another, about which I am less sanguine. It is the supply
of *fuel*, and especially of *water*, to make steam. Such supply is
clearly practicable, but can the expense of it be borne? Steam-
boats live upon the water, and find their fuel at stated places.
Steam mills, and other stationary steam machinery, have their
stationary supplies of fuel and water. Railroad locomotives
have their regular wood and water station. But the steam

plow is less fortunate. It does not live upon the water; and if it be once at a water station, it will work away from it, and when it gets away can not return, without leaving its work, at a great expense of its time and strength. It will occur that a wagon and horse team might be employed to supply it with fuel and water; but this, too, is expensive; and the question recurs, "can the expense be borne?" When this is added to all other expenses, will not the plowing cost more than in the old way?

It is to be hoped that the steam plow will be finally successful, and if it shall be, *"thorough cultivation"*—putting the soil to the top of its capacity—producing the largest crop possible from a given quantity of ground—will be most favorable to it. Doing a large amount of work upon a small quantity of ground, it will be, as nearly as possible, stationary while working, and as free as possible from locomotion; thus expending its strength as much as possible upon its work, and as little as possible in travelling. Our thanks, and something more substantial than thanks, are due to every man engaged in the effort to produce a successful steam plow. Even the unsuccessful will bring something to light, which, in the hands of others, will contribute to the final success. I have not pointed out difficulties, in order to discourage, but in order that being seen, they may be the more readily overcome.

The world is agreed that *labor* is the source from which human wants are mainly supplied. There is no dispute upon this point. From this point, however, men immediately diverge. Much disputation is maintained as to the best way of applying and controlling the labor element. By some it is assumed that labor is available only in connection with capital—that nobody labors, unless somebody else, owning capital, somehow, by the use of that capital, induces him to do it. Having assumed this, they proceed to consider whether it is best that capital shall *hire* laborers, and thus induce them to work by their own consent; or *buy* them, and drive them to it without their consent. Having proceeded so far they naturally conclude that all laborers are necessarily either *hired* laborers, or *slaves*. They further assume that whoever is once a *hired* laborer, is fatally fixed in that condition for life; and thence again that his condition is as bad as, or worse than that of a slave. This is the *"mud-sill"* theory.

But another class of reasoners hold the opinion that there is no *such* relation between capital and labor, as assumed; and that there is no such thing as a freeman being fatally fixed for life, in the condition of a hired laborer, that both these assumptions are false, and all inferences from them groundless. They hold that labor is prior to, and independent of, capital; that, in fact, capital is the fruit of labor, and could never have existed if labor had not *first* existed—that labor can exist without capital, but that capital could never have existed without labor. Hence they hold that labor is the superior—greatly the superior—of capital.

They do not deny that there is, and probably always will be, *a* relation between labor and capital. The error, as they hold, is in assuming that the *whole* labor of the world exists within that relation. A few men own capital; and that few avoid labor themselves, and with their capital, hire, or buy, another few to labor for them. A large majority belong to neither class—neither work for others, nor have others working for them. Even in all our slave States, except South Carolina, a majority of the whole people of all colors, are neither slaves nor masters. In these Free States, a large majority are neither *hirers* nor *hired*. Men, with their families—wives, sons and daughters—work for themselves, on their farms, in their houses and in their shops, taking the whole product to themselves, and asking no favors of capital on the one hand, nor of hirelings or slaves on the other. It is not forgotten that a considerable number of persons mingle their own labor with capital; that is, labor with their own hands, and also buy slaves or hire freemen to labor for them; but this is only a *mixed*, and not a *distinct* class. No principle stated is disturbed by the existence of this mixed class. Again, as has already been said, the opponents of the *"mud-sill"* theory insist that there is not, of necessity, any such thing as the free hired laborer being fixed to that condition for life. There is demonstration for saying this. Many independent men, in this assembly, doubtless a few years ago were hired laborers. And their case is almost if not quite the general rule.

The prudent, penniless beginner in the world, labors for

wages awhile, saves a surplus with which to buy tools or land, for himself; then labors on his own account another while, and at length hires another new beginner to help him. This, say its advocates, is *free* labor—the just and generous, and prosperous system, which opens the way for all—gives hope to all, and energy, and progress, and improvement of condition to all. If any continue through life in the condition of the hired laborer, it is not the fault of the system, but because of either a dependent nature which prefers it, or improvidence, folly, or singular misfortune. I have said this much about the elements of labor generally, as introductory to the consideration of a new phase which that element is in process of assuming. The old general rule was that *educated* people did not perform manual labor. They managed to eat their bread, leaving the toil of producing it to the uneducated. This was not an insupportable evil to the working bees, so long as the class of drones remained very small. But *now*, especially in these free States, nearly all are educated—quite too nearly all, to leave the labor of the uneducated, in any wise adequate to the support of the whole. It follows from this that henceforth educated people must labor. Otherwise, education itself would become a positive and intolerable evil. No country can sustain, in idleness, more than a small per centage of its numbers. The great majority must labor at something productive. From these premises the problem springs, "How can *labor* and *education* be the most satisfactorily combined?"

By the *"mud-sill"* theory it is assumed that labor and education are incompatible; and any practical combination of them impossible. According to that theory, a blind horse upon a tread-mill, is a perfect illustration of what a laborer should be—all the better for being blind, that he could not tread out of place, or kick understandingly. According to that theory, the education of laborers, is not only useless, but pernicious, and dangerous. In fact, it is, in some sort, deemed a misfortune that laborers should have heads at all. Those same heads are regarded as explosive materials, only to be safely kept in damp places, as far as possible from that peculiar sort of fire which ignites them. A Yankee who could invent a strong *handed* man without a head would receive the everlasting gratitude of the "mud-sill" advocates.

But Free Labor says "no!" Free Labor argues that, as the Author of man makes every individual with one head and one pair of hands, it was probably intended that heads and hands should cooperate as friends; and that that particular head, should direct and control that particular pair of hands. As each man has one mouth to be fed, and one pair of hands to furnish food, it was probably intended that that particular pair of hands should feed that particular mouth— that each head is the natural guardian, director, and protector of the hands and mouth inseparably connected with it; and that being so, every head should be cultivated, and improved, by whatever will add to its capacity for performing its charge. In one word Free Labor insists on universal education.

I have so far stated the opposite theories of *"Mud-Sill"* and *"Free Labor"* without declaring any preference of my own between them. On an occasion like this I ought not to declare any. I suppose, however, I shall not be mistaken, in assuming as a fact, that the people of Wisconsin prefer free labor, with its natural companion, education.

This leads to the further reflection, that no other human occupation opens so wide a field for the profitable and agreeable combination of labor with cultivated thought, as agriculture. I know of nothing so pleasant to the mind, as the discovery of anything which is at once *new* and *valuable*— nothing which so lightens and sweetens toil, as the hopeful pursuit of such discovery. And how vast, and how varied a field is agriculture, for such discovery. The mind, already trained to thought, in the country school, or higher school, cannot fail to find there an exhaustless source of profitable enjoyment. Every blade of grass is a study; and to produce two, where there was but one, is both a profit and a pleasure. And not grass alone; but soils, seeds, and seasons—hedges, ditches, and fences, draining, droughts, and irrigation— plowing, hoeing, and harrowing—reaping, mowing, and threshing—saving crops, pests of crops, diseases of crops, and what will prevent or cure them—implements, utensils, and machines, their relative merits, and how to improve them—hogs, horses, and cattle—sheep, goats, and poultry— trees, shrubs, fruits, plants, and flowers—the thousand things of which these are specimens—each a world of study within itself.

In all this, book-learning is available. A capacity, and taste, for reading, gives access to whatever has already been discovered by others. It is the key, or one of the keys, to the already solved problems. And not only so. It gives a relish, and facility, for successfully pursuing the yet unsolved ones. The rudiments of science, are available, and highly valuable. Some knowledge of Botany assists in dealing with the vegetable world—with all growing crops. Chemistry assists in the analysis of soils, selection, and application of manures, and in numerous other ways. The mechanical branches of Natural Philosophy, are ready help in almost everything; but especially in reference to implements and machinery.

The thought recurs that education—cultivated thought—can best be combined with agricultural labor, or any labor, on the principle of *thorough* work—that careless, half performed, slovenly work, makes no place for such combination. And thorough work, again, renders sufficient, the smallest quantity of ground to each man. And this again, conforms to what must occur in a world less inclined to wars, and more devoted to the arts of peace, than heretofore. Population must increase rapidly—more rapidly than in former times—and ere long the most valuable of all arts, will be the art of deriving a comfortable subsistence from the smallest area of soil. No community whose every member possesses this art, can ever be the victim of oppression in any of its forms. Such community will be alike independent of crowned-kings, money-kings, and land-kings.

But, according to your programme, the awarding of premiums awaits the closing of this address. Considering the deep interest necessarily pertaining to that performance, it would be no wonder if I am already heard with some impatience. I will detain you but a moment longer. Some of you will be successful, and such will need but little philosophy to take them home in cheerful spirits; others will be disappointed, and will be in a less happy mood. To such, let it be said, "Lay it not too much to heart." Let them adopt the maxim, "Better luck next time;" and then, by renewed exertion, make that better luck for themselves.

And by the successful, and the unsuccessful, let it be remembered, that while occasions like the present, bring their sober and durable benefits, the exultations and mortifications of them, are but temporary; that the victor shall soon be the vanquished, if he relax in his exertion; and that the vanquished this year, may be victor the next, in spite of all competition.

It is said an Eastern monarch once charged his wise men to invent him a sentence, to be ever in view, and which should be true and appropriate in all times and situations. They presented him the words: *"And this, too, shall pass away."* How much it expresses! How chastening in the hour of pride!— how consoling in the depths of affliction! "And this, too, shall pass away." And yet let us hope it is not *quite* true. Let us hope, rather, that by the best cultivation of the physical world, beneath and around us; and the intellectual and moral world within us, we shall secure an individual, social, and political prosperity and happiness, whose course shall be onward and upward, and which, while the earth endures, shall not pass away.

September 30, 1859

To William E. Frazer

W. E. Frazer, Esq   Springfield, Ills.
Dear Sir: Nov. 1. 1859
Yours of the 24th. ult. was forwarded to me from Chicago. It certainly is important to secure Pennsylvania for the Republicans, in the next Presidential contest; and not unimportant to, also, secure Illinois. As to the ticket you name, I shall be heartily for it, *after* it shall have been fairly nominated by a Republican national convention; and I can not be committed to it *before.* For my single self, I have enlisted for the permanent success of the Republican cause; and, for this object, I shall labor faithfully in the ranks, unless, as I think not probable, the judgment of the party shall assign me a different position. If the Republicans of the great State of Pennsylvania, shall present Mr. Cameron as their candidate for the

Presidency, such an indorsement of his fitness for the place, could scarcely be deemed insufficient. Still, as I would not like the *public* to know, so I would not like *myself* to know I had entered a combination with any man, to the prejudice of all others whose friends respectively may consider them preferable   Yours truly

To William Kellogg

Hon: William Kellogg.   Springfield, Ills.
My dear Sir: Dec. 11. 1859
    I have been a good deal relieved this morning by a sight of Greeley's letter to you, published in the Tribune. Before seeing it, I much feared you had, in charging interviews between Douglas & Greely, stated what you *believed*, but did not certainly *know* to be true; and that it might be untrue, and our enemies would get an advantage of you. However, as G. admits the interviews, I think it will not hurt you that he denies conversing with D. about his re-election to the Senate. G. I think, will not tell a falsehood; and I think he will scarcely deny that he had the interviews with D. in order to assure himself from D's own lips, better than he could from his public acts & declarations, whether to try to bring the Republican party to his support generally, including his re-election to the Senate. What else could the interviews be for? Why immediately followed in the Tribune the advice that all anti-Lecompton democrats should be re-elected? The world will not consider it any thing that D's reelection to the Senate was not specifically talked of by him & G.
    Now, mark, I do not charge that G. was corrupt in this. I do not think he was, or is. It was his judgment that the course he took was the best way of serving the Republican cause. For this reason, and for the further reason, that he is now pulling straight with us, I think, if I were you, I would not pursue him further than necessary to my own justification. If I were you I would however be greatly tempted to ask him if he really thinks D.s advice to his friends to vote for a Lecompton & Slave code man, is very *"plucky"*
    Please excuse what I have said, in the way of unsolicited

advice. I believe you will not doubt the sincerity of my friendship for you. Yours very truly

To George W. Dole, Gurdon S. Hubbard, and William H. Brown

Messrs. Dole, Hubbard & Brown—   Springfield,
Gent.   Dec. 14, 1859

Your favor of the 12th. is at hand, and it gives me pleasure to be able to answer it. It is not my intention to take part in any of the rivalries for the Gubernatorial nomination; but the fear of being misunderstood upon that subject, ought not to deter me from doing justice to Mr. Judd, and preventing a wrong being done to him by the use of my name in connection with alledged wrongs to me.

In answer to your first question as to whether Mr. Judd was guilty of any unfairness to me at the time of Senator Trumbull's election, I answer unhesitatingly in the negative. Mr. Judd owed no political allegiance to any party whose candidate I was. He was in the Senate, holding over, having been elected by a democratic constituency. He never was in any caucus of the friends who sought to make me U.S. Senator— never gave me any promises or pledges to support me—and subsequent events have greatly tended to prove the wisdom, politically, of Mr. Judd's course. The election of Judge Trumbull strongly tended to sustain and preserve the position of that portion of the Democrats who condemned the repeal of the Missouri compromise, and left them in a position of joining with us in forming the Republican party, as was done at the Bloomington convention in 1856.

During the canvass of 1858 for the Senatorship my belief was, and still is, that I had no more sincere and faithful friend than Mr. Judd—certainly none whom I trusted more. His position as Chairman of the State Central committee, led to my greater intercourse with him, and to my giving him a larger share of my confidence, than with, or, to almost any other friend; and I have never suspected that that confidence was, to any degree, misplaced.

My relations with Mr. Judd, since the organization of the Republican party, in our State, in 1856, and, especially since the adjournment of the Legislature in Feb. 1857, have been so very intimate, that I deem it an impossibility that he could have been dealing treacherously with me. He has also, at all times, appeared equally true and faithful to the party. In his position, as Chairman of the Committee, I believe he did all that any man could have done. The best of us are liable to commit errors, which become apparent, by subsequent developement; but I do not now know of a single error, even, committed by Mr. Judd, since he and I have acted together politically.

I had occasionally heard these insinuations against Mr. Judd, before the receipt of your letter; and in no instance have I hesitated to pronounce them wholly unjust, to the full extent of my knowledge and belief. I have been, and still am, very anxious to take no part between the many friends, all good and true, who are mentioned as candidates for a Republican Gubernatorial nomination; but I can not feel that my own honor is quite clear, if I remain silent, when I hear any one of them assailed about matters of which I believe I know more than his assailants.

I take pleasure in adding that of all the avowed friends I had in the canvass of last year, I do not suspect any of having acted treacherously to me, or to our cause; and that there is not one of them in whose honesty, honor, and integrity I, to-day, have greater confidence than I have in those of Mr. Judd.

I dislike to appear before the public, in this matter; but you are at liberty to make such use of this letter as you may think justice requires. Yours very truly

You can use your discretion as to whether you make this public.

To George M. Parsons and Others

Springfield, Ills., Dec. 19, 1859.
Messrs. Geo. M. Parsons and Others, Cent. Ex. Com., &c.
Gentlemen: Your letter of the 7th inst., accompanied by a

similar one from the Governor elect, the Republican State officers, and the Republican members of the State Board of Equalization of Ohio, both requesting of me, for publication in permanent form, copies of the political debates between Senator Douglas and myself, last year, has been received. With my grateful acknowledgments to both you and them, for the very flattering terms in which the request is communicated, I transmit you the copies. The copies I send you are reported and printed, by the respective friends of Senator Douglas and myself, at the time—that is, his by his friends, and mine by mine. It would be an unwarrantable liberty for us to change a word or a letter in his, and the changes I have made in mine, you perceive, are verbal only, and very few in number. I wish the reprint to be precisely as the copies I send, without any comment whatever. Yours very truly,

To Samuel Galloway

Private   Springfield Ill Dec. 19. 1859
Hon Saml Galloway.

This will introduce my friend, Mr. George Nicolay who will deliver to you the copies of the debates you desire. As they cost a good deal of trouble to get them together, some of us have concluded to send them by him at our own expense, rather than risk their loss by any public conveyance. He is a printer I believe & certainly has conducted a newspaper, and can give something of my views a little more in detail than I could write them, and also some mechanical assistance in getting the thing started. He will remain a few days at our expense for that purpose. You will perceive the copies in all of the shapes sent are in a scrapbook, as they stood there, precisely in the shape I would prefer the publication to be made in; but as that includes with the joint debates, six previously made speeches, and the correspondence which led to the joint debates it may make a larger job than you wish to undertake. These six speeches however, are so frequently referred to in the joint debates, as to make them a

very proper, if not indispensable accompaniment. If, however, you publish the joint debates only, then it is my wish
to preserve the scrapbook unbroken, and for that contingency Mr. Nicolay will furnish you another double set of the
joint debates, so that Douglas's speeches may be taken from
the paper friendly to him, and mine from that friendly to
me. Of course I wish the whole to be accurately done, but
especially let there be no color of complaint, that a word, or
letter in Douglas' speeches has been changed. Allow me to
add that I esteem the compliment paid me in this matter, as
the very highest I have ever received, and to assure to the
other kind friends that it shall ever be held in grateful remembrance. Still, I think it would be indelicate in me to
publish the correspondence. You can do that if you desire.
Yours very truly

P.S. I forgot to say in the proper place, that the copies of the
Columbus & Cincinnati speeches are a correction by me.

P.S. Mr. Nicolay is a good Republican, and a good man, and
worthy of any confidence that may be bestowed upon him.

To Jesse W. Fell, Enclosing Autobiography

J. W. Fell, Esq   Springfield,
My dear Sir: Dec. 20. 1859

Herewith is a little sketch, as you requested. There is not
much of it, for the reason, I suppose, that there is not much
of me.

If any thing be made out of it, I wish it to be modest, and
not to go beyond the materials. If it were thought necessary
to incorporate any thing from any of my speeches, I suppose
there would be no objection. Of course it must not appear to
have been written by myself. Yours very truly

I was born Feb. 12, 1809, in Hardin County, Kentucky.
My parents were both born in Virginia, of undistinguished
families—second families, perhaps I should say. My mother,
who died in my tenth year, was of a family of the name of

Hanks, some of whom now reside in Adams, and others in Macon counties, Illinois. My paternal grandfather, Abraham Lincoln, emigrated from Rockingham County, Virginia, to Kentucky, about 1781 or 2, where, a year or two later, he was killed by indians, not in battle, but by stealth, when he was laboring to open a farm in the forest. His ancestors, who were quakers, went to Virginia from Berks County, Pennsylvania. An effort to identify them with the New-England family of the same name ended in nothing more definite, than a similarity of Christian names in both families, such as Enoch, Levi, Mordecai, Solomon, Abraham, and the like.

My father, at the death of his father, was but six years of age; and he grew up, litterally without education. He removed from Kentucky to what is now Spencer county, Indiana, in my eighth year. We reached our new home about the time the State came into the Union. It was a wild region, with many bears and other wild animals still in the woods. There I grew up. There were some schools, so called; but no qualification was ever required of a teacher, beyond *"readin, writin, and cipherin,"* to the Rule of Three. If a straggler supposed to understand latin, happened to sojourn in the neighborhood, he was looked upon as a wizzard. There was absolutely nothing to excite ambition for education. Of course when I came of age I did not know much. Still somehow, I could read, write, and cipher to the Rule of Three; but that was all. I have not been to school since. The little advance I now have upon this store of education, I have picked up from time to time under the pressure of necessity.

I was raised to farm work, which I continued till I was twenty two. At twenty one I came to Illinois, and passed the first year in Macon county. Then I got to New-Salem (at that time in Sangamon, now in Menard county, where I remained a year as a sort of Clerk in a store. Then came the Black-Hawk war; and I was elected a Captain of Volunteers —a success which gave me more pleasure than any I have had since. I went the campaign, was elated, ran for the Legislature the same year (1832) and was beaten—the only time I ever have been beaten by the people. The next, and three succeeding biennial elections, I was elected to the Legislature. I was not a candidate afterwards. During this Legislative period I had studied law, and removed to Springfield to practice it. In 1846 I was once elected to the lower House of Congress. Was not a candidate for re-election. From 1849 to 1854, both inclusive, practiced law more assiduously than ever before. Always a whig in politics, and generally on the whig electoral tickets, making active canvasses. I was losing interest in politics, when the repeal of the Missouri Compromise aroused me again. What I have done since then is pretty well known.

If any personal description of me is thought desirable, it may be said, I am, in height, six feet, four inches, nearly; lean in flesh, weighing, on an average, one hundred and eighty pounds; dark complexion, with coarse black hair, and grey eyes—no other marks or brands recollected. Yours very truly

To James W. Sheahan

Jas. W. Sheahan, Esq   Springfield, Jan. 24. 1860

Dear Sir Yours of the 21st., requesting copies of my speeches now in progress of publication in Ohio, is received. I have no such copies now at my control; having sent the only sett I ever had, to Ohio. Mr. Geo. M. Parsons has taken an active part among those who have the matter in charge, in Ohio; and I understand Messrs. Follett, Foster & Co are to be the publishers. I make no objection to any satisfactory arrangement you may make with Mr. Parsons and the publishers; and, if it will facilitate you, you are at liberty to show them this note.

You labor under a mistake, somewhat injurious to me, if you suppose I have *revised* the speeches, in any just sense of the word. I only made some small verbal corrections, mostly such as an inteligent reader would make for himself; not feeling justified to do more, when republishing the speeches along with those of Senator Douglas—his and mine being mutually answers and replies to one another. Yours truly

To Norman B. Judd

Hon. N. B. Judd,   Springfield Feb. 9. 1860

Dear Sir: I am not in a position where it would hurt much for me to not be nominated on the national ticket; but I am where it would hurt some for me to not get the Illinois delegates. What I expected when I wrote the letter to Messrs Dole and others is now happening. Your discomfitted assailants are most bitter against me; and they will, for revenge upon me, lay to the Bates egg in the South, and to the Seward egg in the North, and go far towards squeezing me out in the middle with nothing. Can you not help me a little in this matter, in your end of the vineyard?

I mean this to be private. Yours as ever

To Oliver P. Hall, Jacob N. Fullinwider, and William F. Correll

Messrs. O. P. Hall   Springfield,
J. R. Fullinwider & W. F. Correll.   Feb. 14. 1860

Gentlemen. Your letter, in which among other things, you ask "what I meant when I said this Union could not stand half slave and half free—and also what I meant when I said a house divided against itself could not stand" is received, and I very cheerfully answer it as plainly as I may be able. You misquote, to some material extent, what I did say; which induces me to think you have not, very carefully read the speech in which the expressions occur which puzzle you to understand. For this reason and because the language I used is as plain as I can make it, I now quote at length the whole paragraph in which the expressions which puzzle you occur. It is as follows: "We are now far into the fifth year since a policy was initiated with the avowed object, and confident promise of putting an end to slavery agitation. Under the operation of that policy that agitation has not only not ceased but constantly augmented. I believe it will not cease until a crisis shall have been reached, and passed. A house divided against itself can not stand. I believe this government can not endure *permanently*, half slave, and half free. I do not expect the Union to be dissolved; I do not expect the house to fall; but I do expect it will cease to be divided. It will become all one thing, or all the other. Either the opponents of slavery will arrest the further spread of it, and place it where the public mind shall rest in the belief that it is in course of ultimate extinction; or it's advocates will push it forward till it will become alike lawful in all the states, old as well as new, North, as well as South."

That is the whole paragraph; and it puzzles me to make my meaning plainer. Look over it carefully, and conclude I meant all I said and did not mean anything I did not say, and you will have my meaning. Douglas attacked me upon this, saying it was a declaration of war between the slave and the free states. You will perceive I said no such thing, and I assure you I thought of no such thing.

If I had said "I believe this government can not *last always*, half slave and half free" would you understand it any better than you do? "Endure permanently" and "last always" have exactly the same meaning.

If you, or any of you, will state to me some meaning which you suppose I had, I can, and will instantly tell you whether that was my meaning. Yours very truly

Address at Cooper Institute, New York City

Mr. President and Fellow-Citizens of New-York: —
The facts with which I shall deal this evening are mainly old
and familiar; nor is there anything new in the general use I
shall make of them. If there shall be any novelty, it will be in
the mode of presenting the facts, and the inferences and observations following that presentation.

In his speech last autumn, at Columbus, Ohio, as reported
in "The New-York Times," Senator Douglas said:

*"Our fathers, when they framed the Government under which
we live, understood this question just as well, and even better, than
we do now."*

I fully indorse this, and I adopt it as a text for this discourse. I so adopt it because it furnishes a precise and an
agreed starting point for a discussion between Republicans
and that wing of the Democracy headed by Senator Douglas.
It simply leaves the inquiry: *"What was the understanding those
fathers had of the question mentioned?"*

What is the frame of Government under which we live?

The answer must be: "The Constitution of the United
States." That Constitution consists of the original, framed in
1787, (and under which the present government first went into
operation,) and twelve subsequently framed amendments, the
first ten of which were framed in 1789.

Who were our fathers that framed the Constitution? I suppose the "thirty-nine" who signed the original instrument
may be fairly called our fathers who framed that part of the
present Government. It is almost exactly true to say they
framed it, and it is altogether true to say they fairly represented the opinion and sentiment of the whole nation at that
time. Their names, being familiar to nearly all, and accessible
to quite all, need not now be repeated.

I take these "thirty-nine" for the present, as being "our
fathers who framed the Government under which we live."

What is the question which, according to the text, those
fathers understood "just as well, and even better than we do
now?"

It is this: Does the proper division of local from federal

authority, or anything in the Constitution, forbid *our Federal Government* to control as to slavery in *our Federal Territories*?

Upon this, Senator Douglas holds the affirmative, and Republicans the negative. This affirmation and denial form an issue; and this issue—this question—is precisely what the text declares our fathers understood "better than we."

Let us now inquire whether the "thirty-nine," or any of them, ever acted upon this question; and if they did, how they acted upon it—how they expressed that better understanding?

In 1784, three years before the Constitution—the United States then owning the Northwestern Territory, and no other, the Congress of the Confederation had before them the question of prohibiting slavery in that Territory; and four of the "thirty-nine," who afterward framed the Constitution, were in that Congress, and voted on that question. Of these, Roger Sherman, Thomas Mifflin, and Hugh Williamson voted for the prohibition, thus showing that, in their understanding, no line dividing local from federal authority, nor anything else, properly forbade the Federal Government to control as to slavery in federal territory. The other of the four—James M'Henry—voted against the prohibition, showing that, for some cause, he thought it improper to vote for it.

In 1787, still before the Constitution, but while the Convention was in session framing it, and while the Northwestern Territory still was the only territory owned by the United States, the same question of prohibiting slavery in the territory again came before the Congress of the Confederation; and two more of the "thirty-nine" who afterward signed the Constitution, were in that Congress, and voted on the question. They were William Blount and William Few; and they both voted for the prohibition—thus showing that, in their understanding, no line dividing local from federal authority, nor anything else, properly forbade the Federal Government to control as to slavery in federal territory. This time the prohibition became a law, being part of what is now well known as the Ordinance of '87.

The question of federal control of slavery in the territories, seems not to have been directly before the Convention which framed the original Constitution; and hence it is not recorded that the "thirty-nine," or any of them, while engaged on that instrument, expressed any opinion of that precise question.

In 1789, by the first Congress which sat under the Constitution, an act was passed to enforce the Ordinance of '87, including the prohibition of slavery in the Northwestern Territory. The bill for this act was reported by one of the "thirty-nine," Thomas Fitzsimmons, then a member of the House of Representatives from Pennsylvania. It went through all its stages without a word of opposition, and finally passed both branches without yeas and nays, which is equivalent to an unanimous passage. In this Congress there were sixteen of the thirty-nine fathers who framed the original Constitution. They were John Langdon, Nicholas Gilman, Wm. S. Johnson, Roger Sherman, Robert Morris, Thos. Fitzsimmons, William Few, Abraham Baldwin, Rufus King, William Paterson, George Clymer, Richard Bassett, George Read, Pierce Butler, Daniel Carroll, James Madison.

This shows that, in their understanding, no line dividing local from federal authority, nor anything in the Constitution, properly forbade Congress to prohibit slavery in the federal territory; else both their fidelity to correct principle, and their oath to support the Constitution, would have constrained them to oppose the prohibition.

Again, George Washington, another of the "thirty-nine," was then President of the United States, and, as such, approved and signed the bill; thus completing its validity as a law, and thus showing that, in his understanding, no line dividing local from federal authority, nor anything in the Constitution, forbade the Federal Government, to control as to slavery in federal territory.

No great while after the adoption of the original Constitution, North Carolina ceded to the Federal Government the country now constituting the State of Tennessee; and a few years later Georgia ceded that which now constitutes the States of Mississippi and Alabama. In both deeds of cession it was made a condition by the ceding States that the Federal Government should not prohibit slavery in the ceded country. Besides this, slavery was then actually in the ceded country. Under these circumstances, Congress, on taking charge of these countries, did not absolutely prohibit slavery within them. But they did interfere with it—take control of it—even there, to a certain extent. In 1798, Congress organized the Territory of Mississippi. In the act of organization, they prohibited the bringing of slaves into the Territory, from any place without the United States, by fine, and giving freedom to slaves so brought. This act passed both branches of Congress without yeas and nays. In that Congress were three of the "thirty-nine" who framed the original Constitution. They were John Langdon, George Read and Abraham Baldwin. They all, probably, voted for it. Certainly they would have placed their opposition to it upon record, if, in their understanding, any line dividing local from federal authority, or anything in the Constitution, properly forbade the Federal Government to control as to slavery in federal territory.

In 1803, the Federal Government purchased the Louisiana country. Our former territorial acquisitions came from certain of our own States; but this Louisiana country was acquired from a foreign nation. In 1804, Congress gave a territorial organization to that part of it which now constitutes the State of Louisiana. New Orleans, lying within that part, was an old and comparatively large city. There were other considerable towns and settlements, and slavery was extensively and thoroughly intermingled with the people. Congress did not, in the Territorial Act, prohibit slavery; but they did interfere with it—take control of it—in a more marked and extensive way than they did in the case of Mississippi. The substance of the provision therein made, in relation to slaves, was:

First. That no slave should be imported into the territory from foreign parts.

Second. That no slave should be carried into it who had been imported into the United States since the first day of May, 1798.

Third. That no slave should be carried into it, except by the owner, and for his own use as a settler; the penalty in all the cases being a fine upon the violator of the law, and freedom to the slave.

This act also was passed without yeas and nays. In the Congress which passed it, there were two of the "thirty-nine." They were Abraham Baldwin and Jonathan Dayton. As stated in the case of Mississippi, it is probable they both voted for it.

They would not have allowed it to pass without recording their opposition to it, if, in their understanding, it violated either the line properly dividing local from federal authority, or any provision of the Constitution.

In 1819–20, came and passed the Missouri question. Many votes were taken, by yeas and nays, in both branches of Congress, upon the various phases of the general question. Two of the "thirty-nine"—Rufus King and Charles Pinckney—were members of that Congress. Mr. King steadily voted for slavery prohibition and against all compromises, while Mr. Pinckney as steadily voted against slavery prohibition and against all compromises. By this, Mr. King showed that, in his understanding, no line dividing local from federal authority, nor anything in the Constitution, was violated by Congress prohibiting slavery in federal territory; while Mr. Pinckney, by his votes, showed that, in his understanding, there was some sufficient reason for opposing such prohibition in that case.

The cases I have mentioned are the only acts of the "thirty-nine," or of any of them, upon the direct issue, which I have been able to discover.

To enumerate the persons who thus acted, as being four in 1784, two in 1787, seventeen in 1789, three in 1798, two in 1804, and two in 1819–20—there would be thirty of them. But this would be counting John Langdon, Roger Sherman, William Few, Rufus King, and George Read, each twice, and Abraham Baldwin, three times. The true number of those of the "thirty-nine" whom I have shown to have acted upon the question, which, by the text, they understood better than we, is twenty-three, leaving sixteen not shown to have acted upon it in any way.

Here, then, we have twenty-three out of our thirty-nine fathers "who framed the Government under which we live," who have, upon their official responsibility and their corporal oaths, acted upon the very question which the text affirms they "understood just as well, and even better than we do now;" and twenty-one of them—a clear majority of the whole "thirty-nine"—so acting upon it as to make them guilty of gross political impropriety and wilful perjury, if, in their understanding, any proper division between local and

federal authority, or anything in the Constitution they had
made themselves, and sworn to support, forbade the Federal
Government to control as to slavery in the federal territories.
Thus the twenty-one acted; and, as actions speak louder than
words, so actions, under such responsibility, speak still
louder.

Two of the twenty-three voted against Congressional prohibition of slavery in the federal territories, in the instances in
which they acted upon the question. But for what reasons
they so voted is not known. They may have done so because
they thought a proper division of local from federal authority,
or some provision or principle of the Constitution, stood in
the way; or they may, without any such question, have voted
against the prohibition, on what appeared to them to be sufficient grounds of expediency. No one who has sworn to support the Constitution, can conscientiously vote for what he
understands to be an unconstitutional measure, however expedient he may think it; but one may and ought to vote
against a measure which he deems constitutional, if, at the
same time, he deems it inexpedient. It, therefore, would be
unsafe to set down even the two who voted against the prohibition, as having done so because, in their understanding,
any proper division of local from federal authority, or anything in the Constitution, forbade the Federal Government to
control as to slavery in federal territory.

The remaining sixteen of the "thirty-nine," so far as I have
discovered, have left no record of their understanding upon
the direct question of federal control of slavery in the federal
territories. But there is much reason to believe that their
understanding upon that question would not have appeared
different from that of their twenty-three compeers, had it
been manifested at all.

For the purpose of adhering rigidly to the text, I have purposely omitted whatever understanding may have been manifested by any person, however distinguished, other than the
thirty-nine fathers who framed the original Constitution; and,
for the same reason, I have also omitted whatever understanding may have been manifested by any of the "thirty-nine"
even, on any other phase of the general question of slavery. If
we should look into their acts and declarations on those other

phases, as the foreign slave trade, and the morality and policy of slavery generally, it would appear to us that on the direct question of federal control of slavery in federal territories, the sixteen, if they had acted at all, would probably have acted just as the twenty-three did. Among that sixteen were several of the most noted anti-slavery men of those times—as Dr. Franklin, Alexander Hamilton and Gouverneur Morris— while there was not one now known to have been otherwise, unless it may be John Rutledge, of South Carolina.

The sum of the whole is, that of our thirty-nine fathers who framed the original Constitution, twenty-one—a clear majority of the whole—certainly understood that no proper division of local from federal authority, nor any part of the Constitution, forbade the Federal Government to control slavery in the federal territories; while all the rest probably had the same understanding. Such, unquestionably, was the understanding of our fathers who framed the original Constitution; and the text affirms that they understood the question "better than we."

But, so far, I have been considering the understanding of the question manifested by the framers of the original Constitution. In and by the original instrument, a mode was provided for amending it; and, as I have already stated, the present frame of "the Government under which we live" consists of that original, and twelve amendatory articles framed and adopted since. Those who now insist that federal control of slavery in federal territories violates the Constitution, point us to the provisions which they suppose it thus violates; and, as I understand, they all fix upon provisions in these amendatory articles, and not in the original instrument. The Supreme Court, in the Dred Scott case, plant themselves upon the fifth amendment, which provides that no person shall be deprived of "life, liberty or property without due process of law;" while Senator Douglas and his peculiar adherents plant themselves upon the tenth amendment, providing that "the powers not delegated to the United States by the Constitution," "are reserved to the States respectively, or to the people."

Now, it so happens that these amendments were framed by the first Congress which sat under the Constitution—the identical Congress which passed the act already mentioned,

enforcing the prohibition of slavery in the Northwestern Territory. Not only was it the same Congress, but they were the
identical, same individual men who, at the same session, and
at the same time within the session, had under consideration,
and in progress toward maturity, these Constitutional amendments, and this act prohibiting slavery in all the territory the
nation then owned. The Constitutional amendments were introduced before, and passed after the act enforcing the Ordinance of '87; so that, during the whole pendency of the act to
enforce the Ordinance, the Constitutional amendments were
also pending.

The seventy-six members of that Congress, including sixteen of the framers of the original Constitution, as before
stated, were preeminently our fathers who framed that part of
"the Government under which we live," which is now claimed
as forbidding the Federal Government to control slavery in
the federal territories.

Is it not a little presumptuous in any one at this day to
affirm that the two things which that Congress deliberately
framed, and carried to maturity at the same time, are absolutely inconsistent with each other? And does not such affirmation become impudently absurd when coupled with the
other affirmation from the same mouth, that those who did
the two things, alleged to be inconsistent, understood
whether they really were inconsistent better than we — better
than he who affirms that they are inconsistent?

It is surely safe to assume that the thirty-nine framers of
the original Constitution, and the seventy-six members of
the Congress which framed the amendments thereto, taken
together, do certainly include those who may be fairly called
"our fathers who framed the Government under which we
live." And so assuming, I defy any man to show that any
one of them ever, in his whole life, declared that, in his understanding, any proper division of local from federal authority, or any part of the Constitution, forbade the Federal
Government to control as to slavery in the federal territories.
I go a step further. I defy any one to show that any living
man in the whole world ever did, prior to the beginning of
the present century, (and I might almost say prior to the beginning of the last half of the present century,) declare that,

in his understanding, any proper division of local from fed-eral authority, or any part of the Constitution, forbade the Federal Government to control as to slavery in the federal territories. To those who now so declare, I give, not only "our fathers who framed the Government under which we live," but with them all other living men within the century in which it was framed, among whom to search, and they shall not be able to find the evidence of a single man agree-ing with them.

Now, and here, let me guard a little against being mis-understood. I do not mean to say we are bound to follow implicitly in whatever our fathers did. To do so, would be to discard all the lights of current experience—to reject all progress—all improvement. What I do say is, that if we would supplant the opinions and policy of our fathers in any case, we should do so upon evidence so conclusive, and argu-ment so clear, that even their great authority, fairly considered and weighed, cannot stand; and most surely not in a case whereof we ourselves declare they understood the question better than we.

If any man at this day sincerely believes that a proper divi-sion of local from federal authority, or any part of the Con-stitution, forbids the Federal Government to control as to slavery in the federal territories, he is right to say so, and to enforce his position by all truthful evidence and fair argument which he can. But he has no right to mislead others, who have less access to history, and less leisure to study it, into the false belief that "our fathers, who framed the Government under which we live," were of the same opinion—thus substi-tuting falsehood and deception for truthful evidence and fair argument. If any man at this day sincerely believes "our fathers who framed the Government under which we live," used and applied principles, in other cases, which ought to have led them to understand that a proper division of local from federal authority or some part of the Constitution, for-bids the Federal Government to control as to slavery in the federal territories, he is right to say so. But he should, at the same time, brave the responsibility of declaring that, in his opinion, he understands their principles better than they did themselves; and especially should he not shirk that responsibility by asserting that they "understood the question just as well, and even better, than we do now."

But enough! *Let all who believe that "our fathers, who framed the Government under which we live, understood this question just as well, and even better, than we do now," speak as they spoke, and act as they acted upon it. This is all Republicans ask—all Republicans desire—in relation to slavery. As those fathers marked it, so let it be again marked, as an evil not to be extended, but to be tolerated and protected only because of and so far as its actual presence among us makes that toleration and protection a necessity. Let all the guaranties those fathers gave it, be, not grudgingly, but fully and fairly maintained.* For this Republicans contend, and with this, so far as I know or believe, they will be content.

And now, if they would listen—as I suppose they will not—I would address a few words to the Southern people.

I would say to them:—You consider yourselves a reasonable and a just people; and I consider that in the general qualities of reason and justice you are not inferior to any other people. Still, when you speak of us Republicans, you do so only to denounce us as reptiles, or, at the best, as no better than outlaws. You will grant a hearing to pirates or murderers, but nothing like it to "Black Republicans." In all your contentions with one another, each of you deems an unconditional condemnation of "Black Republicanism" as the first thing to be attended to. Indeed, such condemnation of us seems to be an indispensable prerequisite—license, so to speak—among you to be admitted or permitted to speak at all. Now, can you, or not, be prevailed upon to pause and to consider whether this is quite just to us, or even to yourselves? Bring forward your charges and specifications, and then be patient long enough to hear us deny or justify.

You say we are sectional. We deny it. That makes an issue; and the burden of proof is upon you. You produce your proof; and what is it? Why, that our party has no existence in your section—gets no votes in your section. The fact is substantially true; but does it prove the issue? If it does, then in case we should, without change of principle, begin to get votes in your section, we should thereby cease to be sectional. You cannot escape this conclusion; and yet, are you willing to abide by it? If you are, you will probably soon find that we have ceased to be sectional, for we shall get votes in your section this very year. You will then begin to discover, as the truth plainly is, that your proof does not touch the issue. The fact that we get no votes in your section, is a fact of your making, and not of ours. And if there be fault in that fact, that fault is primarily yours, and remains so until you show that we repel you by some wrong principle or practice. If we do repel you by any wrong principle or practice, the fault is ours; but this brings you to where you ought to have started—to a discussion of the right or wrong of our principle. If our principle, put in practice, would wrong your section for the benefit of ours, or for any other object, then our principle, and we with it, are sectional, and are justly opposed and denounced as such. Meet us, then, on the question of whether our principle, put in practice, would wrong your section; and so meet us as if it were possible that something may be said on our side. Do you accept the challenge? No! Then you really believe that the principle which "our fathers who framed the Government under which we live" thought so clearly right as to adopt it, and indorse it again and again, upon their official oaths, is in fact so clearly wrong as to demand your condemnation without a moment's consideration.

Some of you delight to flaunt in our faces the warning against sectional parties given by Washington in his Farewell Address. Less than eight years before Washington gave that warning, he had, as President of the United States, approved and signed an act of Congress, enforcing the prohibition of slavery in the Northwestern Territory, which act embodied the policy of the Government upon that subject up to and at the very moment he penned that warning; and about one year after he penned it, he wrote La Fayette that he considered that prohibition a wise measure, expressing in the same connection his hope that we should at some time have a confederacy of free States.

Bearing this in mind, and seeing that sectionalism has since arisen upon this same subject, is that warning a weapon in your hands against us, or in our hands against you? Could Washington himself speak, would he cast the blame of that sectionalism upon us, who sustain his policy, or upon you who repudiate it? We respect that warning of Washington,

and we commend it to you, together with his example pointing to the right application of it.

But you say you are conservative—eminently conservative—while we are revolutionary, destructive, or something
of the sort. What is conservatism? Is it not adherence to the
old and tried, against the new and untried? We stick to, contend for, the identical old policy on the point in controversy
which was adopted by "our fathers who framed the Government under which we live;" while you with one accord reject,
and scout, and spit upon that old policy, and insist upon substituting something new. True, you disagree among yourselves as to what that substitute shall be. You are divided on
new propositions and plans, but you are unanimous in rejecting and denouncing the old policy of the fathers. Some of
you are for reviving the foreign slave trade; some for a Congressional Slave-Code for the Territories; some for Congress
forbidding the Territories to prohibit Slavery within their limits; some for maintaining Slavery in the Territories through
the judiciary; some for the "gur-reat pur-rinciple" that "if one
man would enslave another, no third man should object,"
fantastically called "Popular Sovereignty;" but never a man
among you in favor of federal prohibition of slavery in federal
territories, according to the practice of "our fathers who
framed the Government under which we live." Not one of all
your various plans can show a precedent or an advocate in the
century within which our Government originated. Consider,
then, whether your claim of conservatism for yourselves, and
your charge of destructiveness against us, are based on the
most clear and stable foundations.

Again, you say we have made the slavery question more
prominent than it formerly was. We deny it. We admit that it
is more prominent, but we deny that we made it so. It was
not we, but you, who discarded the old policy of the fathers.
We resisted, and still resist, your innovation; and thence
comes the greater prominence of the question. Would you
have that question reduced to its former proportions? Go
back to that old policy. What has been will be again, under
the same conditions. If you would have the peace of the old
times, readopt the precepts and policy of the old times.

You charge that we stir up insurrections among your slaves.

We deny it; and what is your proof? Harper's Ferry! John Brown!! John Brown was no Republican; and you have failed to implicate a single Republican in his Harper's Ferry enterprise. If any member of our party is guilty in that matter, you know it or you do not know it. If you do know it, you are inexcusable for not designating the man and proving the fact. If you do not know it, you are inexcusable for asserting it, and especially for persisting in the assertion after you have tried and failed to make the proof. You need not be told that persisting in a charge which one does not know to be true, is simply malicious slander.

Some of you admit that no Republican designedly aided or encouraged the Harper's Ferry affair; but still insist that our doctrines and declarations necessarily lead to such results. We do not believe it. We know we hold to no doctrine, and make no declaration, which were not held to and made by "our fathers who framed the Government under which we live." You never dealt fairly by us in relation to this affair. When it occurred, some important State elections were near at hand, and you were in evident glee with the belief that, by charging the blame upon us, you could get an advantage of us in those elections. The elections came, and your expectations were not quite fulfilled. Every Republican man knew that, as to himself at least, your charge was a slander, and he was not much inclined by it to cast his vote in your favor. Republican doctrines and declarations are accompanied with a continual protest against any interference whatever with your slaves, or with you about your slaves. Surely, this does not encourage them to revolt. True, we do, in common with "our fathers, who framed the Government under which we live," declare our belief that slavery is wrong; but the slaves do not hear us declare even this. For anything we say or do, the slaves would scarcely know there is a Republican party. I believe they would not, in fact, generally know it but for your misrepresentations of us, in their hearing. In your political contests among yourselves, each faction charges the other with sympathy with Black Republicanism; and then, to give point to the charge, defines Black Republicanism to simply be insurrection, blood and thunder among the slaves.

Slave insurrections are no more common now than they

were before the Republican party was organized. What induced the Southampton insurrection, twenty-eight years ago,
in which, at least, three times as many lives were lost as at
Harper's Ferry? You can scarcely stretch your very elastic
fancy to the conclusion that Southampton was "got up by
Black Republicanism." In the present state of things in the
United States, I do not think a general, or even a very extensive slave insurrection, is possible. The indispensable concert
of action cannot be attained. The slaves have no means of
rapid communication; nor can incendiary freemen, black or
white, supply it. The explosive materials are everywhere in
parcels; but there neither are, nor can be supplied, the indispensable connecting trains.

Much is said by Southern people about the affection of
slaves for their masters and mistresses; and a part of it, at
least, is true. A plot for an uprising could scarcely be devised
and communicated to twenty individuals before some one of
them, to save the life of a favorite master or mistress, would
divulge it. This is the rule; and the slave revolution in Hayti
was not an exception to it, but a case occurring under peculiar
circumstances. The gunpowder plot of British history, though
not connected with slaves, was more in point. In that case,
only about twenty were admitted to the secret; and yet one of
them, in his anxiety to save a friend, betrayed the plot to that
friend, and, by consequence, averted the calamity. Occasional
poisonings from the kitchen, and open or stealthy assassinations in the field, and local revolts extending to a score or so,
will continue to occur as the natural results of slavery; but no
general insurrection of slaves, as I think, can happen in this
country for a long time. Whoever much fears, or much hopes
for such an event, will be alike disappointed.

In the language of Mr. Jefferson, uttered many years ago,
"It is still in our power to direct the process of emancipation,
and deportation, peaceably, and in such slow degrees, as that
the evil will wear off insensibly; and their places be, *pari passu*,
filled up by free white laborers. If, on the contrary, it is left to
force itself on, human nature must shudder at the prospect
held up."

Mr. Jefferson did not mean to say, nor do I, that the power
of emancipation is in the Federal Government. He spoke of

Virginia; and, as to the power of emancipation, I speak of the slaveholding States only. The Federal Government, however, as we insist, has the power of restraining the extension of the institution—the power to insure that a slave insurrection shall never occur on any American soil which is now free from slavery.

John Brown's effort was peculiar. It was not a slave insurrection. It was an attempt by white men to get up a revolt among slaves, in which the slaves refused to participate. In fact, it was so absurd that the slaves, with all their ignorance, saw plainly enough it could not succeed. That affair, in its philosophy, corresponds with the many attempts, related in history, at the assassination of kings and emperors. An enthusiast broods over the oppression of a people till he fancies himself commissioned by Heaven to liberate them. He ventures the attempt, which ends in little else than his own execution. Orsini's attempt on Louis Napoleon, and John Brown's attempt at Harper's Ferry were, in their philosophy, precisely the same. The eagerness to cast blame on old England in the one case, and on New England in the other, does not disprove the sameness of the two things.

And how much would it avail you, if you could, by the use of John Brown, Helper's Book, and the like, break up the Republican organization? Human action can be modified to some extent, but human nature cannot be changed. There is a judgment and a feeling against slavery in this nation, which cast at least a million and a half of votes. You cannot destroy that judgment and feeling—that sentiment—by breaking up the political organization which rallies around it. You can scarcely scatter and disperse an army which has been formed into order in the face of your heaviest fire; but if you could, how much would you gain by forcing the sentiment which created it out of the peaceful channel of the ballot-box, into some other channel? What would that other channel probably be? Would the number of John Browns be lessened or enlarged by the operation?

But you will break up the Union rather than submit to a denial of your Constitutional rights.

That has a somewhat reckless sound; but it would be palliated, if not fully justified, were we proposing, by the mere force of numbers, to deprive you of some right, plainly written down in the Constitution. But we are proposing no such thing.

When you make these declarations, you have a specific and well-understood allusion to an assumed Constitutional right of yours, to take slaves into the federal territories, and to hold them there as property. But no such right is specifically written in the Constitution. That instrument is literally silent about any such right. We, on the contrary, deny that such a right has any existence in the Constitution, even by implication.

Your purpose, then, plainly stated, is, that you will destroy the Government, unless you be allowed to construe and enforce the Constitution as you please, on all points in dispute between you and us. You will rule or ruin in all events.

This, plainly stated, is your language. Perhaps you will say the Supreme Court has decided the disputed Constitutional question in your favor. Not quite so. But waiving the lawyer's distinction between dictum and decision, the Court have decided the question for you in a sort of way. The Court have substantially said, it is your Constitutional right to take slaves into the federal territories, and to hold them there as property. When I say the decision was made in a sort of way, I mean it was made in a divided Court, by a bare majority of the Judges, and they not quite agreeing with one another in the reasons for making it; that it is so made as that its avowed supporters disagree with one another about its meaning, and that it was mainly based upon a mistaken statement of fact—the statement in the opinion that "the right of property in a slave is distinctly and expressly affirmed in the Constitution."

An inspection of the Constitution will show that the right of property in a slave is not "*distinctly* and *expressly* affirmed" in it. Bear in mind, the Judges do not pledge their judicial opinion that such right is *impliedly* affirmed in the Constitution; but they pledge their veracity that it is "*distinctly* and *expressly*" affirmed there—"distinctly," that is, not mingled with anything else—"expressly," that is, in words meaning just that, without the aid of any inference, and susceptible of no other meaning.

If they had only pledged their judicial opinion that such

right is affirmed in the instrument by implication, it would be open to others to show that neither the word "slave" nor "slavery" is to be found in the Constitution, nor the word "property" even, in any connection with language alluding to the things slave, or slavery, and that wherever in that instrument the slave is alluded to, he is called a "person;"—and wherever his master's legal right in relation to him is alluded to, it is spoken of as "service or labor which may be due,"—as a debt payable in service or labor. Also, it would be open to show, by contemporaneous history, that this mode of alluding to slaves and slavery, instead of speaking of them, was employed on purpose to exclude from the Constitution the idea that there could be property in man.

To show all this, is easy and certain.

When this obvious mistake of the Judges shall be brought to their notice, is it not reasonable to expect that they will withdraw the mistaken statement, and reconsider the conclusion based upon it?

And then it is to be remembered that "our fathers, who framed the Government under which we live"—the men who made the Constitution—decided this same Constitutional question in our favor, long ago—decided it without division among themselves, when making the decision; without division among themselves about the meaning of it after it was made, and, so far as any evidence is left, without basing it upon any mistaken statement of facts.

Under all these circumstances, do you really feel yourselves justified to break up this Government, unless such a court decision as yours is, shall be at once submitted to as a conclusive and final rule of political action? But you will not abide the election of a Republican President! In that supposed event, you say, you will destroy the Union; and then, you say, the great crime of having destroyed it will be upon us! That is cool. A highwayman holds a pistol to my ear, and mutters through his teeth, "Stand and deliver, or I shall kill you, and then you will be a murderer!"

To be sure, what the robber demanded of me—my money—was my own; and I had a clear right to keep it; but it was no more my own than my vote is my own; and the threat of death to me, to extort my money, and the threat of destruction to the Union, to extort my vote, can scarcely be distinguished in principle.

A few words now to Republicans. *It is exceedingly desirable that all parts of this great Confederacy shall be at peace, and in harmony, one with another. Let us Republicans do our part to have it so. Even though much provoked, let us do nothing through passion and ill temper. Even though the southern people will not so much as listen to us, let us calmly consider their demands, and yield to them if, in our deliberate view of our duty, we possibly can.* Judging by all they say and do, and by the subject and nature of their controversy with us, let us determine, if we can, what will satisfy them.

Will they be satisfied if the Territories be unconditionally surrendered to them? We know they will not. In all their present complaints against us, the Territories are scarcely mentioned. Invasions and insurrections are the rage now. Will it satisfy them, if, in the future, we have nothing to do with invasions and insurrections? We know it will not. We so know, because we know we never had anything to do with invasions and insurrections; and yet this total abstaining does not exempt us from the charge and the denunciation.

The question recurs, what will satisfy them? Simply this: We must not only let them alone, but we must, somehow, convince them that we do let them alone. This, we know by experience, is no easy task. We have been so trying to convince them from the very beginning of our organization, but with no success. In all our platforms and speeches we have constantly protested our purpose to let them alone; but this has had no tendency to convince them. Alike unavailing to convince them, is the fact that they have never detected a man of us in any attempt to disturb them.

These natural, and apparently adequate means all failing, what will convince them? This, and this only: cease to call slavery *wrong*, and join them in calling it *right*. And this must be done thoroughly—done in *acts* as well as in *words*. Silence will not be tolerated—we must place ourselves avowedly with them. Senator Douglas's new sedition law must be enacted and enforced, suppressing all declarations that slavery is wrong, whether made in politics, in presses, in pulpits, or in private. We must arrest and return their fugitive slaves with greedy pleasure. We must pull down our Free State constitutions. The whole atmosphere must be disinfected from all taint of opposition to slavery, before they will cease to believe that all their troubles proceed from us.

I am quite aware they do not state their case precisely in this way. Most of them would probably say to us, "Let us alone, *do* nothing to us, and *say* what you please about slavery." But we do let them alone—have never disturbed them—so that, after all, it is what we say, which dissatisfies them. They will continue to accuse us of doing, until we cease saying.

I am also aware they have not, as yet, in terms, demanded the overthrow of our Free-State Constitutions. Yet those Constitutions declare the wrong of slavery, with more solemn emphasis, than do all other sayings against it; and when all these other sayings shall have been silenced, the overthrow of these Constitutions will be demanded, and nothing be left to resist the demand. It is nothing to the contrary, that they do not demand the whole of this just now. Demanding what they do, and for the reason they do, they can voluntarily stop nowhere short of this consummation. Holding, as they do, that slavery is morally right, and socially elevating, they cannot cease to demand a full national recognition of it, as a legal right, and a social blessing.

Nor can we justifiably withhold this, on any ground save our conviction that slavery is wrong. If slavery is right, all words, acts, laws, and constitutions against it, are themselves wrong, and should be silenced, and swept away. If it is right, we cannot justly object to its nationality—its universality; if it is wrong, they cannot justly insist upon its extension—its enlargement. All they ask, we could readily grant, if we thought slavery right; all we ask, they could as readily grant, if they thought it wrong. Their thinking it right, and our thinking it wrong, is the precise fact upon which depends the whole controversy. Thinking it right, as they do, they are not to blame for desiring its full recognition, as being right; but, thinking it wrong, as we do, can we yield to them? Can we cast our votes with their view, and against our own? In view of our moral, social, and political responsibilities, can we do this?

Wrong as we think slavery is, we can yet afford to let it

alone where it is, because that much is due to the necessity arising from its actual presence in the nation; but can we, while our votes will prevent it, allow it to spread into the National Territories, and to overrun us here in these Free States? If our sense of duty forbids this, then let us stand by our duty, fearlessly and effectively. Let us be diverted by none of those sophistical contrivances wherewith we are so industriously plied and belabored—contrivances such as groping for some middle ground between the right and the wrong, vain as the search for a man who should be neither a living man nor a dead man—such as a policy of "don't care" on a question about which all true men do care—such as Union appeals beseeching true Union men to yield to Disunionists, reversing the divine rule, and calling, not the sinners, but the righteous to repentance—such as invocations to Washington, imploring men to unsay what Washington said, and undo what Washington did.

Neither let us be slandered from our duty by false accusations against us, nor frightened from it by menaces of destruction to the Government nor of dungeons to ourselves. LET US HAVE FAITH THAT RIGHT MAKES MIGHT, AND IN THAT FAITH, LET US, TO THE END, DARE TO DO OUR DUTY AS WE UNDERSTAND IT.

February 27, 1860

To Mary Todd Lincoln

Dear Wife: Exeter, N. H. March 4. 1860

When I wrote you before I was just starting on a little speech-making tour, taking the boys with me. On Thursday they went with me to Concord, where I spoke in day-light, and back to Manchester where I spoke at night. Friday we came down to Lawrence—the place of the Pemberton Mill tragedy—where we remained four hours awaiting the train back to Exeter. When it came, we went upon it to Exeter where the boys got off, and I went on to Dover and spoke there Friday evening. Saturday I came back to Exeter, reaching here about noon, and finding the boys all right, having

caught up with their lessons. Bob had a letter from you saying Willie and Taddy were very sick the Saturday night after I
left. Having no despach from you, and having one from
Springfield, of Wednesday, from Mr. Fitzhugh, saying nothing about our family, I trust the dear little fellows are well
again.

This is Sunday morning; and according to Bob's orders, I
am to go to church once to-day. Tomorrow I bid farewell to
the boys, go to Hartford, Conn. and speak there in the
evening; Tuesday at Meriden, Wednesday at New-Haven—
and Thursday at Woonsocket R. I. Then I start home, and
think I will not stop. I may be delayed in New-York City an
hour or two. I have been unable to escape this toil. If I had
foreseen it I think I would not have come East at all. The
speech at New-York, being within my calculation before I
started, went off passably well, and gave me no trouble whatever. The difficulty was to make nine others, before reading
audiences, who have already seen all my ideas in print.

If the trains do not lie over Sunday, of which I do not
know, I hope to be home to-morrow week. Once started I
shall come as quick as possible.

Kiss the dear boys for Father.

Affectionately

Speech at New Haven, Connecticut

MR. PRESIDENT AND FELLOW-CITIZENS OF NEW HAVEN: If the Republican party of this nation shall ever have the national house entrusted to its keeping, it will be the duty of that party to attend to all the affairs of national house-keeping. Whatever matters of importance may come up, whatever difficulties may arise in the way of its administration of the government, that party will then have to attend to. It will then be compelled to attend to other questions, besides this question which now assumes an overwhelming importance—the question of Slavery. It is true that in the organization of the Republican party this question of Slavery was more important than any other; indeed, so much more important has it become that no other national question can even get a hearing just at present. The old question of tariff—a matter that will remain one of the chief affairs of national housekeeping to all time—the question of the management of financial affairs; the question of the disposition of the public domain—how shall it be managed for the purpose of getting it well settled, and of making there the homes of a free and happy people—these will remain open and require attention for a great while yet, and these questions will have to be attended to by whatever party has the control of the government. Yet, just now, they cannot even obtain a hearing, and I do not purpose to detain you upon these topics, or what sort of hearing they should have when opportunity shall come.

For, whether we will or not, the question of Slavery is *the* question, the all absorbing topic of the day. It is true that all of us—and by that I mean, not the Republican party alone, but the whole American people, here and elsewhere—all of us wish this question settled—wish it out of the way. It stands in the way, and prevents the adjustment, and the giving of necessary attention to other questions of national house-keeping. The people of the whole nation agree that this question ought to be settled, and yet it is not settled. And the reason is that they are not yet agreed *how* it shall be settled. All wish it done, but some wish one way and some another, and some a third, or fourth, or fifth; different bodies are pulling in different directions, and none of them having a decided majority, are able to accomplish the common object.

In the beginning of the year 1854 a new policy was inaugurated with the avowed object and confident promise that it would entirely and forever put an end to the Slavery agitation. It was again and again declared that under this policy, when once successfully established, the country would be forever rid of this whole question. Yet under the operation of that policy this agitation has not only not ceased, but it has been constantly augmented. And this too, although, from the day of its introduction, its friends, who promised that it would wholly end all agitation, constantly insisted, down to the time that the Lecompton bill was introduced, that it was working admirably, and that its inevitable tendency was to remove the question forever from the politics of the country. Can you call to mind any Democratic speech, made after the repeal of the Missouri Compromise, down to the time of the Lecompton bill, in which it was not predicted that the Slavery agitation was just at an end; that "the abolition excitement was played out," "the Kansas question was dead," "they have made the most they can out of this question and it is now forever settled." But since the Lecompton bill no Democrat, within my experience, has ever pretended that he could see the end. That cry has been dropped. They themselves do not pretend, now, that the agitation of this subject has come to an end yet. [Applause.]

The truth is, that this question is one of national importance, and we cannot help dealing with it: we must do something about it, whether we will or not. We cannot avoid it; the subject is one we cannot avoid considering; we can no more avoid it than a man can live without eating. It is upon us; it attaches to the body politic as much and as closely as the natural wants attach to our natural bodies. Now I think it important that this matter should be taken up in earnest, and really settled. And one way to bring about a true settlement of the question is to understand its true magnitude.

There have been many efforts to settle it. Again and again it has been fondly hoped that it was settled, but every time it breaks out afresh, and more violently than ever. It was settled, our fathers hoped, by the Missouri Compromise, but it did not stay settled. Then the compromises of 1850 were declared to be a full and final settlement of the question. The two great parties, each in National Convention, adopted resolutions declaring that the settlement made by the Compromise of 1850 was a finality—that it would last forever. Yet how long before it was unsettled again! It broke out again in 1854, and blazed higher and raged more furiously than ever before, and the agitation has not rested since.

These repeated settlements must have some fault about them. There must be some inadequacy in their very nature to the purpose for which they were designed. We can only speculate as to where that fault—that inadequacy, is, but we may perhaps profit by past experience.

I think that one of the causes of these repeated failures is that our best and greatest men have greatly underestimated the size of this question. They have constantly brought forward small cures for great sores—plasters too small to cover the wound. That is one reason that all settlements have proved so temporary—so evanescent. [Applause.]

Look at the magnitude of this subject! One sixth of our population, in round numbers—not quite one sixth, and yet more than a seventh,—about one sixth of the whole population of the United States are slaves! The owners of these slaves consider them property. The effect upon the minds of the owners is that of property, and nothing else—it induces them to insist upon all that will favorably affect its value as property, to demand laws and institutions and a public policy that shall increase and secure its value, and make it durable, lasting and universal. The effect on the minds of the owners is to persuade them that there is no wrong in it. The slaveholder does not like to be considered a mean fellow, for holding that species of property, and hence he has to struggle within himself and sets about arguing himself into the belief that Slavery is right. The property influences his mind. The dissenting minister, who argued some theological point with one of the established church, was always met by the reply, "I can't see it so." He opened the Bible, and pointed him to a passage, but the orthodox minister replied, "I can't see it so." Then he showed him a single word—"Can you see that?" "Yes, I see it," was the reply. The dissenter laid a guinea over the word and asked, "Do you see it now?" [Great laughter.] So here. Whether the owners of this species of property do really see it as it is, it is not for me to say, but if they do, they see it as it is through 2,000,000,000 of dollars, and that is a pretty thick coating. [Laughter.] Certain it is, that they do not see it as we see it. Certain it is, that this two thousand million of dollars, invested in this species of property, all so concentrated that the mind can grasp it at once—this immense pecuniary interest, has its influence upon their minds.

But here in Connecticut and at the North Slavery does not exist, and we see it through no such medium. To us it appears natural to think that slaves are human beings; *men*, not property; that some of the things, at least, stated about men in the Declaration of Independence apply to them as well as to us. [Applause.] I say, we think, most of us, that this Charter of Freedom applies to the slave as well as to ourselves, that the class of arguments put forward to batter down that idea, are also calculated to break down the very idea of a free government, even for white men, and to undermine the very foundations of free society. [Continued applause.] We think Slavery a great moral wrong, and while we do not claim the right to touch it where it exists, we wish to treat it as a wrong in the Territories, where our votes will reach it. We think that a respect for ourselves, a regard for future generations and for the God that made us, require that we put down this wrong where our votes will properly reach it. We think that species of labor an injury to free white men—in short, we think Slavery a great moral, social and political evil, tolerable only because, and so far as its actual existence makes it necessary to tolerate it, and that beyond that, it ought to be treated as a wrong.

Now these two ideas, the property idea that Slavery is right, and the idea that it is wrong, come into collision, and do actually produce that irrepressible conflict which Mr. Seward has been so roundly abused for mentioning. The two ideas conflict, and must conflict.

Again, in its political aspect, does anything in any way

endanger the perpetuity of this Union but that single thing, Slavery? Many of our adversaries are anxious to claim that they are specially devoted to the Union, and take pains to charge upon us hostility to the Union. Now we claim that we are the only true Union men, and we put to them this one proposition: What ever endangered this Union, save and except Slavery? Did any other thing ever cause a moment's fear? All men must agree that this thing alone has ever endangered the perpetuity of the Union. But if it was threatened by any other influence, would not all men say that the best thing that could be done, if we could not or ought not to destroy it, would be at least to keep it from growing any larger? Can any man believe that the way to save the Union is to extend and increase the only thing that threatens the Union, and to suffer it to grow bigger and bigger? [Great applause.]

Whenever this question shall be settled, it must be settled on some philosophical basis. No policy that does not rest upon some philosophical public opinion can be permanently maintained. And hence, there are but two policies in regard to Slavery that can be at all maintained. The first, based on the property view that Slavery is right, conforms to that idea throughout, and demands that we shall do everything for it that we ought to do if it were right. We must sweep away all opposition, for opposition to the right is wrong; we must agree that Slavery is right, and we must adopt the idea that property has persuaded the owner to believe—that Slavery is morally right and socially elevating. This gives a philosophical basis for a permanent policy of encouragement.

The other policy is one that squares with the idea that Slavery is wrong, and it consists in doing everything that we ought to do if it is wrong. Now, I don't wish to be misunderstood, nor to leave a gap down to be misrepresented, even. I don't mean that we ought to attack it where it exists. To me it seems that if we were to form a government anew, in view of the actual presence of Slavery we should find it necessary to frame just such a government as our fathers did; giving to the slaveholder the entire control where the system was established, while we possessed the power to restrain it from going outside those limits. [Applause.] From the necessities of the case we should be compelled to form just such a government as our blessed fathers gave us; and, surely, if they have so made it, that adds another reason why we should let Slavery alone where it exists.

If I saw a venomous snake crawling in the road, any man would say I might seize the nearest stick and kill it; but if I found that snake in bed with my children, that would be another question. [Laughter.] I might hurt the children more than the snake, and it might bite them. [Applause.] Much more, if I found it in bed with my neighbor's children, and I had bound myself by a solemn compact not to meddle with his children under any circumstances, it would become me to let that particular mode of getting rid of the gentleman alone. [Great laughter.] But if there was a bed newly made up, to which the children were to be taken, and it was proposed to take a batch of young snakes and put them there with them, I take it no man would say there was any question how I ought to decide! [Prolonged applause and cheers.]

That is just the case! The new Territories are the newly made bed to which our children are to go, and it lies with the nation to say whether they shall have snakes mixed up with them or not. It does not seem as if there could be much hesitation what our policy should be! [Applause.]

Now I have spoken of a policy based on the idea that Slavery is wrong, and a policy based upon the idea that it is right. But an effort has been made for a policy that shall treat it as neither right or wrong. It is based upon utter indifference. Its leading advocate has said "I don't care whether it be voted up or down." [Laughter.] "It is merely a matter of dollars and cents." "The Almighty has drawn a line across this continent, on one side of which all soil must forever be cultivated by slave labor, and on the other by free;" "when the struggle is between the white man and the negro, I am for the white man; when it is between the negro and the crocodile, I am for the negro." Its central idea is indifference. It holds that it makes no more difference to us whether the Territories become free or slave States, than whether my neighbor stocks his farm with horned cattle or puts it into tobacco. All recognize this policy, the plausible sugar-coated name of which is *"popular sovereignty."* [Laughter.]

This policy chiefly stands in the way of a permanent settlement of the question. I believe there is no danger of its becoming the permanent policy of the country, for it is based on a public indifference. There is nobody that "don't care." ALL THE PEOPLE DO CARE! one way or the other. [Great applause.] I do not charge that its author, when he says he "don't care," states his individual opinion; he only expresses his policy for the government. I understand that he has never said, as an individual, whether he thought Slavery right or wrong—and he is the only man in the nation that has not! Now such a policy may have a temporary run; it may spring up as necessary to the political prospects of some gentleman; but it is utterly baseless; the people are not indifferent; and it can therefore have no durability or permanence.

But suppose it could! Then it could be maintained only by a public opinion that shall say "we don't care." There must be a change in public opinion, the public mind must be so far debauched as to square with this policy of caring not at all. The people must come to consider this as "merely a question of dollars and cents," and to believe that in some places the Almighty has made Slavery necessarily eternal. This policy can be brought to prevail if the people can be brought round to say honestly "we don't care;" if not, it can never be maintained. It is for you to say whether that can be done. [Applause.]

You are ready to say it cannot, but be not too fast! Remember what a long stride has been taken since the repeal of the Missouri Compromise! Do you know of any Democrat, of either branch of the party—do you know one who declares that he believes that the Declaration of Independence has any application to the negro? Judge Taney declares that it has not, and Judge Douglas even vilifies me personally and scolds me roundly for saying that the Declaration applies to all men, and that negroes are men. [Cheers.] Is there a Democrat here who does not deny that the Declaration applies to a negro? Do any of you know of one? Well, I have tried before perhaps fifty audiences, some larger and some smaller than this, to find one such Democrat, and never yet have I found one who said I did not place him right in that. I must assume that Democrats hold that, and now, *not one of these Democrats can show that he said that five years ago!* [Applause.] I venture to defy the whole party to produce one man that ever uttered the belief that the Declaration did not apply to negroes, before the repeal of the Missouri Compromise! Four or five years ago we all thought negroes were men, and that when *"all men"* were named, negroes were included. But *the whole Democratic party has deliberately taken negroes from the class of men and put them in the class of brutes.* [Applause.] Turn it as you will, it is simply the truth! Don't be too hasty then in saying that the people cannot be brought to this new doctrine, but note that long stride. One more as long completes the journey, from where negroes are estimated as men to where they are estimated as mere brutes—as rightful property!

That saying, "in the struggle between the white man and the negro," &c., which I know came from the same source as this policy—that saying marks another step. There is a falsehood wrapped up in that statement. "In the struggle between the white man and the negro" assumes that there is a struggle, in which either the white man must enslave the negro or the negro must enslave the white. There is no such struggle! It is merely an ingenious falsehood, to degrade and brutalize the negro. Let each let the other alone, and there is no struggle about it. If it was like two wrecked seamen on a narrow plank, when each must push the other off or drown himself, I would push the negro off or a white man either, but it is not; the plank is large enough for both. [Applause.] This good earth is plenty broad enough for white man and negro both, and there is no need of either pushing the other off. [Continued applause.]

So that saying, "in the struggle between the negro and the crocodile," &c., is made up from the idea that down where the crocodile inhabits a white man can't labor; it must be nothing else but crocodile or negro; if the negro does not the crocodile must possess the earth; [laughter;] in that case he declares for the negro. The meaning of the whole is just this: As a white man is to a negro, so is a negro to a crocodile; and as the negro may rightfully treat the crocodile, so may the white man rightfully treat the negro. This very dear phrase coined by its author, and so dear that he deliberately repeats it in many speeches, has a tendency to still further brutalize the negro, and to bring public opinion to the point of utter indifference whether men so brutalized are enslaved or not. When that time shall come, if ever, I think that policy to which I refer may prevail. But I hope the good freemen of this country will never allow it to come, and until then the policy can never be maintained.

Now consider the effect of this policy. We in the States are not to care whether Freedom or Slavery gets the better, but the people in the Territories may care. They are to decide, and they may think what they please; it is a matter of dollars and cents! But are not the people of the Territories detailed from the States? If this feeling of indifference—this absence of moral sense about the question—prevails in the States, will it not be carried into the Territories? Will not every man say, "I don't care, it is nothing to me?" If any one comes that wants Slavery, must they not say, "I don't care whether Freedom or Slavery be voted up or voted down?" It results at last in nationalizing the institution of Slavery. Even if fairly carried out, that policy is just as certain to nationalize Slavery as the doctrine of Jeff Davis himself. These are only two roads to the same goal, and "popular sovereignty" is just as sure and almost as short as the other. [Applause.]

What we want, and all we want, is to have with us the men who think slavery wrong. But those who say they hate slavery, and are opposed to it, but yet act with the Democratic party—where are they? Let us apply a few tests. You say that you think slavery is wrong, but you denounce all attempts to restrain it. Is there anything else that you think wrong, that you are not willing to deal with as a wrong? Why are you so careful, so tender of this one wrong and no other? [Laughter.] You will not let us *do* a single thing as if it was wrong; there is no place where you will allow it to be even *called* wrong! We must not call it wrong in the Free States, because it is *not* there, and we must not call it wrong in the Slave States because it *is* there; we must not call it wrong in politics because that is bringing morality into politics, and we must not call it wrong in the pulpit because that is bringing politics into religion; we must not bring it into the Tract Society or the other societies, because those are such unsuitable places, and there is no single place, according to you, where this wrong thing can properly be called wrong! [Continued laughter and applause.]

Perhaps you will plead that if the people of Slave States should themselves set on foot an effort for emancipation, you would wish them success, and bid them God-speed. Let us test that! In 1858, the emancipation party of Missouri, with Frank Blair at their head, tried to get up a movement for that purpose, and having started a party contested the State. Blair was beaten, apparently if not truly, and when the news came to Connecticut, you, who knew that Frank Blair was taking hold of this thing by the right end, and doing the only thing that you say can properly be done to remove this wrong— did you bow your heads in sorrow because of that defeat? Do you, any of you, know one single Democrat that showed sorrow over that result? Not one! On the contrary every man threw up his hat, and hallooed at the top of his lungs, "hooray for Democracy!" [Great laughter and applause.]

Now, gentlemen, *the Republicans desire to place this great question of slavery on the very basis on which our fathers placed it, and no other.* [Applause.] It is easy to demonstrate that "our Fathers, who framed this government under which we live," looked on Slavery as wrong, and so framed it and everything about it as to square with the idea that it was wrong, so far as the necessities arising from its existence permitted. In forming the Constitution they found the slave trade existing; capital invested in it; fields depending upon it for labor, and the whole system resting upon the importation of slave-labor. They therefore did not prohibit the slave trade at once, but they gave the power to prohibit it after twenty years. Why was this? What other foreign trade did they treat in that way? Would they have done this if they had not thought slavery wrong?

Another thing was done by some of the same men who framed the Constitution, and afterwards adopted as their own act by the first Congress held under that Constitution, of which many of the framers were members; they prohibited the spread of Slavery into Territories. Thus the same men, the framers of the Constitution, cut off the supply and prohibited the spread of Slavery, and both acts show conclusively that they considered that the thing was wrong.

If additional proof is wanting it can be found in the phraseology of the Constitution. When men are framing a supreme
law and chart of government, to secure blessings and prosperity to untold generations yet to come, they use language as
short and direct and plain as can be found, to express their
meaning. In all matters but this of Slavery the framers of the
Constitution used the very clearest, shortest, and most direct
language. But the Constitution alludes to Slavery three times
without mentioning it once! The language used becomes am-
biguous, roundabout, and mystical. They speak of the "immigration of persons," and mean the importation of slaves, but
do not say so. In establishing a basis of representation they
say "all other persons," when they mean to say slaves—why
did they not use the shortest phrase? In providing for the
return of fugitives they say "persons held to service or labor."
If they had said slaves it would have been plainer, and less
liable to misconstruction. Why didn't they do it. We cannot
doubt that it was done on purpose. Only one reason is possible, and that is supplied us by one of the framers of the Constitution—and it is not possible for man to conceive of any
other—they expected and desired that the system would
come to an end, and meant that when it did, the Constitution
should not show that there ever had been a slave in this good
free country of ours! [Great applause.]

I will dwell on that no longer. I see the signs of the approaching triumph of the Republicans in the bearing of their
political adversaries. A great deal of their war with us now-
a-days is mere bushwhacking. [Laughter.] At the battle of
Waterloo, when Napoleon's cavalry had charged again and
again upon the unbroken squares of British infantry, at last
they were giving up the attempt, and going off in disorder,
when some of the officers in mere vexation and complete despair fired their pistols at those solid squares. The Democrats
are in that sort of extreme desperation; it is nothing else.
[Laughter.] I will take up a few of these *arguments*.

There is "THE IRREPRESSIBLE CONFLICT." [Applause.]
How they rail at Seward for that saying! They repeat it constantly; and although the proof has been thrust under their
noses again and again, that almost every good man since the
formation of our government has uttered that same senti-

ment, from Gen. Washington, who "trusted that we should yet have a confederacy of Free States," with Jefferson, Jay, Monroe, down to the latest days, yet they refuse to notice that at all, and persist in railing at Seward for saying it. Even Roger A. Pryor, editor of the Richmond Enquirer, uttered the same sentiment in almost the same language, and yet so little offence did it give the Democrats that he was sent for to Washington to edit the States—the Douglas organ there, while Douglas goes into hydrophobia and spasms of rage because Seward dared to repeat it. [Great applause.] This is what I call bushwhacking, a sort of argument that they must know any child can see through.

Another is JOHN BROWN! [Great laughter.] You stir up insurrections, you invade the South! John Brown! Harper's Ferry! Why, John Brown was not a Republican! You have never implicated a single Republican in that Harper's Ferry enterprise. We tell you that if any member of the Republican party is guilty in that matter, you know it or you do not know it. If you do know it, you are inexcusable not to designate the man and prove the fact. If you do not know it, you are inexcusable to assert it, and especially to persist in the assertion after you have tried and failed to make the proof. You need not be told that persisting in a charge which one does not know to be true is simply malicious slander. Some of you admit that no Republican designedly aided or encouraged the Harper's Ferry affair; but still insist that our doctrines and declarations necessarily lead to such results. We do not believe it. We know we hold to no doctrines, and make no declarations, which were not held to and made by our fathers who framed the Government under which we live, and we cannot see how declarations that were patriotic when they made them are villainous when we make them. You never dealt fairly by us in relation to that affair—and I will say frankly that I know of nothing in your character that should lead us to suppose that you would. You had just been soundly thrashed in elections in several States, and others were soon to come. You rejoiced at the occasion, and only were troubled that there were not three times as many killed in the affair. You were in evident glee—there was no sorrow for the killed nor for the peace of Virginia disturbed—you were rejoicing

that by charging Republicans with this thing you might get
an advantage of us in New York, and the other States. You
pulled that string as tightly as you could, but your very
generous and worthy expectations were not quite fulfilled.
[Laughter.] Each Republican knew that the charge was a slander as to himself at least, and was not inclined by it to cast his
vote in your favor. It was mere bushwhacking, because you
had nothing else to do. You are still on that track, and I say,
go on! If you think you can slander a woman into loving you
or a man into voting for you, try it till you are satisfied! [Tre-
mendous applause.]

   Another specimen of this bushwhacking, that "shoe strike."
[Laughter.] Now be it understood that I do not pretend to
know all about the matter. I am merely going to speculate a
little about some of its phases. And at the outset, *I am glad to
see that a system of labor prevails in New England under which
laborers* CAN *strike* when they want to [Cheers,] where they are
not obliged to work under all circumstances, and are not tied
down and obliged to labor whether you pay them or not!
[Cheers.] I *like* the system which lets a man quit when he
wants to, and wish it might prevail everywhere. [Tremendous
applause.] One of the reasons why I am opposed to Slavery is
just here. What is the true condition of the laborer? I take it
that it is best for all to leave each man free to acquire property
as fast as he can. Some will get wealthy. I don't believe in a
law to prevent a man from getting rich; it would do more
harm than good. So while we do not propose any war upon
capital, we do wish to allow the humblest man an equal
chance to get rich with everybody else. [Applause.] When one
starts poor, as most do in the race of life, free society is such
that he knows he can better his condition; he knows that
there is no fixed condition of labor, for his whole life. I am
not ashamed to confess that twenty five years ago I was a
hired laborer, mauling rails, at work on a flat-boat—just what
might happen to any poor man's son! [Applause.] I want
every man to have the chance—and I believe a black man is
entitled to it—in which he *can* better his condition—when
he may look forward and hope to be a hired laborer this year
and the next, work for himself afterward, and finally to hire
men to work for him! That is the true system. Up here in

New England, you have a soil that scarcely sprouts black-eyed beans, and yet where will you find wealthy men so wealthy, and poverty so rarely in extremity? There is not another such place on earth! [Cheers.] I desire that if you get too thick here, and find it hard to better your condition on this soil, you may have a chance to strike and go somewhere else, where you may not be degraded, nor have your family corrupted by forced rivalry with negro slaves. I want you to have a clean bed, and no snakes in it! [Cheers.] Then you can better your condition, and so it may go on and on in one ceaseless round so long as man exists on the face of the earth! [Prolonged applause.]

Now, to come back to this shoe strike,—if, as the Senator from Illinois asserts, this is caused by withdrawal of Southern votes, consider briefly how you will meet the difficulty. You have done nothing, and have protested that you have done nothing, to injure the South. And yet, to get back the shoe trade, you must leave off doing something that you are now doing. What is it? You must stop thinking slavery wrong! Let your institutions be wholly changed; let your State Constitutions be subverted, glorify slavery, and so you will get back the shoe trade—for what? You have brought owned labor with it to compete with your own labor, to underwork you, and to degrade you! Are you ready to get back the trade on those terms?

But the statement is not correct. You have not lost that trade; orders were never better than now! Senator Mason, a Democrat, comes into the Senate in homespun, a proof that the dissolution of the Union has actually begun! but orders are the same. Your factories have not struck work, neither those where they make anything for coats, nor for pants, nor for shirts, nor for ladies' dresses. Mr. Mason has not reached the manufacturers who ought to have made him a coat and pants! To make his proof good for anything he should have come into the Senate barefoot! (Great laughter.)

Another bushwhacking contrivance; simply that, nothing else! I find a good many people who are very much concerned about the loss of Southern trade. Now either these people are sincere or they are not. (Laughter.) I will speculate a little about that. If they are sincere, and are moved by any real danger of the loss of Southern trade, they will simply get their names on the white list, and then, instead of persuading Republicans to do likewise, they will be glad to keep you away! Don't you see they thus shut off competition? They would not be whispering around to Republicans to come in and share the profits with them. But if they are not sincere, and are merely trying to fool Republicans out of their votes, they will grow very anxious about *your* pecuniary prospects; they are afraid you are going to get broken up and ruined; they did not care about Democratic votes—*Oh no, no, no!* You must judge which class those belong to whom you meet; I leave it to you to determine from the facts.

Let us notice some more of the stale charges against Republicans. You say we are sectional. We deny it. That makes an issue; and the burden of proof is upon you. You produce your proof; and what is it? Why, that our party has no existence in your section—gets no votes in your section. The fact is substantially true; but does it prove the issue? If it does, then in case we should, without change of principle, begin to get votes in your section, we should thereby cease to be sectional. You cannot escape this conclusion; and yet, are you willing to abide by it? If you are, you will probably soon find that we have ceased to be sectional, for we shall get votes in your section this very year. [Applause.] The fact that we get no votes in your section is a fact of your making, and not of ours. And if there be fault in that fact, that fault is primarily yours, and remains so until you show that we repel you by some wrong principle or practice. If we do repel you by any wrong principle or practice, the fault is ours; but this brings you to where you ought to have started—to a discussion of the right or wrong of our principle. If our principle, put in practice, would wrong your section for the benefit of ours, or for any other object, then our principle, and we with it, are sectional, and are justly opposed and denounced as such. Meet us, then, on the question of whether our principle, put in practice, would wrong your section; and so meet it as if it were possible that something may be said on our side. Do you accept the challenge? No? Then you really believe that the principle which our fathers who framed the Government under which we live thought so clearly right as to adopt it, and indorse it again and again, upon their official oaths, is, in fact, so clearly wrong as to demand your condemnation without a moment's consideration.

Some of you delight to flaunt in our faces the warning against sectional parties given by Washington in his Farewell address. Less than eight years before Washington gave that warning, he had, as President of the United States, approved and signed an act of Congress, enforcing the prohibition of Slavery in the northwestern Territory, which act embodied the policy of Government upon that subject, up to and at the very moment he penned that warning; and about one year after he penned it he wrote LaFayette that he considered that prohibition a wise measure, expressing in the same connection his hope that we should some time have a confederacy of Free States.

Bearing this in mind, and seeing that sectionalism has since arisen upon this same subject, is that warning a weapon in your hands against us, or in our hands against you? Could Washington himself speak, would he cast the blame of that sectionalism upon us, who sustain his policy, or upon you who repudiate it? We respect that warning of Washington, and we commend it to you, together with his example pointing to the right application of it. [Applause.]

But you say you are conservative—eminently conservative—while we are revolutionary, destructive, or something of the sort. What is conservatism? Is it not adherence to the old and tried, against the new and untried? We stick to, contend for, the identical old policy on the point in controversy which was adopted by our fathers who framed the Government under which we live; while you with one accord reject, and scout, and spit upon that old policy, and insist upon substituting something new. True, you disagree among yourselves as to what that substitute shall be. You have considerable variety of new propositions and plans, but you are unanimous in rejecting and denouncing the old policy of the fathers. Some of you are for reviving the foreign slave-trade; some for a Congressional Slave-Code for the Territories; some for Congress forbidding the Territories to prohibit Slavery within their limits; some for maintaining Slavery in the Territories through the Judiciary; some for the "gur-reat pur-rin-ciple" that "if one man would enslave another, no third man should object," fantastically called "Popular Sovereignty;" [great laughter,] but never a man among you in favor of Federal prohibition of Slavery in Federal Territories, according to the practice of our fathers who framed the Government under which we live. Not one of all your various plans can show a precedent or an advocate in the century within which our Government originated. And yet you draw yourselves up and say "We are eminently conservative!" [Great laughter.]

It is exceedingly desirable that all parts of this great Confederacy shall be at peace, and in harmony, one with another. Let us Republicans do our part to have it so. Even though much provoked, let us do nothing through passion and ill temper. Even though the Southern people will not so much as listen to us, let us calmly consider their demands, and yield to them if, in our deliberate view of our duty, we possibly can. Judging by all they say and do, and by the subject and nature of their controversy with us, let us determine, if we can, what will satisfy them?

Will they be satisfied if the Territories be unconditionally surrendered to them? We know they will not. In all their present complaints against us, the Territories are scarcely mentioned. Invasions and insurrections are the rage now. Will it satisfy them if, in the future, we have nothing to do with invasions and insurrections? We know it will not. We so know because we know we never had anything to do with invasions and insurrections; and yet this total abstaining does not exempt us from the charge and the denunciation.

The question recurs, what will satisfy them? Simply this: we must not only let them alone, but we must, somehow, convince them that we do let them alone. [Applause.] This, we know by experience, is no easy task. We have been so trying to convince them, from the very beginning of our organization, but with no success. In all our platforms and speeches, we have constantly protested our purpose to let them alone; but this has had no tendency to convince them. Alike unavailing to convince them is the fact that they have never detected a man of us in any attempt to disturb them.

These natural and apparently adequate means all failing, what will convince them? This, and this only; cease to call slavery *wrong*, and join them in calling it *right*. And this must be done thoroughly—done in *acts* as well as in *words*. Silence will not be tolerated—we must place ourselves avowedly with them. Douglas's new sedition law must be enacted and enforced, suppressing all declarations that Slavery is wrong, whether made in politics, in presses, in pulpits, or in private. We must arrest and return their fugitive slaves with greedy pleasure. We must pull down our Free State Constitutions. The whole atmosphere must be disinfected of all taint of opposition to Slavery, before they will cease to believe that all their troubles proceed from us. So long as we call Slavery wrong, whenever a slave runs away they will overlook the obvious fact that he ran because he was oppressed, and declare he was stolen off. Whenever a master cuts his slaves with the lash, and they cry out under it, he will overlook the obvious fact that the negroes cry out because they are hurt, and insist that they were *put up to it by some rascally abolitionist*. [Great laughter.]

I am quite aware that they do not state their case precisely in this way. Most of them would probably say to us, "Let us alone, do nothing to us, and say what you please about Slavery." But we do let them alone—have never disturbed them—so that, after all, it is what we say, which dissatisfies them. They will continue to accuse us of doing, until we cease saying.

I am also aware they have not, as yet, in terms, demanded the overthrow of our Free State Constitutions. Yet those Constitutions declare the wrong of Slavery, with more solemn emphasis than do all other sayings against it; and when all these other sayings shall have been silenced, the overthrow of these Constitutions will be demanded, and nothing be left to resist the demand. It is nothing to the contrary, that they do not demand the whole of this just now. Demanding what they do, and for the reason they do, they can voluntarily stop nowhere short of this consummation. Holding as they do, that Slavery is morally right, and socially elevating, they cannot cease to demand a full national recognition of it, as a legal right, and a social blessing.

Nor can we justifiably withhold this, on any ground save our conviction that Slavery is wrong. If Slavery is right, all words, acts, laws, and Constitutions against it, are themselves wrong, and should be silenced, and swept away. If it is right, we cannot justly object to its nationality—its universality; if it is wrong, they cannot justly insist upon its extension—its enlargement. All they ask, we could readily grant, if we thought Slavery right; all we ask, they could as readily grant, if they thought it wrong. Their thinking it right, and our thinking it wrong, is the precise fact upon which depends the whole controversy. Thinking it right as they do, they are not to blame for desiring its full recognition, as being right; but, thinking it wrong, as we do, can we yield to them? Can we cast our votes with their view, and against our own? In view of our moral, social, and political responsibilities, can we do this?

Wrong as we think Slavery is, we can yet afford to let it alone where it is, because that much is due to the necessity arising from its actual presence in the nation; but can we, while our votes will prevent it, allow it to spread into the National Territories, and to overrun us here in these Free States?

If our sense of duty forbids this, then let us stand by our duty, fearlessly and effectively. Let us be diverted by none of those sophistical contrivances wherewith we are so industriously plied and belabored—contrivances such as groping for some middle ground between the right and the wrong, vain as the search for a man who should be neither a living man nor a dead man—such as a policy of "don't care" on a question about which all true men do care—such as Union appeals beseeching true Union men to yield to Disunionists, reversing the divine rule, and calling, not the sinners, but the righteous to repentance—such as invocations of Washington, imploring men to unsay what Washington did.

Neither let us be slandered from our duty by false accusations against us, nor frightened from it by menaces of destruction to the Government, nor of dungeons to ourselves. Let us have faith that right makes might; and in that faith, let us, to the end, dare to do our duty, as we understand it.

March 6, 1860

To Mark W. Delahay

Dear Delahay—   Springfield, Ills— Mar— 16, 1860

I have just returned from the East. Before leaving, I received your letter of Feb. 6; and on my return I find those of the 17th. & 19th. with Genl. Lane's note inclosed in one of them.

I sincerely wish you could be elected one of the first Senators for Kansas; but how to help you I do not know. If it were permissable for me to interfere, I am not personally acquainted with a single member of your Legislature. If my known friendship for you could be of any advantage, that friendship was abundantly manifested by me last December while in Kansas. If any member had written me, as you say some have Trumbull, I would very readily answer him. I shall write Trumbull on the subject at this sitting.

I understood, while in Kansas, that the State Legislature will not meet until the State is admitted. Was that the right understanding?

As to your kind wishes for myself, allow me to say I can not enter the ring on the money basis—first, because, in the main, it is wrong; and secondly, I have not, and can not get, the money. I say, in the main, the use of money is wrong; but for certain objects, in a political contest, the use of some, is both right, and indispensable. With me, as with yourself, this long struggle has been one of great pecuniary loss. I now distinctly say this. If you shall be appointed a delegate to Chicago, I will furnish one hundred dollars to bear the expences of the trip.

Present my respects to Genl. Lane; and say to him, I shall be pleased to hear from him at any time. Your friend, as ever

P.S. I have not yet taken the newspaper slip to the Journal. I shall do that to-morrow; and then send you the paper as requested.

To Samuel Galloway

Hon. Samuel Galloway   Chicago, March 24 1860

My dear Sir: I am here attending a trial in court. Before leaving home I received your kind letter of the 15th. Of course

I am gratified to know I have friends in Ohio who are disposed to give me the highest evidence of their friendship and confidence. Mr Parrott of the Legislature, had written me to the same effect. If I have any chance, it consists mainly in the fact that the *whole* opposition would vote for me if nominated. (I dont mean to include the pro-slavery opposition of the South, of course.) My name is new in the field; and I suppose I am not the *first* choice of a very great many. Our policy, then, is to give no offence to others—leave them in a mood to come to us, if they shall be compelled to give up their first love. This, too, is dealing justly with all, and leaving us in a mood to support heartily whoever shall be nominated. I believe I have once before told you that I especially wish to do no ungenerous thing towards Governor Chase, because he gave us his sympathy in 1858, when scarcely any other distinguished man did. Whatever you may do for me, consistently with these suggestions, will be appreciated, and gratefully remembered.

Please write me again. Yours very truly

To Richard M. Corwine

Hon. R. M. Corwine.   Springfield, Ill., April 6th. 1860.

My Dear Sir   Reaching home yesterday after an absence of more than two weeks, I found your letter of the 24th of March. Remembering that when not a very great man begins to be mentioned for a very great position, his head is very likely to be a little turned, I concluded I am not the fittest person to answer the questions you ask. Making due allowance for this, I think Mr. Seward is the very best candidate we could have for the North of Illinois, and the very *worst* for the South of it. The estimate of Gov. Chase here is neither better nor worse than that of Seward, except that he is a newer man. They are regarded as being almost the same, seniority giving Seward the inside track. Mr. Bates, I think, would be the best man for the South of our State, and the worst for the North of it. If Judge McLean was fifteen, or even ten years younger, I think he would be stronger than either, in our state, taken as a whole; but his great age, and the recollection of the deaths of Harrison and Taylor have, so far, prevented his being much spoken of here.

I really believe we can carry the state for either of them, or for any one who may be nominated; but doubtless it would be easier to do it with some than with others.

I feel myself disqualified to speak of myself in this matter. I feel this letter will be of little value to you; but I can make it no better, under the circumstances. Let it be strictly confidential, not that there is any thing really objectionable in it, but because it might be misconstrued. Yours very truly,

To Cornelius F. McNeill

C. F. McNeill, Esq.—   Springfield, April 6, 1860.

Dear Sir: Reaching home yesterday, I found yours of the 23d. March, inclosing a slip from *The Middleport Press*. It is not true that I ever *charged* anything for a political speech in my life—but this much is true: Last October I was requested, by letter, to deliver some sort of speech in Mr. Beechers church, in Brooklyn, $200 being offered in the first letter. I wrote that I could do it in February, provided they would take a political speech, if I could find time to get up no other. They agreed, and subsequently I informed them the speech would have to be a political one. When I reached New York, I, for the first, learned that the place was changed to "Cooper Institute." I made the speech, and left for New Hampshire, where I have a son at school, neither asking for pay nor having any offered me. Three days after, a check for $200— was sent to me, at N.H., and I took it, *and did not know it was wrong.* My understanding now is, though I knew nothing of it at the time, that they did charge for admittance, at the Cooper Institute, and that they took in more than twice $200.

I have made this explanation to you as a friend; but I wish no explanation made to our enemies. What they want is a squabble and a fuss; and that they can have if we explain; and they can not have if we don't.

When I returned through New York from New England I

was told by the gentlemen who sent me the check, that a drunken vagabond in the Club, having learned something about the $200, made the exhibition out of which *The Herald* manufactured the article quoted by *The Press* of your town.

My judgment is, and therefore my request is, that you give no denial, and no explanations.

Thanking you for your kind interest in the matter, I remain, Yours truly,

To Lyman Trumbull

Hon: L. Trumbull: Springfield,
My dear Sir: April 29. 1860

Yours of the 24th. was duly received; and I have postponed answering it, hoping by the result at Charleston, to know who is to lead our adversaries, before writing. But Charleston hangs fire, and I wait no longer.

As you request, I will be entirely frank. The taste *is* in my mouth a little; and this, no doubt, disqualifies me, to some extent, to form correct opinions. You may confidently rely, however, that by no advice or consent of mine, shall my pretentions be pressed to the point of endangering our common cause.

Now, as to my opinions about the chances of others in Illinois. I think neither Seward nor Bates can carry Illinois if Douglas shall be on the track; and that either of them can, if he shall not be. I rather think McLean could carry it with D. on or off—in other words, I think McLean is stronger in Illinois, taking all sections of it, than either S. or B; and I think S. the weakest of the three. I hear no objection to McLean, except his age; but that objection seems to occur to every one; and it is possible it might leave him no stronger than the others. By the way, if we should nominate him, how would we save to ourselves the chance of filling his vacancy in the Court? Have him hold on up to the moment of his inauguration? Would that course be no draw-back upon us in the canvass?

Recurring to Illinois, we want something here quite as

much as, and which is harder to get than, the electoral vote—
the Legislature. And it is exactly in this point that Seward's
nomination would be hard upon us. Suppose he should gain
us a thousand votes in Winnebago, it would not compensate
for the loss of fifty in Edgar.

A word now for your own special benefit. You better write
no letters which can possibly be distorted into opposition, or
quasi opposition to me. There are men on the constant watch
for such things out of which to prejudice my peculiar friends
against you. While I have no more suspicion of you than I
have of my best friend living, I am kept in a constant struggle
against suggestions of this sort. I have hesitated some to write
this paragraph, lest you should suspect I do it for my own
benefit, and not for yours; but on reflection I conclude you
will not suspect me.

Let no eye but your own see this—not that there is anything wrong, or even ungenerous, in it; but it would be misconstrued. Your friend as ever

To Richard M. Corwine

PRIVATE

Hon: R. M. Corwine   Springfield, Ills. May 2. 1860.

Dear Sir: Yours of the 30th. ult. is just received. After what
you have said, it is perhaps proper I should post you, so far as
I am able, as to the "lay of the land." First then, I think the
Illinois delegation will be unanamous for me at the start; and
no other delegation will. A few individuals in other delegations would like to go for me at the start, but may be restrained by their colleagues. It is represented to me, by men
who ought to know, that the whole of Indiana might not be
difficult to get. You know how it is in Ohio. I am certainly
not the first choice there; and yet I have not heard that any
one makes any positive objection to me. It is just so everywhere so far as I can perceive. Everywhere, except in Illinois,
and possibly Indiana, one or another is prefered to me, but
there is no positive objection. This is the ground as it now
appears. I believe you personally know C. M. Allen, of Vin-

cennes, Ia. He is a delegate, and has notified me that the entire Ia. delegation will be in Chicago the same day you name — Saturday the 12th. My friends Jesse K. Dubois, our Auditor, & Judge David Davis, will probably be there ready to confer with friends from other States. Let me hear from you again when anything occurs. Yours very truly

To Edward Wallace

Dr. Edward Wallace: Springfield, Ills. May 12. 1860

My dear Sir   Your brother, Dr. W. S. Wallace, shows me a letter of yours, in which you request him to inquire if you may use a letter of mine to you, in which something is said upon the Tariff question. I do not precisely remember what I did say in that letter; but I presume I said nothing substantially different from what I shall say now.

In the days of Henry Clay I was a Henry Clay-tariff-man; and my views have undergone no material change upon that subject. I now think the Tariff question ought not to be agitated in the Chicago convention; but that all should be satisfied on that point, with a presidential candidate, whose antecedents give assurance that he would neither seek to force a tariff-law by Executive influence; nor yet to arrest a reasonable one, by a veto, or otherwise. Just such a candidate I desire shall be put in nomination. I really have no objection to these views being publicly known; but I do wish to thrust no letter before the public now, upon any subject. Save me from the appearance of obtrusion; and I do not care who sees this, or my former letter. Yours very truly

Reply to Committee of the Republican National Convention, Springfield, Illinois

Mr. Chairman and gentlemen of the committee, I tender you, and through you the Republican National Convention, and all the people represented in it, my profoundest thanks for the high honor done me, which you now formally announce.

Deeply, and even painfully sensible of the great responsibility which is inseparable from that honor—a responsibility which I could almost wish had fallen upon some one of the far more eminent men and experienced statesmen whose distinguished names were before the Convention, I shall, by your leave, consider more fully the resolutions of the Convention, denominated the platform, and without unseasonable delay, respond to you, Mr. Chairman, in writing—not doubting now, that the platform will be found satisfactory, and the nomination accepted.

And now, I will not longer defer the pleasure of taking you, and each of you, by the hand.

May 19, 1860

To George Ashmun

Hon: George Ashmun: Springfield, Ills. May 23. 1860
President of the Republican National Convention.

Sir: I accept the nomination tendered me by the Convention over which you presided, and of which I am formally apprized in the letter of yourself and others, acting as a committee of the convention, for that purpose.

The declaration of principles and sentiments, which accompanies your letter, meets my approval; and it shall be my care not to violate, or disregard it, in any part.

Imploring the assistance of Divine Providence, and with due regard to the views and feelings of all who were represented in the convention; to the rights of all the states, and territories, and people of the nation; to the inviolability of the constitution, and the perpetual union, harmony, and prosperity of all, I am most happy to co-operate for the practical success of the principles declared by the convention. Your obliged friend, and fellow citizen

To Charles C. Nott

Charles C. Nott, Esq.   Springfield, Ills, May 31, 1860.

My Dear Sir: Yours of the 23rd, accompanied by a copy of the speech delivered by me at the Cooper Institute, and upon which you have made some notes for emendations, was received some days ago. Of course I would not object to, but would be pleased rather, with a more perfect edition of that speech.

I did not preserve memoranda of my investigations; and I could not now re-examine, and make notes, without an expenditure of time which I can not bestow upon it. Some of your notes I do not understand.

So far as it is intended merely to improve in grammar, and elegance of composition, I am quite agreed; but I do not wish the sense changed, or modified, to a hair's breadth. And you, not having studied the particular points so closely as I have, can not be quite sure that you do not change the sense when you do not intend it. For instance, in a note at bottom of first page, you proposed to substitute "Democrats" for "Douglas." But what I am saying there is *true* of Douglas, and is not true of "Democrats" generally; so that the proposed substitution would be a very considerable blunder. Your proposed insertion of "residences" though it would do little or no harm, is not at all necessary to the sense I was trying to convey. On page 5 your proposed grammatical change would certainly do no harm. The *"impudently absurd"* I stick to. The striking out *"he"* and inserting *"we"* turns the sense exactly wrong. The striking out *"upon it"* leaves the sense too general and incomplete. The sense is "act as they acted *upon that question"*—not as they acted generally.

After considering your proposed changes on page 7, I do not think them material, but I am willing to defer to you in relation to them.

On page 9, striking out *"to us"* is probably right. The word *"lawyer's"* I wish retained. The word *"Courts"* struck out twice, I wish reduced to "Court" and retained. "Court" as a collection more properly governs the plural "have" as I understand. "The" preceding "Court," in the latter case, must also be retained. The words "quite," "as," and "or" on the same page, I wish retained. The italicising, and quotation marking, I have no objection to.

As to the note at bottom, I do not think any too much is admitted. What you propose on page 11 is right. I return your copy of the speech, together with one printed here, under my own hasty supervising. That at New York was printed without any supervision by me. If you conclude to publish a new edition, allow me to see the proof-sheets.

And now thanking you for your very complimentary letter, and your interest for me generally, I subscribe myself. Your friend and servant,

Autobiography Written for Campaign

Abraham Lincoln was born Feb. 12, 1809, then in Hardin, now in the more recently formed county of Larue, Kentucky. His father, Thomas, & grand-father, Abraham, were born in Rockingham county Virginia, whither their ancestors had come from Berks county Pennsylvania. His lineage has been traced no farther back than this. The family were originally quakers, though in later times they have fallen away from the peculiar habits of that people. The grand-father Abraham, had four brothers—Isaac, Jacob, John & Thomas. So far as known, the descendants of Jacob and John are still in Virginia. Isaac went to a place near where Virginia, North Carolina, and Tennessee, join; and his decendants are in that region. Thomas came to Kentucky, and after many years, died there, whence his decendants went to Missouri. Abraham, grandfather of the subject of this sketch, came to Kentucky, and was killed by indians about the year 1784. He left a widow, three sons and two daughters. The eldest son, Mordecai, remained in Kentucky till late in life, when he removed to Hancock county, Illinois, where soon after he died, and where several of his descendants still reside. The second son, Josiah, removed at an early day to a place on Blue River, now within Harrison county, Indiana; but no recent information of him, or his family, has been obtained. The eldest sister, Mary, married Ralph Crume and some of her descendants are now known to be in Breckenridge county Kentucky. The second sister, Nancy, married William Brumfield, and her family are not known to have left Kentucky, but there is no recent information from them. Thomas, the youngest son, and father of the present subject, by the early death of his father, and very narrow circumstances of his mother, even in childhood was a wandering laboring boy, and grew up litterally without education. He never did more in the way of writing than to bunglingly sign his own name. Before he was grown, he passed one year as a hired hand with his uncle Isaac on Wataga, a branch of the Holsteen River. Getting back into Kentucky, and having reached his 28th. year, he married Nancy Hanks—mother of the present subject—in the year 1806. She also was born in Virginia; and relatives of hers of the name of Hanks, and of other names, now reside in Coles, in Macon, and in Adams counties, Illinois, and also in Iowa. The present subject has no brother or sister of the whole or half blood. He had a sister, older than himself, who was grown and married, but died many years ago, leaving no child. Also a brother, younger than himself, who died in infancy. Before leaving Kentucky he and his sister were sent for short periods, to A.B.C. schools, the first kept by Zachariah Riney, and the second by Caleb Hazel.

At this time his father resided on Knob-creek, on the road from Bardstown Ky. to Nashville Tenn. at a point three, or three and a half miles South or South-West of Atherton's ferry on the Rolling Fork. From this place he removed to what is now Spencer county Indiana, in the autumn of 1816, A. then being in his eigth year. This removal was partly on account of slavery; but chiefly on account of the difficulty in land titles in Ky. He settled in an unbroken forest; and the clearing away of surplus wood was the great task a head. A. though very young, was large of his age, and had an axe put into his hands at once; and from that till within his twentythird year, he was almost constantly handling that most useful instrument—less, of course, in plowing and harvesting seasons. At this place A. took an early start as a hunter, which was never much improved afterwards. (A few days before the completion of his eigth year, in the absence of his father, a flock of wild turkeys approached the new log-cabin, and A. with a rifle gun, standing inside, shot through a crack, and killed one of them. He has never since pulled a trigger on any larger game.) In the autumn of 1818 his mother died; and a year afterwards his father married Mrs. Sally Johnston, at Elizabeth-Town, Ky— a widow, with three children of her first marriage. She proved a good and kind mother to A. and is still living in Coles Co. Illinois. There were no children of this second marriage. His father's residence continued at the same place in Indiana, till 1830. While here A. went to A.B.C. schools by littles, kept successively by Andrew Crawford, —— Sweeney, and Azel W. Dorsey. He does not remember any other. The family of Mr. Dorsey now reside in Schuyler Co. Illinois. A. now thinks that the agregate of all his schooling did not amount to one year. He was never in a college or Academy as a student; and never inside of a college or accademy building till since he had a law-license. What he has in the way of education, he has picked up. After he was twentythree, and had separated from his father, he studied English grammar, imperfectly of course, but so as to speak and write as well as he now does. He studied and nearly mastered the Six-books of Euclid, since he was a member of Congress. He regrets his want of education, and does what he can to supply the want. In his tenth year he was kicked by a horse, and apparently killed for a time. When he was nineteen, still residing in Indiana, he made his first trip upon a flat-boat to New-Orleans. He was a hired hand merely; and he and a son of the owner, without other assistance, made the trip. The nature of part of the cargo-load, as it was called—made it necessary for them to linger and trade along the Sugar coast—and one night they were attacked by seven negroes with intent to kill and rob them. They were hurt some in the melee, but succeeded in driving the negroes from the boat, and then "cut cable" "weighed anchor" and left.

March 1st. 1830—A. having just completed his 21st. year, his father and family, with the families of the two daughters and sons-in-law, of his step-mother, left the old homestead in Indiana, and came to Illinois. Their mode of conveyance was waggons drawn by ox-teams, or A. drove one of the teams. They reached the county of Macon, and stopped there some time within the same month of March. His father and family settled a new place on the North side of the Sangamon river, at the junction of the timber-land and prairie, about ten miles Westerly from Decatur. Here they built a log-cabin, into which they removed, and made sufficient of rails to fence ten acres of ground, fenced and broke the ground, and raised a crop of sown corn upon it the same year. These are, or are supposed to be, the rails about which so much is being said just now, though they are far from being the first, or only rails ever made by A.

The sons-in-law, were temporarily settled at other places in the county. In the autumn all hands were greatly afflicted with augue and fever, to which they had not been used, and by which they were greatly discouraged—so much so that

they determined on leaving the county. They remained however, through the succeeding winter, which was the winter of
the very celebrated "deep snow" of Illinois. During that winter, A. together with his step-mother's son, John D. Johnston,
and John Hanks, yet residing in Macon county, hired themselves to one Denton Offutt, to take a flat boat from Beardstown Illinois to New-Orleans; and for that purpose, were to
join him—Offut—at Springfield, Ills so soon as the snow
should go off. When it did go off which was about the 1st. of
March 1831—the county was so flooded, as to make traveling
by land impracticable; to obviate which difficulty they purchased a large canoe and came down the Sangamon river in it.
This is the time and the manner of A's first entrance into
Sangamon County. They found Offutt at Springfield, but
learned from him that he had failed in getting a boat at
Beardstown. This lead to their hiring themselves to him at $12
per month, each; and getting the timber out of the trees and
building a boat at old Sangamon Town on the Sangamon
river, seven miles N.W. of Springfield, which boat they took
to New-Orleans, substantially upon the old contract. It was in
connection with this boat that occurred the ludicrous incident
of sewing up the hogs eyes. Offutt bought thirty odd large fat
live hogs, but found difficulty in driving them from where he
purchased them to the boat, and thereupon conceived the
whim that he could sew up their eyes and drive them where
he pleased. No sooner thought of than decided, he put his
hands, including A. at the job, which they completed—all
but the driving. In their blind condition they could not be
driven out of the lot or field they were in. This expedient
failing, they were tied and hauled on carts to the boat. It was
near the Sangamon River, within what is now Menard
county.

During this boat enterprize acquaintance with Offutt, who
was previously an entire stranger, he conceved a liking for A.
and believing he could turn him to account, he contracted
with him to act as clerk for him, on his return from New-
Orleans, in charge of a store and Mill at New-Salem, then in
Sangamon, now in Menard county. Hanks had not gone to
New-Orleans, but having a family, and being likely to be detained from home longer than at first expected, had turned

back from St. Louis. He is the same John Hanks who now engineers the "rail enterprize" at Decatur; and is a first cousin to A's mother. A's father, with his own family & others mentioned, had, in pursuance of their intention, removed from Macon to Coles county. John D. Johnston, the step-mother's son, went to them; and A. stopped indefinitely, and, for the first time, as it were, by himself at New-Salem, before mentioned. This was in July 1831. Here he rapidly made acquaintances and friends. In less than a year Offutt's business was failing—had almost failed,—when the Black-Hawk war of 1832—broke out. A joined a volunteer company, and to his own surprize, was elected captain of it. He says he has not since had any success in life which gave him so much satisfaction. He went the campaign, served near three months, met the ordinary hardships of such an expedition, but was in no battle. He now owns in Iowa, the land upon which his own warrants for this service, were located. Returning from the campaign, and encouraged by his great popularity among his immediate neighbors, he, the same year, ran for the Legislature and was beaten—his own precinct, however, casting it's votes 277 for and 7, against him. And this too while he was an avowed Clay man, and the precinct the autumn afterwards, giving a majority of 115 to Genl. Jackson over Mr. Clay. This was the only time A was ever beaten on a direct vote of the people. He was now without means and out of business, but was anxious to remain with his friends who had treated him with so much generosity, especially as he had nothing elsewhere to go to. He studied what he should do—thought of learning the black-smith trade—thought of trying to study law—rather thought he could not succeed at that without a better education. Before long, strangely enough, a man offered to sell and did sell, to A. and another as poor as himself, an old stock of goods, upon credit. They opened as merchants; and he says that was *the* store. Of course they did nothing but get deeper and deeper in debt. He was appointed Postmaster at New-Salem—the office being too insignificant, to make his politics an objection. The store winked out. The Surveyor of Sangamon, offered to depute to A that portion of his work which was within his part of the county. He accepted, procured a compass and chain, studied Flint, and

Gibson a little, and went at it. This procured bread, and kept soul and body together. The election of 1834 came, and he was then elected to the Legislature by the highest vote cast for any candidate. Major John T. Stuart, then in full practice of the law, was also elected. During the canvass, in a private conversation he encouraged A. to study law. After the election he borrowed books of Stuart, took them home with him, and went at it in good earnest. He studied with nobody. He still mixed in the surveying to pay board and clothing bills. When the Legislature met, the law books were dropped, but were taken up again at the end of the session. He was re-elected in 1836, 1838, and 1840. In the autumn of 1836 he obtained a law licence, and on April 15, 1837 removed to Springfield, and commenced the practice, his old friend, Stuart taking him into partnership. March 3rd. 1837, by a protest entered upon the Ills. House Journal of that date, at pages 817, 818, A. with Dan Stone, another representative of Sangamon, briefly defined his position on the slavery question; and so far as it goes, it was then the same that it is now. The protest is as follows—(Here insert it) In 1838, & 1840 Mr. L's party in the Legislature voted for him as Speaker; but being in the minority, he was not elected. After 1840 he declined a re-election to the Legislature. He was on the Harrison electoral ticket in 1840, and on that of Clay in 1844, and spent much time and labor in both those canvasses. In Nov. 1842 he was married to Mary, daughter of Robert S. Todd, of Lexington, Kentucky. They have three living children, all sons—one born in 1843, one in 1850, and one in 1853. They lost one, who was born in 1846. In 1846, he was elected to the lower House of Congress, and served one term only, commencing in Dec. 1847 and ending with the inauguration of Gen. Taylor, in March 1849. All the battles of the Mexican war had been fought before Mr. L. took his seat in congress, but the American army was still in Mexico, and the treaty of peace was not fully and formally ratified till the June afterwards. Much has been said of his course in Congress in regard to this war. A careful examination of the Journals and Congressional Globe shows, that he voted for all the supply measures which came up, and for all the measures in any way favorable to the officers, soldiers, and their families, who conducted the war through; with this exception that some of these measures passed without yeas and nays, leaving no record as to how particular men voted. The Journals and Globe also show him voting that the war was unnecessarily and unconstitutionally begun by the President of the United States. This is the language of Mr. Ashmun's amendment, for which Mr. L. and nearly or quite all, other whigs of the H. R. voted.

Mr. L's reasons for the opinion expressed by this vote were briefly that the President had sent Genl. Taylor into an inhabited part of the country belonging to Mexico, and not to the U.S. and thereby had provoked the first act of hostility—in fact the commencement of the war; that the place, being the country bordering on the East bank of the Rio Grande, was inhabited by native Mexicans, born there under the Mexican government; and had never submitted to, nor been conquered by Texas, or the U.S. nor transferred to either by treaty—that although Texas claimed the Rio Grande as her boundary, Mexico had never recognized it, the people on the ground had never recognized it, and neither Texas nor the U.S. had ever enforced it—that there was a broad desert between that, and the country over which Texas had actual control—that the country where hostilities commenced, having once belonged to Mexico, must remain so, until it was somehow legally transferred, which had never been done.

Mr. L. thought the act of sending an armed force among the Mexicans, was *unnecessary*, inasmuch as Mexico was in no way molesting, or menacing the U.S. or the people thereof; and that it was *unconstitutional*, because the power of levying war is vested in Congress, and not in the President. He thought the principal motive for the act, was to divert public attention from the surrender of "Fifty-four, forty, or fight" to Great Brittain, on the Oregon boundary question.

Mr. L. was not a candidate for re-election. This was determined upon, and declared before he went to Washington, in accordance with an understanding among whig friends, by which Col. Hardin, and Col. Baker had each previously served a single term in the same District.

In 1848, during his term in congress, he advocated Gen. Taylor's nomination for the Presidency, in opposition to all others, and also took an active part for his election, after his nomination—speaking a few times in Maryland, near Washington, several times in Massachusetts, and canvassing quite fully his own district in Illinois, which was followed by a majority in the district of over 1500 for Gen. Taylor.

Upon his return from Congress he went to the practice of the law with greater earnestness than ever before. In 1852 he was upon the Scott electoral ticket, and did something in the way of canvassing, but owing to the hopelessness of the cause in Illinois, he did less than in previous presidential canvasses.

In 1854, his profession had almost superseded the thought of politics in his mind, when the repeal of the Missouri compromise aroused him as he had never been before.

In the autumn of that year he took the stump with no broader practical aim or object than to secure, if possible, the re-election of Hon Richard Yates to congress. His speeches at once attracted a more marked attention than they had ever before done. As the canvass proceeded, he was drawn to different parts of the state, outside of Mr. Yates' district. He did not abandon the law, but gave his attention, by turns, to that and politics. The State agricultural fair was at Springfield that year, and Douglas was announced to speak there.

In the canvass of 1856, Mr. L. made over fifty speeches, no one of which, so far as he remembers, was put in print. One of them was made at Galena, but Mr. L. has no recollection of any part of it being printed; nor does he remember whether in that speech he said anything about a Supreme court decision. He may have spoken upon that subject; and some of the newspapers may have reported him as saying what is now ascribed to him; but he thinks he could not have expressed himself as represented.

c. June 1860

To Samuel Haycraft

PRIVATE

Hon. Saml. Haycraft.   Springfield, Ills. June 4, 1860

Dear Sir: Your second letter, dated May 31st. is received. You suggest that a visit to the place of my nativity might be pleasant to me. Indeed it would. But would it be safe? Would not the people Lynch me?

The place on Knob Creek, mentioned by Mr. Read, I remember very well; but I was not born there. As my parents have told me, I was born on Nolin, very much nearer Hodgin's-Mill than the Knob Creek place is. My earliest recollection, however, is of the Knob Creek place.

Like yourself I belonged to the whig party from it's origin to it's close. I never belonged to the American party organization; nor ever to a party called a Union party; though I hope I neither am, or ever have been, less devoted to the Union than yourself, or any other patriotic man.

It may not be altogether without interest to let you know that my wife is a daughter of the late Robert S. Todd, of Lexington Ky—and that a half sister of hers is the wife of Ben. Hardin Helm, born and raised at your town, but residing at Louisville now, as I believe. Yours very truly

To Lyman Trumbull

Hon. L. Trumbull   Springfield, Ills. June 5, 1860

My dear Sir: Yours of May 31, inclosing Judge Read's letter, is received.

I see by the papers this morning, that Mr. Fillmore refuses to go with us. What do the New-Yorkers at Washington think of this? Gov. Reeder was here last evening direct from Pennsylvania. He is entirely confident of that state, and of the general result. I do not remember to have heard Gen. Cameron's opinion of Penn. Weed was here, and saw me; but he showed no signs whatever of the intriguer. He asked for nothing; and said N.Y. is safe, without condition.

Remembering that Peter denied his Lord with an oath, after most solemnly protesting that he never would, I will not swear I will make no committals; but I do think I will not.

Write me often. I look with great interest for your letters now. Yours as ever,

To William M. Dickson

Hon: W. M. Dickson.   Springfield, Ills.
My dear Sir: June 7. 1860

Your telegraphic despatch, the day of the nomination, was received; as also was, in due course, your kind letter of May 21st. with Cousin Annie's note at the end of it.

I have just now received a letter from Cincinnati, of which the following is a copy.

"Hon. A. Lincoln   Cincinnati, June 5. 1860

Dr. Sir: We are extremely sorry to be under the necessity of calling your attention to the inclosed bill during your sojourn at the "Burnet" in Sept. last; but it appears there is no remedy left us other than to advise you of it's never having been paid. We relied upon the Republican committee, but as yet have not been able to find any one being willing to take the responsibility of paying same—consequently advise you in the premises. Very Respy. Yours,   Johnson, Saunders & Co"

The inclosed bill is as follows:
                          "Burnet House
                                   Cincinnati, Sept. 19— 1859
Hon: A. Lincoln
          To Johnson, Saunders & Co. Dr.
Board & Parlor self & family   37.50
Extra Suppers. 3.50. Wines, Liquors & cigars 7.50.   11.00
Occupancy of room No. 15. committee.   5.00
                                                       $53.50"

Now this may be right, but I have a slight suspicion of it, for two or three reasons. First, when I left, I called at the office of the Hotel, and was there distinctly told the bill "was settled" "was all right" or words to that effect. Secondly, it seems a little steep that "Board & parlor" from Saturday 7½ P.M. to Monday 10½ A.M. for a man woman and one small child, should be $37.50. Thirdly, we had no extra suppers, unless having tea at our room the first evening, was such. We were in the house over the time of five meals, three only of which we took in the house. We did not once dine in the house. As to wines, liquors & cigars, we had none—absolutely none. These last may have been in room 15, by order of Committee, but I do not recollect them at all.

Please look into this, and write me. I can and will pay it if it is right; but I do not wish to be "diddled!" Please do what you do quietly, having no fuss about it. Yours very truly

To J. Mason Haight

PRIVATE & CONFIDENTIAL.

J. Mason Haight, Esq   Springfield, Ills.
My dear Sir—   June 11. 1860

I think it would be improper for me to write, or say anything to, or for, the public, upon the subject of which you inquire. I therefore wish the letter I do write to be held as strictly confidential. Having kept house sixteen years, and having never held the "cup" to the lips of my friends then, my judgment was that I should not, in my new position, change my habit in this respect. What actually occurred upon the occasion of the Committee visiting me, I think it would be better for others to say   Yours Respectfully

To Samuel Galloway

Especially Confidential

Hon: Saml. Galloway: Springfield, Ills.
My dear Sir   June 19, 1860

Your very kind letter of the 15th. is received. Messrs. Follett, Foster & Co's Life of me is *not* by my authority; and I have scarcely been so much astounded by anything, as by their public announcement that it is authorized by me. They have fallen into some strange misunderstanding. I certainly knew they contemplated publishing a biography, and I certainly did not object to their doing so, *upon their own responsibility.* I even took pains to facilitate them. But, at the same time, I made myself tiresome, if not hoarse, with repeating to Mr. Howard, their only agent seen by me, my protest that I *authorized nothing*—would be *responsible for nothing.* How, they could so misunderstand me, passes comprehension. As a matter, *wholly my own*, I would authorize no biography, without *time*, and *opertunity* to carefully examine and consider every word of it; and, in this case, in the nature of things, I can have no such time and opertunity. But, in my present position, when, by the lessons of the past, and the united voice of all discreet friends, I am neither to write or speak a word for the public, how dare I to send forth, by my authority, a volume of hundreds of pages, for adversaries to make points upon without end. Were I to do so, the convention would have a right to re-assemble, and substitute another name for mine.

For these reasons, I would not look at the proof sheets. I am determined to maintain the position of truly saying I never saw the proof sheets, or any part of their work, before it's publication.

Now, do not mistake me. I feel great kindness for Messrs. F. F. & Co—do not think they have intentionally done wrong. There may be nothing wrong in their proposed book. I sincerely hope there will not. I barely suggest that you, or any of the friends there, on the party account, look it over, & exclude what you may think would embarrass the party— bearing in mind, at all times, that I *authorize nothing*—will be *responsible* for *nothing*. Your friend, as ever

To Anson G. Henry

My dear Doctor: Springfield, Ills. July 4, 1860
Your very agreeable letter of May 15th. was received three days ago. We are just now receiving the first sprinkling of your Oregon election returns—not enough, I think, to indicate the result. We should be too happy if both Logan and Baker should triumph.

Long before this you have learned who was nominated at Chicago. We know not what a day may bring forth; but, today, it looks as if the Chicago ticket will be elected. I think the chances were more than equal that we could have beaten the Democracy *united*. Divided, as it is, it's chance appears indeed very slim. But great is Democracy in resources; and it may yet give it's fortunes a turn. It is under great temptation to do something; but what can it do which was not thought of, and found impracticable, at Charleston and Baltimore? The signs now are that Douglas and Breckenridge will each have a ticket in every state. They are driven to this to keep up their bombastic claims of *nationality*, and to avoid the charge of *sectionalism* which they have so much lavished upon us.

It is an amusing fact, after all Douglas has said about *nationality*, and *sectionalism*, that I had more votes from the Southern section at Chicago, than he had at Baltimore! In fact, there was more of the Southern section represented at Chicago, than in the Douglas rump concern at Baltimore!!

Our boy, in his tenth year, (the baby when you left) has just had a hard and tedious spell of scarlet-fever; and he is not yet beyond all danger. I have a head-ache, and a sore throat upon me now, inducing me to suspect that I have an inferior type of the same thing.

Our eldest boy, Bob, has been away from us nearly a year at school, and will enter Harvard University this month. He promises very well, considering we never controlled him much.

Write again when you receive this. Mary joins in sending our kindest regards to Mrs. H. yourself, and all the family. Your friend, as ever

To Abraham Jonas
Confidential

Hon. A. Jonas: Springfield, Ills.
My dear Sir   July 21, 1860

Yours of the 20th. is received. I suppose as good, or even better, men than I may have been in American, or Know-Nothing lodges; but in point of fact, I never was in one, at Quincy, or elsewhere. I was never in Quincy but one day and two nights, while Know-Nothing lodges were in existence, and you were with me that day and both those nights. I had never been there before in my life; and never afterwards, till the joint debate with Douglas in 1858. It was in 1854, when I spoke in some Hall there, and after the speaking, you, with others, took me to an oyster saloon, passed an hour there, and you walked with me to, and parted with me at, the Quincy-House, quite late at night. I left by stage for Naples before day-light in the morning, having come in by the same route, after dark, the evening previous to the speaking, when I found you waiting at the Quincy House to meet me. A few days after I was there, Richardson, as I understood, started this same story about my having been in a Know-Nothing lodge. When I heard of the charge, as I did soon after, I taxed my recollection for some incident which could have suggested it; and I remembered that on parting with you the last night, I went to the Office of the Hotel to take my stage passage for the morning, was told that no stage office for that line was kept there, and that I must see the driver, before retiring, to insure his calling for me in the morning; and a servant was sent with me to find the driver, who after taking me a square or two, stopped me, and stepped perhaps a dozen steps farther, and in my hearing called to some one, who answered him apparantly from the upper part of a building, and promised to call with the stage for me at the Quincy House. I returned and went to bed; and before day the stage called and took me. This is all.

That I never was in a Know-Nothing lodge in Quincy, I should expect, could be easily proved, by respectable men, who were always in the lodges and never saw me there. An affidavit of one or two such would put the matter at rest.

And now, a word of caution. Our adversaries think they can gain a point, if they could force me to openly deny this charge, by which some degree of offence would be given to the Americans. For this reason, it must not publicly appear that I am paying any attention to the charge. Yours truly

To George C. Latham

My dear George   Springfield, Ills. July 22. 1860.
    I have scarcely felt greater pain in my life than on learning yesterday from Bob's letter, that you had failed to enter

Harvard University. And yet there is very little in it, if you will allow no feeling of *discouragement* to seize, and prey upon you. It is a *certain* truth, that you *can* enter, and graduate in, Harvard University; and having made the attempt, you *must* succeed in it. *"Must"* is the word.

I know not how to aid you, save in the assurance of one of mature age, and much severe experience, that you *can* not fail, if you resolutely determine, that you *will* not.

The President of the institution, can scarcely be other than a kind man; and doubtless he would grant you an interview, and point out the readiest way to remove, or overcome, the obstacles which have thwarted you.

In your temporary failure there is no evidence that you may not yet be a better scholar, and a more successful man in the great struggle of life, than many others, who have entered college more easily.

Again I say let no feeling of discouragement prey upon you, and in the end you are sure to succeed.

With more than a common interest I subscribe myself Very truly your friend,

To Simeon Francis

Friend Francis—   Springfield, Ills. Aug. 4. 1860

I have had three letters from you—one, a long one, received in February; one, telling me of the deputation of Mr. Greely to cast the vote of Oregon, in the Chicago convention, received a few days before that convention; and one written since you knew the result of your Oregon election, received a few days ago. I have not, till now, attempted an answer to any of them, because I disliked to write you a mere note, and because I could not find time to write at length.

Your brother Allen has returned from California, and, I understand, intends remaining here. Josiah is running his J. P. court, about as when you left. We had a storm here last night which did considerable damage, the largest single instance of which, was to the Withies. A wall of their brick shop building was thrown in, and, it is said destroyed ten thousand dollars worth of carriages. I have heard of no personal injury done.

When you wrote, you had not learned of the doings of the democratic convention at Baltimore; but you will be in possession of it all long before this reaches you. I hesitate to say it, but it really appears now, as if the success of the Republican ticket is inevitable. We have no reason to doubt any of the states which voted for Fremont. Add to these, Minnesota, Pennsylvania, and New-Jersey, and the thing is done. Minnesota is as sure as such a thing can be; while the democracy are so divided between Douglas and Breckenridge in Penn. & N.J. that they are scarcely less sure. Our friends are also confident in Indiana and Illinois. I should expect the same division would give us a fair chance in Oregon. Write me what you think on that point.

We were very anxious here for David Logan's election. I think I will write him before long. If you see Col. Baker, give him my respects. I do hope he may not be tricked out of what he has fairly earned.

Make my kindest regards to Mrs. Francis; and tell her I both hope and believe she is not so unhappy as when I saw her last. Your friend, as ever

Remarks at Republican Rally, Springfield, Illinois

My Fellow Citizens:—I appear among you upon this occasion with no intention of making a speech.

It has been my purpose, since I have been placed in my present position, to make no speeches. This assemblage having been drawn together at the place of my residence, it appeared to be the wish of those constituting this vast assembly to see me; and it is certainly my wish to see all of you. I appear upon the ground here at this time only for the purpose of affording myself the best opportunity of seeing you, and enabling you to see me.

I confess with gratitude, be it understood, that I did not suppose my appearance among you would create the tumult which I now witness. I am profoundly gratified for this manifestation of your feelings. I am gratified, because it is a tribute such as can be paid to no man as a man. It is the evidence that four years from this time you will give a like manifestation to the next man who is the representative of the truth on the questions that now agitate the public. And it is because you will then fight for this cause as you do now, or with even greater ardor than now, though I be dead and gone. I most profoundly and sincerely thank you.

Having said this much, allow me now to say that it is my wish that you will hear this public discussion by others of our friends who are present for the purpose of addressing you, and that you will kindly let me be silent.

August 8, 1860

To John B. Fry

Private

John B. Fry, Esq   Springfield, Ills. August 15. 1860

My dear Sir: Yours of the 9th. inclosing the letter of Hon. John M. Botts, was duly received. The latter is herewith returned according to your request. It contains one of the many assurances I receive from the South that in no probable event will there be any very formidable effort to break up the Union. The people of the South have too much of good sense, and good temper, to attempt the ruin of the government, rather than see it administered as it was administered by the men who made it. At least, so I hope and believe.

I thank you both for your own letter, and a sight of that of Mr. Botts. Yours, very truly

To George G. Fogg

PRIVATE

Hon. George G. Fogg—   Springfield, Ills.
My dear Sir: Aug. 16, 1860

I am annoyed some by the printed paragraph below, in relation to myself, taken from the N.Y. Herald's correspondence from this place of August 8th.

He had, he said, on one occasion been invited to go into Kentucky and revisit some of the scenes with whose history his father in his lifetime had been identified. On asking by letter whether Judge Lynch would be present, he received no response; and he therefore came to the conclusion that the invitation was a trap laid by some designing person to inveigle him into a slave State for the purpose of doing violence to his person.

This is decidedly wrong. I did not say it. I do not impugn the correspondent. I suppose he misconceived the statement from the following incident. Soon after the Chicago nomination I was written to by a highly respectable gentleman of Hardin County, Ky, inquiring if I was a son of Thomas Lincoln, whom he had known long ago, in that county. I answered that I was, and that I was myself born there. He wrote again, and, among other things, (did not *invite* me but) simply *inquired* if it would not be agreeable to me to revisit the scenes of my childhood. I replied, among other things, "It would indeed; but would you not Lynch me?" He did not write again.

I have, *playfully*, (and never otherwise) related this incident several times; and I suppose I did so to the Herald correspondent, though I do not remember it. If I did, it is all that I did say, from which the correspondent could have inferred his statement.

Now, I dislike, exceedingly, for Kentuckians to understand that I am charging them with a purpose to inveigle me, and do violence to me. Yet I can not go into the newspapers. Would not the editor of the Herald, upon being shown this letter, insert the short correction, which you find upon the inclosed scrap?

Please try him, unless you perceive some sufficient reason to the contrary. In no event, let my name be publicly used. Yours very truly

CORRECTION

We have such assurance as satisfies us that our correspondent writing from Springfield, Ills, under date of Aug. 8— was mistaken in representing Mr. Lincoln as expressing a suspicion of a design to inveigle him into Kentucky for the purpose of doing him violence. Mr. Lincoln neither entertains, nor has intended to express any such suspicion.

To Charles H. Fisher

Private

C. H. Fisher   Springfield, Ills— Aug. 27, 1860

Dear Sir: Your second note, inclosing the *supposed* speech of Mr. Dallas to Lord Brougham, is received. I have read the speech quite through, together with the real author's introductory, and closing remarks. I have also looked through the long preface of the book to-day. Both seem to be well written, and contain many things with which I could agree, and some with which I could not. A specimen of the latter is the declaration, in the closing remarks upon the "speech" that the institution is a *necessity* imposed on us by the negro race. That the going many thousand miles, seizing a set of savages, bringing them here, and making slaves of them, is a *necessity* imposed on *us* by *them*, involves a species of logic to which my mind will scarcely assent.

To John M. Pomeroy

Private

Hon. John ——,   Springfield, Ills.
My dear Sir: Aug. 31. 1860

Yours of the 27th. is duly received. It consists almost exclusively of a historical detail of some local troubles among some of our friends in Pennsylvania; and I suppose it's object is to guard me against forming a prejudice against Mr. McC——. I have not heard near so much upon that subject as you probably suppose; and I am slow to listen to criminations among friends, and never expose their quarrels on either side. My sincere wish is that both sides will allow by-gones to be by-gones, and look to the present & future only. Yours very truly

To Henry Wilson

Hon. Henry Wilson   Springfield, Ills.
My dear Sir: Sep. 1. 1860

Yours of August 25th. was received yesterday.

The point you press—the importance of thorough organization—is felt, and appreciated by our friends everywhere. And yet it involves so much more of dry, and irksome labor, that most of them shrink from it—preferring parades, and shows, and monster meetings. I know not how this can be helped. I do what I can in my position, for organization; but it does not amount to so much as it should.

I shall be pleased to hear from you at all times. Yours very truly

To Mrs. M. J. Green

Mrs. M. J. Green   Springfield, Ills.
My dear Madam.   Sep. 22. 1860

Your kind congratulatory letter, of August, was received in due course—and should have been answered sooner. The truth is I have never corresponded much with ladies; and hence I postpone writing letters to them, as a business which I do not understand. I can only say now I thank you for the good opinion you express of me, fearing, at the same time, I may not be able to maintain it through life. Yours very truly

To John T. Hanks

Dear John   Springfield, Ills. Sep. 24, 1860

Your letter of July 22— was received a few days ago. If your Father and Mother desire you to come home, it is a delicate matter for me to advise you not to do it. Still, as you ask my advice, it is that if you are doing well, you better stick to it. If you have a good start there, and should give it up, you might not get it again, here, or elsewhere. It can not be other than their first wish that you shall do well.

And now, as to politics, I am very much obliged to you for what you offer to do for me in Oregon. This side of the Rocky Mountains things appear reasonably well for the general result. In opposing David Logan, at the late congressional election in Oregon, I suppose you did what you thought was right; and when a man does what he thinks is right, he does the best he can. Still, I am sorry you did not think differently, as I knew David from his childhood, and he studied law in our office when his father and I were partners.

I heard from our relations over at Charleston, about three weeks ago, and they were well then.

Write me again when you receive this. Your Uncle

To John M. Brockman

J. M. Brockman, Esq   Springfield, Ills. Sep. 25. 1860
Dear Sir: Yours of the 24th. asking "the best mode of obtaining a thorough knowledge of the law" is received. The mode is very simple, though laborious, and tedious. It is only to get the books, and read, and study them carefully. Begin with Blackstone's Commentaries, and after reading it carefully through, say twice, take up Chitty's Pleading, Greenleaf's Evidence, & Story's Equity &c. in succession. Work, work, work, is the main thing. Yours very truly

To Daniel P. Gardner

Professor Gardner   Springfield, Ills.
Dear Sir: Sep. 28. 1860
Some specimens of your Soap have been used at our house and Mrs. L. declares it is a superb article. She at the same time, protests that *I* have never given sufficient attention to the "soap question" to be a competent judge. Yours truly

Imaginary Dialogue Between Douglas and Breckinridge

Louisville, Ky– Sep. 29. 1860

Meeting & Dialogue of Douglas & Breckenridge—

DOUG—Well, you have succeeded in breaking up the Democratic party.

BRECK—Certainly, for the time being, the party is under a cloud, to say the least; but why you should say *I* did it, I do not comprehend.

DOUG—Perhaps I should charge it to your *supporters*, rather than to *you*.

BRECK—The blame, as I conceive, is neither upon my friends or me.

DOUG—They insisted on having a plat-form, upon which *I* could not stand.

BRECK—Aye, and *you* insisted on having a platform upon which *they* could not stand.

DOUG—But *mine* was the true *Democratic* platform.

BRECK—That presents the exact point in dispute; my friends insist that *theirs* is the true Democratic platform.

DOUG—Let us argue it, then.

BRECK—I conceive that argument is exhausted; *you* certainly could advance nothing new, and *I* know not that I could. There is, however, a colatteral point, upon which I would like the exchange of a few words.

DOUG—What is it?

BRECK—It is this: We insisted on Congressional protection of Slave property in the national teritories; and you broke with us professedly because of this.

DOUG—Exactly so; I insisted upon non-intervention.

BRECK—And yet you are forming coalitions, wherever you can, with Bell, who is for this very congressional protection of slavery—for the very thing which you pretend, drove you from us—for Bell, with all his Know-Nothingism, and anti-democracy of every sort.

DOUG—Bell is a good Union-man; and you, and your friends, are a set of disunionists.

BRECK—Bah! You have known us long, and intimately; why

did you never denounce us as disunionists, till since our refusal to support *you* for the Presidency? Why have you never
warned the North against our disunion schemes, till since the
Charleston and Baltimore sessions of the National convention? Will you answer, Senator Douglas?

DOUG—The condition of my throat will not permit me to
carry this conversation any further.

To Grace Bedell

Private

Miss. Grace Bedell   Springfield, Ills.
My dear little Miss.   Oct 19. 1860

Your very agreeable letter of the 15th. is received.

I regret the necessity of saying I have no daughters. I have
three sons—one seventeen, one nine, and one seven, years of
age. They, with their mother, constitute my whole family.

As to the whiskers, having never worn any, do you not
think people would call it a piece of silly affection if I were to
begin it now? Your very sincere well-wisher

To William S. Speer

Confidential.

Wm. S. Speer Esq   Springfield, Ill. Oct 23d 1860.

My dear Sir   Yours of the 13th was duly received. I appreciate your motive when you suggest the propriety of my
writing for the public something disclaiming all intention to
interfere with slaves or slavery in the States; but in my judgment, it would do no good. I have already done this many—
many, times; and it is in print, and open to all who will read.
Those who will not read, or heed, what I have already publicly said, would not read, or heed, a repetition of it.

"If they hear not Moses and the prophets, neither will they
be persuaded though one rose from the dead." Yours Truly

To David Hunter

Private & confidential

Maj. David Hunter: Springfield, Ills. Oct. 26. 1860

My dear Sir: Your very kind letter of the 20th. was duly received, and for which, please accept my thanks.

I have another letter from a writer unknown to me, saying the officers of the Army at Fort Kearney, have determined, in case of Republican success, at the approaching Presidential election, to take themselves, and the arms at that point, South, for the purpose of resistence to the government. While I think there are many chances to one that this is a hum-bug, it occurs to me that any real movement of this sort in the army would leak out and become known to you. In such case, if it would not be unprofessional, or dishonorable (of which you are to be judge) I shall be much obliged if you will apprize me of it. Yours very truly

To George T. M. Davis

Private & confidential.

Geo. T. M. Davis, Esq   Springfield, Ills.

My dear Sir: Oct. 27. 1860

Mr. Dubois has shown me your letter of the 20th.; and I promised him to write you. What is it I could say which would quiet alarm? Is it that no interference by the government, with slaves or slavery within the states, is intended? I have said this so often already, that a repetition of it is but mockery, bearing an appearance of weakness, and cowardice, which perhaps should be avoided. Why do not uneasy men *read* what I have already said? and what our *platform* says? If they will not read, or heed, then, would they read, or heed, a repetition of them? Of course the declaration that there is no intention to interfere with slaves or slavery, in the states, with all that is fairly implied in such declaration, is true; and I should have no objection to make, and repeat the declaration a thousand times, if there were no danger of encouraging bold bad men to believe they are dealing with one who can be scared into anything.

I have some reason to believe the Sub-National committee, at the Astor House, may be considering this question; and if their judgment should be different from mine, mine might be modified by theirs. Yours very truly

To George D. Prentice

Private & confidential

Geo. D. Prentice, Esq   Springfield, Ills. Oct. 29. 1860

My dear Sir: Yours of the 26th. is just received. Your suggestion that I, in a certain event, shall write a letter, setting forth my conservative views and intentions, is certainly a very worthy one. But would it do any good? If I were to labor a month, I could not express my conservative views and intentions more clearly and strongly, than they are expressed in our plat-form, and in my many speeches already in print, and before the public. And yet even you, who do occasionally speak of me in terms of personal kindness, give no prominence to these oft-repeated expressions of conservative views and intentions; but busy yourself with appeals to all conservative men, to vote for Douglas—to vote any way which can possibly defeat me—thus impressing your readers that you think, I am the very worst man living. If what I have already said has failed to convince you, no repetition of it would convince you. The writing of your letter, now before me, gives assurance that you would publish such a letter from me as you suggest; but, till now, what reason had I to suppose the Louisville Journal, even, would publish a *repetition* of that which is already at it's command, and which it does not press upon the public attention?

And, now my friend—for such I esteem you personally—do not misunderstand me. I have not decided that I will not do substantially what you suggest. I will not forbear doing so, merely on *punctilio* and pluck. If I do finally abstain, it will be because of apprehension that it would do harm. For the good men of the South—and I regard the majority of them as such—I have no objection to repeat seventy and seven times. But I have *bad* men also to deal with, both North and

South—men who are eager for something new upon which to base new misrepresentations—men who would like to frighten me, or, at least, to fix upon me the character of timidity and cowardice. They would seize upon almost any letter I could write, as being an *"awful coming down."* I intend keeping my eye upon these gentlemen, and to not unnecessarily put any weapons in their hands. Yours very truly

Confidential

The within letter was written on the day of it's date, and, on reflection, withheld till now. It expresses the views I still entertain.

To Truman Smith

Private & confidential.

Hon. Truman Smith   Springfield Ill Nov 10th 1860.

My dear Sir   This is intended as a strictly private letter to you, and not as an answer to yours brought me by Mr. Sanford. It is with the most profound appreciation of your motive, and highest respect for your judgment too, that I feel constrained, for the present, at least, to make no declaration for the public.

First, I could say nothing which I have not already said, and which is in print, and open for the inspection of all. To press a repetition of this upon those who *have* listened, is useless; to press it upon those who have *refused* to listen, and still refuse, would be wanting in self-respect, and would have an appearance of sycophancy and timidity, which would excite the contempt of good men, and encourage bad ones to clamor the more loudly.

I am not insensible to any commercial or financial depression that may exist; but nothing is to be gained by fawning around the *"respectable scoundrels"* who got it up. Let them go to work and repair the mischief of their own making; and then perhaps they will be less greedy to do the like again. Yours very truly

To Nathaniel P. Paschall

Private & confidential.

N. P. Paschall Esq   Springfield Nov 16th. 1860.

My dear Sir   Mr. Ridgely showed me a letter of yours in which you manifest some anxiety that I should make some public declaration with a view to favorably affect the business of the country. I said to Mr. Ridgely I would write you to-day, which I now do.

I could say nothing which I have not already said, and which is in print and accessible to the public. Please pardon me for suggesting that if the papers, like yours, which heretofore have persistently garbled, and misrepresented what I have said, will now fully and fairly place it before their readers, there can be no further misunderstanding. I beg you to believe me sincere when I declare I do not say this in a spirit of complaint or resentment; but that I urge it as the true cure for any real uneasiness in the country that my course may be other than conservative. The Republican newspapers now, and for some time past, are and have been republishing copious extracts from my many published speeches, which would at once reach the whole public if your class of papers would also publish them.

I am not at liberty to shift my ground—that is out of the question. If I thought a *repetition* would do any good I would make it. But my judgment is it would do positive harm. The secessionists, *per se* believing they had alarmed me, would clamor all the louder. Yours &c

Passage Written for Lyman Trumbull's Speech at Springfield, Illinois

I have labored in, and for, the Republican organization with entire confidence that whenever it shall be in power, each and all of the States will be left in as complete control of their own affairs respectively, and at as perfect liberty to choose, and employ, their own means of protecting property, and preserving peace and order within their respective limits, as they have ever been under any administration. Those who have voted for Mr. Lincoln, have expected, and still expect this; and they would not have voted for him had they expected otherwise. I regard it as extremely fortunate for the peace of the whole country, that this point, upon which the Republicans have been so long, and so persistently misrepresented, is now to be brought to a practical test, and placed beyond the possibility of doubt. Disunionists *per se*, are now in hot haste to get out of the Union, precisely because they perceive they can not, much longer, maintain apprehension among the Southern people that their homes, and firesides, and lives, are to be endangered by the action of the Federal Government. With such *"Now, or never"* is the maxim.

I am rather glad of this military preparation in the South. It will enable the people the more easily to suppress any uprisings there, which their misrepresentations of purposes may have encouraged.

November 20, 1860

Remarks at Bloomington, Illinois

FELLOW-CITIZENS OF BLOOMINGTON AND McLEAN COUNTY: I am glad to meet you after a longer separation than has been common between you and me. I thank you for the good report you made of the election in Old McLean. The people of the country have again fixed up their affairs for a constitutional period of time. By the way, I think very much of the people, as an old friend said he thought of woman. He said when he lost his first wife, who had been a great help to him in his business, he thought he was ruined—that he could never find another to fill her place. At length, however, he married another, who he found did quite as well as the first, and that his opinion now was that any woman would do well who was well done by. So I think of the whole people of this nation—they will ever do well if well done by. We will try to do well by them in all parts of the country, North and South, with entire confidence that all will be well with all of us.

November 21, 1860

To Henry J. Raymond

Private & confidential

Hon. H. J. Raymond   Springfield, Ills.
My dear Sir   Nov. 28. 1860

Yours of the 14th. was received in due course. I have delayed so long to answer it, because my reasons for not coming
before the public in any form just now, had substantially appeared in your paper (The Times), and hence I feared they
were not deemed sufficient by you, else you would not have
written me as you did.

I now think we have a demonstration in favor of my view.
On the 20th. Inst. Senator Trumbull made a short speech
which I suppose you have both seen and approved. Has a
single newspaper, heretofore against us, urged that speech
upon its readers with a purpose to quiet public anxiety? Not
one, so far as I know. On the contrary the Boston Courier,
and its' class, hold me responsible for the speech, and endeavor to inflame the North with the belief that it fore-
shadows an abandonment of Republican ground by the incoming administration; while the Washington Constitution,
and its' class hold the same speech up to the South as an open
declaration of war against them.

This is just as I expected, and just what would happen with
any declaration I could make. These political fiends are not
half sick enough yet. "Party malice" and not "public good"
possesses them entirely. "They seek a sign, and no sign shall
be given them." At least such is my present feeling and purpose. Yours very truly

To William H. Seward

Private & Confidential

Springfield Ills. Dec. 8. 1860

My dear Sir: In addition to the accompanying, and more
formal note, inviting you to take charge of the State Department, I deem it proper to address you this. Rumors have got
into the newspapers to the effect that the Department, named

above, would be tendered you, as a compliment, and with the expectation that you would decline it. I beg you to be assured that I have said nothing to justify these rumors. On the contrary, it has been my purpose, from the day of the nomination at Chicago, to assign you, by your leave, this place in the administration. I have delayed so long to communicate that purpose, in deference to what appeared to me to be a proper caution in the case. Nothing has been developed to change my view in the premises; and I now offer you the place, in the hope that you will accept it, and with the belief that your position in the public eye, your integrity, ability, learning, and great experience, all combine to render it an appointment pre-eminently fit to be made.

One word more. In regard to the patronage, sought with so much eagerness and jealousy, I have prescribed for myself the maxim, "Justice to all"; and I earnestly beseech your co-operation in keeping the maxim good. Your friend, and obedient servant

To Lyman Trumbull

Private

Hon. Lyman Trumbull—   Springfield, Ills. Dec. 8. 1860.

My dear Sir: Yours of the 2nd. is received. I regret exceedingly the anxiety of our friends in New-York, of whom you write; but it seems to me the sentiment in that state which sent a united delegation to Chicago in favor of Gov. S. ought not, and must not be snubbed, as it would be by the omission to offer Gov. S. a place in the cabinet. I will, myself, take care of the question of "corrupt jobs" and see that justice is done to all, our friends, of whom you write, as well as others. I have written Mr. Hamlin, on this very subject of Gov. S. and requested him to consult fully with you. He will show you my note, and inclosures to him; and then please act as therein requested. Yours as ever

To Lyman Trumbull

Private, & confidential

Hon. L. Trumbull.   Springfield, Ills. Dec. 10. 1860

My dear Sir: Let there be no compromise on the question of *extending* slavery. If there be, all our labor is lost, and, ere long, must be done again. The dangerous ground—that into which some of our friends have a hankering to run—is Pop. Sov. Have none of it. Stand firm. The tug has to come, & better now, than any time hereafter. Yours as ever

To William Kellogg

Private & confidential.

Hon. William Kellogg.   Springfield, Ills.
My dear Sir—   Dec. 11. 1860

Entertain no proposition for a compromise in regard to the *extension* of slavery. The instant you do, they have us under again; all our labor is lost, and sooner or later must be done over. Douglas is sure to be again trying to bring in his "Pop. Sov." Have none of it. The tug has to come & better now than later.

You know I think the fugitive slave clause of the constitution ought to be enforced—to put it on the mildest form, ought not to be resisted. In haste   Yours as ever

To John A. Gilmer

Strictly confidential.

Hon. John A. Gilmer: Springfield, Ill. Dec 15, 1860.

My dear Sir—Yours of the 10th is received. I am greatly disinclined to write a letter on the subject embraced in yours; and I would not do so, even privately as I do, were it not that I fear you might misconstrue my silence. Is it desired that I shall shift the ground upon which I have been elected? I can not do it. You need only to acquaint yourself with that ground, and press it on the attention of the South. It is all in print and easy of access. May I be pardoned if I ask whether even you have ever attempted to procure the reading of the Republican platform, or my speeches, by the Southern people? If not, what reason have I to expect that any additional production of mine would meet a better fate? It would make me appear as if I repented for the crime of having been elected, and was anxious to apologize and beg forgiveness. To so represent me, would be the principal use made of any letter I might now thrust upon the public. My old record cannot be so used; and that is precisely the reason that some new declaration is so much sought.

Now, my dear sir, be assured, that I am not questioning *your* candor; I am only pointing out, that, while a new letter would hurt the cause which I think a just one, you can quite as well effect every patriotic object with the old record. Carefully read pages 18, 19, 74, 75, 88, 89, & 267 of the volume of Joint Debates between Senator Douglas and myself, with the Republican Platform adopted at Chicago, and all your questions will be substantially answered. I have no thought of recommending the abolition of slavery in the District of Columbia, nor the slave trade among the slave states, even on the conditions indicated; and if I were to make such recommendation, it is quite clear Congress would not follow it.

As to employing slaves in Arsenals and Dockyards, it is a thing I never thought of in my life, to my recollection, till I saw your letter; and I may say of it, precisely as I have said of the two points above.

As to the use of patronage in the slave states, where there are few or no Republicans, I do not expect to inquire for the politics of the appointee, or whether he does or not own slaves. I intend in that matter to accommodate the people in the several localities, if they themselves will allow me to accommodate them. In one word, I never have been, am not now, and probably never shall be, in a mood of harassing the people, either North or South.

On the territorial question, I am inflexible, as you see my position in the book. On that, there is a difference between you and us; and it is the only substantial difference. You think slavery is right and ought to be extended; we think it is wrong and ought to be restricted. For this, neither has any just occasion to be angry with the other.

As to the state laws, mentioned in your sixth question, I really know very little of them. I never have read one. If any of them are in conflict with the fugitive slave clause, or any other part of the constitution, I certainly should be glad of their repeal; but I could hardly be justified, as a citizen of Illinois, or as President of the United States, to recommend the repeal of a statute of Vermont, or South Carolina.

With the assurance of my highest regards I subscribe myself   Your obt. Servt.,

P.S. The documents referred to, I suppose you will readily find in Washington.

To Thurlow Weed

Private & confidential.

Hon. Thurlow Weed   Springfield, Ills– Dec. 17– 1860

My dear Sir   Yours of the 11th. was received two days ago. Should the convocation of Governors, of which you speak, seem desirous to know my views on the present aspect of things, tell them you judge from my speeches that I will be inflexible on the territorial question; that I probably think either the Missouri line extended, or Douglas' and Eli Thayer's Pop. Sov. would lose us every thing we gained by the election; that filibustering for all South of us, and making slave states of it, would follow in spite of us, under either plan.

Also, that I probably think all opposition, real and apparant, to the fugitive slave clause of the constitution ought to be withdrawn.

I believe you can pretend to find but little, if any thing, in my speeches, about secession; but my opinion is that no state can, in any way lawfully, get out of the Union, without the consent of the others; and that it is the duty of the President, and other government functionaries to run the machine as it is. Yours very truly

To John D. Defrees

Confidential

Hon. Jno. D. Defrees.   Springfield Ills.

My dear Sir   Dec. 18. 1860

Yours of the 15th. is received. I am sorry any republican inclines to dally with Pop. Sov. of any sort. It acknowledges that slavery has equal rights with liberty, and surrenders all we have contended for. Once fastened on us as a settled policy, filibustering for all South of us, and making slave states of it, follows in spite of us, with an early Supreme court decision, holding our free-state constitutions to be unconstitutional.

Would Scott or Stephens go into the cabinet? And if yea, on what terms? Do they come to me? or I go to them? or are we to lead off in open hostility to each other? Yours truly

To Henry J. Raymond

Confidential

Hon. H. J. Raymond   Springfield, Ills.

My dear Sir   Dec. 18, 1860

Yours of the 14th. is received. What a very mad-man your correspondent, Smedes is. Mr. Lincoln is not pledged to the ultimate extinction of slavery; does not hold the black man to be the equal of the white, unqualifiedly as Mr. S. states it; and never did stigmatize their white people as immoral & unchristian; and Mr. S. can not prove one of his assertions true.

Mr. S. seems sensitive on the questions of morals and christianity. What does he think of a man who makes charges against another which he does not know to be true, and could easily learn to be false?

As to the pitcher story, it is a forgery out and out. I never made but one speech in Cincinnati—the last speech in the volume containing the Joint Debates between Senator Douglas and myself. I have never yet seen Gov. Chase. I was never in a meeting of negroes in my life; and never saw a pitcher presented by anybody to anybody.

I am much obliged by your letter, and shall be glad to hear from you again when you have anything of interest. Yours truly

To Alexander H. Stephens

For your own eye only.

Hon. A. H. Stephens—   Springfield, Ills.
My dear Sir   Dec. 22, 1860

Your obliging answer to my short note is just received, and for which please accept my thanks. I fully appreciate the present peril the country is in, and the weight of responsibility on me.

Do the people of the South really entertain fears that a Republican administration would, *directly*, or *indirectly*, interfere with their slaves, or with them, about their slaves? If they do, I wish to assure you, as once a friend, and still, I hope, not an enemy, that there is no cause for such fears.

The South would be in no more danger in this respect, than it was in the days of Washington. I suppose, however, this does not meet the case. You think slavery is *right* and ought to be extended; while we think it is *wrong* and ought to be restricted. That I suppose is the rub. It certainly is the only substantial difference between us. Yours very truly

To James W. Webb

Private

Col. J. W. Webb.   Springfield, Ills.
My dear Sir: Dec. 29. 1860

Yours kindly seeking my view as to the proper mode of dealing with secession, was received several days ago, but, for want of time I could not answer it till now. I think we should hold the forts, or retake them, as the case may be, and collect the revenue. *We* shall have to forego the use of the federal courts, and *they* that of the mails, for a while. We can not fight them in to holding courts, or receiving the mails.

This is an outline of my view; and perhaps suggests sufficiently, the whole of it. Yours very truly

To Simon Cameron

Private   (Copy)

Hon. Simon Cameron   Springfield, Ills. Jan. 3, 1861

My dear Sir   Since seeing you things have developed which make it impossible for me to take you into the cabinet. You will say this comes of an interview with McClure; and this is partly, but not wholly true. The more potent matter is wholly outside of Pennsylvania; and yet I am not at liberty to specify it. Enough that it appears to me to be sufficient. And now I suggest that you write me declining the appointment, in which case I do not object to its being known that it was tendered you. Better do this at once, before things so change, that you can not honorably decline, and I be compelled to openly recall the tender. No person living knows, or has an intimation that I write this letter. Yours truly

P.S. Telegraph, me instantly, on receipt of this, saying "All right"

To Lyman Trumbull

Very Confidential

Hon. Lyman Trumbull   Springfield, Ills.
My dear Sir   Jan. 7. 1861

Yours of the 3rd. is just received. The democrats of our H.R. refused to make a quorum today, trying, as I understand, to prevent your re-election. I trust that before this reaches you, the telegraph will have informed you that they have failed, and you have triumphed.

Gen. C. has not been offered the Treasury, and, I think, will not be. It seems to me not only highly proper, but a *necessity*, that Gov. Chase shall take that place. His ability, firmness, and purity of character, produce the propriety; and that he alone can reconcile Mr. Bryant, and his class, to the appointment of Gov. S. to the State Department produces the necessity. But then comes the danger that the protectionists of Pennsylvania will be dissatisfied; and, to clear this difficulty, Gen. C. must be brought to co-operate. He would readily do this for the War Department. But then comes the fierce opposition to his having any Department, threatening even to send charges into the Senate to procure his rejection by that body. Now, what I would most like, and what I think he should prefer too, under the circumstances, would be to retain his place in the Senate; and if that place has been promised to another, let that other take a respectable, and reasonably lucrative place abroad. Also let Gen. C's friends be, with entire fairness, cared for in Pennsylvania, and elsewhere.

I may mention before closing that besides the very fierce opposition to Gen. C. he is more amply recommended for a place in the cabinet, than any other man.

I have a great notion to post Judd fully in this matter, and get him to visit Washington, and in his quiet way, try to adjust it satisfactorily. Yours as ever

To James T. Hale

Confidential.

Hon. J. T. Hale   Springfield, Ill. Jan'y. 11th 1861.

My dear Sir—Yours of the 6th is received. I answer it only because I fear you would misconstrue my silence. What is our present condition? We have just carried an election on principles fairly stated to the people. Now we are told in advance, the government shall be broken up, unless we surrender to those we have beaten, before we take the offices. In this they are either attempting to play upon us, or they are in dead earnest. Either way, if we surrender, it is the end of us, and of the government. They will repeat the experiment upon us *ad libitum.* A year will not pass, till we shall have to take Cuba as a condition upon which they will stay in the Union. They now have the Constitution, under which we have lived over seventy years, and acts of Congress of their own framing, with no prospect of their being changed; and they can never have a more shallow pretext for breaking up the government, or extorting a compromise, than now. There is, in my judgment, but one compromise which would really settle the slavery question, and that would be a prohibition against acquiring any more territory. Yours very truly,

To William H. Seward

Private & confidential.

Hon. W. H. Seward   Springfield, Ills. Feb. 1. 1861

My dear Sir   On the 21st. ult. Hon. W. Kellogg, a Republican M.C of this state whom you probably know, was here, in a good deal of anxiety, seeking to ascertain to what extent I would be consenting for our friends to go in the way of compromise on the now vexed question. While he was with me I received a despatch from Senator Trumbull, at Washington, alluding to the same question, and telling me to await letters. I thereupon told Mr. Kellogg that when I should receive these letters, posting me as to the state of affairs at Washington, I would write you, requesting you to let him see my letter. To my surprise when the letters mentioned by Judge Trumbull came, they made no allusion to the "vexed question" This baffled me so much that I was near not writing you at all, in compliance with what I had said to Judge Kellogg.

I say now, however, as I have all the while said, that on the territorial question—that is, the question of extending slavery under the national auspices,—I am inflexible. I am for no compromise which *assists* or *permits* the extension of the institution on soil owned by the nation. And any trick by which the nation is to acquire territory, and then allow some local authority to spread slavery over it, is as obnoxious as any other.

I take it that to effect some such result as this, and to put us again on the high-road to a slave empire is the object of all these proposed compromises. I am against it.

As to fugitive slaves, District of Columbia, slave trade among the slave states, and whatever springs of necessity from the fact that the institution is amongst us, I care but little, so that what is done be comely, and not altogether outrageous. Nor do I care much about New-Mexico, if further extension were hedged against. Yours very truly

To Thurlow Weed

Private

Thurlow Weed, Esq   Springfield, Ills. Feb. 4, 1861

My dear Sir. I have both your letter to myself, and that to Judge Davis, in relation to a certain gentleman in your state claiming to dispense patronage in my name, and also to be authorized to use my name to advance the chances of Mr. Greely for an election to the U.S. Senate. It is very strange that such things should be said by any one. The gentleman you mention, did speak to me of Mr. Greely, in connection with the Senatorial election, and I replied in terms of kindness towards Mr. Greely which I really feel, but always with an express protest that my name *must* not be used in the Senatorial election, in favor of, or against any one. Any other representation of me, is a misrepresentation.

As to the matter of dispensing patronage, it perhaps will surprise you to learn, that I have information that *you* claim to have my authority to arrange that matter in N.Y. I do not believe you have so claimed; but still so some men say. On that subject you know all I have said to you is "justice to all," and I beg you to believe I have said nothing more particular to any one. I say this to re-assure you that I have not changed my purpose; in the hope however, that you will not use my name in the matter. Yours truly

Farewell Address at Springfield, Illinois

My friends—No one, not in my situation, can appreciate my feeling of sadness at this parting. To this place, and the kindness of these people, I owe every thing. Here I have lived a quarter of a century, and have passed from a young to an old man. Here my children have been born, and one is buried. I now leave, not knowing when, or whether ever, I may return, with a task before me greater than that which rested upon Washington. Without the assistance of that Divine Being, who ever attended him, I cannot succeed. With that assistance I cannot fail. Trusting in Him, who can go with me, and remain with you and be every where for good, let us confidently hope that all will yet be well. To His care commending you, as I hope in your prayers you will commend me, I bid you an affectionate farewell

February 11, 1861

Reply to Oliver P. Morton at Indianapolis, Indiana

Gov. Morton and Fellow Citizens of the State of Indiana:
Most heartily do I thank you for this magnificent reception, and while I cannot take to myself any share of the compliment thus paid, more than that which pertains to a mere instrument, an accidental instrument, perhaps I should say, of a great cause, I yet must look upon it as a most magnificent reception, and as such, most heartily do I thank you for it.

You have been pleased to address yourselves to me chiefly in behalf of this glorious Union in which we live, in all of which you have my hearty sympathy, and, as far as may be within my power, will have, one and inseparably, my hearty consideration. While I do not expect, upon this occasion, or on any occasion, till after I get to Washington, to attempt any lengthy speech, I will only say that to the salvation of this Union there needs but one single thing—the hearts of a people like yours. [Applause.] When the people rise in masses in behalf of the Union and the liberties of their country, truly may it be said, "The gates of hell shall not prevail against them." [Renewed applause.]

In all the trying positions in which I shall be placed, and doubtless I shall be placed in many trying ones, my reliance will be placed upon you and the people of the United States—and I wish you to remember now and forever, that it is your business, and not mine; that if the union of these States, and the liberties of this people, shall be lost, it is but little to any one man of fifty-two years of age, but a great deal to the thirty millions of people who inhabit these United States, and to their posterity in all coming time. It is your business to rise up and preserve the Union and liberty, for yourselves, and not for me. I desire they shall be constitutionally preserved.

I, as already intimated, am but an accidental instrument, temporary, and to serve but for a limited time, but I appeal to you again to constantly bear in mind that with you, and not with politicians, not with Presidents, not with office-seekers, but with you, is the question, "Shall the Union and shall the liberties of this country be preserved to the latest generation?" [Loud and prolonged applause.]

February 11, 1861

Speech at Indianapolis, Indiana

It is not possible, in my journey to the national capital, to address assemblies like this which may do me the great honor to meet me as you have done, but very briefly. I should be entirely worn out if I were to attempt it. I appear before you now to thank you for this very magnificent welcome which you have given me, and still more for the very generous support which your State recently gave to the political cause of the whole country, and the whole world. [Applause.] Solomon has said, that there is a time to keep silence. [Renewed and deafening applause.] * * * * * We know certain that they mean the same thing while using the same words now, and it perhaps would be as well if they would keep silence.

The words "coercion" and "invasion" are in great use about these days. Suppose we were simply to try if we can, and ascertain what, is the meaning of these words. Let us get, if we can, the exact definitions of these words—not from dictionaries, but from the men who constantly repeat them—what things they mean to express by the words. What, then, is "coercion"? What is "invasion"? Would the marching of an army into South Carolina, for instance, without the consent of her people, and in hostility against them, be coercion or invasion? I very frankly say, I think it would be invasion, and it would be coercion too, if the people of that country were forced to submit. But if the Government, for instance, but simply insists upon holding its own forts, or retaking those forts which belong to it,—[cheers,]—or the enforcement of the laws of the United States in the collection of duties upon foreign importations,—[renewed cheers,]—or even the withdrawal of the mails from those portions of the country where the mails themselves are habitually violated; would any or all of these things be coercion? Do the lovers of the Union contend that they will resist coercion or invasion of any State, understanding that any or all of these would be coercing or invading a State? If they do, then it occurs to me that the means for the preservation of the Union they so greatly love, in their own estimation, is of a very thin and airy character. [Applause.] If sick, they would consider the little pills of the homœopathist as already too large for them to swallow. In their view, the Union, as a family relation, would not be anything like a regular marriage at all, but only as a sort of free-love arrangement,—[laughter,]—to be maintained on what that sect calls passionate attraction. [Continued laughter.] But, my friends, enough of this.

What is the particular sacredness of a State? I speak not of that position which is given to a State in and by the Constitution of the United States, for that all of us agree to—we abide by; but that position assumed, that a State can carry with it out of the Union that which it holds in sacredness by virtue of its connection with the Union. I am speaking of that assumed right of a State, as a primary principle, that the Constitution should rule all that is less than itself, and ruin all that is bigger than itself. [Laughter.] But, I ask, wherein does consist that right? If a State, in one instance, and a county in another, should be equal in extent of territory, and equal in the number of people, wherein is that State any better than the county? Can a change of name change the right? By what principle of original right is it that one-fiftieth or one-ninetieth of a great nation, by calling themselves a State, have the right to break up and ruin that nation as a matter of original principle? Now, I ask the question—I am not deciding anything—[laughter,]—and with the request that you will think somewhat upon that subject and decide for yourselves, if you choose, when you get ready,—where is the mysterious, original right, from principle, for a certain district of country with inhabitants, by merely being called a State, to play tyrant over all its own citizens, and deny the authority of everything greater than itself. [Laughter.] I say I am deciding nothing, but simply giving something for you to reflect upon; and, with having said this much, and having declared, in the start, that I will make no long speeches, I thank you again for this magnificent welcome, and bid you an affectionate farewell. [Cheers.]

February 11, 1861

Speech to Germans at Cincinnati, Ohio

Mr. Chairman: I thank you and those whom you represent, for the compliment you have paid me, by tendering me this address. In so far as there is an allusion to our present national difficulties, which expresses, as you have said, the views of the gentlemen present, I shall have to beg pardon for not entering fully upon the questions, which the address you have now read, suggests.

I deem it my duty—a duty which I owe to my constituents—to you, gentlemen, that I should wait until the last moment, for a development of the present national difficulties, before I express myself decidedly what course I shall pursue. I hope, then, not to be false to anything that you have to expect of me.

I agree with you, Mr. Chairman, that the working men are the basis of all governments, for the plain reason that they are the most numerous, and as you added that those were the sentiments of the gentlemen present, representing not only the working class, but citizens of other callings than those of the mechanic, I am happy to concur with you in these sentiments, not only of the native born citizens, but also of the Germans and foreigners from other countries.

Mr. Chairman, I hold that while man exists, it is his duty to improve not only his own condition, but to assist in ameliorating mankind; and therefore, without entering upon the details of the question, I will simply say, that I am for those means which will give the greatest good to the greatest number.

In regard to the Homestead Law, I have to say that in so far as the Government lands can be disposed of, I am in favor of cutting up the wild lands into parcels, so that every poor man may have a home.

In regard to the Germans and foreigners, I esteem them no better than other people, nor any worse. [Cries of good.] It is not my nature, when I see a people borne down by the weight of their shackles—the oppression of tyranny—to make their life more bitter by heaping upon them greater burdens; but rather would I do all in my power to raise the yoke, than to add anything that would tend to crush them.

Inasmuch as our country is extensive and new, and the countries of Europe are densely populated, if there are any abroad who desire to make this the land of their adoption, it is not in my heart to throw aught in their way, to prevent them from coming to the United States.

Mr. Chairman, and Gentlemen, I will bid you an affectionate farewell.

February 12, 1861

Address to the Ohio Legislature, Columbus, Ohio

MR. PRESIDENT AND MR. SPEAKER AND GENTLEMEN OF THE GENERAL ASSEMBLY: — It is true, as has been said by the President of the Senate, that very great responsibility rests upon me in the position to which the votes of the American people have called me. I am deeply sensible of that weighty responsibility. I cannot but know what you all know, that, without a name, perhaps without a reason why I should have a name, there has fallen upon me a task such as did not rest even upon the Father of his country, and so feeling I cannot but turn and look for the support without which it will be impossible for me to perform that great task. I turn, then, and look to the American people and to that God who has never forsaken them. Allusion has been made to the interest felt in relation to the policy of the new administration. In this I have received from some a degree of credit for having kept silence, and from others some deprecation. I still think that I was right. In the varying and repeatedly shifting scenes of the present, and without a precedent which could enable me to judge by the past, it has seemed fitting that before speaking upon the difficulties of the country, I should have gained a view of the whole field, to be sure, after all, being at liberty to modify and change the course of policy, as future events may make a change necessary. I have not maintained silence from any want of real anxiety. It is a good thing that there is no more than anxiety, for there is nothing going wrong. It is a consoling circumstance that when we look out there is nothing that really hurts anybody. We entertain different views upon political questions, but nobody is suffering anything. This is a most consoling circumstance, and from it we may conclude that all we want is time, patience and a reliance on that God who has never forsaken this people. Fellow citizens, what I have said, I have said altogether extemporaneously, and I will now come to a close.

February 13, 1861

Speech at Cleveland, Ohio

MR. CHAIRMAN AND FELLOW CITIZENS OF CLEVE-LAND: — We have been marching about two miles through snow, rain and deep mud. The large numbers that have turned out under these circumstances testify that you are in earnest about something or other. But do I think so meanly of you as to suppose that that earnestness is about me person-ally? I would be doing you injustice to suppose you did. You have assembled to testify your respect to the Union, the con-stitution and the laws, and here let me say that it is with you, the people, to advance the great cause of the Union and the constitution, and not with any one man. It rests with you alone. This fact is strongly impressed on my mind at present. In a community like this, whose appearance testifies to their intelligence, I am convinced that the cause of liberty and the Union can never be in danger. Frequent allusion is made to the excitement at present existing in our national politics, and it is as well that I should also allude to it here. I think that there is no occasion for any excitement. The crisis, as it is called, is altogether an artificial crisis. In all parts of the nation there are differences of opinion and politics. There are differ-ences of opinion even here. You did not all vote for the per-son who now addresses you. What is happening now will not hurt those who are farther away from here. Have they not all their rights now as they ever have had? Do they not have their fugitive slaves returned now as ever? Have they not the same constitution that they have lived under for seventy odd years? Have they not a position as citizens of this common country, and have we any power to change that position? (Cries of "No.") What then is the matter with them? Why all this excitement? Why all these complaints? As I said before, this crisis is all artificial. It has no foundation in facts. It was not argued up, as the saying is, and cannot, therefore, be argued down. Let it alone and it will go down of itself (Laughter). Mr. Lincoln said they must be content with but a few words from him. He was very much fatigued, and had spoken so frequently that he was already hoarse. He thanked them for the cordial and magnificent reception they had given him. Not less did he thank them for the votes they gave him last fall, and quite as much he thanked them for the efficient aid they had given the cause which he represented—a cause which he would say was a good one. He had one more word to say. He was given to understand that this reception was not tendered by his own party supporters, but by men of all parties. This is as it should be. If Judge Douglas had been elected and had been here on his way to Washington, as I am to-night, the republicans should have joined his supporters in welcoming him, just as his friends have joined with mine to-night. If all do not join now to save the good old ship of the Union this voyage nobody will have a chance to pilot her on another voyage. He concluded by thanking all present for the devotion they have shown to the cause of the Union.

February 15, 1861

Remarks at Syracuse, New York

LADIES AND GENTLEMEN: I see you have erected a very fine and handsome platform here for me, and I presume you expected me to speak from it. If I should go upon it you would imagine that I was about to deliver you a much longer speech than I am. I wish you to understand that I mean no discourtesy to you by thus declining. I intend discourtesy to no one. But I wish you to understand that though I am unwilling to go upon this platform, you are not at liberty to draw any inferences concerning any other platform with which my name has been or is connected. [Laughter and applause.] I wish you a long life and prosperity individually, and pray that with the perpetuity of those institutions under which we have all so long lived and prospered, our happiness may be secured, our future made brilliant, and the glorious destiny of our country established forever. I bid you a kind farewell.

February 18, 1861

Remarks at Little Falls, New York

Ladies and Gentlemen: I appear before you merely for the purpose of greeting you, saying a few words and bidding you farewell. I have no speech to make, and no sufficient time to make one if I had; nor have I the strength to repeat a speech, at all the places at which I stop, even if all the other circumstances were favorable. I have come to see you and allow you to see me (Applause) and in this so far regards the Ladies, I have the best of the bargain on my side. I don't make that acknowledgement to the gentlemen, (Increased laughter) and now I believe I have really made my speech and am ready to bid you farewell when the cars move on.

February 18, 1861

Address to the New Jersey Senate at Trenton, New Jersey

MR. PRESIDENT AND GENTLEMEN OF THE SENATE OF THE STATE OF NEW-JERSEY: I am very grateful to you for the honorable reception of which I have been the object. I cannot but remember the place that New-Jersey holds in our early history. In the early Revolutionary struggle, few of the States among the old Thirteen had more of the battle-fields of the country within their limits than old New-Jersey. May I be pardoned if, upon this occasion, I mention that away back in my childhood, the earliest days of my being able to read, I got hold of a small book, such a one as few of the younger members have ever seen, "Weem's Life of Washington." I remember all the accounts there given of the battle fields and struggles for the liberties of the country, and none fixed themselves upon my imagination so deeply as the struggle here at Trenton, New-Jersey. The crossing of the river; the contest with the Hessians; the great hardships endured at that time, all fixed themselves on my memory more than any single revolutionary event; and you all know, for you have all been boys, how these early impressions last longer than any others. I recollect thinking then, boy even though I was, that there must have been something more than common that those men struggled for. I am exceedingly anxious that that thing which they struggled for; that something even more than National Independence; that something that held out a great promise to all the people of the world to all time to come; I am exceedingly anxious that this Union, the Constitution, and the liberties of the people shall be perpetuated in accordance with the original idea for which that struggle was made, and I shall be most happy indeed if I shall be an humble instrument in the hands of the Almighty, and of this, his almost chosen people, for perpetuating the object of that great struggle. You give me this reception, as I understand, without distinction of party. I learn that this body is composed of a majority of gentlemen who, in the exercise of their best judgment in the choice of a Chief Magistrate, did not think I was the man. I understand, nevertheless, that they came forward here to

209

greet me as the constitutional President of the United States — as citizens of the United States, to meet the man who, for the time being, is the representative man of the nation, united by a purpose to perpetuate the Union and liberties of the people. As such, I accept this reception more gratefully than I could do did I believe it was tendered to me as an individual.

February 21, 1861

Address to the New Jersey General Assembly at Trenton, New Jersey

MR. SPEAKER AND GENTLEMEN: I have just enjoyed the honor of a reception by the other branch of this Legislature, and I return to you and them my thanks for the reception which the people of New-Jersey have given, through their chosen representatives, to me, as the representative, for the time being, of the majesty of the people of the United States. I appropriate to myself very little of the demonstrations of respect with which I have been greeted. I think little should be given to any man, but that it should be a manifestation of adherence to the Union and the Constitution. I understand myself to be received here by the representatives of the people of New-Jersey, a majority of whom differ in opinion from those with whom I have acted. This manifestation is therefore to be regarded by me as expressing their devotion to the Union, the Constitution and the liberties of the people. You, Mr. Speaker, have well said that this is a time when the bravest and wisest look with doubt and awe upon the aspect presented by our national affairs. Under these circumstances, you will readily see why I should not speak in detail of the course I shall deem it best to pursue. It is proper that I should avail myself of all the information and all the time at my command, in order that when the time arrives in which I must speak officially, I shall be able to take the ground which I deem the best and safest, and from which I may have no occasion to swerve. I shall endeavor to take the ground I deem most just to the North, the East, the West, the South, and the whole country. I take it, I hope, in good temper—certainly no malice toward any section. I shall do all that may be in my power to promote a peaceful settlement of all our difficulties. The man does not live who is more devoted to peace than I am. [Cheers.] None who would do more to preserve it. But it may be necessary to put the foot down firmly. [Here the audience broke out into cheers so loud and long that for some moments it was impossible to hear Mr. L.'s voice.] He continued: And if I do my duty, and do right, you will sustain me, will you not? [Loud cheers, and cries of "Yes," "Yes," "We will."] Received, as I am, by the members of a Legislature the majority of whom do not agree with me in political sentiments, I trust that I may have their assistance in piloting the ship of State through this voyage, surrounded by perils as it is; for, if it should suffer attack now, there will be no pilot ever needed for another voyage.

Gentlemen, I have already spoken longer than I intended, and must beg leave to stop here.

February 21, 1861

Reply to Mayor Alexander Henry at Philadelphia, Pennsylvania

Mr. Mayor and Fellow Citizens of Philadelphia—I appear before you to make no lengthy speech. I appear before you to thank you for the reception. The reception you have given me to-night is not to me, the man, the individual, but to the man who temporarily represents, or should represent, the majesty of the nation. (Applause.) It is true, as your worthy Mayor has said, that there is great anxiety amongst the citizens of the United States at this time. I say I deem it a happy circumstance that the dissatisfied portion of our fellow citizens do not point us to anything in which they are being injured, or about to be injured, from which I have felt all the while justified in concluding that the crisis, the panic, the anxiety of the country at this time is artificial. If there be those who differ with me upon this subject, they have not pointed out the substantial difficulty that exists. (Tremendous cheering.)

I do not mean to say that this artificial panic has not done harm. That it has done much harm I do not deny. The hope that has been expressed by your worthy Mayor, that I may be able to restore peace and harmony and prosperity to the country, is most worthy in him; and most happy indeed shall I be if I shall be able to fulfill and verify that hope. (Cheers.)

I promise you in all sincerity, that I bring to the work a sincere heart. Whether I will bring a head equal to that heart, will be for future time to determine. It were useless for me to speak of the details of the plans now. I shall speak officially on next Monday week, if ever. If I should not speak, then it were useless for me to do so now. When I do speak, as your worthy Mayor has expressed the hope, I will take such grounds as I shall deem best calculated to restore peace, harmony and prosperity to the country, and tend to the perpetuity of the nation, and the liberty of these States and all these people. (Applause.)

Your worthy Mayor has expressed the wish, in which I join with him, that if it were convenient for me to remain with you in your city long enough to consult, or, as it were, to listen to those breathings rising within the consecrated walls where the Constitution of the United States, and, I will add, the Declaration of American Independence was originally framed, I would do so.

I assure you and your Mayor that I had hoped on this occasion, and upon all occasions during my life, that I shall do nothing inconsistent with the teachings of those holy and most sacred walls.

I have never asked anything that does not breathe from those walls. All my political warfare has been in favor of the teachings coming forth from that sacred hall. May my right hand forget its cunning and my tongue cleave to the roof of my mouth, if ever I prove false to those teachings.

Fellow citizens, I have addressed you longer than I expected to do, and allow me now to bid you good night.

February 21, 1861

Speech at Independence Hall, Philadelphia, Pennsylvania

Mr. CUYLER:—I am filled with deep emotion at finding myself standing here in the place where were collected together the wisdom, the patriotism, the devotion to principle, from which sprang the institutions under which we live. You have kindly suggested to me that in my hands is the task of restoring peace to our distracted country. I can say in return, sir, that all the political sentiments I entertain have been drawn, so far as I have been able to draw them, from the sentiments which originated, and were given to the world from this hall in which we stand. I have never had a feeling politically that did not spring from the sentiments embodied in the Declaration of Independence. (Great cheering.) I have often pondered over the dangers which were incurred by the men who assembled here and adopted that Declaration of Independence—I have pondered over the toils that were endured by the officers and soldiers of the army, who achieved that Independence. (Applause.) I have often inquired of myself, what great principle or idea it was that kept this Confederacy so long together. It was not the mere matter of the separation of the colonies from the mother land; but something in that Declaration giving liberty, not alone to the people of this country, but hope to the world for all future time. (Great applause.) It was that which gave promise that in due time the weights should be lifted from the shoulders of all men, and that *all* should have an equal chance. (Cheers.) This is the sentiment embodied in that Declaration of Independence.

Now, my friends, can this country be saved upon that basis? If it can, I will consider myself one of the happiest men in the world if I can help to save it. If it can't be saved upon that principle, it will be truly awful. But, if this country cannot be saved without giving up that principle—I was about to say I would rather be assassinated on this spot than to surrender it. (Applause.)

Now, in my view of the present aspect of affairs, there is no need of bloodshed and war. There is no necessity for it. I am not in favor of such a course, and I may say in advance, there will be no blood shed unless it be forced upon the Government. The Government will not use force unless force is used against it. (Prolonged applause and cries of "That's the proper sentiment.")

My friends, this is a wholly unprepared speech. I did not expect to be called upon to say a word when I came here—I supposed I was merely to do something towards raising a flag. I may, therefore, have said something indiscreet, (cries of "no, no"), but I have said nothing but what I am willing to live by, and, in the pleasure of Almighty God, die by.

February 22, 1861

First Inaugural Address

Fellow citizens of the United States:

In compliance with a custom as old as the government itself, I appear before you to address you briefly, and to take, in your presence, the oath prescribed by the Constitution of the United States, to be taken by the President "before he enters on the execution of his office."

I do not consider it necessary, at present, for me to discuss those matters of administration about which there is no special anxiety, or excitement.

Apprehension seems to exist among the people of the Southern States, that by the accession of a Republican Administration, their property, and their peace, and personal security, are to be endangered. There has never been any reasonable cause for such apprehension. Indeed, the most ample evidence to the contrary has all the while existed, and been open to their inspection. It is found in nearly all the published speeches of him who now addresses you. I do but quote from one of those speeches when I declare that "I have no purpose, directly or indirectly, to interfere with the institution of slavery in the States where it exists. I believe I have no lawful right to do so, and I have no inclination to do so." Those who nominated and elected me did so with full knowledge that I had made this, and many similar declarations, and had never recanted them. And more than this, they placed in the platform, for my acceptance, and as a law to themselves, and to me, the clear and emphatic resolution which I now read:

"*Resolved,* That the maintenance inviolate of the rights of the States, and especially the right of each State to order and control its own domestic institutions according to its own judgment exclusively, is essential to that balance of power on which the perfection and endurance of our political fabric depend; and we denounce the lawless invasion by armed force of the soil of any State or Territory, no matter under what pretext, as among the gravest of crimes."

I now reiterate these sentiments: and in doing so, I only press upon the public attention the most conclusive evidence of which the case is susceptible, that the property, peace and security of no section are to be in anywise endangered by the now incoming Administration. I add too, that all the protection which, consistently with the Constitution and the laws, can be given, will be cheerfully given to all the States when lawfully demanded, for whatever cause—as cheerfully to one section, as to another.

There is much controversy about the delivering up of fugitives from service or labor. The clause I now read is as plainly written in the Constitution as any other of its provisions:

"No person held to service or labor in one State, under the laws thereof, escaping into another, shall, in consequence of any law or regulation therein, be discharged from such service or labor, but shall be delivered up on claim of the party to whom such service or labor may be due."

It is scarcely questioned that this provision was intended by those who made it, for the reclaiming of what we call fugitive slaves; and the intention of the law-giver is the law. All members of Congress swear their support to the whole Constitution—to this provision as much as to any other. To the proposition, then, that slaves whose cases come within the terms of this clause, "shall be delivered up," their oaths are unanimous. Now, if they would make the effort in good temper, could they not, with nearly equal unanimity, frame and pass a law, by means of which to keep good that unanimous oath?

There is some difference of opinion whether this clause should be enforced by national or by state authority; but surely that difference is not a very material one. If the slave is to be surrendered, it can be of but little consequence to him, or to others, by which authority it is done. And should any one, in any case, be content that his oath shall go unkept, on a merely unsubstantial controversy as to *how* it shall be kept?

Again, in any law upon this subject, ought not all the safeguards of liberty known in civilized and humane jurisprudence to be introduced, so that a free man be not, in any case, surrendered as a slave? And might it not be well, at the same time, to provide by law for the enforcement of that clause in the Constitution which guarranties that "The citizens of each

State shall be entitled to all previleges and immunities of citizens in the several States?"

I take the official oath to-day, with no mental reservations, and with no purpose to construe the Constitution or laws, by any hypercritical rules. And while I do not choose now to specify particular acts of Congress as proper to be enforced, I do suggest, that it will be much safer for all, both in official and private stations, to conform to, and abide by, all those acts which stand unrepealed, than to violate any of them, trusting to find impunity in having them held to be unconstitutional.

It is seventy-two years since the first inauguration of a President under our national Constitution. During that period fifteen different and greatly distinguished citizens, have, in succession, administered the executive branch of the government. They have conducted it through many perils; and, generally, with great success. Yet, with all this scope for precedent, I now enter upon the same task for the brief constitutional term of four years, under great and peculiar difficulty. A disruption of the Federal Union heretofore only menaced, is now formidably attempted.

I hold, that in contemplation of universal law, and of the Constitution, the Union of these States is perpetual. Perpetuity is implied, if not expressed, in the fundamental law of all national governments. It is safe to assert that no government proper, ever had a provision in its organic law for its own termination. Continue to execute all the express provisions of our national Constitution, and the Union will endure forever—it being impossible to destroy it, except by some action not provided for in the instrument itself.

Again, if the United States be not a government proper, but an association of States in the nature of contract merely, can it, as a contract, be peaceably unmade, by less than all the parties who made it? One party to a contract may violate it— break it, so to speak; but does it not require all to lawfully rescind it?

Descending from these general principles, we find the proposition that, in legal contemplation, the Union is perpetual, confirmed by the history of the Union itself. The Union is much older than the Constitution. It was formed in fact, by

the Articles of Association in 1774. It was matured and continued by the Declaration of Independence in 1776. It was further matured and the faith of all the then thirteen States
expressly plighted and engaged that it should be perpetual, by
the Articles of Confederation in 1778. And finally, in 1787, one
of the declared objects for ordaining and establishing the
Constitution, was *"to form a more perfect union."*

But if destruction of the Union, by one, or by a part only,
of the States, be lawfully possible, the Union is *less* perfect
than before the Constitution, having lost the vital element of
perpetuity.

It follows from these views that no State, upon its own
mere motion, can lawfully get out of the Union,—that *resolves*
and *ordinances* to that effect are legally void; and that acts of
violence, within any State or States, against the authority of
the United States, are insurrectionary or revolutionary, according to circumstances.

I therefore consider that, in view of the Constitution and
the laws, the Union is unbroken; and, to the extent of my
ability, I shall take care, as the Constitution itself expressly
enjoins upon me, that the laws of the Union be faithfully executed in all the States. Doing this I deem to be only a simple
duty on my part; and I shall perform it, so far as practicable,
unless my rightful masters, the American people, shall withhold the requisite means, or, in some authoritative manner,
direct the contrary. I trust this will not be regarded as a menace, but only as the declared purpose of the Union that it *will*
constitutionally defend, and maintain itself.

In doing this there needs to be no bloodshed or violence;
and there shall be none, unless it be forced upon the national
authority. The power confided to me, will be used to hold,
occupy, and possess the property, and places belonging to the
government, and to collect the duties and imposts; but beyond what may be necessary for these objects, there will be no
invasion—no using of force against, or among the people
anywhere. Where hostility to the United States, in any interior locality, shall be so great and so universal, as to prevent
competent resident citizens from holding the Federal offices,
there will be no attempt to force obnoxious strangers among
the people for that object. While the strict legal right may

exist in the government to enforce the exercise of these offices, the attempt to do so would be so irritating, and so nearly impracticable with all, that I deem it better to forego, for the time, the uses of such offices.

The mails, unless repelled, will continue to be furnished in all parts of the Union. So far as possible, the people everywhere shall have that sense of perfect security which is most favorable to calm thought and reflection. The course here indicated will be followed, unless current events, and experience, shall show a modification, or change, to be proper; and in every case and exigency, my best discretion will be exercised, according to circumstances actually existing, and with a view and a hope of a peaceful solution of the national troubles, and the restoration of fraternal sympathies and affections.

That there are persons in one section, or another who seek to destroy the Union at all events, and are glad of any pretext to do it, I will neither affirm or deny; but if there be such, I need address no word to them. To those, however, who really love the Union, may I not speak?

Before entering upon so grave a matter as the destruction of our national fabric, with all its benefits, its memories, and its hopes, would it not be wise to ascertain precisely why we do it? Will you hazard so desperate a step, while there is any possibility that any portion of the ills you fly from, have no real existence? Will you, while the certain ills you fly to, are greater than all the real ones you fly from? Will you risk the commission of so fearful a mistake?

All profess to be content in the Union, if all constitutional rights can be maintained. Is it true, then, that any right, plainly written in the Constitution, has been denied? I think not. Happily the human mind is so constituted, that no party can reach to the audacity of doing this. Think, if you can, of a single instance in which a plainly written provision of the Constitution has ever been denied. If, by the mere force of numbers, a majority should deprive a minority of any clearly written constitutional right, it might, in a moral point of view, justify revolution—certainly would, if such right were a vital one. But such is not our case. All the vital rights of minorities, and of individuals, are so plainly assured to them, by affirmations and negations, guarranties and prohibitions, in the Constitution, that controversies never arise concerning them. But no organic law can ever be framed with a provision specifically applicable to every question which may occur in practical administration. No foresight can anticipate, nor any document of reasonable length contain express provisions for all possible questions. Shall fugitives from labor be surrendered by national or by State authority? The Constitution does not expressly say. *May* Congress prohibit slavery in the territories? The Constitution does not expressly say. *Must* Congress protect slavery in the territories? The Constitution does not expressly say.

From questions of this class spring all our constitutional controversies, and we divide upon them into majorities and minorities. If the minority will not acquiesce, the majority must, or the government must cease. There is no other alternative; for continuing the government, is acquiescence on one side or the other. If a minority, in such case, will secede rather than acquiesce, they make a precedent which, in turn, will divide and ruin them; for a minority of their own will secede from them, whenever a majority refuses to be controlled by such minority. For instance, why may not any portion of a new confederacy, a year or two hence, arbitrarily secede again, precisely as portions of the present Union now claim to secede from it. All who cherish disunion sentiments, are now being educated to the exact temper of doing this. Is there such perfect identity of interests among the States to compose a new Union, as to produce harmony only, and prevent renewed secession?

Plainly, the central idea of secession, is the essence of anarchy. A majority, held in restraint by constitutional checks, and limitations, and always changing easily, with deliberate changes of popular opinions and sentiments, is the only true sovereign of a free people. Whoever rejects it, does, of necessity, fly to anarchy or to despotism. Unanimity is impossible; the rule of a minority, as a permanent arrangement, is wholly inadmissable; so that, rejecting the majority principle, anarchy, or despotism in some form, is all that is left.

I do not forget the position assumed by some, that constitutional questions are to be decided by the Supreme Court;

nor do I deny that such decisions must be binding in any case, upon the parties to a suit, as to the object of that suit, while they are also entitled to very high respect and consideration, in all paralel cases, by all other departments of the government. And while it is obviously possible that such decision may be erroneous in any given case, still the evil effect following it, being limited to that particular case, with the chance that it may be over-ruled, and never become a precedent for other cases, can better be borne than could the evils of a different practice. At the same time the candid citizen must confess that if the policy of the government, upon vital questions, affecting the whole people, is to be irrevocably fixed by decisions of the Supreme Court, the instant they are made, in ordinary litigation between parties, in personal actions, the people will have ceased, to be their own rulers, having, to that extent, practically resigned their government, into the hands of that eminent tribunal. Nor is there, in this view, any assault upon the court, or the judges. It is a duty, from which they may not shrink, to decide cases properly brought before them; and it is no fault of theirs, if others seek to turn their decisions to political purposes.

One section of our country believes slavery is *right*, and ought to be extended, while the other believes it is *wrong*, and ought not to be extended. This is the only substantial dispute. The fugitive slave clause of the Constitution, and the law for the suppression of the foreign slave trade, are each as well enforced, perhaps, as any law can ever be in a community where the moral sense of the people imperfectly supports the law itself. The great body of the people abide by the dry legal obligation in both cases, and a few break over in each. This, I think, cannot be perfectly cured; and it would be worse in both cases *after* the separation of the sections, than before. The foreign slave trade, now imperfectly suppressed, would be ultimately revived without restriction, in one section; while fugitive slaves, now only partially surrendered, would not be surrendered at all, by the other.

Physically speaking, we cannot separate. We cannot remove our respective sections from each other, nor build an impassable wall between them. A husband and wife may be divorced, and go out of the presence, and beyond the reach of each other; but the different parts of our country cannot do this. They cannot but remain face to face; and intercourse, either amicable or hostile, must continue between them. Is it possible then to make that intercourse more advantageous, or more satisfactory, *after* separation than *before*? Can aliens make treaties easier than friends can make laws? Can treaties be more faithfully enforced between aliens, than laws can among friends? Suppose you go to war, you cannot fight always; and when, after much loss on both sides, and no gain on either, you cease fighting, the identical old questions, as to terms of intercourse, are again upon you.

This country, with its institutions, belongs to the people who inhabit it. Whenever they shall grow weary of the existing government, they can exercise their *constitutional* right of amending it, or their *revolutionary* right to dismember, or overthrow it. I can not be ignorant of the fact that many worthy, and patriotic citizens are desirous of having the national constitution amended. While I make no recommendation of amendments, I fully recognize the rightful authority of the people over the whole subject, to be exercised in either of the modes prescribed in the instrument itself; and I should, under existing circumstances, favor, rather than oppose, a fair oppertunity being afforded the people to act upon it.

I will venture to add that, to me, the convention mode seems preferable, in that it allows amendments to originate with the people themselves, instead of only permitting them to take, or reject, propositions, originated by others, not especially chosen for the purpose, and which might not be precisely such, as they would wish to either accept or refuse. I understand a proposed amendment to the Constitution— which amendment, however, I have not seen, has passed Congress, to the effect that the federal government, shall never interfere with the domestic institutions of the States, including that of persons held to service. To avoid misconstruction of what I have said, I depart from my purpose not to speak of particular amendments, so far as to say that, holding such a provision to now be implied constitutional law, I have no objection to its being made express, and irrevocable.

The Chief Magistrate derives all his authority from the

people, and they have conferred none upon him to fix terms for the separation of the States. The people themselves can do this also if they choose; but the executive, as such, has nothing to do with it. His duty is to administer the present government, as it came to his hands, and to transmit it, unimpaired by him, to his successor.

Why should there not be a patient confidence in the ultimate justice of the people? Is there any better, or equal hope, in the world? In our present differences, is either party without faith of being in the right? If the Almighty Ruler of nations, with his eternal truth and justice, be on your side of the North, or on yours of the South, that truth, and that justice, will surely prevail, by the judgment of this great tribunal, the American people.

By the frame of the government under which we live, this same people have wisely given their public servants but little power for mischief; and have, with equal wisdom, provided for the return of that little to their own hands at very short intervals.

While the people retain their virtue, and vigilence, no administration, by any extreme of wickedness or folly, can very seriously injure the government, in the short space of four years.

My countrymen, one and all, think calmly and *well*, upon this whole subject. Nothing valuable can be lost by taking time. If there be an object to *hurry* any of you, in hot haste, to a step which you would never take *deliberately*, that object will be frustrated by taking time; but no good object can be frustrated by it. Such of you as are now dissatisfied, still have the old Constitution unimpaired, and, on the sensitive point, the laws of your own framing under it; while the new administration will have no immediate power, if it would, to change either. If it were admitted that you who are dissatisfied, hold the right side in the dispute, there still is no single good reason for precipitate action. Intelligence, patriotism, Christianity, and a firm reliance on Him, who has never yet forsaken this favored land, are still competent to adjust, in the best way, all our present difficulty.

In *your* hands, my dissatisfied fellow countrymen, and not in *mine*, is the momentous issue of civil war. The government will not assail *you*. You can have no conflict, without being yourselves the aggressors. *You* have no oath registered in Heaven to destroy the government, while *I* shall have the most solemn one to "preserve, protect and defend" it.

I am loth to close. We are not enemies, but friends. We must not be enemies. Though passion may have strained, it must not break our bonds of affection. The mystic chords of memory, streching from every battle-field, and patriot grave, to every living heart and hearthstone, all over this broad land, will yet swell the chorus of the Union, when again touched, as surely they will be, by the better angels of our nature.

March 4, 1861

To Schuyler Colfax

Hon. Schuyler Colfax   Executive Mansion March 8. 1861

My dear Sir: Your letter of the 6th, has just been handed me by Mr. Baker of Minnesota. When I said to you, the other day, that I wished to write you a letter, I had reference, of course, to my not having offered you a cabinet appointment. I meant to say, and now do say, you were most honorably and amply recommended; and a tender of the appointment was not withheld on any ground disparaging to you. Nor was it withheld, in any part, because of anything happening in 1858—indeed, I should have decided as I did, easier than I did, had that matter never existed. I had partly made up my mind in favor of Mr. Smith—not conclusively of course—before your name was mentioned in that connection. When you were brought forward I said "Colfax is a young man—is already in position—is running a brilliant career, and is sure of a bright future in any event." "With Smith, it is now or never." I considered either abundantly competent, and decided on the ground I have stated. I now have to beg that you will not do me the injustice to suppose, for a moment, that I remembered any thing against you in malice. Yours very truly

To Winfield Scott

Executive Mansion, March 9, 1861.

Lieutenant General Scott:

My dear Sir: On the 5th inst. I received from the Hon. Joseph Holt, the then faithful and vigilant Secretary of War, a letter of that date, inclosing a letter and accompanying documents received by him on the 4th inst. from Major Robert Anderson commanding at Fort Sumpter South Carolina; and copies of all which I now transmit. Immediately on the receipt of them by me, I transmitted the whole to you for your consideration; and the same day you returned the package to me with your opinion endorsed upon it, a copy of which opinion I now also transmit to you. Learning from you verbally that since then you have given the subject a more full and thorough consideration, you will much oblige me by giving answers, in writing, to the following interrogatories:

1st To what point of time can Major Anderson maintain his position at Fort Sumpter, without fresh supplies or reinforcement?

2d. Can you, with all the means now in your control, supply or re-inforce Fort Sumpter within that time?

3d If not, what amount of means and of what description, in addition to that already at your control, would enable you to supply and reinforce that fortress within the time?

Please answer these, adding such statements, information, and counsel as your great skill and experience may suggest. Your obedient Servant

To William H. Seward

The Hon. Secretary of State   Executive Mansion
My dear Sir   March 15. 1861

Assuming it to be possible to now provision Fort-Sumpter, under all the circumstances, is it wise to attempt it?

Please give me your opinion, in writing, on this question. Your Obt. Servt.

To John T. Stuart

PRIVATE

Dear Stuart: Washington, March 30, 1861

Cousin Lizzie shows me your letter of the 27th. The question of giving her the Springfield Post-office troubles me. You see I have already appointed William Jayne a territorial governor, and Judge Trumbulls brother to a Land-office. Will it do for me to go on and justify the declaration that Trumbull and I have divided out all the offices among our relatives? Dr. Wallace, you know, is needy, and looks to me; and I personally owe him much.

I see by the papers, a vote is to be taken as to the Post-office. Could you not set up Lizzie and beat them all? She, being here, need know nothing of it, & therefore there would be no indelicacy on her part. Yours as ever

To David D. Porter

Executive Mansion, April 1, 1861.

Sir: You will proceed to New York, and with the least possible delay assume command of any naval steamer available. Proceed to Pensacola Harbor, and at any cost or risk prevent any expedition from the mainland reaching Fort Pickens or Santa Rosa.

You will exhibit this order to any naval officer at Pensacola if you deem it necessary after you have established yourself within the harbor, and will request cooperation by the entrance of at least one other vessel.

This order, its object, and your destination will be communicated to no person whatever until you reach the harbor of Pensacola.

ABRAHAM LINCOLN.

Lieutenant D. D. Porter, U.S. Navy.
Recommended: WM. H. SEWARD.

To Winfield Scott

Lieut General Scott: Executive Mansion April 1st 1861.

Would it impose too much labor on General Scott to make short, comprehensive daily reports to me of what occurs in his Department, including movements by himself, and under his orders, and the receipt of intelligence? If not I will thank him to do so. Your Obedient Servant

To William H. Seward

Hon: W. H. Seward: Executive Mansion April 1, 1861

My dear Sir: Since parting with you I have been considering your paper dated this day, and entitled "Some thoughts for the President's consideration." The first proposition in it is, "1st. We are at the end of a month's administration, and yet without a policy, either domestic or foreign."

At the *beginning* of that month, in the inaugeral, I said "The power confided to me will be used to hold, occupy and possess the property and places belonging to the government, and to collect the duties, and imposts." This had your distinct approval at the time; and, taken in connection with the order I immediately gave General Scott, directing him to employ every means in his power to strengthen and hold the forts, comprises the exact domestic policy you now urge, with the single exception, that it does not propose to abandon Fort Sumpter.

Again, I do not perceive how the re-inforcement of Fort Sumpter would be done on a slavery, or party issue, while that of Fort Pickens would be on a more national, and patriotic one.

The news received yesterday in regard to St. Domingo, certainly brings a new item within the range of our foreign policy; but up to that time we have been preparing circulars, and instructions to ministers, and the like, all in perfect harmony, without even a suggestion that we had no foreign policy.

Upon your closing propositions, that "whatever policy we adopt, there must be an energetic prossecution of it"

"For this purpose it must be somebody's business to pursue and direct it incessantly"

"Either the President must do it himself, and be all the while active in it, or"

"Devolve it on some member of his cabinet"

"Once adopted, debates on it must end, and all agree and abide" I remark that if this must be done, *I* must do it. When a general line of policy is adopted, I apprehend there is no danger of its being changed without good reason, or continuing to be a subject of unnecessary debate; still, upon points arising in its progress, I wish, and suppose I am entitled to have the advice of all the cabinet. Your Obt. Servt.

To Robert Anderson

War Department Washington, April 4. 1861

Sir: Your letter of the 1st. inst. occasions some anxiety to the President.

On the information of Capt. Fox, he had supposed you could hold out till the 15th. inst. without any great inconvenience; and had prepared an expedition to relieve you before that period.

Hoping still that you will be able to sustain yourself till the 11th. or 12th. inst. the expedition will go forward; and, finding your flag flying, will attempt to provision you, and, in case the effort is resisted, will endeavor also to reinforce you.

You will therefore hold out if possible till the arrival of the expedition.

It is not, however, the intention of the President to subject your command to any danger or hardship beyond what, in your judgment, would be usual in military life; and he has entire confidence that you will act as becomes a patriot and a soldier, under all circumstances.

Whenever, if at all, in your judgment, to save yourself and command, a capitulation becomes a necessity, you are authorized to make it. Respectfully   SIMON CAMERON.

To Major Robert Anderson
    U.S. Army

This was sent by Capt. Talbot, on April 6, 1861, to be delivered to Maj. Anderson, if permitted. On reaching Charleston, he was refused permission to deliver it to Major Anderson.

To Robert S. Chew

War Department. Washington, April 6. 1861

Sir—You will proceed directly to Charleston, South Carolina; and if, on your arrival there, the flag of the United States shall be flying over Fort-Sumpter, and the Fort shall not have been attacked, you will procure an interview with Gov. Pickens, and read to him as follows:

"I am directed by the President of the United States to notify you to expect an attempt will be made to supply Fort-Sumpter with provisions only; and that, if such attempt be not resisted, no effort to throw in men, arms, or amunition, will be made, without further notice, or in case of an attack upon the Fort"

After you shall have read this to Governor Pickens, deliver to him the copy of it herein inclosed, and retain this letter yourself.

But if, on your arrival at Charleston, you shall ascertain that Fort Sumpter shall have been already evacuated, or surrendered, by the United States force; or, shall have been attacked by an opposing force, you will seek no interview with Gov. Pickens, but return here forthwith. Respectfully

SIMON CAMERON
Secy of War

Notice carried by R. S. Chew to Gov. Pickens, and his report as to how he gave the notice.

Reply to the Virginia Convention

Hon: William Ballard Preston, Alexander H. H. Stuart,
    & George W. Randolph, Esq—

Gentlemen: As a committee of the Virginia convention, now in session, you present me a preamble and resolution, in these words:

Whereas, in the opinion of this Convention the uncertainty which prevails in the public mind as to the policy which the Federal Executive intends to pursue toward the seceded States is extremely injurious to the industrial and commercial interests of the country; tends to keep up an excitement which is unfavorable to the adjustment of pending difficulties, and threatens a disturbance of the public peace; therefore

Resolved, that a committee of three delegates be appointed by this Convention to wait upon the President of the United States, present to him this preamble and resolution, and respectfully ask of him to communicate to this Convention the policy which the Federal Executive intends to pursue in regard to the Confederate States.

Adopted by the Convention of the State of Virginia, Richmond, April 8th 1861

In pursuance of the foregoing resolution, the following delegates were appointed to constitute said committee.

>Hon. William Ballard Preston.
>Hon. Alexander H. H. Stuart.
>George W. Randolph Esq.

JOHN JANNEY PRESIDENT

JNO. L. EUBANK SECRETARY.

In answer I have to say, that having, at the beginning of my official term, expressed my intended policy, as plainly as I was able, it is with deep regret, and some mortification, I now learn, that there is great, and injurious uncertainty, in the public mind, as to what that policy is, and what course I intend to pursue. Not having, as yet, seen occasion to change, it is now my purpose to pursue the course marked out in the inaugeral address. I commend a careful consideration of the whole document, as the best expression I can give of my purposes. As I then, and therein, said, I now repeat:

"The power confided to me will be used to hold, occupy, and possess, the property, and places belonging to the Government, and to collect the duties, and imposts; but, beyond what is necessary for these objects, there will be no invasion—no using of force against, or among the people anywhere"

By the words "property, and places, belonging to the Government" I chiefly allude to the military posts, and property, which were in the possession of the Government when it came to my hands. But if, as now appears to be true, in pursuit of a purpose to drive the United States authority from these places, an unprovoked assault, has been made upon

Fort-Sumpter, I shall hold myself at liberty to re-possess, if I can, like places which had been seized before the Government was devolved upon me.

And, in every event, I shall, to the extent of my ability, repel force by force.

In case it proves true, that Fort-Sumpter has been assaulted, as is reported, I shall perhaps, cause the United States mails to be withdrawn from all the States which claim to have seceded—believing that the commencement of actual war against the Government, justifies and possibly demands this.

I scarcely need to say that I consider the Military posts and property situated within the states, which claim to have seceded, as yet belonging to the Government of the United States, as much as they did before the supposed secession.

Whatever else I may do for the purpose, I shall not attempt to collect the duties, and imposts, by any armed invasion of any part of the country—not meaning by this, however, that I may not land a force, deemed necessary, to relieve a fort upon a border of the country. From the fact, that I have quoted a part of the inaugeral address, it must not be infered that I repudiate any other part, the whole of which I re-affirm, except so far as what I now say of the mails, may be regarded as a modification.

April 13, 1861

Proclamation Calling Militia and Convening Congress

BY THE PRESIDENT OF THE UNITED STATES

A PROCLAMATION.

Whereas the laws of the United States have been for some time past, and now are opposed, and the execution thereof obstructed, in the States of South Carolina, Georgia, Alabama, Florida, Mississippi, Louisiana and Texas, by combinations too powerful to be suppressed by the ordinary course of judicial proceedings, or by the powers vested in the Marshals by law,

Now therefore, I, Abraham Lincoln, President of the United States, in virtue of the power in me vested by the Constitution, and the laws, have thought fit to call forth, and hereby do call forth, the militia of the several States of the Union, to the aggregate number of seventy-five thousand, in order to suppress said combinations, and to cause the laws to be duly executed. The details, for this object, will be immediately communicated to the State authorities through the War Department.

I appeal to all loyal citizens to favor, facilitate and aid this effort to maintain the honor, the integrity, and the existence of our National Union, and the perpetuity of popular government; and to redress wrongs already long enough endured.

I deem it proper to say that the first service assigned to the forces hereby called forth will probably be to re-possess the forts, places, and property which have been seized from the Union; and in every event, the utmost care will be observed, consistently with the objects aforesaid, to avoid any devastation, any destruction of, or interference with, property, or any disturbance of peaceful citizens in any part of the country.

And I hereby command the persons composing the combinations aforesaid to disperse, and retire peaceably to their respective abodes within twenty days from this date.

Deeming that the present condition of public affairs presents an extraordinary occasion, I do hereby, in virtue of the power in me vested by the Constitution, convene both Houses of Congress. Senators and Representatives are therefore summoned to assemble at their respective chambers, at 12 o'clock, noon, on Thursday, the fourth day of July, next, then and there to consider and determine, such measures, as, in their wisdom, the public safety, and interest may seem to demand.

In Witness Whereof I have hereunto set my hand, and caused the Seal of the United States to be affixed.

Done at the city of Washington this fifteenth day of April in the year of our Lord One thousand, Eight hundred and Sixty-one, and of the Independence of the United States the Eighty-fifth.

ABRAHAM LINCOLN

By the President
WILLIAM H. SEWARD, Secretary of State.

Proclamation of Blockade

BY THE PRESIDENT OF THE UNITED STATES OF AMERICA:

A PROCLAMATION.

Whereas an insurrection against the Government of the United States has broken out in the States of South Carolina, Georgia, Alabama, Florida, Mississippi, Louisiana, and Texas, and the laws of the United States for the collection of the revenue cannot be effectually executed therein comformably to that provision of the Constitution which requires duties to be uniform throughout the United States:

And whereas a combination of persons engaged in such insurrection, have threatened to grant pretended letters of marque to authorize the bearers thereof to commit assaults on the lives, vessels, and property of good citizens of the country lawfully engaged in commerce on the high seas, and in waters of the United States: And whereas an Executive Proclamation has been already issued, requiring the persons engaged in these disorderly proceedings to desist therefrom, calling out a militia force for the purpose of repressing the same, and convening Congress in extraordinary session, to deliberate and determine thereon:

Now, therefore, I, Abraham Lincoln, President of the

United States, with a view to the same purposes before mentioned, and to the protection of the public peace, and the lives and property of quiet and orderly citizens pursuing their lawful occupations, until Congress shall have assembled and deliberated on the said unlawful proceedings, or until the same shall have ceased, have further deemed it advisable to set on foot a blockade of the ports within the States aforesaid, in pursuance of the laws of the United States, and of the law of Nations, in such case provided. For this purpose a competent force will be posted so as to prevent entrance and exit of vessels from the ports aforesaid. If, therefore, with a view to violate such blockade, a vessel shall approach, or shall attempt to leave either of the said ports, she will be duly warned by the Commander of one of the blockading vessels, who will endorse on her register the fact and date of such warning, and if the same vessel shall again attempt to enter or leave the blockaded port, she will be captured and sent to the nearest convenient port, for such proceedings against her and her cargo as prize, as may be deemed advisable.

And I hereby proclaim and declare that if any person, under the pretended authority of the said States, or under any other pretense, shall molest a vessel of the United States, or the persons or cargo on board of her, such person will be held amenable to the laws of the United States for the prevention and punishment of piracy.

In witness whereof, I have hereunto set my hand, and caused the seal of the United States to be affixed.

Done at the City of Washington, this nineteenth day of April, in the year of our Lord one thousand eight hundred and sixty-one, and of the Independence of the United States the eighty-fifth.

ABRAHAM LINCOLN

By the President:
    WILLIAM H. SEWARD, Secretary of State

Inscription in Album
of Mary Rebecca Darby Smith

White House, April 19, 1861.
Whoever in later-times shall see this, and look at the date, will readily excuse the writer for not having indulged in sentiment, or poetry. With all kind regards for Miss Smith.

To Thomas H. Hicks and George W. Brown

Gov. Hicks, & Mayor Brown   Washington, April 20. 1861
Gentlemen: Your letter by Messrs. Bond, Dobbin & Brune, is received. I tender you both my sincere thanks for your efforts to keep the peace in the trying situation in which you are placed. For the future, troops *must* be brought here, but I make no point of bringing them *through* Baltimore. Without any military knowledge myself, of course I must leave details to Gen. Scott. He hastily said, this morning, in presence of these gentlemen, "March them *around* Baltimore, and not through it." I sincerely hope the General, on fuller reflection, will consider this practical and proper, and that you will not object to it. By this, a collision of the people of Baltimore with the troops will be avoided, unless they go out of their way to seek it. I hope you will exert your influence to prevent this.

Now, and ever, I shall do all in my power for peace, consistently with the maintainance of government. Your Obt. Servt.

To Reverdy Johnson

Confidential.

Executive Mansion, April 24th 1861.
Hon. Reverdy Johnson
My dear Sir: Your note of this morning is just received. I forebore to answer yours of the 22d because of my aversion (which I thought you understood,) to getting on paper, and furnishing new grounds for misunderstanding.

I *do* say the sole purpose of bringing troops *here* is to defend this capital.

I *do* say I have no purpose to *invade* Virginia, with them or any other troops, as I understand the word *invasion*. But suppose Virginia sends her troops, or admits others through her borders, to assail this capital, am I not to repel them, even to the crossing of the Potomac if I can?

Suppose Virginia erects, or permits to be erected, batteries on the opposite shore, to bombard the city, are we to stand still and see it done? In a word, if Virginia strikes us, are we not to strike back, and as effectively as we can?

Again, are we not to hold Fort Monroe (for instance) if we can? I have no objection to declare a thousand times that I have no purpose to *invade* Virginia or any other State, but I do not mean to let them invade us without striking back. Yours truly

To Winfield Scott

Lieutenant General Scott   Washington, April 25— 1861.

My dear Sir: The Maryland Legislature assembles tomorrow at Anapolis; and, not improbably, will take action to arm the people of that State against the United States. The question has been submitted to, and considered by me, whether it would not be justifiable, upon the ground of necessary defence, for you, as commander in Chief of the United States Army, to arrest, or disperse the members of that body. I think it would *not* be justifiable; nor, efficient for the desired object.

First, they have a clearly legal right to assemble; and, we can not know in advance, that their action will not be lawful, and peaceful. And if we wait until they shall *have* acted, their arrest, or dispersion, will not lessen the effect of their action.

Secondly, we *can* not permanently prevent their action. If we arrest them, we can not long hold them as prisoners; and when liberated, they will immediately re-assemble, and take their action. And, precisely the same if we simply disperse them. They will immediately re-assemble in some other place.

I therefore conclude that it is only left to the commanding General to watch, and await their action, which, if it shall be to arm their people against the United States, he is to adopt the most prompt, and efficient means to counteract, even, if necessary, to the bombardment of their cities—and in the extremest necessity, the suspension of the writ of habeas corpus. Your Obedient Servant

To Winfield Scott

To the Commanding General of the Army
  of the United States:
You are engaged in repressing an insurrection against the laws of the United States. If at any point on or in the vicinity of the military line, which is now used between the City of Philadelphia and the City of Washington, via Perryville, Annapolis City, and Annapolis Junction, you find resistance which renders it necessary to suspend the writ of Habeas Corpus for the public safety, you, personally or through the officer in command at the point where the resistance occurs, are authorized to suspend that writ.
  April 27, 1861

To Gustavus V. Fox

Capt. G. V. Fox   Washington, D.C.
My dear Sir   May 1, 1861
I sincerely regret that the failure of the late attempt to provision Fort-Sumpter, should be the source of any annoyance to you. The practicability of your plan was not, in fact, brought to a test. By reason of a gale, well known in advance to be possible, and not improbable, the tugs, an essential part of the plan, never reached the ground; while, by an accident, for which you were in no wise responsible, and possibly I, to some extent was, you were deprived of a war vessel with her men, which you deemed of great importance to the enterprize.

I most cheerfully and truly declare that the failure of the undertaking has not lowered you a particle, while the qualities you developed in the effort, have greatly heightened you, in my estimation. For a daring and dangerous enterprize, of a similar character, you would, to-day, be the man, of all my acquaintances, whom I would select.

You and I both anticipated that the cause of the country would be advanced by making the attempt to provision Fort-Sumpter, even if it should fail; and it is no small consolation now to feel that our anticipation is justified by the result. Very truly your friend

To Isham G. Harris

To His Excellency the Governor   Executive Department
    of the State of Tennessee—   Washington, D.C.
        Nashville Tenn.   May 1861

Sir: Yours of the 29th. ultimo, calling my attention to the supposed seizure, near Cairo, Illinois, of the Steamboat C. E. Hillman, and claiming that the said boat and it's cargo are the property of the State of Tennessee and her citizens; and demanding to know whether the seizure was made by the authority of this Government, or is approved by it, is duly received.

In answer I have to say this Government has no official information of such seizure; but assuming that the seizure was made, and that the cargo consisted chiefly of munitions of War owned by the State of Tennessee, and passing into the control of it's Governor, this Government avows the seizure, for the following reasons.

A legal call was recently made upon the said Governor of Tennessee to furnish a quota of militia to suppress an insurrection against the United States, which call said Governor responded to by a refusal, couched in disrespectful and malicious language. This Government therefore infers that munitions of War passing into the hands of said Governor, are intended to be used against the United States; and the government will not indulge the weakness of allowing it, so long as it is in it's power to prevent. This Government will not, at present, question, but that the State of Tennessee, by a majority of it's citizens, is loyal to the Federal Union, and the government holds itself responsible in damages for all injuries it may do to any who may prove to be such.

May 1, 1861, or after

To Salmon P. Chase

Executive Mansion, May 8, 1861.

My dear Sir: I am told there is an office in your department called "The Superintending Architect of the Treasury Department, connected with the Bureau of Construction," which is now held by a man of the name of Young, and wanted by a gentleman of the name of Christopher Adams.

Ought Mr. Young to be removed, and if yea, ought Mr. Adams to be appointed? Mr. Adams is magnificently recommended; but the great point in his favor is that Thurlow Weed and Horace Greeley join in recommending him. I suppose the like never happened before, and never will again; so that it is now or never. What say you? Yours truly,

To Francis P. Blair, Jr.

Private

Hon. F. P. Blair   Washington D.C. May 18. 1861

My Dear Sir. We have a good deal of anxiety here about St. Louis. I understand an order has gone from the War Department to you, to be delivered or withheld in your discretion, relieving Gen. Harney from his command. I was not quite satisfied with the order when it was made, though on the whole I thought it best to make it; but since then I have become more doubtful of its propriety. I do not write now to countermand it; but to say I wish you would withhold it, unless in your judgement the necessity to the contrary is very urgent.

There are several reasons for this. We better have him a *friend* than an *enemy*. It will dissatisfy a good many who otherwise would be quiet. More than all, we first relieved him, then restored him, & now if we relieve him again, the public will ask, "why all this vacillation."

Still if, in your judgment, it is *indispensable* let it be so. Yours very truly

To Salmon P. Chase

Executive Mansion, May 18, 1861.

My dear Sir: The suggestions of your note accompanying the commission for Mr. Dennison as naval officer at New York have been considered in the same spirit of kindness in which I know they were offered. They present the very difficulty which has embarrassed me from the first in the case: that Mr. Dennison has not the position in the public eye which would lead to the expectation of his receiving so high an office. I believe I have told you fully what it was, and is, that pressed me to appoint him: the urgent solicitation of an old friend who has served me all my life, and who has never before received or asked anything in return. His (Mr. Dennison's) good character was vouched for from the start by many at New York, including Mr. Opdyke.

At length, when I was, as it were, in the very act of appointing him, Mr. —— made a general charge of dishonesty against him. I pressed him for particulars, and it turned out that Mr. Dennison in his business as a lawyer had got some printing done for his clients, becoming personally responsible for the work, and had not paid for it when dunned. While this, if true, is certainly not to be commended, I believe the like might, in some cases, be proven upon me. They are a class of debts which our clients ought to pay, and when we are personally dunned for them we sometimes hang fire. Besides, Mr. Dennison went far toward a satisfactory explanation of one case; and while Mr. —— intimated that there were other cases, he did not specify them.

I consider that the charge of dishonesty has failed; and it

now seems to me more difficult to change my purpose than if the charge had never been made. Yours as ever,

To Edwin D. Morgan

His Excellency   Washington, D.C.
Gov. E. D. Morgan   May 20. 1861

My dear Sir: Yours of the 19th. is received. Your letter to the Secretary of War I have not seen.

To not shirk just responsibility, I suppose I ought to admit that I had much to do with the matter of which you complain.

The committee came here some time last week, saying there were fourteen Regiments in N.Y. city, not within the 38 you were organizing; that *something must* be done with them, —that they could not safely keep them longer, nor safely disband them. I could not see—can not yet—how it could wrong you, or the Regiments you were raising, for these 14 to move forward at once, provided yours, too, should be received when ready. But aware of my own ignorance in military matters, I sent to Genl. Scott to get his opinion whether the thing could be safely done, both as to the question of confusion, and also whether the Govt. could advantageously keep and use the *whole*. His answer was that the *whole* should come—of the 14, 5 to come here, & 9 to Fortress Monroe. I thought the whole difficulty was solved, and directed an order to be made accordingly. I was even pleased with it; because I had been trying for two weeks to begin the collecting of a force at Fortress Monroe, and it now appeared as if this would begin.

Next day & after the committee had gone, I was brought to fear that a squabble was to arise between you and the committee, by which neither your Regiments nor theirs, would move in any reasonable time; to avoid which, I wrote one of the committee—Mr. Russell—to send them at once.

I am very loth to do any wrong; but I do not see yet wherein this was a wrong.

I certainly did not know that any Regiments especially

under your control were to be sent forward by the committee; but I do not perceive the *substantial* wrong, even in such a case. That it may be a *technical* wrong, I can readily understand—but we are in no condition to waste time on technicalities.

The enthusiastic uprising of the people in our cause, is our great reliance; and we can not safely give it any check, even though it overflows, and runs in channels not laid down in any chart.

In ordering the 14 Regiments forward, no intimation was intended, that you were failing in activity, or in any duty. On the contrary, I acknowledge you have done, & are doing nobly; and for which I tender you my sincere thanks. Yours very truly

To Ephraim D. and Phoebe Ellsworth

To the Father and Mother of Col.   Washington D.C.
     Elmer E. Ellsworth: May 25. 1861
My dear Sir and Madam,   In the untimely loss of your noble son, our affliction here, is scarcely less than your own. So much of promised usefulness to one's country, and of bright hopes for one's self and friends, have rarely been so suddenly dashed, as in his fall. In size, in years, and in youthful appearance, a boy only, his power to command men, was surpassingly great. This power, combined with a fine intellect, an indomitable energy, and a taste altogether military, constituted in him, as seemed to me, the best natural talent, in that department, I ever knew. And yet he was singularly modest and deferential in social intercourse. My acquaintance with him began less than two years ago; yet through the latter half of the intervening period, it was as intimate as the disparity of our ages, and my engrossing engagements, would permit. To me, he appeared to have no indulgences or pastimes; and I never heard him utter a profane, or an intemperate word. What was conclusive of his good heart, he never forgot his parents. The honors he labored for so laudably, and, in the sad end, so gallantly gave his life, he meant for them, no less than for himself.

In the hope that it may be no intrusion upon the sacredness of your sorrow, I have ventured to address you this tribute to the memory of my young friend, and your brave and early fallen child.

May God give you that consolation which is beyond all earthly power. Sincerely your friend in a common affliction—

To Winfield Scott

Private

Lieut. Genl. Scott   Executive Mansion   June 5. 1861

My dear Sir   Doubtless you begin to understand how disagreeable it is to me to do a thing arbitrarily, when it is unsatisfactory to others associated with me.

I very much wish to appoint Col. Meigs Quarter-Master General, and yet Gen. Cameron does not quite consent. I have come to know Col. Meigs quite well for a short acquaintance, and, so far as I am capable of judging I do not know one who combines the qualities of masculine intellect, learning and experience of the right sort, and physical power of labor and endurance so well as he.

I know he has great confidence in you, always sustaining so far as I have observed, your opinions, against any differing ones.

You will lay me under one more obligation, if you can and will use your influence to remove Gen. Cameron's objection. I scarcely need tell you I have nothing personal in this, having never seen or heard of Col. Meigs, until about the end of last March. Your obt. Servt,

To William P. Dole

Hon. W. P. Dole   Executive Mansion
Comr. of Ind. Affrs.   June, 1861

My dear Sir   Some time ago I directed you to designate a suitable person to be Superintendent of Indian Affairs in Washington Territory, saying I would appoint the person you

would so designate. You designated Anson Dart; and I now
have the following reasons for not appointing him all coming
to my knowledge since I gave you the direction mentioned.

1st.   A member of the present Cabinet tells me that during
Genl. Taylor's administration Dart distinctly tendered money
to him for his influence to get an office from Gen. Taylor.

2nd.   A member of the present H.R. from Wisconsin
writes me over his own name that Dart is an immoral and
dishonest man; and that if nominated, he will go before the
Senate and procure his rejection if possible.

3rd.   One of the Senators from Oregon tells me that
Dart's character is very bad in that county; that he is universally understood out there to have left his family at home, and
kept a prostitute while there; and that, if nominated, he will,
in the Senate, procure his rejection if possible.

4th.   The other Senator from Oregon tells me Dart's character is very odious and bad in that county; and that Dart, last
winter, distinctly proposed to him that if he would procure
his appointment to the Oregon Indian Superintendency, he
would give him a thousand dollars the day the appointment
should be made, and five hundred a year, as long as he should
hold the office.

I presume you knew nothing of these things; and that neither you or I could knowingly be for such a man. Yours truly

June 11, 1861, or after

To Ninian W. Edwards

Hon. N. W. Edwards   Washington D.C.   June 19, 1861

My dear Sir: It pains me to hear you speak of being ruined
in your pecuniary affairs. I still hope you are injured only, and
not ruined. When you wrote me some time ago in reference
to looking up something in the Departments here, I thought
I would inquire into the thing and write you, but the extraordinary pressure upon me diverted me from it, and soon it
passed out of my mind. The thing you proposed, it seemed to
me, I ought to understand myself before it was set on foot by
my direction or permission; and I really had no *time* to make

myself acquainted with it. Nor have I yet. And yet I am un-willing, of course, that you should be deprived of a chance to make something, if it can be done without injustice to the Government, or to any individual. If you choose to come here and point out to me how this can be done, I shall not only not object, but shall be gratified to be able to oblige you. Your friend as ever

Message to Congress in Special Session

Fellow-citizens of the Senate and House of Representatives:

Having been convened on an extraordinary occasion, as authorized by the Constitution, your attention is not called to any ordinary subject of legislation.

At the beginning of the present Presidential term, four months ago, the functions of the Federal Government were found to be generally suspended within the several States of South Carolina, Georgia, Alabama, Mississippi, Louisiana, and Florida, excepting only those of the Post Office Department.

Within these States, all the Forts, Arsenals, Dock-yards, Custom-houses, and the like, including the movable and stationary property in, and about them, had been seized, and were held in open hostility to this Government, excepting only Forts Pickens, Taylor, and Jefferson, on, and near the Florida coast, and Fort Sumter, in Charleston harbor, South Carolina. The Forts thus seized had been put in improved condition; new ones had been built; and armed forces had been organized, and were organizing, all avowedly with the same hostile purpose.

The Forts remaining in the possession of the Federal government, in, and near, these States, were either besieged or menaced by warlike preparations; and especially Fort Sumter was nearly surrounded by well-protected hostile batteries, with guns equal in quality to the best of its own, and outnumbering the latter as perhaps ten to one. A disproportionate share, of the Federal muskets and rifles, had somehow found their way into these States, and had been seized, to be used against the government. Accumulations of the public revenue, lying within them, had been seized for the same object. The Navy was scattered in distant seas; leaving but a very small part of it within the immediate reach of the government. Officers of the Federal Army and Navy, had resigned in great numbers; and, of those resigning, a large proportion had taken up arms against the government. Simultaneously, and in connection, with all this, the purpose to sever the Federal Union, was openly avowed. In accordance with this purpose, an ordinance had been adopted in each of these States, declaring the States, respectively, to be separated from the National Union. A formula for instituting a combined government of these states had been promulgated; and this illegal organization, in the character of confederate States was already invoking recognition, aid, and intervention, from Foreign Powers.

Finding this condition of things, and believing it to be an imperative duty upon the incoming Executive, to prevent, if possible, the consummation of such attempt to destroy the Federal Union, a choice of means to that end became indispensable. This choice was made; and was declared in the Inaugural address. The policy chosen looked to the exhaustion of all peaceful measures, before a resort to any stronger ones. It sought only to hold the public places and property, not already wrested from the Government, and to collect the revenue; relying for the rest, on time, discussion, and the ballot-box. It promised a continuance of the mails, at government expense, to the very people who were resisting the government; and it gave repeated pledges against any disturbance to any of the people, or any of their rights. Of all that which a president might constitutionally, and justifiably, do in such a case, everything was foreborne, without which, it was believed possible to keep the government on foot.

On the 5th of March, (the present incumbent's first full day in office) a letter of Major Anderson, commanding at Fort Sumter, written on the 28th of February, and received at the War Department on the 4th of March, was, by that Department, placed in his hands. This letter expressed the professional opinion of the writer, that re-inforcements could not be thrown into that Fort within the time for his relief, rendered necessary by the limited supply of provisions, and with a view of holding possession of the same, with a force of less than twenty thousand good, and well-disciplined men. This opinion was concurred in by all the officers of his command; and their *memoranda* on the subject, were made enclosures of Major Anderson's letter. The whole was immediately laid before Lieutenant General Scott, who at once concurred with Major Anderson in opinion. On reflection, however, he took full time, consulting with other officers, both of the Army and the Navy; and, at the end of four days, came reluctantly, but decidedly, to the same conclusion as before. He also stated at the same time that no such sufficient force was then at the control of the Government, or could be raised, and brought to the ground, within the time when the provisions in the Fort would be exhausted. In a purely military point of view, this reduced the duty of the administration, in the case, to the mere matter of getting the garrison safely out of the Fort.

It was believed, however, that to so abandon that position, under the circumstances, would be utterly ruinous; that the *necessity* under which it was to be done, would not be fully understood—that, by many, it would be construed as a part of a *voluntary* policy—that, at home, it would discourage the friends of the Union, embolden its adversaries, and go far to insure to the latter, a recognition abroad—that, in fact, it would be our national destruction consummated. This could not be allowed. Starvation was not yet upon the garrison; and ere it would be reached, *Fort Pickens* might be reinforced. This last, would be a clear indication of *policy*, and would better enable the country to accept the evacuation of Fort Sumter, as a military *necessity*. An order was at once directed to be sent for the landing of the troops from the Steamship Brooklyn, into Fort Pickens. This order could not go by land, but must take the longer, and slower route by sea. The first return news from the order was received just one week before the fall of Fort Sumter. The news itself was, that the officer commanding the Sabine, to which vessel the troops had been transferred from the Brooklyn, acting upon some *quasi* armistice of the late administration, (and of the existence of which, the present administration, up to the time the order was despatched, had only too vague and uncertain rumors, to fix attention) had refused to land the troops. To now re-inforce Fort Pickens, before a crisis would be reached at Fort Sumter was impossible—rendered so by the near exhaustion of provisions in the latter-named Fort. In precaution against such a conjuncture, the government had, a few days before, commenced preparing an expedition, as well adapted as might be, to relieve Fort Sumter, which expedition was intended to be ultimately used, or not, according to circumstances. The strongest anticipated case, for using it, was now presented; and it was resolved to send it forward. As had been intended, in this contingency, it was also resolved to notify the Governor of South Carolina, that he might expect an attempt would be made to provision the Fort; and that, if the attempt should not be resisted, there would be no effort to throw in men, arms, or ammunition, without further notice, or in case of an attack upon the Fort. This notice was accordingly given; whereupon the Fort was attacked, and bombarded to its fall, without even awaiting the arrival of the provisioning expedition.

It is thus seen that the assault upon, and reduction of, Fort Sumter, was, in no sense, a matter of self defence on the part of the assailants. They well knew that the garrison in the Fort could, by no possibility, commit aggression upon them. They knew—they were expressly notified—that the giving of bread to the few brave and hungry men of the garrison, was all which would on that occasion be attempted, unless themselves, by resisting so much, should provoke more. They knew that this Government desired to keep the garrison in the Fort, not to assail them, but merely to maintain visible possession, and thus to preserve the Union from actual, and immediate dissolution—trusting, as herein-before stated, to time, discussion, and the ballot-box, for final adjustment; and they assailed, and reduced the Fort, for precisely the reverse object—to drive out the visible authority of the Federal Union, and thus force it to immediate dissolution.

That this was their object, the Executive well understood; and having said to them in the inaugural address, "You can have no conflict without being yourselves the aggressors," he took pains, not only to keep this declaration good, but also to keep the case so free from the power of ingenious sophistry, as that the world should not be able to misunderstand it. By the affair at Fort Sumter, with its surrounding circumstances, that point was reached. Then, and thereby, the assailants of the Government, began the conflict of arms, without a gun in sight, or in expectancy, to return their fire, save only the few in the Fort, sent to that harbor, years before, for their own protection, and still ready to give that protection, in whatever was lawful. In this act, discarding all else, they have forced upon the country, the distinct issue: "Immediate dissolution, or blood."

And this issue embraces more than the fate of these United States. It presents to the whole family of man, the question, whether a constitutional republic, or a democracy—a government of the people, by the same people—can, or cannot, maintain its territorial integrity, against its own domestic foes. It presents the question, whether discontented individuals, too few in numbers to control administration, according to organic law, in any case, can always, upon the pretences made in this case, or on any other pretences, or arbitrarily, without any pretence, break up their Government, and thus practically put an end to free government upon the earth. It forces us to ask: "Is there, in all republics, this inherent, and fatal weakness?" "Must a government, of necessity, be too *strong* for the liberties of its own people, or too *weak* to maintain its own existence?"

So viewing the issue, no choice was left but to call out the war power of the Government; and so to resist force, employed for its destruction, by force, for its preservation.

The call was made; and the response of the country was most gratifying; surpassing, in unanimity and spirit, the most sanguine expectation. Yet none of the States commonly called Slave-states, except Delaware, gave a Regiment through regular State organization. A few regiments have been organized within some others of those states, by individual enterprise, and received into the government service. Of course the seceded States, so called, (and to which Texas had been joined about the time of the inauguration,) gave no troops to the cause of the Union. The border States, so called, were not uniform in their actions; some of them being almost *for* the Union, while in others—as Virginia, North Carolina, Tennessee, and Arkansas—the Union sentiment was nearly repressed, and silenced. The course taken in Virginia was the most remarkable—perhaps the most important. A convention, elected by the people of that State, to consider this very question of disrupting the Federal Union, was in session at the capital of Virginia when Fort Sumter fell. To this body the people had chosen a large majority of *professed* Union men. Almost immediately after the fall of Sumter, many members of that majority went over to the original disunion minority, and, with them, adopted an ordinance for withdrawing the State from the Union. Whether this change was wrought by their great approval of the assault upon Sumter, or their great resentment at the government's resistance to that assault, is not definitely known. Although they submitted the ordinance, for ratification, to a vote of the people, to be taken on a day then somewhat more than a month distant, the convention, and the Legislature, (which was also in session at the same time and place) with leading men of the State, not members of either, immediately commenced acting, as if the State were already out of the Union. They pushed military preparations vigorously forward all over the state. They seized the United States Armory at Harper's Ferry, and the Navy-yard at Gosport, near Norfolk. They received—perhaps invited—into their state, large bodies of troops, with their warlike appointments, from the so-called seceded States. They formally entered into a treaty of temporary alliance, and co-operation with the so-called "Confederate States," and sent members to their Congress at Montgomery. And, finally, they permitted the insurrectionary government to be transferred to their capital at Richmond.

The people of Virginia have thus allowed this giant insurrection to make its nest within her borders; and this government has no choice left but to deal with it, *where* it finds it. And it has the less regret, as the loyal citizens have, in due form, claimed its protection. Those loyal citizens, this government is bound to recognize, and protect, as being Virginia.

In the border States, so called—in fact, the middle states—there are those who favor a policy which they call "armed neutrality"—that is, an arming of those states to prevent the Union forces passing one way, or the disunion, the other, over their soil. This would be disunion completed. Figuratively speaking, it would be the building of an impassable wall along the line of separation. And yet, not quite an impassable one; for, under the guise of neutrality, it would tie the hands of the Union men, and freely pass supplies from among them, to the insurrectionists, which it could not do as an open enemy. At a stroke, it would take all the trouble off the hands of secession, except only what proceeds from the external blockade. It would do for the disunionists that which, of all things, they most desire—feed them well, and give them disunion without a struggle of their own. It recognizes no fidelity to the Constitution, no obligation to maintain the Union; and while very many who have favored it are, doubtless, loyal citizens, it is, nevertheless, treason in effect.

Recurring to the action of the government, it may be stated that, at first, a call was made for seventy-five thousand militia; and rapidly following this, a proclamation was issued for closing the ports of the insurrectionary districts by proceedings in the nature of Blockade. So far all was believed to be strictly legal. At this point the insurrectionists announced their purpose to enter upon the practice of privateering.

Other calls were made for volunteers, to serve three years, unless sooner discharged; and also for large additions to the regular Army and Navy. These measures, whether strictly legal or not, were ventured upon, under what appeared to be a popular demand, and a public necessity; trusting, then as now, that Congress would readily ratify them. It is believed that nothing has been done beyond the constitutional competency of Congress.

Soon after the first call for militia, it was considered a duty to authorize the Commanding General, in proper cases, according to his discretion, to suspend the privilege of the writ of habeas corpus; or, in other words, to arrest, and detain, without resort to the ordinary processes and forms of law, such individuals as he might deem dangerous to the public safety. This authority has purposely been exercised but very sparingly. Nevertheless, the legality and propriety of what has been done under it, are questioned; and the attention of the country has been called to the proposition that one who is sworn to "take care that the laws be faithfully executed," should not himself violate them. Of course some consideration was given to the questions of power, and propriety, before this matter was acted upon. The whole of the laws which were required to be faithfully executed, were being resisted, and failing of execution, in nearly one-third of the States. Must they be allowed to finally fail of execution, even had it been perfectly clear, that by the use of the means necessary to their execution, some single law, made in such extreme tenderness of the citizen's liberty, that practically, it relieves more of the guilty, than of the innocent, should, to a very limited extent, be violated? To state the question more directly, are all the laws, *but one*, to go unexecuted, and the government itself go to pieces, lest that one be violated? Even in such a case, would not the official oath be broken, if the government should be overthrown, when it was believed that disregarding the single law, would tend to preserve it? But it was not believed that this question was presented. It was not believed that any law was violated. The provision of the Constitution that "The privilege of the writ of habeas corpus, shall not be suspended unless when, in cases of rebellion or invasion, the public safety may require it," is equivalent to a provision—is a provision—that such privilege may be suspended when, in cases of rebellion, or invasion, the public safety *does* require it. It was decided that we have a case of rebellion, and that the public safety does require the qualified suspension of the privilege of the writ which was authorized to be made. Now it is insisted that Congress, and not the Executive, is vested with this power. But the Constitution itself, is silent as to which, or who, is to exercise the power; and as the provision was plainly made for a dangerous emergency, it cannot be believed the framers of the instrument intended, that in every case, the danger should run its course, until Congress could be called together; the very assembling of which might be prevented, as was intended in this case, by the rebellion.

No more extended argument is now offered; as an opinion, at some length, will probably be presented by the Attorney General. Whether there shall be any legislation upon the subject, and if any, what, is submitted entirely to the better judgment of Congress.

The forbearance of this government had been so extraordinary, and so long continued, as to lead some foreign nations to shape their action as if they supposed the early destruction of our national Union was probable. While this, on discovery, gave the Executive some concern, he is now happy to say that the sovereignty, and rights of the United States, are now everywhere practically respected by foreign powers; and a general sympathy with the country is manifested throughout the world.

The reports of the Secretaries of the Treasury, War, and the Navy, will give the information in detail deemed necessary, and convenient for your deliberation, and action; while the Executive, and all the Departments, will stand ready to supply omissions, or to communicate new facts, considered important for you to know.

It is now recommended that you give the legal means for making this contest a short, and a decisive one; that you place at the control of the government, for the work, at least four hundred thousand men, and four hundred millions of dollars. That number of men is about one tenth of those of proper ages within the regions where, apparently, *all* are willing to engage; and the sum is less than a twentythird part of the money value owned by the men who seem ready to devote the whole. A debt of six hundred millions of dollars *now*, is a less sum per head, than was the debt of our revolution, when we came out of that struggle; and the money value in the country now, bears even a greater proportion to what it was *then*, than does the population. Surely each man has as strong a motive *now*, to *preserve* our liberties, as each had *then*, to *establish* them.

A right result, at this time, will be worth more to the world, than ten times the men, and ten times the money. The evidence reaching us from the country, leaves no doubt, that the material for the work is abundant; and that it needs only the hand of legislation to give it legal sanction, and the hand of the Executive to give it practical shape and efficiency. One of the greatest perplexities of the government, is to avoid receiving troops faster than it can provide for them. In a word, the people will save their government, if the government itself, will do its part, only indifferently well.

It might seem, at first thought, to be of little difference whether the present movement at the South be called "secession" or "rebellion." The movers, however, well understand the difference. At the beginning, they knew they could never raise their treason to any respectable magnitude, by any name which implies *violation* of law. They knew their people possessed as much of moral sense, as much of devotion to law and order, and as much pride in, and reverence for, the history, and government, of their common country, as any other civilized, and patriotic people. They knew they could make no advancement directly in the teeth of these strong and noble sentiments. Accordingly they commenced by an insidious debauching of the public mind. They invented an ingenious sophism, which, if conceded, was followed by perfectly logical steps, through all the incidents, to the complete destruction of the Union. The sophism itself is, that any state of the Union may, *consistently* with the national Constitution, and therefore *lawfully*, and *peacefully*, withdraw from the Union, without the consent of the Union, or of any other state. The little disguise that the supposed right is to be exercised only for just cause, themselves to be the sole judge of its justice, is too thin to merit any notice.

With rebellion thus sugar-coated, they have been drugging the public mind of their section for more than thirty years; and, until at length, they have brought many good men to a willingness to take up arms against the government the day *after* some assemblage of men have enacted the farcical pretence of taking their State out of the Union, who could have been brought to no such thing the day *before*.

This sophism derives much—perhaps the whole—of its currency, from the assumption, that there is some omnipotent, and sacred supremacy, pertaining to a *State*—to each State of our Federal Union. Our States have neither more, nor less power, than that reserved to them, in the Union, by the Constitution—no one of them ever having been a State *out* of the Union. The original ones passed into the Union even *before* they cast off their British colonial dependence; and the new ones each came into the Union directly from a condition of dependence, excepting Texas. And even Texas, in its temporary independence, was never designated a State. The new ones only took the designation of States, on coming into the Union, while that name was first adopted for the old ones, in, and by, the Declaration of Independence. Therein the "United Colonies" were declared to be "Free and Independent States"; but, even then, the object plainly was not to declare their independence of *one another*, or of the *Union*; but directly the contrary, as their mutual pledge, and their

mutual action, before, at the time, and afterwards, abundantly
show. The express plighting of faith, by each and all of the
original thirteen, in the Articles of Confederation, two years
later, that the Union shall be perpetual, is most conclusive.
Having never been States, either in substance, or in name,
outside of the Union, whence this magical omnipotence of
"State rights," asserting a claim of power to lawfully destroy
the Union itself? Much is said about the "sovereignty" of the
States; but the word, even, is not in the national Constitution; nor, as is believed, in any of the State constitutions.
What is a "sovereignty," in the political sense of the term?
Would it be far wrong to define it "A political community,
without a political superior"? Tested by this, no one of our
States, except Texas, ever was a sovereignty. And even Texas
gave up the character on coming into the Union; by which
act, she acknowledged the Constitution of the United States,
and the laws and treaties of the United States made in pursuance of the Constitution, to be, for her, the supreme law of
the land. The States have their *status* IN the Union, and they
have no other *legal status*. If they break from this, they can
only do so against law, and by revolution. The Union, and
not themselves separately, procured their independence, and
their liberty. By conquest, or purchase, the Union gave each
of them, whatever of independence, and liberty, it has. The
Union is older than any of the States; and, in fact, it created
them as States. Originally, some dependent colonies made the
Union; and, in turn, the Union threw off their old dependence, for them, and made them States, such as they are. Not
one of them ever had a State constitution, independent of the
Union. Of course, it is not forgotten that all the new States
framed their constitutions, before they entered the Union;
nevertheless, dependent upon, and preparatory to, coming
into the Union.

Unquestionably the States have the powers, and rights, reserved to them in, and by the National Constitution; but
among these, surely, are not included all conceivable powers,
however mischievous, or destructive; but, at most, such only,
as were known in the world, at the time, as governmental
powers; and certainly, a power to destroy the government itself, had never been known as a governmental—as a merely

administrative power. This relative matter of National power, and State rights, as a principle, is no other than the principle of *generality*, and *locality*. Whatever concerns the whole, should be confided to the whole—to the general government; while, whatever concerns *only* the State, should be left exclusively, to the State. This is all there is of original principle about it. Whether the National Constitution, in defining boundaries between the two, has applied the principle with exact accuracy, is not to be questioned. We are all bound by that defining, without question.

What is now combatted, is the position that secession is *consistent* with the Constitution—is *lawful*, and *peaceful*. It is not contended that there is any express law for it; and nothing should ever be implied as law, which leads to unjust, or absurd consequences. The nation purchased, with money, the countries out of which several of these States were formed. Is it just that they shall go off without leave, and without refunding? The nation paid very large sums, (in the aggregate, I believe, nearly a hundred millions) to relieve Florida of the aboriginal tribes. Is it just that she shall now be off without consent, or without making any return? The nation is now in debt for money applied to the benefit of these so-called seceding States, in common with the rest. Is it just, either that creditors shall go unpaid, or the remaining States pay the whole? A part of the present national debt was contracted to pay the old debts of Texas. Is it just that she shall leave, and pay no part of this herself?

Again, if one State may secede, so may another; and when all shall have seceded, none is left to pay the debts. Is this quite just to creditors? Did we notify them of this sage view of ours, when we borrowed their money? If we now recognize this doctrine, by allowing the seceders to go in peace, it is difficult to see what we can do, if others choose to go, or to extort terms upon which they will promise to remain.

The seceders insist that our Constitution admits of secession. They have assumed to make a National Constitution of their own, in which, of necessity, they have either *discarded*, or *retained*, the right of secession, as they insist, it exists in ours. If they have discarded it, they thereby admit that, on principle, it ought not to be in ours. If they have retained it,

by their own construction of ours they show that to be consistent they must secede from one another, whenever they
shall find it the easiest way of settling their debts, or effecting
any other selfish, or unjust object. The principle itself is one
of disintegration, and upon which no government can possibly endure.

If all the States, save one, should assert the power to *drive*
that one out of the Union, it is presumed the whole class of
seceder politicians would at once deny the power, and denounce the act as the greatest outrage upon State rights. But
suppose that precisely the same act, instead of being called
"driving the one out," should be called "the seceding of the
others from that one," it would be exactly what the seceders
claim to do; unless, indeed, they make the point, that the one,
because it is a minority, may rightfully do, what the others,
because they are a majority, may not rightfully do. These politicians are subtle, and profound, on the rights of minorities.
They are not partial to that power which made the Constitution, and speaks from the preamble, calling itself "We, the
People."

It may well be questioned whether there is, to-day, a majority of the legally qualified voters of any State, except perhaps South Carolina, in favor of disunion. There is much
reason to believe that the Union men are the majority in
many, if not in every other one, of the so-called seceded
States. The contrary has not been demonstrated in any one
of them. It is ventured to affirm this, even of Virginia and
Tennessee; for the result of an election, held in military
camps, where the bayonets are all on one side of the question voted upon, can scarcely be considered as demonstrat-
ing popular sentiment. At such an election, all that large
class who are, at once, *for* the Union, and *against* coercion,
would be coerced to vote against the Union.

It may be affirmed, without extravagance, that the free
institutions we enjoy, have developed the powers, and
improved the condition, of our whole people, beyond any
example in the world. Of this we now have a striking, and an
impressive illustration. So large an army as the government
has now on foot, was never before known, without a soldier
in it, but who had taken his place there, of his own free

choice. But more than this: there are many single Regiments whose members, one and another, possess full practical knowledge of all the arts, sciences, professions, and whatever else, whether useful or elegant, is known in the world; and there is scarcely one, from which there could not be selected, a President, a Cabinet, a Congress, and perhaps a Court, abundantly competent to administer the government itself. Nor do I say this is not true, also, in the army of our late friends, now adversaries, in this contest; but if it is, so much better the reason why the government, which has conferred such benefits on both them and us, should not be broken up. Whoever, in any section, proposes to abandon such a government, would do well to consider, in deference to what principle it is, that he does it—what better he is likely to get in its stead—whether the substitute will give, or be intended to give, so much of good to the people. There are some foreshadowings on this subject. Our adversaries have adopted some Declarations of Independence; in which, unlike the good old one, penned by Jefferson, they omit the words "all men are created equal." Why? They have adopted a temporary national constitution, in the preamble of which, unlike our good old one, signed by Washington, they omit "We, the People," and substitute "We, the deputies of the sovereign and independent States." Why? Why this deliberate pressing out of view, the rights of men, and the authority of the people?

This is essentially a People's contest. On the side of the Union, it is a struggle for maintaining in the world, that form, and substance of government, whose leading object is, to elevate the condition of men—to lift artificial weights from all shoulders—to clear the paths of laudable pursuit for all—to afford all, an unfettered start, and a fair chance, in the race of life. Yielding to partial, and temporary departures, from necessity, this is the leading object of the government for whose existence we contend.

I am most happy to believe that the plain people understand, and appreciate this. It is worthy of note, that while in this, the government's hour of trial, large numbers of those in the Army and Navy, who have been favored with the offices, have resigned, and proved false to the hand which had pampered them, not one common soldier, or common sailor is known to have deserted his flag.

Great honor is due to those officers who remain true, despite the example of their treacherous associates; but the greatest honor, and most important fact of all, is the unanimous firmness of the common soldiers, and common sailors. To the last man, so far as known, they have successfully resisted the traitorous efforts of those, whose commands, but an hour before, they obeyed as absolute law. This is the patriotic instinct of the plain people. They understand, without an argument, that destroying the government, which was made by Washington, means no good to them.

Our popular government has often been called an experiment. Two points in it, our people have already settled—the successful *establishing*, and the successful *administering* of it. One still remains—its successful *maintenance* against a formidable internal attempt to overthrow it. It is now for them to demonstrate to the world, that those who can fairly carry an election, can also suppress a rebellion—that ballots are the rightful, and peaceful, successors of bullets; and that when ballots have fairly, and constitutionally, decided, there can be no successful appeal, back to bullets; that there can be no successful appeal, except to ballots themselves, at succeeding elections. Such will be a great lesson of peace; teaching men that what they cannot take by an election, neither can they take it by a war—teaching all, the folly of being the beginners of a war.

Lest there be some uneasiness in the minds of candid men, as to what is to be the course of the government, towards the Southern States, *after* the rebellion shall have been suppressed, the Executive deems it proper to say, it will be his purpose then, as ever, to be guided by the Constitution, and the laws; and that he probably will have no different understanding of the powers, and duties of the Federal government, relatively to the rights of the States, and the people, under the Constitution, than that expressed in the inaugural address.

He desires to preserve the government, that it may be administered for all, as it was administered by the men who made it. Loyal citizens everywhere, have the right to claim this of their government; and the government has no right to withhold, or neglect it. It is not perceived that, in giving it, there is any coercion, any conquest, or any subjugation, in any just sense of those terms.

The Constitution provides, and all the States have accepted the provision, that "The United States shall guarantee to every State in this Union a republican form of government." But, if a State may lawfully go out of the Union, having done so, it may also discard the republican form of government; so that to prevent its going out, is an indispensable *means*, to the *end*, of maintaining the guaranty mentioned; and when an end is lawful and obligatory, the indispensable means to it, are also lawful, and obligatory.

It was with the deepest regret that the Executive found the duty of employing the war-power, in defence of the government, forced upon him. He could but perform this duty, or surrender the existence of the government. No compromise, by public servants, could, in this case, be a cure; not that compromises are not often proper, but that no popular government can long survive a marked precedent, that those who carry an election, can only save the government from immediate destruction, by giving up the main point, upon which the people gave the election. The people themselves, and not their servants, can safely reverse their own deliberate decisions. As a private citizen, the Executive could not have consented that these institutions shall perish; much less could he, in betrayal of so vast, and so sacred a trust, as these free people had confided to him. He felt that he had no moral right to shrink; nor even to count the chances of his own life, in what might follow. In full view of his great responsibility, he has, so far, done what he has deemed his duty. You will now, according to your own judgment, perform yours. He sincerely hopes that your views, and your action, may so accord with his, as to assure all faithful citizens, who have been disturbed in their rights, of a certain, and speedy restoration to them, under the Constitution, and the laws.

And having thus chosen our course, without guile, and with pure purpose, let us renew our trust in God, and go forward without fear, and with manly hearts.

July 4, 1861.

To Simon B. Buckner

It is my duty, as I conceive, to suppress an insurrection existing within the United States. I wish to do this with the least possible disturbance, or annoyance to well disposed people anywhere. So far I have not sent an armed force into Kentucky; nor have I any present purpose to do so. I sincerely desire that no necessity for it may be presented; but I mean to say nothing which shall hereafter embarrass me in the performance of what may seem to be my duty.

(Copy of this delivered to Gen. Buckner this 10th. day of July 1861.)

Memoranda on Military Policy

July 23. 1861.

1   Let the plan for making the Blockade effective be pushed forward with all possible despatch.

2   Let the volunteer forces at Fort-Monroe & vicinity— under Genl. Butler—be constantly drilled, disciplined, and instructed without more for the present.

3.   Let Baltimore be held, as now, with a gentle, but firm, and certain hand.

4   Let the force now under Patterson, or Banks, be strengthened, and made secure in it's possition.

5.   Let the forces in Western Virginia act, till further orders, according to instructions, or orders from Gen. Mc-Clellan.

6.   Gen. Fremont push forward his organization, and opperations in the West as rapidly as possible, giving rather special attention to Missouri.

7   Let the forces late before Manassas, except the three months men, be reorganized as rapidly as possible, in their camps here and about Arlington

8.   Let the three months forces, who decline to enter the longer service, be discharged as rapidly as circumstances will permit.

9   Let the new volunteer forces be brought forward as fast

as possible; and especially into the camps on the two sides of the river here.

July 27, 1861

When the foregoing shall have been substantially attended to—

1. Let Manassas junction, (or some point on one or other of the railroads near it;); and Strasburg, be seized, and permanently held, with an open line from Washington to Manassas; and an open line from Harper's Ferry to Strasburg—the military men to find the way of doing these.

2. This done, a joint movement from Cairo on Memphis; and from Cincinnati on East Tennessee.

Proclamation of a National Fast Day

BY THE PRESIDENT OF THE UNITED STATES OF AMERICA:
A PROCLAMATION.

Whereas a joint Committee of both Houses of Congress has waited on the President of the United States, and requested him to "recommend a day of public humiliation, prayer and fasting, to be observed by the people of the United States with religious solemnities, and the offering of fervent supplications to Almighty God for the safety and welfare of these States, His blessings on their arms, and a speedy restoration of peace:"—

And whereas it is fit and becoming in all people, at all times, to acknowledge and revere the Supreme Government of God; to bow in humble submission to his chastisements; to confess and deplore their sins and transgressions in the full conviction that the fear of the Lord is the beginning of wisdom; and to pray, with all fervency and contrition, for the pardon of their past offences, and for a blessing upon their present and prospective action:

And whereas, when our own beloved Country, once, by the blessing of God, united, prosperous and happy, is now afflicted with faction and civil war, it is peculiarly fit for us to recognize the hand of God in this terrible visitation, and in sorrowful remembrance of our own faults and crimes as a nation and as individuals, to humble ourselves before Him, and to pray for His mercy,—to pray that we may be spared further punishment, though most justly deserved; that our arms may be blessed and made effectual for the re-establishment of law, order and peace, throughout the wide extent of our country; and that the inestimable boon of civil and religious liberty, earned under His guidance and blessing, by the labors and sufferings of our fathers, may be restored in all its original excellence:—

Therefore, I, Abraham Lincoln, President of the United States, do appoint the last Thursday in September next, as a day of humiliation, prayer and fasting for all the people of the nation. And I do earnestly recommend to all the People, and especially to all ministers and teachers of religion of all denominations, and to all heads of families, to observe and keep that day according to their several creeds and modes of worship, in all humility and with all religious solemnity, to the end that the united prayer of the nation may ascend to the Throne of Grace and bring down plentiful blessings upon our Country.

In testimony whereof, I have hereunto set my hand, and caused the Seal of the United States to be affixed, this 12th, day of August A.D. 1861, and of the Independence of the United States of America the 86th.

By the President: ABRAHAM LINCOLN.
 WILLIAM H. SEWARD, Secretary of State.

To Beriah Magoffin

To His Excellency   Washington, D.C.
B. Magoffin   August 24. 1861
Governor of the State of Kentucky.

Sir: Your letter of the 19th. Inst. in which you *"urge the removal from the limits of Kentucky of the military force now organized, and in camp within said State"* is received.

I may not possess full and precisely accurate knowledge upon this subject; but I believe it is true that there is a military force in camp within Kentucky, acting by authority of the United States, which force is not very large, and is not now being augmented.

I also believe that some arms have been furnished to this force by the United States.

I also believe this force consists exclusively of Kentuckians, having their camp in the immediate vicinity of their own homes, and not assailing, or menacing, any of the good people of Kentucky.

In all I have done in the premises, I have acted upon the urgent solicitation of many Kentuckians, and in accordance with what I believed, and still believe, to be the wish of a majority of all the Union-loving people of Kentucky.

While I have conversed on this subject with many eminent men of Kentucky, including a large majority of her Members of Congress, I do not remember that any one of them, or any other person, except your Excellency and the bearers of your Excellency's letter, has urged me to remove the military force from Kentucky, or to disband it. One other very worthy citizen of Kentucky did solicit me to have the augmenting of the force suspended for a time.

Taking all the means within my reach to form a judgment, I do not believe it is the popular wish of Kentucky that this force shall be removed beyond her limits; and, with this impression, I must respectfully decline to so remove it.

I most cordially sympathize with your Excellency, in the wish to preserve the peace of my own native State, Kentucky; but it is with regret I search, and can not find, in your not very short letter, any declaration, or intimation, that you entertain any desire for the preservation of the Federal Union. Your Obedient Servant,

To John C. Frémont

Private and confidential.

Major General Fremont: Washington D.C. Sept. 2, 1861.

My dear Sir: Two points in your proclamation of August 30th give me some anxiety. First, should you shoot a man, according to the proclamation, the Confederates would very certainly shoot our best man in their hands in retaliation; and so, man for man, indefinitely. It is therefore my order that you allow no man to be shot, under the proclamation, without first having my approbation or consent.

Secondly, I think there is great danger that the closing paragraph, in relation to the confiscation of property, and the liberating slaves of traiterous owners, will alarm our Southern Union friends, and turn them against us—perhaps ruin our rather fair prospect for Kentucky. Allow me therefore to ask, that you will as of your own motion, modify that paragraph so as to conform to the *first* and *fourth* sections of the act of Congress, entitled, "An act to confiscate property used for insurrectionary purposes," approved August, 6th, 1861, and a copy of which act I herewith send you. This letter is written in a spirit of caution and not of censure.

I send it by a special messenger, in order that it may certainly and speedily reach you. Yours very truly

Copy of letter sent to Gen. Fremont, by special messenger leaving Washington Sep. 3. 1861.

To David Hunter

Major Genl. David Hunter   Washington D.C. Sep. 9. 1861

My dear Sir: Gen. Fremont needs assistance which it is difficult to give him. He is losing the confidence of men near him, whose support any man in his position must have to be successful. His cardinal mistake is that he isolates himself, & allows nobody to see him; and by which he does not know what is going on in the very matter he is dealing with. He needs to have, by his side, a man of large experience. Will you not, for me, take that place? Your rank is one grade too high to be ordered to it; but will you not serve the country, and oblige me, by taking it voluntarily?

To John C. Frémont

Washington, D.C.
Major General John C. Fremont.   Sep. 11. 1861.

Sir: Yours of the 8th. in answer to mine of 2nd. Inst. is just received. Assuming that you, upon the ground, could better judge of the necessities of your position than I could at this distance, on seeing your proclamation of August 30th. I perceived no general objection to it. The particular clause, however, in relation to the confiscation of property and the liberation of slaves, appeared to me to be objectionable, in it's non-conformity to the Act of Congress passed the 6th. of last August upon the same subjects; and hence I wrote you expressing my wish that that clause should be modified accordingly. Your answer, just received, expresses the preference on your part, that I should make an open order for the modification, which I very cheerfully do. It is therefore ordered that the said clause of said proclamation be so modified, held, and construed, as to conform to, and not to transcend, the provisions on the same subject contained in the act of Congress entitled "An Act to confiscate property used for insurrectionary purposes" Approved, August 6. 1861; and that said act be published at length with this order. Your Obt. Servt

To Orville H. Browning

Private & confidential.

Hon. O. H. Browning   Executive Mansion
My dear Sir   Washington Sept 22d 1861.

Yours of the 17th is just received; and coming from you, I confess it astonishes me. That you should object to my adhering to a law, which you had assisted in making, and presenting to me, less than a month before, is odd enough. But this is a very small part. Genl. Fremont's proclamation, as to confiscation of property, and the liberation of slaves, is *purely political*, and not within the range of *military* law, or necessity. If a commanding General finds a necessity to seize the farm of a private owner, for a pasture, an encampment, or a fortification, he has the right to do so, and to so hold it, as long as the necessity lasts; and this is within military law, because within military necessity. But to say the farm shall no longer belong to the owner, or his heirs forever; and this as well when the farm is not needed for military purposes as when it is, is purely political, without the savor of military law about it. And the same is true of slaves. If the General needs them, he can seize them, and use them; but when the need is past, it is not for him to fix their permanent future condition. That must be settled according to laws made by law-makers, and not by military proclamations. The proclamation in the point in question, is simply "dictatorship." It assumes that the general may do *anything* he pleases—confiscate the lands and free the slaves of *loyal* people, as well as of disloyal ones. And going the whole figure I have no doubt would be more popular with some thoughtless people, than that which has been done! But I cannot assume this reckless position; nor allow others to assume it on my responsibility. You speak of it as being the only means of *saving* the government. On the contrary it is itself the surrender of the government. Can it be pretended that it is any longer the government of the U.S. — any government of Constitution and laws, — wherein a General, or a President, may make permanent rules of property by proclamation?

I do not say Congress might not with propriety pass a law, on the point, just such as General Fremont proclaimed. I do not say I might not, as a member of Congress, vote for it. What I object to, is, that I as President, shall expressly or impliedly seize and exercise the permanent legislative functions of the government.

So much as to principle. Now as to policy. No doubt the thing was popular in some quarters, and would have been more so if it had been a general declaration of emancipation. The Kentucky Legislature would not budge till that proclamation was modified; and Gen. Anderson telegraphed me that on the news of Gen. Fremont having actually issued deeds of manumission, a whole company of our Volunteers threw down their arms and disbanded. I was so assured, as to think it probable, that the very arms we had furnished Kentucky would be turned against us. I think to lose Kentucky is nearly the same as to lose the whole game. Kentucky gone, we can not hold Missouri, nor, as I think, Maryland. These all against us, and the job on our hands is too large for us. We would as well consent to separation at once, including the surrender of this capitol. On the contrary, if you will give up your restlessness for new positions, and back me manfully on the grounds upon which you and other kind friends gave me the election, and have approved in my public documents, we shall go through triumphantly.

You must not understand I took my course on the proclamation *because* of Kentucky. I took the same ground in a private letter to General Fremont before I heard from Kentucky.

You think I am inconsistent because I did not also forbid Gen. Fremont to shoot men under the proclamation. I understand that part to be within military law; but I also think, and so privately wrote Gen. Fremont, that it is impolitic in this, that our adversaries have the power, and will certainly exercise it, to shoot as many of our men as we shoot of theirs. I did not say this in the public letter, because it is a subject I prefer not to discuss in the hearing of our enemies.

There has been no thought of removing Gen. Fremont on any ground connected with his proclamation; and if there has been any wish for his removal on any ground, our mutual friend Sam. Glover can probably tell you what it was. I hope no real necessity for it exists on any ground.

Suppose you write to Hurlbut and get him to resign. Your friend as ever

To Oliver P. Morton

Washington, D.C. Sep. 29, 1861

His Excellency Gov. O. P. Morton: Your letter by the hand of Mr. Prunk was received yesterday. I write this letter because I wish you to believe of us (as we certainly believe of you) that we are doing the very best we can. You do not receive arms from us as fast as you need them; but it is because we have not near enough to meet all the pressing demands; and we are obliged to share around what we have, sending the larger share to the points which appear to need them most. We have great hope that our own supply will be ample before long, so that you and all others can have as many as you need. I see an article in an Indianapolis newspaper denouncing me for not answering your letter sent by a special messenger two or three weeks ago. I did make what I thought the best answer I could to that letter. As I remember, it asked for ten heavy guns to be distributed, with some troops, at Lawrenceburgh, Madison, New-Albany and Evansville; and I ordered the guns, and directed you to send the troops if you had them.

As to Kentucky, you do not estimate that state as more important than I do; but I am compelled to watch all points. While I write this I am, if not in *range*, at least in *hearing* of cannon-shot, from an army of enemies more than a hundred thousand strong. I do not expect them to capture this city; but I *know* they would, if I were to send the men and arms from here, to defend Louisville, of which there is not a single hostile armed soldier within forty miles, nor any force known to be moving upon it from any distance.

It is true, the Army in our front may make a half circle around Southward, and move on Louisville; but when they do, we will make a half circle around Northward, and meet them; and in the mean time we will get up what forces we can from other sources to also meet them.

I hope Zollicoffer has left Cumberland Gap (though I fear he has not) because, if he has, I rather infer he did it because of his dred of Camp Dick Robinson, re-inforced from Cincinnati, moving on him, than because of his intention to move on Louisville. But if he does go round and re-inforce Buckner, let Dick Robinson come round and re-inforce Sherman, and the thing is substantially as it was when Zollicoffer left Cumberland Gap. I state this as an illustration; for in fact, I think if the Gap is left open to us Dick Robinson should take it and hold it; while Indiana, and the vicinity of Louisville in Kentucky, can re-inforce Sherman faster than Zollicoffer can Buckner.

You requested that Lt. Col. Wood, of the Army, should be appointed a Brigadier General   I will only say that very formidable objection has been made to this from Indiana. Yours very truly

To Samuel R. Curtis

Brig: Genl. S. R. Curtis   Washington, D.C.
My dear Sir: Oct. 7. 1861.

Without prejudice, and looking to nothing but justice, and the public interest, I am greatly perplexed about Gen: Fremont: In your position, you can not but have a correct judgment in the case; and I beseech you to answer Gen. Cameron, when he hands you this, "Ought Gen: Fremont to be relieved from, or retained in his present command?" It shall be entirely confidential; but you can perceive how indispensable it is to justice & the public service, that I should have, an intelligent

unprejudiced, and judicious opinion from some professional
Military man on the spot, to assist me in the case. Yours very
truly

To George D. Ramsay

Majr. Ramsay   Executive Mansion
My dear Sir   Oct. 17, 1861
    The lady—bearer of this—says she has two sons who want
to work. Set them at it, if possible. Wanting to work is so rare
a merit, that it should be encouraged   Yours truly

To Samuel R. Curtis

                                          Executive Mansion,
Brig: Genl. S. R. Curtis   Washington, Oct. 24, 1861.
    Dear Sir   On receipt of this, with the accompanying in-
closures, you will take safe, certain, and suitable measures to
have the inclosure addressed to Major General Fremont,
delivered to him, with all reasonable despatch—subject to
these conditions only, that if, when Gen. Fremont shall be
reached by the messenger (yourself, or any one sent by you)
he shall then have, in personal command, fought and won a
battle, or shall then be actually in a battle, or shall then be in
the immediate presence of the enemy, in expectation of a
battle, it is not to be delivered, but held for further orders.
After, and not till after, the delivery to Gen. Fremont, let the
inclosure addressed to Gen. Hunter be delivered to him.
Your Obt. Servt.

To David Hunter

                                    Washington, Oct. 24, 1861
    Sir: The command of the Department of the West having
devolved upon you, I propose to offer you a few *suggestions*,

knowing how hazzardous it is to bind down a distant commander in the field to specific lines and operations, as so much always depends on a knowledge of localities & passing events. It is intended therefore, to leave a considerable margin for the exercise of your judgment & discretion.

The main rebel army (Prices) west of the Mississippi, is believed to have passed Dade county, in full retreat upon North-Western Arkansas, leaving Missouri almost freed from the enemy, excepting in the South-East of the State. Assuming this basis of fact, it seems desireable, as you are not likely to overtake Price, and are in danger of making too long a line from your own base of supplies and reinforcements, that you should give up the pursuit, halt your main army, divide it into two corps of observation, one occupying Sedalia, and the other Rolla, the present *termini* of Railroads; then recruit the condition of both corps, by re-establishing, and improving, their discipline and instruction; perfecting their clothing and equipments, and providing less uncomfortable quarters. Of course both Railroads must be guarded, and kept open, judiciously employing just so much force as is necessary for this. From these two points, Sedalia and Rolla, and especially in judicious co-operation with Lane on the Kansas border, it would be so easy to concentrate, and repel any army of the enemy returning on Missouri from the South-West, that it is not probable any such attempt to return will be made before, or during, the approaching cold weather. Before spring the people of Missouri will be in no favorable mood to renew, for next year, the troubles which have so much afflicted, and impoverished them during this.

If you adopt this line of policy, and if, as I anticipate, you will see no enemy in great force approaching, you will have a surplus of force, which you can withdraw from these points and direct to others, as may be needed, the railroads furnishing ready means of re-inforcing these main points, if occasion requires. Doubtless local uprisings, for a time, will continue to occur; but these can be met by detachments, and local forces of our own, and will, ere long, tire out of themselves.

While, as stated at the beginning of this letter, a large discretion must be, and is, left with yourself, I feel sure that an indefinite pursuit of Price, or an attempt, by this long and circuitous route, to reach Memphis, will be exhaustive beyond endurance, and will end in the loss of the whole force engaged in it. Your Obt. Servt.

To the Commander of the Department of the West.

To John A. McClernand

Brigadier General McClernand   Washington. Nov. 10. 1861

My Dear Sir   This is not an official but a social letter. You have had a battle, and without being able to judge as to the precise measure of its value, I think it is safe to say that you, and all with you have done honor to yourselves and the flag and service to the country. Most gratefully do I thank you and them. In my present position, I must care for the whole nation; but I hope it will be no injustice to any other state, for me to indulge a little home pride, that Illinois does not disappoint us.

I have just closed a long interview with Mr. Washburne in which he has detailed the many difficulties you, and those with you labor under. Be assured, we do not forget or neglect you. Much, very much, goes undone: but it is because we have not the power to do it faster than we do. Some of your forces are without arms, but the same is true here, and at every other place where we have considerable bodies of troops. The plain matter-of-fact is, our good people have rushed to the rescue of the Government, faster than the government can find arms to put into their hands.

It would be agreeable to each division of the army to know its own precise destination: but the Government cannot immediately, nor inflexibly at any time, determine as to all; nor if determined, can it tell its *friends* without at the same time telling its *enemies*.

We know you do all as wisely and well as you can; and you will not be deceived if you conclude the same is true of us. Please give my respects and thanks to all   Yours very truly

Reply to Delegation of Baltimore Citizens, Washington, D.C.

GENTLEMEN: I thank you for the address you have presented to me in behalf of the people of Baltimore. I have deplored the calamities which the sympathies of some misguided citizens of Maryland had brought down upon that patriotic and heretofore flourishing State. The prosperity of Baltimore up to the 19th of April last, was one of the wonders produced by the American Union. He who strangles himself, for whatever motive, is not more unreasonable than were those citizens of Baltimore who, in a single night, destroyed the Baltimore and Ohio Railroad, the Northern Pennsylvania Railroad, and the railroad from Baltimore to Philadelphia. From the day when that mad transaction occurred, the Government of the United States has been diligently engaged in endeavoring to restore those great avenues to their former usefulness, and, at the same time, to save Baltimore and Maryland from the danger of complete ruin through an unnecessary and unnatural rebellion.

I congratulate you upon the declaration which the people of Baltimore and Maryland have made in the recent election, of their recent approbation of the Federal Government, and of their enduring loyalty to the Union. I regard the results of these elections as auspicious of returning loyalty throughout all the insurrectionary States.

Your wishes for a fair participation by the mechanics and laboring men of Baltimore in the benefits of supplying the Government with materials and provisions are reasonable and just. They have deserved that participation. Loyalty has involved them in some danger, and has demanded of them some sacrifices. Their wishes, as you have communicated them, shall be referred to the proper Departments, and I am sure that every member of the Administration will cheerfully lend his aid to carry them out so far as it can be done consistently with the prudence and economy which ought always to regulate the public service.

November 15, 1861

Drafts of Bill for Compensated Emancipation in Delaware

Be it enacted by the State of Delaware, that on condition the United States of America will, at the present session of Congress, engage by law to pay, and thereafter faithfully pay to the said State of Delaware, in the six per cent bonds of said United States, the sum of seven hundred and nineteen thousand and two hundred dollars, in five equal annual instalments, there shall be neither slavery nor involuntary servitude, at any time after the first day of January in the year of our Lord one thousand, eight hundred and sixtyseven, within the said State of Delaware, except in the punishment of crime, whereof the party shall have been duly convicted: *Provided*, that said State shall, in good faith prevent, so far as possible, the carrying of any person out of said State, into involuntary servitude, beyond the limits of said State, at any time after the passage of this act; and shall also provide for one fifth of the adult slavery becoming free at the middle of the year one thousand eight hundred and sixtytwo; one fourth of the remainder of said adults, at the middle of the year one thousand eight hundred and sixtythree; one third of the remainder of said adults, at the middle of the year one thousand eight hundred and sixtyfour; one half the remainder of said adults at the middle of the year one thousand eight hundred and sixtyfive; and the entire remainder of adults, together with all minors, at the beginning of the year one thousand eight hundred and sixtyseven, as hereinbefore indicated. And *provided* also that said State may make provision of apprenticeship, not to extend beyond the age of twenty-one years for males, nor eighteen for females, for all minors whose mothers were not free, at the respective births of such minors.

———

Be it enacted by the State of Delaware that on condition the United States of America will, at the present session of Congress, engage by law to pay, and thereafter faithfully pay to the said State of Delaware, in the six per cent bonds of said United States, the sum of seven hundred and nineteen thousand, and two hundred dollars, in thirty one equal annual instalments, there shall be neither slavery nor involuntary servitude, at any time after the first day of January in the year of our Lord one thousand eight hundred and ninety three, within the said State of Delaware, except in the punishment of crime, whereof the party shall have been duly convicted; nor, except in the punishment of crime as aforesaid, shall any person who shall be born after the passage of this act, nor any person above the age of thirty five years, be held in slavery, or to involuntary servitude, within said State of Delaware, at any time after the passage of this act.

And be it further enacted that said State shall, in good faith prevent, so far as possible, the carrying of any person out of said state, into involuntary servitude, beyond the limits of said State, at any time after the passage of this act.

And be it further enacted that said State may make provision of apprenticeship, not to extend beyond the age of twentyone years for males, nor eighteen for females, for all minors whose mothers were not free at the respective births of such minors.

On reflection, I like No. 2 the better. By it the Nation would pay the State $23,200 per annum for thirtyone years — and

All born after the passage of the act would be born free — and

All slaves above the age of 35 years would become free on the passage of the act — and

All others would become free on arriving at the age of 35 years, until January 1893 — when

All remaining of all ages would become free, subject to apprenticeship for minors born of slave mothers, up to the respective ages of 21 and 18.

If the State would desire to have the money sooner, let the bill be altered only in fixing the time of final emancipation earlier, and making the annual instalments correspondingly fewer in number, by which they would also be correspondingly larger in amount. For instance, strike out "1893," and insert "1872"; and strike out "thirtyone" annual instalments, and insert "ten" annual instalments. The instalments would

then be $71,920 instead of $23,200 as now. In all other particulars let the bill stand precisely as it is.

c. late November 1861

Memorandum on Advice to Mrs. Stephen A. Douglas

Executive Mansion, Nov. 27– 1861

Yesterday Mrs. Douglas called, saying she is guardian of the
minor children of her late husband; that she is being urged,
against her inclination, to send them South, on the plea of
avoiding the confiscation of their property there, and asking
my counsel in the case.

I expect the United States will overcome the attempt to
confiscate property, because of loyalty to the government; but
if not, I still do not expect the property of absent minor children will be confiscated. I therefore think Mrs. Douglas may
safely act her pleasure in the premises.

But it is especially dangerous for my name to be connected
with the matter; for nothing would more certainly excite the
secessionists to do the worst they can against the children.

Annual Message to Congress

Fellow Citizens of the Senate and House of Representatives:

In the midst of unprecedented political troubles, we have cause of great gratitude to God for unusual good health, and most abundant harvests.

You will not be surprised to learn that, in the peculiar exigencies of the times, our intercourse with foreign nations has been attended with profound solicitude, chiefly turning upon our own domestic affairs.

A disloyal portion of the American people have, during the whole year, been engaged in an attempt to divide and destroy the Union. A nation which endures factious domestic division, is exposed to disrespect abroad; and one party, if not both, is sure, sooner or later, to invoke foreign intervention.

Nations, thus tempted to interfere, are not always able to resist the counsels of seeming expediency, and ungenerous ambition, although measures adopted under such influences seldom fail to be unfortunate and injurious to those adopting them.

The disloyal citizens of the United States who have offered the ruin of our country, in return for the aid and comfort which they have invoked abroad, have received less patronage and encouragement than they probably expected. If it were just to suppose, as the insurgents have seemed to assume, that foreign nations, in this case, discarding all moral, social, and treaty obligations, would act solely, and selfishly, for the most speedy restoration of commerce, including, especially, the acquisition of cotton, those nations appear, as yet, not to have seen their way to their object more directly, or clearly, through the destruction, than through the preservation, of the Union. If we could dare to believe that foreign nations are actuated by no higher principle than this, I am quite sure a sound argument could be made to show them that they can reach their aim more readily, and easily, by aiding to crush this rebellion, than by giving encouragement to it.

The principal lever relied on by the insurgents for exciting foreign nations to hostility against us, as already intimated, is the embarrassment of commerce. Those nations, however, not improbably, saw from the first, that it was the Union which made as well our foreign, as our domestic, commerce. They can scarcely have failed to perceive that the effort for disunion produces the existing difficulty; and that one strong nation promises more durable peace, and a more extensive, valuable and reliable commerce, than can the same nation broken into hostile fragments.

It is not my purpose to review our discussions with foreign states, because whatever might be their wishes, or dispositions, the integrity of our country, and the stability of our government, mainly depend, not upon them, but on the loyalty, virtue, patriotism, and intelligence of the American people. The correspondence itself, with the usual reservations, is herewith submitted.

I venture to hope it will appear that we have practiced prudence, and liberality towards foreign powers, averting causes of irritation; and, with firmness, maintaining our own rights and honor.

Since, however, it is apparent that here, as in every other state, foreign dangers necessarily attend domestic difficulties, I recommend that adequate and ample measures be adopted for maintaining the public defences on every side. While, under this general recommendation, provision for defending our sea-coast line readily occurs to the mind, I also, in the same connexion, ask the attention of Congress to our great lakes and rivers. It is believed that some fortifications and depots of arms and munitions, with harbor and navigation improvements, all at well selected points upon these, would be of great importance to the national defence and preservation. I ask attention to the views of the Secretary of War, expressed in his report, upon the same general subject.

I deem it of importance that the loyal regions of East Tennessee and western North Carolina should be connected with Kentucky, and other faithful parts of the Union, by railroad. I therefore recommend, as a military measure, that Congress provide for the construction of such road, as speedily as possible. Kentucky, no doubt, will co-operate, and, through her legislature, make the most judicious selection of a line. The northern terminus must connect with some existing railroad; and whether the route shall be from Lexington, or Nicholasville, to the Cumberland Gap; or from Lebanon to the Tennessee line, in the direction of Knoxville; or on some still different line, can easily be determined. Kentucky and the general government co-operating, the work can be completed in a very short time; and when done, it will be not only of vast present usefulness, but also a valuable permanent improvement, worth its cost in all the future.

Some treaties, designed chiefly for the interests of commerce, and having no grave political importance, have been negotiated, and will be submitted to the Senate for their consideration.

Although we have failed to induce some of the commercial powers to adopt a desirable melioration of the rigor of maritime war, we have removed all obstructions from the way of this humane reform, except such as are merely of temporary and accidental occurrence.

I invite your attention to the correspondence between her Britannic Majesty's minister accredited to this government, and the Secretary of State, relative to the detention of the British ship Perthshire in June last, by the United States steamer Massachusetts, for a supposed breach of the blockade. As this detention was occasioned by an obvious misapprehension of the facts, and as justice requires that we should commit no belligerent act not founded in strict right, as sanctioned by public law, I recommend that an appropriation be made to satisfy the reasonable demand of the owners of the vessel for her detention.

I repeat the recommendation of my predecessor, in his annual message to Congress in December last, in regard to the disposition of the surplus which will probably remain after satisfying the claims of American citizens against China, pursuant to the awards of the commissioners under the act of the 3rd of March, 1859. If, however, it should not be deemed advisable to carry that recommendation into effect, I would suggest that authority be given for investing the principal, over the proceeds of the surplus referred to, in good securities, with a view to the satisfaction of such other just claims of our citizens against China as are not unlikely to arise hereafter in the course of our extensive trade with that Empire.

By the act of the 5th of August last, Congress authorized

the President to instruct the commanders of suitable vessels to defend themselves against, and to capture pirates. This authority has been exercised in a single instance only. For the more effectual protection of our extensive and valuable commerce, in the eastern seas especially, it seems to me that it would also be advisable to authorize the commanders of sailing vessels to re-capture any prizes which pirates might make of United States vessels and their cargoes, and the consular courts, now established by law in eastern countries, to adjudicate the cases, in the event that this should not be objected to by the local authorities.

If any good reason exists why we should persevere longer in withholding our recognition of the independence and sovereignty of Hayti and Liberia, I am unable to discern it. Unwilling, however, to inaugurate a novel policy in regard to them without the approbation of Congress, I submit for your consideration the expediency of an appropriation for maintaining a chargé d'affaires near each of those new states. It does not admit of doubt that important commercial advantages might be secured by favorable commercial treaties with them.

The operations of the treasury during the period which has elapsed since your adjournment have been conducted with signal success. The patriotism of the people has placed at the disposal of the government the large means demanded by the public exigencies. Much of the national loan has been taken by citizens of the industrial classes, whose confidence in their country's faith, and zeal for their country's deliverance from present peril, have induced them to contribute to the support of the government the whole of their limited acquisitions. This fact imposes peculiar obligations to economy in disbursement and energy in action.

The revenue from all sources, including loans, for the financial year ending on the 30th June, 1861, was eighty six million, eight hundred and thirty five thousand, nine hundred dollars, and twenty seven cents, ($86,835,900.27,) and the expenditures for the same period, including payments on account of the public debt, were eighty four million, five hundred and seventy eight thousand, eight hundred and thirty four dollars and forty seven cents, ($84,578,834.47;) leaving a balance in the treasury, on the 1st July, of two million, two hundred and fifty seven thousand, sixty five dollars and eighty cents, ($2,257,065.80.) For the first quarter of the financial year, ending on the 30th September, 1861, the receipts from all sources, including the balance of first of July, were $102,532,509.27, and the expenses $98,239,733.09; leaving a balance on the 1st of October, 1861, of $4,292,776.18.

Estimates for the remaining three quarters of the year, and for the financial year 1863, together with his views of ways and means for meeting the demands contemplated by them, will be submitted to Congress by the Secretary of the Treasury. It is gratifying to know that the expenditures made necessary by the rebellion are not beyond the resources of the loyal people, and to believe that the same patriotism which has thus far sustained the government will continue to sustain it till Peace and Union shall again bless the land.

I respectfully refer to the report of the Secretary of War for information respecting the numerical strength of the army, and for recommendations having in view an increase of its efficiency and the well being of the various branches of the service intrusted to his care. It is gratifying to know that the patriotism of the people has proved equal to the occasion, and that the number of troops tendered greatly exceeds the force which Congress authorized me to call into the field.

I refer with pleasure to those portions of his report which make allusion to the creditable degree of discipline already attained by our troops, and to the excellent sanitary condition of the entire army.

The recommendation of the Secretary for an organization of the militia upon a uniform basis, is a subject of vital importance to the future safety of the country, and is commended to the serious attention of Congress.

The large addition to the regular army, in connexion with the defection that has so considerably diminished the number of its officers, gives peculiar importance to his recommendation for increasing the corps of cadets to the greatest capacity of the Military Academy.

By mere omission, I presume, Congress has failed to provide chaplains for hospitals occupied by volunteers. This subject was brought to my notice, and I was induced to draw up the form of a letter, one copy of which, properly addressed, has been delivered to each of the persons, and at the dates respectively named and stated, in a schedule, containing also the form of the letter, marked A, and herewith transmitted.

These gentlemen, I understand, entered upon the duties designated, at the times respectively stated in the schedule, and have labored faithfully therein ever since. I therefore recommend that they be compensated at the same rate as chaplains in the army. I further suggest that general provision be made for chaplains to serve at hospitals, as well as with regiments.

The report of the Secretary of the Navy presents in detail the operations of that branch of the service, the activity and energy which have characterized its administration, and the results of measures to increase its efficiency and power. Such have been the additions, by construction and purchase, that it may almost be said a navy has been created and brought into service since our difficulties commenced.

Besides blockading our extensive coast, squadrons larger than ever before assembled under our flag have been put afloat and performed deeds which have increased our naval renown.

I would invite special attention to the recommendation of the Secretary for a more perfect organization of the navy by introducing additional grades in the service.

The present organization is defective and unsatisfactory, and the suggestions submitted by the department will, it is believed, if adopted, obviate the difficulties alluded to, promote harmony, and increase the efficiency of the navy.

There are three vacancies on the bench of the Supreme Court—two by the decease of Justices Daniel and McLean, and one by the resignation of Justice Campbell. I have so far forborne making nominations to fill these vacancies for reasons which I will now state. Two of the outgoing judges resided within the States now overrun by revolt; so that if successors were appointed in the same localities, they could not now serve upon their circuits; and many of the most competent men there, probably would not take the personal hazard of accepting to serve, even here, upon the supreme bench. I have been unwilling to throw all the appointments northward, thus disabling myself from doing justice to the south on the return of peace; although I may remark that to transfer to the north one which has heretofore been in the south, would not, with reference to territory and population, be unjust.

During the long and brilliant judicial career of Judge McLean his circuit grew into an empire—altogether too large for any one judge to give the courts therein more than a nominal attendance—rising in population from one million four hundred and seventy-thousand and eighteen, in 1830, to six million one hundred and fifty-one thousand four hundred and five, in 1860.

Besides this, the country generally has outgrown our present judicial system. If uniformity was at all intended, the system requires that all the States shall be accommodated with circuit courts, attended by supreme judges, while, in fact, Wisconsin, Minnesota, Iowa, Kansas, Florida, Texas, California, and Oregon, have never had any such courts. Nor can this well be remedied without a change of the system; because the adding of judges to the Supreme Court, enough for the accommodation of all parts of the country, with circuit courts, would create a court altogether too numerous for a judicial body of any sort. And the evil, if it be one, will increase as new States come into the Union. Circuit courts are useful, or they are not useful. If useful, no State should be denied them; if not useful, no State should have them. Let them be provided for all, or abolished as to all.

Three modifications occur to me, either of which, I think, would be an improvement upon our present system. Let the Supreme Court be of convenient number in every event. Then, first, let the whole country be divided into circuits of convenient size, the supreme judges to serve in a number of them corresponding to their own number, and independent circuit judges be provided for all the rest. Or, secondly, let the supreme judges be relieved from circuit duties, and circuit judges provided for all the circuits. Or, thirdly, dispense with circuit courts altogether, leaving the judicial functions wholly to the district courts and an independent Supreme Court.

I respectfully recommend to the consideration of Congress the present condition of the statute laws, with the hope that

Congress will be able to find an easy remedy for many of the inconveniences and evils which constantly embarrass those engaged in the practical administration of them. Since the organization of the government, Congress has enacted some five thousand acts and joint resolutions, which fill more than six thousand closely printed pages, and are scattered through many volumes. Many of these acts have been drawn in haste and without sufficient caution, so that their provisions are often obscure in themselves, or in conflict with each other, or at least so doubtful as to render it very difficult for even the best informed persons to ascertain precisely what the statute law really is.

It seems to me very important that the statute laws should be made as plain and intelligible as possible, and be reduced to as small a compass as may consist with the fullness and precision of the will of the legislature and the perspicuity of its language. This, well done, would, I think, greatly facilitate the labors of those whose duty it is to assist in the administration of the laws, and would be a lasting benefit to the people, by placing before them, in a more accessible and intelligible form, the laws which so deeply concern their interests and their duties.

I am informed by some whose opinions I respect, that all the acts of Congress now in force, and of a permanent and general nature, might be revised and re-written, so as to be embraced in one volume (or at most, two volumes) of ordinary and convenient size. And I respectfully recommend to Congress to consider of the subject, and, if my suggestion be approved, to devise such plan as to their wisdom shall seem most proper for the attainment of the end proposed.

One of the unavoidable consequences of the present insurrection is the entire suppression, in many places, of all the ordinary means of administering civil justice by the officers and in the forms of existing law. This is the case, in whole or in part, in all the insurgent States; and as our armies advance upon and take possession of parts of those States, the practical evil becomes more apparent. There are no courts nor officers to whom the citizens of other States may apply for the enforcement of their lawful claims against citizens of the insurgent States; and there is a vast amount of debt constituting such claims. Some have estimated it as high as two hundred million dollars, due, in large part, from insurgents, in open rebellion, to loyal citizens who are, even now, making great sacrifices in the discharge of their patriotic duty to support the government.

Under these circumstances, I have been urgently solicited to establish, by military power, courts to administer summary justice in such cases. I have thus far declined to do it, not because I had any doubt that the end proposed—the collection of the debts—was just and right in itself, but because I have been unwilling to go beyond the pressure of necessity in the unusual exercise of power. But the powers of Congress I suppose are equal to the anomalous occasion, and therefore I refer the whole matter to Congress, with the hope that a plan may be devised for the administration of justice in all such parts of the insurgent States and Territories as may be under the control of this government, whether by a voluntary return to allegiance and order or by the power of our arms. This, however, not to be a permanent institution, but a temporary substitute, and to cease as soon as the ordinary courts can be re-established in peace.

It is important that some more convenient means should be provided, if possible, for the adjustment of claims against the government, especially in view of their increased number by reason of the war. It is as much the duty of government to render prompt justice against itself, in favor of citizens, as it is to administer the same, between private individuals. The investigation and adjudication of claims, in their nature belong to the judicial department; besides it is apparent that the attention of Congress, will be more than usually engaged, for some time to come, with great national questions. It was intended, by the organization of the court of claims, mainly to remove this branch of business from the halls of Congress; but while the court has proved to be an effective, and valuable means of investigation, it in great degree fails to effect the object of its creation, for want of power to make its judgments final.

Fully aware of the delicacy, not to say the danger, of the subject, I commend to your careful consideration whether this power of making judgments final, may not properly be given to the court, reserving the right of appeal on questions of law to the Supreme Court, with such other provisions as experience may have shown to be necessary.

I ask attention to the report of the Postmaster General, the following being a summary statement of the condition of the department:

The revenue from all sources during the fiscal year ending June 30. 1861, including the annual permanent appropriation of seven hundred thousand dollars ($700,000) for the transportation of "free mail matter," was nine million, forty nine thousand, two hundred and ninety six dollars and forty cents ($9,049,296.40) being about two per cent. less than the revenue for 1860.

The expenditures were thirteen million, six hundred and six thousand, seven hundred and fifty nine dollars and eleven cents. ($13,606,759.11) showing a decrease of more than eight per cent. as compared with those of the previous year, and leaving an excess of expenditure over the revenue for the last fiscal year of four million, five hundred and fifty seven thousand, four hundred and sixty two dollars and seventy one cents ($4,557,462.71.)

The gross revenue for the year ending June 30, 1863, is estimated at an increase of four per cent. on that of 1861, making eight million, six hundred and eighty three thousand dollars ($8,683,000) to which should be added the earnings of the department in carrying free matter, viz: seven hundred thousand dollars ($700,000.) making nine million, three hundred and eighty three thousand dollars, ($9,383,000.)

The total expenditures for 1863 are estimated at $12,528,000, leaving an estimated deficiency of $3,145,000, to be supplied from the treasury, in addition to the permanent appropriation.

The present insurrection shows, I think, that the extension of this District across the Potomac river, at the time of establishing the capital here, was eminently wise, and consequently that the relinquishment of that portion of it which lies within the State of Virginia was unwise and dangerous. I submit for your consideration the expediency of regaining that part of the District, and the restoration of the original boundaries thereof, through negotiations with the State of Virginia.

The report of the Secretary of the Interior, with the accompanying documents, exhibits the condition of the several branches of the public business pertaining to that department. The depressing influences of the insurrection have been especially felt in the operations of the Patent and General Land Offices. The cash receipts from the sales of public lands during the past year have exceeded the expenses of our land system only about $200,000. The sales have been entirely suspended in the southern States, while the interruptions to the business of the country, and the diversion of large numbers of men from labor to military service, have obstructed settlements in the new States and Territories of the northwest.

The receipts of the Patent Office have declined in nine months about $100,000, rendering a large reduction of the force employed necessary to make it self sustaining.

The demands upon the Pension Office will be largely increased by the insurrection. Numerous applications for pensions, based upon the casualties of the existing war, have already been made. There is reason to believe that many who are now upon the pension rolls and in receipt of the bounty of the government, are in the ranks of the insurgent army, or giving them aid and comfort. The Secretary of the Interior has directed a suspension of the payment of the pensions of such persons upon proof of their disloyalty. I recommend that Congress authorize that officer to cause the names of such persons to be stricken from the pension rolls.

The relations of the government with the Indian tribes have been greatly disturbed by the insurrection, especially in the southern superintendency and in that of New Mexico. The Indian country south of Kansas is in the possession of insurgents from Texas and Arkansas. The agents of the United States appointed since the 4th. of March for this superintendency have been unable to reach their posts, while the most of those who were in office before that time have espoused the insurrectionary cause, and assume to exercise the powers of agents by virtue of commissions from the insurrectionists. It has been stated in the public press that a portion of those Indians have been organized as a military force, and are attached to the army of the insurgents. Although the government has no official information upon this subject, letters

have been written to the Commissioner of Indian Affairs by
several prominent chiefs, giving assurance of their loyalty to
the United States, and expressing a wish for the presence of
federal troops to protect them. It is believed that upon the
repossession of the country by the federal forces the Indians
will readily cease all hostile demonstrations, and resume their
former relations to the government.

Agriculture, confessedly the largest interest of the nation,
has, not a department, nor a bureau, but a clerkship only,
assigned to it in the government. While it is fortunate that
this great interest is so independent in its nature as to not
have demanded and extorted more from the government, I
respectfully ask Congress to consider whether something
more cannot be given voluntarily with general advantage.

Annual reports exhibiting the condition of our agriculture,
commerce, and manufactures would present a fund of information of great practical value to the country. While I make
no suggestion as to details, I venture the opinion that an agricultural and statistical bureau might profitably be organized.

The execution of the laws for the suppression of the African
slave trade, has been confided to the Department of the Interior. It is a subject of gratulation that the efforts which have
been made for the suppression of this inhuman traffic, have
been recently attended with unusual success. Five vessels being fitted out for the slave trade have been seized and condemned. Two mates of vessels engaged in the trade, and one
person in equipping a vessel as a slaver, have been convicted
and subjected to the penalty of fine and imprisonment, and
one captain, taken with a cargo of Africans on board his vessel, has been convicted of the highest grade of offence under
our laws, the punishment of which is death.

The Territories of Colorado, Dakotah and Nevada, created
by the last Congress, have been organized, and civil administration has been inaugurated therein under auspices especially
gratifying, when it is considered that the leaven of treason
was found existing in some of these new countries when the
federal officers arrived there.

The abundant natural resources of these Territories, with
the security and protection afforded by organized government, will doubtless invite to them a large immigration when

peace shall restore the business of the country to its accustomed channels. I submit the resolutions of the legislature of Colorado, which evidence the patriotic spirit of the people of the Territory. So far the authority of the United States has been upheld in all the Territories, as it is hoped it will be in the future. I commend their interests and defence to the enlightened and generous care of Congress.

I recommend to the favorable consideration of Congress the interests of the District of Columbia. The insurrection has been the cause of much suffering and sacrifice to its inhabitants, and as they have no representative in Congress, that body should not overlook their just claims upon the government.

At your late session a joint resolution was adopted authorizing the President to take measures for facilitating a proper representation of the industrial interests of the United States at the exhibition of the industry of all nations to be holden at London in the year 1862. I regret to say I have been unable to give personal attention to this subject,—a subject at once so interesting in itself, and so extensively and intimately connected with the material prosperity of the world. Through the Secretaries of State and of the Interior a plan, or system, has been devised, and partly matured, and which will be laid before you.

Under and by virtue of the act of Congress entitled "An act to confiscate property used for insurrectionary purposes," approved August, 6, 1861, the legal claims of certain persons to the labor and service of certain other persons have become forfeited; and numbers of the latter, thus liberated, are already dependent on the United States, and must be provided for in some way. Besides this, it is not impossible that some of the States will pass similar enactments for their own benefit respectively, and by operation of which persons of the same class will be thrown upon them for disposal. In such case I recommend that Congress provide for accepting such persons from such States, according to some mode of valuation, in lieu, *pro tanto*, of direct taxes, or upon some other plan to be agreed on with such States respectively; that such persons, on such acceptance by the general government, be at once deemed free; and that, in any event, steps be taken for colonizing both classes, (or the one first mentioned, if the other shall not be brought into existence,) at some place, or places, in a climate congenial to them. It might be well to consider, too,—whether the free colored people already in the United States could not, so far as individuals may desire, be included in such colonization.

To carry out the plan of colonization may involve the acquiring of territory, and also the appropriation of money beyond that to be expended in the territorial acquisition. Having practiced the acquisition of territory for nearly sixty years, the question of constitutional power to do so is no longer an open one with us. The power was questioned at first by Mr. Jefferson, who, however, in the purchase of Louisiana, yielded his scruples on the plea of great expediency. If it be said that the only legitimate object of acquiring territory is to furnish homes for white men, this measure effects that object; for the emigration of colored men leaves additional room for white men remaining or coming here. Mr. Jefferson, however, placed the importance of procuring Louisiana more on political and commercial grounds than on providing room for population.

On this whole proposition,—including the appropriation of money with the acquisition of territory, does not the expediency amount to absolute necessity—that, without which the government itself cannot be perpetuated? The war continues. In considering the policy to be adopted for suppressing the insurrection, I have been anxious and careful that the inevitable conflict for this purpose shall not degenerate into a violent and remorseless revolutionary struggle. I have, therefore, in every case, thought it proper to keep the integrity of the Union prominent as the primary object of the contest on our part, leaving all questions which are not of vital military importance to the more deliberate action of the legislature.

In the exercise of my best discretion I have adhered to the blockade of the ports held by the insurgents, instead of putting in force, by proclamation, the law of Congress enacted at the late session, for closing those ports.

So, also, obeying the dictates of prudence, as well as the obligations of law, instead of transcending, I have adhered to the act of Congress to confiscate property used for insurrectionary purposes. If a new law upon the same subject shall be proposed, its propriety will be duly considered.

The Union must be preserved, and hence, all indispensable means must be employed. We should not be in haste to determine that radical and extreme measures, which may reach the loyal as well as the disloyal, are indispensable.

The inaugural address at the beginning of the Administration, and the message to Congress at the late special session, were both mainly devoted to the domestic controversy out of which the insurrection and consequent war have sprung. Nothing now occurs to add or subtract, to or from, the principles or general purposes stated and expressed in those documents.

The last ray of hope for preserving the Union peaceably, expired at the assault upon Fort Sumter; and a general review of what has occurred since may not be unprofitable. What was painfully uncertain then, is much better defined and more distinct now; and the progress of events is plainly in the right direction. The insurgents confidently claimed a strong support from north of Mason and Dixon's line; and the friends of the Union were not free from apprehension on the point. This, however, was soon settled definitely and on the right side. South of the line, noble little Delaware led off right from the first. Maryland was made to *seem* against the Union. Our soldiers were assaulted, bridges were burned, and railroads torn up, within her limits; and we were many days, at one time, without the ability to bring a single regiment over her soil to the capital. Now, her bridges and railroads are repaired and open to the government; she already gives seven regiments to the cause of the Union and none to the enemy; and her people, at a regular election, have sustained the Union, by a larger majority, and a larger aggregate vote than they ever before gave to any candidate, or any question. Kentucky, too, for some time in doubt, is now decidedly, and, I think, unchangeably, ranged on the side of the Union. Missouri is comparatively quiet; and I believe cannot again be overrun by the insurrectionists. These three States of Maryland, Kentucky, and Missouri, neither of which would promise a single soldier at first, have now an aggregate of not less than forty thousand in the field, for the Union; while, of their citizens, certainly not more than a third of that number, and they of doubtful whereabouts, and doubtful existence, are in arms against it. After a somewhat bloody struggle of months, winter closes on the Union people of western Virginia, leaving them masters of their own country.

An insurgent force of about fifteen hundred, for months dominating the narrow peninsular region, constituting the counties of Accomac and Northampton, and known as eastern shore of Virginia, together with some contiguous parts of Maryland, have laid down their arms; and the people there have renewed their allegiance to, and accepted the protection of, the old flag. This leaves no armed insurrectionist north of the Potomac, or east of the Chesapeake.

Also we have obtained a footing at each of the isolated points, on the southern coast, of Hatteras, Port Royal, Tybee Island, near Savannah, and Ship Island; and we likewise have some general accounts of popular movements, in behalf of the Union, in North Carolina and Tennessee.

These things demonstrate that the cause of the Union is advancing steadily and certainly southward.

Since your last adjournment, Lieutenant General Scott has retired from the head of the army. During his long life, the nation has not been unmindful of his merit; yet, on calling to mind how faithfully, ably and brilliantly he has served the country, from a time far back in our history, when few of the now living had been born, and thenceforward continually, I cannot but think we are still his debtors. I submit, therefore, for your consideration, what further mark of recognition is due to him, and to ourselves, as a grateful people.

With the retirement of General Scott came the executive duty of appointing, in his stead, a general-in-chief of the army. It is a fortunate circumstance that neither in council nor country was there, so far as I know, any difference of opinion as to the proper person to be selected. The retiring chief repeatedly expressed his judgment in favor of General Mc-Clellan for the position; and in this the nation seemed to give a unanimous concurrence. The designation of General McClellan is therefore in considerable degree, the selection of the Country as well as of the Executive; and hence there is better reason to hope there will be given him, the confidence, and cordial support thus, by fair implication, promised, and without which, he cannot, with so full efficiency, serve the country.

It has been said that one bad general is better than two good ones; and the saying is true, if taken to mean no more than that an army is better directed by a single mind, though inferior, than by two superior ones, at variance, and cross-purposes with each other.

And the same is true, in all joint operations wherein those engaged, *can* have none but a common end in view, and *can* differ only as to the choice of means. In a storm at sea, no one on board *can* wish the ship to sink; and yet, not unfrequently, all go down together, because too many will direct, and no single mind can be allowed to control.

It continues to develop that the insurrection is largely, if not exclusively, a war upon the first principle of popular government—the rights of the people. Conclusive evidence of this is found in the most grave and maturely considered public documents, as well as in the general tone of the insurgents. In those documents we find the abridgement of the existing right of suffrage and the denial to the people of all right to participate in the selection of public officers, except the legislative boldly advocated, with labored arguments to prove that large control of the people in government, is the source of all political evil. Monarchy itself is sometimes hinted at as a possible refuge from the power of the people.

In my present position, I could scarcely be justified were I to omit raising a warning voice against this approach of returning despotism.

It is not needed, nor fitting here, that a general argument should be made in favor of popular institutions; but there is one point, with its connexions, not so hackneyed as most others, to which I ask a brief attention. It is the effort to place *capital* on an equal footing with, if not above *labor*, in the structure of government. It is assumed that labor is available only in connexion with capital; that nobody labors unless somebody else, owning capital, somehow by the use of it, induces him to labor. This assumed, it is next considered whether it is best that capital shall *hire* laborers, and thus induce them to work by their own consent, or *buy* them, and

drive them to it without their consent. Having proceeded so
far, it is naturally concluded that all laborers are either *hired*
laborers, or what we call slaves. And further it is assumed that
whoever is once a hired laborer, is fixed in that condition for
life.

Now, there is no such relation between capital and labor
as assumed; nor is there any such thing as a free man being
fixed for life in the condition of a hired laborer. Both these
assumptions are false, and all inferences from them are
groundless.

Labor is prior to, and independent of, capital. Capital is
only the fruit of labor, and could never have existed if labor
had not first existed. Labor is the superior of capital, and deserves much the higher consideration. Capital has its rights,
which are as worthy of protection as any other rights. Nor is
it denied that there is, and probably always will be, a relation
between labor and capital, producing mutual benefits. The error is in assuming that the whole labor of community exists
within that relation. A few men own capital, and that few
avoid labor themselves, and, with their capital, hire or buy
another few to labor for them. A large majority belong to
neither class—neither work for others, nor have others working for them. In most of the southern States, a majority of the
whole people of all colors are neither slaves nor masters;
while in the northern a large majority are neither hirers nor
hired. Men with their families—wives, sons, and daughters—
work for themselves, on their farms, in their houses, and in
their shops, taking the whole product to themselves, and asking no favors of capital on the one hand, nor of hired laborers
or slaves on the other. It is not forgotten that a considerable
number of persons mingle their own labor with capital—that
is, they labor with their own hands, and also buy or hire others to labor for them; but this is only a mixed, and not a
distinct class. No principle stated is disturbed by the existence
of this mixed class.

Again: as has already been said, there is not, of necessity,
any such thing as the free hired laborer being fixed to that
condition for life. Many independent men everywhere in
these States, a few years back in their lives, were hired laborers. The prudent, penniless beginner in the world, labors for

wages awhile, saves a surplus with which to buy tools or land for himself; then labors on his own account another while, and at length hires another new beginner to help him. This is the just, and generous, and prosperous system, which opens the way to all—gives hope to all, and consequent energy, and progress, and improvement of condition to all. No men living are more worthy to be trusted than those who toil up from poverty—none less inclined to take, or touch, aught which they have not honestly earned. Let them beware of surrendering a political power which they already possess, and which, if surrendered, will surely be used to close the door of advancement against such as they, and to fix new disabilities and burdens upon them, till all of liberty shall be lost.

From the first taking of our national census to the last are seventy years; and we find our population at the end of the period eight times as great as it was at the beginning. The increase of those other things which men deem desirable has been even greater. We thus have at one view, what the popular principle applied to government, through the machinery of the States and the Union, has produced in a given time; and also what, if firmly maintained, it promises for the future. There are already among us those, who, if the Union be preserved, will live to see it contain two hundred and fifty millions. The struggle of today, is not altogether for today—it is for a vast future also. With a reliance on Providence, all the more firm and earnest, let us proceed in the great task which events have devolved upon us.

December 3, 1861

To Mrs. Susannah Weathers

Executive Mansion,
My dear Madam   Washington, Dec. 4, 1861.

I take great pleasure in acknowledging the receipt of your letter of Nov. 26; and in thanking you for the present by which it was accompanied. A pair of socks so fine, and soft, and warm, could hardly have been manufactured in any other way than the old Kentucky fashion. Your letter informs me that your maiden name was Crume, and that you were raised in Washington county, Kentucky, by which I infer that an uncle of mine by marriage was a relative of yours. Nearly, or quite sixty years ago, Ralph Crume married Mary Lincoln, a sister of my father, in Washington county, Kentucky.

Accept my thanks, and believe me   Very truly   Your friend

Draft of Letter to Senate from Ward H. Lamon

To the Senate of the United States

In obedience to the resolution of your Honorable body, a copy of which accompanies this, I have the honor to state that since I have held the office of Marshal of the District of Columbia, three persons claimed to be slaves, have been admitted into the jail of said District on the requests, respectively, of the persons claiming to be their owners; that this has been acquiesced in by me, upon an old and uniform custom here, based as I supposed upon some valid law, but of which supposed law I have made no investigation.

December 16, 1861

To David Hunter

Executive Mansion, Washington,
Major General Hunter.   Dec. 31, 1861.

Dear Sir: Yours of the 23rd. is received; and I am constrained to say it is difficult to answer so ugly a letter in good temper. I am, as you intimate, losing much of the great confidence I placed in you, not from any act or omission of yours touching the public service, up to the time you were sent to Leavenworth, but from the flood of grumbling despatches and letters I have seen from you since. I knew you were being ordered to Leavenworth at the time it was done; and I aver that with as tender a regard for your honor and your sensibilities as I had for my own, it never occurred to me that you were being "humiliated, insulted and disgraced"; nor have I, up to this day, heard an intimation that you have been wronged, coming from any one but yourself. No one has blamed you for the retrograde movement from Springfield, nor for the information you gave Gen. Cameron; and this you could readily understand, if it were not for your unwarranted assumption that the ordering you to Leavenworth must necessarily have been done as a *punishment* for some *fault*. I thought then, and think yet, the position assigned to you is as responsible, and as honorable, as that assigned to Buell. I know that Gen. McClellan expected more important results from it. My impression is that at the time you were assigned to the new Western Department, it had not been determined to re-place Gen. Sherman in Kentucky; but of this I am not certain, because the idea that a command in Kentucky was very desireable, and one in the farther West, very undesireable, had never occurred to me. You constantly speak of being placed in command of only 3000. Now tell me, is not this mere impatience? Have you not known all the while that you are to command four or five times that many?

I have been, and am sincerely your friend; and if, as such, I dare to make a suggestion, I would say you are adopting the best possible way to ruin yourself. "Act well your part, there all the honor lies." He who does *something* at the head of one Regiment, will eclipse him who does *nothing* at the head of a hundred. Your friend as ever,

To Henry W. Halleck

Executive Mansion, Washington, January 1, 1862.
My dear General Halleck: General McClellan is not dangerously ill, as I hope, but would better not to be disturbed with business. I am very anxious that, in case of General Buell's moving toward Nashville, the enemy shall not be greatly re-enforced, and I think there is danger he will be from Columbus. It seems to me that a real or feigned attack

upon Columbus from up-river at the same time would either prevent this or compensate for it by throwing Columbus into our hands. I wrote General Buell a letter similar to this, meaning that he and you shall communicate and act in concert, unless it be your judgment and his that there is no necessity for it. You and he will understand much better than I how to do it. Please do not lose time in this matter. Yours, very truly,

To Don C. Buell

Executive Mansion,
Brig. Gen. Buell   Washington, January 6th, 1862.

My dear Sir   Your despatch of yesterday has been received, and it disappoints and distresses me. I have shown it to Gen. McClellan, who says he will write you to-day. I am not competent to criticise your views; and therefore what I offer is merely in justification of myself. Of the two, I would rather have a point on the Railroad south of Cumberland Gap, than Nashville, first, because it cuts a great artery of the enemies' communication, which Nashville does not, and secondly because it is in the midst of loyal people, who would rally around it, while Nashville is not. Again, I cannot see why the movement on East Tennessee would not be a diversion in your favor, rather than a disadvantage, assuming that a movement towards Nashville is the main object.

But my distress is that our friends in East Tennessee are being hanged and driven to despair, and even now I fear, are thinking of taking rebel arms for the sake of personal protection. In this we lose the most valuable stake we have in the South. My despatch, to which yours is an answer, was sent with the knowledge of Senator Johnson and Representative Maynard of East Tennessee, and they will be upon me to know the answer, which I cannot safely show them. They would despair—possibly resign to go and save their families somehow, or die with them.

I do not intend this to be an order in any sense, but merely, as intimated before, to show you the grounds of my anxiety. Yours very Truly

To Simon Cameron

Private   Executive Mansion,
Dear Sir   Washington, Jan. 11, 1862.

Though I have said nothing hitherto in response to your wish, expressed long since, to resign your seat in the cabinet, I have not been unmindful of it. I have been only unwilling to consent to a change at a time, and under circumstances which might give occasion to misconstruction, and unable, till now to see how such misconstruction could be avoided.

But the desire of Mr. Clay to return home and to offer his services to his country in the field enables me now to gratify your wish, and at the same time evince my personal regard for you, and my confidence in your ability, patriotism, and fidelity to public trust.

I therefore tender to your acceptance, if you still desire to resign your present position, the post of Minister to Russia. Should you accept it, you will bear with you the assurance of my undiminished confidence, of my affectionate esteem, and of my sure expectation that, near the great sovreign whose personal and hereditary friendship for the United States, so much endears him to Americans, you will be able to render services to your country, not less important than those you could render at home. Very sincerely   Your friend

To Don C. Buell

COPY—one also sent to Gen. Halleck.
Brig. Genl. Buell.   Executive Mansion,
My dear Sir: Washington, Jan. 13, 1862.

Your despatch of yesterday is received, in which you say "I have received your letter and Gen. McClellan's; and will, at once devote all my efforts to your views, and his." In the midst of my many cares, I have not seen, or asked to see, Gen. McClellan's letter to you. For my own views, I have not offered, and do not now offer them as orders; and while I am glad to have them respectfully considered, I would blame you to follow them contrary to your own clear judgment—unless I should put them in the form of orders. As to Gen.

McClellan's views, you understand your duty in regard to them better than I do. With this preliminary, I state my general idea of this war to be that we have the *greater* numbers, and the enemy has the *greater* facility of concentrating forces upon points of collision; that we must fail, unless we can find some way of making *our* advantage an over-match for *his*; and that this can only be done by menacing him with superior forces at *different* points, at the *same* time; so that we can safely attack, one, or both, if he makes no change; and if he *weakens* one to *strengthen* the other, forbear to attack the strengthened one, but seize, and hold the weakened one, gaining so much. To illustrate, suppose last summer, when Winchester ran away to re-inforce Mannassas, we had forborne to attack Mannassas, but had seized and held Winchester. I mention this to illustrate, and not to criticise. I did not lose confidence in McDowell, and I think less harshly of Patterson than some others seem to. In application of the general rule I am suggesting, every particular case will have its modifying circumstances, among which the most constantly present, and most difficult to meet, will be the want of perfect knowledge of the enemies' movements. This had it's part in the Bull-Run case; but worse, in that case, was the expiration of the terms of the three months men. Applying the principle to your case, my idea is that Halleck shall menace Columbus, and "down river" generally; while you menace Bowling-Green, and East Tennessee. If the enemy shall concentrate at Bowling-Green, do not retire from his front; yet do not fight him there, either, but seize Columbus and East Tennessee, one or both, left exposed by the concentration at Bowling Green. It is matter of no small anxiety to me and one which I am sure you will not over-look, that the East Tennessee line, is so long, and over so bad a road. Yours very truly

To Henry W. Halleck

                                              Washington, D.C.,
Major-General Halleck: January 15, 1862.
    My dear Sir: This will introduce Gov. G. Koerner, of Illinois, who is my personal friend, and who calls on you at my

particular request. Please open the sealed letter he will hand you before he leaves you and confer with him as to its contents. Yours, very truly,

Executive Mansion,
Major-General Halleck: Washington, January 15, 1862.

My dear Sir: The Germans are true and patriotic, and so far as they have got cross in Missouri it is upon mistake and misunderstanding. Without a knowledge of its contents Governor Koerner, of Illinois, will hand you this letter. He is an educated and talented German gentleman, as true a man as lives. With his assistance you can set everything right with the Germans. I write this without his knowledge, asking him at the same time, by letter, to deliver it. My clear judgment is that, with reference to the German element in your command, you should have Governor Koerner with you; and if agreeable to you and him, I will make him a brigadier-general, so that he can afford to so give his time. He does not wish to command in the field, though he has more military knowledge than many who do. If he goes into the place he will simply be an efficient, zealous, and unselfish assistant to you. I say all this upon intimate personal acquaintance with Governor Koerner. Yours, very truly,

President's General War Order No. 1

President's general⎱ Executive Mansion,
War Order No. 1 ⎰ Washington, January 27, 1862.

Ordered that the 22nd. day of February 1862, be the day for a general movement of the Land and Naval forces of the United States against the insurgent forces.

That especially—

The Army at & about, Fortress Monroe.
The Army of the Potomac.
The Army of Western Virginia
The Army near Munfordsville, Ky.
The Army and Flotilla at Cairo.

And a Naval force in the Gulf of Mexico, be ready
for a movement on that day.

That all other forces, both Land and Naval, with their respective commanders, obey existing orders, for the time, and
be ready to obey additional orders when duly given.

That the Heads of Departments, and especially the Secretaries of War and of the Navy, with all their subordinates; and
the General-in-Chief, with all other commanders and subordinates, of Land and Naval forces, will severally be held to their
strict and full responsibilities, for the prompt execution of this
order.

To George B. McClellan

                                      Executive Mansion,
Major General McClellan   Washington, Feb. 3, 1862.

My dear Sir: You and I have distinct, and different plans for
a movement of the Army of the Potomac—yours to be down
the Chesapeake, up the Rappahannock to Urbana, and across
land to the terminus of the Railroad on the York River—,
mine to move directly to a point on the Railroad South West
of Manassas.

If you will give me satisfactory answers to the following
questions, I shall gladly yield my plan to yours.

1st. Does not your plan involve a greatly larger expenditure
of *time*, and *money* than mine?

2nd. Wherein is a victory *more certain* by your plan than
mine?

3rd. Wherein is a victory *more valuable* by your plan than
mine?

4th. In fact, would it not be *less* valuable, in this, that it
would break no great line of the enemie's communications,
while mine would?

5th. In case of disaster, would not a safe retreat be more
difficult by your plan than by mine? Yours truly

---

1. Suppose the enemy should attack us in force *before* we
reach the Ocoquan, what? In view of the possibility of this,

might it not be safest to have our entire force to move together from above the Ocoquan.

2. Suppose the enemy, in force, shall dispute the crossing of the Ocoquan, what? In view of this, might it not be safest for us to cross the Ocoquan at Colchester rather than at the village of Ocoquan? This would cost the enemy two miles more of travel to meet us, but would, on the contrary, leave us two miles further from our ultimate destination.

3. Suppose we reach Maple valley without an attack, will we not be attacked there, in force, by the enemy marching by the several roads from Manassas? and if so, what?

Stay of Execution for Nathaniel Gordon

Abraham Lincoln,
President of the United States of America,

To all to whom these Presents shall come Greeting:

Whereas, it appears that at a Term of the Circuit Court of the United States of America for the Southern District of New York held in the month of November A.D. 1861, Nathaniel Gordon was indicted and convicted for being engaged in the Slave Trade, and was by the said Court sentenced to be put to death by hanging by the neck, on Friday the 7th. day of February, A.D. 1862;

And whereas, a large number of respectable citizens have earnestly besought me to commute the said sentence of the said Nathaniel Gordon to a term of imprisonment for life, which application I have felt it to be my duty to refuse;

And whereas, it has seemed to me probable that the unsuccessful application made for the commutation of his sentence may have prevented the said Nathaniel Gordon from making the necessary preparation for the awful change which awaits him:

Now, therefore, be it known, that I, Abraham Lincoln, President of the United States of America, have granted and do hereby grant unto him, the said Nathaniel Gordon, a respite of the above recited sentence, until Friday the twenty-first day of February, A.D. 1862, between the hours of twelve o'clock at noon and three o'clock in the afternoon of the said day, when the said sentence shall be executed.

In granting this respite, it becomes my painful duty to admonish the prisoner that, relinquishing all expectation of pardon by Human Authority, he refer himself alone to the mercy of the common God and Father of all men.

In testimony whereof, I have hereunto signed my name and caused the Seal of the United States to be affixed.

Done at the City of Washington, this Fourth day of February A.D. 1862, and of the Independence of the United States the Eighty-sixth.   ABRAHAM LINCOLN.

By the President:

WILLIAM H. SEWARD Secretary of State.

To Henry W. Halleck

Major General Halleck   Executive Mansion,
St. Louis, Mo.   Washington, Feb. 16, 1862

You have Fort Donelson safe, unless Grant shall be overwhelmed from outside, to prevent which latter will, I think, require all the vigilance, energy, and skill of yourself & Buell, acting in full co-operation. Columbus will not get at Grant, but the force from Bowling-Green will. They hold the Railroad from Bowling-Green to within a few miles of Donelson, with the Bridge at Clarksburg undisturbed. It is unsafe to rely that they will not dare to expose Nashville to Buell. A small part of their force can retire slowly towards Nashville, breaking up the Railroad as they go, and keep Buell out of that city twenty days. Mean time Nashville will be abundantly defended by forces from all South & perhaps from here at Manassas. Could not a cavalry force from Gen. Thomas on the upper Cumberland, dash across, almost unresisted, and cut the Railroad at or near Knoxville, Tenn.? In the midst of a bombardment at Donnelson, why could not a Gun-boat run up and destroy the Bridge at Clarksburg? Our success or failure at Donnelson is vastly important; and I beg you to put your soul in the effort. I send a copy to Buell.

Message to Congress

Fellow-citizens of the Senate, and House of Representatives,

I recommend the adoption of a Joint Resolution by your honorable bodies which shall be substantially as follows:

"Resolved that the United States ought to co-operate with any state which may adopt gradual abolishment of slavery, giving to such state pecuniary aid, to be used by such state in it's discretion, to compensate for the inconveniences public and private, produced by such change of system"

If the proposition contained in the resolution does not meet the approval of Congress and the country, there is the end; but if it does command such approval, I deem it of importance that the states and people immediately interested, should be at once distinctly notified of the fact, so that they may begin to consider whether to accept or reject it. The federal government would find it's highest interest in such a measure, as one of the most efficient means of self-preservation. The leaders of the existing insurrection entertain the hope that this government will ultimately be forced to acknowledge the independence of some part of the disaffected region, and that all the slave states North of such part will then say "the Union, for which we have struggled, being already gone, we now choose to go with the Southern section." To deprive them of this hope, substantially ends the rebellion; and the initiation of emancipation completely deprives them of it, as to all the states initiating it. The point is not that *all* the states tolerating slavery would very soon, if at all, initiate emancipation; but that, while the offer is equally made to all, the more Northern shall, by such initiation, make it certain to the more Southern, that in no event, will the former ever join the latter, in their proposed confederacy. I say "initiation" because, in my judgment, gradual, and not sudden emancipation, is better for all. In the mere financial, or pecuniary view, any member of Congress, with the census-tables and Treasury-reports before him, can readily see for himself how very soon the current expenditures of this war would purchase, at fair valuation, all the slaves in any named State. Such a proposition, on the part of

the general government, sets up no claim of a right, by federal authority, to interfere with slavery within state limits, referring, as it does, the absolute control of the subject, in
each case, to the state and it's people, immediately interested. It is proposed as a matter of perfectly free choice with
them.

In the annual message last December, I thought fit to say
"The Union must be preserved; and hence all indispensable
means must be employed." I said this, not hastily, but deliberately. War has been made, and continues to be, an indispensable means to this end. A practical re-acknowledgement
of the national authority would render the war unnecessary,
and it would at once cease. If, however, resistance continues,
the war must also continue; and it is impossible to foresee all
the incidents, which may attend and all the ruin which may
follow it. Such as may seem indispensable, or may obviously
promise great efficiency towards ending the struggle, must
and will come.

The proposition now made, though an offer only, I hope it
may be esteemed no offence to ask whether the pecuniary
consideration tendered would not be of more value to the
States and private persons concerned, than are the institution,
and property in it, in the present aspect of affairs.

While it is true that the adoption of the proposed resolution would be merely initiatory, and not within itself a practical measure, it is recommended in the hope that it would
soon lead to important practical results. In full view of my
great responsibility to my God, and to my country, I earnestly
beg the attention of Congress and the people to the subject.

March 6. 1862.

President's General War Order No. 3

President's General War ⎫   Executive Mansion
Order No. 3   ⎭   Washington, March 8, 1862.

Ordered, that no change of the base of operations of the
Army of the Potomac shall be made without leaving in, and
about Washington, such a force as, in the opinion of the

General-in-chief, and the commanders of all the Army corps, shall leave said City entirely secure.

That not more than two Army corps, (about fifty thousand troops) of said Army of the Potomac, shall be moved *en route* for a new base of operations until the navigation of the Potomac, from Washington to the Chesapeake bay shall be freed from enemies batteries and other obstructions, or, until the President shall hereafter give express permission.

That any movement, as aforesaid, *en route* for a new base of operations, which may be ordered by the General-in-chief, & which may be intended to move upon the Chesapeake-bay, shall begin to move upon the bay as early as the 18th. day of March Inst.; and the General-in-chief shall be responsible that it so move as early as that day.

Ordered that the Army and Navy co-operate in an immediate effort to capture the enemies batteries upon the Potomac between Washington and the Chesapeake-bay.

To Henry J. Raymond

COPY.

Private   Executive Mansion,
Hon. Henry J. Raymond: Washington, March 9, 1862.

My dear Sir: I am grateful to the New-York Journals, and not less so to the Times than to others, for their kind notices of the late special Message to Congress. Your paper, however, intimates that the proposition, though well-intentioned, must fail on the score of expense. I do hope you will reconsider this. Have you noticed the facts that less than one half-day's cost of this war would pay for all the slaves in Delaware, at four hundred dollars per head?—that eighty-seven days cost of this war would pay for all in Delaware, Maryland, District of Columbia, Kentucky, and Missouri at the same price? Were those states to take the step, do you doubt that it would shorten the war more than eighty seven days, and thus be an actual saving of expense. Please look at these things, and consider whether there should not be another article in the Times? Yours very truly,

Speech to a Massachusetts Delegation, Washington, D.C.

I thank you, Mr. TRAIN, for your kindness in presenting me with this truly elegant and highly creditable specimen of the handiwork of the mechanics of your State of Massachusetts, and I beg of you to express my hearty thanks to the donors. It displays a perfection of workmanship which I really wish I had time to acknowledge in more fitting words, and I might then follow your idea that it is suggestive, for it is evidently expected that a good deal of whipping is to be done. But, as we meet here socially, let us not think only of whipping rebels, or of those who seem to think only of whipping negroes, but of those pleasant days which it is to be hoped are in store for us, when, seated behind a good pair of horses, we can crack our whips and drive through a peaceful, happy and prosperous land. With this idea, gentlemen, I must leave you for my business duties.

March 13, 1862

To James A. McDougall

Hon. James A. McDougal   Executive Mansion
U.S. Senate   Washington, March 14, 1862

My dear Sir: As to the expensiveness of the plan of gradual emancipation with compensation, proposed in the late Message, please allow me one or two brief suggestions.

Less than one half-day's cost of this war would pay for all the slaves in Delaware at four hundred dollars per head:

Thus, all the slaves in Delaware,
by the Census of 1860, are.   1798
                                             400
                                    _____
Cost of the slaves, ... $ 719,200.
One day's cost of the war . . . . "2,000,000.

Again, less than eighty seven days cost of this war would, at the same price, pay for all in Delaware, Maryland, District of Columbia, Kentucky, and Missouri.

Thus, slaves in Delaware	1798
" " Maryland	87,188
" " Dis. of Col.	3,181
" " Kentucky	225,490
" " Missouri	114,965
	432,622
	400

Cost of the slaves . . . .$ 173,048,800
Eightyseven days' cost of the war . . . . ."174,000,000.

Do you doubt that taking the initiatory steps on the part of those states and this District, would shorten the war more than eightyseven days, and thus be an actual saving of expense?

A word as to the *time* and *manner* of incurring the expence. Suppose, for instance, a State devises and adopts a system by which the institution absolutely ceases therein by a named day—say January 1st. 1882. Then, let the sum to be paid to such state by the United States, be ascertained by taking from the Census of 1860, the number of slaves within the state, and multiplying that number by four hundred—the United States to pay such sum to the state in twenty equal annual instalments, in six per cent. bonds of the United States.

The sum thus given, as to *time* and *manner*, I think would not be half as onerous, as would be an equal sum, raised *now*, for the indefinite prossecution of the war; but of this you can judge as well as I.

I inclose a Census-table for your convenience. Yours very truly

To Samuel B. Tobey

Executive Mansion,
Dr. Samuel Boyd Tobey: Washington, March 19, 1862.

My dear Sir: A domestic affliction, of which doubtless you are informed, has delayed me so long in making acknowledgment for the very kind and appropriate letter, signed, on behalf, and by direction of a Meeting of the Representatives of the Society of Friends for New-England, held at

Providence, Rhode Island the 8th. of second month 1862, by Samuel Boyce, clerk, and presented to me by yourself and associates.

Engaged, as I am, in a great war, I fear it will be difficult for the world to understand how fully I appreciate the principles of peace, inculcated in this letter, and everywhere, by the Society of Friends. Grateful to the good people you represent for their prayers in behalf of our common country, I look forward hopefully to an early end of war, and return of peace. Your obliged friend

To Horace Greeley

Private

Hon. Horace Greeley—   Executive Mansion,
My dear Sir: Washington, March 24, 1862.

Your very kind letter of the 16th. to Mr. Colfax, has been shown me by him. I am grateful for the generous sentiments and purposes expressed towards the administration. Of course I am anxious to see the policy proposed in the late special message, go forward; but you have advocated it from the first, so that I need to say little to you on the subject. If I were to suggest anything it would be that as the North are already for the measure, we should urge it *persuasively*, and not *menacingly*, upon the South. I am a little uneasy about the abolishment of slavery in this District, not but I would be glad to see it abolished, but as to the time and manner of doing it. If some one or more of the border-states would move fast, I should greatly prefer it; but if this can not be in a reasonable time, I would like the bill to have the three main features—gradual—compensation—and vote of the people—I do not talk to members of congress on the subject, except when they ask me. I am not prepared to make any suggestion about confiscation. I may drop you a line hereafter. Yours truly

To George B. McClellan

Private

Major General McClellan   Executive Mansion,
My dear Sir   Washington, March 31, 1862.

    This morning I felt constrained to order Blenker's Division to Fremont; and I write this to assure you that I did so with great pain, understanding that you would wish it otherwise. If you could know the full pressure of the case, I am confident you would justify it—even beyond a mere acknowledgment that the Commander-in-chief, may order what he pleases. Yours very truly

To George B. McClellan

Major General McClellan.   Washington,
My dear Sir.   April 9. 1862

    Your despatches complaining that you are not properly sustained, while they do not offend me, do pain me very much.

    Blencker's Division was withdrawn from you before you left here; and you knew the pressure under which I did it, and, as I thought, acquiesced in it—certainly not without reluctance.

    After you left, I ascertained that less than twenty thousand unorganized men, without a single field battery, were all you designed to be left for the defence of Washington, and Manassas Junction; and part of this even, was to go to Gen. Hooker's old position. Gen. Banks' corps, once designed for Manassas Junction, was diverted, and tied up on the line of Winchester and Strausburg, and could not leave it without again exposing the upper Potomac, and the Baltimore and Ohio Railroad. This presented, (or would present, when McDowell and Sumner should be gone) a great temptation to the enemy to turn back from the Rappahanock, and sack Washington. My explicit order that Washington should, by the judgment of *all* the commanders of Army corps, be left entirely secure, had been neglected. It was precisely this that drove me to detain McDowell.

    I do not forget that I was satisfied with your arrangement

to leave Banks at Mannassas Junction; but when that arrangement was broken up, and *nothing* was substituted for it, of
course I was not satisfied. I was constrained to substitute
something for it myself. And now allow me to ask "Do you
really think I should permit the line from Richmond, *via*
Mannassas Junction, to this city to be entirely open, except
what resistance could be presented by less than twenty thousand unorganized troops?" This is a question which the country will not allow me to evade.

There is a curious mystery about the *number* of the troops
now with you. When I telegraphed you on the 6th. saying
you had over a hundred thousand with you, I had just obtained from the Secretary of War, a statement, taken as he
said, from your own returns, making 108,000 then with you,
and *en route* to you. You now say you will have but 85,000,
when all *en route* to you shall have reached you. How can the
discrepancy of 23,000 be accounted for?

As to Gen. Wool's command, I understand it is doing for
you precisely what a like number of your own would have to
do, if that command was away.

I suppose the whole force which has gone forward for you,
is with you by this time; and if so, I think it is the precise
time for you to strike a blow. By delay the enemy will relatively gain upon you—that is, he will gain faster, by
fortifications and *re-inforcements*, than you can by re-inforcements alone.

And, once more let me tell you, it is indispensable to *you*
that you strike a blow. *I* am powerless to help this. You will
do me the justice to remember I always insisted, that going
down the Bay in search of a field, instead of fighting at or
near Mannassas, was only shifting, and not surmounting, a
difficulty—that we would find the same enemy, and the same,
or equal, intrenchments, at either place. The country will not
fail to note—is now noting—that the present hesitation to
move upon an intrenched enemy, is but the story of Manassas
repeated.

I beg to assure you that I have never written you, or spoken to you, in greater kindness of feeling than now, nor with
a fuller purpose to sustain you, so far as in my most anxious
judgment, I consistently can. *But you must act.* Yours very truly

To Richard Yates and William Butler

Hon. R. Yates, & Wm. Butler   Washington,
Springfield, Ills.   April 10. 1862

I fully appreciate Gen. Pope's splendid achievements with their invaluable results; but you must know that Major Generalships in the Regular Army, are not as plenty as blackberries.

Message to Congress

Fellow citizens of the Senate, and House of Representatives.

The Act entitled "An Act for the release of certain persons held to service, or labor in the District of Columbia" has this day been approved, and signed.

I have never doubted the constitutional authority of congress to abolish slavery in this District; and I have ever desired to see the national capital freed from the institution in some satisfactory way. Hence there has never been, in my mind, any question upon the subject, except the one of expediency, arising in view of all the circumstances. If there be matters within and about this act, which might have taken a course or shape, more satisfactory to my judgment, I do not attempt to specify them. I am gratified that the two principles of compensation, and colonization, are both recognized, and practically applied in the act.

In the matter of compensation, it is provided that claims may be presented within ninety days from the passage of the act "but not thereafter"; and there is no saving for minors, femes-covert, insane, or absent persons. I presume this is an omission by mere over-sight, and I recommend that it be supplied by an amendatory or supplemental act.

April 16. 1862.

To George B. McClellan

(CYPHER)

Major Gen. McClellan   Executive Mansion,
Near York-Town, Va.   Washington, May 1, 1862.

Your call for Parrott guns from Washington alarms me—chiefly because it argues indefinite procrastination. Is anything to be done?

To George B. McClellan

Major General McClellan.   Fort Monroe, Va.
My dear Sir: May 9, 1862.

I have just assisted the Secretary of War in framing the part of a despatch to you, relating to Army Corps, which despatch of course will have reached you long before this will. I wish to say a few words to you privately on this subject. I ordered the Army Corps organization not only on the unanimous opinion of the twelve Generals whom you had selected and assigned as Generals of Division, but also on the unanimous opinion of every *military man* I could get an opinion from, and every modern military book, yourself only excepted. Of course, I did not, on my own judgment, pretend to understand the subject. I now think it indispensable for you to know how your struggle against it is received in quarters which we cannot entirely disregard. It is looked upon as merely an effort to pamper one or two pets, and to persecute and degrade their supposed rivals. I have had no word from Sumner, Heintzelman, or Keyes. The commanders of these Corps are of course the three highest officers with you, but I am constantly told that you have no consultation or communication with them; that you consult and communicate with nobody but General Fitz John Porter, and perhaps General Franklin. I do not say these complaints are true or just; but at all events it is proper you should know of their existence. Do the Commanders of Corps disobey your orders in any thing?

When you relieved General Hamilton of his command the other day, you thereby lost the confidence of at least one of your best friends in the Senate. And here let me say, not as applicable to you personally, that Senators and Representatives speak of me in their places as they please, without question; and that officers of the army must cease addressing insulting letters to them for taking no greater liberty with them.

But, to return, are you strong enough—are you strong enough, even with my help—to set your foot upon the necks of Sumner, Heintzelman, and Keyes all at once? This is a practical and very serious question for you.

The success of your army and the cause of the country are the same; and of course I only desire the good of the cause. Yours truly

Proclamation Revoking General Hunter's Emancipation Order

BY THE PRESIDENT OF THE UNITED STATES OF AMERICA.

A PROCLAMATION.

Whereas there appears in the public prints, what purports to be a proclamation, of Major General Hunter, in the words and figures following, towit:

> *Headquarters Department of the South,* }
> Hilton Head, S.C., May 9, 1862. }
>
> General Orders No. 11.—The three States of Georgia, Florida and South Carolina, comprising the military department of the south, having deliberately declared themselves no longer under the protection of the United States of America, and having taken up arms against the said United States, it becomes a military necessity to declare them under martial law. This was accordingly done on the 25th day of April, 1862. Slavery and martial law in a free country are altogether incompatible; the persons in these three States—Georgia, Florida and South Carolina—heretofore held as slaves, are therefore declared forever free.
>
> DAVID HUNTER,
>
> (Official)   Major General Commanding.
>
> ED. W. SMITH, Acting Assistant Adjutant General.

And whereas the same is producing some excitement, and misunderstanding: therefore

I, Abraham Lincoln, president of the United States, proclaim and declare, that the government of the United States, had no knowledge, information, or belief, of an intention on the part of General Hunter to issue such a proclamation; nor has it yet, any authentic information that the document is genuine. And further, that neither General Hunter, nor any other commander, or person, has been authorized by the Government of the United States, to make proclamations declaring the slaves of any State free; and that the supposed proclamation, now in question, whether genuine or false, is altogether void, so far as respects such declaration.

I further make known that whether it be competent for me, as Commander-in-Chief of the Army and Navy, to declare the Slaves of any state or states, free, and whether at any time, in any case, it shall have become a necessity indispensable to the maintenance of the government, to exercise such supposed power, are questions which, under my responsibility, I reserve to myself, and which I can not feel justified in leaving to the decision of commanders in the field. These are totally different questions from those of police regulations in armies and camps.

On the sixth day of March last, by a special message, I recommended to Congress the adoption of a joint resolution to be substantially as follows:

> *Resolved,* That the United States ought to co-operate with any State which may adopt a gradual abolishment of slavery, giving to such State pecuniary aid, to be used by such State in its discretion to compensate for the inconveniences, public and private, produced by such change of system.

The resolution, in the language above quoted, was adopted by large majorities in both branches of Congress, and now stands an authentic, definite, and solemn proposal of the nation to the States and people most immediately interested in the subject matter. To the people of those states I now earnestly appeal. I do not argue. I beseech you to make the arguments for yourselves. You can not if you would, be blind to the signs of the times. I beg of you a calm and enlarged consideration of them, ranging, if it may be, far above personal and partizan politics. This proposal makes common cause for a common object, casting no reproaches upon any. It acts not the pharisee. The change it contemplates would come gently as the dews of heaven, not rending or wrecking anything. Will you not embrace it? So much good has not been done, by one effort, in all past time, as, in the providence of God, it is now your high previlege to do. May the vast future not have to lament that you have neglected it.

In witness whereof, I have hereunto set my hand, and caused the seal of the United States to be affixed.

Done at the City of Washington this nineteenth day of May, in the year of our Lord one thousand eight hundred and sixty-two, and of the Independence of the United States the eighty-sixth.   ABRAHAM LINCOLN.

By the President:

WILLIAM H. SEWARD, Secretary of State.

To George B. McClellan

Washington City, D C   May 21, 1862

Major General McClellan: Your long despatch of yesterday just received. You will have just such control of Gen. McDowell and his force as you therein indicate. McDowell can reach you by land sooner than he could get aboard of boats if the boats were ready at Frederick'sburg,—unless his march shall be resisted, in which case, the force resisting him, will certainly not be confronting you at Richmond. By land he can reach you in five days after starting, whereas by water he would not reach you in two weeks, judging by past experience. Franklin's single Division did not reach you in ten days after I ordered it.

To Henry W. Halleck

Major Genl. Halleck   Washington City, D.C.
Near Corinth, Tenn.   May 24, 7½ P.M. 1862

Several despatches from Assistant Secretary Scott, and one from Gov. Morton, asking re-inforcements for you have been received. I beg you to be assured we do the best we can. I mean to cast no blame when I tell you each of our commanders along our line from Richmond to Corinth supposes himself to be confronted by numbers superior to his own. Under this pressure we thinned the line on the upper Potomac until yesterday it was broken, at heavy loss to us, and Gen. Banks put in great peril, out of which he is not yet extricated, and may be actually captured. We need men to repair this breach, and have them not at hand.

My dear general, I feel justified to rely very much on you. I believe you and the brave officers and men with you, can and will get the victory at Corinth.

To George B. McClellan

Washington City, D.C.

Major General McClellan   May 24. 1862

I left Gen. McDowell's camp at dark last evening. Shields' command is there but is so worn that he can not move before Monday morning the (26th.) twenty sixth. We have so thinned our line to get troops for other places that it was broken yesterday at Front-Royal with a probable loss to us of a Regiment infantry, two companies of cavalry, putting Banks in some peril. The enemies forces under Gen. Anderson now opposing Gen. McDowell's advance have, as their line of supply and retreat, the Road to Richmond. If in conjunction with McDowell's movement against Anderson you could send a force from your right to cut off the enemies supplies from Richmond, preserve the Rail Road bridges across the two forks of the Pamunkey and intercept the enemies retreat you will prevent the army now opposed to you from receiving an accession of numbers of nearly fifteen thousand men— and if you succeed in saving the bridges you will secure a line of Rail Road for supplies in addition to the one you now have. Can you not do this almost as well as not, while you are building the Chicahomany bridges? McDowell and Shields both say they can, and positively will, move monday morning. I wish you to move cautiously and safely. You will have command of Gen. McDowell after he joins you, precisely as you indicate in your long despatch to me of the twentyfirst.

To George B. McClellan

Washington City, D.C.

Major Gen. McClellan   May 24. 4. P.M. 1862

In consequence of Gen. Banks' critical position I have been compelled to suspend Gen. McDowell's movement to join you. The enemy are making a desperate push upon Harper's Ferry, and we are trying to throw Fremont's force & part of McDowell's in their rear.

To Irvin McDowell

Major Gen McDowell   Washington City, D.C.
Fredericksburg   24 May 1862

Gen Fremont has been ordered by Telegraph to move from Franklin on Harrisonburg to relieve Gen Banks and capture or destroy Jackson & Ewell's force.

You are instructed laying aside for the present the movement on Richmond to put twenty thousand men (20000) in motion at once for the Shenandoah moving on the line or in advance of the line of the Manassas Gap R Road. Your object will be to capture the forces of Jackson & Ewell, either in cooperation with Gen Fremont or in case want of supplies or of transportation interferes with his movement, it is believed that the force with which you move will be sufficient to accomplish the object alone.

The information thus far received here makes it probable that if the enemy operates actively against Gen Banks you will not be able to count upon much assistance from him but may even have to release him.

Reports received this moment are that Banks is fighting with Ewell (8) Eight miles from Winchester.

To Salmon P. Chase

Secretary Chase   Washington City, D.C.
Fredericksburg, Va.   May 25. 1862

It now appears that Banks got safely in to Winchester last night, and is, this morning, retreating on Harper's Ferry. This justifies the inference that he is pressed by numbers superior to his own. I think it not improbable that Ewell   Jackson and Johnson, are pouring through the gap they made day-before yesterday at Front-Royal, making a dash Northward. It will be a very valuable, and very honorable service for Gen. McDowell to cut them off. I hope he will put all possible energy and speed into the effort.

To George B. McClellan

United States Military Telegraph
War Department, Washington, D.C.
To/   May 25, 1862.

General McClellan: The enemy is moving North in sufficient force to drive Banks before him in precisely what force we can not tell. He is also threatening Leesburgh and Geary on the Manassas Gap Rail Road from both north and south in precisely what force we can not tell. I think the movement is a general and concerted one, such as could not be if he was acting upon the purpose of a very desperate defence of Richmond. I think the time is near when you must either attack Richmond or give up the job and come to the defence of Washington. Let me hear from you instantly.

To George B. McClellan

(Send in Cypher).   War Department
                                  Washington City, D.C.
Major Gen. McClellan   May 25. 1862 8½ P.M.

Your despatch received. Banks was at Strausburg with about six-thousand men, Shields having been taken from him to swell a column for McDowell to aid you at Richmond, and the rest of his force scattered at various places. On the 23rd. a rebel force of seven to ten thousand fell upon one regiment and two companies guarding the bridge at Front-Royal, destroying it entirely, crossed the Shenandoah, and on the 24th. (yesterday) pushed to get North of Banks on the Road to Winchester. Banks ran a race with them, beating them into Winchester yesterday evening. This morning a battle ensued between the two forces in which Banks was beaten back into full retreat towards Martinsburg, and probably is broken up into a total route. Geary, on the Manassas Gap R.R. just now reports that Jackson is now near Front-Royal with ten thousand following up & supporting as I understand, the force now pursuing Banks. Also that another force of ten thousand is near Orleans following on in the same direction. Stripped bare, as we are here, it will be all we can do to prevent them crossing the Potomac at Harper's Ferry, or above. We have about twenty thousand of McDowell's force moving back to the vicinity of Front Royal; and Gen. Fremont, who was at Franklin, is moving to Harrisonburg, both these movements intended to get in the enemies rear. One more of McDowells Brigades is ordered through here to Harper's Ferry. The rest of his force remains, for the present, at Fredericksburg. We are sending such regiments and dribs from here and Baltimore, as we can spare, to Harper's Ferry, supplying their places, in some sort, by calling in Militia from the adjacent States. We also have eighteen cannon on the road to Harper's Ferry of which arm, there is not a single one yet at that point. This is now our situation. If McDowell's force was now beyond our reach, we should be utterly helpless. Apprehension of something like this, and no unwillingness to sustain you, has always been my reason for withholding McDowells force from you. Please understand this, and do the best you can with the force you have.

To the Senate and House of Representatives

To the Senate and House of Representatives:

The insurrection which is yet existing in the United States, and aims at the overthrow of the federal Constitution and the Union, was clandestinely prepared during the winter of 1860 and 1861, and assumed an open organization in the form of a treasonable provisional government at Montgomery, in Alabama, on the 18th day of February, 1861. On the 12th day of April, 1861, the insurgents committed the flagrant act of civil war by the bombardment and capture of Fort Sumter, which cut off the hope of immediate conciliation. Immediately afterwards all the roads and avenues to this city were obstructed, and the capital was put into the condition of a siege. The mails in every direction were stopped, and the lines of telegraph cut off by the insurgents, and military and naval forces, which had been called out by the government for the defence of Washington, were prevented from reaching the city by organized and combined treasonable resistance in the State of Maryland. There was no adequate and effective organization for the public defence. Congress had indefinitely adjourned. There was no time to convene them. It became necessary for me to choose whether, using only the existing means, agencies, and processes which Congress had provided, I should let the government fall at once into ruin, or whether, availing myself of the broader powers conferred by the Constitution in cases of insurrection, I would make an effort to save it with all its blessings for the present age and for posterity.

I thereupon summoned my constitutional advisers, the heads of all the departments, to meet on Sunday, the 20th day of April, 1861, at the office of the Navy Department, and then and there, with their unanimous concurrence, I directed that an armed revenue cutter should proceed to sea, to afford protection to the commercial marine, and especially the California treasure ships then on their way to this coast. I also directed the commandant of the navy yard at Boston to purchase or charter, and arm as quickly as possible, five steamships, for purposes of public defence. I directed the commandant of the navy yard at Philadelphia to purchase, or charter and arm, an equal number for the same purpose. I directed the commandant at New York to purchase, or charter and arm, an equal number. I directed Commander Gillis to purchase, or charter and arm, and put to sea two other vessels. Similar directions were given to Commodore Du-Pont, with a view to the opening of passages by water to and from the capital. I directed the several officers to take the advice and obtain the aid and efficient services in the matter of his excellency Edwin D. Morgan, the governor of New York, or, in his absence, George D. Morgan, William M. Evarts, R. M. Blatchford, and Moses H. Grinnell, who were, by my directions, especially empowered by the Secretary of the Navy to act for his department in that crisis, in matters pertaining to the forwarding of troops and supplies for the public defence.

On the same occasion I directed that Governor Morgan and Alexander Cummings, of the city of New York, should be authorized by the Secretary of War, Simon Cameron, to make all necessary arrangements for the transportation of troops and munitions of war, in aid and assistance of the officers of the army of the United States, until communication by mails and telegraph should be completely re-established between the cities of Washington and New York. No security was required to be given by them, and either of them was authorized to act in case of inability to consult with the other.

On the same occasion I authorized and directed the Secretary of the Treasury to advance, without requiring security, two millions of dollars of public money to John A. Dix, George Opdyke, and Richard M. Blatchford, of New York, to be used by them in meeting such requisitions as should be directly consequent upon the military and naval measures necessary for the defence and support of the government, requiring them only to act without compensation, and to report their transactions when duly called upon.

The several departments of the government at that time contained so large a number of disloyal persons that it would have been impossible to provide safely, through official agents only, for the performance of the duties thus confided to citizens favorably known for their ability, loyalty, and patriotism.

The several orders issued upon these occurrences were transmitted by private messengers, who pursued a circuitous way to the seaboard cities, inland, across the States of Pennsylvania and Ohio and the northern lakes. I believe that by these and other similar measures taken in that crisis, some of which were without any authority of law, the government was saved from overthrow. I am not aware that a dollar of the public funds thus confided without authority of law to unofficial persons was either lost or wasted, although apprehensions of such misdirection occurred to me as objections to those extraordinary proceedings, and were necessarily overruled.

I recall these transactions now because my attention has been directed to a resolution which was passed by the House of Representatives on the 30th day of last month, which is in these words:

"*Resolved,* That Simon Cameron, late Secretary of War, by investing Alexander Cummings with the control of large sums of the public money, and authority to purchase military supplies without restriction, without requiring from him any guarantee for the faithful performance of his duties, when the services of competent public officers were available, and by involving the government in a vast number of contracts with persons not legitimately engaged in the business pertaining to the subject-matter of such contracts, especially in the purchase of arms for future delivery, has adopted a policy highly injurious to the public service, and deserves the censure of the House."

Congress will see that I should be wanting equally in candor and in justice if I should leave the censure expressed in this resolution to rest exclusively or chiefly upon Mr. Cameron. The same sentiment is unanimously entertained by the heads of departments, who participated in the proceedings which the House of Representatives has censured. It is due to Mr. Cameron to say that, although he fully approved the proceedings, they were not moved nor suggested by himself, and that not only the President but all the other heads of departments were at least equally responsible with him for whatever error, wrong, or fault was committed in the premises.

Washington, May 26, 1862.

To Irvin McDowell

Gen. McDowell   Washington,
Mannassas Junction   May 28. 1862. 4. P.M.

You say Gen. Geary's scouts report that they find no enemy this side of the Blue Ridge. Neither do I. Have *they* been *to* the Blue Ridge looking for them?

To George B. McClellan

Washington City, D.C.
Maj. Gen. McClellan   May 28, 1862. 8.40 P.M.

I am very glad of Gen. F. J. Porter's victory. Still, if it was a total rout of the enemy, I am puzzled to know why the Richmond and Fredericksburg Railroad was not seized. Again, as you say you have *all* the Railroads but the Richmond and Fredericksburg, I am puzzled to see how, lacking that, you can have any, except the scrap from Richmond to West-Point. The scrap of the Virginia Central from Richmond to Hanover Junction, without more, is simply nothing.

That the whole force of the enemy is concentrating in Richmond, I think can not be certainly known to you or me. Saxton, at Harper's Ferry, informs us that a large force (supposed to be Jackson's and Ewells) forced his advance from Charlestown to-day. Gen. King telegraphs us from Frederick'sburg that contrabands give certain information that fifteen thousand left Hanover Junction monday morning to re-inforce Jackson. I am painfully impressed with the importance of the struggle before you; and I shall aid you all I can consistently with my view of due regard to all points.

To Edwin M. Stanton

War Department
Hon. Sec. of War.   Washington City, D.C.
My dear Sir   June 5. 1862

Herewith I return you the papers in relation to the proposed re-appointment of William Kellogg, Jr. to a Cadetship. Upon Gen. Totten's statement of the case I think it is natural that he should feel as he expresses himself. And yet the case comes upon me in the very strongest way to be painful to me. Hon. William Kellogg, the father, is not only a member of Congress from my state, but he is my personal friend of more than twenty years' standing, and of whom I had many personal kindnesses. This matter touches him very deeply—the feelings of a father for a child—as he thinks, all the future of his child. I can not be the instrument to crush his heart. According to strict rule he has the right to make the re-nomination. Let the appointment be made. It needs not to become a precedent. Hereafter let no resignation be accepted under demerit amounting to cause for dismissal, unless upon express stipulation in writing that the cadet resigning shall not be re-nominated. In this I mean no censure upon Gen. Totten; and although I have marked this note *"private"* I am quite willing for him to see it. Yours truly

To John C. Frémont

                                                   War Department,
                                           Washington City, D.C.,
Major-General Frémont: June 15, 1862.

My Dear Sir: Your letter of the 12th, by Colonel Zagonyi, is just received. In answer to the principal part of it I repeat the substance of an order of the 8th and one or two telegraphic despatches sent you since.

We have no indefinite power of sending re-enforcements; so that we are compelled rather to consider the proper disposal of the forces we have than of those we could wish to have. We may be able to send you some dribs by degrees, but I do not believe we can do more. As you alone beat Jackson last Sunday I argue that you are stronger than he is to-day, unless he has been re-enforced; and that he cannot have been materially re-enforced, because such re-enforcement could only have come from Richmond, and he is much more likely to go to Richmond than Richmond is to come to him. Neither is very likely. I think Jackson's game—his assigned work—now is to magnify the accounts of his numbers and reports of his movements, and thus by constant alarms keep three or four times as many of our troops away from Richmond as his own force amounts to. Thus he helps his friends at Richmond three or four times as much as if he were there. Our game is not to allow this. Accordingly, by the order of the 8th, I directed you to halt at Harrisonburg, rest your force, and get it well in hand, the objects being to guard against Jackson's returning by the same route to the Upper Potomac, over which you have just driven him out, and at the same time give some protection against a raid into West Virginia. Already I have given you discretion to occupy Mount Jackson instead, if, on full consideration, you think best. I do not believe Jackson will attack you, but certainly he cannot attack you by surprise; and if he comes upon you in superior force you have but to notify us, fall back cautiously, and Banks will join you in due time. But while we know not whether Jackson will move at all, or by what route, we cannot safely put you and Banks both on the Strasburg line, and leave no force on the Front Royal line, the very line upon which he prosecuted his late raid. The true policy is to place one of you on one line and the other on the other, in such positions that you can unite on either once you actually find Jackson moving upon it. And this is precisely what we are doing. This protects that part of our frontier, so to speak, and liberates McDowell to go to the assistance of McClellan. I have arranged this, and am very unwilling to have it deranged. While you have only asked for Sigel I have spoken only of Banks, and this because Sigel's force is now the principal part of Banks's force.

About transferring General Schenck's command, the purchase of supplies, and the promotion and appointment of officers mentioned in your letter, I will consult with the Secretary of War to-morrow. Yours, truly,

To George B. McClellan

War Department
Washington City, D.C.

Major General McClellan   June 15, 1862

My dear Sir: The night between your two late battles of Saturday and Sunday, I went earnestly to work to find a way of putting Gen. Wool's force under your control without wounding any one's feelings. But after all, Gen. Dix was a little hurt at being taken from an independent command and put in a dependent one. I could not help this without giving up the principal object of the move. So soon as you can, (which I do not expect is yet,) I wish you to give me the benefit of your suggestions as to how an independent command can be given him without detriment.

The Secretary of War has turned over to me your despatch about sending McDowell to you by water, instead of by land. I now fear he can not get to you either way in time. Shields' Division has got so terribly out of shape, out at elbows, and out at toes, that it will require a long time to get it in again. I expect to see McDowell within a day or two, when I will again talk with him about the mode of moving.

McCall's Division has nearly or quite reached you by now. This, with what you get from Gen. Wool's old command, and the new regiments sent you, must give you an increase since the late battles of over twenty thousand. Doubtless the battles and other causes have decreased you half as much in the same time; but then the enemy have lost as many in the same way.

I believe I would come and see you, were it not that I fear my presence might divert you and the army from more important matters. Yours truly

To John C. Frémont

"Cypher"

Major General Fremont   Washington City, D.C.
Mount Jackson, Va.   June 16, 1862

Your despatch of yesterday reminding me of a supposed understanding that I would furnish you a corps of thirty five thousand men, and asking of me "the fulfillment of this understanding" is received. I am ready to come to a fair settlement of accounts with you on the fulfillment of understandings.

Early in March last, when I assigned you to the command of the Mountain Department, I did tell you I would give you all the force I could, and that I hoped to make it reach thirty five thousand. You, at the same time told me that, within a reasonable time, you would seize the Railroad at, or East of, Knoxville, Tenn. if you could. There was then in the Department a force supposed to be twentyfive thousand—the exact number as well known to you as to me. After looking about two or three days you called and distinctly told me that if I would add the Blecker Division to the force already in the Department, you would undertake the job. The Blecker division contained ten thousand; and at the expense of great dissatisfaction to Gen. McClellan, I took it from his army, and gave it to you. My promise was litterally fulfilled. I had given you all I could, and I had given you very nearly if not quite thirtyfive thousand.

Now for yours. On the 23rd. of May, largely over two months afterwards, you were at Franklin Va, not within three hundred miles of Knoxville, nor within eighty miles of any part of the Railroad East of it—and not moving forward, but telegraphing here that you could not move for lack of everything. Now, do not misunderstand me. I do not say you have not done all you could. I presume you met unexpected difficulties; and I beg you to believe that as surely as you have done your best, so have I. I have not the power now to fill up your corps to thirtyfive thousand. I am not demanding of you to do the work of thirtyfive thousand. I am only asking of you to stand cautiously on the defensive, get your force in order, and give such protection as you can to the valley of the Shenandoah, and to Western Virginia. Have you received the orders? and will you act upon them?

To Carl Schurz

Brigadier General Schurz. Washington City, D.C.
Mount Jackson, Va. June 16, 1862

Your long letter is received. The information you give is valuable. You say it is fortunate that Fremont did not intercept Jackson—that Jackson had the superior force, and would have overwhelmed him. If this is so, how happened it that Fremont fairly fought and worsted him on the 8th.? Or, is the account that he did fight and worst him, false, and fabricated?

Both Gen. Fremont and you speak of Jackson having beaten Shields. By our accounts, he did not beat Shields. He had no engagement with Shields. He did meet, and drive back with disaster, about two thousand of Shields' advance, till they were met by an additional Brigade of Shields, when Jackson himself turned and retreated. Shields himself, and more than half his force, were not nearer than twenty miles of any of it.

Remarks at Jersey City, New Jersey

When birds and animals are looked at through a fog they are seen to disadvantage, and so it might be with you if I were to attempt to tell you why I went to see Gen. Scott. I can only say that my visit to West Point did not have the importance which has been attached to it; but it concerned matters that you understand quite as well as if I were to tell you all about them. Now, I can only remark that it had nothing whatever to do with making or unmaking any General in the country. [Laughter and applause.] The Secretary of War, you know, holds a pretty tight rein on the Press, so that they shall not tell more than they ought to, and I'm afraid that if I blab too much he might draw a tight rein on me.

June 24, 1862

To George B. McClellan

Washington, June 26, 1862.

Major-General McClellan: Your three dispatches of yesterday in relation to the affair, ending with the statement that you completely succeeded in making your point, are very gratifying. The later one of 6:15 p.m., suggesting the probability of your being overwhelmed by 200,000, and talking of where the responsibility will belong, pains me very much. I give you all I can, and act on the presumption that you will do the best you can with what you have, while you continue, ungenerously I think, to assume that I could give you more if I would. I have omitted and shall omit no opportunity to send you reenforcements whenever I possibly can.

To George B. McClellan

Washington City, D.C.

Major Gen. McClellan   June 28– 1862

Save your Army at all events. Will send re-inforcements as fast as we can. Of course they can not reach you to-day, to-morrow, or next day. I have not said you were ungenerous for saying you needed re-inforcement. I thought you were ungenerous in assuming that I did not send them as fast as I could. I feel any misfortune to you and your Army quite as keenly as you feel it yourself. If you have had a drawn battle, or a repulse, it is the price we pay for the enemy not being in Washington. We protected Washington, and the enemy concentrated on you; had we stripped Washington, he would have been upon us before the troops sent could have got to you. Less than a week ago you notified us that re-inforcements were leaving Richmond to come in front of us. It is the nature of the case, and neither you or the government that is to blame. Please tell at once the present condition and aspect of things.

P.S. Gen. Pope thinks if you fall back, it would be much better towards York River, than towards the James. As Pope now has charge of the Capital, please confer with him through the telegraph.

To William H. Seward

Hon. W. H. Seward   Executive Mansion
My dear Sir   June 28. 1862.

My view of the present condition of the War is about as follows:

The evacuation of Corinth, and our delay by the flood in the Chicahominy, has enabled the enemy to concentrate too much force in Richmond for McClellan to successfully attack. In fact there soon will be no substantial rebel force any where else. But if we send all the force from here to McClellan, the enemy will, before we can know of it, send a force from Richmond and take Washington. Or, if a large part of the Western Army be brought here to McClellan, they will let us have Richmond, and retake Tennessee, Kentucky, Missouri &c. What should be done is to hold what we have in the West, open the Mississippi, and, take Chatanooga & East Tennessee, without more—a reasonable force should, in every event, be kept about Washington for it's protection. Then let the country give us a hundred thousand new troops in the shortest possible time, which added to McClellan, directly or indirectly, will take Richmond, without endangering any other place which we now hold—and will substantially end the war. I expect to maintain this contest until successful, or till I die, or am conquered, or my term expires, or Congress or the country forsakes me; and I would publicly appeal to the country for this new force, were it not that I fear a general panic and stampede would follow—so hard is it to have a thing understood as it really is. I think the new force should be all, or nearly all infantry, principally because such can be raised most cheaply and quickly. Yours very truly

To William H. Seward

Hon. W. H. Seward   Washington City, D.C.
New-York—   June 30 1862

We are yet without communication with Gen. McClellan; and this absence of news, is our point of anxiety. Up to the latest point to which we are posted, he effected everything in such exact accordance with his plan contingently announced to us before the battle began, that we feel justified to hope he has not failed since. He had a severe engagement in getting the part of his army on this side of the Chickahominy over to the other side, in which the enemy lost certainly as much as we did. We are not dissatisfied with this, only that the loss of enemies does not compensate for the loss of friends. The enemy did not come below White-House, certainly is not there now, and probably has abandoned the whole line. Dix' pickets are at New-Kent C.H.

To George B. McClellan

Major Genl. McClellan—   Executive Mansion,
                                            Washington, July 1 1862.

It is impossible to re-inforce you for your present emergency. If we had a million of men we could not get them to you in time. We have not the men to send. If you are not strong enough to face the enemy you must find a place of security, and wait, rest, and repair. Maintain your ground if you can; but save the Army at all events, even if you fall back to Fortress-Monroe. We still have strength enough in the country, and will bring it out.

To George B. McClellan

Major Gen. McClellan   Washington, D.C.,
                                            July 2 1862.

Your despatch of Tuesday morning induces me to hope your Army is having some rest. In this hope, allow me to reason with you a moment. When you ask for fifty thousand men to be promptly sent you, you surely labor under some gross mistake of fact. Recently you sent papers showing your disposal of forces, made last spring, for the defence of Washington, and advising a return to that plan. I find it included in, and about Washington seventyfive thousand men. Now please be assured, I have not men enough to fill that very plan by fifteen thousand. All of Fremont in the valley, all of Banks, all of McDowell, not with you, and all in Washington, taken together do not exceed, if they reach sixty thousand. With Wool and Dix added to those mentioned, I have not, outside of your Army, seventyfive thousand men East of the mountains. Thus, the idea of sending you fifty thousand, or any other considerable force promptly, is simply absurd. If in your frequent mention of responsibility, you have the impression that I blame you for not doing more than you can, please be relieved of such impression. I only beg that in like manner, you will not ask impossibilities of me. If you think you are not strong enough to take Richmond just now, I do not ask you to try just now. Save the Army, material and personal; and I will strengthen it for the offensive again, as fast as I can. The Governors of eighteen states offer me a new levy of three hundred thousand, which I accept.

To George B. McClellan

Washington City, D.C.

Major Genl. McClellan   July 3, 1862.

Yours of 5.30. yesterday is just received. I am satisfied that yourself, officers and men have done the best you could. All accounts say better fighting was never done. Ten thousand thanks for it.

On the 28th. we sent Gen. Burnside an order to send all the force he could spare, to you. We then learned that you had requested him to go to Goldsborough, upon which, we said to him our order was intended for your benefit, and we did not wish to be in conflict with your views. We hope you will have help from him soon. To day we have ordered Gen. Hunter to send you all he can spare. At last advices Halleck thinks he can not send reinforcements, without endangering all he has gained.

To Union Governors

Gov. E. D. Morgan   Washington,
My dear Sir—   July 3. 1862.

I should not want the half of three hundred thousand new troops, if I could have them *now*. If I had fifty thousand additional troops here *now*, I believe I could substantially close the war in two weeks. But *time* is *every-thing*; and if I get fifty thousand new men in a month, I shall have lost twenty thousand old ones during the same month, having gained only thirty thousand, with the difference between old and new troops still against me. The quicker you send, the fewer you will have to send. *Time* is every-thing. Please act in view of this. The enemy having given up Corinth, it is not wonderful that he is thereby enabled to check us for a time at Richmond.

To George B. McClellan

                        War Department   Washington City, D.C.
Major Gen. McClellan: July 4. 1862

I understand your position as stated in your letter, and by Gen. Marcy. To reinforce you so as to enable you to resume the offensive within a month, or even six weeks, is impossible. In addition to that arrived, and now arriving from the Potomac, (about ten thousand, I suppose) and about ten thousand I hope you will have from Burnside very soon, and about five thousand from Hunter a little later, I do not see how I can send you another man within a month. Under these circumstances the defensive, for the present, must be your only care. Save the Army—first, where you are, if you *can*; and secondly, by removal, if you must. You, on the ground, must be the judge as to which you will attempt, and of the means for effecting it. I but give it as opinion, that with the aid of the Gun-Boats, and the re-inforcements mentioned above, you can hold your present position, provided, and so long as, you can keep the James River open below you. If you are not tolerably confident you can keep the James River open, you had better remove as soon as possible. I do not remember that you have expressed any apprehension as to the danger of having your communication cut on the river below you; yet I do not suppose it can have escaped your attention. Yours very truly

P.S. If, at any time, you feel able to take the offensive, you are not restrained from doing so.

To George B. McClellan

Washington City, D.C.

Major Genl. McClellan   July 5, 1862.

A thousand thanks for the relief your two despatches of 12 & 1 P.M. yesterday—give me. Be assured the heroism and skill of yourself, officers, and men, are, and forever will be appreciated. If you can hold your present position, we shall *"hive"* the enemy yet.

Appeal to Border-State Representatives for Compensated Emancipation, Washington, D.C.

Gentlemen. After the adjournment of Congress, now very near, I shall have no opportunity of seeing you for several months. Believing that you of the border-states hold more power for good than any other equal number of members, I feel it a duty which I can not justifiably waive, to make this appeal to you. I intend no reproach or complaint when I assure you that in my opinion, if you all had voted for the resolution in the gradual emancipation message of last March, the war would now be substantially ended. And the plan therein proposed is yet one of the most potent, and swift means of ending it. Let the states which are in rebellion see, definitely and certainly, that, in no event, will the states you represent ever join their proposed Confederacy, and they can not, much longer maintain the contest. But you can not divest them of their hope to ultimately have you with them so long as you show a determination to perpetuate the institution within your own states. Beat them at elections, as you have overwhelmingly done, and, nothing daunted, they still claim you as their own. You and I know what the lever of their power is. Break that lever before their faces, and they can shake you no more forever.

Most of you have treated me with kindness and consideration; and I trust you will not now think I improperly touch what is exclusively your own, when, for the sake of the whole country I ask "Can you, for your states, do better than to take the course I urge?" Discarding *punctillio*, and maxims adapted to more manageable times, and looking only to the unprecedentedly stern facts of our case, can you do better in any possible event? You prefer that the constitutional relation of the states to the nation shall be practically restored, without disturbance of the institution; and if this were done, my whole duty, in this respect, under the constitution, and my oath of office, would be performed. But it is not done, and we are trying to accomplish it by war. The incidents of the war can not be avoided. If the war continue long, as it must, if the object be not sooner attained, the institution in your states will be extinguished by mere friction and abrasion—by the mere incidents of the war. It will be gone, and you will have nothing valuable in lieu of it. Much of it's value is gone already. How much better for you, and for your people, to take the step which, at once, shortens the war, and secures substantial compensation for that which is sure to be wholly lost in any other event. How much better to thus save the money which else we sink forever in the war. How much better to do it while we can, lest the war ere long render us pecuniarily unable to do it. How much better for you, as seller, and the nation as buyer, to sell out, and buy out, that without which the war could never have been, than to sink both the thing to be sold, and the price of it, in cutting one another's throats.

I do not speak of emancipation *at once*, but of a *decision* at once to emancipate *gradually*. Room in South America for colonization, can be obtained cheaply, and in abundance; and when numbers shall be large enough to be company and encouragement for one another, the freed people will not be so reluctant to go.

I am pressed with a difficulty not yet mentioned—one which threatens division among those who, united are none too strong. An instance of it is known to you. Gen. Hunter is an honest man. He was, and I hope, still is, my friend. I valued him none the less for his agreeing with me in the general wish that all men everywhere, could be free. He proclaimed all men free within certain states, and I repudiated the proclamation. He expected more good, and less harm from the measure, than I could believe would follow. Yet in repudiating it, I gave dissatisfaction, if not offence, to many whose support the country can not afford to lose. And this is not the end of it. The pressure, in this direction, is still upon me, and is increasing. By conceding what I now ask, you can relieve me, and much more, can relieve the country, in this important point. Upon these considerations I have again begged your attention to the message of March last. Before leaving the Capital, consider and discuss it among yourselves. You are patriots and statesmen; and, as such, I pray you, consider this proposition; and, at the least, commend it to the consideration of your states and people. As you would perpetuate

popular government for the best people in the world, I beseech you that you do in no wise omit this. Our common
country is in great peril, demanding the loftiest views, and
boldest action to bring it speedy relief. Once relieved, it's
form of government is saved to the world; it's beloved history, and cherished memories, are vindicated; and it's happy
future fully assured, and rendered inconceivably grand. To
you, more than to any others, the previlege is given, to assure
that happiness, and swell that grandeur, and to link your own
names therewith forever.

July 12, 1862

To George B. McClellan

Major General McClellan   Executive Mansion,
My dear Sir—   Washington, July 13 1862.
   I am told that over 160-000 men have gone into your Army
on the Peninsula. When I was with you the other day we
made out 86,500 remaining, leaving 73,500 to be accounted
for. I believe 23,500, will cover all the killed, wounded and
missing in all your battles and skirmishes, leaving 50-000 who
have left otherwise. Not more than 5000 of these have died,
leaving 45,000 of your Army still alive, and not with it. I
believe half, or two thirds of them are fit for duty to-day.
Have you any more perfect knowledge of this than I have? If
I am right, and you had these men with you, you could go
into Richmond in the next three days. How can they be got
to you? and how can they be prevented from getting away in
such numbers for the future?

To Edwin M. Stanton

1.

   Ordered that Military commanders, within the States of
Virginia, South Carolina, Georgia, Florida Alabama, Mississippi, Louisiana, Texas and Arkansas, in an orderly manner,
seize and use any property, real or personal, which may be

necessary or convenient for their several commands, as supplies, or for other military purposes; and that, while property may be destroyed for proper military objects, none shall be destroyed, in wantonness or malice.

2.

That military, and Naval commanders shall employ, as laborers, within, and from said States, so many persons of African descent, as can be advantageously used, for Military or Naval purposes, giving them reasonable wages for their labor.

3.

That as to both property, and persons of African descent, accounts shall be kept, sufficiently accurate, and in detail to show quantities and amounts and from whom, both property, and such persons shall have come, as a basis upon which compensation can be made in proper cases. And the several Departments of this government shall attend to, and perform their appropriate parts towards the execution of these orders.

By order of the President

July 22, 1862

To Reverdy Johnson

PRIVATE

Executive Mansion,
Hon Reverdy Johnson   Washington, July 26, 1862.

My Dear Sir. Yours of the 16th. by the hand of Governor Shepley is received. It seems the Union feeling in Louisiana is being crushed out by the course of General Phelps. Please pardon me for believing that is a false pretense. The people of Louisiana—all intelligent people every where—know full well, that I never had a wish to touch the foundations of their society, or any right of theirs. With perfect knowledge of this, they forced a necessity upon me to send armies among them, and it is their own fault, not mine, that they are annoyed by the presence of General Phelps. They also know the remedy—know how to be cured of General Phelps. Remove the necessity of his presence. And might it not be well for them to consider whether they have not already had *time* enough to do this? If they can conceive of anything worse than General Phelps, within my power, would they not better be looking out for it? They very well know the way to avert all this is simply to take their place in the Union upon the old terms. If they will not do this, should they not receive harder blows rather than lighter ones?

You are ready to say I apply to *friends* what is due only to *enemies*. I distrust the *wisdom* if not the *sincerity* of friends, who would hold my hands while my enemies stab me. This appeal of professed friends has paralyzed me more in this struggle than any other one thing. You remember telling me the day after the Baltimore mob in April 1861, that it would crush all Union feeling in Maryland for me to attempt bringing troops over Maryland soil to Washington. I brought the troops notwithstanding, and yet there was Union feeling enough left to elect a Legislature the next autumn which in turn elected a very excellent Union U.S. Senator!

I am a patient man—always willing to forgive on the Christian terms of repentance; and also to give ample *time* for repentance. Still I must save this government if possible. What I *cannot* do, of course I *will* not do; but it may as well be understood, once for all, that I shall not surrender this game leaving any available card unplayed. Yours truly

To Cuthbert Bullitt

PRIVATE

Cuthbert Bullitt Esq   Washington D.C.
New Orleans   La.   July 28. 1862

Sir: The copy of a letter addressed to yourself by Mr. Thomas J. Durant, has been shown to me. The writer appears to be an able, a dispassionate, and an entirely sincere man. The first part of the letter is devoted to an effort to show that the Secession Ordinance of Louisiana was adopted against the will of a majority of the people. This is probably true; and in that fact may be found some instruction. Why did they allow the Ordinance to go into effect? Why did they not assert themselves? Why stand passive and allow themselves to be trodden down by a minority? Why did they not hold popular meetings, and have a convention of their own, to express and enforce the true sentiment of the state? If preorganization was against them *then*, why not do this *now*, that the United States Army is present to protect them? The paralysis—the dead palsy—of the government in this whole struggle is, that this class of men will do nothing for the government, nothing for themselves, except demanding that the government shall not strike its open enemies, lest they be struck by accident!

Mr. Durant complains that in various ways the relation of master and slave is disturbed by the presence of our Army; and he considers it particularly vexatious that this, in part, is done under cover of an act of Congress, while constitutional guaranties are suspended on the plea of military necessity. The truth is, that what is done, and omitted, about slaves, is done and omitted on the same military necessity. It is a military necessity to have men and money; and we can get neither, in sufficient numbers, or amounts, if we keep from, or drive from, our lines, slaves coming to them. Mr. Durant cannot be ignorant of the pressure in this direction; nor of my efforts to hold it within bounds till he, and such as he shall have time to help themselves.

I am not posted to speak understandingly on all the police regulations of which Mr. Durant complains. If experience shows any one of them to be wrong, let them be set right. I think I can perceive, in the freedom of trade, which Mr. Durant urges, that he would relieve both friends and enemies from the pressure of the blockade. By this he would serve the enemy more effectively than the enemy is able to serve himself. I do not say or believe that to serve the enemy is the purpose of Mr. Durant; or that he is conscious of any purpose, other than national and patriotic ones. Still, if there were a class of men who, having no choice of sides in the contest, were anxious only to have quiet and comfort for themselves while it rages, and to fall in with the victorious side at the end of it, without loss to themselves, their advice as to the mode of conducting the contest would be precisely such as his is. He speaks of no duty—apparently thinks of none—resting upon Union men. He even thinks it injurious to the Union cause that they should be restrained in trade and passage without taking sides. They are to touch neither a sail nor a pump, but to be merely passengers,—dead-heads at that—to be carried snug and dry, throughout the storm, and safely landed right side up. Nay, more; even a mutineer is to go untouched lest these sacred passengers receive an accidental wound.

Of course the rebellion will never be suppressed in Louisiana, if the professed Union men there will neither help to do it, nor permit the government to do it without their help.

Now, I think the true remedy is very different from what is suggested by Mr. Durant. It does not lie in rounding the rough angles of the war, but in removing the necessity for the war. The people of Louisiana who wish protection to person and property, have but to reach forth their hands and take it. Let them, in good faith, reinaugurate the national authority, and set up a State Government conforming thereto under the constitution. They know how to do it, and can have the protection of the Army while doing it. The Army will be withdrawn so soon as such State government can dispense with its presence; and the people of the State can then upon the old Constitutional terms, govern themselves to their own liking. This is very simple and easy.

If they will not do this, if they prefer to hazard all for the sake of destroying the government, it is for them to consider whether it is probable I will surrender the government to save them from losing all. If they decline what I suggest, you scarcely need to ask what I will do. What would you do in my position? Would you drop the war where it is? Or, would you prosecute it in future, with elder-stalk squirts, charged with rose water? Would you deal lighter blows rather than heavier ones? Would you give up the contest, leaving any available means unapplied.

I am in no boastful mood. I shall not do *more* than I can, and I shall do *all* I can to save the government, which is my sworn duty as well as my personal inclination. I shall do nothing in malice. What I deal with is too vast for malicious dealing. Yours truly

To August Belmont

July 31, 1862.

Dear Sir: You send to Mr. W an extract from a letter written at New Orleans the 9th instant, which is shown to me. You do not give the writer's name; but plainly he is a man of ability, and probably of some note. He says: "The time has arrived when Mr. Lincoln must take a decisive course. Trying to please everybody, he will satisfy nobody. A vacillating policy in matters of importance is the very worst. Now is the time, if ever, for honest men who love their country to rally to its support. Why will not the North say officially that it wishes for the restoration of the Union as it was?"

And so, it seems, this is the point on which the writer thinks I have no policy. Why will he not read and understand what I have said?

The substance of the very declaration he desires is in the inaugural, in each of the two regular messages to Congress, and in many, if not all, the minor documents issued by the Executive since the inauguration.

Broken eggs cannot be mended; but Louisiana has nothing to do now but to take her place in the Union as it was, barring the already broken eggs. The sooner she does so, the smaller will be the amount of that which will be past mending. This government cannot much longer play a game in which it stakes all, and its enemies stake nothing. Those enemies must understand that they cannot experiment for ten years trying to destroy the government, and if they fail still come back into the Union unhurt. If they expect in any contingency to ever have the Union as it was, I join with the writer in saying, "Now is the time."

How much better it would have been for the writer to have gone at this, under the protection of the army at New Orleans, than to have sat down in a closet writing complaining letters northward! Yours truly,

To Agénor-Etienne de Gasparin

Executive Mansion   Washington August 4. 1862

Dear Sir: Your very acceptable letter dated Orbe Canton de Vaud, Switzerland 18th of July 1862 is received. The moral effect was the worst of the affair before Richmond; and that has run its course downward; we are now at a stand, and shall soon be rising again, as we hope. I believe it is true that in men and material, the enemy suffered more than we, in that series of conflicts; while it is certain he is less able to bear it.

With us every soldier is a man of character and must be treated with more consideration than is customary in Europe. Hence our great army for slighter causes than could have prevailed there has dwindled rapidly, bringing the necessity for a new call, earlier than was anticipated. We shall easily obtain the new levy, however. Be not alarmed if you shall learn that we shall have resorted to a draft for part of this. It seems strange, even to me, but it is true, that the Government is now pressed to this course by a popular demand. Thousands who wish not to personally enter the service are nevertheless anxious to pay and send substitutes, provided they can have assurance that unwilling persons similarly situated will be compelled to do like wise. Besides this, volunteers mostly choose to enter newly forming regiments, while drafted men can be sent to fill up the old ones, wherein, man for man, they are quite doubly as valuable.

You ask "why is it that the North with her great armies, so often is found, with inferiority of numbers, face to face with the armies of the South?" While I painfully know the fact, a military man, which I am not, would better answer the question. The fact I know, has not been overlooked; and I suppose the cause of its continuance lies mainly in the other facts that the enemy holds the interior, and we the exterior lines; and that we operate where the people convey information to the enemy, while he operates where they convey none to us.

I have received the volume and letter which you did me the honor of addressing to me, and for which please accept my sincere thanks. You are much admired in America for the ability of your writings, and much loved for your generosity to us, and your devotion to liberal principles generally.

You are quite right, as to the importance to us, for its bearing upon Europe, that we should achieve military successes; and the same is true for us at home as well as abroad. Yet it seems unreasonable that a series of successes, extending through half-a-year, and clearing more than a hundred thousand square miles of country, should help us so little, while a single half-defeat should hurt us so much. But let us be patient.

I am very happy to know that my course has not conflicted with your judgement, of propriety and policy.

I can only say that I have acted upon my best convictions without selfishness or malice, and that by the help of God, I shall continue to do so.

Please be assured of my highest respect and esteem.

Address to Union Meeting, Washington, D.C.

FELLOW-CITIZENS: I believe there is no precedent for my appearing before you on this occasion, [applause] but it is also true that there is no precedent for your being here yourselves, [applause and laughter:] and I offer, in justification of myself and of you, that, upon examination, I have found nothing in the Constitution against. [Renewed applause.] I, however, have an impression that there are younger gentlemen who will entertain you better, [voices—"No, no; none can do better than yourself. Go on!"] and better address your understanding, than I will or could, and therefore, I propose but to detain you a moment longer. [Cries—"Go on! Tar and feather the rebels!"]

I am very little inclined on any occasion to say anything unless I hope to produce some good by it. [A voice—"You do that; go on."] The only thing I think of just now not likely to be better said by some one else, is *a matter in which we have heard some other persons blamed for what I did myself.* [Voices—"What is it?"] There has been a very wide-spread attempt to have a quarrel between Gen. McClellan and the Secretary of War. *Now, I occupy a position that enables me to observe, at least, these two gentlemen are not nearly so deep in the quarrel as some pretending to be their friends.* [Cries of "Good."] Gen. McClellan's attitude is such that, in the very selfishness of his nature, he cannot but wish to be successful, and I hope he will—and the Secretary of War is in precisely the same situation. If the military commanders in the field cannot be successful, not only the Secretary of War, but myself for the time being the master of them both, cannot be but failures. [Laughter and applause.] I know Gen. McClellan wishes to be successful, and I know he does not wish it any more than the Secretary of War for him, and both of them together no more than I wish it. [Applause and cries of "Good."] Sometimes we have a dispute about how many men Gen. McClellan has had, and those who would disparage him say that he has had a very large number, and those who would disparage the Secretary of War insist that Gen. McClellan has had a very small number. The basis for this is, *there is always a wide difference, and*

350

on this occasion, perhaps, a wider one between the grand total on McClellan's rolls and the men actually fit for duty; and those who would disparage him talk of the grand total on paper, and those who would disparage the Secretary of War talk of those at present fit for duty. Gen. McClellan *has sometimes asked for things that the Secretary of War did not give him.* Gen. McClellan is not to blame for asking what he wanted and needed, and the Secretary of War *is not to blame for not giving when he had none to give.* [Applause, laughter, and cries of "Good, good."] And I say here, as far as I know, *the Secretary of War has withheld no one thing at any time in my power to give him.* [Wild applause, and a voice—"Give him enough now!"] I have no accusation against him. *I believe he is a brave and able man,* [applause,] and I stand here, as justice requires me to do, *to take upon myself what has been charged on the Secretary of War, as withholding from him.*

I have talked longer than I expected to do, [cries of "No, no—go on,"] and now I avail myself of my privilege of saying no more.

August 6, 1862

To John M. Clay

Mr. John M. Clay.   Executive Mansion,
My dear Sir: Washington, August 9, 1862.

The snuff-box you sent, with the accompanying note, was received yesterday.

Thanks for this *memento* of your great and patriotic father. Thanks also for the assurance that, in these days of dereliction, you remain true to his principles. In the concurrent sentiment of your venerable mother, so long the partner of his bosom and his honors, and lingering now, where he *was*, but for the call to rejoin him where he *is*, I recognize his voice, speaking as it ever spoke, for the Union, the Constitution, and the freedom of mankind. Your Obt. Servt.

To Edwin M. Stanton

Hon Sec of War   Executive Mansion
Sir   Washington Aug 9 1862

I have examined and seen tried the "Rafael Repeater" and consider it a decided improvement upon what was called the "Coffee Mill Gun" in these particulars that it dispenses with the great cost and liability to loss of the Steel cartridges and that it is better arranged to prevent the escape of gas. Other advantages are claimed for it upon which I cannot so well speak. While I do not order it into the service I think it well worthy of the attention of the Ordnance Bureau and should be rather pleased if it should be decided to put it into the service   Yours Truly

To John A. Andrew

Gov. Andrew,   Washington, D.C.,
Boston, Mass.   Aug. 12 1862.

Your despatch saying "I cant get those regts. off because I cant get quick work out of the U.S. disbursing officer & the Paymaster" is received.

Please say to these gentlemen that if they do not work quickly I will make quick work with them. In the name of all that is reasonable, how long does it take to pay a couple of Regts.?

We were never more in need of the arrival of Regts. than now—even to-day.

Address on Colonization to a Committee of Colored Men, Washington, D.C.

This afternoon the President of the United States gave audience to a Committee of colored men at the White House. They were introduced by the Rev. J. Mitchell, Commissioner of Emigration. E. M. Thomas, the Chairman, remarked that they were there by invitation to hear what the Executive had to say to them. Having all been seated, the President, after a few preliminary observations, informed them that a sum of money had been appropriated by Congress, and placed at his disposition for the purpose of aiding the colonization in some country of the people, or a portion of them, of African descent, thereby making it his duty, as it had for a long time been his inclination, to favor that cause; and why, he asked, should the people of your race be colonized, and where? Why should they leave this country? This is, perhaps, the first question for proper consideration. You and we are different races. We have between us a broader difference than exists between almost any other two races. Whether it is right or wrong I need not discuss, but this physical difference is a great disadvantage to us both, as I think your race suffer very greatly, many of them by living among us, while ours suffer from your presence. In a word we suffer on each side. If this is admitted, it affords a reason at least why we should be separated. You here are freemen I suppose.

A Voice: Yes, sir.

The President—Perhaps you have long been free, or all your lives. Your race are suffering, in my judgment, the greatest wrong inflicted on any people. But even when you cease to be slaves, you are yet far removed from being placed on an equality with the white race. You are cut off from many of the advantages which the other race enjoy. The aspiration of men is to enjoy equality with the best when free, but on this broad continent, not a single man of your race is made the equal of a single man of ours. Go where you are treated the best, and the ban is still upon you.

I do not propose to discuss this, but to present it as a fact with which we have to deal. I cannot alter it if I would. It is a fact, about which we all think and feel alike, I and you. We look to our condition, owing to the existence of the two races on this continent. I need not recount to you the effects upon white men, growing out of the institution of Slavery. I believe in its general evil effects on the white race. See our present condition—the country engaged in war!—our white men cutting one another's throats, none knowing how far it will extend; and then consider what we know to be the truth. But for your race among us there could not be war, although many men engaged on either side do not care for you one way or the other. Nevertheless, I repeat, without the institution of Slavery and the colored race as a basis, the war could not have an existence.

It is better for us both, therefore, to be separated. I know that there are free men among you, who even if they could better their condition are not as much inclined to go out of the country as those, who being slaves could obtain their freedom on this condition. I suppose one of the principal difficulties in the way of colonization is that the free colored man cannot see that his comfort would be advanced by it. You may believe you can live in Washington or elsewhere in the United States the remainder of your life, perhaps more so than you can in any foreign country, and hence you may come to the conclusion that you have nothing to do with the idea of going to a foreign country. This is (I speak in no unkind sense) an extremely selfish view of the case.

But you ought to do something to help those who are not so fortunate as yourselves. There is an unwillingness on the part of our people, harsh as it may be, for you free colored people to remain with us. Now, if you could give a start to white people, you would open a wide door for many to be made free. If we deal with those who are not free at the beginning, and whose intellects are clouded by Slavery, we have very poor materials to start with. If intelligent colored men, such as are before me, would move in this matter, much might be accomplished. It is exceedingly important that we have men at the beginning capable of thinking as white men, and not those who have been systematically oppressed.

There is much to encourage you. For the sake of your race you should sacrifice something of your present comfort for the purpose of being as grand in that respect as the white people. It is a cheering thought throughout life that something can be done to ameliorate the condition of those who have been subject to the hard usage of the world. It is difficult to make a man miserable while he feels he is worthy of himself, and claims kindred to the great God who made him. In the American Revolutionary war sacrifices were made by men engaged in it; but they were cheered by the future. Gen. Washington himself endured greater physical hardships than if he had remained a British subject. Yet he was a happy man, because he was engaged in benefiting his race—something for the children of his neighbors, having none of his own.

The colony of Liberia has been in existence a long time. In a certain sense it is a success. The old President of Liberia, Roberts, has just been with me—the first time I ever saw him. He says they have within the bounds of that colony between 300,000 and 400,000 people, or more than in some of our old States, such as Rhode Island or Delaware, or in some of our newer States, and less than in some of our larger ones. They are not all American colonists, or their descendants. Something less than 12,000 have been sent thither from this country. Many of the original settlers have died, yet, like people elsewhere, their offspring outnumber those deceased.

The question is if the colored people are persuaded to go anywhere, why not there? One reason for an unwillingness to do so is that some of you would rather remain within reach of the country of your nativity. I do not know how much attachment you may have toward our race. It does not strike me that you have the greatest reason to love them. But still you are attached to them at all events.

The place I am thinking about having for a colony is in Central America. It is nearer to us than Liberia—not much more than one-fourth as far as Liberia, and within seven days' run by steamers. Unlike Liberia it is on a great line of travel—it is a highway. The country is a very excellent one for any people, and with great natural resources and advantages, and especially because of the similarity of climate with your native land—thus being suited to your physical condition.

The particular place I have in view is to be a great highway from the Atlantic or Caribbean Sea to the Pacific Ocean, and this particular place has all the advantages for a colony. On both sides there are harbors among the finest in the world. Again, there is evidence of very rich coal mines. A certain amount of coal is valuable in any country, and there may be more than enough for the wants of the country. Why I attach so much importance to coal is, it will afford an opportunity to the inhabitants for immediate employment till they get ready to settle permanently in their homes.

If you take colonists where there is no good landing, there is a bad show; and so where there is nothing to cultivate, and of which to make a farm. But if something is started so that you can get your daily bread as soon as you reach there, it is a great advantage. Coal land is the best thing I know of with which to commence an enterprise.

To return, you have been talked to upon this subject, and told that a speculation is intended by gentlemen, who have an interest in the country, including the coal mines. We have been mistaken all our lives if we do not know whites as well as blacks look to their self-interest. Unless among those deficient of intellect everybody you trade with makes something. You meet with these things here as elsewhere.

If such persons have what will be an advantage to them, the question is whether it cannot be made of advantage to you. You are intelligent, and know that success does not as much depend on external help as on self-reliance. Much, therefore, depends upon yourselves. As to the coal mines, I think I see the means available for your self-reliance.

I shall, if I get a sufficient number of you engaged, have provisions made that you shall not be wronged. If you will engage in the enterprise I will spend some of the money intrusted to me. I am not sure you will succeed. The Government may lose the money, but we cannot succeed unless we try; but we think, with care, we can succeed.

The political affairs in Central America are not in quite as satisfactory condition as I wish. There are contending factions in that quarter; but it is true all the factions are agreed alike on the subject of colonization, and want it, and are more generous than we are here. To your colored race they have no objection. Besides, I would endeavor to have you made equals, and have the best assurance that you should be the equals of the best.

The practical thing I want to ascertain is whether I can get a number of able-bodied men, with their wives and children, who are willing to go, when I present evidence of encouragement and protection. Could I get a hundred tolerably intelligent men, with their wives and children, to "cut their own fodder," so to speak? Can I have fifty? If I could find twenty-five able-bodied men, with a mixture of women and children, good things in the family relation, I think I could make a successful commencement.

I want you to let me know whether this can be done or not. This is the practical part of my wish to see you. These are subjects of very great importance, worthy of a month's study, instead of a speech delivered in an hour. I ask you then to consider seriously not pertaining to yourselves merely, nor for your race, and ours, for the present time, but as one of the things, if successfully managed, for the good of mankind—not confined to the present generation, but as

> "From age to age descends the lay,
>   To millions yet to be,
>   Till far its echoes roll away,
>   Into eternity."

The above is merely given as the substance of the President's remarks.

The Chairman of the delegation briefly replied that "they would hold a consultation and in a short time give an answer." The President said: "Take your full time—no hurry at all."

The delegation then withdrew.

August 14, 1862

To Horace Greeley

Hon. Horace Greely: Executive Mansion,
Dear Sir   Washington, August 22, 1862.

I have just read yours of the 19th. addressed to myself through the New-York Tribune. If there be in it any statements, or assumptions of fact, which I may know to be erroneous, I do not, now and here, controvert them. If there be in it any inferences which I may believe to be falsely drawn, I do not now and here, argue against them. If there be perceptable in it an impatient and dictatorial tone, I waive it in deference to an old friend, whose heart I have always supposed to be right.

As to the policy I "seem to be pursuing" as you say, I have not meant to leave any one in doubt.

I would save the Union. I would save it the shortest way under the Constitution. The sooner the national authority can be restored; the nearer the Union will be "the Union as it was." If there be those who would not save the Union, unless they could at the same time *save* slavery, I do not agree with them. If there be those who would not save the Union unless they could at the same time *destroy* slavery, I do not agree with them. My paramount object in this struggle *is* to save the Union, and is *not* either to save or to destroy slavery. If I could save the Union without freeing *any* slave I would do it, and if I could save it by freeing *all* the slaves I would do it; and if I could save it by freeing some and leaving others alone I would also do that. What I do about slavery, and the colored race, I do because I believe it helps to save the Union; and what I forbear, I forbear because I do *not* believe it would help to save the Union. I shall do *less* whenever I shall believe what I am doing hurts the cause, and I shall do *more* whenever I shall believe doing more will help the cause. I shall try to correct errors when shown to be errors; and I shall adopt new views so fast as they shall appear to be true views.

I have here stated my purpose according to my view of *official* duty; and I intend no modification of my oft-expressed *personal* wish that all men every where could be free. Yours,

To David Davis

Hon. David Davis   Executive Mansion,
My dear Sir   Washington, Aug. 27, 1862.

My mind is made up to appoint you Supreme Judge; but I am so anxious that Mr. Bradley, present clerk at Chicago, shall be retained, that I think it no dishonor for me to ask, and for you to tell me, that you will not remove him. Please answer. Yours truly

Meditation on the Divine Will

The will of God prevails. In great contests each party claims to act in accordance with the will of God. Both *may* be, and one *must* be wrong. God can not be *for*, and *against* the same thing at the same time. In the present civil war it is quite possible that God's purpose is something different from the purpose of either party—and yet the human instrumentalities, working just as they do, are of the best adaptation to effect His purpose. I am almost ready to say this is probably true—that God wills this contest, and wills that it shall not end yet. By his mere quiet power, on the minds of the now contestants, He could have either *saved* or *destroyed* the Union without a human contest. Yet the contest began. And having begun He could give the final victory to either side any day. Yet the contest proceeds.

c. early September 1862

To Jeremiah T. Boyle

Gen. Boyle—   Washington,
Louisville, Ky.   Sep. 12. 1862

Your despatch of last evening received. Where is the enemy which you dread in Louisville? How near to you? What is Gen. Gilbert's opinion? With all possible respect for you, I must think Gen. Wright's military opinion is the better. He is as much responsible for Louisville, as for Cincinnati. Gen. Halleck telegraphed him on this very subject yesterday; and I telegraph him now; but for us here, to control him there on the ground would be a Babel of confusion which would be utterly ruinous. Where do you understand Buell to be? and what is he doing?

To Andrew G. Curtin

Hon. A. G. Curtin   Washington, D.C.,
Harrisburg, Penn.   Sep. 12. 10/35 1862.

Your despatch asking for eighty thousand disciplined troops to be sent to Pennsylvania is received. Please consider. We have not to exceed eighty thousand disciplined troops, properly so called, this side of the mountains, and most of them, with many of the new regiments, are now close in the rear of the enemy supposed to be invading Pennsylvania. Start half of them to Harrisburg, and the enemy will turn upon and beat the remaining half, and then reach Harrisburg before the part going there, and beat it too when it comes. The best possible security for Pennsylvania is putting the strongest force possible into the enemies rear.

Reply to Chicago Emancipation Memorial, Washington, D.C.

"The subject presented in the memorial is one upon which I have thought much for weeks past, and I may even say for months. I am approached with the most opposite opinions and advice, and that by religious men, who are equally certain that they represent the Divine will. I am sure that either the one or the other class is mistaken in that belief, and perhaps in some respects both. I hope it will not be irreverent for me to say that if it is probable that God would reveal his will to others, on a point so connected with my duty, it might be supposed he would reveal it directly to me; for, unless I am more deceived in myself than I often am, it is my earnest desire to know the will of Providence in this matter. *And if I can learn what it is I will do it!* These are not, however, the days of miracles, and I suppose it will be granted that I am not to expect a direct revelation. I must study the plain physical facts of the case, ascertain what is possible and learn what appears to be wise and right. The subject is difficult, and good men do not agree. For instance, the other day four gentlemen of standing and intelligence (naming one or two of the number) from New York called, as a delegation, on business connected with the war; but, before leaving, two of them earnestly beset me to proclaim general emancipation, upon which the other two at once attacked them! You know, also, that the last session of Congress had a decided majority of anti-slavery men, yet they could not unite on this policy. And the same is true of the religious people. Why, the rebel soldiers are praying with a great deal more earnestness, I fear, than our own troops, and expecting God to favor their side; for one of our soldiers, who had been taken prisoner, told Senator Wilson, a few days since, that he met with nothing so discouraging as the evident sincerity of those he was among in their prayers. But we will talk over the merits of the case.

"What *good* would a proclamation of emancipation from me do, especially as we are now situated? I do not want to issue a document that the whole world will see must necessarily be inoperative, like the Pope's bull against the comet!

361

Would *my word* free the slaves, when I cannot even enforce
the Constitution in the rebel States? Is there a single court, or
magistrate, or individual that would be influenced by it there?
And what reason is there to think it would have any greater
effect upon the slaves than the late law of Congress, which I
approved, and which offers protection and freedom to the
slaves of rebel masters who come within our lines? Yet I cannot learn that that law has caused a single slave to come over
to us. And suppose they could be induced by a proclamation
of freedom from me to throw themselves upon us, *what should
we do with them?* How can we feed and care for such a multitude? Gen. Butler wrote me a few days since that he was issuing more rations to the slaves who have rushed to him than to
all the white troops under his command. They *eat*, and that is
all, though it is true Gen. Butler is feeding the whites also by
the thousand; for it nearly amounts to a famine there. If,
now, the pressure of the war should call off our forces from
New Orleans to defend some other point, what is to prevent
the masters from reducing the blacks to slavery again; for I
am told that whenever the rebels take any black prisoners, free
or slave, they immediately auction them off! They did so with
those they took from a boat that was aground in the Tennessee river a few days ago. And then *I am very ungenerously
attacked for it!* For instance, when, after the late battles at and
near Bull Run, an expedition went out from Washington
under a flag of truce to bury the dead and bring in the
wounded, and the rebels seized the blacks who went along to
help and sent them into slavery, Horace Greeley said in his
paper that the Government would probably do nothing about
it. What *could* I do? [Here your delegation suggested that this
was a gross outrage on a flag of truce, which covers and protects all over which it waves, and that whatever he could do if
white men had been similarly detained he *could* do in this
case.]

   "Now, then, tell me, if you please, what possible result of
good would follow the issuing of such a proclamation as you
desire? Understand, I raise no objections against it on legal or
constitutional grounds; for, as commander-in-chief of the
army and navy, in time of war, I suppose I have a right to
take any measure which may best subdue the enemy. Nor do

I urge objections of a moral nature, in view of possible consequences of insurrection and massacre at the South. I view the matter as a practical war measure, to be decided upon according to the advantages or disadvantages it may offer to the suppression of the rebellion."

Thus invited, your delegation very willingly made reply to the following effect; it being understood that a portion of the remarks were intermingled by the way of conversation with those of the President just given.

We observed (taking up the President's ideas in order) that good men indeed differed in their opinions on this subject; nevertheless *the truth was somewhere*, and it was a matter of solemn moment for him to ascertain it; that we had not been so wanting in respect, alike to ourselves and to him, as to come a thousand miles to bring merely *our opinion* to be set over against the *opinion* of other parties; that the memorial contained facts, principles, and arguments which appealed to the intelligence of the President and to his faith in Divine Providence; that he could not deny that the Bible denounced oppression as one of the highest of crimes, and threatened Divine judgments against nations that practice it; that our country had been exceedingly guilty in this respect, both at the North and South; that our just punishment has come by a slaveholder's rebellion; that the virus of secession is found wherever the virus of slavery extends, and no farther; so that there is the amplest reason for expecting to avert Divine judgments by putting away the sin, and for hoping to remedy the national troubles by striking at their cause.

We observed, further, that we freely admitted the probability, and even the certainty, that God would reveal the path of duty to the President as well as to others, provided he sought to learn it in the appointed way; but, as according to his own remark, Providence wrought by means and not miraculously, it might be, God would use the suggestions and arguments of other minds to secure that result. We felt the deepest personal interest in the matter as of national concern, and would fain aid the thoughts of our President by communicating the convictions of the Christian community from which we came, with the ground upon which they were based.

That it was true he could not now enforce the Constitution

at the South; but we could see in that fact no reason whatever for not proclaiming emancipation, but rather the contrary. The two appealed to different classes; the latter would aid, and in truth was necessary to re-establish the former; and the two could be made operative together as fast as our armies fought their way southward; while we had yet to hear that he proposed to abandon the Constitution because of the present difficulty of enforcing it.

As to the inability of Congress to agree on this policy at the late session, it was quite possible, in view of subsequent events, there might be more unanimity at another meeting. The members have met their constituents and learned of marvellous conversions to the wisdom of emancipation, especially since late reverses have awakened thought as to the extreme peril of the nation, and made bad men as well as good men realize that we have to deal with God in this matter. Men of the most opposite previous views were now uniting in calling for this measure.

That to proclaim emancipation would secure the sympathy of Europe and the whole civilized world, which now saw no other reason for the strife than national pride and ambition, an unwillingness to abridge our domain and power. No other step would be so potent to prevent foreign intervention.

Furthermore, it would send a thrill through the entire North, firing every patriotic heart, giving the people a glorious principle for which to suffer and to fight, and assuring them that the work was to be so thoroughly done as to leave our country free forever from danger and disgrace in this quarter.

We added, that when the proclamation should become widely known (as the law of Congress has *not* been) it would withdraw the slaves from the rebels, leaving them without laborers, and giving us *both laborers and soldiers*. That the difficulty experienced by Gen. Butler and other Generals arose from the fact that *half-way measures could never avail*. It is the inherent vice of half-way measures that they create as many difficulties as they remove. It is folly merely to receive and feed the slaves. They should be welcomed and fed, and then, according to Paul's doctrine, that they who eat must work, be made to labor and to fight for their liberty and ours. With such a policy the blacks would be no incumbrance and their rations no waste. In this respect we should follow the ancient maxim, and learn of the enemy. What the rebels most fear is what we should be most prompt to do; and what they most fear is evident from the hot haste with which, on the first day of the present session of the Rebel Congress, bills were introduced threatening terrible vengeance if we used the blacks in the war.

The President rejoined from time to time in about these terms:

"I admit that slavery is the root of the rebellion, or at least its *sine qua non*. The ambition of politicians may have instigated them to act, but they would have been impotent without slavery as their instrument. I will also concede that emancipation would help us in Europe, and convince them that we are incited by something more than ambition. I grant further that it would help *somewhat* at the North, though not so much, I fear, as you and those you represent imagine. Still, some additional strength would be added in that way to the war. And then unquestionably it would weaken the rebels by drawing off their laborers, which is of great importance. But I am not so sure we could do much with the blacks. If we were to arm them, I fear that in a few weeks the arms would be in the hands of the rebels; and indeed thus far we have not had arms enough to equip our white troops. I will mention another thing, though it meet only your scorn and contempt: There are fifty thousand bayonets in the Union armies from the Border Slave States. It would be a serious matter if, in consequence of a proclamation such as you desire, they should go over to the rebels. I do not think they all would — not so many indeed as a year ago, or as six months ago — not so many to-day as yesterday. Every day increases their Union feeling. They are also getting their pride enlisted, and want to beat the rebels. Let me say one thing more: I think you should admit that we already have an important principle to rally and unite the people in the fact that constitutional government is at stake. This is a fundamental idea, going down about as deep as any thing."

We answered that, being fresh from the people, we were naturally more hopeful than himself as to the necessity and probable effect of such a proclamation. The value of constitutional government is indeed a grand idea for which to contend; but the people know that *nothing else has put constitutional government in danger but slavery*; that the toleration of that aristocratic and despotic element among our free institutions was the inconsistency that had nearly wrought our ruin and caused free government to appear a failure before the world, and therefore the people demand emancipation to preserve and perpetuate constitutional government. Our idea would thus be found to go deeper than this, and to be armed with corresponding power. ("Yes," interrupted Mr. Lincoln, "that is the true ground of our difficulties.") That a proclamation of general emancipation, "giving Liberty and Union" as the national watch-word, would rouse the people and rally them to his support beyond any thing yet witnessed—appealing alike to conscience, sentiment, and hope. He must remember, too, that present manifestations are no index of what would then take place. If the leader will but utter a trumpet call the nation will respond with patriotic ardor. No one can tell the power of the right word from the right man to develop the latent fire and enthusiasm of the masses. ("I know it," exclaimed Mr. Lincoln.) That good sense must of course be exercised in drilling, arming, and using black as well as white troops to make them efficient; and that in a scarcity of arms it was at least worthy of inquiry whether it were not wise to place a portion of them in the hands of those nearest to the seat of the rebellion and able to strike the deadliest blow.

That in case of a proclamation of emancipation we had no fear of serious injury from the desertion of Border State troops. The danger was greatly diminished, as the President had admitted. But let the desertions be what they might, the increased spirit of the North would replace them two to one. One State alone, if necessary, would compensate the loss, were the whole 50,000 to join the enemy. The struggle has gone too far, and cost too much treasure and blood, to allow of a partial settlement. Let the line be drawn at the same time between freedom and slavery, and between loyalty and treason. The sooner we know who are our enemies the better.

In bringing our interview to a close, after an hour of

earnest and frank discussion, of which the foregoing is a specimen, Mr. Lincoln remarked: "Do not misunderstand me, because I have mentioned these objections. They indicate the difficulties that have thus far prevented my action in some such way as you desire. I have not decided against a proclamation of liberty to the slaves, but hold the matter under advisement. And I can assure you that the subject is on my mind, by day and night, more than any other. Whatever shall appear to be God's will I will do. I trust that, in the freedom with which I have canvassed your views, I have not in any respect injured your feelings."

September 13, 1862

To George B. McClellan

Washington, D.C.,
Major General McClellan.   Sep. 15, 2/45 1862.
    Your despatches of to-day received. God bless you, and all with you. Destroy the rebel army, if possible.

To Edwin M. Stanton

Hon. Sec. of War   Executive Mansion,
Dear Sir.   Washington, Sep. 20, 1862.
    I know it is your purpose to send the paroled prisoners to the seat of the Indian difficulties; and I write this only to urge that this be done with all possible despatch. Gen. Wool telegraphs that including those from Harper's Ferry, there are now twenty thousand at Anapolis, requiring four good unparoled regiments to guard them. This should not be endured beyond the earliest moment possible to change it. Arm them and send them away just as fast as the Railroads will carry them. Each regiment arriving on the frontier will relieve a new regiment to come forward. Yours truly

Preliminary Emancipation Proclamation

BY THE PRESIDENT OF THE UNITED STATES OF AMERICA
A PROCLAMATION.

I, Abraham Lincoln, President of the United States of America, and Commander-in-chief of the Army and Navy thereof, do hereby proclaim and declare that hereafter, as heretofore, the war will be prossecuted for the object of practically restoring the constitutional relation between the United States, and each of the states, and the people thereof, in which states that relation is, or may be suspended, or disturbed.

That it is my purpose, upon the next meeting of Congress to again recommend the adoption of a practical measure tendering pecuniary aid to the free acceptance or rejection of all slave-states, so called, the people whereof may not then be in rebellion against the United States, and which states, may then have voluntarily adopted, or thereafter may voluntarily adopt, immediate, or gradual abolishment of slavery within their respective limits; and that the effort to colonize persons of African descent, with their consent, upon this continent, or elsewhere, with the previously obtained consent of the Governments existing there, will be continued.

That on the first day of January in the year of our Lord, one thousand eight hundred and sixty-three, all persons held as slaves within any state, or designated part of a state, the people whereof shall then be in rebellion against the United States shall be then, thenceforward, and forever free; and the executive government of the United States, including the military and naval authority thereof, will recognize and maintain the freedom of such persons, and will do no act or acts to repress such persons, or any of them, in any efforts they may make for their actual freedom.

That the executive will, on the first day of January aforesaid, by proclamation, designate the States, and parts of states, if any, in which the people thereof respectively, shall then be in rebellion against the United States; and the fact that any state, or the people thereof shall, on that day be, in good faith represented in the Congress of the United States, by members chosen thereto, at elections wherein a majority of the qualified voters of such state shall have participated, shall, in the absence of strong countervailing testimony, be deemed conclusive evidence that such state and the people thereof, are not then in rebellion against the United States.

That attention is hereby called to an act of Congress entitled "An act to make an additional Article of War" approved March 13, 1862, and which act is in the words and figure following:

Be it enacted by the Senate and House of Representatives of the United States of America in Congress assembled, That hereafter the following shall be promulgated as an additional article of war for the government of the army of the United States, and shall be obeyed and observed as such:

Article—. All officers or persons in the military or naval service of the United States are prohibited from employing any of the forces under their respective commands for the purpose of returning fugitives from service or labor, who may have escaped from any persons to whom such service or labor is claimed to be due, and any officer who shall be found guilty by a court-martial of violating this article shall be dismissed from the service.

SEC. 2. *And be it further enacted,* That this act shall take effect from and after its passage.

Also to the ninth and tenth sections of an act entitled "An Act to suppress Insurrection, to punish Treason and Rebellion, to seize and confiscate property of rebels, and for other purposes," approved July 17, 1862, and which sections are in the words and figures following:

SEC. 9. *And be it further enacted,* That all slaves of persons who shall hereafter be engaged in rebellion against the government of the United States, or who shall in any way give aid or comfort thereto, escaping from such persons and taking refuge within the lines of the army; and all slaves captured from such persons or deserted by them and coming under the control of the government of the United States; and all slaves of such persons found *on* (or) being within any place occupied by rebel forces and afterwards occupied by the forces of the United States, shall be deemed captives of war, and shall be forever free of their servitude and not again held as slaves.

SEC. 10. *And be it further enacted,* That no slave escaping into any State, Territory, or the District of Columbia, from any other State, shall be delivered up, or in any way impeded or hindered of his liberty, except for crime, or some offence against the laws, unless the person claiming said fugitive shall first make oath that the person to whom the labor or service of such fugitive is alleged to be due is his lawful owner, and has not borne arms against the United States in the present rebellion, nor in any way given aid and comfort thereto; and no person engaged in the military or naval service of the United States shall, under any pretence whatever, assume to decide on the validity of the claim of any person to the service or labor of any other person, or surrender up any such person to the claimant, on pain of being dismissed from the service.

And I do hereby enjoin upon and order all persons engaged in the military and naval service of the United States to observe, obey, and enforce, within their respective spheres of service, the act, and sections above recited.

And the executive will in due time recommend that all citizens of the United States who shall have remained loyal thereto throughout the rebellion, shall (upon the restoration of the constitutional relation between the United States, and their respective states, and people, if that relation shall have been suspended or disturbed) be compensated for all losses by acts of the United States, including the loss of slaves.

In witness whereof, I have hereunto set my hand, and caused the seal of the United States to be affixed.

Done at the City of Washington, this twenty second day of September, in the year of our Lord, one thousand eight hundred and sixty two, and of the Independence of the United States, the eighty seventh.

ABRAHAM LINCOLN

By the President:
    WILLIAM H. SEWARD, Secretary of State.

Proclamation Suspending the Writ of Habeas Corpus

BY THE PRESIDENT OF THE UNITED STATES OF AMERICA:
A PROCLAMATION.

Whereas, it has become necessary to call into service not only volunteers but also portions of the militia of the States by draft in order to suppress the insurrection existing in the United States, and disloyal persons are not adequately restrained by the ordinary processes of law from hindering this measure and from giving aid and comfort in various ways to the insurrection;

Now, therefore, be it ordered, first, that during the existing insurrection and as a necessary measure for suppressing the same, all Rebels and Insurgents, their aiders and abettors within the United States, and all persons discouraging volunteer enlistments, resisting militia drafts, or guilty of any disloyal practice, affording aid and comfort to Rebels against the authority of the United States, shall be subject to martial law and liable to trial and punishment by Courts Martial or Military Commission:

Second. That the Writ of Habeas Corpus is suspended in respect to all persons arrested, or who are now, or hereafter during the rebellion shall be, imprisoned in any fort, camp, arsenal, military prison, or other place of confinement by any military authority or by the sentence of any Court Martial or Military Commission.

In witness whereof, I have hereunto set my hand, and caused the seal of the United States to be affixed.

Done at the City of Washington this twenty fourth day of September, in the year of our Lord one thousand eight hundred and sixty-two, and of the Independence of the United States the 87th.   ABRAHAM LINCOLN.

By the President:
    WILLIAM H. SEWARD, Secretary of State.

Response to Serenade, Washington, D.C.

FELLOW-CITIZENS: I appear before you to do little more

than acknowledge the courtesy you pay me, and to thank you for it. I have not been distinctly informed why it is this occasion you appear to do me this honor, though I suppose [interruptions] it is because of the proclamation. [Cries of "Good," and applause.] I was about to say, I suppose I understand it. [Laughter—Voices: "That you do," "You thoroughly understand it."] What I did, I did after very full deliberation, and under a very heavy and solemn sense of responsibility. [Cries of "Good," "Good," "Bless you," and applause.]

I can only trust in God I have made no mistake. [Cries "No mistake—all right; you've made no mistakes yet. Go ahead, you're right."] I shall make no attempt on this occasion to sustain what I have done or said by any comment. [Voices—"That's unnecessary; we understand it."] It is now for the country and the world to pass judgment on it, and, may be, take action upon it. I will say no more upon this subject. In my position I am environed with difficulties. [A voice—"That's so."]

Yet they are scarcely so great as the difficulties of those who, upon the battle field, are endeavoring to purchase with their blood and their lives the future happiness and prosperity of this country. [Applause, long and continued.] Let us never forget them. On the 14th and 17th days of the present month there have been battles bravely, skillfully and successfully fought. [Applause.] We do not yet know the particulars. Let us be sure that in giving praise to particular individuals, we do no injustice to others. I only ask you, at the conclusion of these few remarks, to give three hearty cheers to all good and brave officers and men who fought those successful battles.

September 24, 1862

To John Ross

John Ross   Executive Mansion,
Principal Chief of the   Washington,
Cherokee Nation   Sept. 25, 1862.

Sir: Your letter of the 16th. Inst. was received two days ago. In the multitude of cares claiming my constant attention I have been unable to examine and determine the exact treaty relations between the United States and the Cherokee Nation. Neither have I been able to investigate and determine the exact state of facts claimed by you as constituting a failure of treaty obligation on our part, excusing the Cherokee Nation for making a treaty with a portion of the people of the United States in open rebellion against the government thereof. This letter therefore, must not be understood to decide anything upon these questions. I shall, however, cause a careful investigation of them to be made. Meanwhile the Cherokee people remaining practically loyal to the federal Union will receive all the protection which can be given them consistently with the duty of the government to the whole country. I sincerely hope the Cherokee country may not again be over-run by the enemy; and I shall do all I consistently can to prevent it. Your Obt. Servt.

Record of Dismissal of John J. Key

September 26–27, 1862

We have reason to believe that the following is an exact copy of the record upon which Major John J. Key was dismissed from the military service of the United States.

Executive Mansion
Major John J. Key   Washington, Sept. 26. 1862.

Sir: I am informed that in answer to the question "Why was not the rebel army bagged immediately after the battle near Sharpsburg?" propounded to you by Major Levi C. Turner, Judge Advocate &c. you answered "That is not the game" "The object is that neither army shall get much advantage of the other; that both shall be kept in the field till they are exhausted, when we will make a compromise and save slavery."

I shall be very happy if you will, within twentyfour hours from the receipt of this, prove to me by Major Turner, that you did not, either litterally, or in substance, make the answer stated. Yours,

A. LINCOLN

(Indorsed as follows)

"Copy delivered to Major Key at 10.25 A.M. September 27th. 1862.

JOHN HAY."

At about 11 o'clock, A.M. Sept. 27. 1862, Major Key and Major Turner appear before me. Major Turner says: "As I remember it, the conversation was, I asked the question why we did not bag them after the battle at Sharpsburg? Major Key's reply was that was not the game, that we should tire the rebels out, and ourselves, that that was the only way the Union could be preserved, we come together fraternally, and slavery be saved"

On cross-examination, Major Turner says he has frequently heard Major Key converse in regard to the present troubles, and never heard him utter a sentiment unfavorable to the maintainance of the Union. He has never uttered anything which he Major T. would call disloyalty. The particular conversation detailed was a private one

A. LINCOLN.

(Indorsed on the above)

In my view it is wholly inadmissable for any gentleman holding a military commission from the United States to utter such sentiments as Major Key is within proved to have done. Therefore let Major John J. Key be forthwith dismissed from the Military service of the United States.

A LINCOLN.

The foregoing is the whole record, except the simple order of dismissal at the War Department. At the interview of Major Key and Major Turner with the President, Major Key did not attempt to controvert the statement of Major Turner; but simply insisted, and sought to prove, that he was true to the Union. The substance of the President's reply was that if there was a "game" ever among Union men, to have our army not take an advantage of the enemy when it could, it was his object to break up that game.

To Hannibal Hamlin

(*Strictly private.*)

Executive Mansion,
Washington, September 28, 1862.

My Dear Sir: Your kind letter of the 25th is just received. It is known to some that while I hope something from the proclamation, my expectations are not as sanguine as are those of some friends. The time for its effect southward has not come; but northward the effect should be instantaneous.

It is six days old, and while commendation in newspapers and by distinguished individuals is all that a vain man could wish, the stocks have declined, and troops come forward more slowly than ever. This, looked soberly in the face, is not very satisfactory. We have fewer troops in the field at the end of six days than we had at the beginning—the attrition among the old outnumbering the addition by the new. The North responds to the proclamation sufficiently in breath; but breath alone kills no rebels.

I wish I could write more cheerfully; nor do I thank you the less for the kindness of your letter. Yours very truly,

Remarks at Frederick, Maryland

FELLOW-CITIZENS: I see myself surrounded by soldiers, and a little further off I note the citizens of this good city of Frederick, anxious to hear something from me. I can only say, as I did five minutes ago, it is not proper for me to make speeches in my present position. I return thanks to our soldiers for the good service they have rendered, for the energies they have shown, the hardships they have endured, and the blood they have so nobly shed for this dear Union of ours; and I also return thanks not only to the soldiers, but to the good citizens of Maryland, and to all the good men and women in this land, for their devotion to our glorious cause. I say this without any malice in my heart to those who have done otherwise. May our children and our children's children to a thousand generations, continue to enjoy the benefits conferred upon us by a united country, and have cause yet to rejoice under those glorious institutions bequeathed us by Washington and his compeers. Now, my friends, soldiers and citizens, I can only say once more, farewell.

October 4, 1862

To Thomas H. Clay

Thomas H. Clay.   Washington, D.C.,
Cincinnati O.   Oct. 8 1862.

You *can not* have reflected seriously when you ask that I shall order Gen. Morgan's command to Kentucky as a favor, because they have marched from Cumberland Gap. The precedent established by it would instantly break up the whole army. Buell's old troops now in pursuit of Bragg, have done more hard marching recently. And, in fact, if you include marching and fighting, there are scarcely any old troops East or West of the mountains that have not done as hard service.

I sincerely wish war was an easier and pleasanter business than it is; but it does not admit of holy-days. On Morgan's command, where it is now sent, as I understand, depends the question whether the enemy will get to the Ohio River in another place.

To George B. McClellan

Major General McClellan   Executive Mansion,
My dear Sir   Washington, Oct. 13, 1862.

You remember my speaking to you of what I called your over-cautiousness. Are you not over-cautious when you assume that you can not do what the enemy is constantly doing? Should you not claim to be at least his equal in prowess, and act upon the claim?

As I understand, you telegraph Gen. Halleck that you can not subsist your army at Winchester unless the Railroad from Harper's Ferry to that point be put in working order. But the enemy does now subsist his army at Winchester at a distance nearly twice as great from railroad transportation as you would have to do without the railroad last named. He now wagons from Culpepper C.H. which is just about twice as far as you would have to do from Harper's Ferry. He is certainly not more than half as well provided with wagons as you are. I certainly should be pleased for you to have the advantage of the Railroad from Harper's Ferry to Winchester, but it wastes all the remainder of autumn to give it to you; and, in fact ignores the question of *time*, which can not, and must not be ignored.

Again, one of the standard maxims of war, as you know, is "to operate upon the enemy's communications as much as possible without exposing your own." You seem to act as if this applies *against* you, but can not apply in your *favor*. Change positions with the enemy, and think you not he would break your communication with Richmond within the next twentyfour hours? You dread his going into Pennsylvania. But if he does so in full force, he gives up his communications to you absolutely, and you have nothing to do but to follow, and ruin him; if he does so with less than full force, fall upon, and beat what is left behind all the easier.

Exclusive of the water line, you are now nearer Richmond than the enemy is by the route that you *can*, and he *must* take. Why can you not reach there before him, unless you admit that he is more than your equal on a march. His route is the arc of a circle, while yours is the chord. The roads are as good on yours as on his.

You know I desired, but did not order, you to cross the Potomac below, instead of above the Shenandoah and Blue Ridge. My idea was that this would at once menace the enemies' communications, which I would seize if he would permit. If he should move Northward I would follow him closely, holding his communications. If he should prevent our seizing his communications, and move towards Richmond, I would press closely to him, fight him if a favorable opportunity should present, and, at least, try to beat him to Richmond on the inside track. I say "try"; if we never try, we shall never succeed. If he make a stand at Winchester, moving neither North or South, I would fight him there, on the idea that if we can not beat him when he bears the wastage of coming to us, we never can when we bear the wastage of going to him. This proposition is a simple truth, and is too important to be lost sight of for a moment. In coming to us, he tenders us an advantage which we should not waive. We should not so operate as to merely drive him away. As we must beat him somewhere, or fail finally, we can do it, if at all, easier near to us, than far away. If we can not beat the enemy where he now is, we never can, he again being within the entrenchments of Richmond.

Recurring to the idea of going to Richmond on the inside track, the facility of supplying from the side away from the enemy is remarkable—as it were, by the different spokes of a wheel extending from the hub towards the rim—and this whether you move directly by the chord, or on the inside arc, hugging the Blue Ridge more closely. The chord-line, as you see, carries you by Aldie, Hay-Market, and Fredericksburg; and you see how turn-pikes, railroads, and finally, the Potomac by Acquia Creek, meet you at all points from Washington. The same, only the lines lengthened a little, if you press closer to the Blue Ridge part of the way. The gaps through the Blue Ridge I understand to be about the following distances from Harper's Ferry, towit: Vestal's five miles; Gregorie's, thirteen, Snicker's eighteen, Ashby's, twenty-eight, Mannassas, thirty-eight, Chester fortyfive, and Thornton's fifty-three. I should think it preferable to take the route nearest the enemy, disabling him to make an important move without your knowledge, and compelling him to keep his forces together, for dread of you. The gaps would enable you to attack if you should wish. For a great part of the way, you would be practically between the enemy and both Washington and Richmond, enabling us to spare you the greatest number of troops from here. When at length, running for Richmond ahead of him enables him to move this way; if he does so, turn and attack him in rear. But I think he should be engaged long before such point is reached. It is all easy if our troops march as well as the enemy; and it is unmanly to say they can not do it.

This letter is in no sense an order. Yours truly

To Benjamin F. Butler, George F. Shepley, and Others

(Copy).

Executive Mansion,
Washington, October 14. 1862

Major General Butler, Governor Shepley, & all having military and naval authority under the United States within the State of Louisiana.

The bearer of this, Hon. John E. Bouligny, a citizen of Louisiana, goes to that State seeking to have such of the people thereof as desire to avoid the unsatisfactory prospect before them, and to have peace again upon the old terms under the constitution of the United States, to manifest such desire by elections of members to the Congress of the United States particularly, and perhaps a legislature, State officers, and United States Senators friendly to their object. I shall be glad for you and each of you, to aid him and all others acting for this object, as much as possible. In all available ways give the people a chance to express their wishes at these elections. Follow forms of law as far as convenient, but at all events get the expression of the largest number of the people possible. All see how such action will connect with, and affect the proclamation of September 22nd. Of course the men elected should be gentlemen of character, willing to swear support to the constitution, as of old, and known to be above reasonable suspicion of duplicity. Yours very Respectfully

Similar letter to Gen. Grant, Gov. Johnson & others in Tenn. dated Oct. 21. 1862.
And to, Steele, Phelps & others in Arkansas.
    Nov. 18, 1862

To George B. McClellan

Washington City, D.C.

Majr. Genl. McClellan   Oct. 24. 1862

I have just read your despatch about sore tongued and fatiegued horses. Will you pardon me for asking what the horses of your army have done since the battle of Antietam that fatigue anything?

October 25, 1862

To George B. McClellan

Executive Mansion, Washington,
Majr. Gen. McClellan.   Oct. 27. 1862

Yours of yesterday received. Most certainly I intend no injustice to any; and if I have done any, I deeply regret it. To be told after more than five weeks total inaction of the Army, and during which period we had sent to that Army every fresh horse we possibly could, amounting in the whole to 7918 that the cavalry horses were too much fatiegued to move, presented a very cheerless, almost hopeless, prospect for the future; and it may have forced something of impatience into my despatches. If not recruited, and rested then, when could they ever be? I suppose the river is rising, and I am glad to believe you are crossing.

To John Pope

Major General Pope   Executive Mansion,
St. Paul, Minnesota   Washington, Nov. 10. 1862.

Your despatch giving the names of three hundred Indians condemned to death, is received. Please forward, as soon as possible, the full and complete record of these convictions. And if the record does not fully indicate the more guilty and influential, of the culprits, please have a careful statement made on these points and forwarded to me. Send all by mail.

To Carl Schurz

"Private & confidential"
Gen. Schurz.   Executive Mansion,
My dear Sir   Washington, Nov. 10. 1862.

Yours of the 8th. was, to-day, read to me by Mrs. S. We

have lost the elections; and it is natural that each of us will believe, and say, it has been because his peculiar views was not made sufficiently prominent. I think I know what it was, but I may be mistaken. Three main causes told the whole story. 1. The democrats were left in a majority by our friends going to the war. 2. The democrats observed this & determined to re-instate themselves in power, and 3. Our newspaper's, by vilifying and disparaging the administration, furnished them all the weapons to do it with. Certainly, the ill-success of the war had much to do with this.

You give a different set of reasons. If you had not made the following statements, I should not have suspected them to be true. "The defeat of the administration is the administrations own fault." (opinion) "It admitted its professed opponents to its counsels" (Asserted as a fact) "It placed the Army, now a great power in this Republic, into the hands of its' enemys" (Asserted as a fact) "In all personal questions, to be hostile to the party of the Government, seemed, to be a title to consideration." (Asserted as a fact) "If to forget the great rule, that if you are true to your friends, your friends will be true to you, and that you make your enemies stronger by placing them upon an equality with your friends." "Is it surprising that the opponents of the administration should have got into their hands the government of the principal states, after they have had for a long time the principal management of the war, the great business of the national government."

I can not dispute about the matter of opinion. On the three matters (stated as facts) I shall be glad to have your evidence upon them when I shall meet you. The plain facts, as they appear to me, are these. The administration came into power, very largely in a minority of the popular vote. Notwithstanding this, it distributed to it's party friends as nearly all the civil patronage as any administration ever did. The war came. The administration could not even start in this, without assistance outside of it's party. It was mere nonsense to suppose a minority could put down a majority in rebellion. Mr. Schurz (now Gen. Schurz) was about here then & I do not recollect that he then considered all who were not republicans, were enemies of the government, and that none of them must be appointed to military positions. He will correct me if I am mistaken. It so happened that very few of our friends had a military education or were of the profession of arms. It would have been a question whether the war should be conducted on military knowledge, or on political affinity, only that our own friends (I think Mr. Schurz included) seemed to think that such a question was inadmissable. Accordingly I have scarcely appointed a democrat to a command, who was not urged by many republicans and opposed by none. It was so as to McClellan. He was first brought forward by the Republican Governor of Ohio, & claimed, and contended for at the same time by the Republican Governor of Pennsylvania. I received recommendations from the republican delegations in congress, and I believe every one of them recommended a majority of democrats. But, after all many Republicans were appointed; and I mean no disparagement to them when I say I do not see that their superiority of success has been so marked as to throw great suspicion on the good faith of those who are not Republicans. Yours truly,

Order for Sabbath Observance

Executive Mansion, Washington, November 15, 1862.

The President, Commander-in-Chief of the Army and Navy, desires and enjoins the orderly observance of the Sabbath by the officers and men in the military and naval service. The importance for man and beast of the prescribed weekly rest, the sacred rights of Christian soldiers and sailors, a becoming deference to the best sentiment of a Christian people, and a due regard for the Divine will, demand that Sunday labor in the Army and Navy be reduced to the measure of strict necessity.

The discipline and character of the national forces should not suffer, nor the cause they defend be imperiled, by the profanation of the day or name of the Most High. "At this time of public distress"—adopting the words of Washington in 1776—"men may find enough to do in the service of God and their country without abandoning themselves to vice and immorality." The first General Order issued by the Father of his Country after the Declaration of Independence, indicates the spirit in which our institutions were founded and should ever be defended: *"The General hopes and trusts that every officer and man will endeavor to live and act as becomes a Christian soldier defending the dearest rights and liberties of his country."*

To Samuel Treat

PRIVATE

Judge S. Treat   Executive Mansion,
St. Louis, Mo.   Washington, Nov. 19, 1862.

My dear Sir   Your very patriotic and judicious letter, addressed to Judge Davis, in relation to the Mississippi, has been left with me by him for perusal. You do not estimate the value of the object you press, more highly than it is estimated here. It is now the object of particular attention. It has not been neglected, as you seem to think, because the West was divided into different military Departments. The cause is much deeper. The country will not allow us to send our whole Western force down the Mississippi, while the enemy sacks Louisville and Cincinnati. Possibly it would be better if the country would allow this, but it will not. I confidently believed, last September that we could end the war by allowing the enemy to go to Harrisburg and Philadelphia, only that we could not keep down mutiny, and utter demoralization among the Pennsylvanians. And this, though very unhandy sometimes, is not at all strange. I presume if an army was starting to-day for New-Orleans, and you confidently believed that St. Louis would be sacked in consequence, you would be in favor of stopping such army.

We are compelled to watch all these things. With great respect   Your Obt. Servt

To George Robertson

PRIVATE

Hon. George Robertson   Executive Mansion,
My dear Sir.   Washington, Nov. 20. 1862.

Your despatch of yesterday is just received. I believe you are acquainted with the American Classics, (if there be such) and probably remember a speech of Patrick Henry, in which he represented a certain character in the revolutionary times, as totally disregarding all questions of country, and "hoarsely bawling, beef! beef!! beef!!!"

Do you not know that I may as well surrender this contest, directly, as to make any order, the obvious purpose of which would be to return fugitive slaves? Yours very truly

To George F. Shepley

Hon. G. F. Shepley   Executive Mansion,
Dear Sir.   Washington, Nov. 21. 1862.

Dr. Kennedy, bearer of this, has some apprehension that Federal officers, not citizens of Louisiana, may be set up as candidates for Congress in that State. In my view, there could be no possible object in such an election. We do not particularly need members of congress from there to enable us to get along with legislation here. What we do want is the conclusive evidence that respectable citizens of Louisiana, are willing to be members of congress & to swear support to the constitution; and that other respectable citizens there are willing to vote for them and send them. To send a parcel of Northern men here, as representatives, elected as would be understood, (and perhaps really so,) at the point of the bayonet, would be disgusting and outrageous; and were I a member of congress here I would vote against admitting any such man to a seat. Yours very truly

To George F. Shepley

Hon. G. F. Shepley   Executive Mansion,
My dear Sir   Washington, Nov. 21. 1862.

Your letter of the 6th. Inst. to the Secretary of War has been placed in my hands; and I am annoyed to learn from it that, at it's date, nothing had been done about congressional elections. On the 14th. of October I addressed a letter to Gen.

Butler, yourself and others upon this very subject, sending it by Hon. Mr. Bouligny. I now regret the necessity of inferring that you had not seen this letter up to the 6th. Inst. I inclose you a copy of it, and also a copy of another addressed to yourself this morning, upon the same general subject, and placed in the hands of Dr. Kennedy. I ask attention to both.

I wish elections for Congressmen to take place in Louisiana; but I wish it to be a movement of the people of the Districts, and not a movement of our military and quasi-military, authorities there. I merely wish our authorities to give the people a chance—to protect them against secession interference. Of course the election can not be according to strict law—by state law, there is, I suppose, no election day, before January; and the regular election officers will not act, in many cases, if in any. These knots must be cut, the main object being to get an expression of the people. If they would fix a day and a way, for themselves, all the better; but if they stand idle not seeming to know what to do, do you fix these things for them by proclamation. And do not waste a day about it; but, fix the election day early enough that we can hear the result here by the first of January. Fix a day for an election in all the Districts, and have it held in as many places as you can. Yours very truly

To Nathaniel P. Banks

Executive Mansion,
My dear General Banks   Washington, Nov. 22, 1862.

Early last week you left me in high hope with your assurance that you would be off with your expedition at the end of that week, or early in this. It is now the end of this, and I have just been overwhelmed and confounded with the sight of a requisition made by you, which, I am assured, can not be filled, and got off within an hour short of two months! I inclose you a copy of the requisition, in some hope that it is not genuine—that you have never seen it.

My dear General, this expanding, and piling up of *impedimenta*, has been, so far, almost our ruin, and will be our final ruin if it is not abandoned. If you had the articles of this requisition upon the wharf, with the necessary animals to make them of any use, and forage for the animals, you could not get vessels together in two weeks to carry the whole, to say nothing of your twenty thousand men; and, having the vessels, you could not put the cargoes aboard in two weeks more. And, after all, where you are going, you have no use for them. When you parted with me, you had no such idea in your mind. I know you had not, or you could not have expected to be off so soon as you said. You must get back to something like the plan you had then, or your expedition is a failure before you start. You must be off before Congress meets. You would be better off any where, and especially where you are going, for not having a thousand wagons, doing nothing but hauling forage to feed the animals that draw them, and taking at least two thousand men to care for the wagons and animals, who otherwise might be two thousand good soldiers.

Now dear General, do not think this is an ill-natured letter—it is the very reverse. The simple publication of this requisition would ruin you. Very truly your friend

To William L. Vance

Mr. W. L. Vance   Executive Mansion,
Sir: Washington, Nov. 22, 1862.

You tell me you have in your hands some two hundred and seventy thousand dollars of "Confederate Scrip" which was forced upon Union men of Kentucky, in exchange for supplies, by the rebels during their late raid into that State; and you wish government authority for you to take this Scrip into the Cotten-States, exchange it for cotten if found practicable, and to bring the cotten out.

While I have felt great anxiety to oblige you, and your friends, in this matter, I feel constrained to decline it. It would come to something, or it would come to nothing— that is, you would get cotten for the Scrip, or you would not. If you should get none, the effort would have been a useless failure. If you should get *any*, to precisely that extent, this government would have aided in giving currency to this Scrip—that is, men seeing that the Scrip would bring cotten, would gladly give produce for the scrip; and hence a scramble for it, as for gold would ensue. If your two hundred and seventy thousand dollars, was to be the sole instance, I would gladly risk it. But it would not be the beginning, or, at most, only the beginning. Having begun, I could not stop. What I had done for some, I must do for others. All that sort of Scrip now in Kentucky, and much not yet in Kentucky, would find it's way into Union-hands and be presented under the rule. We all know how easily oaths are furnished, when required, in transactions of this sort. And the thing would become even broader yet. Men who have been robbed out-right by the rebels, without even receiving scrip would appeal, (and with quite as equitable a case) to be permitted a means of indemnity, by leave to go in and bring out cotten. This would run till at length I should have to abandon all restraint, or put a stop to what it is now much easier to not begin.

To John J. Key

Major John J. Key   Executive Mansion,
Dear Sir: Washington, Nov. 24, 1862

A bundle of letters including one from yourself, was, early last week, handed me by Gen. Halleck, as I understood, at your request. I sincerely sympathise with you in the death of your brave and noble son.

In regard to my dismissal of yourself from the military service, it seems to me you misunderstand me. I did not charge, or intend to charge you with disloyalty. I had been brought to fear that there was a class of officers in the army, not very inconsiderable in numbers, who were playing a game to not beat the enemy when they could, on some peculiar notion as to the proper way of saving the Union; and when you were proved to me, in your own presence, to have avowed yourself in favor of that "game," and did not attempt to controvert the proof, I dismissed you as an example and a warning to that supposed class. I bear you no ill will; and I regret that I could not have the example without wounding you personally. But can I now, in view of the public interest, restore you to the service, by which the army would understand that I indorse and approve that game myself? If there was any doubt of your having made the avowal, the case would be different. But when it was proved to me, in your presence, you did not deny or attempt to deny it, but confirmed it in my mind, by attempting to sustain the position by argument.

I am really sorry for the pain the case gives you, but I do not see how, consistently with duty, I can change it. Yours, &c.

To Carl Schurz

Gen. Carl Schurz   Executive Mansion,
My dear Sir   Washington, Nov. 24. 1862.

I have just received, and read, your letter of the 20th. The purport of it is that we lost the late elections, and the administration is failing, because the war is unsuccessful; and that I must not flatter myself that I am not justly to blame for it. I certainly know that if the war fails, the administration fails, and that I *will* be blamed for it, whether I deserve it or not. And I ought to be blamed, if I could do better. You think I could do better; therefore you blame me already. I think I could not do better; therefore I blame you for blaming me. I understand you *now* to be willing to accept the help of men, who are not republicans, provided they have "heart in it." Agreed. I want no others. But who is to be the judge of hearts, or of "heart in it"? If I must discard my own judgment, and take yours, I must also take that of others; and by the time I should reject all I should be advised to reject, I should have none left, republicans, or others—not even yourself. For, be assured, my dear sir, there are men who have "heart in it" that think you are performing your part as poorly as you think I am performing mine. I certainly have been dissatisfied with the slowness of Buell and McClellan; but before I relieved them I had great fears I should not find successors to them, who would do better; and I am sorry to add, that I have seen little since to relieve those fears. I do not clearly see the prospect of any more rapid movements. I fear we shall at last find out that the difficulty is in our case, rather than in particular generals. I wish to disparage no one—certainly not those who sympathize with me; but I must say I need success more than I need sympathy, and that I have not seen the so much greater evidence of getting success from my sympathizers, than from those who are denounced as the contrary. It does seem to me that in the field the two classes have been very much alike, in what they have done, and what they have failed to do. In sealing their faith with their blood, Baker, and Lyon, and Bohlen, and Richardson, republicans, did all that men could do; but did they any more than Kearney, and Stevens, and Reno, and Mansfield, none of whom were republicans, and some, at least of whom, have been bitterly, and repeatedly, denounced to me as secession sympathizers? I will not perform the ungrateful task of comparing cases of failure.

In answer to your question "Has it not been publicly stated in the newspapers, and apparently proved as a fact, that from the commencement of the war, the enemy was continually supplied with information by some of the confidential subordinates of as important an officer as Adjutant General Thomas?" I must say "no" so far as my knowledge extends. And I add that if you can give any tangible evidence upon that subject, I will thank you to come to the City and do so. Very truly Your friend

To George Robertson

Private

Executive Mansion,
Hon. George Robertson,   Washington, Nov. 26, 1862.

My dear Sir: A few days since I had a despatch from you which I did not answer. If I were to be wounded personally, I think I would not shun it. But it is the life of the nation. I now understand the trouble is with Col. Utley; that he has five slaves in his camp, four of whom belong to rebels, and one belonging to you. If this be true, convey yours to Col. Utley, so that he can make him free, and I will pay you any sum not exceeding five hundred dollars. Yours, &c.

To Henry W. Halleck

Major General Halleck
Sir:

Steamer Baltimore
Off Acquia Creek, Va
Nov. 27. 1862

I have just had a long conference with Gen. Burnside. He believes that Gen. Lees whole army, or nearly the whole of it is in front of him, at and near Fredericksburg. Gen. B. says he could take into battle now any day, about, one hundred and ten thousand men, that his army is in good spirit, good condition, good moral, and that in all respects he is satisfied with officers and men; that he does not want more men with him, because he could not handle them to advantage; that he thinks he can cross the river in face of the enemy and drive him away, but that, to use his own expression, it is somewhat risky. I wish the case to stand more favorable than this in two respects. First, I wish his crossing of the river to be nearly free from risk; and secondly, I wish the enemy to be prevented from falling back, accumulating strength as he goes, into his intrenchments at Richmond. I therefore propose that Gen. B. shall not move immediately; that we accumulate a force on the South bank of the Rappahanock—at, say, Port-Royal, under protection of one or two gun-boats, as nearly up to twenty-five thousand strong as we can. At the same time another force of about the same strength as high up the Pamunkey, as can be protected by gunboats. These being ready, let all three forces move simultaneously, Gen. B.'s force in it's attempt to cross the river, the Rappahanock force moving directly up the South side of the river to his assistance, and ready, if found admissable, to deflect off to the turnpike bridge over the Mattapony in the direction of Richmond. The Pamunkey force to move as rapidly as possible up the North side of the Pamunkey, holding all the bridges, and especially the turnpike bridge immediately North of Hanover C.H; hurry North, and seize and hold the Mattapony bridge before mentioned, and also, if possible, press higher up the streams and destroy the railroad bridges. Then, if Gen. B. succeeds in driving the enemy from Fredericksburg, he the enemy no longer has the road to Richmond, but we have it and can march into the city. Or, possibly, having forced the enemy from his line, we could move upon, and destroy his army. Gen. B.'s main army would have the same line of supply and retreat as he has now provided; the Rappahanock force would have that river for supply, and gun-boats to fall back upon; and the Pamunkey force would have that river for supply, and a line between the two rivers— Pamunkey & Mattapony—along which to fall back upon it's gun-boats. I think the plan promises the best results, with the least hazzard, of any now conceiveable.

Note— The above plan, proposed by me, was rejected by Gen. Halleck & Gen. Burnside, on the ground that we could not raise and put in position, the Pamunkey force without too much waste of time

To Edward Bates

Executive Mansion, Washington,

Hon. Attorney General   Nov. 29, 1862.

My dear Sir: Few things perplex me more than this question between Gov. Gamble, and the War Department, as to whether the peculiar force organized by the former in Missouri are "State troops," or "United States troops." Now, this is either an immaterial, or a mischievous question. First, if no more is desired than to have it settled what name the forces is to be called by, it is immaterial. Secondly, if it is desired for more than the fixing a name, it can only be to get a position from which to draw practical inferences, then it is mischievous. Instead of settling one dispute by deciding the question, I should merely furnish a nest full of eggs for hatching new disputes. I believe the force is not strictly either "State troops" or "United States troops." It is of mixed character. I therefore think it is safer when a practical question arises, to decide that question directly, and not indirectly, by deciding a general abstraction supposed to include it, and also including a great deal more. Without dispute, Gov. Gamble appoints the officers of this force, and fills vacancies when they occur. The question now practically in dispute is "Can Gov. Gamble make a vacancy, by removing an officer, or accepting a resignation?" Now, while it is proper that this question shall be settled, I do not perceive why either Gov. Gamble, or the government here, should care which way it is settled. I am perplexed with it only because there seems to be pertinacity about it. It seems to me that it might be either way without injury to the service; or that the offer of the Secretary of War to let Gov. Gamble make vacancies, and he, the Secretary, to ratify the making of them, ought to be satisfactory.

Annual Message to Congress

Fellow-citizens of the Senate and House of Representatives:

Since your last annual assembling another year of health and bountiful harvests has passed. And while it has not pleased the Almighty to bless us with a return of peace, we can but press on, guided by the best light He gives us, trusting that in His own good time, and wise way, all will yet be well.

The correspondence touching foreign affairs which has taken place during the last year is herewith submitted, in virtual compliance with a request to that effect, made by the House of Representatives near the close of the last session of Congress.

If the condition of our relations with other nations is less gratifying than it has usually been at former periods, it is certainly more satisfactory than a nation so unhappily distracted as we are, might reasonably have apprehended. In the month of June last there were some grounds to expect that the maritime powers which, at the beginning of our domestic difficulties, so unwisely and unnecessarily, as we think, recognized the insurgents as a belligerent, would soon recede from that position, which has proved only less injurious to themselves, than to our own country. But the temporary reverses which afterwards befell the national arms, and which were exaggerated by our own disloyal citizens abroad have hitherto delayed that act of simple justice.

The civil war, which has so radically changed for the moment, the occupations and habits of the American people, has necessarily disturbed the social condition, and affected very deeply the prosperity of the nations with which we have carried on a commerce that has been steadily increasing throughout a period of half a century. It has, at the same time, excited political ambitions and apprehensions which have produced a profound agitation throughout the civilized world. In this unusual agitation we have forborne from taking part in any controversy between foreign states, and between parties or factions in such states. We have attempted no propagandism, and acknowledged no revolution. But we have left to every nation the exclusive conduct and management of its own affairs. Our struggle has been, of course, contemplated by foreign nations with reference less to its own merits, than to its supposed, and often exaggerated effects and consequences resulting to those nations themselves. Nevertheless, complaint on the part of this government, even if it were just, would certainly be unwise.

The treaty with Great Britain for the suppression of the slave trade has been put into operation with a good prospect of complete success. It is an occasion of special pleasure to acknowledge that the execution of it, on the part of Her Majesty's government, has been marked with a jealous respect for the authority of the United States, and the rights of their moral and loyal citizens.

The convention with Hanover for the abolition of the stade dues has been carried into full effect, under the act of Congress for that purpose.

A blockade of three thousand miles of sea-coast could not be established, and vigorously enforced, in a season of great commercial activity like the present, without committing occasional mistakes, and inflicting unintentional injuries upon foreign nations and their subjects.

A civil war occurring in a country where foreigners reside and carry on trade under treaty stipulations, is necessarily fruitful of complaints of the violation of neutral rights. All such collisions tend to excite misapprehensions, and possibly to produce mutual reclamations between nations which have a common interest in preserving peace and friendship. In clear cases of these kinds I have, so far as possible, heard and redressed complaints which have been presented by friendly powers. There is still, however, a large and an augmenting number of doubtful cases upon which the government is unable to agree with the governments whose protection is demanded by the claimants. There are, moreover, many cases in which the United States, or their citizens, suffer wrongs from the naval or military authorities of foreign nations, which the governments of those states are not at once prepared to redress. I have proposed to some of the foreign states, thus interested, mutual conventions to examine and adjust such complaints. This proposition has been made especially to

Great Britain, to France, to Spain, and to Prussia. In each case it has been kindly received, but has not yet been formally adopted.

I deem it my duty to recommend an appropriation in behalf of the owners of the Norwegian bark Admiral P. Tordenskiold, which vessel was, in May, 1861, prevented by the commander of the blockading force off Charleston from leaving that port with cargo, notwithstanding a similar privilege had, shortly before, been granted to an English vessel. I have directed the Secretary of State to cause the papers in the case to be communicated to the proper committees.

Applications have been made to me by many free Americans of African descent to favor their emigration, with a view to such colonization as was contemplated in recent acts of Congress. Other parties, at home and abroad—some from interested motives, others upon patriotic considerations, and still others influenced by philanthropic sentiments—have suggested similar measures; while, on the other hand, several of the Spanish-American republics have protested against the sending of such colonies to their respective territories. Under these circumstances, I have declined to move any such colony to any state, without first obtaining the consent of its government, with an agreement on its part to receive and protect such emigrants in all the rights of freemen; and I have, at the same time, offered to the several states situated within the tropics, or having colonies there, to negotiate with them, subject to the advice and consent of the Senate, to favor the voluntary emigration of persons of that class to their respective territories, upon conditions which shall be equal, just, and humane. Liberia and Hayti are, as yet, the only countries to which colonists of African descent from here, could go with certainty of being received and adopted as citizens; and I regret to say such persons, contemplating colonization, do not seem so willing to migrate to those countries, as to some others, nor so willing as I think their interest demands. I believe, however, opinion among them, in this respect, is improving; and that, ere long, there will be an augmented, and considerable migration to both these countries, from the United States.

The new commercial treaty between the United States and the Sultan of Turkey has been carried into execution.

A commercial and consular treaty has been negotiated, subject to the Senate's consent, with Liberia; and a similar negotiation is now pending with the republic of Hayti. A considerable improvement of the national commerce is expected to result from these measures.

Our relations with Great Britain, France, Spain, Portugal, Russia, Prussia, Denmark, Sweden, Austria, the Netherlands, Italy, Rome, and the other European states, remain undisturbed. Very favorable relations also continue to be maintained with Turkey, Morocco, China and Japan.

During the last year there has not only been no change of our previous relations with the independent states of our own continent, but, more friendly sentiments than have heretofore existed, are believed to be entertained by these neighbors, whose safety and progress, are so intimately connected with our own. This statement especially applies to Mexico, Nicaragua, Costa Rica, Honduras, Peru, and Chile.

The commission under the convention with the republic of New Granada closed its session, without having audited and passed upon, all the claims which were submitted to it. A proposition is pending to revive the convention, that it may be able to do more complete justice. The joint commission between the United States and the republic of Costa Rica has completed its labors and submitted its report.

I have favored the project for connecting the United States with Europe by an Atlantic telegraph, and a similar project to extend the telegraph from San Francisco, to connect by a Pacific telegraph with the line which is being extended across the Russian empire.

The Territories of the United States, with unimportant exceptions, have remained undisturbed by the civil war, and they are exhibiting such evidence of prosperity as justifies an expectation that some of them will soon be in a condition to be organized as States, and be constitutionally admitted into the federal Union.

The immense mineral resources of some of those Territories ought to be developed as rapidly as possible. Every step in that direction would have a tendency to improve the revenues of the government, and diminish the burdens of the people. It is worthy of your serious consideration whether some extraordinary measures to promote that end cannot be adopted. The means which suggests itself as most likely to be effective, is a scientific exploration of the mineral regions in those Territories, with a view to the publication of its results at home and in foreign countries—results which cannot fail to be auspicious.

The condition of the finances will claim your most diligent consideration. The vast expenditures incident to the military and naval operations required for the suppression of the rebellion, have hitherto been met with a promptitude, and certainty, unusual in similar circumstances, and the public credit has been fully maintained. The continuance of the war, however, and the increased disbursements made necessary by the augmented forces now in the field, demand your best reflections as to the best modes of providing the necessary revenue, without injury to business and with the least possible burdens upon labor.

The suspension of specie payments by the banks, soon after the commencement of your last session, made large issues of United States notes unavoidable. In no other way could the payment of the troops, and the satisfaction of other just demands, be so economically, or so well provided for. The judicious legislation of Congress, securing the receivability of these notes for loans and internal duties, and making them a legal tender for other debts, has made them an universal currency; and has satisfied, partially, at least, and for the time, the long felt want of an uniform circulating medium, saving thereby to the people, immense sums in discounts and exchanges.

A return to specie payments, however, at the earliest period compatible with due regard to all interests concerned, should ever be kept in view. Fluctuations in the value of currency are always injurious, and to reduce these fluctuations to the lowest possible point will always be a leading purpose in wise legislation. Convertibility, prompt and certain convertibility into coin, is generally acknowledged to be the best and surest safeguard against them; and it is extremely doubtful whether a circulation of United States notes, payable in coin, and sufficiently large for the wants of the people, can be permanently, usefully and safely maintained.

Is there, then, any other mode in which the necessary provision for the public wants can be made, and the great advantages of a safe and uniform currency secured?

I know of none which promises so certain results, and is, at the same time, so unobjectionable, as the organization of banking associations, under a general act of Congress, well guarded in its provisions. To such associations the government might furnish circulating notes, on the security of United States bonds deposited in the treasury. These notes, prepared under the supervision of proper officers, being uniform in appearance and security, and convertible always into coin, would at once protect labor against the evils of a vicious currency, and facilitate commerce by cheap and safe exchanges.

A moderate reservation from the interest on the bonds would compensate the United States for the preparation and distribution of the notes and a general supervision of the system, and would lighten the burden of that part of the public debt employed as securities. The public credit, moreover, would be greatly improved, and the negotiation of new loans greatly facilitated by the steady market demand for government bonds which the adoption of the proposed system would create.

It is an additional recommendation of the measure, of considerable weight, in my judgment, that it would reconcile, as far as possible, all existing interests, by the opportunity offered to existing institutions to reorganize under the act, substituting only the secured uniform national circulation for the local and various circulation, secured and unsecured, now issued by them.

The receipts into the treasury from all sources, including loans and balance from the preceding year, for the fiscal year ending on the 30th June, 1862, were $583,885,247 06, of which sum $49,056,397 62 were derived from customs; $1,795,331,73 from the direct tax; from public lands $152,203,77; from miscellaneous sources, $931,787 64; from loans in all forms, $529,692,460 50. The remainder, $2,257,065 80, was the balance from last year.

The disbursements during the same period were for congressional, executive, and judicial purposes, $5,939,009 29; for foreign intercourse, $1,339,710,35; for miscellaneous expenses, including the mints, loans, post office deficiencies, collection of revenue, and other like charges, $14,129,771 50; for expenses under the Interior Department, $3,102,985 52; under the War Department, $394,368,407,36; under the Navy Department, $42,674,569 69; for interest on public debt, $13,190,324 45; and for payment of public debt, including reimbursement of temporary loan, and redemptions, $96,096,922 09; making an aggregate of $570,841,700 25; and leaving a balance in the treasury on the first day of July, 1862, of $13,043,546,81.

It should be observed that the sum of $96,096,922 09, expended for reimbursements and redemption of public debt, being included also in the loans made, may be properly deducted, both from receipts and expenditures, leaving the actual receipts for the year $487,788,324 97; and the expenditures, $474,744,778 16.

Other information on the subject of the finances will be found in the report of the Secretary of the Treasury, to whose statements and views I invite your most candid and considerate attention.

The reports of the Secretaries of War, and of the Navy, are herewith transmitted. These reports, though lengthy, are scarcely more than brief abstracts of the very numerous and extensive transactions and operations conducted through those departments. Nor could I give a summary of them here, upon any principle, which would admit of its being much shorter than the reports themselves. I therefore content myself with laying the reports before you, and asking your attention to them.

It gives me pleasure to report a decided improvement in the financial condition of the Post Office Department, as compared with several preceding years. The receipts for the fiscal year 1861 amounted to $8,349,296 40, which embraced the revenue from all the States of the Union for three quarters of that year. Notwithstanding the cessation of revenue from the so-called seceded States during the last fiscal year, the increase of the correspondence of the loyal States has been sufficient to produce a revenue during the same year of $8,299,820 90, being only $50,000 less than was derived from all the States of the Union during the previous year. The expenditures show a still more favorable result. The amount expended in 1861 was $13,606,759 11. For the last year the amount has been reduced to $11,125,364 13, showing a decrease of about $2,481,000 in the expenditures as compared with the preceding year and about $3,750,000 as compared with the fiscal year 1860. The deficiency in the department for the previous year was $4,551,966.98. For the last fiscal year it was reduced to $2,112,814.57. These favorable results are in part owing to the cessation of mail service in the insurrectionary States, and in part to a careful review of all expenditures in that department in the interest of economy. The efficiency of the postal service, it is believed, has also been much improved. The Postmaster General has also opened a correspondence, through the Department of State, with foreign governments, proposing a convention of postal representatives for the purpose of simplifying the rates of foreign postage, and to expedite the foreign mails. This proposition, equally important to our adopted citizens, and to the commercial interests of this country, has been favorably entertained, and agreed to, by all the governments from whom replies have been received.

I ask the attention of Congress to the suggestions of the Postmaster General in his report respecting the further legislation required, in his opinion, for the benefit of the postal service.

The Secretary of the Interior reports as follows in regard to the public lands:

"The public lands have ceased to be a source of revenue. From the 1st July, 1861, to the 30th September, 1862, the entire cash receipts from the sale of lands were $137,476 26—a sum much less than the expenses of our land system during the same period. The homestead law, which will take effect on the 1st of January next, offers such inducements to settlers, that sales for cash cannot be expected, to an extent sufficient to meet the expenses of the General Land Office, and the cost of surveying and bringing the land into market"

The discrepancy between the sum here stated as arising from the sales of the public lands, and the sum derived from the same source as reported from the Treasury Department arises, as I understand, from the fact that the periods of time, though apparently, were not really, coincident at the beginning point—the Treasury report including a considerable sum now, which had previously been reported from the Interior—sufficiently large to greatly overreach the sum derived from the three months now reported upon by the Interior, and not by the Treasury.

The Indian tribes upon our frontiers have, during the past year, manifested a spirit of insubordination, and, at several points, have engaged in open hostilities against the white settlements in their vicinity. The tribes occupying the Indian country south of Kansas, renounced their allegiance to the United States, and entered into treaties with the insurgents. Those who remained loyal to the United States were driven from the country. The chief of the Cherokees has visited this city for the purpose of restoring the former relations of the tribe with the United States. He alleges that they were constrained, by superior force, to enter into treaties with the insurgents, and that the United States neglected to furnish the protection which their treaty stipulations required.

In the month of August last the Sioux Indians, in Minnesota, attacked the settlements in their vicinity with extreme ferocity, killing, indiscriminately, men, women, and children. This attack was wholly unexpected, and, therefore, no means of defence had been provided. It is estimated that not less than eight hundred persons were killed by the Indians, and a large amount of property was destroyed. How this outbreak was induced is not definitely known, and suspicions, which may be unjust, need not to be stated. Information was received by the Indian bureau, from different sources, about the time hostilities were commenced, that a simultaneous attack was to be made upon the white settlements by all the tribes between the Mississippi river and the Rocky mountains. The State of Minnesota has suffered great injury from this Indian war. A large portion of her territory has been depopulated, and a severe loss has been sustained by the destruction of property. The people of that State manifest much anxiety for the removal of the tribes beyond the limits of the State as a guarantee against future hostilities. The Commissioner of Indian Affairs will furnish full details. I submit for your especial consideration whether our Indian system shall not be remodelled. Many wise and good men have impressed me with the belief that this can be profitably done.

I submit a statement of the proceedings of commissioners, which shows the progress that has been made in the enterprise of constructing the Pacific railroad. And this suggests the earliest completion of this road, and also the favorable action of Congress upon the projects now pending before them for enlarging the capacities of the great canals in New York and Illinois, as being of vital, and rapidly increasing importance to the whole nation, and especially to the vast interior region hereinafter to be noticed at some greater length. I purpose having prepared and laid before you at an early day some interesting and valuable statistical information upon this subject. The military and commercial importance of enlarging the Illinois and Michigan canal, and improving the Illinois river, is presented in the report of Colonel Webster to the Secretary of War, and now transmitted to Congress. I respectfully ask attention to it.

To carry out the provisions of the act of Congress of the 15th of May last, I have caused the Department of Agriculture of the United States to be organized.

The Commissioner informs me that within the period of a few months this department has established an extensive system of correspondence and exchanges, both at home and abroad, which promises to effect highly beneficial results in the development of a correct knowledge of recent improvements in agriculture, in the introduction of new products, and in the collection of the agricultural statistics of the different States.

Also that it will soon be prepared to distribute largely seeds, cereals, plants and cuttings, and has already published, and liberally diffused, much valuable information in anticipation of a more elaborate report, which will in due time be furnished, embracing some valuable tests in chemical science now in progress in the laboratory.

The creation of this department was for the more immediate benefit of a large class of our most valuable citizens; and I trust that the liberal basis upon which it has been organized will not only meet your approbation, but that it will realize, at no distant day, all the fondest anticipations of its most sanguine friends, and become the fruitful source of advantage to all our people.

On the twenty-second day of September last a proclamation was issued by the Executive, a copy of which is herewith submitted.

In accordance with the purpose expressed in the second paragraph of that paper, I now respectfully recall your attention to what may be called "compensated emancipation."

A nation may be said to consist of its territory, its people, and its laws. The territory is the only part which is of certain durability. "One generation passeth away, and another generation cometh, but the earth abideth forever." It is of the first importance to duly consider, and estimate, this ever-enduring part. That portion of the earth's surface which is owned and inhabited by the people of the United States, is well adapted to be the home of one national family; and it is not well adapted for two, or more. Its vast extent, and its variety of climate and productions, are of advantage, in this age, for one people, whatever they might have been in former ages. Steam, telegraphs, and intelligence, have brought these, to be an advantageous combination, for one united people.

In the inaugural address I briefly pointed out the total inadequacy of disunion, as a remedy for the differences between the people of the two sections. I did so in language which I cannot improve, and which, therefore, I beg to repeat:

"One section of our country believes slavery is *right*, and ought to be extended, while the other believes it is *wrong*, and ought not to be extended. This is the only substantial dispute. The fugitive slave clause of the Constitution, and the law for the suppression of the foreign slave trade, are each as well enforced, perhaps, as any law can ever be in a community where the moral sense of the people imperfectly supports the law itself. The great body of the people abide by the dry legal obligation in both cases, and a few break over in each. This, I think, cannot be perfectly cured; and it would be worse in both cases *after* the separation of the sections, than before. The foreign slave trade, now imperfectly suppressed, would be ultimately revived without restriction in one section; while fugitive slaves, now only partially surrendered, would not be surrendered at all by the other.

"Physically speaking, we cannot separate. We cannot remove our respective sections from each other, nor build an impassable wall between them. A husband and wife may be divorced, and go out of the presence, and beyond the reach of each other; but the different parts of our country cannot do this. They cannot but remain face to face; and intercourse, either amicable or hostile, must continue between them. Is it possible, then, to make that intercourse more advantageous, or more satisfactory, *after* separation than *before*? Can aliens make treaties, easier than friends can make laws? Can treaties be more faithfully enforced between aliens, than laws can among friends? Suppose you go to war, you cannot fight always; and when, after much loss on both sides, and no gain on either, you cease fighting, the identical old questions, as to terms of intercourse, are again upon you."

There is no line, straight or crooked, suitable for a national boundary, upon which to divide. Trace through, from east to west, upon the line between the free and slave country, and we shall find a little more than one-third of its length are rivers, easy to be crossed, and populated, or soon to be populated, thickly upon both sides; while nearly all its remaining length, are merely surveyor's lines, over which people may walk back and forth without any consciousness of their presence. No part of this line can be made any more difficult to pass, by writing it down on paper, or parchment, as a national boundary. The fact of separation, if it comes, gives up, on the part of the seceding section, the fugitive slave clause, along with all other constitutional obligations upon the section seceded from, while I should expect no treaty stipulation would ever be made to take its place.

But there is another difficulty. The great interior region, bounded east by the Alleghanies, north by the British dominions, west by the Rocky mountains, and south by the line along which the culture of corn and cotton meets, and which includes part of Virginia, part of Tennessee, all of Kentucky, Ohio, Indiana, Michigan, Wisconsin, Illinois, Missouri, Kansas, Iowa, Minnesota and the Territories of Dakota, Nebraska, and part of Colorado, already has above ten millions of

people, and will have fifty millions within fifty years, if not
prevented by any political folly or mistake. It contains more
than one-third of the country owned by the United States—
certainly more than one million of square miles. Once half as
populous as Massachusetts already is, it would have more
than seventy-five millions of people. A glance at the map
shows that, territorially speaking, it is the great body of the
republic. The other parts are but marginal borders to it, the
magnificent region sloping west from the rocky mountains to
the Pacific, being the deepest, and also the richest, in undevel-
oped resources. In the production of provisions, grains,
grasses, and all which proceed from them, this great interior
region is naturally one of the most important in the world.
Ascertain from the statistics the small proportion of the region which has, as yet, been brought into cultivation, and
also the large and rapidly increasing amount of its products,
and we shall be overwhelmed with the magnitude of the prospect presented. And yet this region has no sea-coast, touches
no ocean anywhere. As part of one nation, its people now
find, and may forever find, their way to Europe by New York,
to South America and Africa by New Orleans, and to Asia by
San Francisco. But separate our common country into two
nations, as designed by the present rebellion, and every man
of this great interior region is thereby cut off from some one
or more of these outlets, not, perhaps, by a physical barrier,
but by embarrassing and onerous trade regulations.

And this is true, *wherever* a dividing, or boundary line, may
be fixed. Place it between the now free and slave country, or
place it south of Kentucky, or north of Ohio, and still the
truth remains, that none south of it, can trade to any port or
place north of it, and none north of it, can trade to any port
or place south of it, except upon terms dictated by a government foreign to them. These outlets, east, west, and south,
are indispensable to the well-being of the people inhabiting,
and to inhabit, this vast interior region. *Which* of the three
may be the best, is no proper question. All, are better than
either, and all, of right, belong to that people, and to their
successors forever. True to themselves, they will not ask *where*
a line of separation shall be, but will vow, rather, that there
shall be no such line. Nor are the marginal regions less inter-

ested in these communications to, and through them, to the great outside world. They too, and each of them, must have access to this Egypt of the West, without paying toll at the crossing of any national boundary.

Our national strife springs not from our permanent part; not from the land we inhabit; not from our national homestead. There is no possible severing of this, but would multiply, and not mitigate, evils among us. In all its adaptations and aptitudes, it demands union, and abhors separation. In fact, it would, ere long, force reunion, however much of blood and treasure the separation might have cost.

Our strife pertains to ourselves—to the passing generations of men; and it can, without convulsion, be hushed forever with the passing of one generation.

In this view, I recommend the adoption of the following resolution and articles amendatory to the Constitution of the United States:

"Resolved by the Senate and House of Representatives of the United States of America in Congress assembled, (two thirds of both houses concurring,) That the following articles be proposed to the legislatures (or conventions) of the several States as amendments to the Constitution of the United States, all or any of which articles when ratified by three-fourths of the said legislatures (or conventions) to be valid as part or parts of the said Constitution, viz:

"Article——.

"Every State, wherein slavery now exists, which shall abolish the same therein, at any time, or times, before the first day of January, in the year of our Lord one thousand and nine hundred, shall receive compensation from the United States as follows, to wit:

"The President of the United States shall deliver to every such State, bonds of the United States, bearing interest at the rate of —— per cent, per annum, to an amount equal to the aggregate sum of   for each slave shown to have been therein, by the eighth census of the United States, said bonds to be delivered to such State by instalments, or in one parcel, at the completion of the abolishment, accordingly as the same shall have been gradual, or at one time, within such State; and interest shall begin to run upon any such bond, only from the proper time of its delivery as aforesaid. Any State having received bonds as aforesaid, and afterwards reintroducing or tolerating slavery therein, shall refund to the United States the bonds so received, or the value thereof, and all interest paid thereon.

"Article ——.

"All slaves who shall have enjoyed actual freedom by the chances of the war, at any time before the end of the rebellion, shall be forever free; but all owners of such, who shall not have been disloyal, shall be compensated for them, at the same rates as is provided for States adopting abolishment of slavery, but in such way, that no slave shall be twice accounted for.

"Article ——.

"Congress may appropriate money, and otherwise provide, for colonizing free colored persons, with their own consent, at any place or places without the United States."

I beg indulgence to discuss these proposed articles at some length. Without slavery the rebellion could never have existed; without slavery it could not continue.

Among the friends of the Union there is great diversity, of sentiment, and of policy, in regard to slavery, and the African race amongst us. Some would perpetuate slavery; some would abolish it suddenly, and without compensation; some would abolish it gradually, and with compensation; some would remove the freed people from us, and some would retain them with us; and there are yet other minor diversities. Because of these diversities, we waste much strength in struggles among ourselves. By mutual concession we should harmonize, and act together. This would be compromise; but it would be compromise among the friends, and not with the enemies of the Union. These articles are intended to embody a plan of such mutual concessions. If the plan shall be adopted, it is assumed that emancipation will follow, at least, in several of the States.

As to the first article, the main points are: first, the emancipation; secondly, the length of time for consummating it—thirty-seven years; and thirdly, the compensation.

The emancipation will be unsatisfactory to the advocates of perpetual slavery; but the length of time should greatly mitigate their dissatisfaction. The time spares both races from the evils of sudden derangement—in fact, from the necessity of any derangement—while most of those whose habitual course of thought will be disturbed by the measure will have passed away before its consummation. They will never see it. Another class will hail the prospect of emancipation, but will deprecate the length of time. They will feel that it gives too little to the now living slaves. But it really gives them much. It saves them from the vagrant destitution which must largely attend immediate emancipation in localities where their numbers are very great; and it gives the inspiring assurance that their posterity shall be free forever. The plan leaves to each State, choosing to act under it, to abolish slavery now, or at the end of the century, or at any intermediate time, or by degrees, extending over the whole or any part of the period; and it obliges no two states to proceed alike. It also provides for compensation, and generally the mode of making it. This, it would seem, must further mitigate the dissatisfaction of those who favor perpetual slavery, and especially of those who are to receive the compensation. Doubtless some of those who are to pay, and not to receive will object. Yet the measure is both just and economical. In a certain sense the liberation of slaves is the destruction of property—property acquired by descent, or by purchase, the same as any other property. It is no less true for having been often said, that the people of the south are not more responsible for the original introduction of this property, than are the people of the north; and when it is remembered how unhesitatingly we all use cotton and sugar, and share the profits of dealing in them, it may not be quite safe to say, that the south has been more responsible than the north for its continuance. If then, for a common object, this property is to be sacrificed is it not just that it be done at a common charge?

And if, with less money, or money more easily paid, we can preserve the benefits of the Union by this means, than we can by the war alone, is it not also economical to do it? Let us consider it then. Let us ascertain the sum we have expended in the war since compensated emancipation was proposed last March, and consider whether, if that measure had been promptly accepted, by even some of the slave States, the same sum would not have done more to close the war, than has been otherwise done. If so the measure would save money, and, in that view, would be a prudent and economical measure. Certainly it is not so easy to pay *something* as it is to pay *nothing*; but it is easier to pay a *large* sum than it is to pay a larger one. And it is easier to pay any sum *when* we are able, than it is to pay it *before* we are able. The war requires large sums, and requires them at once. The aggregate sum necessary for compensated emancipation, of course, would be large. But it would require no ready cash; nor the bonds even, any faster than the emancipation progresses. This might not, and probably would not, close before the end of the thirty-seven years. At that time we shall probably have a hundred millions of people to share the burden, instead of thirty one millions, as now. And not only so, but the increase of our population may be expected to continue for a long time after that period, as rapidly as before; because our territory will not have become full. I do not state this inconsiderately. At the same ratio of increase which we have maintained, on an average, from our first national census, in 1790, until that of 1860, we should, in 1900, have a population of 103,208,415. And why may we not continue that ratio far beyond that period? Our abundant room—our broad national homestead—is our ample resource. Were our territory as limited as are the British Isles, very certainly our population could not expand as stated. Instead of receiving the foreign born, as now, we should be compelled to send part of the native born away. But such is not our condition. We have two millions nine hundred and sixty-three thousand square miles. Europe has three millions and eight hundred thousand, with a population averaging seventy-three and one-third persons to the square mile. Why may not our country, at some time, average as many? Is it less fertile? Has it more waste surface, by mountains, rivers, lakes, deserts, or other causes? Is it inferior to Europe in any natural advantage? If, then, we are, at some time, to be as populous as Europe, how soon? As to when this *may* be, we can judge by the past and the present; as to when it *will* be, if ever, depends much on whether we maintain the Union. Several of our States are already above the average of Europe—seventy three and a third to the square mile. Massachusetts has 157; Rhode Island, 133; Connecticut, 99; New York and New Jersey, each, 80; also two other great States, Pennsylvania and Ohio, are not far below, the former having 63, and the latter 59. The States already above the European average, except New York, have increased in as rapid a ratio, since passing that point, as ever before; while no one of them is equal to some other parts of our country, in natural capacity for sustaining a dense population.

Taking the nation in the aggregate, and we find its population and ratio of increase, for the several decennial periods, to be as follows:—

1790	3,929,827		
1800	5,305,937	35.02 per cent.	{ratio of increase
1810	7,239,814	36.45	"
1820	9,638,131	33.13	"
1830	12,866,020	33.49	"
1840	17,069,453	32.67	"
1850	23,191,876	35.87	"
1860	31,443,790	35.58	"

This shows an average decennial increase of 34.60 per cent. in population through the seventy years from our first, to our last census yet taken. It is seen that the ratio of increase, at no one of these seven periods, is either two per cent. below, or two per cent. above, the average; thus showing how inflexible, and, consequently, how reliable, the law of increase, in our case, is. Assuming that it will continue, gives the following results:—

1870	42,323,341	1910	138,918,526
1880	56,967,216	1920	186,984,335
1890	76,677,872	1930	251,680,914
1900	103,208,415		

These figures show that our country *may* be as populous as Europe now is, at some point between 1920 and 1930—say about 1925—our territory, at seventy-three and a third persons to the square mile, being of capacity to contain 217,186,000.

And we *will* reach this, too, if we do not ourselves relinquish the chance, by the folly and evils of disunion, or by long and exhausting war springing from the only great element of national discord among us. While it cannot be foreseen exactly how much one huge example of secession, breeding lesser ones indefinitely, would retard population, civilization, and prosperity, no one can doubt that the extent of it would be very great and injurious.

The proposed emancipation would shorten the war, perpetuate peace, insure this increase of population, and proportionately the wealth of the country. With these, we should pay all the emancipation would cost, together with our other debt, easier than we should pay our other debt, without it. If we had allowed our old national debt to run at six per cent. per annum, simple interest, from the end of our revolutionary struggle until to day, without paying anything on either principal or interest, each man of us would owe less upon that debt now, than each man owed upon it then; and this because our increase of men, through the whole period, has been greater than six per cent.; has run faster than the interest upon the debt. Thus, time alone relieves a debtor nation, so long as its population increases faster than unpaid interest accumulates on its debt.

This fact would be no excuse for delaying payment of what is justly due; but it shows the great importance of time in this connexion—the great advantage of a policy by which we shall not have to pay until we number a hundred millions, what, by a different policy, we would have to pay now, when we number but thirty one millions. In a word, it shows that a dollar will be much harder to pay for the war, than will be a dollar for emancipation on the proposed plan. And then the latter will cost no blood, no precious life. It will be a saving of both.

As to the second article, I think it would be impracticable to return to bondage the class of persons therein contemplated. Some of them, doubtless, in the property sense, belong to loyal owners; and hence, provision is made in this article for compensating such.

The third article relates to the future of the freed people. It does not oblige, but merely authorizes, Congress to aid in colonizing such as may consent. This ought not to be regarded as objectionable, on the one hand, or on the other, in so much as it comes to nothing, unless by the mutual consent of the people to be deported, and the American voters, through their representatives in Congress.

I cannot make it better known than it already is, that I strongly favor colonization. And yet I wish to say there is an objection urged against free colored persons remaining in the country, which is largely imaginary, if not sometimes malicious.

It is insisted that their presence would injure, and displace white labor and white laborers. If there ever could be a proper time for mere catch arguments, that time surely is not now. In times like the present, men should utter nothing for which they would not willingly be responsible through time and in eternity. Is it true, then, that colored people can displace any more white labor, by being free, than by remaining slaves? If they stay in their old places, they jostle no white laborers; if they leave their old places, they leave them open to white laborers. Logically, there is neither more nor less of it. Emancipation, even without deportation, would probably enhance the wages of white labor, and, very surely, would not reduce them. Thus, the customary amount of labor would still have to be performed; the freed people would surely not do more than their old proportion of it, and very probably, for a time, would do less, leaving an increased part to white laborers, bringing their labor into greater demand, and, consequently, enhancing the wages of it. With deportation, even to a limited extent, enhanced wages to white labor is mathematically certain. Labor is like any other commodity in the market—increase the demand for it, and you increase the price of it. Reduce the supply of black labor, by colonizing the black laborer out of the country, and, by precisely so much, you increase the demand for, and wages of, white labor.

But it is dreaded that the freed people will swarm forth, and cover the whole land? Are they not already in the land? Will liberation make them any more numerous? Equally distributed among the whites of the whole country, and there would be but one colored to seven whites. Could the one, in any way, greatly disturb the seven? There are many communities now, having more than one free colored person, to seven whites; and this, without any apparent consciousness of evil from it. The District of Columbia, and the States of Maryland and Delaware, are all in this condition. The District has more than one free colored to six whites; and yet, in its frequent petitions to Congress, I believe it has never presented the presence of free colored persons as one of its grievances. But why should emancipation south, send the free people north? People, of any color, seldom run, unless there be something to run from. *Heretofore* colored people, to some extent, have fled north from bondage; and *now*, perhaps, from both bondage and destitution. But if gradual emancipation and deportation be adopted, they will have neither to flee from. Their old masters will give them wages at least until new laborers can be procured; and the freed men, in turn, will gladly give their labor for the wages, till new homes can be found for them, in congenial climes, and with people of their own blood and race. This proposition can be trusted on the mutual interests involved. And, in any event, cannot the north decide for itself, whether to receive them?

Again, as practice proves more than theory, in any case, has there been any irruption of colored people northward, because of the abolishment of slavery in this District last spring?

What I have said of the proportion of free colored persons to the whites, in the District, is from the census of 1860, having no reference to persons called contrabands, nor to those made free by the act of Congress abolishing slavery here.

The plan consisting of these articles is recommended, not but that a restoration of the national authority would be accepted without its adoption.

Nor will the war, nor proceedings under the proclamation of September 22, 1862, be stayed because of the *recommendation* of this plan. Its timely *adoption*, I doubt not, would bring restoration and thereby stay both.

And, notwithstanding this plan, the recommendation that Congress provide by law for compensating any State which may adopt emancipation, before this plan shall have been acted upon, is hereby earnestly renewed. Such would be only an advance part of the plan, and the same arguments apply to both.

This plan is recommended as a means, not in exclusion of, but additional to, all others for restoring and preserving the national authority throughout the Union. The subject is presented exclusively in its economical aspect. The plan would, I am confident, secure peace more speedily, and maintain it more permanently, than can be done by force alone; while all it would cost, considering amounts, and manner of payment, and times of payment, would be easier paid than will be the additional cost of the war, if we rely solely upon force. It is much—very much—that it would cost no blood at all.

The plan is proposed as permanent constitutional law. It cannot become such without the concurrence of, first, two-thirds of Congress, and, afterwards, three-fourths of the States. The requisite three-fourths of the States will necessarily include seven of the Slave states. Their concurrence, if obtained, will give assurance of their severally adopting emancipation, at no very distant day, upon the new constitutional terms. This assurance would end the struggle now, and save the Union forever.

I do not forget the gravity which should characterize a paper addressed to the Congress of the nation by the Chief Magistrate of the nation. Nor do I forget that some of you are my seniors, nor that many of you have more experience than I, in the conduct of public affairs. Yet I trust that in view of the great responsibility resting upon me, you will perceive no want of respect to yourselves, in any undue earnestness I may seem to display.

Is it doubted, then, that the plan I propose, if adopted, would shorten the war, and thus lessen its expenditure of money and of blood? Is it doubted that it would restore the national authority and national prosperity, and perpetuate both indefinitely? Is it doubted that we here—Congress and Executive—can secure its adoption? Will not the good people respond to a united, and earnest appeal from us? Can we, can they, by any other means, so certainly, or so speedily, assure these vital objects? We can succeed only by concert. It is not "can *any* of us *imagine* better?" but "can we *all* do better?" Object whatsoever is possible, still the question recurs "can we do better?" The dogmas of the quiet past, are inadequate to the stormy present. The occasion is piled high with difficulty, and we must rise with the occasion. As our case is new, so we must think anew, and act anew. We must disenthrall ourselves, and then we shall save our country.

Fellow-citizens, *we* cannot escape history. We of this Congress and this administration, will be remembered in spite of ourselves. No personal significance, or insignificance, can spare one or another of us. The fiery trial through which we pass, will light us down, in honor or dishonor, to the latest generation. We *say* we are for the Union. The world will not forget that we say this. We know how to save the Union. The world knows we do know how to save it. We—even *we here*—hold the power, and bear the responsibility. In *giving* freedom to the *slave*, we *assure* freedom to the *free*—honorable alike in what we give, and what we preserve. We shall nobly save, or meanly lose, the last best, hope of earth. Other means may succeed; this could not fail. The way is plain, peaceful, generous, just—a way which, if followed, the world will forever applaud, and God must forever bless.

December 1, 1862.

Message to Senate on Minnesota Indians

To the Senate of the United States:

In compliance with your resolution of December 5th, 1862, requesting the President "to furnish the Senate with all information in his possession touching the late Indian barbarities in the State of Minnesota, and also the evidence in his possession upon which some of the principal actors and head men were tried and condemned to death," I have the honor to state, that on receipt of said resolution I transmitted the same to the Secretary of the Interior, accompanied by a note, a copy of which is herewith inclosed, marked "A.," and in response to which I received, through that Department, a letter of the Commissioner of Indian Affairs, a copy of which is herewith inclosed, marked "B."

I further state, that on the 8th. day of November last I received a long telegraphic dispatch from Major General Pope, at St. Paul, Minnesota, simply announcing the names of the persons sentenced to be hanged. I immediately telegraphed to have transcripts of the records in all the cases forwarded to me, which transcripts, however, did not reach me until two or three days before the present meeting of Congress. Meantime I received, through telegraphic dispatches and otherwise, appeals in behalf of the condemned, appeals for their execution, and expressions of opinion as to proper policy in regard to them, and to the Indians generally in that vicinity, none of which, as I understand, falls within the scope of your inquiry. After the arrival of the transcripts of records, but before I had sufficient opportunity to examine them, I received a joint letter from one of the Senators and two of the Representatives from Minnesota, which contains some statements of fact not found in the records of the trials, and for which reason I herewith transmit a copy, marked "C." I also, for the same reason, inclose a printed memorial of the citizens of St Paul, addressed to me, and forwarded with the letter aforesaid.

Anxious to not act with so much clemency as to encourage another outbreak on the one hand, nor with so much severity as to be real cruelty on the other, I caused a careful examination of the records of trials to be made, in view of first ordering the execution of such as had been proved guilty of violating females. Contrary to my expectations, only two of this class were found. I then directed a further examination, and a classification of all who were proven to have participated in *massacres*, as distinguished from participation in *battles*. This class numbered forty, and included the two convicted of female violation. One of the number is strongly recommended by the Commission which tried them, for commutation to ten years' imprisonment. I have ordered the other thirty-nine to be executed on Friday, the 19th. instant. The order was dispatched from here on Monday, the 8th. instant, by a messenger to General Sibley; and a copy of which order is herewith transmitted, marked "D."

An abstract of the evidence as to the forty is herewith enclosed, marked "E."

To avoid the immense amount of copying, I lay before the Senate the original transcripts of the records of trials, as received by me.

This is as full and complete a response to the resolution as it is in my power to make.

December 11, 1862

To Fernando Wood

Executive Mansion, Washington,
Hon. Fernando Wood December 12, 1862.
My dear Sir   Your letter of the 8th. with the accompanying note of same date, was received yesterday. The most important paragraph in the letter, as I consider, is in these words: "On the 25th. November last I was advised by an authority which I deemed likely to be well informed, as well as reliable and truthful, that the Southern States would send representatives to the next congress, provided that a full and general amnesty should permit them to do so. No guarranties or terms were asked for other than the amnesty referred to."

I strongly suspect your information will prove to be groundless; nevertheless I thank you for communicating it to me.

Understanding the phrase in the paragraph above quoted "the Southern States would send representatives to the next congress" to be substantially the same as that "the people of the Southern States would cease resistance, and would reinaugerate, submit to, and maintain the national authority, within the limits of such states under the Constitution of the United States," I say, that in such case, the war would cease on the part of the United States; and that, if within a reasonable time "a full and general amnesty" were necessary to such end, it would not be withheld.

I do not think it would be proper now for me to communicate this, formally or informally, to the people of the Southern States. My belief is that they already know it; and when they choose, if ever, they can communicate with me unequivocally. Nor do I think it proper now to suspend military operations to try any experiment of negotiation.

I should, nevertheless, receive with great pleasure the exact information you now have, and also such other as you may in any way obtain. Such information might be more valuable before the first of January than afterwards.

While there is nothing in this letter which I shall dread to see in history, it is, perhaps, better for the present, that it's existence should not become public.

I therefore have to request that you will regard it as confidential. Your Obt. Servt

To Thomas J. Henderson

                                    Executive Mansion, Washington,
Hon. T. J. Henderson.   December 20, 1862.
My dear Sir:— Your letter of the 8th to Hon. William Kellogg has just been shown me. You can scarcely overestimate the pleasure it would give me to oblige you, but nothing is operating so ruinously upon us everywhere as "absenteeism." It positively will not do for me to grant leaves of absence in cases not sufficient to procure them under the regular rules.

It would astonish you to know the extent of the evil of

"absenteeism." We scarcely have more than half the men we are paying on the spot for service anywhere. Yours very truly,

To William H. Seward and Salmon P. Chase

(COPY)

Hon. William H. Seward, &   Executive Mansion,
Hon. Salmon P. Chase.   Washington, December 20. 1862.

Gentlemen: You have respectively tendered me your resignations, as Secretary of State, and Secretary of the Treasury of the United States. I am apprised of the circumstances which may render this course personally desireable to each of you; but, after most anxious consideration, my deliberate judgment is, that the public interest does not admit of it. I therefore have to request that you will resume the duties of your Departments respectively. Your Obt. Servt.

P.S. Same as above sent to Gov. Chase

P.S. Same as above sent to Gov. Seward.

Note—Postscripts, like the above are to respective letters.

Message to the Army of the Potomac

Executive Mansion, Washington, December 22, 1862.

To the Army of the Potomac: I have just read your Commanding General's preliminary report of the battle of Fredericksburg. Although you were not successful, the attempt was not an error, nor the failure other than an accident. The courage with which you, in an open field, maintained the contest against an entrenched foe, and the consummate skill and success with which you crossed and re-crossed the river, in face of the enemy, show that you possess all the qualities of a great army, which will yet give victory to the cause of the country and of popular government. Condoling with the mourners for the dead, and sympathizing with the severely wounded, I congratulate you that the number of both is comparatively so small.

I tender to you, officers and soldiers, the thanks of the nation.

To Fanny McCullough

                                          Executive Mansion,
Dear Fanny   Washington, December 23, 1862.

It is with deep grief that I learn of the death of your kind
and brave Father; and, especially, that it is affecting your
young heart beyond what is common in such cases. In this
sad world of ours, sorrow comes to all; and, to the young, it
comes with bitterest agony, because it takes them unawares.
The older have learned to ever expect it. I am anxious to afford some alleviation of your present distress. Perfect relief is
not possible, except with time. You can not now realize that
you will ever feel better. Is not this so? And yet it is a mistake.
You are sure to be happy again. To know this, which is certainly true, will make you some less miserable now. I have
had experience enough to know what I say; and you need
only to believe it, to feel better at once. The memory of your
dear Father, instead of an agony, will yet be a sad sweet feeling in your heart, of a purer, and holier sort than you have
known before.

Please present my kind regards to your afflicted mother.
                                          Your sincere friend

To Hiram Walbridge

General Hiram Walbridge   Executive Mansion
My Dear Sir   Washington December 28th. 1862.

I have twice declined to see you on the ground that I understood the object of your desired interview, and that it was
a matter of embarrassment to me. My real respect and esteem
for you makes me unwilling to leave the matter in quite so
abrupt a form. My embarrassment is that the place you seek
not selfishly I think, is greedily sought by many others; and
there is sure to be opposition both fierce and plausible to the
appointment of any one who up to this time has not been in
the military service. What answer to it will I make? Shall I say
I did it for political influence? That will be the more loudly
objected to. I need not point out to you where this objection
will come from. It will come from your competitors; it will

come from party spirit; it will come from indignant members of Congress who will perceive in it an attempt of mine to set a guardian over them.

The longer I can get along without a formal appointment the better. Yours Very truly

Opinion on Admission of West Virginia into the Union

The consent of the Legislature of Virginia is constitutionally necessary to the bill for the admission of West-Virginia becoming a law. A body claiming to be such Legislature has given it's consent. We can not well deny that it is such, unless we do so upon the outside knowledge that the body was chosen at elections, in which a majority of the qualified voters of Virginia did not participate. But it is a universal practice in the popular elections in all these states, to give no legal consideration whatever to those who do not choose to vote, as against the effect of the votes of those, who do choose to vote. Hence it is not the qualified voters, but the qualified voters, *who choose to vote*, that constitute the political power of the state. Much less than to non-voters, should any consideration be given to those who did not vote, *in this case*: because it is also matter of outside knowledge, that they were not merely neglectful of their rights under, and duty to, this government, but were also engaged in open rebellion against it. Doubtless among these non-voters were some Union men whose voices were smothered by the more numerous secessionists; but we know too little of their number to assign them any appreciable value. Can this government stand, if it indulges constitutional constructions by which men in open rebellion against it, are to be accounted, man for man, the equals of those who maintain their loyalty to it? Are they to be accounted even better citizens, and more worthy of consideration, than those who merely neglect to vote? If so, their treason against the constitution, enhances their constitutional value! Without braving these absurd conclusions, we can not deny that the body which consents to the admission of West-

Virginia, is the Legislature of Virginia. I do not think the plural form of the words "Legislatures" and "States" in the phrase of the constitution "without the consent of the Legislatures of the States concerned &c" has any reference to the *new* State concerned. That plural form sprang from the contemplation of two or more old States contributing to form a new one. The idea that the new state was in danger of being admitted without its own consent, was not provided against, because it was not thought of, as I conceive. It is said, the devil takes care of his own. Much more should a good spirit—the spirit of the Constitution and the Union—take care of it's own. I think it can not do less, and live.

But is the admission into the Union, of West-Virginia, expedient. This, in my general view, is more a question for Congress, than for the Executive. Still I do not evade it. More than on anything else, it depends on whether the admission or rejection of the new state would under all the circumstances tend the more strongly to the restoration of the national authority throughout the Union. That which helps most in this direction is the most expedient at this time. Doutless those in remaining Virginia would return to the Union, so to speak, less reluctantly without the division of the old state than with it; but I think we could not save as much in this quarter by rejecting the new state, as we should lose by it in West-Virginia. We can scarcely dispense with the aid of West-Virginia in this struggle; much less can we afford to have her against us, in congress and in the field. Her brave and good men regard her admission into the Union as a matter of life and death. They have been true to the Union under very severe trials. We have so acted as to justify their hopes; and we can not fully retain their confidence, and co-operation, if we seem to break faith with them. In fact, they could not do so much for us, if they would.

Again, the admission of the new state, turns that much slave soil to free; and thus, is a certain, and irrevocable encroachment upon the cause of the rebellion.

The division of a State is dreaded as a precedent. But a measure made expedient by a war, is no precedent for times of peace. It is said that the admission of West-Virginia, is secession, and tolerated only because it is our secession. Well, if we call it by that name, there is still difference enough between secession against the constitution, and secession in favor of the constitution.

I believe the admission of West-Virginia into the Union is expedient.

c. late December 1862

Final Emancipation Proclamation

BY THE PRESIDENT OF THE UNITED STATES OF AMERICA:
A PROCLAMATION.

Whereas, on the twentysecond day of September, in the year of our Lord one thousand eight hundred and sixty two, a proclamation was issued by the President of the United States, containing, among other things, the following, towit:

"That on the first day of January, in the year of our Lord one thousand eight hundred and sixty-three, all persons held as slaves within any State or designated part of a State, the people whereof shall then be in rebellion against the United States, shall be then, thenceforward, and forever free; and the Executive Government of the United States, including the military and naval authority thereof, will recognize and maintain the freedom of such persons, and will do no act or acts to repress such persons, or any of them, in any efforts they may make for their actual freedom.

"That the Executive will, on the first day of January aforesaid, by proclamation, designate the States and parts of States, if any, in which the people thereof, respectively, shall then be in rebellion against the United States; and the fact that any State, or the people thereof, shall on that day be, in good faith, represented in the Congress of the United States by members chosen thereto at elections wherein a majority of the qualified voters of such State shall have participated, shall, in the absence of strong countervailing testimony, be deemed conclusive evidence that such State, and the people thereof, are not then in rebellion against the United States."

Now, therefore I, Abraham Lincoln, President of the United States, by virtue of the power in me vested as Commander-in-Chief, of the Army and Navy of the United States in time of actual armed rebellion against authority and government of the United States, and as a fit and necessary war measure for suppressing said rebellion, do, on this first day of January, in the year of our Lord one thousand eight hundred and sixty three, and in accordance with my purpose so to do publicly proclaimed for the full period of one hundred days, from the day first above mentioned, order and designate as the States and parts of States wherein the people thereof respectively, are this day in rebellion against the United States, the following, towit:

Arkansas, Texas, Louisiana, (except the Parishes of St. Bernard, Plaquemines, Jefferson, St. Johns, St. Charles, St. James, Ascension, Assumption, Terrebonne, Lafourche, St. Mary, St. Martin, and Orleans, including the City of New-Orleans) Mississippi, Alabama, Florida, Georgia, South-Carolina, North-Carolina, and Virginia, (except the fortyeight counties designated as West Virginia, and also the counties of Berkley, Accomac, Northampton, Elizabeth-City, York, Princess Ann, and Norfolk, including the cities of Norfolk & Portsmouth); and which excepted parts are, for the present, left precisely as if this proclamation were not issued.

And by virtue of the power, and for the purpose aforesaid, I do order and declare that all persons held as slaves within said designated States, and parts of States, are, and henceforward shall be free; and that the Executive government of the United States, including the military and naval authorities thereof, will recognize and maintain the freedom of said persons.

And I hereby enjoin upon the people so declared to be free to abstain from all violence, unless in necessary self-defence; and I recommend to them that, in all cases when allowed, they labor faithfully for reasonable wages.

And I further declare and make known, that such persons of suitable condition, will be received into the armed service of the United States to garrison forts, positions, stations, and other places, and to man vessels of all sorts in said service.

And upon this act, sincerely believed to be an act of justice, warranted by the Constitution, upon military necessity, I invoke the considerate judgment of mankind, and the gracious favor of Almighty God.

In witness whereof, I have hereunto set my hand and caused the seal of the United States to be affixed.

Done at the City of Washington, this first day of January, in the year of our Lord one thousand eight hundred and sixty three, and of the Independence of the United States of America the eighty-seventh.

By the President: ABRAHAM LINCOLN
    WILLIAM H. SEWARD, Secretary of State.

To Henry W. Halleck

Major Gen. Halleck   Executive Mansion,
My dear Sir: Washington, January 1. 1863.

Gen. Burnside wishes to cross the Rappahannock with his army, but his Grand Division commanders all oppose the movement. If in such a difficulty as this you do not help, you fail me precisely in the point for which I sought your assistance. You know what Gen. Burnside's plan is; and it is my wish that you go with him to the ground, examine it as far as practicable, confer with the officers, getting their judgment, and ascertaining their temper, in a word, gather all the elements for forming a judgment of your own; and then tell Gen. Burnside that you *do* approve, or that you do *not* approve his plan. Your military skill is useless to me, if you will not do this. Yours very truly

Withdrawn, because considered harsh by Gen. Halleck.
    Jan. 1. 1862

To Samuel R. Curtis

                    Executive Mansion,
Major General Curtis   Washington, January 2, 1863.

My dear Sir: Yours of Dec. 29th. by the hand of Mr. Strong is just received. The day I telegraphed you suspending the order in relation to Dr. McPheters, he, with Mr. Bates, the Attorney General, appeared before me, and left with me a copy of the order mentioned. The Dr. also showed me the copy of an oath which he said he had taken, which is, indeed, very strong, and specific. He also verbally assured me that he had constantly prayed in church for the President and Government, as he had always done before the present war. In looking over the recitals in your order, I do not see that this matter of the prayer, as he states it, is negatived; nor that any violation of his oath is charged; nor, in fact, that any thing specific is alledged against him. The charges are all general— that he has a rebel wife & rebel relations, that he sympathizes with rebels, and that he exercises rebel influence. Now, after talking with him, I tell you frankly, I believe he does sympathize with the rebels; but the question remains whether such a man, of unquestioned good moral character, who has taken such an oath as he has, and can not even be charged of violating it, and who can be charged with no other specific act or omision, can, with safety to the government be exiled, upon the suspicion of his secret sympathies. But I agree that this must be left to you who are on the spot; and if, after all, you think the public good requires his removal, my suspension of the order is withdrawn, only with this qualification that the time during the suspension, is not to be counted against him. I have promised him this.

But I must add that the U.S. government must not, as by this order, undertake to run the churches. When an individual, in a church or out of it, becomes dangerous to the public interest, he must be checked; but let the churches, as such take care of themselves. It will not do for the U.S. to appoint Trustees, Supervisors, or other agents for the churches. Yours very truly

P.S. The committee composed of Messrs. Yeatman & Filley (Mr. Brodhead not attending) has presented your letter and the memorial of sundry citizens. On the whole subject embraced, exercise your best judgment, with a sole view to the public interest, and I will not interfere without hearing you.

Jan. 3, 1863.

To William S. Rosecrans

Major General W. S. Rosecrans   Executive Mansion,
Murfreesboro, Tenn.   Washington, Jan. 5. 1863

Your despatch announcing retreat of enemy has just reached here. God bless you, and all with you! Please tender to all, and accept for yourself, the Nation's gratitude for yours, and their, skill, endurance, and dantless courage.

To John A. McClernand

                                        Executive Mansion,
Major General McClernand   Washington, January 8. 1863.

My dear Sir   Your interesting communication by the hand

of Major Scates is received. I never did ask more, nor ever was willing to accept less, than for all the States, and the people thereof, to take and hold their places, and their rights, in the Union, under the Constitution of the United States. For this alone have I felt authorized to struggle; and I seek neither more nor less now. Still, to use a coarse, but an expressive figure, broken eggs can not be mended. I have issued the emancipation proclamation, and I can not retract it.

After the commencement of hostilities I struggled nearly a year and a half to get along without touching the "institution"; and when finally I conditionally determined to touch it, I gave a hundred days fair notice of my purpose, to all the States and people, within which time they could have turned it wholly aside, by simply again becoming good citizens of the United States. They chose to disregard it, and I made the peremptory proclamation on what appeared to me to be a military necessity. And being made, it must stand. As to the States not included in it, of course they can have their rights in the Union as of old. Even the people of the states included, if they choose, need not to be hurt by it. Let them adopt systems of apprenticeship for the colored people, conforming substantially to the most approved plans of gradual emancipation; and, with the aid they can have from the general government, they may be nearly as well off, in this respect, as if the present trouble had not occurred, and much better off than they can possibly be if the contest continues persistently.

As to any dread of my having a "purpose to enslave, or exterminate, the whites of the South," I can scarcely believe that such dread exists. It is too absurd. I believe you can be my personal witness that no man is less to be dreaded for undue severity, in any case.

If the friends you mention really wish to have peace upon the old terms, they should act at once. Every day makes the case more difficult. They can so act, with entire safety, so far as I am concerned.

I think you would better not make this letter public; but you may rely confidently on my standing by whatever I have said in it. Please write me if any thing more comes to light. Yours very truly

To John A. Dix

Private & confidential

Major General Dix   Executive Mansion,
My dear Sir: Washington, January 14, 1863.

The proclamation has been issued. We were not succeeding—at best, were progressing too slowly—without it. Now,
that we have it, and bear all the disadvantage of it, (as we do
bear some in certain quarters) we must also take some benefit
from it, if practicable. I therefore will thank you for your well
considered opinion whether Fortress-Monroe, and York-
Town, one or both, could not, in whole or in part, be garri-
soned by colored troops, leaving the white forces now
necessary at those places, to be employed elsewhere. Yours
very truly

To the Senate and House of Representatives

To the Senate and House of Representatives:

I have signed the Joint Resolution to provide for the immediate payment of the army and navy of the United States, passed by the House of Representatives on the 14th, and by the Senate on the 15th instant.

The Joint Resolution is a simple authority, amounting however, under existing circumstances, to a direction to the Secretary of the Treasury to make an additional issue of one hundred millions of dollars in United States notes if so much money is needed for the payment of the army and navy.

My approval is given in order that every possible facility may be afforded for the prompt discharge of all arrears of pay due to our soldiers and our sailors.

While giving this approval, however, I think it my duty to express my sincere regret that it has been found necessary to authorize so large an additional issue of United States notes, when this circulation, and that of the suspended banks together have become already so redundant as to increase prices beyond real values, thereby augmenting the cost of living to the injury of labor, and the cost of supplies to the injury of the whole country.

It seems very plain that continued issues of United States notes, without any check to the issues of suspended banks, and without adequate provision for the raising of money by loans, and for funding the issues so as to keep them within due limits, must soon produce disastrous consequences. And this matter appears to me so important that I feel bound to avail myself of this occasion to ask the special attention of Congress to it.

That Congress has power to regulate the currency of the country, can hardly admit of doubt; and that a judicious measure to prevent the deterioration of this currency, by a reasonable taxation of bank circulation or otherwise is needed, seems equally clear. Independently of this general consideration, it would be unjust to the people at large, to exempt banks, enjoying the special privilege of circulation, from their just proportion of the public burdens.

In order to raise money by way of loans most easily and cheaply, it is clearly necessary to give every possible support to the public credit. To that end, a uniform currency, in which taxes, subscriptions to loans, and all other ordinary public dues, as well as all private dues may be paid, is almost, if not quite indispensable. Such a currency can be furnished by banking associations, organized under a general act of Congress, as suggested in my message at the beginning of the present session. The securing of this circulation, by the pledge of United States bonds, as therein suggested, would still further facilitate loans, by increasing the present and causing a future demand for such bonds.

In view of the actual financial embarrassments of the government, and of the greater embarrassments sure to come, if the necessary means of relief be not afforded, I feel that I should not perform my duty by a simple announcement of my approval of the Joint Resolution which proposes relief only by increasing circulation, without expressing my earnest desire that measures, such in substance as those I have just referred to, may receive the early sanction of Congress.

By such measures, in my opinion, will payment be most certainly secured, not only to the army and navy, but to all honest creditors of the government, and satisfactory provision made for future demands on the treasury.

January 17. 1863.

To the Workingmen of Manchester, England

Executive Mansion, Washington,
To the workingmen of Manchester: January 19, 1863.

I have the honor to acknowledge the receipt of the address and resolutions which you sent to me on the eve of the new year.

When I came, on the fourth day of March, 1861, through a free and constitutional election, to preside in the government of the United States, the country was found at the verge of civil war. Whatever might have been the cause, or whosoever the fault, one duty paramount to all others was before me, namely, to maintain and preserve at once the Constitution and the integrity of the federal republic. A conscientious purpose to perform this duty is a key to all the measures of administration which have been, and to all which will hereafter be pursued. Under our form of government, and my official oath, I could not depart from this purpose if I would. It is not always in the power of governments to enlarge or restrict the scope of moral results which follow the policies that they may deem it necessary for the public safety, from time to time, to adopt.

I have understood well that the duty of self-preservation rests solely with the American people. But I have at the same time been aware that favor or disfavor of foreign nations might have a material influence in enlarging and prolonging the struggle with disloyal men in which the country is engaged. A fair examination of history has seemed to authorize a belief that the past action and influences of the United States were generally regarded as having been beneficent towards mankind. I have therefore reckoned upon the forbearance of nations. Circumstances, to some of which you kindly allude, induced me especially to expect that if justice and good faith should be practiced by the United States, they would encounter no hostile influence on the part of Great Britain. It is now a pleasant duty to acknowledge the demonstration you have given of your desire that a spirit of peace and amity towards this country may prevail in the councils of your Queen, who is respected and esteemed in your own country only more than she is by the kindred nation which has its home on this side of the Atlantic.

I know and deeply deplore the sufferings which the workingmen at Manchester and in all Europe are called to endure in this crisis. It has been often and studiously represented that the attempt to overthrow this government, which was built upon the foundation of human rights, and to substitute for it one which should rest exclusively on the basis of human slavery, was likely to obtain the favor of Europe. Through the actions of our disloyal citizens the workingmen of Europe have been subjected to a severe trial, for the purpose of forcing their sanction to that attempt. Under these circumstances, I cannot but regard your decisive utterance upon the question as an instance of sublime Christian heroism which has not been surpassed in any age or in any country. It is, indeed, an energetic and reinspiring assurance of the inherent power of truth and of the ultimate and universal triumph of justice, humanity, and freedom. I do not doubt that the sentiments you have expressed will be sustained by your great nation, and, on the other hand, I have no hesitation in assuring you that they will excite admiration, esteem, and the most reciprocal feelings of friendship among the American people. I hail this interchange of sentiment, therefore, as an augury that, whatever else may happen, whatever misfortune may befall your country or my own, the peace and friendship which now exist between the two nations will be, as it shall be my desire to make them, perpetual.

To John A. McClernand

Major Gen. McClernand   Executive Mansion,
My dear Sir: Washington, January 22. 1863.
    Yours of the 7th. was received yesterday. I need not recite, because you remember the contents. The charges, in their nature, are such that I must know as much about the facts involved, as you can. I have too many *family* controversies, (so to speak) already on my hands, to voluntarily, or so long as I can avoid it, take up another. You are now doing well—well for the country, and well for yourself—much better than you could possibly be, if engaged in open war with Gen. Halleck. Allow me to beg, that for your sake, for my sake, & for the country's sake, you give your whole attention to the better work.
    Your success upon the Arkansas, was both brilliant and valuable, and is fully appreciated by the country and government. Yours truly

To Joseph Hooker

Major General Hooker: Executive Mansion,
General.   Washington, January 26, 1863.
    I have placed you at the head of the Army of the Poto-

mac. Of course I have done this upon what appear to me to be sufficient reasons. And yet I think it best for you to know that there are some things in regard to which, I am not quite satisfied with you. I believe you to be a brave and a skilful soldier, which, of course, I like. I also believe you do not mix politics with your profession, in which you are right. You have confidence in yourself, which is a valuable, if not an indispensable quality. You are ambitious, which, within reasonable bounds, does good rather than harm. But I think that during Gen. Burnside's command of the Army, you have taken counsel of your ambition, and thwarted him as much as you could, in which you did a great wrong to the country, and to a most meritorious and honorable brother officer. I have heard, in such way as to believe it, of your recently saying that both the Army and the Government needed a Dictator. Of course it was not *for* this, but in spite of it, that I have given you the command. Only those generals who gain successes, can set up dictators. What I now ask of you is military success, and I will risk the dictatorship. The government will support you to the utmost of it's ability, which is neither more nor less than it has done and will do for all commanders. I much fear that the spirit which you have aided to infuse into the Army, of criticising their Commander, and withholding confidence from him, will now turn upon you. I shall assist you as far as I can, to put it down. Neither you, nor Napoleon, if he were alive again, could get any good out of an army, while such a spirit prevails in it.

And now, beware of rashness. Beware of rashness, but with energy, and sleepless vigilance, go forward, and give us victories. Yours very truly

To Franz Sigel

I believe an increased Cavalry force would be valuable, but I have not promised that, to suit the convenience of any officer, I would, however inconvenient to the government, raise one immediately. I have tried, in regard to Gen. Schurz & Gen.

Stahl, to oblige all around; but it seems to get worse & worse. If Gen. Sigel would say distinctly, and unconditionally, what he desires done, about the command of the forces he has, I should try to do it; but when he has plans, conditioned upon my raising new forces, which is inconvenient for me to do, it is drawing upon me too severely.

Jan. 26. 1863.

To Ambrose E. Burnside

Major Gen. Burnside   Executive Mansion, Washington,
My dear Sir   January 28. 1862.

Gen. Humphreys is now with me saying that you told him that you had strongly urged upon me, his, Gen. H's promotion, and that I in response had used such strong language, that you were sure his name would be sent to the Senate. I remember nothing of your speaking to me; or I to you, about Gen. H. still this is far from conclusive that nothing was said. I will now thank you to drop me a note, saying what you think is right and just about Gen. Humphreys. Yours as ever

January 28, 1863

To Franz Sigel

                                                    Executive Mansion,
Major General Sigel   Washington, February 5. 1863.

My dear Sir   Gen. Schurz thinks I was a little cross in my late note to you. If I was, I ask pardon. If I do get up a little temper I have no sufficient time to keep it up.

I believe I will not now issue any new order in relation to the matter in question; but I will be obliged, if Gen. Hooker consistently can, and will give an increased Cavalry command to Gen. Stahl. You may show Gen. Hooker this letter if you choose. Yours truly

To William S. Rosecrans

Executive Mansion, Washington,
Major General Rosecrans.   February 17, 1863.

My dear Sir: In no other way does the enemy give us so much trouble, at so little expence to himself, as by the *raids* of rapidly moving small bodies of troops (largely, if not wholly, mounted) harrassing, and discouraging loyal residents, supplying themselves with provisions, clothing, horses, and the like, surprising and capturing small detachments of our forces, and breaking our communications. And this will increase just in proportion as his larger armies shall weaken, and wane. Nor can these raids be successfully met by even larger forces of our own, of the same kind, acting merely on the *defensive.* I think we should organize proper forces, and make *counter-raids.* We should not capture so much of supplies from them, as they have done from us; but it would trouble them more to repair railroads and bridges than it does us. What think you of trying to get up such a corps in your army? Could you do it without any, or many additional troops (which we have not to give you) provided we furnish horses, suitable arms, and other appointments? Please consider this, not as an order, but as a suggestion. Yours truly

While I wish the required arms to be furnished to Gen. Rosecrans, I have made no promise on the subject, except what you can find in the within copy of letter

March 27, 1863.

To Mrs. L. H. Phipps

Executive Mansion,
Mrs. L. H. Phipps   Washington, March 9, 1863.

Yours of the 8th. is received. It is difficult for you to understand, what is, nevertheless true, that the bare reading of a letter of that length requires more than any one person's share of my time. And when read, what is it but an evidence that you intend to importune me for one thing, and another, and another, until, in self-defence, I must drop all and devote myself to find a place, even though I remove somebody else to do it, and thereby turn him & his friends upon me for indefinite future importunity, and hindrance from the legitimate duties for which I am supposed to be placed here? Yours &c.

To Edwin M. Stanton

Hon. Sec. of War: Executive Mansion,
Dear Sir   Washington, March 9. 1863.

A few days since I gave the lady, bearer of this, Mrs. Phipps, some sort of writing, favoring the appointment of her husband to be an Additional PayMaster. She thinks she failed because the application was made as from Pennsylvania, and says that it could & can be justly made from Tennessee. Please let her have it, if you consistently can either from Tennessee or any where else. Yours truly

To William S. Rosecrans

                                           Executive Mansion,
Major General Rosecrans   Washington, March 17, 1863.

My dear Sir. I have just received your telegram saying that "The Secy. of War telegraphed after the battle of Stone River" 'Anything you & your command want, you can have,' " and then specifying several things you have requested, and have not received.

The promise of the Secretary, as you state it, is certainly pretty broad; nevertheless it accords with the feeling of the whole government here towards you. I know not a single enemy of yours here. Still the promise must have a reasonable construction. We know you will not purposely make an unreasonable request; nor persist in one after it shall appear to be such.

Now, as to the matter of a Pay-Master. You desired one to be permanently attached to your Army, and, as I understand, desired that Major Larned should be the man. This was denied you; and you seem to think it was denied, partly to disoblige you, and partly to disoblige Major Larned—the latter, as you suspect, at the instance of Paymaster-General Andrews. On the contrary, the Secretary of War assures me the request was refused on no personal ground, whatever, but because to grant it, would derange, and substantially break up the whole pay-system as now organized, and so organized on very full consideration, and sound reason as believed. There is powerful temptation in money; and it was and is believed that nothing can prevent the Pay-Masters speculating upon the soldiers, but a system by which each is to pay certain regiments so soon after he has notice that he is to pay those particular regiments that he has no time or opportunity to lay plans for speculating upon them. This precaution is all lost, if Paymasters respectively are to serve permanently with the same regiments, and pay them over and over during the war. No special application of this has been intended to be made to Major Larned, or to your Army.

And as to Gen. Andrews, I have, in another connection, felt a little agrieved, at what seemed to me, his implicit following the advice and suggestions of Major Larned—so ready are we all to cry out, and ascribe motives, when our own toes are pinched.

Now, as to your request that your Commission should date from December 1861. Of course you expected to *gain* something by this; but you should remember that precisely so much as you should gain by it others would lose by it. If the thing you sought had been exclusively ours, we would have given it cheerfully; but being the right of other men, we having a merely arbitrary power over it, the taking it from them and giving it to you, became a more delicate matter, and more deserving of consideration. Truth to speak, I do not appreciate this matter of rank on paper, as you officers do. The world will not forget that you fought the battle of "Stone River" and it will never care a fig whether you rank Gen. Grant on paper, or he so, ranks you.

As to the appointment of an aid contrary to your wishes, I knew nothing of it until I received your despatch; and the Secretary of War tells me he has known nothing of it, but will trace it out. The examination of course will extend to the case of R. S. Thoms, whom you say you wish appointed.

And now be assured, you wrong both yourself and us, when you even suspect there is not the best disposition on the part of us all here to oblige you. Yours very truly

To Henry W. Davis

Hon. H. W. Davis   Executive Mansion,
My dear Sir   Washington, March 18. 1863.

There will be, in the new House of Representatives, as there were in the old, some members openly opposing the war, some supporting it *unconditionally*, and some supporting it with "buts" and "ifs" and "ands." They will divide on the organization of the House—on the election of Speaker.

As you ask my opinion, I give it that the supporters of the war should send no man to congress who will not go into caucus with the unconditional supporters of the war, and abide the action of such caucus, and support in the House, the person therein nominated for Speaker. Let the friends of the government first save the government, and then administer it to their own liking. Yours truly

P.S. This is not for publication, but to prevent any misunderstanding of what I verbally said to you yesterday.

To Horatio Seymour

Private & Confidential

His Excellency   Executive Mansion,
Gov. Seymour   Washington, March 23, 1863.

Dear Sir: You and I are substantially strangers; and I write this chiefly that we may become better acquainted. I, for the time being, am at the head of a nation which is in great peril; and you are at the head of the greatest State of that nation. As to maintaining the nation's life, and integrity, I assume, and believe, there can not be a difference of *purpose* between you and me. If we should differ as to the *means*, it is important that such difference should be as small as possible—that it should not be enhanced by unjust suspicions on one side or the other. In the performance of my duty, the co-operation of your State, as that of others, is needed—in fact, is indispensable. This alone is a sufficient reason why I should wish to be at a good understanding with you. Please write me at least as long a letter as this—of course, saying in it, just what you think fit. Yours very truly

Commutation of Sentence of James S. Pleasants

March 25, 1863.

The sentence of death in this case is hereby commuted to imprisonment for during the war, in one of the military prisons to be designated by the Secretary of War.

To Andrew Johnson

Private

Hon. Andrew Johnson   Executive Mansion,
My dear Sir: Washington, March 26. 1863.

I am told you have at least *thought* of raising a negro military force. In my opinion the country now needs no specific thing so much as some man of your ability, and position, to go to this work. When I speak of your position, I mean that of an eminent citizen of a slave-state, and himself a slaveholder. The colored population is the great *available* and yet *unavailed* of, force for restoring the Union. The bare sight of fifty thousand armed, and drilled black soldiers on the banks of the Mississippi, would end the rebellion at once. And who doubts that we can present that sight, if we but take hold in earnest? If you *have* been thinking of it please do not dismiss the thought. Yours truly

Speech to Indian Chiefs, Washington, D.C.

"You have all spoken of the strange sights you see here, among your pale-faced brethren; the very great number of people that you see; the big wigwams; the difference between our people and your own. But you have seen but a very small part of the pale-faced people. You may wonder when I tell you that there are people here in this wigwam, now looking at you, who have come from other countries a great deal farther off than you have come.

"We pale-faced people think that this world is a great, round ball, and we have people here of the pale-faced family who have come almost from the other side of it to represent their nations here and conduct their friendly intercourse with us, as you now come from your part of the round ball."

Here a globe was introduced, and the President, laying his hand upon it, said:

"One of our learned men will now explain to you our notions about this great ball, and show you where you live."

Professor Henry then gave the delegation a detailed and interesting explanation of the formation of the earth, showing how much of it was water and how much was land; and pointing out the countries with which we had intercourse. He also showed them the position of Washington and that of their own country, from which they had come.

The President then said:

"We have people now present from all parts of the globe— here, and here, and here. There is a great difference between this pale-faced people and their red brethren, both as to numbers and the way in which they live. We know not whether your own situation is best for your race, but this is what has made the difference in our way of living.

"The pale-faced people are numerous and prosperous because they cultivate the earth, produce bread, and depend upon the products of the earth rather than wild game for a subsistence.

"This is the chief reason of the difference; but there is another. Although we are now engaged in a great war between one another, we are not, as a race, so much disposed to fight and kill one another as our red brethren.

"You have asked for my advice. I really am not capable of advising you whether, in the providence of the Great Spirit, who is the great Father of us all, it is best for you to maintain the habits and customs of your race, or adopt a new mode of life.

"I can only say that I can see no way in which your race is to become as numerous and prosperous as the white race except by living as they do, by the cultivation of the earth.

"It is the object of this Government to be on terms of peace with you, and with all our red brethren. We constantly endeavor to be so. We make treaties with you, and will try to observe them; and if our children should sometimes behave badly, and violate these treaties, it is against our wish.

"You know it is not always possible for any father to have his children do precisely as he wishes them to do.

"In regard to being sent back to your own country, we have an officer, the Commissioner of Indian Affairs, who will take charge of that matter, and make the necessary arrangements."

The President's remarks were received with frequent marks of applause and approbation. "Ugh," "Aha" sounded along the line as the interpreter proceeded, and their countenances gave evident tokens of satisfaction.

March 27, 1863

To Nathaniel P. Banks

Private

Major General Banks   Executive Mansion,
My dear Sir: Washington, March 29, 1863.

Hon. Daniel Ullmann, with a commission of Brigadier General, and two or three hundred other gentlemen as officers, goes to your department and reports to you, for the purpose of raising a colored brigade. To now avail ourselves of this element of force, is very important, if not indispensable. I therefore will thank you to help Gen. Ullmann forward with his undertaking, as much, and as rapidly, as you can; and also to carry the general object beyond his particular organization if you find it practicable. The necessity of this is palpable if, as I understand, you are now unable to effect anything with your present force; and which force is soon to be greatly diminished by the expiration of terms of service, as well as by ordinary causes. I shall be very glad if you will take hold of the matter in earnest.

You will receive from the Department a regular order upon this subject. Yours truly

To David Hunter

Private   Executive Mansion
Major General Hunter   Washington D.C. April 1. 1863.

My dear Sir: I am glad to see the accounts of your colored force at Jacksonville, Florida. I see the enemy are driving at them fiercely, as is to be expected. It is important to the enemy that such a force shall *not* take shape, and grow, and thrive, in the South; and in precisely the same proportion, it is important to us that it *shall*. Hence the utmost caution and vigilance is necessary on our part. The enemy will make extra efforts to destroy them; and we should do the same to preserve and increase them. Yours truly

Memorandum on Hooker's Plan of Campaign

My opinion is, that just now, with the enemy directly ahead of us, there is *no* eligible route for us into Richmond; and consequently a question of preference between the Rappahannock route, and the James River route is a contest about nothing. Hence our prime object is the enemies' army in front of us, and is not with, or about, Richmond—at all, unless it be incidental to the main object.

What then? The two armies are face to face with a narrow river between them. Our communications are shorter and safer than are those of the enemy. For this reason, we can, with equal powers fret him more than he can us. I do not think that by raids towards Washington he can derange the Army of the Potomac at all. He has no distant opperations which can call any of the Army of the Potomac away; we have such operations which may call him away, at least in part. While he remains in tact, I do not think we should take the disadvantage of attacking him in his entrenchments; but we should continually harrass and menace him, so that he shall have no leisure, nor safety in sending away detachments. If he weakens himself, then pitch into him.

c. early April 1863

To Joseph Hooker

Executive Mansion,
Major General Hooker   Washington, April 15. 1863
    It is now 10-15. P.M. An hour ago I received your letter of this morning, and a few minutes later your despatch of this evening. The latter gives me considerable uneasiness. The rain and mud, of course, were to be calculated upon. Gen. S. is not moving rapidly enough to make the expedition come to any thing. He has now been out three days, two of which were unusually fine weather, and all three without hindrance from the enemy, and yet he is not twentyfive miles from where he started. To reach his point, he still has sixty to go; another river, the Rapidan, to cross, and will be hindered by the enemy. By arithmetic, how many days will it take him to do it? I do not know that any better can be done, but I greatly fear it is another failure already. Write me often. I am very anxious. Yours truly

Resolution on Slavery

Whereas, while *heretofore*, States, and Nations, have tolerated slavery, *recently*, for the first in the world, an attempt has been made to construct a new Nation, upon the basis of, and with the primary, and fundamental object to maintain, enlarge, and perpetuate human slavery, therefore,

Resolved, That no such embryo State should ever be recognized by, or admitted into, the family of christian and civilized nations; and that all christian and civilized men everywhere should, by all lawful means, resist to the utmost, such recognition or admission.

April 15, 1863

Memorandum on Patronage in St. Louis, Missouri

In answer to the within question "Shall we be sustained by you?" I have to answer that at the beginning of the administration I appointed one whom I understood to be an editor of the "Democrat" to be Post-Master at St. Louis—the best office in my gift within Missouri. Soon after this, our friends at St. Louis, must needs break into factions, the Democrat being, in my opinion, justly chargeable with a full share of the blame for it. I have stoutly tried to keep out of the quarrel, and so mean to do. As to contracts, and jobs, I understand that, by the law, they are awarded to the best bidders; and if the government agents at St. Louis do differently, it would be good ground to prossecute them upon.

April 16. 1863.

Commutation of Sentence of John A. Chase

April 28, 1863.

The sentence of death in this case is commuted to imprisonment at hard labor, with ball and chain attached to his leg, during the remainder of the present war; all to be in Fort Delaware.

Memorandum on Francis L. Capen's Weather Forecasts

It seems to me Mr. Capen knows nothing about the weather, in advance. He told me three days ago that it would not rain again till the 30th. of April or 1st. of May. It is raining now & has been for ten hours. I can not spare any more time to Mr. Capen.

April. 28. 1863.

To David Hunter

PRIVATE   Executive Mansion,
Major General Hunter   Washington, April 30, 1863.

My dear Sir   This morning I was presented an order of yours dismissing from the service, subject to my approval, a Captain Schaadt, of one of the Pennsylvania regiments. Disloyalty, without any statement of the evidence supposed to have proved it, is assigned as the cause of the dismissal; and he represents at home, as I am told, that the sole evidence was his refusal to sanction a resolution (indorsing the emancipation proclamation I believe); and our friends assure me that this statement is doing the Union cause great harm in his neighborhood and county, especially as he is a man of character, did good service in raising troops for us last fall, and still declares for the Union & his wish to fight for it. On this state of case I wrote a special indorsement on the order, which I suppose he will present to you; and I write this merely to assure you that no censure is intended upon you; but that it is hoped that you will inquire into the case more minutely, and that if there be no evidence, but his refusal to sanction the resolution, you will restore him. Yours as ever

Regarding the Case of David Schaadt

Executive Mansion, Washington, April 30, 1863.
Such facts are brought to my notice as induce me to withhold, my approval of the dismissal of Capt. Schaadt, named within. He is satisfactorily proved to me to be of good character for candor and manliness, and generally; and that he was most active and efficient, in Pennsylvania last autumn, in raising troops for the Union. All this should not retain him in the

service, if, since then, he has given himself, in any way, to the injury of the service. How this is I must understand better than I now do, before I can approve his dismissal. What has he done? What has he said? If, as is claimed for him, he is guilty of nothing, but the withholding his vote or sanction, from a certain resolution or resolutions, I think his dismissal is wrong, even though I might think the resolution itself right, and very proper to be adopted by such as choose. Capt. Schaadt will report himself to Gen. Hunter, and deliver him this paper, for his further action.

To Joseph Hooker

	Head-Quarters,
Major General Hooker.	Army of the Potomac,
My dear Sir	May. 7 1863.

The recent movement of your army is ended without effecting it's object, except perhaps some important breakings of the enemies communications. What next? If possible I would be very glad of another movement early enough to give us some benefit from the fact of the enemies communications being broken, but neither for this reason or any other, do I wish anything done in desperation or rashness. An early movement would also help to supersede the bad moral effect of the recent one, which is sure to be considerably injurious. Have you already in your mind a plan wholly, or partially formed? If you have, prossecute it without interference from me. If you have not, please inform me, so that I, incompetent as I may be, can try assist in the formation of some plan for the Army. Yours as ever

To Joseph Hooker

| | Executive Mansion, Washington, |
| Major General Hooker | May 14. 1863. |

My dear Sir: When I wrote you on the 7th. I had an impression that possibly, by an early movement, you could get some advantage from the supposed facts that the enemies communications were disturbed and that he was somewhat deranged in position. That idea has now passed away, the enemy having re-established his communications, regained his positions and actually received re-inforcements. It does not now appear probable to me that you can gain any thing by an early renewal of the attempt to cross the Rappahannock. I therefore shall not complain, if you do no more, for a time, than to keep the enemy at bay, and out of other mischief, by menaces and occasional cavalry raids, if practicable; and to put your own army in good condition again. Still, if in your own clear judgment, you can renew the attack successfully, I do not mean to restrain you. Bearing upon this last point, I must tell you I have some painful intimations that some of your corps and Division Commanders are not giving you their entire confidence. This would be ruinous, if true; and you should therefore, first of all, ascertain the real facts beyond all possibility of doubt. Yours truly

To Henry T. Blow, Charles D. Drake, and Others

Hon. H. T. Blow   Executive Mansion,
C. D. Drake & others   Washington,
St. Louis, Mo   May 15, 1863.
   Your despatch of to-day is just received. It is very painful to me that you in Missouri can not, or will not, settle your factional quarrel among yourselves. I have been tormented with it beyond endurance for months, by both sides. Neither side pays the least respect to my appeals to your reason. I am now compelled to take hold of the case.

To Isaac N. Arnold

Private & confidential

Hon. I. N. Arnold.   Executive Mansion,
My dear Sir: Washington, May 26. 1863.
   Your letter advising me to dismiss Gen. Halleck is received. If the public believe, as you say, that he has driven

Fremont, Butler, and Sigel from the service, they believe what I know to be false; so that if I were to yield to it, it would only be to be instantly beset by some other demand based on another falsehood equally gross. You know yourself that Fremont was relieved at his own request, before Halleck could have had any thing to do with it—went out near the end of June, while Halleck only came in near the end of July. I know equally well that no wish of Halleck's had any thing to do with the removal of Butler or Sigel. Sigel, like Fremont, was relieved at his own request, pressed upon me almost constantly for six months, and upon complaints that could have been made as justly by almost any corps commander in the army, and more justly by some. So much for the way they got out. Now a word as to their not getting back. In the early Spring, Gen. Fremont sought active service again; and, as it seemed to me, sought it in a very good, and reasonable spirit. But he holds the highest rank in the Army, except McClellan, so that I could not well offer him a subordinate command. Was I to displace Hooker, or Hunter, or Rosecrans, or Grant, or Banks? If not, what was I to do? And similar to this, is the case of both the others. One month after Gen. Butler's return, I offered him a position in which I thought and still think, he could have done himself the highest credit, and the country the greatest service, but he declined it. When Gen. Sigel was relieved, at his own request as I have said, of course I had to put another in command of his corps. Can I instantly thrust that other out to put him in again?

And now my good friend, let me turn your eyes upon another point. Whether Gen. Grant shall or shall not consummate the capture of Vicksburg, his campaign from the beginning of this month up to the twenty second day of it, is one of the most brilliant in the world. His corps commanders, & Division commanders, in part, are McClernand, McPherson, Sherman, Steele, Hovey, Blair, & Logan. And yet taking Gen. Grant & these seven of his generals, and you can scarcely name one of them that has not been constantly denounced and opposed by the same men who are now so anxious to get Halleck out, and Fremont & Butler & Sigel in. I believe no one of them went through the Senate easily, and certainly one failed to get through at all. I am compelled to take a more impartial and unprejudiced view of things. Without claiming to be your superior, which I do not, my position enables me to understand my duty in all these matters better than you possibly can, and I hope you do not yet doubt my integrity. Your friend, as ever

To John M. Schofield

Executive Mansion,
Gen. J. M. Schofield   Washington, May 27. 1863.

My dear Sir: Having relieved Gen. Curtis and assigned you to the command of the Department of the Missouri—I think it may be of some advantage for me to state to you why I did it. I did not relieve Gen. Curtis because of any full conviction that he had done wrong by commission or omission. I did it because of a conviction in my mind that the Union men of Missouri, constituting, when united, a vast majority of the whole people, have entered into a pestilent factional quarrel among themselves, Gen. Curtis, perhaps not of choice, being the head of one faction, and Gov. Gamble that of the other. After months of labor to reconcile the difficulty, it seemed to grow worse and worse until I felt it my duty to break it up some how; and as I could not remove Gov. Gamble, I had to remove Gen. Curtis. Now that you are in the position, I wish you to undo nothing merely because Gen. Curtis or Gov. Gamble did it; but to exercise your own judgment, and do *right* for the public interest. Let your military measures be strong enough to repel the invader and keep the peace, and not so strong as to unnecessarily harrass and persecute the people. It is a difficult *role*, and so much greater will be the honor if you perform it well. If both factions, or neither, shall abuse you, you will probably be about right. Beware of being assailed by one, and praised by the other. Yours truly

To Ambrose E. Burnside

"Cypher"

Major General Burnside—   Washington, D.C.
Cincinnati, O.   May 29. 1863

Your despatch of to-day received. When I shall wish to supersede you I will let you know. All the cabinet regretted the necessity of arresting, for instance, Vallandigham, some perhaps, doubting, that there was a real necessity for it—but, being done, all were for seeing you through with it.

To William T. Otto

I must repeat now in writing what I have told Mr. Kelly verbally, that the courts and not the President, must decide questions of land titles. There may be some questions in regard to pre-emptions, which by law, are to be decided through the Department, with appeal to me, and when such a case shall come regularly to me, I shall hear it. But I must now say, once for all, that mere vague assertions that the decisions of the Courts are fraudulent, with appeals to me to reverse them, can not be entertained.

June 1, 1863

To Edwin M. Stanton

                                               Executive Mansion,
Hon. Secretary of War: Washington, D.C., June 4, 1863.

My dear Sir: I have received additional dispatches which, with former ones, induce me to believe we should revoke or suspend the order suspending the Chicago Times, and if you concur in opinion, please have it done. Yours, truly,

To Joseph Hooker

                                          Washington, D.C.,
Major General Hooker   June 5. 1863

Yours of to-day was received an hour ago. So much of professional military skill is requisite to answer it, that I have turned the task over to Gen. Halleck. He promises to perform it with his utmost care. I have but one idea which I think worth suggesting to you, and that is in case you find Lee coming to the North of the Rappahannock, I would by no means cross to the South of it. If he should leave a rear force at Fredericksburg, tempting you to fall upon it, it would fight in intrenchments, and have you at disadvantage, and so, man for man, worst you at that point, while his main force would in some way be getting an advantage of you Northward. In one word, I would not take any risk of being entangled upon the river, like an ox jumped half over a fence, and liable to be torn by dogs, front and rear, without a fair chance to gore one way or kick the other. If Lee would come to my side of the river, I would keep on the same side & fight him, or act on the defence, according as might be my estimate of his strength relatively to my own. But these are mere suggestions which I desire to be controlled by the judgment of yourself and Gen. Halleck.

Draft of Anonymous Letter to the Washington Chronicle

Executive Mansion,

Editor of the Chronicle.   Washington, June 6. 1863.

In your issue of this morning, you have an article on the "Chicago Times." Being an Illinoisian, I happen to know that much of the article is incorrect. As I remember, upon the repeal of the Missouri Compromise, the democratic newspapers at Chicago went over to the opposition. Thereupon the Times was established by the friends of the administration, Senator Douglas being the most prominent in establishing it. A man by the name of James Sheahan, from this city, was it's first, and only editor, nearly if not quite all the remainder of the Senator's life. On the political separation between Mr. Buchanan and Senator Douglas, the Times adhered to the Senator, and was the ablest paper in his support through his senatorial contest with Mr. Lincoln. Since the last Presidential election certainly, perhaps since Senator Douglas' death, Mr.

Sheahan left the Times; and the Times since then, has been identical with the Times before then, in little more than the name. The writer hereof is not well enough posted to say but that your article in other respects is correct.

To Samuel R. Curtis

Major General Curtis   Executive Mansion,
My dear Sir: Washington, June 8. 1863.

I have scarcely supposed it possible that you would entirely understand my feelings and motives in making the late change of commander for the Department of the Missouri. I inclose you a copy of a letter which I recently addressed to Gen. Schofield, & which will explain the matter in part. It became almost a matter of personal self-defence to somehow break up the state of things in Missouri. I did not mean to cast any censure upon you, nor to indorse any of the charges made against you by others. With me the presumption is still in your favor that you are honest, capable, faithful, and patriotic. Yours very truly

To Mary Todd Lincoln

Mrs. Lincoln   Executive Mansion,
Philadelphia, Pa.   Washington, June 9. 1863.

Think you better put "Tad's" pistol away. I had an ugly dream about him.

To Joseph Hooker

"Cypher"   United States Military Telegraph
                    War Department. Washington DC.
Major General Hooker   June 10. 1863.

Your long despatch of to-day is just received. If left to me, I would not go South of the Rappahannock, upon Lee's moving North of it. If you had Richmond invested to-day, you would not be able to take it in twenty days; meanwhile, your communications, and with them, your army would be ruined. I think *Lee's* Army, and not *Richmond*, is your true objective point. If he comes towards the Upper Potomac, follow on his flank, and on the inside track, shortening your lines, whilst he lengthens his. Fight him when oppertunity offers. If he stays where he is, fret him, and fret him.

To Erastus Corning and Others

EXECUTIVE MANSION
Washington.

Hon. ERASTUS CORNING *and others:*   June 12, 1863.

GENTLEMEN: Your letter of May 19, inclosing the resolutions of a public meeting held at Albany, N. Y., on the 16th of the same month, was received several days ago.

The resolutions, as I understand them, are resolvable into two propositions—first, the expression of a purpose to sustain the cause of the Union, to secure peace through victory, and to support the Administration in every constitutional and lawful measure to suppress the Rebellion; and secondly, a declaration of censure upon the Administration for supposed unconstitutional action, such as the making of military arrests. And, from the two propositions, a third is deduced, which is that the gentlemen composing the meeting are resolved on doing their part to maintain our common government and country, despite the folly or wickedness, as they may conceive, of any Administration. This position is eminently patriotic, and as such I thank the meeting and congratulate the nation for it. My own purpose is the same; so that the meeting and myself have a common object, and can have no difference, except in the choice of means or measures for effecting that object.

And here I ought to close this paper, and would close it, if there were no apprehension that more injurious consequences than any merely personal to myself might follow the censures systematically cast upon me for doing what, in my view of duty, I could not forbear. The resolutions promise to support me in every constitutional and lawful measure to suppress the Rebellion; and I have not knowingly employed, nor shall knowingly employ, any other. But the meeting, by their resolutions, assert and argue that certain military arrests, and proceedings following them, for which I am ultimately responsible, are unconstitutional. I think they are not. The resolutions quote from the Constitution the definition of treason, and also the limiting safeguards and guarantees therein provided for the citizen on trials for treason, and on his being held to answer for capital or otherwise infamous crimes, and, in criminal prosecutions, his right to a speedy and public trial by an impartial jury. They proceed to resolve "that these safeguards of the rights of the citizen against the pretensions of arbitrary power were intended more *especially* for his protection in times of civil commotion." And, apparently to demonstrate the proposition, the resolutions proceed: "They were secured substantially to the English people *after* years of protracted civil war, and were adopted into our Constitution at the *close* of the Revolution." Would not the demonstration have been better if it could have been truly said that these safeguards had been adopted and applied *during* the civil wars and *during* our Revolution, instead of *after* the one and at the *close* of the other? I, too, am devotedly for them *after* civil war, and *before* civil war, and at all times, "except when, in cases of rebellion or invasion, the public safety may require" their suspension. The resolutions proceed to tell us that these safeguards "have stood the test of seventy-six years of trial, under our republican system, under circumstances which show that, while they constitute the foundation of all free government, they are the elements of the enduring stability of the Republic." No one denies that they have so stood the test up to the beginning of the present Rebellion, if we except a certain occurrence at New-Orleans; nor does any one question that they will stand the same test much longer after the Rebellion closes. But these provisions of the Constitution have no application to the case we have in hand, because the arrests complained of were not made for treason—that is, not for *the* treason defined in the Constitution, and upon conviction of which the punishment is death—nor yet were they made to hold persons to answer for any capital or otherwise infamous crimes; nor were the proceedings following, in any constitutional or legal sense, "criminal prosecutions." The arrests were made on totally different grounds, and the proceedings following accorded with the grounds of the arrests. Let us consider the real case with which we are dealing, and apply to it the parts of the Constitution plainly made for such cases.

Prior to my installation here, it had been inculcated that any State had a lawful right to secede from the national Union, and that it would be expedient to exercise the right whenever the devotees of the doctrine should fail to elect a President to their own liking. I was elected contrary to their liking; and, accordingly, so far as it was legally possible, they had taken seven States out of the Union, had seized many of the United States forts, and had fired upon the United States flag, all before I was inaugurated, and, of course, before I had done any official act whatever. The Rebellion thus began soon ran into the present Civil War; and, in certain respects, it began on very unequal terms between the parties. The insurgents had been preparing for it more than thirty years, while the Government had taken no steps to resist them. The former had carefully considered all the means which could be turned to their account. It undoubtedly was a well-pondered reliance with them that, in their own unrestricted efforts to destroy Union, Constitution, and law, all together, the Government would, in great degree, be restrained by the same Constitution and law from arresting their progress. Their sympathizers pervaded all departments of the Government and nearly all communities of the people. From this material, under cover of "liberty of speech," "liberty of the press," and "habeas corpus," they hoped to keep on foot among us a most efficient corps of spies, informers, suppliers, and aiders and abettors of their cause in a thousand ways. They knew that in times such as they were inaugurating, by the Constitution itself, the "habeas corpus" might be suspended; but they also knew they had friends who would make a question as to *who* was to suspend it; meanwhile, their spies and others might remain at large to help on their cause. Or, if, as has happened, the Executive should suspend the writ, without ruinous waste of time, instances of arresting innocent persons might occur, as are always likely to occur in such cases; and then a clamor could be raised in regard to this, which might be, at least, of some service to the insurgent cause. It needed no very keen perception to discover this part of the enemy's programme, so soon as, by open hostilities, their machinery was fairly put in motion. Yet, thoroughly imbued with a reverence for the guaranteed rights of individuals, I was slow to adopt the strong measures which by degrees I have been forced to regard as being within the exceptions of the Constitution, and as indispensable to the public safety. Nothing is better known to history than that courts of justice are utterly incompetent to such cases. Civil courts are organized chiefly for trials of individuals, or, at most, a few individuals acting in concert; and this in quiet times, and on charges of crimes well defined in the law. Even in times of peace, bands of horse-thieves and robbers frequently grow too numerous and powerful for the ordinary courts of justice. But what comparison, in numbers have such bands ever borne to the insurgent sympathizers, even in many of the loyal States? Again: a jury too frequently has at least one member more ready to hang the panel than to hang the traitor. And yet, again, he who dissuades one man from volunteering, or induces one soldier to desert, weakens the Union cause as much as he who kills a Union soldier in battle. Yet this dissuasion or inducement may be so conducted as to be no defined crime of which any civil court would take cognizance.

Ours is a case of rebellion—so called by the resolutions before me—in fact, a clear, flagrant, and gigantic case of rebellion; and the provision of the Constitution that "the privilege of the writ of habeas corpus shall not be suspended, unless when, in cases of rebellion or invasion, the public safety may require it," is *the* provision which specially applies to our present case. This provision plainly attests the understanding of those who made the Constitution, that ordinary courts of justice are inadequate to "cases of rebellion"—attests their purpose that, in such cases, men may be held in custody whom the courts, acting on ordinary rules, would discharge. Habeas corpus does not discharge men who are proved to be guilty of defined crime; and its suspension is allowed by the Constitution on purpose that men may be arrested and held who cannot be proved to be guilty of defined crime, "when, in cases of rebellion or invasion, the public safety may require it." This is precisely our present case—a case of rebellion, wherein the public safety *does* require the suspension. Indeed, arrests by process of courts, and arrests in cases of rebellion, do not proceed altogether upon the same basis. The former is directed at the small per centage of ordinary and continuous perpetration of crime; while the latter is directed at sudden and extensive uprisings against the Government, which at most, will succeed or fail in no great length of time. In the latter case, arrests are made, not so much for what has been done, as for what probably would be done. The latter is more for the preventive and less for the vindictive than the former. In such cases, the purposes of men are much more easily understood than in cases of ordinary crime. The man who stands by and says nothing when the peril of his Government is discussed, cannot be misunderstood. If not hindered, he is sure to help the enemy; much more, if he talks ambiguously—talks for his country with "buts" and "ifs" and "ands." Of how little value the constitutional provisions I have quoted will be rendered, if arrests shall never be made until defined crimes shall have been committed, may be illustrated by a few notable examples. Gen. John C. Breckinridge, Gen. Robert E. Lee, Gen. Joseph E. Johnston, Gen. John B. Magruder, Gen. William B. Preston, Gen. Simon B. Buckner, and Commodore Franklin Buchanan, now occupying the very highest places in the Rebel war service, were all within the power of the Government since the Rebellion began, and were nearly as well known to be traitors then as now. Unquestionably if we had seized and held them, the insurgent cause would be much weaker. But no one of them had then committed any crime defined in the law. Every one of them, if arrested, would have been discharged on *habeas corpus* were the writ allowed to operate. In view of these and similar cases, I think the time not unlikely to come when I shall be blamed for having made too few arrests rather than too many.

By the third resolution, the meeting indicate their opinion that military arrests may be constitutional in localities where rebellion actually exists, but that such arrests are unconstitutional in localities where rebellion or insurrection does *not* actually exist. They insist that such arrests shall not be made "outside of the lines of necessary military occupation, and the scenes of insurrection." Inasmuch, however, as the Constitution itself makes no such distinction, I am unable to believe that there *is* any such constitutional distinction. I concede that the class of arrests complained of can be constitutional only when, in cases of rebellion or invasion, the public safety may require them; and I insist that in such cases they are constitutional *wherever* the public safety does require them; as well in places to which they may prevent the Rebellion extending as in those where it may be already prevailing; as well where they may restrain mischievous interference with the raising and supplying of armies to suppress the Rebellion, as where the Rebellion may actually be; as well where they may restrain the enticing men out of the army, as where they would prevent mutiny in the army; equally constitutional at all places where they will conduce to the public safety, as against the dangers of rebellion or invasion. Take the particular case mentioned by the meeting. It is asserted, in substance, that Mr. Vallandigham was, by a military commander, seized and tried "for no other reason than words addressed to a public meeting, in criticism of the course of the Administration, and in condemnation of the Military orders of the General." Now, if there be no mistake about this; if this assertion is the truth and the whole truth; if there was no other reason for the arrest, then I concede that the arrest was wrong. But the arrest, as I understand, was made for a very different reason. Mr. Vallandigham avows his hostility to the War on the part of the Union; and his arrest was made because he was laboring, with some effect, to prevent the raising of troops; to encourage desertions from the army; and to leave the Rebellion without an adequate military force to suppress it. He was not arrested because he was damaging the political prospects of the Administration, or the personal interests of the Commanding General, but because he was damaging the Army, upon the existence and vigor of which the life of the Nation depends. He was warring upon the Military, and this gave the Military constitutional jurisdiction to lay hands upon him. If Mr. Vallandigham was not damaging the military power of the country, then his arrest was made on mistake of fact, which I would be glad to correct on reasonably satisfactory evidence.

I understand the meeting, whose resolutions I am considering, to be in favor of suppressing the Rebellion by military force—by armies. Long experience has shown that armies cannot be maintained unless desertions shall be punished by the severe penalty of death. The case requires, and the law and the Constitution sanction, this punishment. Must I shoot a simple-minded soldier boy who deserts, while I must not touch a hair of a wily agitator who induces him to desert? This is none the less injurious when effected by getting a father, or brother, or friend, into a public meeting, and there working upon his feelings till he is persuaded to write the soldier boy that he is fighting in a bad cause, for a wicked Administration of a contemptible Government, too weak to arrest and punish him if he shall desert. I think that in such a case to silence the agitator, and save the boy is not only constitutional, but withal a great mercy.

If I be wrong on this question of constitutional power, my error lies in believing that certain proceedings are constitutional when, in cases of rebellion or invasion, the public safety requires them, which would not be constitutional when, in the absence of rebellion or invasion, the public safety does *not* require them: in other words, that the Constitution is not, in its application, in all respects the same, in cases of rebellion or invasion involving the public safety, as it is in time of profound peace and public security. The Constitution itself makes the distinction; and I can no more be persuaded that the Government can constitutionally take no strong measures in time of rebellion, because it can be shown that the same could not be lawfully taken in time of peace, than I can be persuaded that a particular drug is not good medicine for a sick man, because it can be shown not to be good food for a well one. Nor am I able to appreciate the danger apprehended by the meeting that the American people will, by means of military arrests during the Rebellion, lose the right of Public Discussion, the Liberty of Speech and the Press, the Law of Evidence, Trial by Jury, and Habeas Corpus, throughout the indefinite peaceful future, which I trust lies before them, any more than I am able to believe that a man could contract so strong an appetite for emetics during temporary illness as to persist in feeding upon them during the remainder of his healthful life.

In giving the resolutions that earnest consideration which you request of me, I cannot overlook the fact that the meeting speak as "Democrats." Nor can I, with full respect for their known intelligence, and the fairly presumed deliberation with which they prepared their resolutions, be permitted to suppose that this occurred by accident, or in any way other than that they preferred to designate themselves "Democrats" rather than "American citizens." In this time of national peril, I would have preferred to meet you upon a level one step higher than any party platform; because I am sure that, from such more elevated position, we could do better battle for the country we all love than we possibly can from those lower ones where, from the force of habit, the prejudices of the past, and selfish hopes of the future, we are sure to expend much of our ingenuity and strength in finding fault with, and aiming blows at each other. But, since you have denied me this, I will yet be thankful, for the country's sake, that not all Democrats have done so. He on whose discretionary judgment Mr. Vallandigham was arrested and tried is a Democrat, having no old party affinity with me; and the judge who rejected the constitutional view expressed in these resolutions, by refusing to discharge Mr. Vallandigham on habeas corpus, is a Democrat of better days than these, having received his judicial mantle at the hands of President Jackson. And still more, of all those Democrats who are nobly exposing their lives and shedding their blood on the battle-field, I have learned that many approve the course taken with Mr. Vallandigham, while I have not heard of a single one condemning it. I cannot assert that there are none such. And the name of President Jackson recalls an instance of pertinent history: After the battle of New-Orleans, and while the fact that the treaty of peace had been concluded was well known in the city, but before official knowledge of it had arrived, Gen. Jackson still maintained martial or military law. Now, that it could be said the war was over, the clamor against martial law, which had existed from the first, grew more furious. Among other things, a Mr. Louiallier published a denunciatory newspaper article. Gen. Jackson arrested him. A lawyer by the name of Morel procured the United States Judge Hall to issue a writ of habeas corpus to release Mr. Louiallier. Gen. Jackson arrested both the lawyer and the judge. A Mr. Hollander ventured to say of some part of the matter that "it was a dirty trick." Gen. Jackson arrested him. When the officer undertook to serve the writ of habeas corpus, Gen. Jackson took it from him, and sent him away with a copy. Holding the judge in custody a few days, the General sent him beyond the limits of his encampment, and set him at liberty, with an order to remain till the ratification of peace should be regularly announced, or until the British should have left the Southern coast. A day or two more elapsed, the ratification of a treaty of peace was regularly announced, and the judge and others were fully liberated. A few days more, and the judge called Gen. Jackson into court and fined him $1,000 for having arrested him and the others named. The General paid the fine, and there the matter rested for nearly thirty years, when Congress refunded principal and interest. The late Senator Douglas, then in the House of Representatives, took a leading part in the debates, in which the constitutional question was much discussed. I am not prepared to say whom the journals would show to have voted for the measure.

It may be remarked: First, that we had the same Constitution then as now; secondly, that we then had a case of invasion, and now we have a case of rebellion; and, thirdly, that the permanent right of the People to Public Discussion, the Liberty of Speech and the Press, the Trial by Jury, the Law of Evidence, and the Habeas Corpus, suffered no detriment whatever by that conduct of Gen. Jackson, or its subsequent approval by the American Congress.

And yet, let me say that, in my own discretion, I do not know whether I would have ordered the arrest of Mr. Vallandigham. While I cannot shift the responsibility from myself, I hold that, as a general rule, the commander in the field is the better judge of the necessity in any particular case. Of course, I must practice a general directory and revisory power in the matter.

One of the resolutions expresses the opinion of the meeting that arbitrary arrests will have the effect to divide and distract those who should be united in suppressing the Rebellion, and I am specifically called on to discharge Mr. Vallandigham. I regard this as, at least, a fair appeal to me on the expediency of exercising a Constitutional power which I think exists. In response to such appeal, I have to say, it gave me pain when I learned that Mr. Vallandigham had been arrested—that is, I was pained that there should have seemed to be a necessity for arresting him—and that it will afford me great pleasure to discharge him so soon as I can, by any means, believe the public safety will not suffer by it. I further say that, as the war progresses, it appears to me, opinion, and action, which were in great confusion at first, take shape, and fall into more regular channels, so that the necessity for strong dealing with them gradually decreases. I have every reason to desire that it should cease altogether, and far from the least is my regard for the opinions and wishes of those who, like the meeting at Albany, declare their purpose to sustain the Government in every constitutional and lawful measure to suppress the Rebellion. Still, I must continue to do so much as may seem to be required by the public safety.

To Joseph Hooker

Washington, June 14, 1863—5.50 p.m.
Major-General Hooker: So far as we can make out here, the enemy have Milroy surrounded at Winchester, and Tyler at Martinsburg. If they could hold out a few days, could you help them? If the head of Lee's army is at Martinsburg and the tail of it on the Plank road between Fredericksburg and Chancellorsville, the animal must be very slim somewhere. Could you not break him?

To Joseph Hooker

(*Private.*)
Executive Mansion, Washington, D.C., June 16, 1863.
My dear General: I send you this by the hand of Captain Dahlgren. Your despatch of 11:30 A.M. to-day is just received. When you say I have long been aware that you do not enjoy

the confidence of the major-general commanding, you state the case much too strongly.

You do not lack his confidence in any degree to do you any harm. On seeing him, after telegraphing you this morning, I found him more nearly agreeing with you than I was myself. Surely you do not mean to understand that I am withholding my confidence from you when I happen to express an opinion (certainly never discourteously) differing from one of your own.

I believe Halleck is dissatisfied with you to this extent only, that he knows that you write and telegraph ("report," as he calls it) to me. I think he is wrong to find fault with this; but I do not think he withholds any support from you on account of it. If you and he would use the same frankness to one another, and to me, that I use to both of you, there would be no difficulty. I need and must have the professional skill of both, and yet these suspicions tend to deprive me of both.

I believe you are aware that since you took command of the army I have not believed you had any chance to effect anything till now. As it looks to me, Lee's now returning toward Harper's Ferry gives you back the chance that I thought McClellan lost last fall. Quite possibly I was wrong both then and now; but, in the great responsibility resting upon me, I cannot be entirely silent. Now, all I ask is that you will be in such mood that we can get into our action the best cordial judgment of yourself and General Halleck, with my poor mite added, if indeed he and you shall think it entitled to any consideration at all. Yours as ever,

To Joseph Hooker

                              Executive Mansion, Washington,
Major General Hooker.   June 16. 1863.

To remove all misunderstanding, I now place you in the strict military relation to Gen. Halleck, of a commander of one of the armies, to the General-in-Chief of all the armies. I have not intended differently; but as it seems to be differently understood, I shall direct him to give you orders, and you to obey them.

To John M. Schofield

Gen. John M. Schofield.   Executive Mansion,
My dear Sir: Washington, June 22, 1863.

Your despatch, asking in substance, whether, in case Missouri shall adopt gradual emancipation, the general government will protect slave owners in that species of property during the short time it shall be permitted by the State to exist within it, has been received. Desirous as I am, that emancipation shall be adopted by Missouri, and believing as I do, that *gradual* can be made better than *immediate* for both black and white, except when military necessity changes the case, my impulse is to say that such protection would be given. I can not know exactly what shape an act of emancipation may take. If the period from the initiation to the final end, should be comparatively short, and the act should prevent persons being sold, during that period, into more lasting slavery, the whole would be easier. I do not wish to pledge the general government to the affirmative support of even temporary slavery, beyond what can be fairly claimed under the constitution. I suppose, however, this is not desired; but that it is desired for the Military force of the United States, while in Missouri, to not be used in subverting the temporarily reserved legal rights in slaves during the progress of emancipation. This I would desire also. I have very earnestly urged the slave-states to adopt emancipation; and it ought to be, and is an object with me not to overthrow, or thwart what any of them may in good faith do, to that end.

You are therefore authorized to act in the spirit of this letter, in conjunction with what may appear to be the military necessities of your Department.

Although this letter will become public at some time, it is not intended to be made so now. Yours truly

Reply to the Ohio Democratic Convention

Washington, D.C. June 29, 1863
Messrs M. Birchard   David A Houk   Geo. Bliss   T. W.
Bartley   W. J. Gordon   Jno. O'Neill   C. A. White

W. E. Finck   Alexander Long   J. W White   Geo. H.
Pendleton   Geo L. Converse   Warren P. Noble   Jas. R.
Morris   W. A. Hutchins   Abner L. Backus   J. F.
McKinney   F. C. Le Blond   Louis Schaefer

Gentlemen: The resolutions of the Ohio Democratic State
convention which you present me, together with your introductory and closing remarks, being in position and argument, mainly the same as the resolutions of the Democratic
meeting at Albany, New-York, I refer you to my response to
the latter, as meeting most of the points in the former. This
response you evidently used in preparing your remarks, and
I desire no more than that it be used with accuracy. In a
single reading of your remarks I only discovered one inaccu-
racy in matter which I suppose you took from that paper.
It is when you say "The undersigned are unable to agree
with you in the opinion you have expressed that the constitution is different in time of insurrection or invasion from
what it is in time of peace & public security." A recurrence
to the paper will show you that I have not expressed the
opinion you suppose. I expressed the opinion that the constitution is different, *in its application* in cases of Rebellion or
Invasion, involving the Public Safety, from what it is in
times of profound peace and public security; and this opinion I adhere to, simply because, by the constitution itself,
things may be done in the one case which may not be done
in the other.

I dislike to waste a word on a merely personal point; but I
must respectfully assure you that you will find yourselves at
fault should you ever seek for evidence to prove your assumption that I "opposed, in discussions before the people, the
policy of the Mexican war."

You say "Expunge from the constitution this limitation
upon the power of congress to suspend the writ of Habeas
corpus, and yet the other guarranties of personal liberty
would remain unchanged." Doubtless if this clause of the
constitution, improperly called, as I think, a limitation upon
the power of congress, were expunged, the other guarranties
would remain the same; but the question is, not how those
guarranties would stand, with that clause *out* of the constitution, but how they stand with that clause remaining in it—

in cases of Rebellion or Invasion, involving the public Safety. If the liberty could be indulged, of expunging that clause letter & spirit, I really think the constitutional argument would be with you. My general view on this question was stated in the Albany response, and hence I do not state it now. I only add that, as seems to me, the benefit of the writ of Habeas corpus, is the great means through which the guarranties of personal liberty are conserved, and made available in the last resort; and coroborative of this view, is the fact that Mr. V. in the very case in question, under the advice of able lawyers, saw not where else to go but to the Habeas Corpus. But by the constitution the benefit of the writ of Habeas corpus itself may be suspended when in cases of Rebellion or Invasion the public Safety may require it.

You ask, in substance, whether I really claim that I may override all the guarrantied rights of individuals, on the plea of conserving the public safety—when I may choose to say the public safety requires it. This question, divested of the phraseology calculated to represent me as struggling for an arbitrary personal prerogative, is either simply a question *who* shall decide, or an affirmation that *nobody* shall decide, what the public safety does require, in cases of Rebellion or Invasion. The constitution contemplates the question as likely to occur for decision, but it does not expressly declare who is to decide it. By necessary implication, when Rebellion or Invasion comes, the decision is to be made, from time to time; and I think the man whom, for the time, the people have, under the constitution, made the commander-in-chief, of their Army and Navy, is the man who holds the power, and bears the responsibility of making it. If he uses the power justly, the same people will probably justify him; if he abuses it, he is in their hands, to be dealt with by all the modes they have reserved to themselves in the constitution.

The earnestness with which you insist that persons can only, in times of rebellion, be lawfully dealt with, in accordance with the rules for criminal trials and punishments in times of peace, induces me to add a word to what I said on that point, in the Albany response. You claim that men may, if they choose, embarrass those whose duty it is, to combat a giant rebellion, and then be dealt with in turn, only as if there was no rebellion. The constitution itself rejects this view. The military arrests and detentions, which have been made, including those of Mr. V. which are not different in principle from the others, have been for *prevention*, and not for *punishment*—as injunctions to stay injury, as proceedings to keep the peace—and hence, like proceedings in such cases, and for like reasons, they have not been accompanied with indictments, or trials by juries, nor, in a single case by any punishment whatever, beyond what is purely incidental to the prevention. The original sentence of imprisonment in Mr. V.'s case, was to prevent injury to the Military service only, and the modification of it was made as a less disagreeable mode to him, of securing the same prevention.

I am unable to perceive an insult to Ohio in the case of Mr. V. Quite surely nothing of the sort was or is intended. I was wholly unaware that Mr. V. was at the time of his arrest a candidate for the democratic nomination for Governor until so informed by your reading to me the resolutions of the convention. I am grateful to the State of Ohio for many things, especially for the brave soldiers and officers she has given in the present national trial, to the armies of the Union.

You claim, as I understand, that according to my own position in the Albany response, Mr. V. should be released; and this because, as you claim, he has not damaged the military service, by discouraging enlistments, encouraging desertions, or otherwise; and that if he had, he should have been turned over to the civil authorities under recent acts of congress. I certainly do not *know* that Mr. V. has specifically, and by direct language, advised against enlistments, and in favor of desertion, and resistance to drafting. We all know that combinations, armed in some instances, to resist the arrest of deserters, began several months ago; that more recently the like has appeared in resistance to the enrolment preparatory to a draft; and that quite a number of assassinations have occurred from the same animus. These had to be met by military force, and this again has led to bloodshed and death. And now under a sense of responsibility more weighty and enduring than any which is merely official, I solemnly declare my belief that this hindrance, of the military, including maiming and murder, is due to the course in which Mr. V. has been engaged, in a greater degree than to any other cause; and is due to him personally, in a greater degree than to any other one man. These things have been notorious, known to all, and of course known to Mr. V. Perhaps I would not be wrong to say they originated with his special friends and adhereants. With perfect knowledge of them, he has frequently, if not constantly made speeches, in congress, and before popular assemblies; and if it can be shown that, with these things staring him, in the face, he has ever uttered a word of rebuke, or counsel against them, it will be a fact greatly in his favor with me, and one of which, as yet I, am totally ignorant. When it is known that the whole burthen of his speeches has been to stir up men against the prossecution of the war, and that in the midst of resistance to it, he has not been known, in any instance, to counsel against such resistance, it is next to impossible to repel the inference that he has counselled directly in favor of it. With all this before their eyes the convention you represent have nominated Mr. V. for Governor of Ohio; and both they and you, have declared the purpose to sustain the national Union by all constitutional means. But, of course, they and you, in common, reserve to yourselves to decide what are constitutional means; and, unlike the Albany meeting, you omit to state, or intimate, that in your opinion, an army is a constitutional means of saving the Union against a rebellion; or even to intimate that you are conscious of an existing rebellion being in progress with the avowed object of destroying that very Union. At the same time your nominee for Governor, in whose behalf you appeal, is known to you, and to the world, to declare against the use of an army to suppress the rebellion. Your own attitude, therefore, encourages desertion, resistance to the draft and the like, because it teaches those who incline to desert, and to escape the draft, to believe it is your purpose to protect them, and to hope that you will become strong enough to do so. After a short personal intercourse with you gentlemen of the committee, I can not say I think you desire this effect to follow your attitude; but I assure you that both friends and enemies of the

Union look upon it in this light. It is a substantial hope, and by consequence, a real strength to the enemy. If it is a false hope, and one which you would willingly dispel, I will make the way exceedingly easy. I send you duplicates of this letter, in order that you, or a majority of you, may if you choose, indorse your names upon one of them, and return it thus indorsed to me, with the understanding that those signing, are thereby committed to the following propositions, and to nothing else.

1   That there is now a rebellion in the United States, the object and tendency of which is to destroy the national Union; and that in your opinion, an army and navy are constitutional means for suppressing that rebellion.

2.   That no one of you will do any thing which in his own judgment, will tend to hinder the increase, or favor the decrease, or lessen the efficiency of the army or navy, while engaged in the effort to suppress that rebellion; and,

3.   That each of you will, in his sphere, do all he can to have the officers, soldiers, and seamen of the army and navy, while engaged in the effort to suppress the rebellion, paid, fed, clad, and otherwise well provided and supported.

And with the further understanding that upon receiving the letter and names thus indorsed, I will cause them to be published, which publication shall be within itself, a revocation of the order in relation to Mr. V.

It will not escape observation that I consent to the release of Mr. V. upon terms, not embracing any pledge from him, or from others as to what he will, or will not do. I do this because he is not present to speak for himself, or to authorize others to speak for him; and because I should expect that on his returning, he would not put himself practically in antagonism with the position of his friends. But I do it chiefly because I thereby prevail on other influential gentlemen of Ohio to so define their position, as to be of immense value to the Army—thus more than compensating for the consequences of any mistake in allowing Mr. V. to return; and so that, on the whole, the public safety will not have suffered by it. Still, in regard to Mr. V. and all others, I must hereafter as heretofore, do so much as the public safety may seem to require. I have the honor to be respectfully yours, &c.,

To William Kellogg

Hon. Wm. Kellogg.   Executive Mansion,
My dear Sir: Washington, June 29. 1863.

I have received, and read, your pencil note. I think you do not know how embarrassing your request is. Few things are so troublesome to the government as the fierceness with which the profits of trading in cotten are sought. The temptation is so great that nearly every body wishes to be in it; and when in, the question of profit controls all, regardless of whether the cotten seller is loyal or rebel, or whether he is paid in corn-meal or gun-powder. The officers of the army, in numerous instances, are believed to connive and share the profits, and thus the army itself is diverted from fighting the rebels to speculating in cotten; and steam-boats and wagons in the pay of the government, are set to gathering and carrying cotten, and the soldiers to loading cotten-trains and guarding them.

The matter deeply affects the Treasury and War Departments, and has been discussed again and again in the cabinet. What can, and what can not be done, has, for the time been settled, and it seems to me I can not safely break over it. I know it is thought that one case is not much, but how can I favor one and deny another. One case can not be kept a secret. The authority given would be utterly ineffectual until it is shown; and when shown, every body knows of it. The administration would do for you as much as for any other man; and I personally would do some more than for most others; but really I can not involve myself and the Government as this would do. Yours as ever

To Robert H. Milroy

PRIVATE

Major General Milroy   Executive Mansion,
My dear Sir: Washington, June 29. 1863.

Your letters to Mr. Blair and to myself, are handed to me by him. I have never doubted your courage and devotion to the cause. But you have just lost a Division, and *prima facie* the fault is upon you; and while that remains unchanged, for me to put you in command again, is to justly subject me to the charge of having put you there on purpose to have you lose another. If I knew facts sufficient to satisfy me that you were not in fault, or error, the case would be different. But the facts I do know, while they are not at all conclusive, and I hope they may never prove so, tend the other way.

First, I have scarcely seen anything from you at any time, that did not contain imputations against your superiors, and a chafing against acting the part they had assigned you. You have constantly urged the idea that you were persecuted because you did not come from West-Point, and you repeat it in these letters. This, my dear general, is I fear, the rock on which you have split.

In the Winchester case, you were under General Schenck, and he under Gen. Halleck. I know by Gen. Hallecks orderbook, that he, on the 11th. of June advised Gen. Schenck to call you in from Winchester to Harper's Ferry; and I have been told, but do not know, that Gen. Schenck gave you the order accordingly, on the same day—and I have been told, but do not know, that on receiving it, instead of obeying it, you sent by mail a written protest against obeying it, which did not reach him until you were actually beleagered at Winchester. I say I do not know this. You hate West-Point generally, and General Halleck particularly; but I do know that it is not his fault that you were at Winchester on the 13th. 14th. and morning of the 15th.—the days of your disaster. If Gen. Schenck gave the order on the 11th. as Gen. Halleck advised, it was an easy matter for you to have been off at least on the 12th. The case is inevitably between Gen. Schenck & you. Neither Gen. Halleck, nor any one else, so far as I know, required you to stay and fight 60,000, with 6,000, as you insinuate. I know Gen. Halleck, through Gen. Schenck required you to get away, & that in abundant time for you to have done it. Gen. Schenck is not a West-Pointer & has no prejudice against you on that score. Yours very truly

To Alexander K. McClure

A. K. McClure   Washington City,
Philadelphia   June 30 1863
Do we gain anything by opening one leak to stop another?
Do we gain any thing by quieting one clamor, merely to open
another, and probably a larger one?

To Joel Parker

Gov. Parker   Executive Mansion,
Trenton, N.J.   Washington, June 30, 1863.
Your despatch of yesterday received. I really think the attitude of the enemies' army in Pennsylvania, presents us the
best opportunity we have had since the war began. I think
you will not see the foe in New-Jersey. I beg you to be assured that no one out of my position can know so well as if
he were in it, the difficulties and involvements of replacing
Gen. McClellan in command—and this aside from any imputations upon him.
Please accept my sincere thanks for what you have done,
and are doing to get troops forward.

To Samuel P. Lee

Rr. Adml.   Navy Department
   S. P. Lee.   Washington, D.C. July 1863
Your despatch transmitting a note from Mr. Alexander H.
Stephens has been received. You will not permit Mr. Stephens
to proceed to Washington, or to pass the blockade. He does
not make known the subjects to which the communication in
writing from Mr. Davis relates, which he bears, and seeks to
deliver in person to the President, and upon which he desires
to confer. Those subjects can only be Military, or not Military, or partly both. Whatever may be military will be readily
received, if offered through the well understood Military
channel. Of course nothing else, will be received by the Pres-

ident, when offered, as in this case, in terms assuming the independence of the so-called Confederate States; and anything will be received and carefully considered by him, when offered by any influential person or persons, in terms not assuming the independence of the so-called Confederate States.

July 4, 1863

To Samuel P. Lee

War Department, Washington, D.C., July 4, 1863.
Rear-Admiral S. P. Lee: The request of A. H. Stephens is inadmissible. The customary agents and channels are adequate for all needful communication and conference between the United States forces and the insurgents.

To Henry W. Halleck

Soldiers' Home,
July 6, 1863– 7 p.m.
Major-General Halleck: I left the telegraph office a good deal dissatisfied. You know I did not like the phrase, in Orders, No. 68, I believe, "Drive the invaders from our soil." Since that, I see a dispatch from General French, saying the enemy is crossing his wounded over the river in flats, without saying why he does not stop it, or even intimating a thought that it ought to be stopped. Still later, another dispatch from General Pleasonton, by direction of General Meade, to General French, stating that the main army is halted because it is believed the rebels are concentrating "on the road toward Hagerstown, beyond Fairfield," and is not to move until it is ascertained that the rebels intend to evacuate Cumberland Valley.

These things all appear to me to be connected with a purpose to cover Baltimore and Washington, and to get the enemy across the river again without a further collision, and they do not appear connected with a purpose to prevent his crossing and to destroy him. I do fear the former purpose is acted upon and the latter is rejected.

If you are satisfied the latter purpose is entertained and is judiciously pursued, I am content. If you are not so satisfied, please look to it. Yours, truly,

To Henry W. Halleck

Major-General Halleck:

We have certain information that Vicksburg surrendered to General Grant on the 4th of July. Now, if General Meade can complete his work, so gloriously prosecuted thus far, by the literal or substantial destruction of Lee's army, the rebellion will be over. Yours, truly,

July 7, 1863

Response to Serenade, Washington, D.C.

Fellow-citizens: I am very glad indeed to see you to-night, and yet I will not say I thank you for this call, but I do most sincerely thank Almighty God for the occasion on which you have called. [Cheers.] How long ago is it?—eighty odd years—since on the Fourth of July for the first time in the history of the world a nation by its representatives, assembled and declared as a self-evident truth that "all men are created equal." [Cheers.] That was the birthday of the United States of America. Since then the Fourth of July has had several peculiar recognitions. The two most distinguished men in the framing and support of the Declaration were Thomas Jefferson and John Adams—the one having penned it and the other sustained it the most forcibly in debate—the only two of the fifty-five who sustained it being elected President of the United States. Precisely fifty years after they put their hands to the paper it pleased Almighty God to take both from the stage of action. This was indeed an extraordinary and remarkable event in our history. Another President, five years after, was called from this stage of existence on the same day and month of the year; and now, on this last Fourth of July just passed, when we have a gigantic Rebellion, at the bottom of which is an effort to overthrow the principle that all men were created equal, we have the surrender of a most powerful position and army on that very day, [cheers] and not only so, but in a succession of battles in Pennsylvania, near to us, through three days, so rapidly fought that they might be called one great battle on the 1st, 2d and 3d of the month of July; and on the 4th the cohorts of those who opposed the declaration that all men are created equal, "turned tail" and run. [Long and continued cheers.] Gentlemen, this is a glorious theme, and the occasion for a speech, but I am not prepared to make one worthy of the occasion. I would like to speak in terms of praise due to the many brave officers and soldiers who have fought in the cause of the Union and liberties of the country from the beginning of the war. There are trying occasions, not only in success, but for the want of success. I dislike to mention the name of one single officer lest I might do wrong to those I might forget. Recent events bring up glorious names, and particularly prominent ones, but these I will not mention. Having said this much, I will now take the music.

July 7, 1863

To Lorenzo Thomas

Gen. Thomas   Washington, D.C.,
Harrisburg, Penn.   July 8 1863

Your despatch of this morning to the Sec. of War is before me. The forces you speak of, will be of no immagineable service, if they can not go forward with a little more expedition. Lee is now passing the Potomac faster than the forces you mention are passing Carlyle. Forces now beyond Carlyle, to be joined by regiments still at Harrisburg, and the united force again to join Pierce somewhere, and the whole to move down the Cumberland Valley, will, in my unprofessional opinion, be quite as likely to capture the Man-in-the-Moon, as any part of Lee's Army

To Jesse K. Dubois

Hon. J. K. Dubois   Washington City, D.C.
Springfield, Ills —   July 11 1863

It is certain that after three days fighting at Gettysburg, Lee withdrew and made for the Potomac; that he found the river so swollen as to prevent his crossing, that he is still this side near Hagerstown and Williamsport, preparing to defend himself; and that Meade is close upon him preparing to attack him, heavy skirmishing having occurred nearly all day yesterday. I am more than satisfied with what has happened North of the Potomac so far, and am anxious and hopeful for what is to come.

To Henry T. Blow

War Department, Washington, July 13, 1863.

Hon. H. T. Blow, St. Louis, Mo.: I saw your dispatch to the Secretary of War. The publication of a letter without the leave of the writer or the receiver I think cannot be justified, but in this case I do not think it of sufficient consequence to justify an arrest; and again, the arrest being, through a parole, merely nominal, does not deserve the importance sought to be attached to it. Cannot this small matter be dropped on both sides without further difficulty?

To Ulysses S. Grant

Major General Grant   Executive Mansion,
My dear General   Washington, July 13, 1863.

I do not remember that you and I ever met personally. I write this now as a grateful acknowledgment for the almost inestimable service you have done the country. I wish to say a word further. When you first reached the vicinity of Vicksburg, I thought you should do, what you finally did — march the troops across the neck, run the batteries with the transports, and thus go below; and I never had any faith, except a general hope that you knew better than I, that the Yazoo Pass expedition, and the like, could succeed. When you got below, and took Port-Gibson, Grand Gulf, and vicinity, I thought you should go down the river and join Gen. Banks; and when you turned Northward East of the Big Black, I feared it was a mistake. I now wish to make the personal acknowledgment that you were right, and I was wrong.   Yours very truly

To John M. Schofield

Gen. Schofield   Washington City, D.C.
St. Louis, Mo.   July 13 1863
    I regret to learn of the arrest of the Democrat editor. I fear this loses you the middle position I desired you to occupy. I have not learned which of the two letters I wrote you, it was that the Democrat published; but I care very little for the publication of any letter I have written. Please spare me the trouble this is likely to bring

To George G. Meade

                                        Executive Mansion,
Major General Meade   Washington, July 14, 1863.
    I have just seen your despatch to Gen. Halleck, asking to be relieved of your command, because of a supposed censure of mine. I am very—*very*—grateful to you for the magnificient success you gave the cause of the country at Gettysburg; and I am sorry now to be the author of the slightest pain to you. But I was in such deep distress myself that I could not restrain some expression of it. I had been oppressed nearly ever since the battles at Gettysburg, by what appeared to be evidences that yourself, and Gen. Couch, and Gen. Smith, were not seeking a collision with the enemy, but were trying to get him across the river without another battle. What these evidences were, if you please, I hope to tell you at some time, when we shall both feel better. The case, summarily stated is this. You fought and beat the enemy at Gettysburg; and, of course, to

say the least, his loss was as great as yours. He retreated; and you did not, as it seemed to me, pressingly pursue him; but a flood in the river detained him, till, by slow degrees, you were again upon him. You had at least twenty thousand veteran troops directly with you, and as many more raw ones within supporting distance, all in addition to those who fought with you at Gettysburg; while it was not possible that he had received a single recruit; and yet you stood and let the flood run down, bridges be built, and the enemy move away at his leisure, without attacking him. And Couch and Smith! The latter left Carlisle in time, upon all ordinary calculation, to have aided you in the last battle at Gettysburg; but he did not arrive. At the end of more than ten days, I believe twelve, under constant urging, he reached Hagerstown from Carlisle, which is not an inch over fiftyfive miles, if so much. And Couch's movement was very little different.

Again, my dear general, I do not believe you appreciate the magnitude of the misfortune involved in Lee's escape. He was within your easy grasp, and to have closed upon him would, in connection with our other late successes, have ended the war. As it is, the war will be prolonged indefinitely. If you could not safely attack Lee last monday, how can you possibly do so South of the river, when you can take with you very few more than two thirds of the force you then had in hand? It would be unreasonable to expect, and I do not expect you can now effect much. Your golden opportunity is gone, and I am distressed immeasureably because of it.

I beg you will not consider this a prossecution, or persecution of yourself. As you had learned that I was dissatisfied, I have thought it best to kindly tell you why.

To Simon Cameron

"Cypher"

Hon. Simon Cameron   Washington City,
Harrisburg, Penn.   July 15, 1863.

Your despatch of yesterday received. Lee was already across the river when you sent it. I would give much to be relieved of the impression that Meade, Couch, Smith and all, since the battle at Gettysburg, have striven only to get Lee over the river without another fight. Please tell me, if you know, who was the one corps commander who was for fighting, in the council of War on Sunday-night.

To Joseph Holt

Let him fight instead of being shot
   July 18. 1863.

Verse on Lee's Invasion of the North

Gen. Lees invasion of the North written by himself—

> In eighteen sixty three, with pomp,
>   and mighty swell,
> Me and Jeff's Confederacy, went
>   forth to sack Phil-del,
> The Yankees they got arter us, and
>   giv us particular hell,
> And we skedaddled back again,
>   and didn't sack Phil-del.

July 19, 1863

To John M. Schofield

                                    Executive Mansion,
My Dear General   Washington, July 20th, 1863.
   I have received and read your letter of the 14th of July.
   I think the suggestion you make, of discontinuing proceedings against Mr. McKee, a very proper one. While I admit that there is an apparent impropriety in the publication of the letter mentioned without my consent or yours, it is still a case where no evil could result, and which I am entirely willing to overlook. Yours truly
   To Gen Schofield

To Oliver O. Howard

Executive Mansion,
My dear General Howard   Washington, July 21. 1863.

Your letter of the 18th. is received. I was deeply mortified by the escape of Lee across the Potomac, because the substantial destruction of his army would have ended the war, and because I believed, such destruction was perfectly easy— believed that Gen. Meade and his noble army had expended all the skill, and toil, and blood, up to the ripe harvest, and then let the crop go to waste. Perhaps my mortification was heightened because I had always believed—making my belief a hobby possibly—that the main rebel army going North of the Potomac, could never return, if well attended to; and because I was so greatly flattered in this belief, by the operations at Gettysburg. A few days having passed, I am now profoundly grateful for what was done, without criticism for what was not done. Gen. Meade has my confidence as a brave and skillful officer, and a true man. Yours very truly

To Edwin M. Stanton

Hon. Sec. of War   Executive Mansion,
My dear Sir: Washington, July 21, 1863.

I desire that a renewed and vigorous effort be made to raise colored forces along the shores of the Missippi.

Please consult the General-in-Chief; and if it is perceived that any acceleration of the matter can be effected, let it be done.

I think the evidence is nearly conclusive that Gen. Thomas is one of the best, if not the very best, instruments for this service. Yours truly

To Hamilton R. Gamble

His Excellency   Executive Mansion,
H. R. Gamble   Washington, July 23, 1863.

Sir My Private Secretary has just brought me a letter saying it is a very *"cross"* one from you, about mine to Gen.

Schofield, recently published in the Democrat. As I am trying to preserve my own temper, by avoiding irritants, so far as practicable, I have declined to read the cross letter. I think fit to say, however, that when I wrote the letter to Gen. Schofield, I was totally unconscious of any malice, or disrespect towards you, or of using any expression which should offend you, if seen by you. I have not seen the document in the Democrat, and therefore can not say whether it is a correct copy. Your Obt. Servt.

To Montgomery Blair

Hon. Post-Master-General   Executive Mansion,
Sir: Washington, July 24, 1863.

Yesterday little indorsements of mine went to you in two cases of Post-Masterships sought for widows whose husbands have fallen in the battles of this war. These cases occurring on the same day, brought me to reflect more attentively than I had before done, as to what is fairly due from us here, in the dispensing of patronage, towards the men who, by fighting our battles, bear the chief burthen of saving our country. My conclusion is that, other claims and qualifications being equal, they have the better right; and this is especially applicable to the disabled soldier, and the deceased soldier's family. Your Obt. Servt.

To Ambrose E. Burnside

Major General Burnside   Washington, D.C.,
Cincinnati, O   July 27 1863

Let me explain. In Gen. Grant's first despatch after the fall of Vicksburg, he said, among other things, he would send the Ninth Corps to you. Thinking it would be pleasant to you, I asked the Secretary of War to telegraph you the news. For some reason, never mentioned to us by Gen. Grant, they have not been sent, though we have seen out-side intimations that they took part in the expedition against Jackson. Gen. Grant is a copious worker, and fighter, but a very meagre writer, or telegrapher. No doubt he changed his purpose in regard to the Ninth Corps, for some sufficient reason, but has forgotten to notify us of it.

To George G. Meade

Private   Executive Mansion,
Major General Meade: Washington, July 27, 1863.
   I have not thrown Gen. Hooker away; and therefore I would like to know whether, it would be agreeable to you, all things considered, for him to take a corps under you, if he himself is willing to do so. Write me, in perfect freedom, with the assurance that I will not subject you to any embarrassment, by making your letter, or its contents, known to any one. I wish to know your wishes before I decide whether to break the subject to him. Do not lean a hair's breadth against your own feelings, or your judgment of the public service, on the idea of gratifying me. Yours truly

To Edwin M. Stanton

Hon Secretary of War   Executive Mansion
My dear Sir: Washington July 28 1863
   A young son of the Senator Brown of Mississippi, not yet twenty, as I understand, was wounded, and made a prisoner at Gettysburg. His mother is sister of Mrs P. R. Fendall, of this city. Mr Fendall, on behalf of himself and family, asks that he and they may have charge of the boy, to cure him up, being responsible for his person and good behavior. Would it not be rather a grateful and graceful thing to let them have him? Yours truly

To Henry W. Halleck

                                                         Executive Mansion,
Major General Halleck: Washington, July 29, 1863.
   Seeing Gen. Meade's despatch of yesterday to yourself,

causes, me to fear that he supposes the government here is demanding of him to bring on a general engagement with Lee as soon as possible. I am claiming no such thing of him. In fact, my judgment is against it; which judgment, of course, I will yield if yours and his are the contrary. If he could not safely engage Lee at Williamsport, it seems absurd to suppose he can safely engage him now, when he has scarcely more than two thirds of the force he had at Williamsport, while it must be, that Lee has been re-inforced. True, I desired Gen. Meade to pursue Lee across the Potomac, hoping, as has proved true, that he would thereby clear the Baltimore and Ohio Railroad, and get some advantages by harrassing him on his retreat. These being past, I am unwilling he should now get into a general engagement on the impression that we here are pressing him; and I shall be glad for you to so inform him, unless your own judgment is against it. Yours truly

Order of Retaliation

Executive Mansion, Washington D.C July 30. 1863

It is the duty of every government to give protection to its citizens, of whatever class, color, or condition, and especially to those who are duly organized as soldiers in the public service. The law of nations and the usages and customs of war as carried on by civilized powers, permit no distinction as to color in the treatment of prisoners of war as public enemies. To sell or enslave any captured person, on account of his color, and for no offence against the laws of war, is a relapse into barbarism and a crime against the civilization of the age.

The government of the United States will give the same protection to all its soldiers, and if the enemy shall sell or enslave anyone because of his color, the offense shall be punished by retaliation upon the enemy's prisoners in our possession.

It is therefore ordered that for every soldier of the United States killed in violation of the laws of war, a rebel soldier shall be executed; and for every one enslaved by the enemy or sold into slavery, a rebel soldier shall be placed at hard labor on the public works and continued at such labor until the other shall be released and receive the treatment due to a prisoner of war

To Stephen A. Hurlbut

Executive Mansion,
My dear General Hurlbut: Washington, July 31, 1863.

Your letter by Mr. Dana was duly received. I now learn that your resignation has reached the War Department. I also learn that an active command has been assigned you by Gen. Grant. The Secretary of War and Gen. Halleck are very partial to you, as you know I also am. We all wish you to re-consider the question of resigning; not that we would wish to retain you greatly against your wish and interest, but that your decision may be at least a very well considered one.

I understand that Senator Sebastian of Arkansas thinks of offering to resume his place in the Senate. Of course the Senate, and not I, would decide whether to admit or reject him. Still I should feel great interest in the question. It may be so presented as to be one of the very greatest national importance; and it may be otherwise so presented, as to be of no more than temporary personal consequence to him.

The emancipation proclamation applies to Arkansas. I think it is valid in law, and will be so held by the courts. I think I shall not retract or repudiate it. Those who shall have tasted actual freedom I believe can never be slaves, or quasi slaves again. For the rest, I believe some plan, substantially being gradual emancipation, would be better for both white and black. The Missouri plan, recently adopted, I do not object to on account of the time for *ending* the institution; but I am sorry the *beginning* should have been postponed for seven years, leaving all that time to agitate for the repeal of the whole thing. It should begin at once, giving at least the new-born, a vested interest in freedom, which could not be taken away. If Senator Sebastian could come with something of this sort from Arkansas, I at least should take great interest in his case; and I believe a single individual will have scarcely done

the world so great a service. See him, if you can, and read this
to him; but charge him to not make it public for the present.
Write me again. Yours very truly.

To John G. Foster

Executive Mansion, Washington, August 3, 1863.
Major General Foster, or whoever may be in command of the
Military Department, with Head Quarters at Fort-Monroe, Va.

If Dr. Wright, on trial at Norfolk, has been, or shall be
convicted, send me a transcript of his trial and conviction, and
do not let execution be done upon him, until my further
order.

To Nathaniel P. Banks

Executive Mansion, Washington,
My dear General Banks   August 5, 1863.
Being a poor correspondent is the only apology I offer for
not having sooner tendered my thanks for your very successful, and very valuable military operations this year. The final
stroke in opening the Mississippi never should, and I think
never will, be forgotten.

Recent events in Mexico, I think, render early action in Texas
more important than ever. I expect, however, the General-
in-Chief, will address you more fully upon this subject.

Governor Boutwell read me to-day that part of your letter
to him, which relates to Louisiana affairs. While I very well
know what I would be glad for Louisiana to do, it is quite a
different thing for me to assume direction of the matter. I
would be glad for her to make a new Constitution recognizing the emancipation proclamation, and adopting emancipation in those parts of the state to which the proclamation does
not apply. And while she is at it, I think it would not be
objectionable for her to adopt some practical system by which
the two races could gradually live themselves out of their old
relation to each other, and both come out better prepared for
the new. Education for young blacks should be included in
the plan. After all, the power, or element, of "contract" may

be sufficient for this probationary period; and, by it's simplicity, and flexibility, may be the better.

As an anti-slavery man I have a motive to desire emancipation, which pro-slavery men do not have; but even they have strong enough reason to thus place themselves again under the shield of the Union; and to thus perpetually hedge against the recurrence of the scenes through which we are now passing.

Gov. Shepley has informed me that Mr. Durant is now taking a registry, with a view to the election of a Constitutional convention in Louisiana. This, to me, appears proper. If such convention were to ask my views, I could present little else than what I now say to you. I think the thing should be pushed forward, so that if possible, it's mature work may reach here by the meeting of Congress.

For my own part I think I shall not, in any event, retract the emancipation proclamation; nor, as executive, ever return to slavery any person who is free by the terms of that proclamation, or by any of the acts of Congress.

If Louisiana shall send members to Congress, their admission to seats will depend, as you know, upon the respective Houses, and not upon the President.

If these views can be of any advantage in giving shape, and impetus, to action there, I shall be glad for you to use them prudently for that object. Of course you will confer with intelligent and trusty citizens of the State, among whom I would suggest Messrs. Flanders, Hahn, and Durant; and to each of whom I now think I may send copies of this letter. Still it is perhaps better to not make the letter generally public. Yours very truly

Copies sent to Messrs. Flanders, Hahn & Durant, each indorsed as follows.
The within is a copy of a letter to Gen. Banks. Please observe my directions to him. Do not mention the paragraph about Mexico.
Aug. 6. 1863.

To Horatio Seymour

His Excellency Horatio Seymour   Executive Mansion,
Governor of New-York   Washington, August 7, 1863.

Your communication of the 3rd. Inst. has been received, and attentively considered.

I can not consent to suspend the draft in New-York, as you request, because, among other reasons, *time* is too important.

By the figures you send, which I presume are correct, the twelve Districts represented fall into two classes of eight, and four respectively. The disparity of the quotas for the draft, in these two classes is certainly very striking, being the difference between an average of 2200 in one class, and 4864 in the other. Assuming that the Districts are equal, one to another, in entire population, as required by the plan on which they were made, this disparity is such as to require attention. Much of it, however, I suppose will be accounted for by the fact that so many more persons fit for soldiers, are in the city than are in the country, who have too recently arrived from other parts of the United States and from Europe to be either included in the Census of 1860, or to have voted in 1862. Still, making due allowance for this, I am yet unwilling to stand upon it as an entirely sufficient explanation of the great disparity.

I shall direct the draft to proceed in all the Districts, drawing however, at first, from each of the four Districts, towit: the second, fourth, sixth, and eighth, only 2200, being the average quota of the other class. After this drawing, these four Districts, and also the seventeenth and twentyninth, shall be carefully re-enrolled, and, if you please, agents of yours may witness every step of the process. Any deficiency which may appear by the new enrollment will be supplied by a special draft for that object, allowing due credit for volunteers who may be obtained from these Districts respectively, during the interval. And at all points, so far as consistent, with practical convenience, due credits will be given for volunteers; and your Excellency shall be notified of the time fixed for commencing a draft in each District.

I do not object to abide a decision of the United States Supreme Court, or of the judges thereof, on the constitutionality of the draft law. In fact, I should be willing to facilitate the obtaining of it; but I can not consent to lose the *time* while it is being obtained. We are contending with an enemy who, as I understand, drives every able bodied man he can reach, into his ranks, very much as a butcher drives bullocks into a slaughter-pen. No time is wasted, no argument is used.

This produces an army which will soon turn upon our now victorious soldiers already in the field, if they shall not be sustained by recruits, as they should be. It produces an army with a rapidity not to be matched on our side, if we first waste time to re-experiment with the volunteer system, already deemed by congress, and palpably, in fact, so far exhausted, as to be inadequate; and then more time, to obtain a court decision, as to whether a law is constitutional, which requires a part of those not now in the service, to go to the aid of those who are already in it; and still more time, to determine with absolute certainty, that we get those, who are to go, in the precisely legal proportion, to those who are not to go.

My purpose is to be, in my action, just and constitutional; and yet practical, in performing the important duty, with which I am charged, of maintaining the unity, and the free principles of our common country. Your Obt. Servt.

To Mary Todd Lincoln

Executive Mansion, Washington, August 8, 1863.

My dear Wife. All as well as usual, and no particular trouble any way. I put the money into the Treasury at five per cent, with the previlege of withdrawing it any time upon thirty days' notice. I suppose you are glad to learn this. Tell dear Tad, poor "Nanny Goat," is lost; and Mrs. Cuthbert & I are in distress about it. The day you left Nanny was found resting herself, and chewing her little cud, on the middle of Tad's bed. But now she's gone! The gardener kept complaining that she destroyed the flowers, till it was concluded to bring her down to the White House. This was done, and the second day she had disappeared, and has not been heard of since. This is the last we know of poor "Nanny"

The weather continues dry, and excessively warm here.

Nothing very important occurring. The election in Kentucky has gone very strongly right. Old Mr. Wickliffe got ugly, as you know, ran for Governor, and is terribly beaten. Upon Mr. Crittendens death, Brutus Clay, Cassius' brother, was put on the track for Congress, and is largely elected. Mr. Menzies, who, as we thought, behaved very badly last session of Congress, is largely beaten in the District opposite Cincinnati, by Green Clay Smith, Cassius Clay's nephew. But enough. Affectionately

To Ulysses S. Grant

Executive Mansion,
My dear General Grant: Washington, August 9, 1863.

I see by a despatch of yours that you incline quite strongly towards an expedition against Mobile. This would appear tempting to me also, were it not that in view of recent events in Mexico, I am greatly impressed with the importance of re-establishing the national authority in Western Texas as soon as possible. I am not making an order, however. That I leave, for the present at least, to the General-in-Chief.

A word upon another subject. Gen. Thomas has gone again to the Mississippi Valley, with the view of raising colored troops. I have no reason to doubt that you are doing what you reasonably can upon the same subject. I believe it is a resource which, if vigorously applied now, will soon close the contest. It works doubly, weakening the enemy and strengthening us. We were not fully ripe for it until the river was opened. Now, I think at least a hundred thousand can, and ought to be rapidly organized along it's shores, relieving all the white troops to serve elsewhere.

Mr. Dana understands you as believing that the emancipation proclamation has helped some in your military operations. I am very glad if this is so. Did you receive a short letter from me, dated the 13th. of July? Yours very truly

To William S. Rosecrans

Executive Mansion,
My Dear General Rosecrans Washington, August 10, 1863.

Yours of the 1st was received two days ago. I think you

must have inferred more than Gen Halleck has intended, as to any dissatisfaction of mine with you. I am sure you, as a reasonable man, would not have been wounded, could you have heard all my words and seen all my thoughts, in regard to you. I have not abated in my kind feeling for and confidence in you. I have seen most of your despatches to General Halleck—probably all of them. After Grant invested Vicksburg, I was very anxious lest Johnston should overwhelm him from the outside, and when it appeared certain that part of Bragg's force had gone, and was going to Johnston, it did seem to me, it was the exactly proper time for you to attack Bragg with what force he had left. In all kindness, let me say, it so seems to me yet. Finding from your despatches to General Halleck that your judgement was different, and being very anxious for Grant, I, on one occasion told Gen. Halleck, I thought he should direct you to decide at once, to immediately attack Bragg or to stand on the defensive, and send part of your force to Grant. He replied he had already so directed, in substance. Soon after, despatches from Grant abated my anxiety for him, and in proportion abated my anxiety about any movement of yours. When afterwards, however, I saw a despatch of yours arguing that the right time for you to attack Bragg was not before but would be after the fall of Vicksburg, it impressed me very strangely; and I think I so stated to the Secretary of War and General Halleck. It seemed no other than the proposition that you could better fight Bragg *when* Johnston should be at liberty to return and assist him, than you could *before* he could so return to his assistance.

Since Grant has been entirely relieved by the fall of Vicksburg, by which Johnston is also relieved, it has seemed to me that your chance for a stroke, has been considerably diminished, and I have not been pressing you directly or indirectly. True, I am very anxious for East Tennessee to be occupied by us; but I see and appreciate the difficulties you mention. The question occurs, Can the thing be done at all? Does preparation advance at all? Do you not consume supplies as fast as you get them forward? Have you more animals today than you had at the battle of Stone River? and yet have not more been furnished you since then than your entire present stock? I ask the same questions as to your mounted force.

Do not misunderstand. I am not casting blame upon you. I rather think, by great exertion, you can get to East Tennessee. But a very important question is, "Can you stay there?" I make no order in the case—that I leave to General Halleck and yourself.

And now, be assured once more, that I think of you in all kindness and confidence: and that I am not watching you with an evil-eye. Yours very truly

To John A. McClernand

Major General McClernand: Executive Mansion,
My dear Sir: Washington, August 12, 1863.
Our friend, William G. Greene, has just presented a kind letter in regard to yourself, addressed to me by our other friends, Yates, Hatch, and Dubois. I doubt whether your present position is more painful to you than to myself. Grateful for the patriotic stand so early taken by you in this life-and-death struggle of the nation, I have done whatever has appeared practicable to advance you and the public interest together. No charges, with a view to a trial, have been preferred against you by any one; nor do I suppose any will be. All there is, so far as I have heard, is Gen. Grant's statement of his reasons for relieving you. And even this I have not seen or sought to see; because it is a case, as appears to me, in which I could do nothing without doing harm. Gen. Grant and yourself have been conspicuous in our most important successes; and for me to interfere, and thus magnify a breach between you, could not but be of evil effect. Better leave it where the law of the case has placed it. For me to force you back upon Gen. Grant, would be forcing him to resign. I can not give you a new command, because we have no forces except such as already have commanders. I am constantly pressed by those who *scold* before they *think*, or without thinking at all, to give commands respectively to Fremont, McClellan, Butler, Sigel, Curtis, Hunter, Hooker, and perhaps others; when, all else out of the way, I have no commands to give them. This is now your case, which, as I have before said, pains me, not less than it does you.

My belief is that the permanent estimate of what a general does in the field, is fixed by the "cloud of witnesses" who have been with him in the field; and that relying on these, he who has the right needs not to fear. Your friend as ever

To James H. Hackett

Executive Mansion,
My dear Sir: Washington, August 17, 1863.

Months ago I should have acknowledged the receipt of your book, and accompanying kind note; and I now have to beg your pardon for not having done so.

For one of my age, I have seen very little of the drama. The first presentation of Falstaff I ever saw was yours here, last winter or spring. Perhaps the best compliment I can pay is to say, as I truly can, I am very anxious to see it again. Some of Shakspeare's plays I have never read; while others I have gone over perhaps as frequently as any unprofessional reader. Among the latter are Lear, Richard Third, Henry Eighth, Hamlet, and especially Macbeth. I think nothing equals Macbeth. It is wonderful. Unlike you gentlemen of the profession, I think the soliloquy in Hamlet commencing "O, my offence is rank" surpasses that commencing "To be, or not to be." But pardon this small attempt at criticism. I should like to hear you pronounce the opening speech of Richard the Third. Will you not soon visit Washington again? If you do, please call and let me make your personal acquaintance. Yours truly

To James G. Blunt

Executive Mansion,
Major General Blunt: Washington, August 18, 1863.

Yours of July 31st is received. Governor Carney did leave some papers with me concerning you; but they made no great impression upon me; and I believe they are not altogether such as you seem to think. As I am not proposing to act upon them, I do not now take the time to re-examine them.

I regret to find you denouncing so many persons as liars, scoundrels, fools, thieves, and persecutors of yourself. Your military position looks critical, but did any body *force* you into it? Have you been *ordered* to confront and fight ten thousand men, with three thousand men? The Government cannot make men; and it is very easy, when a man has been given the highest commission, for him to turn on those who gave it and vilify them for not giving him a command according to his rank.

My appointment of you first as a Brigadier, and then as a Major General, was evidence of my appreciation of your service; and I have not since marked but one thing in connection with you, with which to be dissatisfied. The sending a military order twenty five miles outside of your lines, and all military lines, to take men charged with no offence against the military, out of the hands of the courts, to be turned over to a mob to be hanged, can find no precedent or principle to justify it. Judge Lynch sometimes takes jurisdiction of cases which prove too strong for the courts; but this is the first case within my knowledge, wherein the court being able to maintain jurisdiction against Judge Lynch, the military has come to the assistance of the latter. I take the facts of this case as you state them yourself, and not from any report of Governor Carney, or other person. Yours truly

To George G. Meade

Major General Meade   Executive Mansion,
Warrenton, Va   Washington, Aug. 21, 1863.

At this late moment I am appealed to in behalf of William Thompson of Co. K. 3rd. Maryland Volunteers, in 12th. Army Corps said to be at Kelly's Ford, under sentence to be shot to-day as a deserter. He is represented to me to be very young, with symptoms of insanity. Please postpone the execution till further order

To Edwin M. Stanton

Hon. Secretary of War: Executive Mansion,
My dear Sir: Washington, August 21. 1863.

In the autumn of 1861, certain persons in armed rebellion,

against the United States, within the counties of Acomac and Northampton, laid down their arms upon certain terms then proposed to them by Genl. Dix, in and by a certain proclamation. It is now said that these persons or some of them, are about to be forced into the military lines of the existing rebellion, unless they will take an oath prescribed to them since, and not included in, Gen. Dix' proclamation referred to. Now, my judgment is that no one of these men should be forced from his home, who has not broken faith with the government, according to the terms fixed by Gen. Dix and these men. It is bad faith in the government to force new terms upon such as have kept faith with it. At least so it seems to me.

To James C. Conkling

Hon. James C. Conkling   Executive Mansion,
My Dear Sir.   Washington, August 26, 1863.

Your letter inviting me to attend a mass-meeting of unconditional Union-men, to be held at the Capital of Illinois, on the 3d day of September, has been received.

It would be very agreeable to me, to thus meet my old friends, at my own home; but I can not, just now, be absent from here, so long as a visit there, would require.

The meeting is to be of all those who maintain unconditional devotion to the Union; and I am sure my old political friends will thank me for tendering, as I do, the nation's gratitude to those other noble men, whom no partizan malice, or partizan hope, can make false to the nation's life.

There are those who are dissatisfied with me. To such I would say: You desire peace; and you blame me that we do not have it. But how can we attain it? There are but three conceivable ways. First, to suppress the rebellion by force of arms. This, I am trying to do. Are you for it? If you are, so far we are agreed. If you are not for it, a second way is, to give up the Union. I am against this. Are you for it? If you are, you should say so plainly. If you are not for *force*, nor yet for *dissolution*, there only remains some imaginable *compromise.* I do not believe any compromise, embracing the maintenance of the Union, is now possible. All I learn, leads to a directly opposite belief. The strength of the rebellion, is its military—its army. That army dominates all the country, and all the people, within its range. Any offer of terms made by any man or men within that range, in opposition to that army, is simply nothing for the present; because such man or men, have no power whatever to enforce their side of a compromise, if one were made with them. To illustrate— Suppose refugees from the South, and peace men of the North, get together in convention, and frame and proclaim a compromise embracing a restoration of the Union; in what way can that compromise be used to keep Lee's army out of Pennsylvania? Meade's army can keep Lee's army out of Pennsylvania; and, I think, can ultimately drive it out of existence. But no paper compromise, to which the controllers of Lee's army are not agreed, can, at all, affect that army. In an effort at such compromise we should waste time, which the enemy would improve to our disadvantage; and that would be all. A compromise, to be effective, must be made either with those who control the rebel army, or with the people first liberated from the domination of that army, by the success of our own army. Now allow me to assure you, that no word or intimation, from that rebel army, or from any of the men controlling it, in relation to any peace compromise, has ever come to my knowledge or belief. All charges and insinuations to the contrary, are deceptive and groundless. And I promise you, that if any such proposition shall hereafter come, it shall not be rejected, and kept a secret from you. I freely acknowledge myself the servant of the people, according to the bond of service—the United States constitution; and that, as such, I am responsible to them.

But, to be plain, you are dissatisfied with me about the negro. Quite likely there is a difference of opinion between you and myself upon that subject. I certainly wish that all men could be free, while I suppose you do not. Yet I have neither adopted, nor proposed any measure, which is not consistent with even your view, provided you are for the Union. I suggested compensated emancipation; to which you replied you wished not to be taxed to buy negroes. But I had not asked you to be taxed to buy negroes, except in such way, as to save you from greater taxation to save the Union exclusively by other means.

You dislike the emancipation proclamation; and, perhaps, would have it retracted. You say it is unconstitutional— I think differently. I think the constitution invests its commander-in-chief, with the law of war, in time of war. The most that can be said, if so much, is, that slaves are property. Is there—has there ever been—any question that by the law of war, property, both of enemies and friends, may be taken when needed? And is it not needed whenever taking it, helps us, or hurts the enemy? Armies, the world over, destroy enemies' property when they can not use it; and even destroy their own to keep it from the enemy. Civilized belligerents do all in their power to help themselves, or hurt the enemy, except a few things regarded as barbarous or cruel. Among the exceptions are the massacre of vanquished foes, and non-combatants, male and female.

But the proclamation, as law, either is valid, or is not valid. If it is not valid, it needs no retraction. If it is valid, it can not be retracted, any more than the dead can be brought to life. Some of you profess to think its retraction would operate favorably for the Union. Why better *after* the retraction, than *before* the issue? There was more than a year and a half of trial to suppress the rebellion before the proclamation issued, the last one hundred days of which passed under an explicit notice that it was coming, unless averted by those in revolt, returning to their allegiance. The war has certainly progressed as favorably for us, since the issue of the proclamation as before. I know as fully as one can know the opinions of others, that some of the commanders of our armies in the field who have given us our most important successes, believe the emancipation policy, and the use of colored troops, constitute the heaviest blow yet dealt to the rebellion; and that, at least one of those important successes, could not have been achieved when it was, but for the aid of black soldiers. Among the commanders holding these views are some who have never had any affinity with what is called abolitionism, or with republican party politics; but who hold them purely as military opinions. I submit these opinions as being entitled to some weight against the objections, often urged, that emancipation, and arming the blacks, are unwise as military measures, and were not adopted, as such, in good faith.

You say you will not fight to free negroes. Some of them seem willing to fight for you; but, no matter. Fight you, then, exclusively to save the Union. I issued the proclamation on purpose to aid you in saving the Union. Whenever you shall have conquered all resistance to the Union, if I shall urge you to continue fighting, it will be an apt time, then, for you to declare you will not fight to free negroes.

I thought that in your struggle for the Union, to whatever extent the negroes should cease helping the enemy, to that extent it weakened the enemy in his resistance to you. Do you think differently? I thought that whatever negroes can be got to do as soldiers, leaves just so much less for white soldiers to do, in saving the Union. Does it appear otherwise to you? But negroes, like other people, act upon motives. Why should they do any thing for us, if we will do nothing for them? If they stake their lives for us, they must be prompted by the strongest motive—even the promise of freedom. And the promise being made, must be kept.

The signs look better. The Father of Waters again goes un-vexed to the sea. Thanks to the great North-West for it. Nor yet wholly to them. Three hundred miles up, they met New-England, Empire, Key-Stone, and Jersey, hewing their way right and left. The Sunny South too, in more colors than one, also lent a hand. On the spot, their part of the history was jotted down in black and white. The job was a great national one; and let none be banned who bore an honorable part in it. And while those who have cleared the great river may well be proud, even that is not all. It is hard to say that anything has been more bravely, and well done, than at Antietam, Murfreesboro, Gettysburg, and on many fields of lesser note. Nor must Uncle Sam's Web-feet be forgotten. At all the wa-tery margins they have been present. Not only on the deep sea, the broad bay, and the rapid river, but also up the narrow muddy bayou, and wherever the ground was a little damp, they have been, and made their tracks. Thanks to all. For the great republic—for the principle it lives by, and keeps alive—for man's vast future,—thanks to all.

Peace does not appear so distant as it did. I hope it will come soon, and come to stay; and so come as to be worth the keeping in all future time. It will then have been proved that, among free men, there can be no successful appeal from the ballot to the bullet; and that they who take such appeal are sure to lose their case, and pay the cost. And then, there will be some black men who can remember that, with silent tongue, and clenched teeth, and steady eye, and well-poised bayonet, they have helped mankind on to this great consummation; while, I fear, there will be some white ones, unable to forget that, with malignant heart, and deceitful speech, they have strove to hinder it.

Still let us not be over-sanguine of a speedy final triumph. Let us be quite sober. Let us diligently apply the means, never doubting that a just God, in his own good time, will give us the rightful result. Yours very truly

To George G. Meade

Major General Meade   Washington, D.C.,
Warrenton Va   August 27 1863

Walter, Rainese, Faline, Lae, & Kuhne appeal to me for mercy, without giving any ground for it whatever. I understand these are very flagrant cases, and that you deem their punishment as being indispensable to the service. If I am not mistaken in this, please let them know at once that their appeal is denied.

To William S. Rosecrans

Executive Mansion, Washington,
My dear General Rosecrans   August 31. 1863.

Yours of the 22nd. was received yesterday. When I wrote you before, I did not intend, nor do I now, to engage in an argument with you on military questions. You had informed me you were impressed, through Gen. Halleck, that I was dissatisfied with you; and I could not bluntly deny that I was, without unjustly implicating him. I therefore concluded to tell you the plain truth, being satisfied the matter would thus appear much smaller than it would if seen by mere glimpses. I repeat that my appreciation of you has not abated. I can never forget, whilst I remember anything, that about the end of last year, and beginning of this, you gave us a hard earned victory which, had there been a defeat instead, the nation could scarcely have lived over. Neither can I forget the check you so opportunely gave to a dangerous sentiment which was spreading in the North. Yours as ever

To Edwin M. Stanton

Hon. Secretary of War   Executive Mansion,
Dear Sir   Washington, Sept. 1, 1863.

I am quite satisfied that it will be good policy for us to suspend until further order, the collection of the assessment levied to indemnify the government for destruction and spoliation of property at and about the Light-House on Smith Island, Virginia. Please let an order be made accordingly. Yours truly

To Edwin M. Stanton

Hon. Sec. of War   Executive Mansion,
My dear Sir: Washington, Sep 1, 1863.

I am now informed, contrary to my impression when I last talked with you, that the order compelling the four hundred on Eastern Shore of Virginia to take the oath or be sent away, is about being carried into execution. As this, and also the assessment for damage done to, and at the light house, are very strong measures, and as I have to bear the responsibility of them, I wish them suspended till I can at least be better satisfied of their propriety than I now am. Yours truly

To Salmon P. Chase

Hon. S. P. Chase.   Executive Mansion,
My dear Sir: Washington, September 2. 1863.

Knowing your great anxiety that the emancipation proclamation shall now be applied to certain parts of Virginia and Louisiana which were exempted from it last January, I state briefly what appear to me to be difficulties in the way of such a step. The original proclamation has no constitutional or legal justification, except as a military measure. The exemptions were made because the military necessity did not apply to the exempted localities. Nor does that necessity apply to them now any more than it did then. If I take the step must I not do so, without the argument of military necessity, and so, without any argument, except the one that I think the measure politically expedient, and morally right? Would I not thus give up all footing upon constitution or law? Would I not thus be in the boundless field of absolutism? Could this pass unnoticed, or unresisted? Could it fail to be perceived that without any further stretch, I might do the same in Delaware, Maryland, Kentucky, Tennessee, and Missouri; and even change any law in any state? Would not many of our own friends shrink away appalled? Would it not lose us the elections, and with them, the very cause we seek to advance?

To Edwin M. Stanton

Hon. Sec. of War   Executive Mansion,
Dear Sir   Washington, Sept. 2. 1863.
    This woman says her husband and two sons are in the war; that the youngest son W. J. Klaproth, is a private in Co. D, of 143rd. Pennsylvania, volunteers, was wounded, made a prisoner & paroled at Gettysburg, and is now at Center-Street hospital, New-Jersey; and that he was under eighteen when he entered the service without the consent of his father or herself. She says she is destitute, and she asks that he may be discharged   If she makes satisfactory proof of the above let it be done.

To Joseph Segar

Hon. Joseph Segar: Washington, D.C.,
Fort-Monroe—Va   Sept. 5 1863
    I have just seen your despatch to the Secretary of War,

who is absent. I also send a despatch from Major Hayner of the 3rd. showing that he had notice of my order, and stating that the people were jubilant over it, as a victory over the government extorted by fear, and that he had already collected about four thousand of the money. If he has proceeded since I shall hold him accountable for his contumacy. On the contrary no dollar shall be refunded by my order, until it shall appear that my act in the case has been accepted in the right spirit.

To Edwin M. Stanton

                    Executive Mansion, Washington,
Honorable Secretary of War.   September 7, 1863.
    My dear Sir: This lady says her husband, Theophilus Brown, and his brother, George E. Brown, are in the Old Capitol Prison as prisoners of war, that they were conscripted into the rebel army, and were never for the rebel cause, and are now willing to do anything reasonable to be at liberty. This may be true, and if true they should be liberated. Please take hold of the case, and do what may seem proper in it. Yours truly,

To John P. Gray

Dr. John P. Gray   Executive Mansion,
Sir,   Washington, September 10th. 1863.
    Dr. David M. Wright is in military custody at Norfolk, Virginia, having been, by a military commission, tried for murder, and sentenced to death, his execution awaiting the order of the Major General in command of that Military Department, or of the President of the United States. The record is before me; and a question is made as to the sanity of the accused. You will please proceed to the Military Department whose head-quarters are at Fort-Monroe, and take in writing all evidence which may be offered on behalf of Dr. Wright and against him, and any, in addition, which you may find

within your reach, and deem pertinent; all said evidence to be directed to the question of Dr. Wright's sanity or insanity, and not to any other questions; you to preside, with power to exclude evidence which shall appear to you clearly not pertinent to the question.

When the taking of the evidence shall be closed, you will report the same to me, together with your own conclusions, as to Dr. Wright's sanity, both at the time of the homocide, and the time of your examination. On reaching Fort-Monroe, you will present this letter to the officer then commanding that Department, and deliver to him a copy of the same; upon which he is hereby directed to notify Hon. L. J. Bowden, and Hon. L. H. Chandler, of the same; to designate some suitable person in his command to appear for the government, as Judge Advocate or Prossecuting Attorney; to provide for the attendance of all such witnesses before you as may be desired by either party, or by yourself, and who may be within convenient reach of you; to furnish you a suitable place, or places for conducting the examination; and to render you such other reasonable assistance in the premises as you may require. If you deem it proper, you will examine Dr. Wright personally, and you may, in your discretion, require him to be present during the whole, or any part, of the taking of the evidence. The Military are hereby charged to see that an escape does not occur. Yours truly.

To Andrew Johnson

Private

Hon. Andrew Johnson: Executive Mansion,
My dear Sir: Washington, September 11, 1863.

All Tennessee is now clear of armed insurrectionists. You need not to be reminded that it is the nick of time for re-inaugerating a loyal State government. Not a moment should be lost. You, and the co-operating friends there, can better judge of the ways and means, than can be judged by any here. I only offer a few suggestions. The re-inauguration must not be such as to give control of the State, and it's representation in Congress, to the enemies of the Union, driving it's friends there into political exile. The whole struggle for Tennessee will have been profitless to both State and Nation, if it so ends that Gov. Johnson is put down, and Gov. Harris is put up. It must not be so. You must have it otherwise. Let the reconstruction be the work of such men only as can be trusted for the Union. Exclude all others, and trust that your government, so organized, will be recognized here, as being the one of republican form, to be guarranteed to the state, and to be protected against invasion and domestic violence.

It is something on the question of *time*, to remember that it can not be known who is next to occupy the position I now hold, nor what he will do.

I see that you have declared in favor of emancipation in Tennessee, for which, may God bless you. Get emancipation into your new State government—Constitution—and there will be no such word as fail for your case.

The raising of colored troops I think will greatly help every way. Yours very truly

Opinion on the Draft

It is at all times proper that misunderstanding between the public and the public servant should be avoided; and this is far more important now, than in times of peace and tranquility. I therefore address you without searching for a precedent upon which to do so. Some of you are sincerely devoted to the republican institutions, and territorial integrity of our country, and yet are opposed to what is called the draft, or conscription.

At the beginning of the war, and ever since, a variety of motives pressing, some in one direction and some in the other, would be presented to the mind of each man physically fit for a soldier, upon the combined effect of which motives, he would, or would not, voluntarily enter the service. Among these motives would be patriotism, political bias, ambition, personal courage, love of adventure, want of employment, and convenience, or the opposites of some of these. We already have, and have had in the service, as appears, substantially all that can be obtained upon this voluntary weighing of motives. And yet we must somehow obtain more, or relinquish the original object of the contest, together with all the blood and treasure already expended in the effort to secure it. To meet this necessity the law for the draft has been enacted. You who do not wish to be soldiers, do not like this law. This is natural; nor does it imply want of patriotism. Nothing can be so just, and necessary, as to make us like it, if it is disagreeable to us. We are prone, too, to find false arguments with which to excuse ourselves for opposing such disagreeable things. In this case those who desire the rebellion to succeed, and others who seek reward in a different way, are very active in accomodating us with this class of arguments. They tell us the law is unconstitutional. It is the first instance, I believe, in which the power of congress to do a thing has ever been questioned, in a case when the power is given by the constitution in express terms. Whether a power can be implied, when it is not expressed, has often been the subject of controversy; but this is the first case in which the degree of effrontery has been ventured upon, of denying a power which is plainly and distinctly written down in the constitution. The constitution declares that "The congress shall have power . . . To raise and support armies; but no appropriation of money to that use shall be for a longer term than two years." The whole scope of the conscription act is "to raise and support armies." There is nothing else in it. It makes no appropriation of money; and hence the money clause just quoted, is not touched by it. The case simply is the constitution provides that the congress shall have power to raise and support armies; and, by this act, the congress has exercised the power to raise and support armies. This is the whole of it. It is a law made in litteral pursuance of this part of the United States Constitution; and another part of the same constitution declares that "This constitution, and the laws made in pursuance thereof . . . shall be the supreme law of the land, and the judges in every state shall be bound thereby, anything in the constitution or laws of any state to the contrary notwithstanding."

Do you admit that the power is given to raise and support armies, and yet insist that by this act congress has not exercised the power in a constitutional mode?—has not done the thing, in the right way? Who is to judge of this? The constitution gives congress the power, but it does not prescribe the mode, or expressly declare who shall prescribe it. In such case congress must prescribe the mode, or relinquish the power. There is no alternative. Congress could not exercise the power to do the thing, if it had not the power of providing a way to do it, when no way is provided by the constitution for doing it. In fact congress would not have the power to raise and support armies, if even by the constitution, it were left to the option of any other, or others, to give or withhold the only mode of doing it. If the constitution had prescribed a mode, congress could and must follow that mode; but as it is, the mode necessarily goes to congress, with the power expressly given. The power is given fully, completely, unconditionally. It is not a power to raise armies *if* State authorities consent; nor *if* the men to compose the armies are entirely willing; but it is a power to raise and support armies given to congress by the constitution, without an if.

It is clear that a constitutional law may not be expedient or proper. Such would be a law to raise armies when no armies were needed. But this is not such. The republican institutions, and territorial integrity of our country can not be maintained without the further raising and supporting of armies. There can be no army without men. Men can be had only voluntarily, or involuntarily. We have ceased to obtain them voluntarily; and to obtain them involuntarily, is the draft—the conscription. If you dispute the fact, and declare that men can still be had voluntarily in sufficient numbers prove the assertion by yourselves volunteering in such numbers, and I shall gladly give up the draft. Or if not a sufficient number, but any one of you will volunteer, he for his single self, will escape all the horrors of the draft; and will thereby do only what each one of at least a million of his manly brethren have already done. Their toil and blood have been given as much for you as for themselves. Shall it all be lost rather than you too, will bear your part?

I do not say that all who would avoid serving in the war,

are unpatriotic; but I do think every patriot should willingly take his chance under a law made with great care in order to secure entire fairness. This law was considered, discussed, modified, and amended, by congress, at great length, and with much labor; and was finally passed, by both branches, with a near approach to unanimity. At last, it may not be exactly such as any one man out of congress, or even in congress, would have made it. It has been said, and I believe truly, that the constitution itself is not altogether such as any one of it's framers would have preferred. It was the joint work of all; and certainly the better that it was so.

Much complaint is made of that provision of the conscription law which allows a drafted man to substitute three hundred dollars for himself; while, as I believe, none is made of that provision which allows him to substitute another man for himself. Nor is the three hundred dollar provision objected to for unconstitutionality; but for inequality—for favoring the rich against the poor. The substitution of men is the provision if any, which favors the rich to the exclusion of the poor. But this being a provision in accordance with an old and well known practice, in the raising of armies, is not objected to. There would have been great objection if that provision had been omitted. And yet being in, the money provision really modifies the inequality which the other introduces. It allows men to escape the service, who are too poor to escape but for it. Without the money provision, competition among the more wealthy might, and probably would, raise the price of substitutes above three hundred dollars, thus leaving the man who could raise only three hundred dollars, no escape from personal service. True, by the law as it is, the man who can not raise so much as three hundred dollars, nor obtain a personal substitute for less, can not escape; but he can come quite as near escaping as he could if the money provision were not in the law. To put it another way, is an unobjectionable law which allows only the man to escape who can pay a thousand dollars, made objectionable by adding a provision that any one may escape who can pay the smaller sum of three hundred dollars? This is the exact difference at this point between the present law and all former draft laws. It is true that by this law a some what larger number will escape than could under a law allowing personal substitutes only; but each additional man thus escaping will be a poorer man than could have escaped by the law in the other form. The money provision enlarges the class of exempts from actual service simply by admitting poorer men into it. How, then can this money provision be a wrong to the poor man? The inequality complained of pertains in greater degree to the substitution of men, and is really modified and lessened by the money provision. The inequality could only be perfectly cured by sweeping both provisions away. This being a great innovation, would probably leave the law more distasteful than it now is.

The principle of the draft, which simply is involuntary, or enforced service, is not new. It has been practiced in all ages of the world. It was well known to the framers of our constitution as one of the modes of raising armies, at the time they placed in that instrument the provision that "the congress shall have power to raise and support armies." It has been used, just before, in establishing our independence; and it was also used under the constitution in 1812. Wherein is the peculiar hardship now? Shall we shrink from the necessary means to maintain our free government, which our grand-fathers employed to establish it, and our own fathers have already employed once to maintain it? Are we degenerate? Has the manhood of our race run out?

Again, a law may be both constitutional and expedient, and yet may be administered in an unjust and unfair way. This law belongs to a class, which class is composed of those laws whose object is to distribute burthens or benefits on the principle of equality. No one of these laws can ever be practically administered with that exactness which can be conceived of in the mind. A tax law, the principle of which is that each owner shall pay in proportion to the value of his property, will be a dead letter, if no one can be compelled to pay until it can be shown that every other one will pay in precisely the same proportion according to value; nay even, it will be a dead letter, if no one can be compelled to pay until it is certain that every other one will pay at all—even in unequal proportion. Again the United States House of representatives is constituted on the principle that each member is sent by the same number of people that each other one is sent by; and yet in practice no two of the whole number, much less the whole number, are ever sent by precisely the same number of constituents. The Districts can not be made precisely equal in population at first, and if they could, they would become unequal in a single day, and much more so in the ten years, which the Districts, once made, are to continue. They can not be re-modelled every day; nor, without too much expence and labor, even every year.

This sort of difficulty applies in full force, to the practical administration of the draft law. In fact the difficulty is greater in the case of the draft law. First, it starts with all the inequality of the congressional Districts; but these are based on entire population, while the draft is based upon those only who are fit for soldiers, and such may not bear the same proportion to the whole in one District, that they do in another. Again, the facts must be ascertained, and credit given, for the unequal numbers of soldiers which have already gone from the several Districts. In all these points errors will occur in spite of the utmost fidelity. The government is bound to administer the law with such an approach to exactness as is usual in analagous cases, and as entire good faith and fidelity will reach. If so great departures as to be inconsistent with such good faith and fidelity, or great departures occurring in any way, be pointed out, they shall be corrected; and any agent shown to have caused such departures intentionally, shall be dismissed.

With these views, and on these principles, I feel bound to tell you it is my purpose to see the draft law faithfully executed.

c. mid-September 1863

To Jesse K. Dubois and Ozias M. Hatch

"Cypher"

Hon. J. K. Dubois &   Executive Mansion,
Hon. O. M. Hatch   Washington, Sept. 15, 1863.

What nation do you desire Gen. Allen to be made Quarter-Master-General of? This nation already has a Quarter-Master-General.

To Henry W. Halleck

Executive Mansion,
Major General Halleck: Washington, Sept. 15. 1863.

If I did not misunderstand Gen. Meade's last despatch, he posts you on facts as well as he can, and desires your views and those of the government, as to what he shall do. My opinion is that he should move upon Lee at once in manner of general attack, leaving to developements, whether he will make it a real attack. I think this would develope Lee's real condition and purposes better than the cavalry alone can do. Of course my opinion is not to control you and Gen. Meade. Yours truly

Proclamation Suspending Writ of Habeas Corpus

BY THE PRESIDENT OF THE UNITED STATES OF AMERICA.

A PROCLAMATION.

Whereas the Constitution of the United States has ordained that the privilege of the Writ of Habeas Corpus shall not be suspended unless when in cases of rebellion or invasion the public safety may require it, And whereas a rebellion was existing on the third day of March, 1863, which rebellion is still existing; and whereas by a statute which was approved on that day, it was enacted by the Senate and House of Representatives of the United States in Congress assembled, that, during the present insurrection, the President of the United States, whenever, in his judgment, the Public safety may require, is authorized to suspend the privilege of the Writ of Habeas Corpus in any case throughout the United States or any part thereof; and whereas in the judgment of the President the public safety does require that the privilege of the said writ shall now be suspended throughout the United States in the cases where, by the authority of the President of the United States, military, naval and civil officers of the United States or any of them hold persons under their command or in their custody either as prisoners of war, spies, or aiders or abettors of the enemy; or officers, soldiers or seamen enrolled or drafted or mustered or enlisted in or belonging to the land or naval forces of the United States or as deserters therefrom or otherwise amenable to military law, or the Rules and Articles of War or the rules or regulations prescribed for the military or naval services by authority of the President of the United States or for resisting a draft or for any other offence against the military or naval service. Now, therefore, I, Abraham Lincoln, President of the United States, do hereby proclaim and make known to all whom it may concern, that the privilege of the Writ of Habeas Corpus is suspended throughout the United States in the several cases before mentioned, and that this suspension will continue throughout the duration of the said rebellion, or until this proclamation shall, by a subsequent one to be issued by the President of the

United States, be modified or revoked. And I do hereby require all magistrates, attorneys and other civil officers within the United States, and all officers and others in the military and naval services of the United States, to take distinct notice of this suspension, and to give it full effect, and all citizens of the United States to conduct and govern themselves accordingly and in conformity with the Constitution of the United States and the laws of Congress in such case made and provided.

In testimony whereof, I have hereunto set my hand, and caused the Seal of the United States to be affixed, this Fifteenth day of September, in the year of our Lord one thousand eight hundred and sixty three and of the Independence of the United States of America the Eighty-eighth.

By the President: ABRAHAM LINCOLN
    WILLIAM H. SEWARD, Secretary of State.

Draft of Order Concerning Writ of Habeas Corpus

Please order each Military officer of the United States, that, whenever he shall have in his custody any person, by the authority of the United States and any writ of *habeas corpus* shall be served upon him, commanding him to produce such person before any court or judge, he, the said Military officer, make known to the court or judge issuing such writ, by a proper return thereto, that he holds such person by the authority of the President of the United States, acting as the Commander-in-Chief, of the Army of the United States in time of actual rebellion and war against the United States; and that, thereupon he do not produce such person according said writ, but that he deal with him according to the orders of his military superiors; and that, having made known to such court or judge, the cause of holding said person as aforesaid, if said court or judge, shall issue any process for his, said officer's, arrest, he refuse obedience thereto; and that, in case there shall be any attempt, to take such person from the custody of such officer, or to arrest such officer, he resist such attempt, calling to his aid any force that may be necessary to make such resistance effectual.

September 17, 1863

To Henry W. Halleck

Executive Mansion
Major General Halleck: Washington, Sept. 19. 1863.

By Gen. Mcade's despatch to you of yesterday it appears that he desires your views and those of the government, as to whether he shall advance upon the enemy. I am not prepared to order, or even advise an advance in this case, wherein I know so little of particulars, and wherein he, in the field, thinks the risk is so great, and the promise of advantage so small. And yet the case presents matter for very serious consideration in another aspect. These two armies confront each other across a small river, substantially midway between the two Capitals, each defending it's own Capital, and menacing the other. Gen. Meade estimates the enemies infantry in front of him at not less than forty thousand. Suppose we add fifty per cent to this, for cavalry, artillery, and extra duty men stretching as far as Richmond, making the whole force of the enemy sixty thousand. Gen. Meade, as shown by the returns, has with him, and between him and Washington, of the same classes of well men, over ninety thousand. Neither can bring the whole of his men into a battle; but each can bring as large a per centage in as the other. For a battle, then, Gen. Meade has three men to Gen. Lee's two. Yet, it having been determined that choosing ground, and standing on the defensive, gives so great advantage that the three can not safely attack the two, the three are left simply standing on the defensive also. If the enemies sixty thousand are sufficient to keep our ninety thousand away from Richmond, why, by the same rule, may not forty thousand of ours keep their sixty thousand away from Washington, leaving us fifty thousand to put to some other use? Having practically come to the mere defensive, it seems to be no economy at all to employ twice as many men for that object as are needed. With no object, certainly, to mislead myself, I can perceive no fault in this statement, unless we admit we are not the equal of the enemy man for man. I hope you will consider it.

To avoid misunderstanding, let me say that to attempt to fight the enemy slowly back into his intrenchments at Richmond, and there to capture him, is an idea I have been trying to repudiate for quite a year. My judgment is so clear against it, that I would scarcely allow the attempt to be made, if the general in command should desire to make it. My last attempt upon Richmond was to get McClellan, when he was nearer there than the enemy was, to run in ahead of him. Since then I have constantly desired the Army of the Potomac, to make Lee's army, and not Richmond, it's objective point. If our army can not fall upon the enemy and hurt him where he is, it is plain to me it can gain nothing by attempting to follow him over a succession of intrenched lines into a fortified city. Yours truly

To Ozias M. Hatch and Jesse K. Dubois

Hon O. M. Hatch &   Executive Mansion,
Hon. J. K. Dubois: Washington, Sep. 22, 1863.
Springfield, Ills.

Your letter is just received. The particular form of my despatch was jocular, which I supposed you gentlemen knew me well enough to understand. Gen. Allen is considered here as a very faithful and capable officer; and one who would be at least thought of for Quarter-Master-General if that office were vacant

To Mary Todd Lincoln

Mrs. A. Lincoln,   Washington, D.C.,
Fifth Avenue Hotel New York—   Sep. 24 1863

We now have a tolerably accurate summing up of the late battle between Rosecrans and Bragg. The result is that we are worsted, if at all, only in the fact that we, after the main fighting was over, yielded the ground, thus leaving considerable of our artillery and wounded to fall into the enemies' hands, for which we got nothing in turn. We lost, in general officers, one killed, and three or four wounded, all Brigadiers; while according to rebel accounts, which we have, they lost six killed, and eight wounded. Of the killed, one Major Genl. and five Brigadiers, including your brother-in-law, Helm; and of the wounded, three Major Generals, and five Brigadiers. This list may be reduced two in number, by correction of confusion in names. At 11/40 A.M. yesterday Gen. Rosecrans telegraphed from Chattanooga "We hold this point, and I can not be dislodged, except by very superior numbers, and after a great battle" A despatch leaving there after night yesterday says, "No fight to-day"

To Ambrose E. Burnside

Office U.S. Military Telegraph,
War Department, Washington, D.C.,
Major General Burnside   Sep. 25. 1863

Yours of the 23rd. is just received, and it makes me doubt whether I am awake or dreaming. I have been struggling for ten days, first through Gen. Halleck, and then directly, to get you to go to assist Gen. Rosecrans in an extremity, and you have repeatedly declared you would do it, and yet you steadily move the contrary way. On the 19th. you telegraph once from Knoxville, and twice from Greenville, acknowledging receipt of order, and saying you will hurry support to Rosecrans. On the 20th. you telegraph again from Knoxville, saying you will do all you can, and are hurrying troops to Rosecrans. On the 21st. you telegraph from Morristown, saying you will hurry support to Rosecrans; and now your despatch of the 23rd. comes in from Carter's Station, still farther away from Rosecrans, still saying you will assist him, but giving no account of any progress made towards assisting him

You came in upon the Tennessee River at Kingston, Loudon, and Knoxville; and what bridges or the want of them upon the Holston, can have to do in getting the troops towards Rosecrans at Chattanooga is incomprehensible. They were already many miles nearer Chattanooga than any part of the Holston river is, and on the right side of it. If they are now on the wrong side of it, they can only have got so by going from the direction of Chattanooga, and that too, since you have assured us you would move to Chattanooga; while it would seem too, that they could re-cross the Holston, by whatever means they crossed it going East.

To William S. Rosecrans

My Dear General   Executive Mansion,
  Rosecrans   Washington, September 28, 1863.
  We are sending you two small corps, one under General Howard, and one under General Slocum, and the whole under General Hooker. Unfortunately the relations between Generals Hooker and Slocum are not such as to promise good, if their present relative positions remain. Therefore let me beg,—almost enjoin upon you—that on their reaching you, you will make a transposition by which Gen. Slocum with his corps, may pass from under the command of Gen. Hooker, and Gen. Hooker, in turn, receive some other equal force. It is important for this to be done, though we could not well arrange it here. Please do it. Yours very truly

Reply to Sons of Temperance, Washington, D.C.

As a matter of course, it will not be possible for me to make a response coextensive with the address which you have presented to me. If I were better known than I am, you would not need to be told that in the advocacy of the cause of temperance you have a friend and sympathizer in me. [Applause.]
  When I was a young man, long ago, before the Sons of Temperance as an organization, had an existence, I in an humble way, made temperance speeches, [applause] and I think I may say that to this day I have never, by my example, belied what I then said. [Loud applause.]
  In regard to the suggestions which you make for the purpose of the advancement of the cause of temperance in the army, I cannot make particular responses to them at this time. To prevent intemperance in the army is even a part of the

articles of war. It is part of the law of the land—and was so, I presume, long ago—to dismiss officers for drunkenness. I am not sure that consistently with the public service, more can be done than has been done. All, therefore, that I can promise you is, (if you will be pleased to furnish me with a copy of your address) to have it submitted to the proper Department and have it considered, whether it contains any suggestions which will improve the cause of temperance and repress the cause of drunkenness in the army any better than it is already done. I can promise no more than that.

I think that the reasonable men of the world have long since agreed that intemperance is one of the greatest, if not the very greatest of all evils amongst mankind. That is not a matter of dispute, I believe. That the disease exists, and that it is a very great one is agreed upon by all.

The mode of cure is one about which there may be differences of opinion. You have suggested that in an army—our army—drunkenness is a great evil, and one which, while it exists to a very great extent, we cannot expect to overcome so entirely as to have such successes in our arms as we might have without it. This undoubtedly is true, and while it is, perhaps, rather a bad source to derive comfort from, nevertheless, in a hard struggle, I do not know but what it is some consolation to be aware that there is some intemperance on the other side, too, and that they have no right to beat us in physical combat on that ground. [Laughter and applause.]

But I have already said more than I expected to be able to say when I began, and if you please to hand me a copy of your address it shall be considered. I thank you very heartily, gentlemen, for this call, and for bringing with you these very many pretty ladies.

September 29, 1863

To John M. Schofield

Executive Mansion
Gen. John M. Schofield   Washington, D.C. Oct. 1. 1863.

There is no organized military force in avowed opposition to the general government, now in Missouri; and if any such shall reappear, your duty in regard to it will be too plain to require any special instruction. Still the condition of things, both there and elsewhere, is such as to render it indispensable to maintain for a time, the United States Military establishment in that State, as well as to rely upon it for a fair contribution of support to that establishment generally.

Your immediate duty, in regard to Missouri, now is to advance the efficiency of that establishment, and to so use it, as far as practicable, to compel the excited people there to leave one another alone.

Under your recent order, which I have approved, you will only arrest individuals, and suppress assemblies, or newspapers, when they may be working *palpable* injury to the Military in your charge; and, in no other case will you interfere with the expression of opinion in any form, or allow it to be interfered with violently by others. In this, you have a discretion to exercise with great caution, calmness, and forbearance.

With the matters of removing the inhabitants of certain counties *en masse*; and of removing certain individuals from time to time, who are supposed to be mischievous, I am not now interfering, but am leaving to your own discretion

Nor am I interfering with what may still seem to you to be necessary restrictions upon trade and intercourse.

I think proper, however, to enjoin upon you the following:

Allow no part of the Military under your command, to be engaged in either returning fugitive slaves, or in forcing, or enticing slaves from their homes; and, so far as practicable, enforce the same forbearance upon the people.

Report to me your opinion upon the availibility for good, of the enrolled militia of the State.

Allow no one to enlist colored troops, except upon orders from you, or from here through you.

Allow no one to assume the functions of confiscating property, under the law of congress, or other wise, except upon orders from here.

At elections, see that those, and only those are allowed to vote, who are entitled to do so, by the laws of Missouri, including as of those laws, the restriction laid by the Missouri convention upon those who may have participated in the rebellion.

So far as practicable you will, by means of your military force, expel guerrillas, marauders, and murderers, and all who are known to harbor, aid, or abet them. But, in like manner, you will repress assumptions of unauthorized individuals to perform the same service; because under pretence of doing this, they become marauders and murderers themselves. To now restore peace, let the military obey orders; and those not of the military, leave each other alone; thus not breaking the peace themselves.

In giving the above directions, it is not intended to restrain you in other expedient and necessary matters not falling within their range. Your Obt. Servt.

Proclamation of Thanksgiving

BY THE PRESIDENT OF THE UNITED STATES OF AMERICA.

A PROCLAMATION.

The year that is drawing towards its close, has been filled with the blessings of fruitful fields and healthful skies. To these bounties, which are so constantly enjoyed that we are prone to forget the source from which they come, others have been added, which are of so extraordinary a nature, that they cannot fail to penetrate and soften even the heart which is habitually insensible to the ever watchful providence of Almighty God. In the midst of a civil war of unequalled magnitude and severity, which has sometimes seemed to foreign States to invite and to provoke their aggression, peace has been preserved with all nations, order has been maintained, the laws have been respected and obeyed, and harmony has prevailed everywhere except in the theatre of military conflict; while that theatre has been greatly contracted by the advancing armies and navies of the Union. Needful diversions of wealth and of strength from the fields of peaceful industry to the national defence, have not arrested the plough, the shuttle or the ship; the axe has enlarged the borders of our settlements, and the mines, as well of iron and coal as of the precious metals, have yielded even more abundantly than heretofore. Population has steadily increased, notwithstanding the waste that has been made in the camp, the siege and the battle-field; and the country, rejoicing in the consciousness of augmented strength and vigor, is permitted to expect continuance of years with large increase of freedom. No human counsel hath devised nor hath any mortal hand worked out these great things. They are the gracious gifts of the Most High God, who, while dealing with us in anger for our sins, hath nevertheless remembered mercy. It has seemed to me fit and proper that they should be solemnly, reverently and gratefully acknowledged as with one heart and one voice by the whole American People. I do therefore invite my fellow citizens in every part of the United States, and also those who are at sea and those who are sojourning in foreign lands, to set apart and observe the last Thursday of November next, as a day of Thanksgiving and Praise to our beneficent Father who dwelleth in the Heavens. And I recommend to them that while offering up the ascriptions justly due to Him for such singular deliverances and blessings, they do also, with humble penitence for our national perverseness and disobedience, commend to His tender care all those who have become widows, orphans, mourners or sufferers in the lamentable civil strife in which we are unavoidably engaged, and fervently implore the interposition of the Almighty Hand to heal the wounds of the nation and to restore it as soon as may be consistent with the Divine purposes to the full enjoyment of peace, harmony, tranquillity and Union.

In testimony whereof, I have hereunto set my hand and caused the Seal of the United States to be affixed.

Done at the city of Washington, this Third day of October, in the year of our Lord one thousand eight hundred and sixty-three, and of the Independence of the United States the Eighty-eighth.

By the President: ABRAHAM LINCOLN
    WILLIAM H. SEWARD, Secretary of State.

To William S. Rosecrans

Major General Rosecrans: Washington, D.C.,
Chattanooga, Tenn.   Oct 4. 1863

Yours of yesterday received. If we can hold Chattanooga, and East Tennessee, I think the rebellion must dwindle and die. I think you and Burnside can do this; and hence doing so is your main object. Of course, to greatly damage, or destroy, the enemy in your front would be a greater object, because it would include the former, and more; but it is not so certainly within your power. I understand the main body of the enemy is very near you—so near that you could "board at home" so to speak, and menace or attack him any day. Would not the doing of this, be your best mode of counteracting his raids on your communications? But this is not an order. I intend doing something like what you suggest, whenever the case shall appear ripe enough to have it accepted in the true understanding, rather than as a confession of weakness and fear.

To Charles D. Drake and Others

Hon. Charles D. Drake &   Executive Mansion
others, Committee   Washington D.C. Oct. 5. 1863

Gentlemen   Your original address, presented on the 30th. ultimo, and the four supplementary ones, presented on the 3rd. inst. have been carefully considered.

I hope you will regard the other duties claiming my attention, together with the great length and importance of these documents as constituting a sufficient apology for my not having responded sooner.

These papers, framed for a common object, consist of the things demanded, and the reasons for demanding them. The things demanded are:

First: That General Schofield shall be relieved, and General Butler be appointed, as commander of the Military Department of Missouri.

Second: That the system of Enrolled Militia in Missouri may be broken up, and national forces be substituted for it, and

Third: That at elections, persons may not be allowed to vote who are not entitled by law to do so.

Among the reasons given, enough of suffering and wrong to Union men is certainly, and I suppose truly stated. Yet the whole case, as presented, fails to convince me, that Gen. Schofield, or the Enrolled Militia, is responsible for that suffering and wrong. The whole can be explained on a more charitable, and, as I think, a more rational hypothesis. We are in civil war. In such cases there always is a main question; but in this case that question is a perplexing compound—Union and Slavery. It thus becomes a question not of two sides merely, but of at least four sides, even among those who are for the Union, saying nothing of those who are against it. Thus, those who are for the Union *with*, but not *without* slavery—those for it *without*, but not *with*—those for it *with* or *without*, but prefer it *with*—and those for it *with* or *without*, but prefer it *without*. Among these again, is a subdivision of those who are for *gradual* but not for *immediate*, and those who are for *immediate*, but not for *gradual* extinction of slavery. It is easy to conceive that all these shades of opinion, and even more, may be sincerely entertained by honest and truthful men. Yet, all being for the Union, by reason of these differences, each will prefer a different way of sustaining the Union. At once sincerity is questioned, and motives are assailed. Actual war coming, blood grows hot, and blood is spilled. Thought is forced from old channels into confusion. Deception breeds and thrives. Confidence dies, and universal suspicion reigns. Each man feels an impulse to kill his neighbor, lest he be first killed by him. Revenge and retaliation follow. And all this, as before said, may be among honest men only. But this is not all. Every foul bird comes abroad, and every dirty reptile rises up. These add crime to confusion. Strong measures, deemed indispensable but harsh at best, such men make worse by mal-administration. Murders for old grudges, and murders for pelf, proceed under any cloak that will best cover for the ocasion. These causes amply account for what has occurred in Missouri, without ascribing it to the weakness, or wickedness of any general. The newspaper files, those chroniclers of current events, will show that the evils now complained of were quite as prevalent under Fremont, Hunter, Halleck, and Curtis, as under Schofield. If the former had greater force opposed to them, they also had greater force with which to meet it. When the organized rebel army left the state, the main federal force had to go also, leaving the Department commander at home relatively no stronger than before. Without disparaging any, I affirm with confidence that no commander of that Department has, in proportion to his means, done better than Gen. Schofield.

The first specific charge against Gen. Schofield is that the Enrolled Militia was placed under his command, whereas it had not been placed under the command of Gen. Curtis. The fact I believe is true; but you do not point out, nor can I conceive, how that did, or could injure loyal men, or the Union cause.

You charge that upon Gen. Curtis being superseded by Gen. Schofield, Franklin A. Dick was superseded by James O. Brodhead, as Provost Marshal-General. No very specific showing is made as to how this did, or could injure the Union cause. It recalls, however, the condition of things, as presented to me, which led to a change of commander for that Department.

To restrain contraband intelligence and trade, a system of searches, seizures, permits, and passes, had been introduced, I think, by Gen. Fremont. When Gen. Halleck came, he found, and continued this system, and added an order applicable to some parts of the State, to levy and collect contributions from noted rebels, to compensate losses, and relieve destitution caused by the rebellion. The action of Gen. Fremont and Gen. Halleck, as stated, constituted a sort of system, which Gen. Curtis found in full operation when he took command of the Department. That there was a necessity for something of the sort was clear; but that it could only be justified by stern necessity, and that it was liable to great abuse in administration, was equally clear. Agents to execute it, contrary to the great Prayer, were led into temptation. Some might, while others would not resist that temptation. It was not possible to hold any to a very strict accountability; and those yielding to the temptation, would sell permits and passes to those who would pay most, and most readily for them; and would seize property, and collect levies in the aptest way to fill their own pockets. Money being the object, the man having money, whether loyal or disloyal, would be a victim. This practice doubtless existed to some extent, and it was a real additional evil, that it could be and was, plausably charged to exist in greater extent than it did.

When Gen. Curtis took command of the Department, Mr. Dick, against whom I never knew anything to allege, had general charge of this system. A controversy in regard to it rapidly grew into almost unmanageable proportions. One side ignored the *necessity*, and magnified the evils of the system; while the other ignored the evils, and magnified the necessity; and each bitterly assailed the motives of the other. I could not fail to see that the controversy enlarged in the same proportion as the professed Union-men there distinctly took sides in two opposing political parties. I exhausted my wits, and very nearly my patience also, in efforts to convince both that the evils they charged on each other, were inherent in the case, and could not be cured by giving either party a victory over the other.

Plainly the irritating system was not to be perpetual; and it was plausably urged that it could be modified at once with advantage. The case could scarcely be worse, and whether it could be made better, could only be determined by a trial. In this view, and not to ban, or brand, Gen. Curtis, or to give a victory to any party, I made the change of commander for the Department. I now learn that soon after this change, Mr. Dick was removed, and that Mr. Brodhead, a gentleman of no less good character, was put in the place. The mere fact of this change is more distinctly complained of, than is any conduct of the new officer, or other consequence, of the change.

I gave the new commander no instructions as to the administration of the system mentioned, beyond what is contained in the private letter, afterwards surreptitiously published, in which I directed him to act solely for the public good, and independently of both parties. Neither anything you have presented me, nor anything I have otherwise learned, has convinced me that he has been unfaithful to this charge.

Imbecility is urged as one cause for removing Gen. Schofield; and the late massacre at Lawrence, Kansas, is pressed as evidence of that imbecility. To my mind that fact scarcely tends to prove the proposition. That massacre is only an example, of what Grierson, John Morgan, and many others, might have repeatedly done, on their respective raids, had they chose to incur the personal hazard, and possessed the fiendish hearts to do it.

The charge is made that Gen. Schofield, on purpose to protect the Lawrence murderers, would not allow them to be pursued into Missouri. While no punishment could be too sudden, or too severe for those murderers, I am well satisfied that the preventing of the threatened remedial raid into Missouri, was the only safe way to avoid an indiscriminate massacre there, including probably more innocent than guilty. Instead of condemning, I therefore approve what I understand Gen. Schofield did in that respect.

The charges that Gen. Schofield has purposely withheld protection from loyal people, and purposely facilitated the objects of the disloyal, are altogether beyond my power of belief. I do not arraign the veracity of gentlemen as to the facts complained of; but I do more than question the judgment which would infer that those facts occurred in accordance with the *purposes* of Gen. Schofield.

With my present views I must decline to remove Gen. Schofield. In this I decide nothing against Gen. Butler. I sincerely wish it were convenient to assign him a suitable command.

In order to meet some existing evils I have addressed a letter of instructions to Gen. Schofield, a copy of which I inclose to you.

As to the "Enrolled Militia" I shall endeavor to ascertain, better than I now know, what is it's exact value.

Let me say now, however, that your proposal to substitute national force for the "Enrolled Militia" implies that in your judgment the latter is doing something which needs to be done; and if so, the proposition to throw that force away, and to supply its place by bringing other forces from the field where they are urgently needed seems to me very extraordinary. Whence shall they come? Shall they be withdrawn from Banks, or Grant, or Steele, or Rosecrans? Few things have been so grateful to my anxious feeling as when, in June last, the local force in Missouri aided Gen. Schofield to so promptly send a large general force to the relief of Gen. Grant, then investing Vicksburg, and menaced from without by Gen. Johnston. Was this all wrong? Should the Enrolled Militia then have been broken up, and Gen. Herron kept from Grant, to police Missouri? So far from finding cause to object, I confess to a sympathy for whatever relieves our general force in Missouri, and allows it to serve elsewhere. I therefore, as at present advised, can not attempt the destruction of the Enrolled Militia of Missouri. I may add that the force being under the national military control, it is also within the proclamation in regard to the *Habeas Corpus*.

I concur in the propriety of your request in regard to elections, and have, as you see, directed Gen. Schofield accordingly.

I do not feel justified to enter upon the broad field you present in regard to the political differences between radicals and conservatives. From time to time I have done and said what appeared to me proper to do and say. The public knows it all. It obliges nobody to follow me, and I trust it obliges me to follow nobody. The radicals and conservatives, each agree with me in some things, and disagree in others. I could wish both to agree with me in all things; for then they would agree with each other, and would be too strong for any foe from any quarter. They, however, choose to do otherwise, and I do not question their right. I too shall do what seems to be my duty. I hold whoever commands in Missouri, or elsewhere, responsible to me, and not to either radicals or conservatives. It is my duty to hear all; but at last, I must, within my sphere, judge what to do, and what to forbear. Your Obt. Servt.

Approval of Sentence of David M. Wright

October 7, 1863

Upon the presentation of the record in this case and the examination thereof, aided by the report thereon of the Judge-Advocate-General, and on full hearing of counsel for the accused, being satisfied that no proper question remained open except as to the insanity of the accused, I caused a very full examination to be made on that question, upon a great amount of evidence, including all offered by counsel of accused, by an expert of high reputation in that professional department, who thereon reports to me, as his opinion, that the accused Dr. David M. Wright, was not insane prior to or on the 11th day of July, 1863, the date of the homicide of Lieutenant Sanborn; that he has not been insane since, and is not insane now (October 7, 1863). I therefore approve the finding and sentence of the military commission, and direct that the major-general in command of the department including the place of trial, and wherein the convict is now in custody, appoint time and place and carry said sentence into execution.

To George G. Meade

Major General Meade   Washington, D.C.,
Army of Potomac   Oct. 8 1863

I am appealed to in behalf of John Murphy, to be shot to-morrow. His Mother says he is but seventeen. Please answer.

To George G. Meade

Major General Meade   Executive Mansion,
Army of Potomac   Washington, Oct. 12, 1863.

The father and mother of John Murphy of the 119th. Pennsylvania Vols. have filed their own affidavits that he was born June 22, 1846; and also the affidavits of three other persons who all swear that they remember the circumstance of his birth and that it was in the year 1846, though they do not remember the particular day. I therefore, on account of his tender age, have concluded to pardon him, and to leave it to yourself whether to discharge him, or continue him in the service.

To William S. Rosecrans

Major General Rosecrans   Washington, D.C.,
Chattanooga, Tenn.   Oct. 12. 8/35 A.M. 1863

As I understand, Burnside is menaced from the East, and so can not go to you without surrendering East Tennessee. I now think the enemy will not attack Chattanooga; and I think you have to look out for his making a concentrated drive at Burnside. You and Burnside now have him by the throat, and he must break your hold, or perish. I therefore think you better to try to hold the river up to Kingston, leaving Burnside to what is above there. Sherman *is* coming to you, though gaps in the telegraph prevent our knowing how far he is advanced. He and Hooker will so support you on the West & North-West, as to enable you to look East & North East. This is not an order. Gen. Halleck will give his views.

To John G. Foster

Major General Foster   Washington, D.C.,
Fort-Monroe, Va   Oct. 15 1863

Postpone the execution of Dr. Wright to Friday the 23rd. Inst. (October). This is intended for his preparation and is final.

To Henry W. Halleck

Executive Mansion,
Major General Halleck   Washington, Oct. 16. 1863.

I do not believe Lee can have over sixty thousand effective men. Longstreet's corps would not be sent away, to bring an equal force back upon the same road; and there is no other direction for them to have come from. Doubtless, in making the present movement Lee gathered in all available scraps, and added them to Hills & Ewell's corps; but that is all. And he made the movement in the belief that *four* corps had left Gen. Meade; and Gen. Meade's apparantly avoiding a collision with him has confirmed him in that belief. If Gen. Meade can now attack him on a field no worse than equal for us, and will do so with all the skill and courage, which he, his officers and men possess, the honor will be his if he succeeds, and the blame may be mine if he fails. Yours truly,

To John G. Foster

Major General Foster   Washington, D.C.,
Fort-Monroe, Va   Oct. 17. 1863

It would be useless for Mrs. Dr. Wright to come here. The subject is a very painful one, but the case is settled.

Remarks to Baltimore Presbyterian Synod, Washington, D.C.

Gentlemen of the Baltimore Synod: I can only say that in this case, as in many others, I am profoundly grateful for the support given me in every field of labor in which it can be given, and which has ever been extended to me by the religious community of the country. I saw before taking my position here that I was to have an administration, if it could be called such, of extraordinary difficulty, and it seems to me that it was ever present with me as an extraordinary matter that in the time of the greatest difficulty that this country had ever experienced, or was likely to experience, the man who, at the least of it, gave poor promise of ability, was brought out for duty at that time. I was early brought to the living reflection that there was nothing in the arms of this man, however there might be in others, to rely upon for such difficulties, and that without the direct assistance of the Almighty I was certain of failing. I sincerely wish that I was a more devoted man than I am. Sometimes in my difficulties I have been driven to the last resort to say God is still my only hope. It is still all the world to me.

I again say that I thank you in the name of the religious people of the country generally, and in the name of our common Father of returning you my thanks for the encouraging and most unanimous support that has been constantly given me. I know not that I can say more.

October 24, 1863

To James M. Cutts, Jr.

Executive Mansion,
Capt. James M. Cutts.   Washington, Oct 26, 1863.

Although what I am now to say is to be, in form, a reprimand, it is not intended to add a pang to what you have already suffered upon the subject to which it relates. You have too much of life yet before you, and have shown too much of promise as an officer, for your future to be lightly surrendered. You were convicted of two offences. One of them, not of great enormity, and yet greatly to be avoided, I feel sure you are in no danger of repeating. The other you are not so well assured against. The advice of a father to his son "Beware of entrance to a quarrel, but being in, bear it that the opposed may beware of thee," is good, and yet not the best. Quarrel not at all. No man resolved to make the most of himself, can spare time for personal contention. Still less can he afford to take all the consequences, including the vitiating of his temper, and the loss of self-control. Yield larger things to which you can show no more than equal right; and yield lesser ones, though clearly your own. Better give your path to a dog, than be bitten by him in contesting for the right. Even killing the dog would not cure the bite.

In the mood indicated deal henceforth with your fellow men, and especially with your brother officers; and even the unpleasant events you are passing from will not have been profitless to you.

To Montgomery Blair

Hon. Montgomery Blair: Executive Mansion,
My dear Sir.   Washington, Nov. 2. 1863.

Some days ago I understood you to say that your brother, Gen. Frank Blair, desires to be guided by my wishes as to whether he will occupy his seat in congress or remain in the field. My wish, then, is compounded of what I believe will be best for the country, and best for him. And it is, that he will come here, put his military commission in my hands, take his seat, go into caucus with our friends, abide the nominations, help elect the nominees, and thus aid to organize a House of Representatives which will really support the government in the war. If the result shall be the election of himself as Speaker, let him serve in that position; if not, let him re-take his commission, and return to the Army. For the country this will heal a dangerous schism; for him, it will relieve from a dangerous position. By a misunderstanding, as I think, he is in danger of being permanently separated from those with whom only he can ever have a real sympathy—the sincere opponents of slavery. It will be a mistake if he shall allow the provocations offered him by insincere time-servers, to drive him out of the house of his own building. He is young yet. He has abundant talent—quite enough to occupy all his time, without devoting any to temper. He is rising in military skill and usefulness. His recent appointment to the command of a corps, by one so competent to judge as Gen. Sherman, proves this. In that line he can serve both the country and himself more profitably than he could as a member of congress on the floor. The foregoing is what I would say, if Frank Blair were my brother instead of yours. Yours very truly

To James H. Hackett

Private

James H. Hackett   Executive Mansion,
My dear Sir: Washington, Nov. 2. 1863.

Yours of Oct. 22nd. is received, as also was, in due course, that of Oct. 3rd. I look forward with pleasure to the fulfilment of the promise made in the former.

Give yourself no uneasiness on the subject mentioned in that of the 22nd.

My note to you I certainly did not expect to see in print; yet I have not been much shocked by the newspaper comments upon it. Those comments constitute a fair specimen of what has occurred to me through life. I have endured a great deal of ridicule without much malice; and have received a great deal of kindness, not quite free from ridicule. I am used to it. Yours truly

Memorandum on Testing Diller's Powder

I select you to make the test of the new gun-powder, according to the foregoing documents. Having expended some five thousand dollars to be prepared for making the test, it is desired that it be most carefully and thoroughly made, and answers thereupon given to all the following questions, and any others which may occur to you as pertinent.

Does this powder contain saltpetre or sulphur?

Does it bear any relation to gun-cotten?

Can the ingredients for making it always be obtained in sufficient quantity in the United States?

Is it's manufacture simple, requiring no complicated apparatus, and is it attended with less danger than the manufacture of ordinary gun-powder?

Do atmospheric changes, whether of moisture or heat, injure the powder?

Will it explode with as little or less pressure than ordinary gun-powder?

Will it ignite under 300°. Celsius?

Will it ignite by a spark, or percussion-cap, like common gun-powder?

Are *seven* parts of it, in weight, as effective in smooth bored guns as *nine* parts of common gun-powder?

Is *one* part of it, in weight, as effective in rifled guns, as *two* parts of common powder?

Will it, or the ingredients of it, deteriorate in store?

Will it heat a gun less than common powder? and in what proportion?

Does it give a weaker report?

Does it make less smoke?

Does it foul a gun less?

Is it less liable to burst or damage a gun?

In proportion to effect produced, is it cheaper than common gun-powder?

Has it any fault or faults not stated, or suggested in and by the answers to the foregoing questions? and if so, what?

November 2, 1863, or after

To Nathaniel P. Banks

Executive Mansion,
Major General Banks Washington, Nov. 5. 1863.

Three months ago to-day I wrote you about Louisiana affairs, stating, on the word of Gov. Shepley, as I understood him, that Mr. Durant was taking a registry of citizens, preparatory to the election of a constitutional convention for that State. I sent a copy of the letter to Mr. Durant; and I now have his letter, written two months after, acknowledging receipt, and saying he is not taking such registry; and he does not let me know that he personally is expecting to do so. Mr. Flanders, to whom I also sent a copy, is now here, and he says nothing has yet been done. This disappoints me bitterly; yet I do not throw blame on you or on them. I do however, urge both you and them, to lose no more time. Gov. Shepley has special instructions from the War Department. I wish him—these gentlemen and others co-operating—without waiting for more territory, to go to work and give me a tangible nucleus which the remainder of the State may rally around as fast as it can, and which I can at once recognize and sustain as the true State government. And in that work I wish you, and all under your command, to give them a hearty sympathy and support. The instruction to Gov. Shepley bases the movement (and rightfully too) upon the loyal element. Time is important. There is danger, even now, that the adverse element seeks insidiously to pre-occupy the ground. If a few professedly loyal men shall draw the disloyal about them, and colorably set up a State government, repudiating the emancipation proclamation, and re-establishing slavery, I can not recognize or sustain their work. I should fall powerless in the attempt. This government, in such an attitude, would be a house divided against itself. I have said, and say again, that if a new State government, acting in harmony with this government, and consistently with general freedom, shall think best to adopt a reasonable temporary arrangement, in relation to the landless and homeless freed people, I do not object; but my word is out to be *for* and not *against* them on the question of their permanent freedom. I do not insist upon such temporary arrangement, but only say such would not be objectionable to me. Yours very truly

To Benjamin F. Flanders

Hon. B. F. Flanders   Executive Mansion
My dear Sir: Washington, D.C. Nov. 9. 1863
    In a conversation with Gen. Butler he made a suggestion which impressed me a good deal at the time. It was that, as a preliminary step, a vote be taken, yea or nay, whether there shall be a State convention to repeal the Ordinance of secession, and remodel the State constitution. I send it merely as a suggestion for your consideration, not having considered it maturely myself. The point which impressed me was, not so much the questions to be voted on, as the effect of chrystallizing, so to speak, in taking such popular vote on any proper question. In fact, I have always thought the act of secession is legally nothing, and needs no repealing. Turn the thought over in your mind, and see if in your own judgment, you can make any thing of it. Yours very truly

To Edwin M. Stanton

Hon. Secretary of War.   Executive Mansion,
My dear Sir: Washington, Nov. 11, 1863.

I personally wish Jacob R. Freese, of New-Jersey to be appointed a Colonel for a colored regiment—and this regardless of whether he can tell the exact shade of Julius Caesar's hair. Yours truly

Address at Gettysburg, Pennsylvania

Address delivered at the dedication of the Cemetery at Gettysburg.

Four score and seven years ago our fathers brought forth on this continent, a new nation, conceived in Liberty, and dedicated to the proposition that all men are created equal.

Now we are engaged in a great civil war, testing whether that nation, or any nation so conceived and so dedicated, can long endure. We are met on a great battle-field of that war. We have come to dedicate a portion of that field, as a final resting place for those who here gave their lives that that nation might live. It is altogether fitting and proper that we should do this.

But, in a larger sense, we can not dedicate—we can not consecrate—we can not hallow—this ground. The brave men, living and dead, who struggled here, have consecrated it, far above our poor power to add or detract. The world will little note, nor long remember what we say here, but it can never forget what they did here. It is for us the living, rather, to be dedicated here to the unfinished work which they who fought here have thus far so nobly advanced. It is rather for us to be here dedicated to the great task remaining before us—that from these honored dead we take increased devotion to that cause for which they gave the last full measure of devotion—that we here highly resolve that these dead shall not have died in vain—that this nation, under God, shall have a new birth of freedom—and that government of the people, by the people, for the people, shall not perish from the earth.

November 19. 1863.

To Zachariah Chandler

Private

Hon. Z. Chandler   Executive Mansion,
My dear Sir: Washington, Nov. 20. 1863.
    Your letter of the 15th. marked *"private"* was received to-

day. I have seen Gov. Morgan and Thurlow Weed, separately, but not together, within the last ten days; but neither of them mentioned the forthcoming message, or said anything, so far as I can remember, which brought the thought of the Message to my mind.

I am very glad the elections this autumn have gone favorably, and that I have not, by native depravity, or under evil influences, done anything bad enough to prevent the good result.

I hope to "stand firm" enough to not go backward, and yet not go forward fast enough to wreck the country's cause. Yours truly

To Edward Everett

Hon. Edward Everett.   Executive Mansion,
My dear Sir: Washington, Nov. 20, 1863.

Your kind note of to-day is received. In our respective parts yesterday, you could not have been excused to make a short address, nor I a long one. I am pleased to know that, in your judgment, the little I did say was not entirely a failure. Of course I knew Mr. Everett would not fail; and yet, while the whole discourse was eminently satisfactory, and will be of great value, there were passages in it which transcended my expectation. The point made against the theory of the general government being only an agency, whose principals are the States, was new to me, and, as I think, is one of the best arguments for the national supremacy. The tribute to our noble women for their angel-ministering to the suffering soldiers, surpasses, in its way, as do the subjects of it, whatever has gone before.

Our sick boy, for whom you kindly inquire, we hope is past the worst. Your Obt. Servt.

Annual Message to Congress

Fellow citizens of the Senate and House of Representatives:

Another year of health, and of sufficiently abundant harvests has passed. For these, and especially for the improved condition of our national affairs, our renewed, and profoundest gratitude to God is due.

We remain in peace and friendship with foreign powers.

The efforts of disloyal citizens of the United States to involve us in foreign wars, to aid an inexcusable insurrection, have been unavailing. Her Britannic Majesty's government, as was justly expected, have exercised their authority to prevent the departure of new hostile expeditions from British ports. The Emperor of France has, by a like proceeding, promptly vindicated the neutrality which he proclaimed at the beginning of the contest. Questions of great intricacy and importance have arisen out of the blockade, and other belligerent operations, between the government and several of the maritime powers, but they have been discussed, and, as far as was possible, accommodated in a spirit of frankness, justice, and mutual good will. It is especially gratifying that our prize courts, by the impartiality of their adjudications, have commanded the respect and confidence of maritime powers.

The supplemental treaty between the United States and Great Britain for the suppression of the African slave trade, made on the 17th. day of February last, has been duly ratified, and carried into execution. It is believed that, so far as American ports and American citizens are concerned, that inhuman and odious traffic has been brought to an end.

I shall submit, for the consideration of the Senate, a convention for the adjustment of possessory claims in Washington Territory, arising out of the treaty of the 15th. June, 1846, between the United States and Great Britain, and which have been the source of some disquiet among the citizens of that now rapidly improving part of the country.

A novel and important question, involving the extent of the maritime jurisdiction of Spain in the waters which surround the island of Cuba, has been debated without reaching an agreement, and it is proposed in an amicable spirit to refer it to the arbitrament of a friendly power. A convention for that purpose will be submitted to the Senate.

I have thought it proper, subject to the approval of the Senate, to concur with the interested commercial powers in an arrangement for the liquidation of the Scheldt dues upon the principles which have been heretofore adopted in regard to the imposts upon navigation in the waters of Denmark.

The long pending controversy between this government and that of Chili touching the seizure at Sitana, in Peru, by Chilian officers, of a large amount in treasure belonging to citizens of the United States, has been brought to a close by the award of His Majesty, the King of the Belgians, to whose arbitration the question was referred by the parties. The subject was thoroughly and patiently examined by that justly respected magistrate, and although the sum awarded to the claimants may not have been as large as they expected, there is no reason to distrust the wisdom of his Majesty's decision. That decision was promptly complied with by Chili, when intelligence in regard to it reached that country.

The joint commission, under the act of the last session, for carrying into effect the convention with Peru on the subject of claims, has been organized at Lima, and is engaged in the business intrusted to it.

Difficulties concerning inter-oceanic transit through Nicaragua are in course of amicable adjustment.

In conformity with principles set forth in my last annual message, I have received a representative from the United States of Colombia, and have accredited a minister to that republic.

Incidents occurring in the progress of our civil war have forced upon my attention the uncertain state of international questions, touching the rights of foreigners in this country and of United States citizens abroad. In regard to some governments these rights are at least partially defined by treaties. In no instance, however, is it expressly stipulated that, in the event of civil war, a foreigner residing in this country, within the lines of the insurgents, is to be exempted from the rule which classes him as a belligerent, in whose behalf the government of his country cannot expect any privileges or immunities distinct from that character. I regret to say, however, that such claims have been put forward, and, in some instances, in behalf of foreigners who have lived in the United States the greater part of their lives.

There is reason to believe that many persons born in foreign countries, who have declared their intention to become citizens, or who have been fully naturalized, have evaded the military duty required of them by denying the fact, and thereby throwing upon the government the burden of proof. It has been found difficult or impracticable to obtain this proof from the want of guides to the proper sources of information. These might be supplied by requiring clerks of courts, where declarations of intention may be made or naturalizations effected, to send, periodically, lists of the names of the persons naturalized, or declaring their intention to become citizens, to the Secretary of the Interior, in whose department those names might be arranged and printed for general information.

There is also reason to believe that foreigners frequently become citizens of the United States for the sole purpose of evading duties imposed by the laws of their native countries, to which, on becoming naturalized here, they at once repair, and though never returning to the United States, they still claim the interposition of this government as citizens. Many altercations and great prejudices have heretofore arisen out of this abuse. It is therefore, submitted to your serious consideration. It might be advisable to fix a limit, beyond which no Citizen of the United States residing abroad may claim the interposition of his government.

The right of suffrage has often been assumed and exercised by aliens, under pretences of naturalization, which they have disavowed when drafted into the military service. I submit the expediency of such an amendment of the law as will make the fact of voting an estoppel against any plea of exemption from military service, or other civil obligation, on the ground of alienage.

In common with other western powers, our relations with Japan have been brought into serious jeopardy, through the perverse opposition of the hereditary aristocracy of the empire, to the enlightened and liberal policy of the Tycoon designed to bring the country into the society of nations. It is hoped, although not with entire confidence, that these difficulties may be peacefully overcome. I ask your attention to the claim of the Minister residing there for the damages he sustained in the destruction by fire of the residence of the legation at Yedo.

Satisfactory arrangements have been made with the Emperor of Russia, which, it is believed, will result in effecting a continuous line of telegraph through that empire from our Pacific coast.

I recommend to your favorable consideration the subject of an international telegraph across the Atlantic ocean; and also of a telegraph between this capital and the national forts along the Atlantic seaboard and the Gulf of Mexico. Such communications, established with any reasonable outlay, would be economical as well as effective aids to the diplomatic, military, and naval service.

The consular system of the United States, under the enactments of the last Congress, begins to be self-sustaining; and there is reason to hope that it may become entirely so, with the increase of trade which will ensue whenever peace is restored. Our ministers abroad have been faithful in defending American rights. In protecting commercial interests, our Consuls have necessarily had to encounter increased labors and responsibilities, growing out of the war. These they have, for the most part, met and discharged with zeal and efficiency. This acknowledgment justly includes those Consuls who, residing in Morocco, Egypt, Turkey, Japan, China, and other oriental countries, are charged with complex functions and extraordinary powers.

The condition of the several organized Territories is generally satisfactory, although Indian disturbances in New Mexico have not been entirely suppressed. The mineral resources of Colorado, Nevada, Idaho, New Mexico, and Arizona are proving far richer than has been heretofore understood. I lay before you a communication on this subject from the governor of New Mexico. I again submit to your consideration the expediency of establishing a system for the encouragement of immigration. Although this source of national wealth and strength is again flowing with greater freedom than for several years before the insurrection occurred, there is still a great deficiency of laborers in every field of industry, especially in agriculture and in our mines, as well of iron and coal as of the precious metals. While the demand for labor is thus increased here, tens of thousands of persons, destitute of remunerative occupation, are thronging our foreign consulates, and offering to emigrate to the United States if essential, but very cheap, assistance can be afforded them. It is easy to see that, under the sharp discipline of civil war, the nation is beginning a new life. This noble effort demands the aid, and ought to receive the attention and support of the government.

Injuries, unforseen by the government and unintended, may, in some cases, have been inflicted on the subjects or citizens of foreign countries, both at sea and on land, by persons in the service of the United States. As this government expects redress from other powers when similar injuries are inflicted by persons in their service upon citizens of the United States, we must be prepared to do justice to foreigners. If the existing judicial tribunals are inadequate to this purpose, a special court may be authorized, with power to hear and decide such claims of the character referred to as may have arisen under treaties and the public law. Conventions for adjusting the claims by joint commission have been proposed to some governments, but no definitive answer to the proposition has yet been received from any.

In the course of the session I shall probably have occasion to request you to provide indemnification to claimants where decrees of restitution have been rendered, and damages awarded by admiralty courts; and in other cases where this government may be acknowledged to be liable in principle, and where the amount of that liability has been ascertained by an informal arbitration.

The proper officers of the treasury have deemed themselves required, by the law of the United States upon the subject, to demand a tax upon the incomes of foreign consuls in this country. While such a demand may not, in strictness, be in derogation of public law, or perhaps of any existing treaty between the United States and a foreign country, the expediency of so far modifying the act as to exempt from tax the income of such consuls as are not citizens of the United States, derived from the emoluments of their office, or from property not situated in the United States, is submitted to your serious consideration. I make this suggestion upon the ground that a comity which ought to be reciprocated exempts our Consuls, in all other countries, from taxation to the extent thus indicated. The United States, I think, ought not to be exceptionally illiberal to international trade and commerce.

The operations of the treasury during the last year have been successfully conducted. The enactment by Congress of a national banking law has proved a valuable support of the public credit; and the general legislation in relation to loans has fully answered the expectations of its favorers. Some amendments may be required to perfect existing laws; but no change in their principles or general scope is believed to be needed.

Since these measures have been in operation, all demands on the treasury, including the pay of the army and navy, have been promptly met and fully satisfied. No considerable body of troops, it is believed, were ever more amply provided, and more liberally and punctually paid; and it may be added that by no people were the burdens incident to a great war ever more cheerfully borne.

The receipts during the year from all sources, including loans and the balance in the treasury at its commencement, were $901,125,674.86, and the aggregate disbursements $895,796,630.65, leaving a balance on the 1st. July, 1863, of $5,329,044.21. Of the receipts there were derived from customs, $69,059,642.40; from internal revenue, $37,640,787.95; from direct tax, $1,485,103.61; from lands, $167,617.17; from miscellaneous sources, $3,046,615.35; and from loans, $776,682,361.57; making the aggregate, $901,125,674.86. Of the disbursements there were for the civil service, $23,253,922.08; for pensions and Indians, $4,216,520.79; for interest on public debt, $24,729,846.51; for the War Department, $599,298,600.83; for the Navy Department, $63,211,105.27; for payment of funded and temporary debt, $181,086,635.07; making the aggregate, $895,796,630.65, and leaving the balance of $5,329,044.21. But the payment of funded and temporary debt, having been made from moneys borrowed during the year, must be regarded as merely nominal payments, and the moneys borrowed to make them as merely nominal receipts;

and their amount, $181,086,635.07, should therefore be deducted both from receipts and disbursements. This being done, there remains as actual receipts $720,039,039.79; and the actual disbursements, $714,709,995.58, leaving the balance as already stated.

The actual receipts and disbursements for the first quarter, and the estimated receipts and disbursements for the remaining three quarters, of the current fiscal year, 1864, will be shown in detail by the report of the Secretary of the Treasury, to which I invite your attention. It is sufficient to say here that it is not believed that actual results will exhibit a state of the finances less favorable to the country than the estimates of that officer heretofore submitted; while it is confidently expected that at the close of the year both disbursements and debt will be found very considerably less than has been anticipated.

The report of the Secretary of War is a document of great interest. It consists of—

1. The military operations of the year, detailed in the report of the general-in-chief.

2. The organization of colored persons into the war service.

3. The exchange of prisoners, fully set forth in the letter of General Hitchcock.

4. The operations under the act for enrolling and calling out the national forces, detailed in the report of the provost marshal general.

5. The organization of the invalid corps; and

6. The operation of the several departments of the quartermaster general, commissary general, paymaster general, chief of engineers, chief of ordnance, and surgeon general.

It has appeared impossible to make a valuable summary of this report except such as would be too extended for this place, and hence I content myself by asking your careful attention to the report itself.

The duties devolving on the naval branch of the service during the year, and throughout the whole of this unhappy contest, have been discharged with fidelity and eminent success. The extensive blockade has been constantly increasing in efficiency, as the navy has expanded; yet on so long a line it has so far been impossible to entirely suppress illicit trade.

From returns received at the Navy Department, it appears that more than one thousand vessels have been captured since the blockade was instituted, and that the value of prizes already sent in for adjudication amounts to over thirteen millions of dollars.

The naval force of the United States consists at this time of five hundred and eighty-eight vessels, completed and in the course of completion, and of these seventy-five are iron-clad or armored steamers. The events of the war give an increased interest and importance to the navy which will probably extend beyond the war itself.

The armored vessels in our navy completed and in service, or which are under contract and approaching completion, are believed to exceed in number those of any other power. But while these may be relied upon for harbor defence and coast service, others of greater strength and capacity will be necessary for cruising purposes, and to maintain our rightful position on the ocean.

The change that has taken place in naval vessels and naval warfare, since the introduction of steam as a motive-power for ships-of-war, demands either a corresponding change in some of our existing navy yards, or the establishment of new ones, for the construction and necessary repair of modern naval vessels. No inconsiderable embarrassment, delay, and public injury have been experienced from the want of such governmental establishments. The necessity of such a navy yard, so furnished, at some suitable place upon the Atlantic seaboard, has on repeated occasions been brought to the attention of Congress by the Navy Department, and is again presented in the report of the Secretary which accompanies this communication. I think it my duty to invite your special attention to this subject, and also to that of establishing a yard and depot for naval purposes upon one of the western rivers. A naval force has been created on those interior waters, and under many disadvantages, within little more than two years, exceeding in numbers the whole naval force of the country at the commencement of the present administration. Satisfactory and important as have been the performances of the heroic men of the navy at this interesting period, they are scarcely more wonderful than the success of our mechanics and artisans in the production of war vessels which has created a new form of naval power.

Our country has advantages superior to any other nation in our resources of iron and timber, with inexhaustible quantities of fuel in the immediate vicinity of both, and all available and in close proximity to navigable waters. Without the advantage of public works the resources of the nation have been developed and its power displayed in the construction of a navy of such magnitude which has, at the very period of its creation, rendered signal service to the Union.

The increase of the number of seamen in the public service, from seven thousand five hundred men, in the spring of 1861, to about thirty four thousand at the present time has been accomplished without special legislation, or extraordinary bounties to promote that increase. It has been found, however, that the operation of the draft, with the high bounties paid for army recruits, is beginning to affect injuriously the naval service, and will, if not corrected, be likely to impair its efficiency, by detaching seamen from their proper vocation and inducing them to enter the Army. I therefore respectfully suggest that Congress might aid both the army and naval services by a definite provision on this subject, which would at the same time be equitable to the communities more especially interested.

I commend to your consideration the suggestions of the Secretary of the Navy in regard to the policy of fostering and training seamen, and also the education of officers and engineers for the naval service. The Naval Academy is rendering signal service in preparing midshipmen for the highly responsible duties which in after life they will be required to perform. In order that the country should not be deprived of the proper quota of educated officers, for which legal provision has been made at the naval school, the vacancies caused by the neglect or omission to make nominations from the States in insurrection have been filled by the Secretary of the Navy.

The school is now more full and complete than at any former period, and in every respect entitled to the favorable consideration of Congress.

During the past fiscal year the financial condition of the Post office Department has been one of increasing prosperity, and I am gratified in being able to state that the actual postal revenue has nearly equalled the entire expenditures; the latter amounting to $11,314,206.84, and the former to $11,163,789 59, leaving a deficiency of but $150,417 25. In 1860, the year immediately preceding the rebellion the deficiency amounted to $5,656,705 49, the postal receipts of that year being $2,645,722 19 less than those of 1863. The decrease since 1860 in the annual amount of transportation has been only about 25 per cent, but the annual expenditure on account of the same has been reduced 35 per cent. It is manifest, therefore, that the Post Office Department may become self-sustaining in a few years, even with the restoration of the whole service.

The international conference of postal delegates from the principal countries of Europe and America, which was called at the suggestion of the Postmaster General, met at Paris on the 11th of May last, and concluded its deliberations on the 8th of June. The principles established by the conference as best adapted to facilitate postal intercourse between nations, and as the basis of future postal conventions, inaugurate a general system of uniform international charges, at reduced rates of postage, and cannot fail to produce beneficial results.

I refer you to the report of the Secretary of the Interior, which is herewith laid before you, for useful and varied information in relation to the public lands, Indian affairs, patents, pensions, and other matters of public concern pertaining to his department.

The quantity of land disposed of during the last and the first quarter of the present fiscal years was three million eight hundred and forty one thousand five hundred and forty nine acres, of which one hundred and sixty one thousand nine hundred and eleven acres were sold for cash, one million four hundred and fifty six thousand five hundred and fourteen acres were taken up under the homestead law, and the residue disposed of under laws granting lands for military bounties, for railroad and other purposes. It also appears that the sale of the public lands is largely on the increase.

It has long been a cherished opinion of some of our wisest statesmen that the people of the United States had a higher and more enduring interest in the early settlement and substantial cultivation of the public lands than in the amount of direct revenue to be derived from the sale of them. This opinion has had a controlling influence in shaping legislation upon the subject of our national domain. I may cite, as evidence of this, the liberal measures adopted in reference to actual settlers; the grant to the States of the overflowed lands within their limits in order to their being reclaimed and rendered fit for cultivation; the grants to railway companies of alternate sections of land upon the contemplated lines of their roads which, when completed, will so largely multiply the facilities for reaching our distant possessions. This policy has received its most signal and beneficent illustration in the recent enactment granting homesteads to actual settlers.

Since the first day of January last the before-mentioned quantity of one million four hundred and fifty-six thousand five hundred and fourteen acres of land have been taken up under its provisions. This fact and the amount of sales furnish gratifying evidence of increasing settlement upon the public lands, notwithstanding the great struggle in which the energies of the nation have been engaged, and which has required so large a withdrawal of our citizens from their accustomed pursuits. I cordially concur in the recommendation of the Secretary of the Interior suggesting a modification of the act in favor of those engaged in the military and naval service of the United States. I doubt not that Congress will cheerfully adopt such measures as will, without essentially changing the general features of the system, secure to the greatest practicable extent, its benefits to those who have left their homes in the defence of the country in this arduous crisis.

I invite your attention to the views of the Secretary as to the propriety of raising by appropriate legislation a revenue from the mineral lands of the United States.

The measures provided at your last session for the removal of certain Indian tribes have been carried into effect. Sundry treaties have been negotiated which will, in due time, be submitted for the constitutional action of the Senate. They contain stipulations for extinguishing the possessory rights of the Indians to large and valuable tracts of land. It is hoped that the effect of these treaties will result in the establishment of permanent friendly relations with such of these tribes as have been brought into frequent and bloody collision with our outlying settlements and emigrants.

Sound policy and our imperative duty to these wards of the government demand our anxious and constant attention to their material well-being, to their progress in the arts of civilization, and, above all, to that moral training which, under the blessing of Divine Providence, will confer upon them the elevated and sanctifying influences, the hopes and consolation of the Christian faith.

I suggested in my last annual message the propriety of remodelling our Indian system. Subsequent events have satisfied me of its necessity. The details set forth in the report of the Secretary evince the urgent need for immediate legislative action.

I commend the benevolent institutions, established or patronized by the government in this District, to your generous and fostering care.

The attention of Congress, during the last session, was engaged to some extent with a proposition for enlarging the water communication between the Mississippi river and the northeastern seaboard, which proposition, however, failed for the time. Since then, upon a call of the greatest respectability a convention has been held at Chicago upon the same subject, a summary of whose views is contained in a memorial addressed to the President and Congress, and which I now have the honor to lay before you. That this interest is one which, ere long, will force its own way, I do not entertain a doubt, while it is submitted entirely to your wisdom as to what can be done now. Augmented interest is given to this subject by the actual commencement of work upon the Pacific railroad, under auspices so favorable to rapid progress and completion. The enlarged navigation becomes a palpable need to the great road.

I transmit the second annual report of the Commissioner of the Department of Agriculture, asking your attention to the developments in that vital interest of the nation.

When Congress assembled a year ago the war had already lasted nearly twenty months, and there had been many conflicts on both land and sea, with varying results.

The rebellion had been pressed back into reduced limits;

yet the tone of public feeling and opinion, at home and abroad, was not satisfactory. With other signs, the popular elections, then just past, indicated uneasiness among ourselves, while amid much that was cold and menacing the kindest words coming from Europe were uttered in accents of pity, that we were too blind to surrender a hopeless cause. Our commerce was suffering greatly by a few armed vessels built upon and furnished from foreign shores, and we were threatened with such additions from the same quarter as would sweep our trade from the sea and raise our blockade. We had failed to elicit from European governments anything hopeful upon this subject. The preliminary emancipation proclamation, issued in September, was running its assigned period to the beginning of the new year. A month later the final proclamation came, including the announcement that colored men of suitable condition would be received into the war service. The policy of emancipation, and of employing black soldiers, gave to the future a new aspect, about which hope, and fear, and doubt contended in uncertain conflict. According to our political system, as a matter of civil administration, the general government had no lawful power to effect emancipation in any State, and for a long time it had been hoped that the rebellion could be suppressed without resorting to it as a military measure. It was all the while deemed possible that the necessity for it might come, and that if it should, the crisis of the contest would then be presented. It came, and as was anticipated, it was followed by dark and doubtful days. Eleven months having now passed, we are permitted to take another review. The rebel borders are pressed still further back, and by the complete opening of the Mississippi the country dominated by the rebellion is divided into distinct parts, with no practical communication between them. Tennessee and Arkansas have been substantially cleared of insurgent control, and influential citizens in each, owners of slaves and advocates of slavery at the beginning of the rebellion, now declare openly for emancipation in their respective States. Of those States not included in the emancipation proclamation, Maryland, and Missouri, neither of which three years ago would tolerate any restraint upon the extension of slavery into new territories, only dispute now as to the best mode of removing it within their own limits.

Of those who were slaves at the beginning of the rebellion, full one hundred thousand are now in the United States military service, about one-half of which number actually bear arms in the ranks; thus giving the double advantage of taking so much labor from the insurgent cause, and supplying the places which otherwise must be filled with so many white men. So far as tested, it is difficult to say they are not as good soldiers as any. No servile insurrection, or tendency to violence or cruelty, has marked the measures of emancipation and arming the blacks. These measures have been much discussed in foreign countries, and contemporary with such discussion the tone of public sentiment there is much improved. At home the same measures have been fully discussed, supported, criticised, and denounced, and the annual elections following are highly encouraging to those whose official duty it is to bear the country through this great trial. Thus we have the new reckoning. The crisis which threatened to divide the friends of the Union is past.

Looking now to the present and future, and with reference to a resumption of the national authority within the States wherein that authority has been suspended, I have thought fit to issue a proclamation, a copy of which is herewith transmitted. On examination of this proclamation it will appear, as is believed, that nothing is attempted beyond what is amply justified by the Constitution. True, the form of an oath is given, but no man is coerced to take it. The man is only promised a pardon in case he voluntarily takes the oath. The Constitution authorizes the Executive to grant or withhold the pardon at his own absolute discretion; and this includes the power to grant on terms, as is fully established by judicial and other authorities.

It is also proffered that if, in any of the States named, a State government shall be, in the mode prescribed, set up, such government shall be recognized and guarantied by the United States, and that under it the State shall, on the constitutional conditions, be protected against invasion and domestic violence. The constitutional obligation of the United States to guaranty to every State in the Union a republican form of government, and to protect the State, in the cases stated, is explicit and full. But why tender the benefits of this provision only to a State government set up in this particular way? This section of the Constitution contemplates a case wherein the element within a State, favorable to republican government, in the Union, may be too feeble for an opposite and hostile element external to, or even within the State; and such are precisely the cases with which we are now dealing.

An attempt to guaranty and protect a revived State government, constructed in whole, or in preponderating part, from the very element against whose hostility and violence it is to be protected, is simply absurd. There must be a test by which to separate the opposing elements, so as to build only from the sound; and that test is a sufficiently liberal one, which accepts as sound whoever will make a sworn recantation of his former unsoundness.

But if it be proper to require, as a test of admission to the political body, an oath of allegiance to the Constitution of the United States, and to the Union under it, why also to the laws and proclamations in regard to slavery? Those laws and proclamations were enacted and put forth for the purpose of aiding in the suppression of the rebellion. To give them their fullest effect, there had to be a pledge for their maintenance. In my judgment they have aided, and will further aid, the cause for which they were intended. To now abandon them would be not only to relinquish a lever of power, but would also be a cruel and an astounding breach of faith. I may add at this point, that while I remain in my present position I shall not attempt to retract or modify the emancipation proclamation; nor shall I return to slavery any person who is free by the terms of that proclamation, or by any of the acts of Congress. For these and other reasons it is thought best that support of these measures shall be included in the oath; and it is believed the Executive may lawfully claim it in return for pardon and restoration of forfeited rights, which he has clear constitutional power to withhold altogether, or grant upon the terms which he shall deem wisest for the public interest. It should be observed, also, that this part of the oath is subject to the modifying and abrogating power of legislation and supreme judicial decision.

The proposed acquiescence of the national Executive in any reasonable temporary State arrangement for the freed people is made with the view of possibly modifying the confusion and destitution which must, at best, attend all classes by a total revolution of labor throughout whole States. It is hoped that the already deeply afflicted people in those States may be somewhat more ready to give up the cause of their affliction, if, to this extent, this vital matter be left to themselves; while no power of the national Executive to prevent an abuse is abridged by the proposition.

The suggestion in the proclamation as to maintaining the political framework of the States on what is called reconstruction, is made in the hope that it may do good without danger of harm. It will save labor and avoid great confusion.

But why any proclamation now upon this subject? This question is beset with the conflicting views that the step might be delayed too long or be taken too soon. In some States the elements for resumption seem ready for action, but remain inactive, apparently for want of a rallying point—a plan of action. Why shall A adopt the plan of B, rather than B that of A? And if A and B should agree, how can they know but that the general government here will reject their plan? By the proclamation a plan is presented which may be accepted by them as a rallying point, and which they are assured in advance will not be rejected here. This may bring them to act sooner than they otherwise would.

The objections to a premature presentation of a plan by the national Executive consists in the danger of committals on points which could be more safely left to further developments. Care has been taken to so shape the document as to avoid embarrassments from this source. Saying that, on certain terms, certain classes will be pardoned, with rights restored, it is not said that other classes, or other terms, will never be included. Saying that reconstruction will be accepted if presented in a specified way, it is not said it will never be accepted in any other way.

The movements, by State action, for emancipation in several of the States, not included in the emancipation proclamation, are matters of profound gratulation. And while I do not repeat in detail what I have heretofore so earnestly urged upon this subject, my general views and feelings remain unchanged; and I trust that Congress will omit no fair opportunity of aiding these important steps to a great consummation.

In the midst of other cares, however important, we must not lose sight of the fact that the war power is still our main reliance. To that power alone can we look, yet for a time, to give confidence to the people in the contested regions, that the insurgent power will not again overrun them. Until that confidence shall be established, little can be done anywhere for what is called reconstruction. Hence our chiefest care must still be directed to the army and navy, who have thus far borne their harder part so nobly and well. And it may be esteemed fortunate that in giving the greatest efficiency to these indispensable arms, we do also honorably recognize the gallant men, from commander to sentinel, who compose them, and to whom, more than to others, the world must stand indebted for the home of freedom disenthralled, regenerated, enlarged, and perpetuated.

Washington, December 8, 1863.

Proclamation of Amnesty and Reconstruction

BY THE PRESIDENT OF THE UNITED STATES OF AMERICA:
A PROCLAMATION.

Whereas, in and by the Constitution of the United States, it is provided that the President "shall have power to grant reprieves and pardons for offences against the United States, except in cases of impeachment;" and

Whereas a rebellion now exists whereby the loyal State governments of several States have for a long time been subverted, and many persons have committed and are now guilty of treason against the United States; and

Whereas, with reference to said rebellion and treason, laws have been enacted by Congress declaring forfeitures and confiscation of property and liberation of slaves, all upon terms and conditions therein stated, and also declaring that the President was thereby authorized at any time thereafter, by proclamation, to extend to persons who may have participated in the existing rebellion, in any State or part thereof, pardon and amnesty, with such exceptions and at such times and on such conditions as he may deem expedient for the public welfare; and

Whereas the congressional declaration for limited and conditional pardon accords with well-established judicial exposition of the pardoning power; and

Whereas, with reference to said rebellion, the President of the United States has issued several proclamations, with provisions in regard to the liberation of slaves; and

Whereas it is now desired by some persons heretofore engaged in said rebellion to resume their allegiance to the United States, and to reinaugurate loyal State governments within and for their respective States; therefore,

I, Abraham Lincoln, President of the United States, do proclaim, declare, and make known to all persons who have, directly or by implication, participated in the existing rebellion, except as hereinafter excepted, that a full pardon is hereby granted to them and each of them, with restoration of all rights of property, except as to slaves, and in property cases where rights of third parties shall have intervened, and upon the condition that every such person shall take and subscribe an oath, and thenceforward keep and maintain said oath inviolate; and which oath shall be registered for permanent preservation, and shall be of the tenor and effect following, to wit:

"I, ——, do solemnly swear, in presence of Almighty God, that I will henceforth faithfully support, protect and defend the Constitution of the United States, and the union of the States thereunder; and that I will, in like manner, abide by and faithfully support all acts of Congress passed during the existing rebellion with reference to slaves, so long and so far as not repealed, modified or held void by Congress, or by decision of the Supreme Court; and that I will, in like manner, abide by and faithfully support all proclamations of the President made during the existing rebellion having reference to slaves, so long and so far as not modified or declared void by decision of the Supreme Court. So help me God."

The persons excepted from the benefits of the foregoing provisions are all who are, or shall have been, civil or diplomatic officers or agents of the so-called confederate government; all who have left judicial stations under the United States to aid the rebellion; all who are, or shall have been, military or naval officers of said so-called confederate government above the rank of colonel in the army, or of lieutenant in the navy; all who left seats in the United States Congress to aid the rebellion; all who resigned commissions in the army or navy of the United States, and afterwards aided the rebellion; and all who have engaged in any way in treating colored persons or white persons, in charge of such, otherwise than lawfully as prisoners of war, and which persons may have been found in the United States service, as soldiers, seamen, or in any other capacity.

And I do further proclaim, declare, and make known, that whenever, in any of the States of Arkansas, Texas, Louisiana, Mississippi, Tennessee, Alabama, Georgia, Florida, South Carolina, and North Carolina, a number of persons, not less than one-tenth in number of the votes cast in such State at the Presidential election of the year of our Lord one thousand eight hundred and sixty, each having taken the oath aforesaid and not having since violated it, and being a qualified voter by the election law of the State existing immediately before the so-called act of secession, and excluding all others, shall re-establish a State government which shall be republican, and in no wise contravening said oath, such shall be recognized as the true government of the State, and the State shall receive thereunder the benefits of the constitutional provision which declares that "The United States shall guaranty to every State in this union a republican form of government, and shall protect each of them against invasion; and, on application of the legislature, or the executive, (when the legislature cannot be convened,) against domestic violence."

And I do further proclaim, declare, and make known that any provision which may be adopted by such State government in relation to the freed people of such State, which shall recognize and declare their permanent freedom, provide for their education, and which may yet be consistent, as a temporary arrangement, with their present condition as a laboring, landless, and homeless class, will not be objected to by the national Executive. And it is suggested as not improper, that, in constructing a loyal State government in any State, the name of the State, the boundary, the subdivisions, the constitution, and the general code of laws, as before the rebellion, be maintained, subject only to the modifications made necessary by the conditions hereinbefore stated, and such others, if any, not contravening said conditions, and which may be deemed expedient by those framing the new State government.

To avoid misunderstanding, it may be proper to say that this proclamation, so far as it relates to State governments, has no reference to States wherein loyal State governments have all the while been maintained. And for the same reason, it may be proper to further say that whether members sent to Congress from any State shall be admitted to seats, constitutionally rests exclusively with the respective Houses, and not to any extent with the Executive. And still further, that this proclamation is intended to present the people of the States wherein the national authority has been suspended, and loyal State governments have been subverted, a mode in and by which the national authority and loyal State governments may be re-established within said States, or in any of them; and, while the mode presented is the best the Executive can suggest, with his present impressions, it must not be understood that no other possible mode would be acceptable.

Given under my hand at the city, of Washington, the 8th. day of December, A.D. one thousand eight hundred and sixty-three, and of the independence of the United States of America the eighty-eighth.

By the President: ABRAHAM LINCOLN
WILLIAM H. SEWARD, Secretary of State.

Amnesty for Emily T. Helm

Executive Mansion, Washington, December 14. 1863.

Mrs. Emily T. Helm, not being excepted from the benefits of the proclamation by the President of the United States issued on the 8th. day of December. 1863, and having on this day taken and subscribed the oath according to said proclamation, she is fully relieved of all penalties and forfeitures, and remitted to all her rights, all according to said proclamation, and not otherwise; and, in regard to said restored rights of person and property, she is to be protected and afforded facilities as a loyal person.

P.S. Mrs. Helm claims to own some cotten at Jackson, Mississippi, and also some in Georgia; and I shall be glad, upon either place being brought within our lines, for her to be afforded the proper facilities to show her ownership, and take her property.

Oath Written for Emily T. Helm

District of Columbia ⎫
Washington County ⎭ SS

I, Emily T. Helm, do solemnly swear in presence of Almighty God that I will henceforth faithfully support, protect and defend the Constitution of the United States, and the union of the States thereunder; and that I will, in like manner, abide by, and faithfully support all acts of Congress passed during the existing rebellion with reference to slaves, so long and so far as not repealed, modified, or held void by Congress, or by decision of the Supreme Court; and that I will, in like manner, abide by, and faithfully support all proclamations of the President, made during the existing rebellion, having reference to slaves so long and so far as not modified, or declared void by the Supreme Court. So help me God.

December 14, 1863

Pass for Emily T. Helm

Executive Mansion,
Whom it may concern   Washington, December 14. 1863.

It is my wish that Mrs. Emily T. Helm, (widow of the late Gen. B. H. Helm, who fell in the Confederate service) now returning to Kentucky, may have protection of person and property, except as to slaves, of which I say nothing.

To Thomas Cottman

Dr. Thomas Cottman   Executive Mansion,
My Dear Sir   Washington, December 15, 1863.

You were so kind as to say this morning that you desire to return to Louisiana, and to be guided by my wishes, to some extent, in the part you may take in bringing that state to resume her rightful relation to the general government.

My wishes are in a general way expressed as well as I can express them, in the Proclamation issued on the 8th of the present month, and in that part of the annual message which relates to that proclamation. It there appears that I deem the sustaining of the emancipation proclamation, where it applies, as indispensable; and I add here that I would esteem it fortunate, if the people of Louisiana should themselves place the remainder of the state upon the same footing, and then, if in their discretion it should appear best, make some temporary provision for the whole of the freed people, substantially as suggested in the last proclamation. I have not put forth the plan in that proclamation, as a Procrustean bed, to which exact conformity is to be indispensable; and in Louisiana particularly, I wish that labor already done, which varies from that plan in no important particular, may not be thrown away.

The strongest wish I have, not already publicly expressed, is that in Louisiana and elsewhere, all sincere Union men would stoutly eschew cliqueism, and, each yielding something in minor matters, all work together. Nothing is likely to be so baleful in the great work before us, as stepping aside of the main object to consider who will get the offices if a small matter shall go thus, and who else will get them, if it shall go otherwise. It is a time now for real patriots to rise above all this. As to the particulars of what I may think best to be done in any state, I have publicly stated certain points, which I have thought indispensable to the reestablishment and maintenance of the national authority; and I go no further than this because I wish to avoid both the substance and the appearance of dictation.

To Stephen A. Hurlbut

"*Cypher*"

Major General Hurlbut   Executive Mansion
Memphis, Tenn.   Washington, D.C. Dec. 17. 1863.

I understand you have, under sentence of death, a tall old man, by the name of Henry F. Luckett. I personally knew him, and did not think him a bad man. Please do not let him be executed, unless upon further order from me, and, in the mean time, send me a transcript of the record.

To Edwin M. Stanton

Hon. Sec. of War: Executive Mansion,
My dear Sir   Washington, Dec. 18. 1863.

I believe Gen. Schofield must be relieved from command of the Department of Missouri, otherwise a question of veracity, in relation to his declarations as to his interfering, or not, with the Missouri Legislature, will be made with him, which will create an additional amount of trouble, not to be overcome by even a correct decision of the question. The question itself must be avoided. Now for the mode. Senator Henderson, his friend, thinks he can be induced to ask to be relieved, if he shall understand he will be generously treated; and, on this latter point, Gratz Brown will help his nomination, as a Major General, through the Senate. In no other way can he be confirmed; and upon his rejection alone, it would be difficult for me to sustain him as Commander of the Department. Besides, his being relieved from command of the Department, and at the same time confirmed as a Major General, will be the means of Henderson and Brown leading off together as friends, and will go far to heal the Missouri difficulty.

Another point. I find it is scarcely less than indispensable for me to do something for Gen. Rosecrans; and I find Henderson and Brown will agree to him for the commander of their Department.

Again, I have received such evidence and explanations, in regard to the supposed cotten transactions of Gen. Curtis, as fully restores in my mind the fair presumption of his innocence; and, as he is my friend, and, what is more, as I think, the countries friend, I would be glad to relieve him from the impression that I think him dishonest, by giving him a command. Most of the Iowa and Kansas delegations, a large part of that of Missouri, and the delegates from Nebraska, and Colorado, ask this in behalf of Gen. C. and suggest Kansas and other contiguous territory West of Missouri, as a Department for him.

In a purely military point of view it may be that none of these things is indispensable, or perhaps, advantageous; but in another aspect, scarcely less important, they would give great relief, while, at the worst, I think they could not injure the military service much. I therefore shall be greatly obliged if yourself and Gen. Halleck can give me your hearty cooperation, in making the arrangement. Perhaps the first thing would be to send Gen. Schofield's nomination to me. Let me hear from you before you take any actual step in the matter. Yours very truly

To Oliver D. Filley

O. D. Filley   Executive Mansion,
St. Louis, Mo.   Washington, Dec. 22. 1863.

I have just looked over a petition signed by some three dozen citizens of St. Louis, and three accompanying letters, one by yourself, one by a Mr. Nathan Ranney, and one by a Mr. John D. Coalter, the whole relating to the Rev. Dr. McPheeters. The petition prays, in the name of justice and mercy that I will restore Dr. McPheeters to all his ecclesiastical rights.

This gives no intimation as to what ecclesiastical rights are withheld. Your letter states that Provost Marshal Dick, about a year ago, ordered the arrest of Dr. McPheters, Pastor of the Vine Street Church, prohibited him from officiating, and placed the management of the affairs of the church out of the control of it's chosen Trustees; and near the close you state that a certain course "would insure his release." Mr. Ranney's letter says "Dr. Saml. S. McPheeters is enjoying all the rights of a civilian, but can not preach the gospel!!!" Mr. Coalter, in his letter, asks "Is it not a strange illustration of the condition of things that the question of who shall be allowed to preach in a church in St. Louis, shall be decided by the *President* of *the United States?*"

Now, all this sounds very strangely; and withal, a little as if you gentlemen making the application, do not understand the case alike, one affirming that the Dr. is enjoying all the rights of a civilian, and another pointing out to me what will secure his *release*! On the 2nd. day of January last I wrote Gen. Curtis in relation to Mr. Dick's order upon Dr. McPheeters, and, as I suppose the Dr. is enjoying all the rights of a civilian, I only quote that part of my letter which relates to the church. It is as follows: "But I must add that the U.S. government must not, as by this order, undertake to run the churches. When an individual, in a church or out of it, becomes dangerous to the public interest, he must be checked; but the churches, as such must take care of themselves. It will not do for the U.S. to appoint Trustees, Supervisors, or other agents for the churches." This letter going to Gen. Curtis, then in command there I supposed of course it was obeyed, especially as I heard no further complaint from Dr. M. or his friends for nearly an entire year.

I have never interfered, nor thought of interfering as to who shall or shall not preach in any church; nor have I knowingly, or believingly, tolerated any one else to so interfere by my authority. If any one is so interfering, by color of my authority, I would like to have it specifically made known to me.

If, after all, what is now sought, is to have me put Dr. M. back, over the heads of a majority of his own congregation, that too, will be declined. I will not have control of any church on any side. Yours Respectfully

Endorsement on Petition Concerning Samuel B. McPheeters

The assumptions of this paper, so far as I know, or believe are entirely false. I have never deprived Dr. McPheters of any ecclesiastical right, or authorized, or excused its' being done by any one deriving authority from me. On the contrary, in regard to this very case, I directed, a long time ago, that Dr. McPheters was to be arrested, or remain at large, upon the same rule as any one else; and that, in no event, was any one to interfere by my authority, as to who should, or should not preach in any church. This was done, I think, in a letter, in the nature of an order, to Mr. Dick. The assumption that I am keeping Dr. M. from preaching in his church is monstrous. If any one is doing this, by pretense of my authority, I will thank any one who can, to make out and present me, a specific case against him. If, after all, the Dr. is kept out by the majority of his own parishioners, and my official power is sought to force him in over their heads, I decline that also.

Dec. 22. 1863.

To Nathaniel P. Banks

Executive Mansion,
Major General Banks   Washington, December 24. 1863.
Yours of the 6th. Inst. has been received, and fully con-

sidered. I deeply regret to have said or done anything which could give you pain, or uneasiness. I have all the while intended you to be *master*, as well in regard to re-organizing a State government for Louisiana, as in regard to the military matters of the Department; and hence my letters on reconstruction have nearly if not quite all been addressed to you. My error has been that it did not occur to me that Gov. Shepley or any one else would set up a claim to act independently of you; and hence I said nothing expressly upon the point. Language has not been guarded at a point where no danger was thought of. I now tell you that in every dispute, with whomsoever, you are master. Gov. Shepley was appointed to *assist* the Commander of the Department, and not to thwart him, or act independently of him. Instructions have been given directly to him, merely to spare you detail labor, and not to supersede your authority. This, in it's liability to be misconstrued, it now seems was an error in us. But it is past. I now distinctly tell you that you are master of all, and that I wish you to take the case as you find it, and give us a free-state re-organization of Louisiana, in the shortest possible time. What I say here is to have a reasonable construction. I do not mean that you are to withdraw from Texas, or abandon any other military measure which you may deem important. Nor do I mean that you are to throw away available work already done for re-construction; or that war is to be made upon Gov. Shepley, or upon any one else, unless it be found that they will not co-operate with you, in which case, and in all cases, you are master while you remain in command of the Department.

My thanks for your successful and valuable operations in Texas. Yours as ever

To Bayard Taylor

Hon. Bayard Taylor: Executive Mansion,
My dear Sir: Washington, Dec. 25. 1863.
    I think a good lecture or two on "Serfs, Serfdom, and Emancipation in Russia" would be both interesting and valuable. Could not you get up such a thing? Yours truly

Endorsement Concerning Henry Andrews

The case of Andrews is really a very bad one, as appears by the record already before me. Yet before receiving this I had ordered his punishment commuted to imprisonment for during the war at hard labor, and had so telegraphed. I did this, not on any merit in the case, but because I am trying to evade the butchering business lately.

January 7, 1864

To Crafts J. Wright and Charles K. Hawkes

Executive Mansion,
Gentlemen: Washington, Jany. 7, 1864.
    You have presented me a plan for getting cotten and other products, from within the rebel lines, from which you think the United States will derive some advantage.
    Please carefully and considerately, answer me the following questions.
    1. If now, without any new order or rule, a rebel should come into our lines with cotten, and offer to take the oath of Dec. 8th. what do you understand would be done with him and his cotten?
    2. How will the physical difficulty, and danger, of getting cotten from within the rebel lines be lessened by your plan? or how will the owners motive to surmount that difficulty and danger, be heightened by it?
    3. If your plan be adopted, *where* do you propose putting the cotten &c. into market? how assure the government of your good faith in the business? and how be compensated for your services? Very Respectfully

To Mrs. Esther Stockton

Executive Mansion,
Mrs. Esther Stockton.   Washington Jany. 8, 1864.
    Madam: Learning that you who have passed the eighty-fourth year of life, have given to the soldiers, some three

hundred pairs of stockings, knitted by yourself, I wish to offer you my thanks. Will you also convey my thanks to those young ladies who have done so much in feeding our soldiers while passing through your city? Yours truly,

To Quincy A. Gillmore

Executive Mansion,
Major General Gillmore   Washington, January 13, 1864.

I understand an effort is being made by some worthy gentlemen to reconstruct a loyal state government in Florida. Florida is in your department, and it is not unlikely that you may be there in person. I have given Mr. Hay a commission of Major, and sent him to you with some blank books and other blanks, to aid in the reconstruction. He will explain, as to the manner of using the blanks, and also my general views on the subject. It is desirable for all to cooperate; but if irreconcileable differences of opinion shall arise, you are master. I wish the thing done in the most speedy way possible, so that, when done, it lie within the range of the late proclamation on the subject. The detail labor, of course, will have to be done by others; but I shall be greatly obliged if you will give it such general supervision as you can find consistent with your more strictly military duties   Yours very truly

To William Crosby and Henry P. Nichols

Messrs Crosby & Nichols.   Executive Mansion,
Gentlemen   Washington, January 16, 1864.

The number for this month and year of the North American Review was duly received, and, for which, please accept my thanks. Of course I am not the most impartial judge; yet with due allowance for this, I venture to hope that the artical entitled the "Presidents Policy" will be of value to the country. I fear I am not quite worthy of all which is therein kindly said of me personally.

The sentence of twelve lines commencing at the top of page

252, I could wish to be not exactly as it is. In what is there expressed, the writer has not correctly understood me. I have never had a theory that secession could absolve States or people from their obligations. Precisely the contrary is asserted in the inaugeral address; and it was because of my belief in the continuation of these *obligations*, that I was puzzled, for a time, as to denying the legal *rights* of those citizens who remained individually innocent of treason or rebellion. But I mean no more now than to merely call attention to this point. Yours Respectfully

To Frederick Steele

Executive Mansion Washington, D.C.
Major General Steele   Jan. 20. 1864.
   Sundry citizens of the State of Arkansas petition me that an election may be held in that State, at which to elect a Governor thereof;

that it be assumed at said election, and thenceforward, that the constitution and laws of the State, as before the rebellion, are in full force, except that the constitution is so modified as to declare that "There shall be neither slavery nor involuntary servitude, except in the punishment of crime whereof the party shall have been duly convicted; but the General Assembly may make such provision for the freedpeople as shall recognize and declare their permanent freedom, provide for their education, and which may yet be consistent, as a temporary arrangement, with their present condition as a laboring, landless, and homeless class"; and also except that all now existing laws in relation to slaves are inoperative and void; that said election be held on the twenty-eighth day of March next, at all the usual voting places of the State, or all such as voters may attend for that purpose; that the voters attending at each place, at eight o'clock in the morning of said day, may choose Judges and Clerks of election for that place; that all persons qualified by said constitution and laws, and taking the oath prescribed in the Presidents proclamation of December the 8th. 1863, either before or at the election, and none others, may be voters provided that persons having the qualifications aforesaid, and being in the Volunteer military service of the United States, may vote once wherever this may be at voting places; that each sett of Judges and Clerks may make return directly to you, on or before the eleventh day of April next; that in all other respects said election may be conducted according to said modified constitution, and laws; that, on receipt of said returns, you count said votes, and that, if the number shall reach, or exceed, five thousand four hundred and six, you canvass said votes and ascertain who shall thereby appear to have been elected Governor; and that on the eighteenth day of April next, the person so appearing to have been elected, and appearing before you at Little Rock, to have, by you, administered to him, an oath to support the constitution of the United States and said modified constitution of the State of Arkansas, and actually taking said oath, be by you declared qualified, and be enjoined to immediately enter upon the duties of the office of Governor of said State; and that you thereupon declare the constitution of the State of Arkansas to have been modified and amended as aforesaid, by the action of the people as aforesaid.

You will please order an election immediately, and perform the other parts assigned you, with necessary incidentals, all according to the foregoing. Yours truly

To Alpheus Lewis

Alpheus Lewis, Esq.   Executive Mansion,
My dear Sir   Washington, January 23. 1864.

You have enquired how the government would regard and treat cases wherein the owners of plantations, in Arkansas, for instance, might fully recognize the freedom of those formerly slaves, and by fair contracts of hire with them, re-commence the cultivation of their plantations. I answer I should regard such cases with great favor, and should, as the principle, treat them precisely as I would treat the same number of free white people in the same relation and condition. Whether white or black, reasonable effort should be made to give government protection. In neither case should the giving of aid and comfort to the rebellion, or other practices injurious to the government, be allowed on such plantations; and in either, the government would claim the right to take if necessary those of proper ages and conditions into the military service. Such plan must not be used to break up existing leases or arrangements of abandoned plantations which the government may have made to give employment and sustenance to the idle and destitute people. With the foregoing qualifications and explanations, and in view of it's tendency to advance freedom, and restore peace and prosperity, such hireing and employment of the freed people, would be regarded by me with rather especial favor. Yours truly

P.S. To be more specific I add that all the Military, and others acting by authority of the United States, are to favor and facilitate the introduction and carrying forward, in good faith, the free-labor system as above indicated, by allowing the necessary supplies therefor to be procured and taken to the proper points, and by doing and forbearing whatever will advance it; *provided* that existing military and trade regulations be not transcended thereby. I shall be glad to learn that planters adopting this system shall have employed one so zealous and active as yourself to act as an agent in relation thereto.

This P.S. is in the body of the letter given

To Frederick Steele

Executive Mansion, Washington,
Major General Steele: January 27, 1864.
    I have addressed a letter to you, and put it in the hands of Mr. Gantt and other Arkansas gentlemen, containing a programme for an election in that State. This letter will be handed you by some of these gentlemen. Since writing, it I see that a convention in Arkansas, having the same general object, has taken some action, which I am afraid may clash somewhat with my programme. I therefore can do no better

than to ask you to see Mr. Gantt immediately on his return, and with him, do what you and he may deem necessary to harmonize the two plans into one, and then put it through with all possible vigor. Be sure to retain the free State constitutional provision in some unquestionable form, and you and he can fix the rest. The points I have made in the programme have been well considered. Take hold with an honest heart and a strong hand. Do not let any questionable man control or influence you. Yours truly

To Frederick Steele

                         Executive Mansion, Washington,
Major General Steele   January 30. 1864.
    Since writing mine of the 27th. seeing still further accounts of the action of the convention in Arkansas, induces me to write you yet again. They seem to be doing so well, that possibly the best you can do would be to help them on their own plan—but of this, you must confer with them, and be the judge. Of all things, avoid if possible, a dividing into cliques among the friends of the common object. Be firm and resolute against such as you can perceive would make confusion and division. Yours truly

To Nathaniel P. Banks

                         Executive Mansion, Washington,
Major General Banks   January 31, 1864.
    Yours of the 22nd. Inst. is just received. In the proclamation of Dec. 8. and which contains the oath that you say some loyal people wish to avoid taking, I said:

And still further, that this proclamation is intended to present the people of the States wherein the national authority has been suspended, and loyal State governments have been subverted, a mode in and by which the national authority and loyal State governments may be re-established within said States, or in any of them; and, while the mode presented is the best the Executive can suggest, with his present impressions, it must not be understood that no other possible mode would be acceptable.

And speaking of this in the Message, I said:

Saying that reconstruction will be accepted if presented in a specified way, it is not said it will never be accepted in any other way.

These things were put into these documents on purpose that some conformity to circumstances should be admissable; and when I have, more than once, said to you in my letters that available labor already done should not be thrown away, I had in my mind the very class of cases you now mention. So you see it is not even a modification of anything I have heretofore said when I tell you that you are at liberty to adopt any rule which shall admit to vote any unquestionably loyal free-state men and none others. And yet I do wish they would all take the oath. Yours truly,

To Edwin M. Stanton

Executive Mansion, February 1, 1864.

Sir: You are directed to have a transport (either a steam or sailing vessel as may be deemed proper by the Quartermaster-General) sent to the colored colony established by the United States at the island of Vache, on the coast of San Domingo, to bring back to this country such of the colonists there as desire to return. You will have the transport furnished with suitable supplies for that purpose, and detail an officer of the Quartermaster's Department who, under special instructions to be given, shall have charge of the business. The colonists will be brought to Washington, unless otherwise hereafter directed, and be employed and provided for at the camps for colored persons around that city. Those only will be brought from the island who desire to return, and their effects will be brought with them.

Permit to Christopher F. Field and Christopher F. Clay

Executive Mansion, Washington, 1864.

Confiding in the representations and assurances made and given by Hon. Brutus J. Clay of Kentucky, that if permitted, and afforded reasonable protection and facilities by the government, his brother-in-law, Christopher F. Field, and his son, Christopher F. Clay, having, prior to the rebellion, had ownership and lawful control, of several plantations in Mississippi and Arkansas would put said plantations into cultivation, upon the system of free hired labor, recognizing and acknowledging the freedom of the laborers, and totally excluding from said plantations, the slave system of labor and all actual slavery, and would neither do or permit anything on said plantations which would aid the rebellion, it is hereby ordered that said Christopher F. Field, and Christopher F. Clay, or either of them, be permitted to so put said plantations, or any of them, into cultivation; and that the Military, and all others acting by the authority of the United States, are to favor and facilitate said Field and Clay in the carrying forward said business in good faith, by giving them protection, and allowing them to procure, and take to the proper points, the necessary supplies of all kinds, and by doing and forbearing in whatever way will advance the object aforesaid; *provided* that existing Military or Trade regulations, nor any military necessity, be transcended or over-ridden thereby.

ABRAHAM LINCOLN

I have made the representations and given the assurances as within indicated.

Feb. 1. 1864   BRUTUS J. CLAY

To Edwin M. Stanton

Submitted to the Sec. of War. On principle I dislike an oath which requires a man to swear he *has* not done wrong. It rejects the Christian principle of forgiveness on terms of repentance. I think it is enough if the man does no wrong *hereafter*.

Feb. 5. 1864

To Edwin M. Stanton

Hon. Secretary of War   Executive Mansion,
My dear Sir   Washington, Feb. 11, 1864.

In January 1863, the Provost-Marshal at St. Louis, having taken the control of a certain church from one set of men and given it to another, I wrote Gen. Curtis on the subject, as follows:

"the U.S. Government must not, as by this order, undertake to run the churches. When an individual, in a church or out of it, becomes dangerous to the public interest, he must be checked; but the churches, as such, must take care of themselves. It will not do for the U.S. to appoint trustees, Supervisors, or other agents for the churches."

Some trouble remaining in this same case, I, on the 22nd. of Dec. 1863, in a letter to Mr. O. D. Filley, repeated the above language; and, among other things, added "I have never interfered, nor thought of interfering as to who shall or shall not preach in any church; nor have I knowingly, or believingly, tolerated any one else to so interfere by my authority. If any one is so interfering by color of my authority, I would like to have it specifically made known to me. . . . I will not have control of any church on any side."

After having made these declarations in good faith, and in writing, you can conceive of my embarrassment at now having brought to me what purports to be a formal order of the War Department, bearing date Nov. 30th. 1863, giving Bishop Ames control and possession of all the Methodist churches in certain Southern Military Departments, whose pastors have not been appointed by a loyal Bishop or Bishops, and ordering the Military to aid him against any resistance which may be made to his taking such possession and control. What is to be done about it? Yours truly

To Daniel E. Sickles

                    Executive Mansion, Washington,
Major General Sickles: February 15. 1864.

I wish you to make a tour for me (principally for observation and information) by way of Cairo and New-Orleans, and returning by the Gulf and Ocean. All Military and Naval officers are to facilitate you with suitable transportation, and by conferring with you, and imparting, so far as they can, the information herein indicated, but you are not to command any of them. You will call at Memphis, Helena, Vicksburg, New-Orleans, Pensacola, Key-West, Charleston-Harbor, and such intermediate points as you may think important. Please ascertain at each place what is being done, if anything, for reconstruction—how the Amnesty proclamation works, if at all—what practical hitches, if any, there are about it—whether deserters come in from the enemy, what number has come in at each point since the Amnesty, and whether the ratio of their arrival is any greater *since* than before the Amnesty—what deserters report generally, and particularly, whether, and to what extent, the Amnesty is known within the rebel lines. Also learn what you can as to the colored people—how they get along as soldiers, as laborers in our service, on leased plantations, and as hired laborers with their old masters, if there be such cases. Also learn what you can about the colored people within the rebel lines. Also get any other information you may consider interesting, and, from time to time, send me what you may deem important to be known here at once, and be ready to make a general report on your return. Yours truly

To Frederick Steele

Major General Steele   Executive Mansion,
Little-Rock, Ark.   Washington, Feb. 17, 1864.

The day fixed by the Convention for the election is probably the best, but you, on the ground, and in consultation with gentlemen there, are to decide. I should have fixed no day for an election—presented no plan for reconstruction—had I known the convention was doing the same things. It is probably best that you merely assist the convention on their own plan, as to election day & all other matters. I have already written and telegraphed this half a dozen times.

To John A. Andrew

His Excellency. John A. Andrew   Executive Mansion,
Governor of Massachusetts   Washington, February 18. 1864.

Yours of the 12th. was received yesterday. If I were to judge from the letter, without any external knowledge, I should suppose that all the colored people South of Washington were struggling to get to Massachusetts; that Massachusetts was anxious to receive and retain the whole of them as permanent citizens; and that the United States Government here was interposing and preventing this. But I suppose these are neither really the facts, nor meant to be asserted as true by you. Coming down to what I suppose to be the real facts, you are engaged in trying to raise colored troops for the U.S. and wish to take recruits from Virginia, through Washington, to Massachusetts for that object; and the loyal Governor of Virginia, also trying to raise troops for us, objects to your taking his material away; while we, having to care for all, and being responsible alike to all, have to do as much for him, as we would have to do for you, if he was, by our authority, taking men from Massachusetts to fill up Virginia regiments. No more than this has been intended by me; nor, as I think, by the Secretary of War. There may have been some abuses of this, as a rule, which, if known, should be prevented in future.

If, however, it be really true that Massachusetts wishes to afford a permanent home within her borders, for all, or even a large number of colored persons who will come to her, I shall be only too glad to know it. It would give relief in a very difficult point; and I would not for a moment hinder from going, any person who is free by the terms of the proclamation or any of the acts of Congress.

To Benjamin F. Loan

Hon. B. Loan   War Department
Dear Sir: Washington, Feb. 22, 1864

At your instance I directed a part of the advertising for this Department to be done in the St. Joseph Tribune. I have just been informed that the Tribune openly avows it's determination that in no event will it support the re-election of the President. As you probably know, please inform me whether this is true. The President's wish is that no objection shall be made to any paper respectfully expressing it's preference for the *nomination* of any candidate; but that the patronage of the government shall be given to none which engages in cultivating a sentiment to oppose the *election* of any when he shall have been fairly nominated by the regular Union National Convention.

To Edwin M. Stanton

I am told there are one hundred colored men at Alexandria, Va. who wish to go to Massachusetts; with their own consent and the consent of Gov. Pierpoint, let them go.

Feby 25. 1864.

To Salmon P. Chase

Hon. Secretary of the Treasury   Executive Mansion,
My dear Sir: Washington, February 29. 1864.
I would have taken time to answer yours of the 22nd. sooner, only that I did not suppose any evil could result from the delay, especially as, by a note, I promptly acknowledged the receipt of yours, and promised a fuller answer. Now, on consideration, I find there is really very little to say. My knowledge of Mr. Pomeroy's letter having been made *public* came to me only the day you wrote; but I had, in spite of myself, known of it's *existence* several days before. I have not yet read it, and I think I shall not. I was not shocked, or surprised by the appearance of the letter, because I had had knowledge of Mr. Pomeroy's Committee, and of secret issues which I supposed came from it, and of secret agents who I supposed were sent out by it, for several weeks. I have known just as little of these things as my own friends have allowed me to know. They bring the documents to me, but I do not read them—they tell me what they think fit to tell me, but I

do not inquire for more. I fully concur with you that neither of us can be justly held responsible for what our respective friends may do without our instigation or countenance; and I assure you, as you have assured me, that no assault has been made upon you by my instigation, or with my countenance.

Whether you shall remain at the head of the Treasury Department is a question which I will not allow myself to consider from any stand-point other than my judgment of the public service; and, in that view, I do not perceive occasion for a change. Yours truly

To Edwin M. Stanton

Hon. Sec. of War—   Executive Mansion,
My dear Sir: Washington, March. 1, 1864.
A poor widow, by the name of Baird, has a son in the Army, that for some offence has been sentenced to serve a long time without pay, or at most, with very little pay. I do not like this punishment of withholding pay—it falls so very hard upon poor families. After he has been serving in this way for several months, at the tearful appeal of the poor Mother, I made a direction that he be allowed to enlist for a new term, on the same conditions as others. She now comes, and says she can not get it acted upon. Please do it. Yours truly

To John A. J. Creswell

Hon. John A. J. Creswell   Executive Mansion,
My dear Sir: Washington, March 7, 1864.
I am very anxious for emancipation to be effected in Maryland in some substantial form. I think it probable that my expressions of a preference for *gradual* over *immediate* emancipation, are misunderstood. I had thought the *gradual* would produce less confusion, and destitution, and therefore would be more satisfactory; but if those who are better acquainted with the subject, and are more deeply interested in it, prefer the *immediate*, most certainly I have no objection to their

judgment prevailing. My wish is that all who are for emancipation *in any form*, shall co-operate, all treating all respectfully, and all adopting and acting upon the major opinion, when fairly ascertained. What I have dreaded is the danger that by jealousies, rivalries, and consequent ill-blood— driving one another out of meetings and conventions—perchance from the polls—the friends of emancipation themselves may divide, and lose the measure altogether. I wish this letter to not be made public; but no man representing me as I herein represent myself, will be in any danger of contradiction by me. Yours truly

Presentation of Commission to Ulysses S. Grant, Washington, D.C.

General Grant

The nation's appreciation of what you have done, and it's reliance upon you for what remains to do, in the existing great struggle, are now presented with this commission, constituting you Lieutenant General in the Army of the United States. With this high honor devolves upon you also, a corresponding responsibility. As the country herein trusts you, so, under God, it will sustain you. I scarcely need to add that with what I here speak for the nation goes my own hearty personal concurrence.

March 9, 1864

To George D. Ramsay

I think the Absterdam projectile is too good a thing to be lost to the service, and if offered at the Hotchkiss prices, and not in excessive quantities, nor unreasonable terms in other respects, by either or both parties to the patent controversy, take it, so that the test be fully made. I am for the government having the best articles, in spite of patent controversies.

March. 10. 1864.

To Michael Hahn

Private

Hon. Michael Hahn

My dear Sir:

Executive Mansion,

Washington,

March 13. 1864.

I congratulate you on having fixed your name in history as the first-free-state Governor of Louisiana. Now you are about to have a Convention which, among other things, will probably define the elective franchise. I barely suggest for your private consideration, whether some of the colored people may not be let in—as, for instance, the very intelligent, and especially those who have fought gallantly in our ranks. They would probably help, in some trying time to come, to keep the jewel of liberty within the family of freedom. But this is only a suggestion, not to the public, but to you alone. Yours truly

To Carl Schurz

Private.

Major General Schurz

My dear Sir:

Executive Mansion,

Washington,

March 13, 1864.

Yours of February 29th, reached me only four days ago; but the delay was of little consequence, because I found, on feeling around, I could not invite you here without a difficulty which at least would be unpleasant, and perhaps would be detrimental to the public service. Allow me to suggest that if you wish to remain in the military service, it is very dangerous for you to get temporarily out of it; because, with a Major General once out, it is next to impossible for even the President to get him in again. With my appreciation of your ability, and correct principle, of course I would be very glad to have your service for the country in the approaching political canvass; but I fear we can not properly have it, without separating you from the military. Yours truly

Endorsement Concerning New Orleans Churches

While I leave this case to the discretion of Gen. Banks, my view is, that the U.S. should not appoint trustees for or in any way take charge of any church as such. If the building is needed for military purposes, take it; if it is not so needed, let its church people have it, dealing with any disloyal people among them, as you deal with other disloyal people.

March 15th. 1864

To John A. J. Creswell

Hon. John A. J. Creswell   Executive Mansion,
My dear Sir: Washington, March 17, 1864.

It needs not to be a secret, that I wish success to emancipation in Maryland. It would aid much to end the rebellion. Hence it is a matter of national consequence, in which every national man, may rightfully feel a deep interest. I sincerely hope the friends of the measure will allow no minor considerations to divide and distract them. Yours truly

Remarks at Closing of Sanitary Fair, Washington, D.C.

Ladies and Gentlemen: I appear to say but a word. This extraordinary war in which we are engaged falls heavily upon all classes of people, but the most heavily upon the soldier. For it has been said, all that a man hath will he give for his life; and while all contribute of their substance the soldier puts his life at stake, and often yields it up in his country's cause. The highest merit, then, is due to the soldier. [Cheers.]

In this extraordinary war extraordinary developments have manifested themselves, such as have not been seen in former wars; and amongst these manifestations nothing has been more remarkable than these fairs for the relief of suffering soldiers and their families. And the chief agents in these fairs are the women of America. [Cheers.]

I am not accustomed to the use of language of eulogy; I have never studied the art of paying compliments to women; but I must say that if all that has been said by orators and poets since the creation of the world in praise of woman were applied to the women of America, it would not do them justice for their conduct during this war. I will close by saying God bless the women of America! [Great applause.]

March 18, 1864

To Edwin M. Stanton

Hon. Secretary of War: Executive Mansion,
My dear Sir: Washington, March 18. 1864.
I am so pressed in regard to prisoners of war in our custody, whose homes are within our lines, and who wish to not be exchanged, but to take the oath and be discharged, that I hope you will pardon me for again calling up the subject. My impression is that we will not ever force the exchange of any of this class; that taking the oath, and being discharged, none of them will again go to the rebellion, but the rebellion again coming to them, a considerable per centage of them, probably not a majority, would rejoin it; that by a cautious discrimination the number so discharged would not be large enough to do any considerable mischief in any event; would relieve distress in, at least some meritorious cases; and would give me some relief from an intolerable pressure. I shall be glad therefore to have your cheerful assent to the discharge of those whose names I may send, which I will only do with circumspection. Yours truly

Remainder of Draft of Letter to Stanton

In using the strong hand, as now compelled to do, the government has a difficult duty to perform. At the very best, it will by turns do both too little and too much. It can properly have no motive of revenge, no purpose to punish merely for punishment's sake. While we must, by all available means, prevent the overthrow of the government, we should avoid planting and cultivating too many thorns in the bosom of society. These general remarks apply to several classes of cases, on each of which I wish to say a word.

First, the dismissal of officers when neither incompetency, nor intentional wrong, nor real injury to the service, is imputed. In such cases it is both cruel and impolitic, to crush the man, and make him and his friends permanent enemies to the administration if not to the government itself. I think of two instances. One wherein a Surgeon, for the benefit of patients in his charge, needed some lumber, and could only get it by making a false certificate wherein the lumber was denominated "butter & eggs" and he was dismissed for the false certificate. The other a Surgeon by the name of Owen who served from the beginning of the war till recently, with two servants, and without objection, when upon discovery that the servants were his own *sons*, he was dismissed.

Another class consists of those who are known or strongly suspected, to be in sympathy with the rebellion. An instance of this is the family of Southern, who killed a recruiting officer last autumn, in Maryland. He fled, and his family are driven from their home, without a shelter or crumb, except when got by burthening our friends more than our enemies. Southern had no justification to kill the officer; and yet he would not have been killed if he had proceeded in the temper and manner agreed upon by yourself and Gov. Bradford. But this is past. What is to be done with the family? Why can they not occupy their old home, and excite much less opposition to the government than the manifestation of their distress is now doing? If the house is really needed for the public service; or if it has been regularly confiscated and the title transferred, the case is different.

Again, the cases of persons, mostly women, wishing to pass our lines, one way or the other. We have, in some cases, been apparantly, if not really, inconsistent upon this subject—that is, we have forced some to go who wished to stay, and forced others to stay who wished to go. Suppose we allow all females, with ungrown children of either sex, to go South, if they desire, upon absolute prohibition against returning during the war; and all to come North upon the same condition of not returning during the war, and the additional condition of taking the oath.

I wish to mention two special cases—both of which you well remember. The first is that of Yocum. He was unquestionably guilty. No one asking for his pardon pretends the contrary. What he did, however, was perfectly lawful, only a short while before, and the change making it unlawful had not, even then been fully accepted in the public mind. It is doubtful whether Yocum did not suppose it was really lawful to return a slave to a loyal owner, though it is certain he did the thing secretly, in the belief that his superiors would not allow it if known to them. But the great point with me is that the severe punishment of five years at hard labor in the Penitentiary is not at all necessary to prevent the repetition of the crime by himself or by others. If the offence was one of frequent recurrence, the case would be different; but this case of Yocum is the single instance which has come to my knowledge. I think that for all public purposes, and for all proper purposes, he has suffered enough.

The case of Smithson is troublesome. His wife and children are quartered mostly on our friends, and exciting a great deal of sympathy, which will soon tell against us. What think you of sending him and his family South, holding the sentence over him to be re-inforced if he returns during the war.

March 18, 1864

To Carl Schurz

                              Executive Mansion Washington,
Major General Schurz.   March 23. 1864

My dear Sir: The letter, of which the above is a copy, was sent to you, before Mr. Willmann saw me; and now yours of the 19th. tells me you did not receive it.

I do not wish to be more specific about the difficulty of your coming to Washington. I think you can easily conjecture it. I perceive no objection to your making a political speech when you are where one is to be made; but quite surely speaking in the North, and fighting in the South, at the same time, are not possible. Nor could I be justified to detail any officer to the political campaign during it's continuance, and then return him to the Army

To Benjamin B. French

Private

	Executive Mansion,
Hon. B. B. French	Washington,
My dear Sir:	March 25, 1864.

I understand a Bill is before Congress, by your instigation, for taking your office from the control of the Department of the Interior, and considerably enlarging the powers and patronage of your office. The proposed change may be right for aught I know; and it certainly is right for Congress to do as it thinks proper in the case. What I wish to say is that if the change is made, I do not think I can allow you to retain the office; because that would be encouraging officers to be constantly intriguing, to the detriment of the public interest, in order to profit themselves. Yours truly

To George G. Meade

| Major General Meade | Executive Mansion, |
| My dear Sir: | Washington, March 29. 1864. |

Your letter to Col. Townsend, inclosing a slip from the Herald, and asking a Court of Inquiry, has been laid before me by the Secretary of War, with the request that I would consider it. It is quite natural that you should feel some sensibility on the subject; yet I am not impressed, nor do I think the country is impressed, with the belief that your honor demands, or the public interest demands, such an Inquiry. The country knows that, at all events, you have done good service; and I believe it agrees with me that it is much better for you to be engaged in trying to do more, than to be diverted, as you necessarily would be, by a Court of Inquiry. Yours truly

To Albert G. Hodges

A. G. Hodges, Esq   Executive Mansion,
Frankfort, Ky.   Washington, April 4, 1864.
My dear Sir: You ask me to put in writing the substance of what I verbally said the other day, in your presence, to Governor Bramlette and Senator Dixon. It was about as follows:

"I am naturally anti-slavery. If slavery is not wrong, nothing is wrong. I can not remember when I did not so think, and feel. And yet I have never understood that the Presidency conferred upon me an unrestricted right to act officially upon this judgment and feeling. It was in the oath I took that I would, to the best of my ability, preserve, protect, and defend the Constitution of the United States. I could not take the office without taking the oath. Nor was it my view that I might take an oath to get power, and break the oath in using the power. I understood, too, that in ordinary civil administration this oath even forbade me to practically indulge my primary abstract judgment on the moral question of slavery. I had publicly declared this many times, and in many ways. And I aver that, to this day, I have done no official act in mere deference to my abstract judgment and feeling on slavery. I did understand however, that my oath to preserve the constitution to the best of my ability, imposed upon me the duty of preserving, by every indispensable means, that government—that nation—of which that constitution was the organic law. Was it possible to lose the nation, and yet preserve the constitution? By general law life *and* limb must be protected; yet often a limb must be amputated to save a life; but a life is never wisely given to save a limb. I felt that measures, otherwise unconstitutional, might become lawful, by becoming indispensable to the preservation of the constitution, through the preservation of the nation. Right or wrong, I assumed this ground, and now avow it. I could not feel that, to the best of my ability, I had even tried to preserve the constitution, if, to save slavery, or any minor matter, I should permit the wreck of government, country, and Constitution all together. When, early in the war, Gen. Fremont attempted military emancipation, I forbade it, because I did not then think it an indispensable necessity. When a little later, Gen.

Cameron, then Secretary of War, suggested the arming of the blacks, I objected, because I did not yet think it an indispensable necessity. When, still later, Gen. Hunter attempted military emancipation, I again forbade it, because I did not yet think the indispensable necessity had come. When, in March, and May, and July 1862 I made earnest, and successive appeals to the border states to favor compensated emancipation, I believed the indispensable necessity for military emancipation, and arming the blacks would come, unless averted by that measure. They declined the proposition; and I was, in my best judgment, driven to the alternative of either surrendering the Union, and with it, the Constitution, or of laying strong hand upon the colored element. I chose the latter. In choosing it, I hoped for greater gain than loss; but of this, I was not entirely confident. More than a year of trial now shows no loss by it in our foreign relations, none in our home popular sentiment, none in our white military force,—no loss by it any how or any where. On the contrary, it shows a gain of quite a hundred and thirty thousand soldiers, seamen, and laborers. These are palpable facts, about which, as facts, there can be no cavilling. We have the men; and we could not have had them without the measure.

"And now let any Union man who complains of the measure, test himself by writing down in one line that he is for subduing the rebellion by force of arms; and in the next, that he is for taking these hundred and thirty thousand men from the Union side, and placing them where they would be but for the measure he condemns. If he can not face his case so stated, it is only because he can not face the truth."

I add a word which was not in the verbal conversation. In telling this tale I attempt no compliment to my own sagacity. I claim not to have controlled events, but confess plainly that events have controlled me. Now, at the end of three years struggle the nation's condition is not what either party, or any man devised, or expected. God alone can claim it. Whither it is tending seems plain. If God now wills the removal of a great wrong, and wills also that we of the North as well as you of the South, shall pay fairly for our complicity in that wrong, impartial history will find therein new cause to attest and revere the justice and goodness of God. Yours truly

To Mrs. Horace Mann

Mrs. Horace Mann,   Executive Mansion,
Madam,   Washington, April 5, 1864.

The petition of persons under eighteen, praying that I would free all slave children, and the heading of which petition it appears you wrote, was handed me a few days since by Senator Sumner. Please tell these little people I am very glad their young hearts are so full of just and generous sympathy, and that, while I have not the power to grant all they ask, I trust they will remember that God has, and that, as it seems, He wills to do it. Yours truly

Letter Concerning Mrs. Daniel Hunt

                                 Executive Mansion,
Whom it may concern   Washington, April 11. 1864.

I know nothing on the subject of the attached letter, except as therein stated. Neither do I personally know Mrs. Hunt. She has, however, from the beginning of the war, been constantly represented to me as an open, and somewhat influential friend of the Union. It has been said to me, (I know not whether truly) that her husband is in the rebel army, that she avows her purpose to not live with him again, and that she refused to see him when she had an opportunity during one of John Morgan's raids into Kentucky. I would not offer her, or any wife, a temptation to a permanent separation from her husband; but if she shall avow that her mind is already, independently and fully made up to such separation, I shall be glad for the property sought by her letter, to be delivered to her, upon her taking the oath of December 8, 1863.

Draft of Address for Sanitary Fair at Baltimore, Maryland

Mr. Webster once stated the proposition that a President could not be so applauded, and ministered unto, when his term of office, and with it, his power to confer favors, drew near to it's close, as he had been in the hey-day of his inauger-ation. To illustrate this, he said: "Politicians—office-seekers—are not sun-flowers; they do not turn upon their god when he sets, the same look they gave when he rose." This may be a general truth; but, to my personal knowledge it is not partic-ularly true in Baltimore. For instance, on the 22nd. or 23rd. of February 1861 (so near the end of one and the beginning of the other, as to be doubtful which) I passed through Balti-more, rich with honorable and fat offices, soon to be dis-pensed, and not one hand reached forth to greet me, not one voice broke the stillness to cheer me. Now, three years having past, and offices having passed away, Baltimore marks my coming, and cheers me when I come. Traitorous malice has sought to wrong Baltimore herein, ascribing to one cause what is justly due to another. For instance the Richmond, alluding to that passage through Baltimore, said: "We have no fear of any bold action by the federal government; we re-member Baltimore, and our faith is unwavering in Lincoln's cowardice" Now this is hugely unjust to Baltimore. I take it to be unquestionable that what happened here three years ago, and what happens here now, was contempt of office then, and is purely appreciation of merit now.

before April 18, 1864

Address at Sanitary Fair, Baltimore, Maryland

Ladies and Gentlemen—Calling to mind that we are in Baltimore, we can not fail to note that the world moves. Looking upon these many people, assembled here, to serve, as they best may, the soldiers of the Union, it occurs at once that three years ago, the same soldiers could not so much as pass through Baltimore. The change from then till now, is both great, and gratifying. Blessings on the brave men who have wrought the change, and the fair women who strive to reward them for it.

But Baltimore suggests more than could happen within Baltimore. The change within Baltimore is part only of a far wider change. When the war began, three years ago, neither party, nor any man, expected it would last till now. Each looked for the end, in some way, long ere to-day. Neither did any anticipate that domestic slavery would be much affected by the war. But here we are; the war has not ended, and slavery has been much affected—how much needs not now to be recounted. So true is it that man proposes, and God disposes.

But we can see the past, though we may not claim to have directed it; and seeing it, in this case, we feel more hopeful and confident for the future.

The world has never had a good definition of the word liberty, and the American people, just now, are much in want of one. We all declare for liberty; but in using the same *word* we do not all mean the same *thing*. With some the word liberty may mean for each man to do as he pleases with himself, and the product of his labor; while with others the same word may mean for some men to do as they please with other men, and the product of other men's labor. Here are two, not only different, but incompatable things, called by the same name— liberty. And it follows that each of the things is, by the respective parties, called by two different and incompatable names—liberty and tyranny.

The shepherd drives the wolf from the sheep's throat, for which the sheep thanks the shepherd as a *liberator*, while the

589

wolf denounces him for the same act as the destroyer of liberty, especially as the sheep was a black one. Plainly the sheep
and the wolf are not agreed upon a definition of the word
liberty; and precisely the same difference prevails to-day
among us human creatures, even in the North, and all professing to love liberty. Hence we behold the processes by
which thousands are daily passing from under the yoke of
bondage, hailed by some as the advance of liberty, and be-
wailed by others as the destruction of all liberty. Recently, as
it seems, the people of Maryland have been doing something
to define liberty; and thanks to them that, in what they have
done, the wolf's dictionary, has been repudiated.

It is not very becoming for one in my position to make
speeches at great length; but there is another subject upon
which I feel that I ought to say a word. A painful rumor, true
I fear, has reached us of the massacre, by the rebel forces, at
Fort Pillow, in the West end of Tennessee, on the Mississippi
river, of some three hundred colored soldiers and white
officers, who had just been overpowered by their assailants.
There seems to be some anxiety in the public mind whether
the government is doing it's duty to the colored soldier, and
to the service, at this point. At the beginning of the war, and
for some time, the use of colored troops was not contemplated; and how the change of purpose was wrought, I will
not now take time to explain. Upon a clear conviction of duty
I resolved to turn that element of strength to account; and I
am responsible for it to the American people, to the christian
world, to history, and on my final account to God. Having
determined to use the negro as a soldier, there is no way but
to give him all the protection given to any other soldier. The
difficulty is not in stating the principle, but in practically applying it. It is a mistake to suppose the government is indifferent to this matter, or is not doing the best it can in regard
to it. We do not to-day *know* that a colored soldier, or white
officer commanding colored soldiers, has been massacred by
the rebels when made a prisoner. We fear it, believe it, I may
say, but we do not *know* it. To take the life of one of their
prisoners, on the assumption that they murder ours, when it
is short of certainty that they do murder ours, might be too
serious, too cruel a mistake. We are having the Fort-Pillow

affair thoroughly investigated; and such investigation will probably show conclusively how the truth is. If, after all that has been said, it shall turn out that there has been no massacre at Fort-Pillow, it will be almost safe to say there has been none, and will be none elsewhere. If there has been the massacre of three hundred there, or even the tenth part of three hundred, it will be conclusively proved; and being so proved, the retribution shall as surely come. It will be matter of grave consideration in what exact course to apply the retribution; but in the supposed case, it must come.

April 18, 1864

To Isaac Murphy

Governor Murphy   Office U.S. Military Telegraph,
Little-Rock,   War Department,
Arkansas.   Washington, D.C., April 27. 1864.

I am much gratified to learn that you got out so large a vote, so nearly all the right way, at the late election; and not less so, that your State-Government, including the Legislature, is organized, and in good working order. Whatever I can, I will do, to protect you; meanwhile you must do your utmost to protect yourselves. Present my greeting to all

To Ulysses S. Grant

Executive Mansion Washington,
Lieutenant General Grant.   April 30, 1864

Not expecting to see you again before the Spring campaign opens, I wish to express, in this way, my entire satisfaction with what you have done up to this time, so far as I understand it. The particulars of your plans I neither know, or seek to know. You are vigilant and self-reliant; and, pleased with this, I wish not to obtrude any constraints or restraints upon you. While I am very anxious that any great disaster, or the capture of our men in great numbers, shall be avoided, I know these points are less likely to escape your attention than they would be mine. If there is anything wanting which is within my power to give, do not fail to let me know it.

And now with a brave Army, and a just cause, may God sustain you. Yours very truly

To Cabinet Members

Sir:

Executive Mansion,
Washington, May 3, 1864.

It is now quite certain that a large number of our colored soldiers, with their white officers, were, by the rebel force, massacred after they had surrendered, at the recent capture of Fort-Pillow. So much is known, though the evidence is not yet quite ready to be laid before me. Meanwhile I will thank you to prepare, and give me in writing your opinion as to what course, the government should take in the case. Yours truly

Response to Serenade, Washington, D.C.

FELLOW-CITIZENS: I am very much obliged to you for the compliment of this call, though I apprehend it is owing more to the good news received to-day from the army than to a desire to see me. I am, indeed, very grateful to the brave men who have been struggling with the enemy in the field, to their noble commanders who have directed them, and especially to our Maker. Our commanders are following up their victories resolutely and successfully. I think, without knowing the particulars of the plans of Gen. Grant, that what has been accomplished is of more importance than at first appears. I believe I know, (and am especially grateful to know) that Gen. Grant has not been jostled in his purposes; that he has made all his points, and to-day he is on his line as he purposed before he moved his armies. I will volunteer to say that I am very glad at what has happened; but there is a great deal still to be done. While we are grateful to all the brave men and officers for the events of the past few days, we should, above all, be very grateful to Almighty God, who gives us victory.

There is enough yet before us requiring all loyal men and patriots to perform their share of the labor and follow the example of the modest General at the head of our armies, and sink all personal considerations for the sake of the country. I commend you to keep yourselves in the same tranquil mood that is characteristic of that brave and loyal man. I have said more than I expected when I came before you; repeating my thanks for this call, I bid you good-bye. [Cheers.]

May 9, 1864

To Samuel C. Pomeroy

Hon. Senator Pomeroy   Executive Mansion
Sir—   Washington May 12. 1864
    I did not doubt yesterday that you desired to see me about the appointment of Assessor in Kansas. I wish you and Lane would make a sincere effort to get out of the mood you are in. It does neither of you any good—it gives you the means of tormenting my life out of me, and nothing else. Yours &c

To Thomas Carney

The within letter is, to my mind, so obviously intended as a page for a political record, as to be difficult to answer in a straight-forward business-like way. The merits of the Kansas people need not to be argued to me. They are just as good as any other loyal and patriotic people; and, as such, to the best of my ability, I have always treated them, and intend to treat them. It is not my recollection that I said to you Senator Lane would probably oppose raising troops in Kansas, because it would confer patronage upon you. What I did say was that he would probably oppose it because he and you were in a mood of each opposing whatever the other should propose. I did argue generally too, that, in my opinion, there is not a more foolish or demoralizing way of conducting a political rivalry, than these fierce and bitter struggles for patronage.
    As to your demand that I will accept or reject your propo-

sition to furnish troops, made to me yesterday, I have to say I took the proposition under advisement, in good faith, as I believe you know; that you can withdraw it if you wish, but that while it remains before me, I shall neither accept or reject it, until, with reference to the public interest, I shall feel that I am ready. Yours truly

May 14, 1864

To Edwin M. Stanton

Hon. Secretary of War: Executive Mansion
Sir.   Washington, D.C. May 17. 1864

Please notify the insurgents, through the proper military channels and forms, that the government of the United States has satisfactory proof of the massacre, by insurgent forces, at Fort-Pillow, on the 12th. and 13th. days of April last, of fully   white and colored officers and soldiers of the United States, after the latter had ceased resistance, and asked quarter of the former.

That with reference to said massacre, the government of the United States has assigned and set apart by name   insurgent officers, theretofore, and up to that time, held by said government as prisoners of war.

That, as blood can not restore blood, and government should not act for revenge, any assurance, as nearly perfect as the case admits, given on or before the first day of July next, that there shall be no similar massacre, nor any officer or soldier of the United States, whether white or colored, now held, or hereafter captured by the insurgents, shall be treated other than according to the laws of war, will insure the re-placing of said   insurgent officers in the simple condition of prisoners of war.

That the insurgents having refused to exchange, or to give any account or explanation in regard to colored soldiers of the United States captured by them, a number of insurgent prisoners equal to the number of such colored soldiers supposed to have been captured by said insurgents will, from time to time, be assigned and set aside, with reference to such captured colored soldiers, and will, if the insurgents assent, be exchanged for such colored soldiers; but that if no satisfactory attention shall be given to this notice, by said insurgents, on or before the first day of July next, it will be assumed by the government of the United States, that said captured colored troops shall have been murdered, or subjected to Slavery, and that said government will, upon said assumption, take such action as may then appear expedient and just.

To Charles Sumner

Hon. Charles Sumner,   Executive Mansion,
My dear Sir: Washington, May 19, 1864.
    The bearer of this is the widow of Major Booth, who fell at Fort-Pillow. She makes a point, which I think very worthy of consideration which is, widows and children *in fact*, of colored soldiers who fall in our service, be placed in law, the same as if their marriages were legal, so that they can have the benefit of the provisions made the widows & orphans of white soldiers. Please see & hear Mrs. Booth. Yours truly

To Isaac N. Arnold

Hon. I. N. Arnold.   Executive Mansion,
My dear Sir.   Washington, May 25, 1864.
    In regard to the order of General Burnside suspending the Chicago Times now nearly a year ago, I can only say I was embarrassed with the question between what was due to the Military service on the one hand, and the Liberty of the Press on the other, and I believe it was the despatch of Senator Trumbull and yourself, added to the proceedings of the meeting which it brought me, that turned the scale in favor of my revoking the order. I am far from certain to-day that the revocation was not right; and I am very sure the small part you took in it, is no just ground to disparage your judgment, much less to impugn your motives. I take it that your devotion to the Union and the Administration can not be questioned by any sincere man. Yours truly

To John H. Bryant

Hon. John H Bryant   Executive Mansion,
My dear Sir.   Washington, May 30, 1864.

Yours of the 14th. Inst. inclosing a card of invitation to a preliminary meeting contemplating the erection of a Monument to the memory of Hon. Owen Lovejoy, was duly received.

As you anticipate, it will be out of my power to attend. Many of you have known Mr. Lovejoy longer than I have, and are better able than I to do his memory complete justice. My personal acquaintance with him commenced only about ten years ago, since when it has been quite intimate; and every step in it has been one of increasing respect and esteem, ending, with his life, in no less than affection on my part. It can be truly said of him that while he was personally ambitious, he bravely endured the obscurity which the unpopularity of his principles imposed, and never accepted official honors, until those honors were ready to admit his principles with him. Throughout my heavy, and perplexing responsibilities here, to the day of his death, it would scarcely wrong any other to say, he was my most generous friend. Let him have the marble monument, along with the well-assured and more enduring one in the hearts of those who love liberty, unselfishly, for all men. Yours truly

To George B. Ide, James R. Doolittle, and A. Hubbell

Rev. Dr. Ide   ⎫   Executive Mansion,
Hon. J. R. Doolittle ⎬ Committee   Washington,
& Hon. A. Hubbell ⎭   May 30, 1864.

In response to the preamble and resolutions of the American Baptist Home Mission Society, which you did me the honor to present, I can only thank you for thus adding to the effective and almost unanamous support which the Christian communities are so zealously giving to the country, and to liberty. Indeed it is difficult to conceive how it could be otherwise with any one professing christianity, or even having ordinary perceptions of right and wrong. To read in the Bible, as the word of God himself, that "In the sweat of *thy* face shalt thou eat bread," and to preach therefrom that, "In the sweat of *other mans* faces shalt thou eat bread," to my mind can scarcely be reconciled with honest sincerity. When brought to my final reckoning, may I have to answer for robbing no man of his goods; yet more tolerable even this, than for robbing one of himself, and all that was his. When, a year or two ago, those professedly holy men of the South, met in the semblance of prayer and devotion, and, in the name of Him who said "As ye would all men should do unto you, do ye even so unto them" appealed to the christian world to aid them in doing to a whole race of men, as they would have no man do unto themselves, to my thinking, they contemned and insulted God and His church, far more than did Satan when he tempted the Saviour with the Kingdoms of the earth. The devils attempt was no more false, and far less hypocritical. But let me forbear, remembering it is also written "Judge not, lest ye be judged."

Endorsement Concerning Leonard Swett and Joseph Holt

Swett is unquestionably all right. Mr. Holt is a good man, but I had not heard or thought of him for V.P. Wish not to interfere about V.P. Can not interfere about platform. Convention must judge for itself.

June 6, 1864

Reply to Committee of the National Union Convention, Washington, D.C.

Gentlemen of the Committee: I will neither conceal my gratification, nor restrain the expression of my gratitude, that the Union people, through their convention, in their continued effort to save, and advance the nation, have deemed me not unworthy to remain in my present position.

I know no reason to doubt that I shall accept the nomination tendered; and yet perhaps I should not declare definitely before reading and considering what is called the Platform.

I will say now, however, I approve the declaration in favor of so amending the Constitution as to prohibit slavery throughout the nation. When the people in revolt, with a hundred days of explicit notice, that they could, within those days, resume their allegiance, without the overthrow of their institution, and that they could not so resume it afterwards, elected to stand out, such amendment of the Constitution as now proposed, became a fitting, and necessary conclusion to the final success of the Union cause. Such alone can meet and cover all cavils. Now, the unconditional Union men, North and South, perceive its importance, and embrace it. In the joint names of Liberty and Union, let us labor to give it legal form, and practical effect.

June 9, 1864

Reply to Delegation
from the National Union League,
Washington, D.C.

Gentlemen: I can only say, in response to the kind remarks of your chairman, as I suppose, that I am very grateful for the renewed confidence which has been accorded to me, both by the convention and by the National League. I am not insensible at all to the personal compliment there is in this; yet I do not allow myself to believe that any but a small portion of it is to be appropriated as a personal compliment. The convention and the nation, I am assured, are alike animated by a higher view of the interests of the country for the present and the great future, and that part I am entitled to appropriate as a compliment is only that part which I may lay hold of as being the opinion of the convention and of the League, that I am not entirely unworthy to be intrusted with the place I have occupied for the last three years. I have not permitted myself, gentlemen, to conclude that I am the best man in the country;

but I am reminded, in this connection, of a story of an old Dutch farmer, who remarked to a companion once that "it was not best to swap horses when crossing streams."

June 9, 1864

Speech at Great Central Sanitary Fair, Philadelphia, Pennsylvania

I suppose that this toast was intended to open the way for me to say something. [Laughter.] War, at the best, is terrible, and this war of ours, in its magnitude and in its duration, is one of the most terrible. It has deranged business, totally in many localities, and partially in all localities. It has destroyed property, and ruined homes; it has produced a national debt and taxation unprecedented, at least in this country. It has carried mourning to almost every home, until it can almost be said that the "heavens are hung in black." Yet it continues, and several relieving coincidents have accompanied it from the very beginning, which have not been known, as I understood, or have any knowledge of, in any former wars in the history of the world. The Sanitary Commission, with all its benevolent labors, the Christian Commission, with all its Christian and benevolent labors, and the various places, arrangements, so to speak, and institutions, have contributed to the comfort and relief of the soldiers. You have two of these places in this city—the Cooper-Shop and Union Volunteer Refreshment Saloons. [Great applause and cheers.] And lastly, these fairs, which, I believe, began only in last August, if I mistake not, in Chicago; then at Boston, at Cincinnati, Brooklyn, New York, at Baltimore, and those at present held at St. Louis, Pittsburg, and Philadelphia. The motive and object that lie at the bottom of all these are most worthy; for, say what you will, after all the most is due to the soldier, who takes his life in his hands and goes to fight the battles of his country. [Cheers.] In what is contributed to his comfort when he passes to and fro, and in what is contributed to him when he is sick and wounded, in whatever shape it comes, whether from the fair and tender hand of woman, or from any other source, is much, very much; but, I think there is still that which has as much value to him—he is not forgotten. [Cheers.] Another view of these various institutions is worthy of consideration, I think; they are voluntary contributions, given freely, zealously, and earnestly, on top of all the disturbances of business, the taxation and burdens that the war has imposed upon us, giving proof that the national resources are not at all exhausted, [cheers;] that the national spirit of patriotism is even stronger than at the commencement of the rebellion.

It is a pertinent question often asked in the mind privately, and from one to the other, when is the war to end? Surely I feel as deep an interest in this question as any other can, but I do not wish to name a day, or month, or a year when it is to end. I do not wish to run any risk of seeing the time come, without our being ready for the end, and for fear of disappointment, because the time had come and not the end. We accepted this war for an object, a worthy object, and the war will end when that object is attained. Under God, I hope it never will until that time. [Great cheering.] Speaking of the present campaign, General Grant is reported to have said, I am going through on this line if it takes all summer. [Cheers.] This war has taken three years; it was begun or accepted upon the line of restoring the national authority over the whole national domain, and for the American people, as far as my knowledge enables me to speak, I say we are going through on this line if it takes three years more. [Cheers.] My friends, I did not know but that I might be called upon to say a few words before I got away from here, but I did not know it was coming just here. [Laughter.] I have never been in the habit of making predictions in regard to the war, but I am almost tempted to make one.—If I were to hazard it, it is this: That Grant is this evening, with General Meade and General Hancock, of Pennsylvania, and the brave officers and soldiers with him, in a position from whence he will never be dislodged until Richmond is taken [loud cheering], and I have but one single proposition to put now, and, perhaps, I can best put it in form of an interrogative. If I shall discover that General Grant and the noble officers and men under him can be greatly facilitated in their work by a sudden pouring forward of men and assistance, will you give them to me? [Cries of "yes."] Then, I say, stand ready, for I am watching for the chance. [Laughter and cheers.] I thank you, gentlemen.

June 16, 1864

To Edward Bates

Hon Attorney General   Executive Mansion,
Sir: Washington, June 24th. 1864.

By authority of the Constitution, and moved thereto by the fourth section of the act of Congress entitled "An act making appropriations for the support of the Army for the year ending the thirtieth of June, Eighteen hundred and sixty five, and for other purposes," approved, June 15th. 1864, I require your opinion in writing as to what pay, bounty, and clothing are allowed by law to persons of color who were free on the 19th. day of April, 1861, and who have been enlisted and mustered into the military service of the United States between the month of December, 1862 and the 16th. of June 1864.

Please answer as you would do, on my requirement, if the Act of June 15th. 1864 had not been passed; and I will so use your opinion as to satisfy that act. Your obt Servt

To William Dennison and Others

                                         Executive Mansion,
                                         Washington, June 27, 1864.
Hon. William Dennison & others, a Committee
of the National Union Convention.

Gentlemen: Your letter of the 14th. Inst. formally notifying me that I have been nominated by the convention you represent for the Presidency of the United States for four years from the fourth of March next has been received. The nomination is gratefully accepted, as the resolutions of the convention, called the platform, are heartily approved.

While the resolution in regard to the supplanting of republican government upon the Western continent is fully concurred in, there might be misunderstanding were I not to say that the position of the government, in relation to the action of France in Mexico, as assumed through the State Department, and approved and indorsed by the convention, among the measures and acts of the Executive, will be faithfully maintained, so long as the state of facts shall leave that position pertinent and applicable.

I am especially gratified that the soldier and the seaman were not forgotten by the convention, as they forever must and will be remembered by the grateful country for whose salvation they devote their lives.

Thanking you for the kind and complimentary terms in which you have communicated the nomination and other proceedings of the convention, I subscribe myself Your Obt. Servt.

To Frederick Steele

Executive Mansion, Washington,
Major General Steele   June 29, 1864

I understand that Congress declines to admit to seats the persons sent as Senators and Representatives from Arkansas. These persons apprehend that, in consequence, you may not support the new State Government then as you otherwise would. My wish is that you give that government and the people there, the same support and protection that you would if the members had been admitted, because in no event, nor in any view of the case, can this do any harm, while it will be the best you can do towards suppressing the rebellion   Yours truly

To Salmon P. Chase

Hon. Salmon P. Chase   Executive Mansion,
My dear Sir.   Washington, June 30, 1864.

Your resignation of the office of Secretary of the Treasury, sent me yesterday, is accepted. Of all I have said in commendation of your ability and fidelity, I have nothing to unsay; and yet you and I have reached a point of mutual embarrassment in our official relation which it seems can not be overcome, or longer sustained, consistently with the public service. Your Obt. Servt.

To John L. Scripps

To —— Esq.   Executive Mansion, July 4th, 1864.

Dear Sir: Complaint is made to me that you are using your official power to defeat Mr. ——'s nomination to Congress. I am well satisfied with Mr. —— as a member of Congress, and I do not know that the man who might supplant him would be as satisfactory. But the correct principle I think is, that all our friends should have *absolute freedom* of choice among our friends. My wish therefore is, that you will do just as you think fit with your own suffrage in the case, and not constrain any of your subordinates to other than he thinks fit with his. This is precisely the rule I inculcated and adhered to on my part, when a *certain* other nomination now recently made, was being canvassed for. Yours, very truly,

Proclamation Concerning Reconstruction

BY THE PRESIDENT OF THE UNITED STATES.

A PROCLAMATION.

Whereas, at the late Session, Congress passed a Bill, "To guarantee to certain States, whose governments have been usurped or overthrown, a republican form of Government," a copy of which is hereunto annexed:

And whereas, the said Bill was presented to the President of the United States, for his approval, less than one hour before the *sine die* adjournment of said Session, and was not signed by him:

And whereas, the said Bill contains, among other things, a plan for restoring the States in rebellion to their proper practical relation in the Union, which plan expresses the sense of Congress upon that subject, and which plan it is now thought fit to lay before the people for their consideration:

Now, therefore, I, Abraham Lincoln, President of the United States, do proclaim, declare, and make known, that, while I am, (as I was in December last, when by proclamation I propounded a plan for restoration) unprepared, by a formal approval of this Bill, to be inflexibly committed to any single plan of restoration; and, while I am also unprepared to declare, that the free-state constitutions and governments, already adopted and installed in Arkansas and Louisiana, shall be set aside and held for nought, thereby repelling and discouraging the loyal citizens who have set up the same, as to further effort; or to declare a constitutional competency in Congress to abolish slavery in States, but am at the same time sincerely hoping and expecting that a constitutional amendment, abolishing slavery throughout the nation, may be adopted, nevertheless, I am fully satisfied with the system for restoration contained in the Bill, as one very proper plan for the loyal people of any State choosing to adopt it; and that I am, and at all times shall be, prepared to give the Executive aid and assistance to any such people, so soon as the military resistance to the United States shall have been suppressed in any such State, and the people thereof shall have sufficiently returned to their obedience to the Constitution and the laws of the United States,—in which cases, military Governors will be appointed, with directions to proceed according to the Bill.

In testimony whereof, I have hereunto set my hand and caused the Seal of the United States to be affixed.

Done at the City of Washington this eighth day of July, in the year of Our Lord, one thousand eight hundred and sixty-four, and of the Independence of the United States the eighty-ninth.

By the President: ABRAHAM LINCOLN.
     WILLIAM H. SEWARD, Secretary of State.

To Horace Greeley

Hon. Horace Greely   Washington, D.C.
Dear Sir   July 9. 1864

Your letter of the 7th., with inclosures, received. If you can find, any person anywhere professing to have any proposition of Jefferson Davis in writing, for peace, embracing the restoration of the Union and abandonment of slavery, what ever else it embraces, say to him he may come to me with you, and that if he really brings such proposition, he shall, at the least, have safe conduct, with the paper (and without publicity, if he choose) to the point where you shall have met him. The same, if there be two or more persons. Yours truly

To Thomas Swann and Others

Thomas Swan &   Office U.S. Military Telegraph,
     others   War Department, Washington, D.C.,
Baltimore, Md.   July 10. 9/20 A.M. 1864.

Yours of last night received. I have not a single soldier but whom is being disposed by the Military for the best protection of all. By latest account the enemy is moving on Washington. They can not fly to either place. Let us be vigilant but keep cool. I hope neither Baltimore or Washington will be sacked.

To Ulysses S. Grant

"Cypher"

War Department

Lieut. Gen. Grant   Washington City,

City-Point, Va   July 10– 2.P.M. 1864

Your despatch to Gen. Halleck, referring to what I may think in the present emergency, is shown me. Gen. Halleck says we have absolutely no force here fit to go to the field. He thinks that with the hundred day-men, and invalids we have here, we can defend Washington, and scarcely Baltimore. Besides these, there are about eight thousand not very reliable, under Howe at Harper's Ferry, with Hunter approaching that point very slowly, with what number I suppose you know better than I. Wallace with some odds and ends, and part of what came up with Ricketts, was so badly beaten yesterday at Monocacy, that what is left can attempt no more than to defend Baltimore. What we shall get in from Penn. & N.Y. will scarcely be worth counting, I fear. Now what I think is that you should provide to retain your hold where you are certainly, and bring the rest with you personally, and make a vigorous effort to destroy the enemie's force in this vicinity. I think there is really a fair chance to do this if the movement is prompt. This is what I think, upon your suggestion, and is not an order

To Edwin M. Stanton

Hon. Secretary of War   Executive Mansion,

Sir.   Washington, July 14. 1864.

Your note of to-day, inclosing Gen. Halleck's letter of yesterday, relative to offensive remarks supposed to have been made by the Post-Master-General concerning the Military officers on duty about Washington, is received. The General's letter, in substance demands of me that if I approve the remarks, I shall strike the names of those officers from the rolls; and that if I do not approve them, the Post-Master-General shall be dismissed from the Cabinet. Whether the remarks were really made I do not know; nor do I suppose such knowledge is necessary to a correct response. If they were made I do *not* approve them; and yet, under the circumstances, I would not dismiss a member of the Cabinet therefor. I do not consider what may have been hastily said in a moment of vexation at so severe a loss, is sufficient ground for so grave a step. Besides this, *truth* is generally the best vindication against slander. I propose continuing to be myself the judge as to when a member of the Cabinet shall be dismissed. Yours truly

To Horace Greeley

Hon. Horace Greeley   Executive Mansion
New-York   Washington, July 15, 1864

I suppose you received my letter of the 9th. I have just received yours of the 13 and am disappointed by it. I was not expecting you to *send* me a letter, but to *bring* me a man, or men. Mr. Hay goes to you with my answer to yours of the 13th.

To Horace Greeley

Hon. Horace Greeley   Executive Mansion,
My dear Sir   Washington, July 15. 1864.

Yours of the 13th, is just received; and I am disappointed that you have not already reached here with those Commissioners, if they would consent to come, on being shown my letter to you of the 9th. Inst. Show that and this to them; and if they will come on the terms stated in the former, bring them. I not only intend a sincere effort for peace, but I intend that you shall be a personal witness that it is made. Yours truly

To Ulysses S. Grant

United States Military Telegraph,

Lieut. Gen. Grant   War Department.

City Point, Va.   July 17. 11/25. AM. 1864

In your despatch of yesterday to Gen. Sherman, I find the following, towit: "I shall make a desparate effort to get a position here which will hold the enemy without the necessity of so many men."

Pressed as we are by lapse of time, I am glad to hear you say this; and yet I do hope you may find a way that the effort shall not be desparate in the sense of great loss of life.

Proclamation Calling for 500,000 Volunteers

BY THE PRESIDENT OF THE UNITED STATES OF AMERICA:

A PROCLAMATION

Whereas, by the act approved July 4, 1864, entitled "an act further to regulate and provide for the enrolling and calling out the National forces and for other purposes," it is provided that the President of the United States may, "at his discretion, at any time hereafter, call for any number of men as volunteers, for the respective terms of one, two and three years for military service," and "that in case the quota of or any part thereof, of any town, township, ward of a city, precinct, or election district, or of a county not so subdivided, shall not be filled within the space of fifty days after such call, then the President shall immediately order a draft for one year to fill such quota or any part thereof which may be unfilled."

And whereas, the new enrolment, heretofore ordered, is so far completed as that the aforementioned act of Congress may now be put in operation for recruiting and keeping up the strength of the armies in the field for garrisons, and such military operations as may be required for the purpose of suppressing the rebellion, and restoring the authority of the United States Government in the insurgent States:

Now, therefore, I, Abraham Lincoln, President of the United States, do issue this my call for five hundred thousand volunteers for the military service, Provided, nevertheless, that this call shall be reduced by all credits which may be established under section 8 of the aforesaid act on account of persons who have entered the naval service during the present rebellion, and by credits for men furnished to the military service in excess of calls heretofore made. Volunteers will be accepted under this call for one, two, or three years, as they may elect, and will be entitled to the bounty provided by the law, for the period of service for which they enlist.

And I hereby proclaim, order and direct, that immediately after the fifth day of September, 1864, being fifty days from the date of this call, a draft for troops to serve for one year shall be had in every town, township, ward of a city, precinct or election district or county not so subdivided to fill the quota which shall be assigned to it under this call, or any part thereof, which may be unfilled, by volunteers on the said fifth day of September 1864.

In testimony whereof, I have hereunto set my hand and caused the seal of the United States to be affixed.

Done at the city of Washington, this eighteenth day of July, in the year of our Lord one thousand eight hundred and sixty four, and of the Independence of the United States the eighty-ninth.

By the President: ABRAHAM LINCOLN

     WILLIAM H. SEWARD Secretary of State.

To William T. Sherman

Major General Sherman   Executive Mansion,
Chattahoochee River, Ga.   Washington, July 18. 1864.

I have seen your despatches objecting to agents of Northern States opening recruiting stations near your camps. An act of congress authorizes this, giving the appointment of agents to the States, and not to this Executive government. It is not for the War Department, or myself, to restrain, or modify the law, in it's execution, further than actual necessity may require. To be candid, I was for the passage of the law, not apprehending at the time that it would produce such inconvenience to the armies in the field, as you now cause me to fear. Many of the States were very anxious for it, and I hoped that, with their State bounties, and active exertions, they would get out substantial additions to our colored forces, which, unlike white recruits, help us where they come from, as well as where they go to. I still hope advantage from the law; and being a law, it must be treated as such by all of us. We here, will do what we consistently can to save you from difficulties arising out of it. May I ask therefore that you will give your hearty co-operation?

Offer of Safe Conduct for Peace Negotiators

                      Executive Mansion,
To Whom it may concern: Washington, July 18, 1864.

Any proposition which embraces the restoration of peace,

the integrity of the whole Union, and the abandonment of slavery, and which comes by and with an authority that can control the armies now at war against the United States will be received and considered by the Executive government of the United States, and will be met by liberal terms on other substantial and collateral points; and the bearer, or bearers thereof shall have safe-conduct both ways.

Memorandum on Clement C. Clay

Executive Mansion,
Washington, 1864

Hon. Clement C. Clay, one of the Confederate gentlemen who recently, at Niagara Falls, in a letter to Mr. Greeley, declared that they were *not* empowered to negotiate for peace, but that they *were*, however, in the confidential employment of their government, has prepared a Platform and an Address to be adopted by the Democracy at the Chicago Convention, the preparing of these, and conferring with the democratic leaders in regard to the same, being the confidential employment of their government, in which he, and his confreres are engaged. The following planks are in the Platform—

5. The war to be further prossecuted only to restore the *Union as it was*, and only in such manner, that no further detriment to slave property shall be effected.

6. All negro soldiers and seamen to be at once disarmed and degraded to menial service in the Army and Navy; and no additional negroes to be, on any pretence whatever, taken from their masters.

7 All negroes not having enjoyed actual freedom during the war to be held permanently as slaves; and whether those who shall have enjoyed actual freedom during the war, shall be free to be a legal question.

The following paragraphs are in the Address—

"Let all who are in favor of peace; of arresting the slaughter of our countrymen, of saving the country from bankruptcy & ruin, of securing food & raiment & good wages for the laboring classes; of disappointing the enemies of Democratic &

Republican Government who are rejoicing in the overthrow of their proudest monuments; of vindicating our capacity for self-government, arouse and maintain these principles, and elect these candidates."

                    +   +   +   +   +

"The stupid tyrant who now disgraces the Chair of Washington and Jackson could, any day, have peace and restoration of the Union; and would have them, only that he persists in the war merely to free the slaves."

The convention may not litterally adopt Mr. Clay's Platform and Address, but we predict it will do so substantially. We shall see.

Mr. Clay confesses to his Democratic friends that he is for *peace* and *disunion*; but, he says "You can not elect without a cry of war for the union; but, once elected, we are friends, and can adjust matters somehow." He also says "You will find some difficulty in proving that Lincoln could, if he would, have peace and re-union, because Davis has not said so, and will not say so; but you must assert it, and re-assert it, and stick to it, and it will pass as at least half proved."

c. late July 1864

To Abram Wakeman

Private

                                              Executive Mansion,
Abram Wakeman, Esq   Washington,
My dear Sir: July 25, 1864.

I feel that the subject which you pressed upon my attention in our recent conversation is an important one. The men of the South, recently (and perhaps still) at Niagara Falls, tell us distinctly that they *are* in the confidential employment of the rebellion; and they tell us as distinctly that they are *not* empowered to offer terms of peace. Does any one doubt that what they *are* empowered to do, is to assist in selecting and arranging a candidate and a platform for the Chicago convention? Who could have given them this confidential employment but he who only a week since declared to Jaquess and

Gilmore that he had no terms of peace but the independence of the South—the dissolution of the Union? Thus the present presidential contest will almost certainly be no other than a contest between a Union and a Disunion candidate, disunion certainly following the success of the latter. The issue is a mighty one for all people and all time; and whoever aids the right, will be appreciated and remembered. Yours truly

To James C. Welling

J. C. Welling, Esq   Executive Mansion,
Sir   Washington, July 25. 1864.
     According to the request contained in your note, I have placed Mr. Gibson's letter of resignation in the hands of the President. He has read the letter, and says he accepts the resignation, as he will be glad to do with any other which may be tendered, as this is, for the purpose of taking an attitude of hostility against him. He says he was not aware that he was so much indebted to Mr. Gibson for having accepted the office at first, not remembering that he ever pressed him to do so, or that he gave it otherwise than as was usual, upon request made on behalf of Mr. Gibson. He thanks Mr. Gibson for his acknowledgment that he has been treated with personal kindness and consideration; and he says he knows of but two small draw-backs upon Mr. Gibson's right to still receive such treatment, one of which is that he never could learn of his giving much attention to the duties of his office, and the other is this studied attempt of Mr. Gibson's to stab him
     I am very truly, Your obedient servant   JOHN HAY.

To Edwin M. Stanton

I know not how much is within the legal power of the government in this case; but it is certainly true in equity, that the laboring women in our employment, should be paid at the least as much as they were at the beginning of the war. Will the Secretary of War please have the case fully examined, and so much relief given as can be consistently with the law and the public service.

July 27. 1864

To Ulysses S. Grant

Cypher.

                                    Office U.S. Military Telegraph,
Lieut. Genl. Grant   War Department,
City-Point, Va.   Washington, D.C., August 3, 1864.

I have seen your despatch in which you say "I want Sheridan put in command of all the troops in the field, with instructions to put himself South of the enemy, and follow him to the death. Wherever the enemy goes, let our troops go also." This, I think, is exactly right, as to how our forces should move. But please look over the despatches you may have receved from here, even since you made that order, and discover, if you can, that there is any idea in the head of any one here, of "putting our army *South* of the enemy" or of "following him to the *death*" in any direction. I repeat to you it will neither be done nor attempted unless you watch it every day, and hour, and force it.

To John McMahon

John McMahon   Washington, D.C.
Harmbrook, Bradford Co Penn.   Aug. 6. 1864

The President has received yours of yesterday, and is kindly paying attention to it. As it is my business to assist him whenever I can, I will thank you to inform me, for his use, whether you are either a white man or black one, because in either case, you can not be regarded as an entirely impartial judge. It may be that you belong to a third or fourth class of *yellow* or *red* men, in which case the impartiality of your judgment would be more apparant.

To Stephen G. Burbridge

Major General   Office U.S. Military Telegraph,
   Burbridge   War Department,
Lexington, Ky.   Washington, D.C., August 8.th. 1864.

Last December Mrs. Emily T. Helm, half-sister of Mrs. L. and widow of the rebel general Ben. Hardin Helm stopped here on her way from Georgia to Kentucky, and I gave her a paper, as I remember, to protect her against the mere fact of her being Gen. Helm's widow. I hear a rumor to-day that you recently sought to arrest her, but was prevented by her presenting the paper from me. I do not intend to protect her against the consequences of disloyal words or acts, spoken or done by her since her return to Kentucky, and if the paper given her by me can be construed to give her protection for such words or acts, it is hereby revoked *pro tanto*. Deal with her for current conduct, just as you would with *any other*.

To Nathaniel P. Banks

                              Executive Mansion, Washington,
Major General Banks.   August 9. 1864.

I have just seen the new Constitution adopted by the Convention of Louisiana; and I am anxious that it shall be ratified by the people. I will thank you to let the civil officers in Louisiana, holding under me, know that this, is my wish, and to let me know at once who of them openly declare for the constitution, and who of them, if any, decline to so declare. Yours truly

To Benjamin F. Butler

                              Executive Mansion, Washington,
Major General Butler: August 9, 1864.

Your paper of the   about Norfolk matters is received, as also was your other, on the same general subject dated, I believe some time in February last. This subject has caused considerable trouble, forcing me to give a good deal of time and reflection to it. I regret that crimination and recrimination are mingled in it. I surely need not to assure you that I have no doubt of your loyalty and devoted patriotism; and I must tell you that I have no less confidence in those of Gov. Pierpoint and the Attorney General. The former, at first, as the loyal governor of all Virginia, including that which is now West-Virginia; in organizing and furnishing troops, and in all other proper matters, was as earnest, honest, and efficient to the extent of his means, as any other loyal governor. The inauguration of West-Virginia as a new State left to him, as he assumed, the remainder of the old State; and the insignificance of the parts which are outside of the rebel lines, and consequently within his reach, certainly gives a somewhat farcical air to his dominion; and I suppose he, as well as I, has considered that it could be useful for little else than as a nucleous to add to. The Attorney General only needs to be known to be relieved from all question as to loyalty and thorough devotion to the national cause; constantly restraining as he does, my tendency to clemency for rebels and rebel sympathizers. But he is the Law-Officer of the government, and a believer in the virtue of adhering to law.

Coming to the question itself, the Military occupancy of Norfolk is a necessity with us. If you, as Department commander, find the cleansing of the City necessary to prevent pestilence in your army—street lights, and a fire department, necessary to prevent assassinations and incendiarism among your men and stores—wharfage necessary to land and ship men and supplies—a large pauperism, badly conducted, at a needlessly large expense to the government, and find also that these things, or any of them, are not reasonably well attended to by the civil government, you rightfully may, and must take them into your own hands. But you should do so on your own avowed judgment of a military necessity, and not seem to admit that there is no such necessity, by taking a vote of the people on the question. Nothing justifies the suspending of the civil by the military authority, but military necessity, and of the existence of that necessity the military commander, and not a popular vote, is to decide. And whatever is not within such necessity should be left undisturbed. In your paper of February you fairly notified me that you contemplated taking a popular vote; and, if fault there be, it was my fault that I did not object then, which I probably should have done, had I studied the subject as closely as I have since done. I now think you would better place whatever you feel is necessary to be done, on this distinct ground of military necessity, openly discarding all reliance for what you do, on any election. I also think you should so keep accounts as to show every item of money received and how expended.

The course here indicated does not touch the case when the military commander finding no friendly civil government existing, may, under the sanction or direction of the President, give assistance to the people to inaugerate one.

To Horace Greeley

Private

Hon. Horace Greeley,   Executive Mansion,
Dear Sir: Washington, August 9, 1864.

Herewith is a full copy of the correspondence, and which I have had privately printed, but not made public. The parts of your letters which I wish suppressed, are only those which, as I think, give too gloomy an aspect to our cause, and those which present the carrying of elections as a motive of action. I have, as you see, drawn a red pencil over the parts I wish suppressed.

As to the A. H. Stephens matter, so much pressed by you, I can only say that he sought to come to Washington in the name of the "Confederate States," in a vessel of "The Confederate States Navy," and with no pretence even, that he would bear any proposal for peace; but with language showing that his mission would be Military, and not civil, or diplomatic. Nor has he at any time since pretended that he had terms of peace, so far as I know, or believe. On the contrary, Jefferson Davis has, in the most formal manner, declared that Stephens had no terms of peace. I thought we could not afford to give this quasi acknowledgement of the independence of the Confederacy, in a case where there was not even an intimation of any thing for our good. Still, as the parts of your letters relating to Stephens contain nothing worse than a questioning of my action, I do not ask a suppression of those parts. Yours truly

To Ulysses S. Grant

"*Cypher*"   Office U.S. Military Telegraph,
Lieut. Genl. Grant   War Department,
City-Point, Va.   Washington, D.C., August 14 1864.

The Secretary of War and I concur that you better confer with Gen. Lee and stipulate for a mutual discontinuance of house-burning and other destruction of private property. The time and manner of conference, and particulars of stipulation we leave, on our part, to your convenience and judgment.

To Henry J. Raymond

Hon. Henry J. Raymond   Executive Mansion,
My dear Sir   Washington, August 15, 1864.

I have proposed to Mr Greely that the Niagara correspondence be published, suppressing only the parts of his letters over which the red-pencil is drawn in the copy which I herewith send. He declines giving his consent to the publication of his letters unless these parts be published with the rest. I have concluded that it is better for *me* to submit, for the time, to the consequences of the false position in which I consider he has placed me, than to subject the *country* to the consequences of publishing these discouraging and injurious parts. I send you this, and the accompanying copy, not for publication, but merely to explain to you, and that you may preserve them until their proper time shall come. Yours truly

To Ulysses S. Grant

"Cypher"

Lieut. Gen. Grant   Executive Mansion,
City Point, Va.   Washington, August 17. 1864.

I have seen your despatch expressing your unwillingness to break your hold where you are. Neither am I willing. Hold on with a bull-dog gripe, and chew & choke, as much as possible.

To Charles D. Robinson

Hon. Charles D. Robinson   Executive Mansion,
My dear Sir: Washington, August 17, 1864.

Your letter of the 7th. was placed in my hand yesterday by Gov. Randall.

To me it seems plain that saying re-union and abandonment of slavery would be considered, if offered, is not saying that nothing *else* or *less* would be considered, if offered. But I will not stand upon the mere construction of language. It is true, as you remind me, that in the Greeley letter of 1862, I said: "If I could save the Union without freeing any slave I would do it; and if I could save it by freeing all the slaves I would do it; and if I could save it by freeing some, and leaving others alone I would also do that." I continued in the same letter as follows: "What I do about slavery and the colored race, I do because I believe it helps to save the Union; and what I forbear I forbear because I do not believe it would help to save the Union. I shall do less whenever I shall believe what I am doing hurts the cause; and I shall do more whenever I shall believe doing more will help the cause." All this I said in the utmost sincerity; and I am as true to the whole of it now, as when I first said it. When I afterwards proclaimed emancipation, and employed colored soldiers, I only followed the declaration just quoted from the Greeley letter that "I shall do *more* whenever I shall believe *doing* more will help the cause" The way these measures were to help the cause, was not to be by magic, or miracles, but by inducing the colored people to come bodily over from the rebel side to ours. On this point, nearly a year ago, in a letter to Mr. Conkling, made public at once, I wrote as follows: "But negroes, like other people, act upon motives. Why should they do anything for us if we will do nothing for them? If they stake their lives for us they must be prompted by the strongest motive—even the promise of freedom. And the promise, being made, must be kept." I am sure you will not, on due reflection, say that the promise being made, must be *broken* at the first opportunity. I am sure you would not desire me to say, or to leave an inference, that I am ready, whenever convenient, to join in re-enslaving those who shall have served us in consideration of our promise. As matter of morals, could such treachery by any possibility, escape the curses of Heaven, or of any good man? As matter of policy, to *announce* such a purpose, would ruin the Union cause itself. All recruiting of colored men would instantly cease, and all colored men now in our service, would instantly desert us. And rightfully too. Why should they give their lives for us, with full notice of our purpose to betray them? Drive back to the support of the rebellion the physical force which the colored people now give, and promise us, and neither the present, nor any coming administration, *can* save the Union. Take from us, and give to the enemy, the hundred and thirty, forty, or fifty thousand colored persons now serving us as soldiers, seamen, and laborers, and we can not longer maintain the contest. The party who could elect a President on a War & Slavery Restoration platform, would, of necessity, lose the colored force; and that force being lost, would be as powerless to save the Union as to do any other impossible thing. It is not a question of sentiment or taste, but one of physical force, which may be measured, and estimated as horse-power, and steam power, are measured and estimated. And by measurement, it is more than we can lose, and live. Nor can we, by discarding it, get a white force in place of it. There is a witness in every white mans bosom that he would rather go to the war having the negro to help him, than to help the enemy against him. It is not the giving of one class for another. It is simply giving a large force to the enemy, for *nothing* in return.

In addition to what I have said, allow me to remind you that no one, having control of the rebel armies, or, in fact, having any influence whatever in the rebellion, has offered, or intimated a willingness to, a restoration of the Union, in any event, or on any condition whatever. Let it be constantly borne in mind that no such offer has been made or intimated. Shall we be weak enough to allow the enemy to distract us with an abstract question which he himself refuses to present as a practical one? In the Conkling letter before mentioned, I said: "Whenever you shall have conquered all resistance to the Union, if I shall urge you to continue fighting, it will be an apt time *then* to declare that you will not fight to free negroes." I repeat this now. If Jefferson Davis wishes, for himself, or for the benefit of his friends at the North, to know what I would do if he were to offer peace and re-union, saying nothing about slavery, let him try me.

Speech to the 164th Ohio Regiment, Washington, D.C.

SOLDIERS—You are about to return to your homes and your friends, after having, as I learn, performed in camp a comparatively short term of duty in this great contest. I am greatly obliged to you, and to all who have come forward at the call of their country. I wish it might be more generally and universally understood what the country is now engaged in. We have, as all will agree, a free Government, where every man has a right to be equal with every other man. In this great struggle, this form of Government and every form of human right is endangered if our enemies succeed. There is more involved in this contest than is realized by every one. There is involved in this struggle the question whether your children and my children shall enjoy the privileges we have enjoyed. I say this in order to impress upon you, if you are not already so impressed, that no small matter should divert us from our great purpose. There may be some irregularities in the practical application of our system. It is fair that each man shall pay taxes in exact proportion to the value of his property; but if we should wait before collecting a tax to adjust the taxes upon each man in exact proportion with every other man, we should never collect any tax at all. There may be mistakes made sometimes; things may be done wrong while the officers of the Government do all they can to prevent mistakes. But I beg of you, as citizens of this great Republic, not to let your minds be carried off from the great work we have before us. This struggle is too large for you to be diverted from it by any small matter. When you return to your homes rise up to the height of a generation of men worthy of a free Government, and we will carry out the great work we have commenced. I return to you my sincere thanks, soldiers, for the honor you have done me this afternoon.

August 18, 1864

Speech to the 166th Ohio Regiment, Washington, D.C.

I suppose you are going home to see your families and friends. For the service you have done in this great struggle in which we are engaged I present you sincere thanks for myself and the country. I almost always feel inclined, when I happen to say anything to soldiers, to impress upon them in a few brief remarks the importance of success in this contest. It is not merely for to-day, but for all time to come that we should perpetuate for our children's children this great and free government, which we have enjoyed all our lives. I beg you to remember this, not merely for my sake, but for yours. I happen temporarily to occupy this big White House. I am a living witness that any one of your children may look to come here as my father's child has. It is in order that each of you may have through this free government which we have enjoyed, an open field and a fair chance for your industry, enterprise and intelligence; that you may all have equal privileges in the race of life, with all its desirable human aspirations. It is for this the struggle should be maintained, that we may not lose our birthright—not only for one, but for two or three years. The nation is worth fighting for, to secure such an inestimable jewel.

August 22, 1864

Memorandum on Probable Failure of Re-election

Executive Mansion
Washington, Aug. 23, 1864.

This morning, as for some days past, it seems exceedingly probable that this Administration will not be re-elected. Then it will be my duty to so co-operate with the President elect, as to save the Union between the election and the inauguration; as he will have secured his election on such ground that he can not possibly save it afterwards.

To Henry J. Raymond

Executive Mansion,
Sir: Washington, August 24. 1864.

You will proceed forthwith and obtain, if possible, a conference for peace with Hon. Jefferson Davis, or any person by him authorized for that purpose.

You will address him in entirely respectful terms, at all events, and in any that may be indispensable to secure the conference.

At said conference you will propose, on behalf this government, that upon the restoration of the Union and the national authority, the war shall cease at once, all remaining questions to be left for adjustment by peaceful modes. If this be accepted hostilities to cease at once.

If it be not accepted, you will then request to be informed what terms, if any embracing the restoration of the Union, would be accepted. If any such be presented you in answer, you will forthwith report the same to this government, and await further instructions.

If the presentation of any terms embracing the restoration of the Union be declined, you will then request to be informed what terms of peace would, be accepted; and on receiving any answer, report the same to this government, and await further instructions.

Speech to the 148th Ohio Regiment, Washington, D.C.

SOLDIERS OF THE 148TH OHIO:—I am most happy to meet you on this occasion. I understand that it has been your honorable privilege to stand, for a brief period, in the defense of your country, and that now you are on your way to your homes. I congratulate you, and those who are waiting to bid you welcome home from the war; and permit me, in the name of the people, to thank you for the part you have taken in this struggle for the life of the nation. You are soldiers of the Republic, everywhere honored and respected. Whenever I appear before a body of soldiers, I feel tempted to talk to them of the nature of the struggle in which we are engaged. I look upon it as an attempt on the one hand to overwhelm and destroy the national existence, while, on our part, we are striving to maintain the government and institutions of our fathers, to enjoy them ourselves, and transmit them to our children and our children's children forever.

To do this the constitutional administration of our government must be sustained, and I beg of you not to allow your minds or your hearts to be diverted from the support of all necessary measures for that purpose, by any miserable picayune arguments addressed to your pockets, or inflammatory appeals made to your passions or your prejudices.

It is vain and foolish to arraign this man or that for the part he has taken, or has not taken, and to hold the government responsible for his acts. In no administration can there be perfect equality of action and uniform satisfaction rendered by all. But this government must be preserved in spite of the acts of any man or set of men. It is worthy your every effort. Nowhere in the world is presented a government of so much liberty and equality. To the humblest and poorest amongst us are held out the highest privileges and positions. The present moment finds me at the White House, yet there is as good a chance for your children as there was for my father's.

Again I admonish you not to be turned from your stern purpose of defending your beloved country and its free institutions by any arguments urged by ambitious and designing men, but stand fast to the Union and the old flag. Soldiers, I bid you God-speed to your homes.

August 31, 1864

To Eliza P. Gurney

Eliza P. Gurney.   Executive Mansion,
My esteemed friend.   Washington, September 4. 1864.

I have not forgotten—probably never shall forget—the very impressive occasion when yourself and friends visited me on a Sabbath forenoon two years ago. Nor has your kind letter, written nearly a year later, ever been forgotten. In all, it has been your purpose to strengthen my reliance on God. I am much indebted to the good christian people of the country for their constant prayers and consolations; and to no one of them, more than to yourself. The purposes of the Almighty are perfect, and must prevail, though we erring mortals may fail to accurately perceive them in advance. We hoped for a happy termination of this terrible war long before this; but God knows best, and has ruled otherwise. We shall yet acknowledge His wisdom and our own error therein. Meanwhile we must work earnestly in the best light He gives us, trusting that so working still conduces to the great ends He ordains. Surely He intends some great good to follow this mighty convulsion, which no mortal could make, and no mortal could stay.

Your people—the Friends—have had, and are having, a very great trial. On principle, and faith, opposed to both war and oppression, they can only practically oppose oppression by war. In this hard dilemma, some have chosen one horn and some the other. For those appealing to me on conscientious grounds, I have done, and shall do, the best I could and can, in my own conscience, under my oath to the law. That you believe this I doubt not; and believing it, I shall still receive, for our country and myself, your earnest prayers to our Father in Heaven. Your sincere friend

Response to Presentation of a Bible by the Loyal Colored People of Baltimore, Washington, D.C.

This occasion would seem fitting for a lengthy response to the address which you have just made. I would make one, if prepared; but I am not. I would promise to respond in writing, had not experience taught me that business will not allow me to do so. I can only now say, as I have often before said, it has always been a sentiment with me that all mankind should be free. So far as able, within my sphere, I have always acted as I believed to be right and just; and I have done all I could for the good of mankind generally. In letters and documents sent from this office I have expressed myself better than I now can. In regard to this Great Book, I have but to say, it is the best gift God has given to man.

All the good the Saviour gave to the world was communicated through this book. But for it we could not know right from wrong. All things most desirable for man's welfare, here and hereafter, are to be found portrayed in it. To you I return my most sincere thanks for the very elegant copy of the great Book of God which you present.

September 7, 1864

Memorandum Concerning Ward H. Lamon

The President has known me intimately for nearly twenty years, and has often heard me sing little ditties. The battle of Antietam was fought on the 17th. day of September 1862. On the first day of October, just two weeks after the battle, the President, with some others including myself, started from Washington to visit the Army, reaching Harper's Ferry at noon of that day. In a short while Gen. McClellan came from his Head Quarters near the battle ground, joined the President, and with him, reviewed, the troops at Bolivar Heights that afternoon; and, at night, returned to his Head Quarters, leaving the President at Harper's Ferry. On the morning of the second, the President, with Gen. Sumner, reviewed the troops respectively at Loudon Heights and Maryland Heights, and at about noon, started to Gen. McClellan's Head Quarters, reaching there only in time to see very little before night. On the morning of the third all started on a review of the three corps, and the Cavalry, in the vicinity of the Antietam battle ground. After getting through with Gen. Burnsides Corps, at the suggestion of Gen. McClellan, he and the President left their horses to be led, and went into an ambulance or ambulances to go to Gen. Fitz John Porter's Corps, which was two or three miles distant. I am not sure whether the President and Gen. Mc. were in the same ambulance, or in different ones; but myself and some others were in the same with the President. On the way, and on no part of the battle-ground, and on what suggestion I do not remember, the President asked me to sing the little sad song, that follows, which he had often heard me sing, and had always seemed to like very much. I sang them. After it was over, some one of the party, (I do not think it was the President) asked me to sing something else; and I sang two or three little comic things of which Picayune Butler was one. Porter's Corps was reached and reviewed; then the battle ground was passed over, and the most noted parts examined; then, in succession the Cavalry, and Franklin's Corps were reviewed, and the President and party returned to Gen. McClellan's Head Quarters at the end of a very hard, hot, and dusty day's work. Next day, the 4th. the President and Gen. Mc. visited such of the wounded as still remained in the vicinity, including the now lamented Gen. Richardson; then proceeded to and examined the South-Mountain battle ground, at which point they parted, Gen. McClellan returning to his Camp, and the President returning to Washington, seeing, on the way, Gen Hartsuff, who lay wounded at Frederick Town. This is the whole story of the singing and it's surroundings. Neither Gen. McClellan or any one else made any objection to the singing; the place was not on the battle field, the time was sixteen days after the battle, no dead body was seen during the whole time the president was absent from Washington, nor even a grave that had not been rained on since it was made.

WARD H LAMON

c. September 12, 1864

To Ulysses S. Grant

Executive Mansion, Washington,
Lieut. Genl. Grant   Sep. 12. 1864.

Sheridan and Early are facing each other at a dead lock. Could we not pick up a regiment here and there, to the number of say ten thousand men, and quietly, but suddenly concentrate them at Sheridan's camp and enable him to make a strike? This is but a suggestion. Yours Truly

Draft of Letter to Isaac M. Schermerhorn

Isaac M. Schemerhorn   Executive Mansion,
My dear Sir.   Washington, Sept. 12. 1864.

Yours inviting me to attend a Union Mass Meeting at Buffalo is received. Much is being said about peace; and no man desires peace more ardently than I. Still I am yet unprepared to give up the Union for a peace which, so achieved, could not be of much duration. The preservation of our Union was *not* the sole avowed object for which the war was commenced. It was commenced for precisely the reverse object — *to destroy our Union.* The insurgents commenced it by firing upon the Star of the West, and on Fort Sumpter, and by other similar acts. It is true, however, that the administration accepted the war thus commenced, for the sole avowed object of preserving our Union; and it is not true that it has since been, or will be, prossecuted by this administration, for any other object. In declaring this, I only declare what I can know, and do know to be true, and what no other man can know to be false.

In taking the various steps which have led to my present position in relation to the war, the public interest and my private interest, have been perfectly paralel, because in no other way could I serve myself so well, as by truly serving the Union. The whole field has been open to me, where to choose. No place-hunting necessity has been upon me urging me to seek a position of antagonism to some other man, irrespective of whether such position might be favorable or un-favorable to the Union.

Of course I may err in judgment, but my present position in reference to the rebellion is the result of my best judgment, and according to that best judgment, it is the only position upon which any Executive can or could save the Union. Any substantial departure from it insures the success of the rebellion. An armistice—a cessation of hostilities—is the end of the struggle, and the insurgents would be in peaceable possession of all that has been struggled for. Any different policy in regard to the colored man, deprives us of his help, and this is more than we can bear. We can not spare the hundred and forty or fifty thousand now serving us as soldiers, seamen, and laborers. This is not a question of sentiment or taste, but one of physical force which may be measured and estimated as horse-power and Steam-power are measured and estimated. Keep it and you can save the Union. Throw it away, and the Union goes with it. Nor is it possible for any Administration to retain the service of these people with the express or implied understanding that upon the first convenient occasion, they are to be re-inslaved. It *can* not be; and it *ought* not to be.

To Isaac M. Schermerhorn

Private.

Executive Mansion,
Isaac M. Schemerhorn, Pres't &c.   Washington,
Buffalo, N.Y.   September 12th. 1864.

My dear Sir: Your letter, mentioned in your two telegrams, has not reached me; so that I am without knowledge of its particulars. I beg you to pardon me for having concluded that it is not best for me now to write a general letter to a political meeting. First, I believe it is not customary for one holding the office, and being a candidate for re-election, to do so; and secondly, a public letter must be written with some care, and at some expense of time, so that having begun with your meeting, I could not well refuse others, and yet could not get through with all having equal claims. Please tender to those you represent my sincere thanks for the invitation, and my appeal to their indulgence for having declined their request. Yours very truly.

To William T. Sherman

Executive Mansion, Washington, D.C.
Major General Sherman,   September 19th, 1864.

The State election of Indiana occurs on the 11th. of October, and the loss of it to the friends of the Government would go far towards losing the whole Union cause. The bad effect upon the November election, and especially the giving the State Government to those who will oppose the war in every possible way, are too much to risk, if it can possibly be avoided. The draft proceeds, notwithstanding its strong tendency to lose us the State. Indiana is the only important State, voting in October, whose soldiers cannot vote in the field. Any thing you can safely do to let her soldiers, or any part of them, go home and vote at the State election, will be greatly in point. They need not remain for the Presidential election, but may return to you at once. This is, in no sense, an order, but is merely intended to impress you with the importance, to the army itself, of your doing all you safely can, yourself being the judge of what you can safely do. Yours truly

To Montgomery Blair

Hon. Montgomery Blair   Executive Mansion,
My dear Sir.   Washington, Sep. 23. 1864.

You have generously said to me more than once, that whenever your resignation could be a relief to me, it was at my disposal. The time has come. You very well know that this proceeds from no dissatisfaction of mine with you personally or officially. Your uniform kindness has been unsurpassed by that of any friend; and, while it is true that the war does not so greatly add to the difficulties of your Department, as to those of some others, it is yet much to say, as I most truly can, that in the three years and a half during which you have administered the General Post-Office, I remember no single complaint against you in connection therewith. Yours

To William S. Rosecrans

Executive Mansion,
Major General Rosecrans,   Washington, Sep. 26, 1864

One can not always safely disregard a report, even which one may not believe. I have a report that you incline to deny the soldiers the right of attending the election in Missouri, on the assumed ground that they will get drunk and make disturbance. Last year I sent Gen. Schofield a letter of instruction, dated October 1st, 1863, which I suppose you will find on the files of the Department, and which contains, among other things, the following:

"At elections see that those and only those, are allowed to vote, who are entitled to do so by the laws of Missouri, including as of those laws, the restrictions laid by the Missouri Convention upon those who may have participated in the rebellion."

This I thought right then, and think right now; and I may add I do not remember that either party complained after the election, of Gen. Schofield's action under it. Wherever the law allows soldiers to vote, their officers must also allow it. Please write me on this subject. Yours truly,

To Ulysses S. Grant

"Cypher"   Office U.S. Military Telegraph,
Lieut. Gen. Grant   War Department,
City-Point, Va   Washington, D.C., Sep. 29 1864.

I hope it will lay no constraint on you, nor do harm any way, for me to say I am a little afraid lest Lee sends reenforcements to Early, and thus enables him to turn upon Sheridan.

To Henry W. Hoffman

Executive Mansion,
Hon. Henry W Hoffman   Washington,
My dear Sir: October 10, 1864.

A convention of Maryland has framed a new constitution for the State; a public meeting is called for this evening, at Baltimore, to aid in securing its ratification by the people; and you ask a word from me, for the occasion. I presume the only feature of the instrument, about which there is serious controversy, is that which provides for the extinction of slavery. It needs not to be a secret, and I presume it is no secret, that I wish success to this provision. I desire it on every consideration. I wish all men to be free. I wish the material prosperity of the already free which I feel sure the extinction of slavery would bring. I wish to see, in process of disappearing, that only thing which ever could bring this nation to civil war. I attempt no argument. Argument upon the question is already exhausted by the abler, better informed, and more immediately interested sons of Maryland herself. I only add that I shall be gratified exceedingly if the good people of the State shall, by their votes, ratify the new constitution. Yours truly

Response to Serenade, Washington, D.C.

Friends and Fellow-citizens:

I am notified that this is a compliment paid me by the loyal Marylanders, resident in this District. I infer that the adoption of the new constitution for the State, furnishes the occasion; and that, in your view, the extirpation of slavery constitutes the chief merit of the new constitution. Most heartily do I congratulate you, and Maryland, and the nation, and the world, upon the event. I regret that it did not occur two years sooner, which I am sure would have saved to the nation more money than would have met all the private loss incident to the measure. But it has come at last, and I sincerely hope it's friends may fully realize all their anticipations of good from it; and that it's opponents may, by it's effects, be agreeably and profitably, disappointed.

A word upon another subject.

Something said by the Secretary of State in his recent speech at Auburn, has been construed by some into a threat that, if I shall be beaten at the election, I will, between then and the end of my constitutional term, do what I may be able, to ruin the government.

Others regard the fact that the Chicago Convention adjourned, not *sine die*, but to meet again, if called to do so by a particular individual, as the intimation of a purpose that if their nominee shall be elected, he will at once seize control of the government. I hope the good people will permit themselves to suffer no uneasiness on either point. I am struggling to maintain government, not to overthrow it. I am struggling especially to prevent others from overthrowing it. I therefore say, that if I shall live, I shall remain President until the fourth of next March; and that whoever shall be constitutionally elected therefor in November, shall be duly installed as President on the fourth of March; and that in the interval I shall do my utmost that whoever is to hold the helm for the next voyage, shall start with the best possible chance to save the ship.

This is due to the people both on principle, and under the constitution. Their will, constitutionally expressed, is the ultimate law for all. If they should deliberately resolve to have immediate peace even at the loss of their country, and their liberty, I know not the power or the right to resist them. It is their own business, and they must do as they please with their own. I believe, however, they are still resolved to preserve their country and their liberty; and in this, in office or out of it, I am resolved to stand by them.

I may add that in this purpose to save the country and it's liberties, no classes of people seem so nearly unanamous as the soldiers in the field and the seamen afloat. Do they not have the hardest of it? Who should quail while they do not?

God bless the soldiers and seamen, with all their brave commanders.

October 19, 1864

Proclamation of Thanksgiving

By the President of the United States of America:
a proclamation.

It has pleased Almighty God to prolong our national life another year, defending us with his guardian care against unfriendly designs from abroad, and vouchsafing to us in His mercy many and signal victories over the enemy, who is of our own household. It has also pleased our Heavenly Father to favor as well our citizens in their homes as our soldiers in their camps and our sailors on the rivers and seas with unusual health. He has largely augmented our free population by emancipation and by immigration, while he has opened to us new sources of wealth, and has crowned the labor of our working men in every department of industry with abundant rewards. Moreover, He has been pleased to animate and inspire our minds and hearts with fortitude, courage and resolution sufficient for the great trial of civil war into which we have been brought by our adherence as a nation to the cause of Freedom and Humanity, and to afford to us reasonable hopes of an ultimate and happy deliverance from all our dangers and afflictions.

Now, therefore, I, Abraham Lincoln, President of the United States, do, hereby, appoint and set apart the last Thursday in November next as a day, which I desire to be observed by all my fellow-citizens wherever they may then be as a day of Thanksgiving and Praise to Almighty God the beneficent Creator and Ruler of the Universe. And I do farther recommend to my fellow-citizens aforesaid that on that occasion they do reverently humble themselves in the dust and from thence offer up penitent and fervent prayers and supplications to the Great Disposer of events for a return of the inestimable blessings of Peace, Union and Harmony throughout the land, which it has pleased him to assign as a dwelling place for ourselves and for our posterity throughout all generations.

In testimony whereof, I have hereunto set my hand and caused the seal of the United States to be affixed.

Done at the city of Washington this twentieth day of

October, in the year of our Lord one thousand eight hundred and sixty four, and, of the Independence of the United States the eighty-ninth.

By the President: ABRAHAM LINCOLN
    WILLIAM H SEWARD Secretary of State.

Speech to the 189th New York Volunteers, Washington, D.C.

SOLDIERS: I am exceedingly obliged to you for this mark of respect. It is said that we have the best Government the world ever knew, and I am glad to meet you, the supporters of that Government. To you who render the hardest work in its support should be given the greatest credit. Others who are connected with it, and who occupy higher positions, their duties can be dispensed with, but we cannot get along without your aid. While others differ with the Administration, and, perhaps, honestly, the soldiers generally have sustained it; they have not only fought right, but, so far as could be judged from their actions, they have voted right, and I for one thank you for it. I know you are en route for the front, and therefore do not expect me to detain you long, and will therefore bid you good morning.

October 24, 1864

To Stephen G. Burbridge

                                        Executive Mansion
Major General Burbridge   Washington, Oct. 27. 1864
    It is represented to me that an officer has, by your authority, assessed and collected considerable sums of money from citizens of Allen and Barren counties, Kentucky, to compensate Union men for depredations committed upon them in the vicinity by rebels; and I am petitioned to order the money to be refunded. At most I could not do this without hearing both sides, which, as yet, I have not. I write now to say, that,

in my opinion, in some extreme cases, this class of proceedings becomes a necessity; but that it is liable to—almost inseparable from—great abuses, and therefore should only be sparingly resorted to, and be conducted with great caution; that you, in your department, must be the judge of the proper localities and occasions for applying it; and that it will be well for you to see that your subordinates be at all times ready to account for every dollar, as to why collected, of whom, and how applied. Without this, you will soon find some of them making assessments and collections merely to put money in their own pockets, and it will also be impossible to correct errors in future and better times.

In the case I have mentioned, such good men as Hon. J. R. Underwood & Hon. Henry Grider though not personally interested, have appealed to me in behalf of others. So soon as you can, consistently with your other duties, I will thank you to acquaint yourself with the particulars of this case, and make any correction which may seem to be proper. Yours truly

Endorsement Concerning Thomas Berington

I do not think a man offering himself a volunteer when he could receive a bounty & being rejected for disability should afterwards be compelled to serve without bounty as a drafted man. Let this man be discharged.

Oct. 29. 1864

Speech to the 42nd Massachusetts Regiment, Washington, D.C.

You have completed a term of service in the cause of your country, and on behalf of the nation and myself I thank you. You are going home; I hope you will find all your friends well. I never see a Massachusetts regiment but it reminds me of the difficulty a regiment from that State met with on its passage through Baltimore; but the world has moved since then, and I congratulate you upon having a better time to-day in Baltimore than that regiment had.

To-night, midnight, slavery ceases in Maryland, and this state of things in Maryland is due greatly to the soldiers. Again I thank you for the services you have rendered the country.

October 31, 1864

Response to Serenade, Washington, D.C.

FRIENDS AND FELLOW-CITIZENS: Even before I had been informed by you that this compliment was paid me by loyal citizens of Pennsylvania friendly to me, I had inferred that you were of that portion of my countrymen who think that the best interests of the nation are to be subserved by the support of the present Administration. I do not pretend to say that you who think so embrace all the patriotism and loyalty of the country. But I do believe, and I trust, without personal interest, that the welfare of the country does require that such support and indorsement be given. I earnestly believe that the consequences of this day's work, if it be as you assure me and as now seems probable, will be to the lasting advantage, if not to the very salvation, of the country. I cannot at this hour say what has been the result of the election; but, whatever it may be, I have no desire to modify this opinion—that all who have labored to-day in behalf of the Union organization, have wrought for the best interests of their country and the world, not only for the present, but for all future ages. I am thankful to God for this approval of the people. But while deeply grateful for this mark of their confidence in me, if I know my heart, my gratitude is free from any taint of personal triumph. I do not impugn the motives of any one opposed to me. It is no pleasure to me to triumph over any one; but I give thanks to the Almighty for this evidence of the people's resolution to stand by free government and the rights of humanity.

November 8, 1864

Response to Serenade, Washington, D.C.

It has long been a grave question whether any government, not *too* strong for the liberties of its people, can be strong *enough* to maintain its own existence, in great emergencies.

On this point the present rebellion brought our republic to a severe test; and a presidential election occurring in regular course during the rebellion added not a little to the strain. If the loyal people, *united*, were put to the utmost of their strength by the rebellion, must they not fail when *divided*, and partially paralized, by a political war among themselves?

But the election was a necessity.

We can not have free government without elections; and if the rebellion could force us to forego, or postpone a national election, it might fairly claim to have already conquered and ruined us. The strife of the election is but human-nature practically applied to the facts of the case. What has occurred in this case, must ever recur in similar cases. Human-nature will not change. In any future great national trial, compared with the men of this, we shall have as weak, and as strong; as silly and as wise; as bad and good. Let us, therefore, study the incidents of this, as philosophy to learn wisdom from, and none of them as wrongs to be revenged.

But the election, along with its incidental, and undesirable strife, has done good too. It has demonstrated that a people's government can sustain a national election, in the midst of a great civil war. Until now it has not been known to the world that this was a possibility. It shows also how *sound*, and how *strong* we still are. It shows that, even among candidates of the same party, he who is most devoted to the Union, and most opposed to treason, can receive most of the people's votes. It shows also, to the extent yet known, that we have more men now, than we had when the war began. Gold is good in its place; but living, brave, patriotic men, are better than gold.

But the rebellion continues; and now that the election is over, may not all, having a common interest, re-unite in a common effort, to save our common country? For my own part I have striven, and shall strive to avoid placing any obstacle in the way. So long as I have been here I have not willingly planted a thorn in any man's bosom.

While I am deeply sensible to the high compliment of a re-election; and duly grateful, as I trust, to Almighty God for having directed my countrymen to a right conclusion, as I think, for their own good, it adds nothing to my satisfaction that any other man may be disappointed or pained by the result.

May I ask those who have not differed with me, to join with me, in this same spirit towards those who have?

And now, let me close by asking three hearty cheers for our brave soldiers and seamen and their gallant and skilful commanders.

November 10, 1864

To Stephen A. Hurlbut

Private

Executive Mansion
Major General Hurlbut   Washington, Nov. 14. 1864

Few things, since I have been here, have impressed me more painfully than what, for four or five months past, has appeared as bitter military opposition to the new State Government of Louisiana. I still indulged some hope that I was mistaken in the fact; but copies of a correspondence on the subject, between Gen. Canby and yourself, and shown me today, dispel that hope. A very fair proportion of the people of Louisiana have inaugerated a new State Government, making an excellent new constitution—better for the poor black man than we have in Illinois. This was done under military protection, directed by me, in the belief, still sincerely entertained, that with such a nucleous around which to build, we could get the State into position again sooner than otherwise. In this belief a general promise of protection and support, applicable alike to Louisiana and other states, was given in the last annual message. During the formation of the new government and constitution, they were supported by nearly every loyal person and opposed by every secessionist. And this support, and this opposition, from the respective stand points of the parties, was perfectly consistent and logical. Every Unionist ought to wish the new government to succeed; and every disunionist must desire it to fail. It's failure would gladden the heart of Slidell in Europe, and of every enemy of the old flag in the world. Every advocate of slavery naturally desires to see blasted, and crushed, the liberty promised the black man by the new constitution. But why Gen. Canby and Gen. Hurlbut should join on the same side is to me incomprehensible.

Of course, in the condition of things at New-Orleans, the military must not be thwarted by the civil authority; but when the constitutional convention, for what it deems a breach of previlege, arrests an editor, in no way connected with the military, the military necessity for insulting the Convention, and forcibly discharging the editor, is difficult to perceive. Neither is the military necessity for protecting the people against paying large salaries, fixed by a Legislature of their own choosing, very apparant. Equally difficult to perceive is the military necessity for forcibly interposing to prevent a bank from loaning it's own money to the State. These things, if they have occurred, are, at the best, no better than gratuitous hostility. I wish I could hope that they may be shown to not have occurred. To make assurance against misunderstanding, I repeat that in the existing condition of things in Louisiana, the military must not be thwarted by the civil authority; and I add that on points of difference the commanding general must be judge and master. But I also add that in the exercise of this judgment and control, a purpose, obvious, and scarcely unavowed, to transcend all military necessity, in order to crush out the civil government, will not be overlooked. Yours truly

To William S. Rosecrans

Executive Mansion, Washington,
Major General Rosecrans.   Nov. 19, 1864.

A Major Wolf, as it seems, was under sentence, in your Department, to be executed in retaliation for the murder of a Major Wilson; and I, without any particular knowledge of the facts, was induced by appeals for mercy, to order the suspension of his execution until further order. Understanding that you so desire, this letter places the case again within your control, with the remark only that I wish you to do nothing merely for revenge, but that what you may do, shall be solely done with reference to the security of the future. Yours truly

To Mrs. Lydia Bixby

Executive Mansion,
Washington, Nov. 21, 1864.

Dear Madam,—I have been shown in the files of the War Department a statement of the Adjutant General of Massachusetts, that you are the mother of five sons who have died gloriously on the field of battle.

I feel how weak and fruitless must be any words of mine which should attempt to beguile you from the grief of a loss so overwhelming. But I cannot refrain from tendering to you the consolation that may be found in the thanks of the Republic they died to save.

I pray that our Heavenly Father may assuage the anguish of your bereavement, and leave you only the cherished memory of the loved and lost, and the solemn pride that must be yours, to have laid so costly a sacrifice upon the altar of Freedom. Yours, very sincerely and respectfully,

To John Phillips

Executive Mansion. Washington,

My dear Sir   21st. November, 1864

I have heard of the incident at the polls in your town, in which you bore so honored a part, and I take the liberty of writing to you to express my personal gratitude for the compliment paid me by the suffrage of a citizen so venerable.

The example of such devotion to civic duties in one whose days have already extended an average life time beyond the

Psalmist's limit, cannot but be valuable and fruitful. It is not for myself only, but for the country which you have in your sphere served so long and so well, that I thank you. Your friend and Servant

Annual Message to Congress

Fellow-citizens of the Senate and House of Representatives:

Again the blessings of health and abundant harvests claim our profoundest gratitude to Almighty God.

The condition of our foreign affairs is reasonably satisfactory.

Mexico continues to be a theatre of civil war. While our political relations with that country have undergone no change, we have, at the same time, strictly maintained neutrality between the belligerents.

At the request of the states of Costa Rica and Nicaragua, a competent engineer has been authorized to make a survey of the river San Juan and the port of San Juan. It is a source of much satisfaction that the difficulties which for a moment excited some political apprehensions, and caused a closing of the inter-oceanic transit route, have been amicably adjusted, and that there is a good prospect that the route will soon be reopened with an increase of capacity and adaptation. We could not exaggerate either the commercial or the political importance of that great improvement.

It would be doing injustice to an important South American state not to acknowledge the directness, frankness, and cordiality with which the United States of Colombia have entered into intimate relations with this government. A claims convention has been constituted to complete the unfinished work of the one which closed its session in 1861.

The new liberal constitution of Venezuela having gone into effect with the universal acquiescence of the people, the government under it has been recognized, and diplomatic intercourse with it has opened in a cordial and friendly spirit. The long-deferred Aves Island claim has been satisfactorily paid and discharged.

Mutual payments have been made of the claims awarded by the late joint commission for the settlement of claims between the United States and Peru. An earnest and cordial friendship continues to exist between the two countries, and such efforts as were in my power have been used to remove misunderstanding and avert a threatened war between Peru and Spain.

Our relations are of the most friendly nature with Chile, the Argentine Republic, Bolivia, Costa Rica, Paraguay, San Salvador, and Hayti.

During the past year no differences of any kind have arisen with any of those republics, and, on the other hand, their sympathies with the United States are constantly expressed with cordiality and earnestness.

The claim arising from the seizure of the cargo of the brig Macedonian in 1821 has been paid in full by the government of Chile.

Civil war continues in the Spanish part of San Domingo, apparently without prospect of an early close.

Official correspondence has been freely opened with Liberia, and it gives us a pleasing view of social and political progress in that Republic. It may be expected to derive new vigor from American influence, improved by the rapid disappearance of slavery in the United States.

I solicit your authority to furnish to the republic a gunboat at moderate cost, to be reimbursed to the United States by instalments. Such a vessel is needed for the safety of that state against the native African races; and in Liberian hands it would be more effective in arresting the African slave trade than a squadron in our own hands. The possession of the least organized naval force would stimulate a generous ambition in the republic, and the confidence which we should manifest by furnishing it would win forbearance and favor towards the colony from all civilized nations.

The proposed overland telegraph between America and Europe, by the way of Behring's Straits and Asiatic Russia, which was sanctioned by Congress at the last session, has been undertaken, under very favorable circumstances, by an association of American citizens, with the cordial good-will and support as well of this government as of those of Great Britain and Russia. Assurances have been received from most of the South American States of their high appreciation of the enterprise, and their readiness to co-operate in constructing lines tributary to that world-encircling communication. I

learn, with much satisfaction, that the noble design of a telegraphic communication between the eastern coast of America
and Great Britain has been renewed with full expectation of
its early accomplishment.

Thus it is hoped that with the return of domestic peace the
country will be able to resume with energy and advantage its
former high career of commerce and civilization.

Our very popular and estimable representative in Egypt
died in April last. An unpleasant altercation which arose
between the temporary incumbent of the office and the
government of the Pacha resulted in a suspension of intercourse. The evil was promptly corrected on the arrival of the
successor in the consulate, and our relations with Egypt, as
well as our relations with the Barbary powers, are entirely
satisfactory.

The rebellion which has so long been flagrant in China, has
at last been suppressed, with the co-operating good offices of
this government, and of the other western commercial states.
The judicial consular establishment there has become very
difficult and onerous, and it will need legislative revision to
adapt it to the extension of our commerce, and to the more
intimate intercourse which has been instituted with the government and people of that vast empire. China seems to be
accepting with hearty good-will the conventional laws which
regulate commercial and social intercourse among the western
nations.

Owing to the peculiar situation of Japan, and the anomalous form of its government, the action of that empire in performing treaty stipulations is inconstant and capricious.
Nevertheless, good progress has been effected by the western
powers, moving with enlightened concert. Our own pecuniary claims have been allowed, or put in course of settlement,
and the inland sea has been reopened to commerce. There is
reason also to believe that these proceedings have increased
rather than diminished the friendship of Japan towards the
United States.

The ports of Norfolk, Fernandina, and Pensacola have been
opened by proclamation. It is hoped that foreign merchants
will now consider whether it is not safer and more profitable
to themselves, as well as just to the United States, to resort to

these and other open ports, than it is to pursue, through many hazards, and at vast cost, a contraband trade with other ports which are closed, if not by actual military occupation, at least by a lawful and effective blockade.

For myself, I have no doubt of the power and duty of the Executive, under the law of nations, to exclude enemies of the human race from an asylum in the United States. If Congress should think that proceedings in such cases lack the authority of law, or ought to be further regulated by it, I recommend that provision be made for effectually preventing foreign slave traders from acquiring domicile and facilities for their criminal occupation in our country.

It is possible that, if it were a new and open question, the maritime powers, with the lights they now enjoy, would not concede the privileges of a naval belligerent to the insurgents of the United States, destitute, as they are, and always have been, equally of ships-of-war and of ports and harbors. Disloyal emissaries have been neither less assiduous nor more successful during the last year than they were before that time in their efforts, under favor of that privilege, to embroil our country in foreign wars. The desire and determination of the governments of the maritime states to defeat that design are believed to be as sincere as, and cannot be more earnest than our own. Nevertheless, unforeseen political difficulties have arisen, especially in Brazilian and British ports, and on the northern boundary of the United States, which have required, and are likely to continue to require, the practice of constant vigilance, and a just and conciliatory spirit on the part of the United States as well as of the nations concerned and their governments.

Commissioners have been appointed under the treaty with Great Britain on the adjustment of the claims of the Hudson's Bay and Puget's Sound Agricultural Companies, in Oregon, and are now proceeding to the execution of the trust assigned to them.

In view of the insecurity of life and property in the region adjacent to the Canadian border, by reason of recent assaults and depredations committed by inimical and desperate persons, who are harbored there, it has been thought proper to give notice that after the expiration of six months, the period conditionally stipulated in the existing arrangement with Great Britain, the United States must hold themselves at liberty to increase their naval armament upon the lakes, if they shall find that proceeding necessary. The condition of the border will necessarily come into consideration in connection with the question of continuing or modifying the rights of transit from Canada through the United States, as well as the regulation of imposts, which were temporarily established by the reciprocity treaty of the 5th of June, 1854.

I desire, however, to be understood, while making this statement, that the Colonial authorities of Canada are not deemed to be intentionally unjust or unfriendly towards the United States; but, on the contrary, there is every reason to expect that, with the approval of the imperial government, they will take the necessary measures to prevent new incursions across the border.

The act passed at the last session for the encouragement of emigration has, so far as was possible, been put into operation. It seems to need amendment which will enable the officers of the government to prevent the practice of frauds against the immigrants while on their way and on their arrival in the ports, so as to secure them here a free choice of avocations and places of settlement. A liberal disposition towards this great national policy is manifested by most of the European States, and ought to be reciprocated on our part by giving the immigrants effective national protection. I regard our emigrants as one of the principal replenishing streams which are appointed by Providence to repair the ravages of internal war, and its wastes of national strength and health. All that is necessary is to secure the flow of that stream in its present fullness, and to that end the government must, in every way, make it manifest that it neither needs nor designs to impose involuntary military service upon those who come from other lands to cast their lot in our country.

The financial affairs of the government have been successfully administered during the last year. The legislation of the last session of Congress has beneficially affected the revenues, although sufficient time has not yet elapsed to experience the full effect of several of the provisions of the acts of Congress imposing increased taxation.

The receipts during the year, from all sources, upon the basis of warrants signed by the Secretary of the Treasury, including loans and the balance in the treasury on the first day of July, 1863, were $1,394,796,007 62; and the aggregate disbursements, upon the same basis, were $1,298,056,101 89, leaving a balance in the treasury, as shown by warrants, of $96,739,905 73.

Deduct from these amounts the amount of the principal of the public debt redeemed, and the amount of issues in substitution therefor, and the actual cash operations of the treasury were: receipts, $884,076,646 57; disbursements $865,234,087 86; which leaves a cash balance in the treasury of $18,842,558 71.

Of the receipts, there were derived from customs, $102,316,152 99; from lands, $588,333 29; from direct taxes, $475,648 96; from internal revenue, $109,741,134 10; from miscellaneous sources, $47,511,448 10; and from loans applied to actual expenditures, including former balance, $623,443,929 13.

There were disbursed, for the civil service, $27,505,599 46; for pensions and Indians, $7,517,930 97; for the War Department $690,791,842 97; for the Navy Department $85,733,292 77; for interest of the public debt $53,685,421 69; —making an aggregate of $865,234,087.86, and leaving a balance in the treasury of $18,842,558.71, as before stated.

For the actual receipts and disbursements for the first quarter, and the estimated receipts and disbursements for the three remaining quarters of the current fiscal year, and the general operations of the treasury in detail, I refer you to the report of the Secretary of the Treasury. I concur with him in the opinion that the proportion of moneys required to meet the expenses consequent upon the war derived from taxation should be still further increased; and I earnestly invite your attention to this subject, to the end that there may be such additional legislation as shall be required to meet the just expectations of the Secretary.

The public debt on the first day of July last, as appears by the books of the treasury, amounted to $1,740,690 489 49. Probably, should the war continue for another year, that amount may be increased by not far from five hundred millions. Held as it is, for the most part, by our own people, it has become a substantial branch of national, though private, property. For obvious reasons, the more nearly this property can be distributed among all the people the better. To favor such general distribution, greater inducements to become owners might, perhaps, with good effect, and without injury, be presented to persons of limited means. With this view, I suggest whether it might not be both competent and expedient for Congress to provide that a limited amount of some future issue of public securities might be held by any bona fide purchaser exempt from taxation, and from seizure for debt, under such restrictions and limitations as might be necessary to guard against abuse of so important a privilege. This would enable every prudent person to set aside a small annuity against a possible day of want.

Privileges like these would render the possession of such securities, to the amount limited, most desirable to every person of small means who might be able to save enough for the purpose. The great advantage of citizens being creditors as well as debtors, with relation to the public debt, is obvious. Men readily perceive that they cannot be much oppressed by a debt which they owe to themselves.

The public debt on the first day of July last, although somewhat exceeding the estimate of the Secretary of the Treasury made to Congress at the commencement of the last session, falls short of the estimate of that officer made in the preceding December, as to its probable amount at the beginning of this year, by the sum of $3,995,097 31. This fact exhibits a satisfactory condition and conduct of the operations of the Treasury.

The national banking system is proving to be acceptable to capitalists and to the people. On the twenty-fifth day of November five hundred and eighty-four national banks had been organized, a considerable number of which were conversions from State banks. Changes from State systems to the national system are rapidly taking place, and it is hoped that, very soon, there will be in the United States, no banks of issue not authorized by Congress, and no bank-note circulation not secured by the government. That the government and the people will derive great benefit from this change in the banking systems of the country can hardly be questioned. The national system will create a reliable and permanent influence in support of the national credit, and protect the people against losses in the use of paper money. Whether or not any further legislation is advisable for the suppression of State bank issues, it will be for Congress to determine. It seems quite clear that the treasury cannot be satisfactorily conducted unless the government can exercise a restraining power over the bank-note circulation of the country.

The report of the Secretary of War and the accompanying documents will detail the campaigns of the armies in the field since the date of the last annual message, and also the operations of the several administrative bureaus of the War Department during the last year. It will also specify the measures deemed essential for the national defence, and to keep up and supply the requisite military force.

The report of the Secretary of the Navy presents a comprehensive and satisfactory exhibit of the affairs of that Department and of the naval service. It is a subject of congratulation and laudable pride to our countrymen that a navy of such vast proportions has been organized in so brief a period, and conducted with so much efficiency and success.

The general exhibit of the navy, including vessels under construction on the 1st. of December, 1864, shows a total of 671 vessels, carrying 4,610 guns, and of 510,396 tons, being an actual increase during the year, over and above all losses by shipwreck or in battle, of 83 vessels, 167 guns, and 42,427 tons.

The total number of men at this time in the naval service, including officers, is about 51,000.

There have been captured by the navy during the year 324 vessels, and the whole number of naval captures since hostilities commenced is 1,379, of which 267 are steamers.

The gross proceeds arising from the sale of condemned prize property, thus far reported, amount to $14,396,250 51. A large amount of such proceeds is still under adjudication and yet to be reported.

The total expenditures of the Navy Department of every description, including the cost of the immense squadrons that have been called into existence from the 4th of March, 1861, to the 1st. of November, 1864, are $238,647,262 35.

Your favorable consideration is invited to the various

recommendations of the Secretary of the Navy, especially in regard to a navy yard and suitable establishment for the construction and repair of iron vessels, and the machinery and armature for our ships, to which reference was made in my last annual message.

Your attention is also invited to the views expressed in the report in relation to the legislation of Congress at its last session in respect to prize on our inland waters.

I cordially concur in the recommendation of the Secretary as to the propriety of creating the new rank of vice-admiral in our naval service.

Your attention is invited to the report of the Postmaster General for a detailed account of the operations and financial condition of the Post Office Department.

The postal revenues for the year ending June 30, 1864, amounted to $12,438,253.78 and the expenditures to $12,644,786.20; the excess of expenditures over receipts being $206,652.42.

The views presented by the Postmaster General on the subject of special grants by the government in aid of the establishment of new lines of ocean mail steamships and the policy he recommends for the development of increased commercial intercourse with adjacent and neighboring countries, should receive the careful consideration of Congress.

It is of noteworthy interest that the steady expansion of population, improvement and governmental institutions over the new and unoccupied portions of our country have scarcely been checked, much less impeded or destroyed, by our great civil war, which at first glance would seem to have absorbed almost the entire energies of the nation.

The organization and admission of the State of Nevada has been completed in conformity with law, and thus our excellent system is firmly established in the mountains, which once seemed a barren and uninhabitable waste between the Atlantic States and those which have grown up on the coast of the Pacific ocean.

The territories of the Union are generally in a condition of prosperity and rapid growth. Idaho and Montana, by reason of their great distance and the interruption of communication with them by Indian hostilities, have been only partially organized; but it is understood that these difficulties are about to disappear, which will permit their governments, like those of the others, to go into speedy and full operation.

As intimately connected with, and promotive of, this material growth of the nation, I ask the attention of Congress to the valuable information and important recommendations relating to the public lands, Indian affairs, the Pacific railroad, and mineral discoveries contained in the report of the Secretary of the Interior, which is herewith transmitted, and which report also embraces the subjects of patents, pensions and other topics of public interest pertaining to his department.

The quantity of public land disposed of during the five quarters ending on the 30th of September last was 4,221,342 acres, of which 1,538,614 acres were entered under the homestead law. The remainder was located with military land warrants, agricultural scrip certified to States for railroads, and sold for cash. The cash received from sales and location fees was $1,019,446.

The income from sales during the fiscal year, ending June 30, 1864, was $678,007,21, against $136,077,95 received during the preceding year. The aggregate number of acres surveyed during the year has been equal to the quantity disposed of; and there is open to settlement about 133,000,000 acres of surveyed land.

The great enterprise of connecting the Atlantic with the Pacific States by railways and telegraph lines has been entered upon with a vigor that gives assurance of success, notwithstanding the embarrassments arising from the prevailing high prices of materials and labor. The route of the main line of the road has been definitely located for one hundred miles westward from the initial point at Omaha City, Nebraska, and a preliminary location of the Pacific railroad of California has been made from Sacramento eastward to the great bend of the Truckee river in Nevada.

Numerous discoveries of gold, silver and cinnabar mines have been added to the many heretofore known and the country occupied by the Sierra Nevada and Rocky mountains, and the subordinate ranges, now teems with enterprising labor, which is richly remunerative. It is believed that the product of the mines of precious metals in that region has, during the year, reached, if not exceeded, one hundred millions in value.

It was recommended in my last annual message that our Indian system be remodelled. Congress, at its last session, acting upon the recommendation, did provide for reorganizing the system in California, and it is believed that under the present organization the management of the Indians there will be attended with reasonable success. Much yet remains to be done to provide for the proper government of the Indians in other parts of the country to render it secure for the advancing settler, and to provide for the welfare of the Indian. The Secretary reiterates his recommendations, and to them the attention of Congress is invited.

The liberal provisions made by Congress for paying pensions to invalid soldiers and sailors of the republic, and to the widows, orphans, and dependent mothers of those who have fallen in battle, or died of disease contracted, or of wounds received in the service of their country, have been diligently administered. There have been added to the pension, rolls, during the year ending the 30th day of June last, the names of 16,770 invalid soldiers, and of 271 disabled seamen, making the present number of army invalid pensioners 22,767, and of navy invalid pensioners 712.

Of widows, orphans and mothers, 22 198 have been placed on the army pension rolls, and 248 on the navy rolls. The present number of army pensioners of this class is 25,433, and of navy pensioners 793. At the beginning of the year the number of revolutionary pensioners was 1,430; only twelve of them were soldiers, of whom seven have since died. The remainder are those who, under the law, receive pensions because of relationship to revolutionary soldiers. During the year ending the 30th of June, 1864, $4,504,616,92 have been paid to pensioners of all classes.

I cheerfully commend to your continued patronage the benevolent institutions of the District of Columbia which have hitherto been established or fostered by Congress, and respectfully refer, for information concerning them, and in relation to the Washington aqueduct, the Capitol and other matters of local interest, to the report of the Secretary.

The Agricultural Department, under the supervision of its

present energetic and faithful head, is rapidly commending itself to the great and vital interest it was created to advance. It is peculiarly the people's department, in which they feel more directly concerned than in any other. I commend it to the continued attention and fostering care of Congress.

The war continues. Since the last annual message all the important lines and positions then occupied by our forces have been maintained, and our arms have steadily advanced; thus liberating the regions left in rear, so that Missouri, Kentucky, Tennessee and parts of other States have again produced reasonably fair crops.

The most remarkable feature in the military operations of the year is General Sherman's attempted march of three hundred miles directly through the insurgent region. It tends to show a great increase of our relative strength that our General-in-Chief should feel able to confront and hold in check every active force of the enemy, and yet to detach a well-appointed large army to move on such an expedition. The result not yet being known, conjecture in regard to it is not here indulged.

Important movements have also occurred during the year to the effect of moulding society for durability in the Union. Although short of complete success, it is much in the right direction, that twelve thousand citizens in each of the States of Arkansas and Louisiana have organized loyal State governments with free constitutions, and are earnestly struggling to maintain and administer them. The movements in the same direction, more extensive, though less definite in Missouri, Kentucky and Tennessee, should not be overlooked. But Maryland presents the example of complete success. Maryland is secure to Liberty and Union for all the future. The genius of rebellion will no more claim Maryland. Like another foul spirit, being driven out, it may seek to tear her, but it will woo her no more.

At the last session of Congress a proposed amendment of the Constitution abolishing slavery throughout the United States, passed the Senate, but failed for lack of the requisite two-thirds vote in the House of Representatives. Although the present is the same Congress, and nearly the same members, and without questioning the wisdom or patriotism of those who stood in opposition, I venture to recommend the reconsideration and passage of the measure at the present session. Of course the abstract question is not changed; but an intervening election shows, almost certainly, that the next Congress will pass the measure if this does not. Hence there is only a question of *time* as to when the proposed amendment will go to the States for their action. And as it is to so go, at all events, may we not agree that the sooner the better? It is not claimed that the election has imposed a duty on members to change their views or their votes, any further than, as an additional element to be considered, their judgment may be affected by it. It is the voice of the people now, for the first time, heard upon the question. In a great national crisis, like ours, unanimity of action among those seeking a common end is very desirable—almost indispensable. And yet no approach to such unanimity is attainable, unless some deference shall be paid to the will of the majority, simply because it is the will of the majority. In this case the common end is the maintenance of the Union; and, among the means to secure that end, such will, through the election, is most clearly declared in favor of such constitutional amendment.

The most reliable indication of public purpose in this country is derived through our popular elections. Judging by the recent canvass and its result, the purpose of the people, within the loyal States, to maintain the integrity of the Union, was never more firm, nor more nearly unanimous, than now. The extraordinary calmness and good order with which the millions of voters met and mingled at the polls, give strong assurance of this. Not only all those who supported the Union ticket, so called, but a great majority of the opposing party also, may be fairly claimed to entertain, and to be actuated by, the same purpose. It is an unanswerable argument to this effect, that no candidate for any office whatever, high or low, has ventured to seek votes on the avowal that he was for giving up the Union. There have been much impugning of motives, and much heated controversy as to the proper means and best mode of advancing the Union cause; but on the distinct issue of Union or no Union, the politicians have shown their instinctive knowledge that there is no diversity among the people. In affording the people the fair opportunity of showing, one to another and to the world, this firmness and unanimity of purpose, the election has been of vast value to the national cause.

The election has exhibited another fact not less valuable to be known—the fact that we do not approach exhaustion in the most important branch of national resources—that of living men. While it is melancholy to reflect that the war has filled so many graves, and carried mourning to so many hearts, it is some relief to know that, compared with the surviving, the fallen have been so few. While corps, and divisions, and brigades, and regiments have formed, and fought, and dwindled, and gone out of existence, a great majority of the men who composed them are still living. The same is true of the naval service. The election returns prove this. So many voters could not else be found. The States regularly holding elections, both now and four years ago, to wit, California, Connecticut, Delaware, Illinois, Indiana, Iowa, Kentucky, Maine, Maryland, Massachusetts, Michigan, Minnesota, Missouri, New Hampshire, New Jersey, New York, Ohio, Oregon, Pennsylvania, Rhode Island, Vermont, West Virginia, and Wisconsin cast 3.982.011 votes now, against 3.870.222 cast then, showing an aggregate now of 3.982.011. To this is to be added 33.762 cast now in the new States of Kansas and Nevada, which States did not vote in 1860, thus swelling the aggregate to 4.015.773 and the net increase during the three years and a half of war to 145.551. A table is appended showing particulars. To this again should be added the number of all soldiers in the field from Massachusetts, Rhode Island, New Jersey, Delaware, Indiana, Illinois, and California, who, by the laws of those States, could not vote away from their homes, and which number cannot be less than 90.000. Nor yet is this all. The number in organized Territories is triple now what it was four years ago, while thousands, white and black, join us as the national arms press back the insurgent lines. So much is shown, affirmatively and negatively, by the election. It is not material to inquire *how* the increase has been produced, or to show that it would have been *greater* but for the war, which is probably true. The important fact remains demonstrated, that we have *more* men *now* than we had when the war *began*; that we are not exhausted, nor in process of exhaustion; that we are *gaining* strength, and may, if need be, maintain the contest indefinitely. This as to men. Material resources are now more complete and abundant than ever.

The national resources, then, are unexhausted, and, as we believe, inexhaustible. The public purpose to re-establish and maintain the national authority is unchanged, and, as we believe, unchangeable. The manner of continuing the effort remains to choose. On careful consideration of all the evidence accessible it seems to me that no attempt at negotiation with the insurgent leader could result in any good. He would accept nothing short of severance of the Union—precisely what we will not and cannot give. His declarations to this effect are explicit and oft-repeated. He does not attempt to deceive us. He affords us no excuse to deceive ourselves. He cannot voluntarily reaccept the Union; we cannot voluntarily yield it. Between him and us the issue is distinct, simple, and inflexible. It is an issue which can only be tried by war, and decided by victory. If we yield, we are beaten; if the Southern people fail him, he is beaten. Either way, it would be the victory and defeat following war. What is true, however, of him who heads the insurgent cause, is not necessarily true of those who follow. Although he cannot reaccept the Union, they can. Some of them, we know, already desire peace and reunion. The number of such may increase. They can, at any moment, have peace simply by laying down their arms and submitting to the national authority under the Constitution. After so much, the government could not, if it would, maintain war against them. The loyal people would not sustain or allow it. If questions should remain, we would adjust them by the peaceful means of legislation, conference, courts, and votes, operating only in constitutional and lawful channels. Some certain, and other possible, questions are, and would be, beyond the Executive power to adjust; as, for instance, the admission of members into Congress, and whatever might require the appropriation of money. The Executive power itself would be greatly diminished by the cessation of actual war. Pardons and remissions of forfeitures, however, would still be within Executive control. In what spirit and temper this control would be exercised can be fairly judged of by the past.

A year ago general pardon and amnesty, upon specified terms, were offered to all, except certain designated classes; and, it was, at the same time, made known that the excepted classes were still within contemplation of special clemency. During the year many availed themselves of the general provision, and many more would, only that the signs of bad faith in some led to such precautionary measures as rendered the practical process less easy and certain. During the same time also special pardons have been granted to individuals of the excepted classes, and no voluntary application has been denied. Thus, practically, the door has been, for a full year, open to all, except such as were not in condition to make free choice—that is, such as were in custody or under constraint. It is still so open to all. But the time may come—probably will come—when public duty shall demand that it be closed; and that, in lieu, more rigorous measures than heretofore shall be adopted.

In presenting the abandonment of armed resistance to the national authority on the part of the insurgents, as the only indispensable condition to ending the war on the part of the government, I retract nothing heretofore said as to slavery. I repeat the declaration made a year ago, that "while I remain in my present position I shall not attempt to retract or modify the emancipation proclamation, nor shall I return to slavery any person who is free by the terms of that proclamation, or by any of the Acts of Congress." If the people should, by whatever mode or means, make it an Executive duty to re-enslave such persons, another, and not I, must be their instrument to perform it.

In stating a single condition of peace, I mean simply to say that the war will cease on the part of the government, whenever it shall have ceased on the part of those who began it.

December 6. 1864.

Table showing the aggregate votes in the States named, at the presidential election respectively in 1860 and 1864.

	1860.	1864.
California	118,840	*110,000
Connecticut	77,246	86,616
Delaware	16,039	16,924
Illinois	339,693	348,235
Indiana	272,143	280,645
Iowa	128,331	143,331
Kentucky	146,216	*91,300
Maine	97,918	115,141
Maryland	92,502	72,703
Massachusetts	169,533	175,487
Michigan	154,747	162,413
Minnesota.	34,799	42,534
Missouri	165,538	*90,000
New Hampshire	65,953	69,111
New Jersey	121,125	128,680
New York	675,156	730,664
Ohio	442,441	470,745
Oregon	14,410	†14,410
Pennsylvania.	476,442	572,697
Rhode Island	19,931	22,187
Vermont	42,844	55,811
West Virginia	46,195	33,874
Wisconsin.	152,180	148,513
	3,870,222	3,982,011
Kansas.		17,234
Nevada		16,528
		33,762
		3,982,011
Total		4,015,773
		3,870,222
Net increase		145,551

*Nearly   †Estimated.

Reply to a Southern Woman

THE PRESIDENT'S LAST, SHORTEST, AND BEST SPEECH.

On thursday of last week two ladies from Tennessee came before the President asking the release of their husbands held as prisoners of war at Johnson's Island. They were put off till friday, when they came again; and were again put off to saturday. At each of the interviews one of the ladies urged that her husband was a religious man. On saturday the President ordered the release of the prisoners, and then said to this lady "You say your husband is a religious man; tell him when you meet him, that I say I am not much of a judge of religion, but that, in my opinion, the religion that sets men to rebel and fight against their government, because, as they think, that government does not sufficiently help *some* men to eat their bread on the sweat of *other* men's faces, is not the sort of religion upon which people can get to heaven!"

December 6, 1864, or before

Response to Serenade, Washington, D.C.

FRIENDS AND FELLOW-CITIZENS: I believe I shall never be old enough to speak without embarrassment when I have anything to talk about. [Laughter and cheering.] I have no good news to tell you, and yet I have no bad news to tell. We have talked of elections until there is nothing more to say about them. The most interesting news we now have is from Sherman. We all know where he went in at, but I can't tell where he will come out at. [Cheers and cries, "He'll come out all right."] I will now close by proposing three cheers for Gen. Sherman and the army.

December 6, 1864

To Edward R. S. Canby

                            Executive Mansion, Washington,
Major General Canby: Dec 12, 1864.
I think it is probable that you are laboring under some mis-apprehension as to the purpose, or rather the motive of the

government on two points—*Cotton*, and the new *Louisiana State* Government. It is conceded that the military operations are the *first* in importance; and as to what is indispensable to these operations, the Department Commander must be judge and master. But the other matters mentioned, I suppose to be of public importance also; and what I have attempted in regard to them, is not merely a concession to private interest and pecuniary greed.

As to cotton. By the external blockade, the price is made certainly six times as great as it was. And yet the enemy gets through at least one sixth part as much in a given period, say a year, as if there were no blockade, and receives as much for it, as he would for a full crop in time of peace. The effect in substance is, that we give him six ordinary crops, without the trouble of producing any but the first; and at the same time leave his fields and his laborers free to produce provisions. You know how this keeps up his armies at home, and procures supplies from abroad. For other reasons we cannot give up the blockade, and hence it becomes immensely important to us to get the cotton away from him. Better give him *guns* for it, than let him, as now, get both guns and ammunition for it. But even this only presents part of the public interest to get out cotton. Our finances are greatly involved in the matter. The way cotton goes now carries so much gold out of the country as to leave us paper currency only, and that so far depreciated, as that for every hard dollar's worth of supplies we obtain, we contract to pay two and a half hard dollars hereafter. This is much to be regretted; and while I believe we can live through it at all events, it demands an earnest effort on the part of all to correct it. And if pecuniary greed can be made to aid us in such effort, let us be thankful that so much good can be got out of pecuniary greed.

As to the new State Government of Louisiana. Most certainly there is no worthy object in getting up a piece of machinery merely to pay salaries, and give political consideration to certain men. But it is a worthy object to again get Louisiana into proper practical relations with the nation; and we can never finish this, if we never begin it. Much good work is already done, and surely nothing can be gained by throwing it away.

I do not wish either cotton or the new State Government to take precedence of the military, while the necessity for the military remains; but there is a strong public reason for treating each with so much favor as may not be substantially detrimental to the military.

Allow me a word of explanation in regard to the telegram which you kindly forwarded to Admiral Faragut for me. That telegram was prompted by a piece of secret information inducing me to suspect that the use of a forged paper might be attempted on the Admiral, in order to base a claim that we had raised our own blockade.

I am happy in the hope that you are almost well of your late and severe wound   Yours very truly,

To William T. Sherman

Executive Mansion, Washington,
My dear General Sherman.   Dec. 26, 1864.

Many, many, thanks for your Christmas-gift—the capture of Savannah.

When you were about leaving Atlanta for the Atlantic coast, I was *anxious*, if not fearful; but feeling that you were the better judge, and remembering that "nothing risked, nothing gained" I did not interfere. Now, the undertaking being a success, the honor is all yours; for I believe none of us went farther than to acquiesce. And, taking the work of Gen. Thomas into the count, as it should be taken, it is indeed a great success. Not only does it afford the obvious and immediate military advantages; but, in showing to the world that your army could be divided, putting the stronger part to an important new service, and yet leaving enough to vanquish the old opposing force of the whole—Hood's army—it brings those who sat in darkness, to see a great light. But what next? I suppose it will be safer if I leave Gen. Grant and yourself to decide.

Please make my grateful acknowledgments to your whole army, officers and men. Yours very truly

To Edwin M. Stanton

Executive Mansion, Washington,
Hon. Secretary of War.   Dec. 31, 1864.

You may remember that some time in June last (I think) an Assistant Inspector General on Col. Speer's staff, in Gen. Butler's army, by name Andrew J. Smith, was convicted of a rape upon a colored girl. Gen. Butler, Mr. Holt, and yourself, each in turn, on examination of the evidence, thought there was no doubt of his guilt, while I thought there was some slight room for doubt on the question of personal identification. I concluded however, to let him suffer a while, and then discharge him. Twice within two or three weeks I made a short order for his pardon for the unexecuted part of the sentence, which, however it seems has not yet been done. Let it be done now. Yours truly

Reply to Delegation of Kentuckians, Washington, D.C.

You howled when Butler went to New-Orleans. Others howled when he was removed from that command. Somebody has been howling ever since at his assignment to military command. How long will it be before you, who are howling for his assignment to rule Kentucky, will be howling to me to remove him?

January 2, 1865

To Edwin M. Stanton

Hon. Sec. of War   Executive Mansion,
Dear Sir,   Washington, Jan. 5, 1865.

Since parting with you, it has occurred to me to say that while Gen. Sherman's *"get a good ready"* is appreciated, and is not to be overlooked, *time*, now that the enemy is wavering, is more important than ever before. Being on the down-hill, & some what confused, keeping him going. Please say so much to Genl. S. Yours truly

To Grenville M. Dodge

Major General Dodge.   Executive Mansion
St. Louis, Mo.   Washington, January 15, 1865

It is represented to me that there is so much irregular violence in Northern Missouri as to be driving away the people and almost depopulating it. Please gather information, and consider whether an appeal to the people there to go to their homes, and let one another alone, recognizing as a full right of protection for each, that he lets others alone, and banning only him who refuses to let others alone, may not enable you to withdraw the troops, their presence itself a cause of irritation and constant apprehension, and thus restore peace and quiet & returning prosperity. Please consider this and telegraph or write me.

To Ulysses S. Grant

                        Executive Mansion, Washington,
Lieut. General Grant: Jan. 19, 1865.

Please read and answer this letter as though I was not President, but only a friend. My son, now in his twenty second year, having graduated at Harvard, wishes to see something of the war before it ends. I do not wish to put him in the ranks, nor yet to give him a commission, to which those who have already served long, are better entitled, and better qualified to hold. Could he, without embarrassment to you, or detriment to the service, go into your Military family with some nominal rank, I, and not the public, furnishing his necessary means? If no, say so without the least hesitation, because I am as anxious, and as deeply interested, that you shall not be encumbered as you can be yourself. Yours truly

To Joseph J. Reynolds

                        Executive Mansion Washington,
Major General Reynolds.   Jan. 20. 1865

It would appear by the accompanying papers that Mrs. Mary E. Morton is the owner, independently of her husband, of a certain building, premises and furniture, which she, with her children, has been occupying and using peaceably during the war, until recently, when the Provost-Marshal, has, in the name of the U.S. government, seized the whole of said property, and ejected her from it. It also appears by her statement to me, that her husband went off in the rebellion at the beginning, wherein he still remains.

It would seem that this seizure has not been made for any Military object, as for a place of storage, a hospital, or the like, because this would not have required the seizure of the furniture, and especially not the return of furniture previously taken away.

The seizure must have been on some claim of *confiscation*, a matter of which the courts, and *not* the Provost-Marshals, or other military officers are to judge. In this very case, would probably be the questions "Is either the husband or wife a traitor?" "Does the property belong to the husband or to the wife?" "Is the property of the wife confiscable for the treason of the husband?" and other similar questions, all which it is ridiculous for a Provost-Marshal to assume to decide.

The true rule for the Military is to seize such property as is needed for Military uses and reasons, and let the rest alone. Cotton and other staple articles of commerce are seizable for military reasons. Dwelling-houses & furniture are seldom so. If Mrs. Morton is playing traitor, to the extent of practical injury, seize her, but leave her house to the courts. Please revise and adjust this case upon these principles. Yours &c

Reply to Philadelphia Delegation, Washington, D.C.

REVEREND SIR, AND LADIES AND GENTLEMEN: I accept, with emotions of profoundest gratitude, the beautiful gift you have been pleased to present to me. You will, of course, expect that I acknowledge it. So much has been said about Gettysburg, and so well said, that for me to attempt to say more may, perhaps, only serve to weaken the force of that which has already been said. A most graceful and eloquent tribute was paid to the patriotism and self-denying labors of the American ladies, on the occasion of the consecration of the National Cemetery at Gettysburg, by our illustrious friend, Edward Everett, now, alas! departed from earth. His life was a truly great one, and, I think, the greatest part of it was that which crowned its closing years. I wish you to read, if you have not already done so, the glowing, and eloquent, and truthful words which he then spoke of the women of America. Truly, the services they have rendered to the defenders of our country in this perilous time, and are yet rendering, can never be estimated as they ought to be. For your kind wishes to me, personally, I beg leave to render you, likewise, my sincerest thanks. I assure you they are reciprocated. And now, gentlemen and ladies, may God bless you all.

January 24, 1865

Response to Serenade, Washington, D.C.

The President said he supposed the passage through Congress of the Constitutional amendment for the abolishment of Slavery throughout the United States, was the occasion to which he was indebted for the honor of this call. [Applause.] The occasion was one of congratulation to the country and to the whole world. But there is a task yet before us—to go forward and consummate by the votes of the States that which Congress so nobly began yesterday. [Applause and cries—"They will do it," &c.] He had the honor to inform those present that Illinois had already to-day done the work. [Applause.] Maryland was about half through; but he felt proud that Illinois was a little ahead. He thought this measure was a very fitting if not an indispensable adjunct to the winding up of the great difficulty. He wished the reunion of all the States perfected and so effected as to remove all causes of disturbance in the future; and to attain this end it was necessary that the original disturbing cause should, if possible, be rooted out. He thought all would bear him witness that he had never shrunk from doing all that he could to eradicate Slavery by issuing an emancipation proclamation. [Applause.] But that proclamation falls far short of what the amendment will be when fully consummated. A question might be raised whether the proclamation was legally valid. It might be added that it only aided those who came into our lines and that it was inoperative as to those who did not give themselves up, or that it would have no effect upon the children of the slaves born hereafter. In fact it would be urged that it did not meet the evil. But this amendment is a King's cure for all the evils. [Applause.] It winds the whole thing up. He would repeat that it was the fitting if not indispensable adjunct to the consummation of the great game we are playing. He could not but congratulate all present, himself, the country and the whole world upon this great moral victory.

February 1, 1865

To the Senate and House of Representatives

Fellow citizens of the Senate, and House of Representatives.

I respectfully recommend that a Joint Resolution, substantially as follows, be adopted so soon as practicable, by your honorable bodies.

"Resolved by the Senate and House of Representatives, of the United States of America in congress assembled: That the President of the United States is hereby empowered, in his discretion, to pay four hundred millions of dollars to the States of Alabama, Arkansas, Delaware, Florida, Georgia, Kentucky, Louisiana, Maryland Mississippi, Missouri, North Carolina, South Carolina, Tennessee, Texas, Virginia, and West-Virginia, in the manner, and on the conditions following, towit: The payment to be made in six per cent government bonds, and to be distributed among said States *pro rata* on their respective slave populations, as shown by the census of 1860; and no part of said sum to be paid unless all resistance to the national authority shall be abandoned and cease, on or before the first day of April next; and upon such abandonment and ceasing of resistance, one half of said sum to be paid in manner aforesaid, and the remaining half to be paid only upon the amendment of the national constitution recently proposed by congress, becoming valid law, on or before the first day of July next, by the action thereon of the requisite number of States"

The adoption of such resolution is sought with a view to embody it, with other propositions, in a proclamation looking to peace and re-union.

Whereas a Joint Resolution has been adopted by congress in the words following, towit

Now therefore I, Abraham Lincoln, President of the United States, do proclaim, declare, and make known, that on the conditions therein stated, the power conferred on the Executive in and by said Joint Resolution, will be fully exercised; that war will cease, and armies be reduced to a basis of peace; that all political offences will be pardoned; that all property, except slaves, liable to confiscation or forfeiture, will be released therefrom, except in cases of intervening interests of third parties; and that liberality will be recommended to congress upon all points not lying within executive control.

Feb. 5. 1865

To-day these papers, which explain themselves, were drawn up and submitted to the Cabinet & unanamously disapproved by them.

To William Lloyd Garrison

Executive Mansion, Washington,

My Dear Mr. Garrison   7 February, 1865.

I have your kind letter of the 21st of January, and can only beg that you will pardon the seeming neglect occasioned by my constant engagements. When I received the spirited and admirable painting "Waiting for the Hour" I directed my Secretary not to acknowledge its arrival at once, preferring to make my personal acknowledgment of the thoughtful kindness of the donors; and waiting for some leisure hour, I have committed the discourtesy of not replying at all.

I hope you will believe that my thanks though late, are most cordial, and I request that you will convey them to those associated with you in this flattering and generous gift.

I am very truly   Your friend and Servant

To John Glenn

"Cypher"

Lt. Col. Glenn.   Executive Mansion
Commanding Post at   Washington,
Henderson, Ky.   Feb. 7. 1865

Complaint is made to me that you are forcing negroes into the Military service, and even torturing them—riding them on rails and the like—to extort their consent. I hope this may be a mistake. The like must not be done by you, or any one under you. You must not force negroes any more than white men. Answer me on this.

To the Senate and House of Representatives

To the Honorable, the Senate and House of Representatives:

The Joint Resolution entitled, "Joint Resolution declaring certain States not entitled to representation in the Electoral College," has been signed by the Executive, in deference to the view of Congress implied in its passage and presentation to him. In his own view, however, the two Houses of Congress, convened under the Twelfth Article of the Constitution, have complete power to exclude from counting all electoral votes deemed by them to be illegal; and it is not competent for the Executive to defeat or obstruct that power by a veto, as would be the case if his action were at all essential in the matter. He disclaims all right of the Executive to interfere in any way in the matter of canvassing or counting electoral votes; and he also disclaims that by signing said Resolution he has expressed any opinion on the recitals of the preamble or any judgment of his own upon the subject of the Resolution.

Executive Mansion
February 8, 1865.

To the House of Representatives

To the Honorable, the House of Representatives.

In response to your resolution of the 8th. Inst. requesting information in relation to a conference recently held in Hampton Roads I have the honor to state that on the day of the date I gave Francis P. Blair *senr* a card written on as follows, towit:

> Allow the bearer, F. P. Blair, Senr. to pass our lines, go South and return
>
> Dec. 28. 1864   A. LINCOLN

That at the time I was informed that Mr. Blair sought the card as a means of getting to Richmond, Va. but he was given no authority to speak or act for the government; nor was I informed of any thing he would say or do on his own account, or otherwise. Afterwards Mr. Blair told me that he had been to Richmond, and had seen Mr. Jefferson Davis; and he Mr. B. at the same time left with me a manuscript letter, as follows, towit:

> F. P. Blair Esqr.   Richmond Va
> Sir: 12 Jany 65
>
> I have deemed it proper and probably desirable to you to give you in this form the substance of remarks made by me to be repeated by you to Presdt. Lincoln &c &c
>
> I have no disposition to find obstacles in forms, and am willing now as heretofore to enter into negociations for the restoration of Peace; am ready to send a commission whenever I have reason to suppose it will be received, or to receive a commission if the U.S. Govt. shall choose to send one. That notwithstanding the rejection of our former offers, I would if you could promise, that a Commissioner, Minister or other Agent would be received, appoint one immediately and renew the effort to enter into conference with a view to secure peace to the two countries. Yrs &c   JEFFN DAVIS

Afterwards, and with the view that it should be shown to Mr. Davis I wrote and delivered to Mr. Blair a letter as follows, to-wit:

> F. P. Blair, Esq   Washington,
> Sir: Jan. 18. 1865
>
> Your having shown me Mr. Davis' letter to you of the 12th. Inst. you may say to him that I have constantly been, am now, and shall con-

tinue, ready to receive any agent whom he, or any other influential person now resisting the national authority, may informally send to me with the view of securing peace to the people of our one common country. Yours &c   A. LINCOLN.

Afterwards Mr. Blair dictated for and authorized me to make an entry on the back of my retained copy of the letter last above recited, which entry is as follows.

January 28. 1865
To-day Mr. Blair tells me that on the 21st. Inst. he delivered to Mr. Davis the original of which the within is a copy, and left it with him; that at the time of delivering it, Mr. Davis read it over twice in Mr. Blair's presence, at the close of which he, Mr. B. remarked that the part about "our one common country" related to the part of Mr. D's letter about "the two countries" to which Mr. D. replied that he so understood it.
                                                                    A. LINCOLN

Afterwards the Secretary of War placed in my hands the following telegram, indorsed by him, as appears.

Office U.S. Military Telegraph,
Cipher   War Department.
    The following Telegram received at Washington, M. Jan 29. 1865.
            From Hd Qrs Army of James 6.30 pm 1865.
Hon. Edwin M. Stanton. Secretary of War.   Jan. 29.
    The following dispatch just rec'd from Maj. Gen. Parke, who refers it to me for my action. I refer it to you in Lieut Gen. Grant's absence.
                        E. O. C. ORD   Maj. Gen. Comd'g

                            "Hd Qrs A of Potomac 4 P.M. Jan. 29. 1865.
Maj. Gen. E. O. C. Ord   Hd Qrs A of J.
    The following dispatch is forwarded to you, for your action. Since I have no knowledge of Gen. Grant's having had any understanding of this kind I refer the matter to you as the ranking officer present in the two Armies.   Signed JNO. G. PARKE "Maj. Gen. Comd'g"

                    "From Hd Qrs 9th A. Corps 29.
Maj. Gen. Jno. G. Parke, Hd Qrs A. of P.
    Alex H. Stevens, R. M. T. Hunter & W. J. A. Campbell desire to cross my lines in accordance with an understanding claimed to exist with Lt. Gen Grant, on their way to Washington as peace Commissioners. Shall they be admitted? They desire an early answer to come through immediately   Would like to reach City Point tonight if they can. If they cannot do this they would like to come through at 10 A.M. to-morrow morning.
            Signed   O. B. WILCOX   Maj Gen. Cmdg   "9th Corps"

Respectfully referred to the President for his instructions as he may be
pleased to give   EDWIN M STANTON   Sec of War
   8.30 PM Jan 29. 1865

It appears that about the time of placing the foregoing telegram in my hands, the Secretary of War despached Gen. Ord
as follows, to-wit:

Copy   War Department Washington City
Maj Gen Ord.   Jany 29th 1865 10. P.M.
   This Department has no knowledge of any understanding by Genl
Grant to allow any person to come within his lines as commissioners of
any sort. You will therefore allow no one to come into your lines under
such character or profession, until you receive the President's instruc-
tions, to whom your telegram will be submitted for his directions
                         (signed) EDWIN M. STANTON   Sec'y of War
   Sent in Cipher at 2. A.M. 30th

Afterwards, by my direction, the Secretary of War telegraphed
Gen. Ord as follows, towit:

Copy.
Maj. Gen. E. O. C. Ord,   War Department   Washington D.C.
Hd. Qrs. Army James.   10.30 A.M. January 30. 1865.
   By direction of the President you are instructed to inform the three
gentlemen, Messrs Stephens, Hunter and Campbell, that a messenger
will be dispatched to them at, or near where they now are, without
unnecessary delay.   Signed EDWIN M. STANTON   Secretary of War.

Afterwards I prepared and put into the hands of Major
Thomas T. Eckert, the following instructions and message.

Major T. T. Eckert   Executive Mansion
Sir.   Washington, Jan. 30. 1865
   You will proceed with the documents placed in your hands; and, on
reaching Gen. Ord, will deliver him the letter addressed to him by the
Secretary of War; then, by Gen. Ord's assistance, procure an interview
with Messrs. Stephens Hunter and Campbell, or any of them, deliver to
him or them the paper on which your own letter is written, note on the
copy which you retain, the time of delivery and to whom delivered, receive their answer in writing waiting a reasonable time for it, and which,
if it contain their decision to come through, without further condition,
will be your warrant to ask Gen Ord to pass them through as directed in
the letter of the Secretary of War to him. If by their answer they decline
to come, or propose other terms, do not have them passed through. And
this being your whole duty, return and report to me. Yours truly
                                            A. LINCOLN

Messrs Alex H. Stephens, J. A. Campbell & R. M. T. Hunter

Gentlemen: I am instructed by the President of the United States to place this paper in your hands with the information that if you pass through the U.S. Military lines it will be understood that you do so for the purpose of an informal conference, on the basis of the letter, a copy of which is on the reverse side of this sheet, and that if you choose to pass on such understanding, and so notify me in writing, I will procure the Commanding General to pass you through the lines, and to Fortress-Monroe, under such military precautions as he may deem prudent; and, at which place you will be met in due time by some person or persons for the purpose of such informal conference. And further that you shall have protection, safe-conduct, and safe return, in all events.   THOS. T. ECKERT.

City Point Va.   Maj & A.D.C.
February 1st. 1865.

Afterwards, but before Major Eckert had departed, the following despatch was received from Gen. Grant

                                        Office U.S. Military Telegraph,
            Cipher   War Department.
The following Telegram received at Washington, M. Jan. 31. 1865.
His Excellency Abraham Lincoln.   From City Point Va.
President of the U.S.   10.30 AM Jan. 31. 1865.

The following communication was received here last evening.
"Lieut. Gen. U.S. Grant   Petersburg Va.
        Comd'g Armies U.S.   Jan. 30. 1865.
Sir: We desire to pass your lines under safe conduct and to proceed to Washington to hold a conference with President Lincoln upon the subject of the existing war, and with a view of ascertaining upon what terms it may be terminated, in pursuance of the course indicated by him in his letter to Mr Blair of January 18th. 1865, of which we presume you have a copy, and if not, we wish to see you in person if convenient, and to confer with you upon the subject. Signed, Very Respy Yours
                                        ALEXANDER STEVENS
                                        J. A. CAMPBELL
                                        R. M. T. HUNTER"
I have sent directions to receive these gentlemen and expect to have them at my Quarters this evening awaiting your instructions.
            U. S. GRANT   Lieut Genl   Comdg Armies US

This, it will be perceived, transferred Gen. Ord's agency in the matter to Gen. Grant. I resolved, however to send Major Eckert forward with his Message, and accordingly telegraphed Gen. Grant as follows, towit:

Telegram   Copy.

Lieut Genl Grant   Executive Mansion
City Point Va.   Washington Jany 31st. 1865

A messenger is coming to you on the business contained in your despatch. Detain the gentlemen in comfortable quarters until he arrives and then act upon the message he brings, as far as applicable, it having been made up to pass through Genl Ord's hands, and when the gentlemen were supposed to be beyond our lines   (signed)   A. LINCOLN

Sent in Cipher at 1.30. P.M.

When Major Eckert departed he bore with him a letter of the Secretary of War to Gen. Grant as follows, towit:

Letter   Copy   War Department   Washington D.C.
Lt Genl Grant   Comd'g &c.   Jany 30th 1865

General: The President desires that you will please procure for the bearer, Major Thomas T. Eckert, an interview with Messrs Stephens, Hunter, & Campbell,—and if on his return to you he requests it—pass them through our lines to Fortress Monroe by such route and under such Military precautions as you may deem prudent, giving them protection & comfortable quarters while there; and that you let none of this, have any effect upon your movements or plans.

By order of the President
                    (signed)   EDWIN M. STANTON   Secretary of War

Supposing the proper point to be then reached I despatched the Secretary of State with the following instructions, Major Eckert, however, going ahead of him.

Hon. William H. Seward.   Executive Mansion
Secretary of State.   Washington, Jan. 31. 1865

You will proceed to Fortress-Monroe, Virginia, there to meet, and informally confer with Messrs. Stephens, Hunter, and Campbell, on the basis of my letter to F. P. Blair, Esq. of Jan. 18. 1865, a copy of which you have.

You will make known to them that three things are indispensable, towit:

1   The restoration of the National authority throughout all the States.
2   No receding by the Executive of the United States, on the Slavery question, from the position assumed thereon, in the late Annual Message to Congress, and on preceding documents.
3. No cessation of hostilities short of an end of the war, and the disbanding of all forces hostile to the government.

You will inform them that all propositions of theirs, not inconsistent with the above, will be considered and passed upon, in a spirit of sincere liberality.

You will hear all they may choose to say, and report it to me.

You will not assume to definitely consummate any thing. Yours &c
ABRAHAM LINCOLN.

On the day of it's date the following telegram was sent to Gen. Grant.

Telegram   Copy.
Lieut Genl Grant   War Department   Washington D.C.
City Point Va.   Feby 1st. 1865
    Let nothing which is transpiring, change, hinder, or delay your Military movements, or plans   (signed) A. LINCOLN
    Sent in cipher at 9.30 a.m

Afterwards the following despatch was received from Gen. Grant.

In Cipher   Office U.S. Military Telegraph,
                                            War Department.
The following Telegram received at Washington,
    2.30 P.M. Feby 1st. 1865
His Excellency A. Lincoln   From City Point Va
Prest U.S.   Feb'y 1st. 12.30 P.M 1865
    Your despatch received; there will be no armistice in consequence of the presence of Mr Stephens and others within our lines. The troops are kept in readiness to move at the shortest notice if occasion should justify it   U.S. GRANT   Lieut Genl

To notify Major Eckert that the Secretary of State would be at Fortress-Monroe, and to put them in communication the following despatch was sent.

Telegram   Copy
Maj T. T. Eckert   War Department Washington D.C.
Care Genl Grant   City Point Va.   Feby 1st. 1865
    Call at Fortress Monroe & put yourself under direction of Mr S. whom you will find there   (signed) A. LINCOLN
    Sent in cipher at 5.30 P.M.

On the morning of the 2nd. Inst. the following telegrams were received by me respectively from the Secretary of State and Major Eckert.

Recd 4 30 AM   Feb 2nd   United States Military Telegraph,
    In cipher   War Department.
The President U.S.   Fort Monroe Va 11 30 PM Feb 1. 1865
    Arrived at ten (10) this evening. Richmond party not here. I remain here.   WM H. SEWARD

Recd   United States Military Telegraph,
In cipher Feb 2nd.   War Department.
His Excellency A Lincoln   City Point Va
President U.S.   10 PM Feb 1. 1865
    I have the honor to report the delivery of your communication and my
letter at four fifteen 4.15 this afternoon, to which I received a reply at six
(6) P.M, but not satisfactory.
    At eight (8) PM the following note addressed to Genl Grant was re-
ceived.

To "Lt Gen Grant,   City Point Va
Sir,   Feb 1. 1865"
    "We desire to go to Washington City to confer informally with the
President personally in reference to the matters mentioned in his letter to
Mr Blair of the eighteenth 18th January ultimo, without any personal
compromise on any question in the letter.
    "We have the permission to do so from the authorities in Richmond."
Very Respectfully Yours"   (signed)   "ALEX H. STEPHENS
                                              "R. M T. HUNTER
                                              "J. A CAMPBELL"

At nine thirty (9.30) P.M I notified them that they could not proceed
further unless they complied with the terms expressed in my letter. The
point of meeting designated, in above note, would not in my opinion, be
insisted upon   Think Fort Monroe would be acceptable. Having complied with my instructions, I will return to Washington to-morrow unless otherwise ordered.   THOS T. ECKERT   Maj &c

On reading this despatch of Major Eckert I was about to recall him and the Secretary of State when the following telegram of Gen. Grant to the Secretary of War was shown me.

                                  Office U.S. Military Telegraph,
In cipher   War Department.
The following Telegram received at Washington,
    4.35 A.M. Feby 2nd. 1865
        From City Point Va. Feby 1st. 10.30 P.M 1865
Hon Edwin M Stanton   Secy of War.
    Now that the interview between Maj. Eckert, under his written in-
structions, and Mr Stevens & party, has ended I will state confidentially,
but not officially to become a matter of record, that I am convinced,
upon conversation with Messrs Stevens & Hunter that their intentions
are good and their desire sincere to restore peace and union. I have not
felt myself at liberty to express even views of my own or to account for
my reticency. This has placed me in an awkward position which I could
have avoided by not seeing them in the first instance. I fear now their
going back without any expression from any one in authority will have a

bad influence. At the same time I recognize the difficulties in the way of receiving these informal commissioners at this time and do not know what to recommend. I am sorry however that Mr Lincoln cannot have an interview with the two named in this despatch if not all three now within our lines. Their letter to me was all that the Presidents instructions contemplated, to secure their safe conduct if they had used the same language to Maj Eckert   (signed)   U.S. GRANT   Lt Genl

This despatch of Gen. Grant changed my purpose; and, accordingly, I telegraphed him and the Secretary of State respectively as follow.

Copy.   War Department
Lieut Genl Grant   Washington D.C.
City Point Va.   Feby 2nd. 1865
    Say to the gentlemen I will meet them personally at Fortress Monroe
as soon as I can get there   (signed)   A. LINCOLN
    sent in cipher at 9. A.M.

Copy.   War Department
Hon Wm H. Seward   Washington D.C.
Fortress Monroe Va.   Feby 2nd. 1865
    Induced by a despatch from Genl Grant, I join you at Fort Monroe as
soon as I can come   (signed)   A. LINCOLN
    Sent in cipher at 9. A.M.

Before starting the following despatch was shown me; I proceeded nevertheless.

                                        Office U.S. Military Telegraph,
        Cipher   War Department.
The following Telegram received at Washington, M. Feby. 2d. 1865
                From City Point Va 9 A.M. Feby. 2d. 1865
Hon Wm. H. Seward   Secretary of State   Ft. Monroe
Copy to Hon. Edwin M. Stanton   Secretary of War   Wash.
    The gentlemen here have accepted the proposed terms and will leave
for Ft. Monroe at 9.30 A.M.   U. S. GRANT   Lt. Genl.

On the night of the 2nd. I reached Hampton Roads found the Secretary of State and Major Eckert on a Steamer anchored off shore, and learned of them that the Richmond gentlemen were on another Steamer also anchored off shore in the Roads, and that the Secretary of State had not yet seen, or communicated with them. Here I ascertained that Major Eckert had litterally complied with his instructions and I saw, for the first, the answer of the Richmond gentlemen to him, which in his despatch to me of the 1st. he characterizes as "not satisfactory." That answer is as follows, towit:

Copy

Thomas J. [T.] Eckert   City Point Va.

Major & A.D.C.   Feby 1st. 1865

Major.   Your note delivered by yourself this day has been considered. In reply we have to say that we were furnished with a copy of the letter of President Lincoln to Francis P. Blair Esq of the 18th of Jany ult. another copy of which is appended to your note.

Our instructions are contained in a letter of which the following is a copy.

"Richmond Jany 28th 1865

"In conformity with the letter of Mr Lincoln of which the foregoing is a copy, you are to proceed to Washington City for informal conference with him upon the issues involved in the existing war and for the purpose of securing peace to the two countries. With great respect Your ob't Servt   (signed) JEFFERSON DAVIS"

The substantial object to be obtained by the informal conference is, to ascertain upon what terms the existing war can be terminated honorably.

Our instructions contemplate a personal interview between President Lincoln and ourselves at Washington City, but with this explanation we are ready to meet any person or persons that President Lincoln may appoint, at such place as he may designate.

Our earnest desire is that a just and honorable peace may be agreed upon, and we are prepared to receive or to submit propositions which may, possibly, lead to the attainment of that end. Very Respectfully Yours   (signed) ALEXANDER H. STEPHENS
                                                           R. M. T. HUNTER
                                                           JOHN A. CAMPBELL

A note of these gentlemen, subsequently addressed to Gen. Grant, has already been given in Major Eckert's despatch of the 1st. Inst. I also here saw, for the first, the following note addressed by the Richmond gentlemen to Major Eckert:

Copy.

Thomas C. [T.] Eckert   City Point Va.

Major & A.D.C.   Feby 2nd. 1865

Major.   In reply to your verbal statement that your instructions did not allow you to alter the conditions upon which a passport could be given to us, we say that we are willing to proceed to Fortress Monroe and there to have an informal conference with any person or persons that President Lincoln may appoint on the basis of his letter to Francis P. Blair of the 18th of Jan'y ult. or upon any other terms, or conditions that he may hereafter propose not inconsistent with the essential principles of self government and popular rights upon which our institutions are founded.

It is our earnest wish to ascertain after a free interchange of ideas and information, upon what principles and terms, if any, a just and honorable peace can be established without the further effusion of blood, and to contribute our utmost efforts to accomplish such a result.

We think it better to add that in accepting your passport we are not to be understood as committing ourselves to anything, but to carry to this informal conference the views and feelings above expressed. Very Respectfully   Yours &c   (signed)   ALEXANDER H. STEPHENS
                                                    J. A. CAMPBELL
                                                    R. M. T. HUNTER

Note

The above communication was delivered to me at Fort Monroe at 4.30 P.M. Feby 2nd. by Lieut Col Babcock of Gen'l Grants Staff
                        (signed)   THOS T. ECKERT   Maj & A.D.C

On the morning of the 3rd., the three gentlemen, Messrs Stephens, Hunter and Campbell, came aboard of our Steamer and had an interview with the Secretary of State and myself of several hours duration. No question of preliminaries to the meeting was then and there made or mentioned. No other person was present; no papers were exchanged, or produced; and it was, in advance, agreed that the conversation was to be informal, and verbal merely. On our part, the whole substance of the instructions to the Secretary of State, herein before recited, was stated and insisted upon, and nothing was said inconsistently therewith; while, by the other party it was not said that, in any event, or on any condition, they *ever* would consent to re-union, and yet they equally omitted to declare that they *never* would so consent. They seemed to desire a postponement of that question, and the adoption of some other course first, which, as some of them, seemed to argue, might, or might not, lead to re-union, but which course, we thought, would amount to an indefinite postponement. The conferrence ended without result. The foregoing, containing, as is believed, all the information sought, is respectfully submitted.

Executive Mansion,
February 10th, 1865.

To Thomas C. Fletcher

His Excellency
Gov. Fletcher,

Executive Mansion
Washington Feb 20 1865

It seems that there is now no organized military force of the enemy in Missouri and yet that destruction of property and life is rampant every where. Is not the cure for this within easy reach of the people themselves? It cannot but be that every man, not naturally a robber or cut-throat would gladly put an end to this state of things. A large majority in every locality must feel alike upon this subject; and if so they only need to reach an understanding one with another. Each leaving all others alone solves the problem. And surely each would do this but for his apprehension that others will not leave him alone. Can not this mischievous distrust be removed? Let neighborhood meetings be every where called and held, of all entertaining a sincere purpose for mutual security in the future, whatever they may heretofore have thought, said or done about the war or about anything else. Let all such meet and waiving all else pledge each to cease harassing others and to make common cause against whomever persists in making, aiding or encouraging further disturbance. The practical means they will best know how to adopt and apply. At such meetings old friendships will cross the memory; and honor and Christian Charity will come in to help.

Please consider whether it may not be well to suggest this to the now afflicted people of Missouri. Yours truly

Reply to Notification Committee, Washington, D.C.

Having served four years in the depths of a great, and yet unended national peril, I can view this call to a second term, in nowise more flatteringly to myself, than as an expression of the public judgment, that I may better finish a difficult work, in which I have labored from the first, than could any one less severely schooled to the task.

In this view, and with assured reliance on that Almighty Ruler who has so graceously sustained us thus far; and with increased gratitude to the generous people for their continued confidence, I accept the renewed trust, with it's yet onerous and perplexing duties and responsibilities.

Please communicate this to the two Houses of Congress.

March 1, 1865

To Ulysses S. Grant

Lieutenant General Grant   March 3. 1865

The President directs me to say to you that he wishes you to have no conference with General Lee unless it be for the capitulation of Gen. Lee's army, or on some minor, and purely, military matter. He instructs me to say that you are not to decide, discuss, or confer upon any political question. Such questions the President holds in his own hands; and will submit them to no military conferences or conventions. Meantime you are to press to the utmost, your military advantages.   EDWIN M STANTON

Secretary of War

Second Inaugural Address

Fellow Countrymen:

At this second appearing to take the oath of the presidential office, there is less occasion for an extended address than there was at the first. Then a statement, somewhat in detail, of a course to be pursued, seemed fitting and proper. Now, at the expiration of four years, during which public declarations have been constantly called forth on every point and phase of the great contest which still absorbs the attention, and engrosses the energies of the nation, little that is new could be presented. The progress of our arms, upon which all else chiefly depends, is as well known to the public as to myself; and it is, I trust, reasonably satisfactory and encouraging to all. With high hope for the future, no prediction in regard to it is ventured.

On the occasion corresponding to this four years ago, all thoughts were anxiously directed to an impending civil-war. All dreaded it—all sought to avert it. While the inaugeral address was being delivered from this place, devoted altogether to *saving* the Union without war, insurgent agents were in the city seeking to *destroy* it without war—seeking to dissolve the Union, and divide effects, by negotiation. Both parties deprecated war; but one of them would *make* war rather than let the nation survive; and the other would *accept* war rather than let it perish. And the war came.

One eighth of the whole population were colored slaves, not distributed generally over the Union, but localized in the Southern part of it. These slaves constituted a peculiar and powerful interest. All knew that this interest was, somehow, the cause of the war. To strengthen, perpetuate, and extend this interest was the object for which the insurgents would rend the Union, even by war; while the government claimed no right to do more than to restrict the territorial enlargement of it. Neither party expected for the war, the magnitude, or the duration, which it has already attained. Neither anticipated that the *cause* of the conflict might cease with, or even before, the conflict itself should cease. Each looked for an easier triumph, and a result less fundamental and astounding.

Both read the same Bible, and pray to the same God; and each invokes His aid against the other. It may seem strange that any men should dare to ask a just God's assistance in wringing their bread from the sweat of other men's faces; but let us judge not that we be not judged. The prayers of both could not be answered; that of neither has been answered fully. The Almighty has His own purposes. "Woe unto the world because of offences! for it must needs be that offences come; but woe to that man by whom the offence cometh!" If we shall suppose that American Slavery is one of those offences which, in the providence of God, must needs come, but which, having continued through His appointed time, He now wills to remove, and that He gives to both North and South, this terrible war, as the woe due to those by whom the offence came, shall we discern therein any departure from those divine attributes which the believers in a Living God always ascribe to Him? Fondly do we hope—fervently do we pray—that this mighty scourge of war may speedily pass away. Yet, if God wills that it continue, until all the wealth piled by the bond-man's two hundred and fifty years of unrequited toil shall be sunk, and until every drop of blood drawn with the lash, shall be paid by another drawn with the sword, as was said three thousand years ago, so still it must be said "the judgments of the Lord, are true and righteous altogether"

With malice toward none; with charity for all; with firmness in the right, as God gives us to see the right, let us strive on to finish the work we are in; to bind up the nation's wounds; to care for him who shall have borne the battle, and for his widow, and his orphan—to do all which may achieve and cherish a just, and a lasting peace, among ourselves, and with all nations.

March 4, 1865

To Charles Sumner

Hon. C. Sumner.   Executive Mansion
My dear Sir   Washington, March 5/65
   I should be pleased for you to accompany us to-morrow

evening at ten o'clock, on a visit of half an hour to the Inaugeral-ball. I inclose a ticket. Our carriage will call for you at half past nine. Yours truly

To Ulysses S. Grant

Office U.S. Military Telegraph,
Lieut. Genl. Grant   War Department,
City Point, Va.   Washington, D.C., March 9. 1865

    I see your despatch to the Sec. of War, objecting to rebel prisoners being allowed to take the oath and go free. Supposing that I am responsible for what is done in this way, I think fit to say that there is no general rule, or action, allowing prisoners to be discharged merely on taking the oath. What has been done is that Members of Congress come to me from time to time with lists of names alleging that from personal knowledge, and evidence of reliable persons they are satisfied that it is safe to discharge the particular persons named on the lists, and I have ordered their discharge. These Members are chiefly from the border states; and those they get discharged are their neighbors and neighbors sons. They tell me that they do not bring to me one tenth of the names which are brought to them, bringing only such as their knowledge or the proof satisfies them about. I have, on the same principle, discharged some on the representations of others than Members of Congress, as, for instance, Gov. Johnson of Tennessee. The number I have discharged has been rather larger than I liked— reaching I should think an average of fifty a day, since the recent general exchange commenced. On the same grounds, last year, I discharged quite a number at different times, aggregating perhaps a thousand, Missourians and Kentuckians; and their Members returning here since the prisoner's return to their homes, report to me only two cases of proving false. Doubtless some more have proved false; but, on the whole I believe what I have done in this way has done good rather than harm.

To Thurlow Weed

Thurlow Weed, Esq   Executive Mansion,
My dear Sir.   Washington, March 15, 1865.

Every one likes a compliment. Thank you for yours on my little notification speech, and on the recent Inaugeral Address. I expect the latter to wear as well as—perhaps better than—any thing I have produced; but I believe it is not immediately popular. Men are not flattered by being shown that there has been a difference of purpose between the Almighty and them. To deny it, however, in this case, is to deny that there is a God governing the world. It is a truth which I thought needed to be told; and as whatever of humiliation there is in it, falls most directly on myself, I thought others might afford for me to tell it. Yours truly

Speech to the 140th Indiana Regiment, Washington, D.C.

FELLOW CITIZENS—It will be but a very few words that I shall undertake to say. I was born in Kentucky, raised in Indiana and lived in Illinois. (Laughter.) And now I am here, where it is my business to care equally for the good people of all the States. I am glad to see an Indiana regiment on this day able to present the captured flag to the Governor of Indiana. (Applause.) I am not disposed, in saying this, to make a distinction between the States, for all have done equally well. (Applause.) There are but few views or aspects of this great war upon which I have not said or written something whereby my own opinions might be known. But there is one—the recent attempt of our erring brethren, as they are sometimes called—(laughter)—to employ the negro to fight for them. I have neither written nor made a speech on that subject, because that was their business, not mine; and if I had a wish upon the subject I had not the power to introduce it, or make it effective. The great question with them was, whether the negro, being put into the army, would fight for them. I do not know, and therefore cannot decide. (Laughter.) They ought to know better than we. I have in my lifetime heard many arguments why the negroes ought to be slaves; but if they fight for those who would keep them in slavery it will be a better argument than any I have yet heard. (Laughter and applause.) He who will fight for that ought to be a slave. (Applause.) They have concluded at last to take one out of four of the slaves, and put them in the army; and that one out of the four who will fight to keep the others in slavery ought to be a slave himself unless he is killed in a fight. (Applause.) While I have often said that all men ought to be free, yet I would allow those colored persons to be slaves who want to be; and next to them those white persons who argue in favor of making other people slaves. (Applause.) I am in favor of giving an opportunity to such white men to try it on for themselves. (Applause.) I will say one thing in regard to the negro being employed to fight for them. I do know he cannot fight and stay at home and make bread too—(laughter and applause)—and as one is about as important as the other to them, I don't care which they do. (Renewed applause.) I am rather in favor of having them try them as soldiers. (Applause.) They lack one vote of doing that, and I wish I could send my vote over the river so that I might cast it in favor of allowing the negro to fight. (Applause.) But they cannot fight and work both. We must now see the bottom of the enemy's resources. They will stand out as long as they can, and if the negro will fight for them, they must allow him to fight. They have drawn upon their last branch of resources. (Applause.) And we can now see the bottom. (Applause.) I am glad to see the end so near at hand. (Applause.) I have said now more than I intended, and will therefore bid you goodby.

March 17, 1865

Order Annulling Sentence of Benjamin G. and Franklin W. Smith

I am unwilling for the sentence to stand and be executed, to any extent in this case. In the absence of a more adequate motive than the evidence discloses, I am wholly unable to believe in the existence of criminal or fraudulent intent on the part of one of such well established good character as is the accused. If the evidence went as far toward establishing a guilty profit of one or two hundred thousand dollars, as it does of one or two hundred dollars, the case would, on the question of guilt, bear a far different aspect. That on this contract, involving from one million to twelve hundred thousand dollars, the contractors should attempt a fraud which at the most could profit them only one or two hundred, or even one thousand dollars, is to my mind beyond the power of rational belief. That they did not, in such a case, strike for greater gains proves that they did not, with guilty, or fraudulent intent, strike at all. The judgment and sentence are disapproved, and declared null, and the accused ordered to be discharged.

March 18. 1865

To Edwin M. Stanton

City Point, Va., March 30, 1865–7.30 p.m.

Hon. Secretary of War: I begin to feel that I ought to be at home, and yet I dislike to leave without seeing nearer to the end of General Grant's present movement. He has now been out since yesterday morning, and although he has not been diverted from his programme, no considerable effect has yet been produced, so far as we know here. Last night at 10.15, when it was dark as a rainy night without a moon could be, a furious cannonade, soon joined in by a heavy musketry-fire, opened near Petersburg and lasted about two hours. The sound was very distinct here, as also were the flashes of the guns upon the clouds. It seemed to me a great battle, but the older hands here scarcely noticed it, and, sure enough, this morning it was found that very little had been done.

To Edwin M. Stanton

Hon. Edwin M. Stanton,   City Point, Va.,
Secretary of War: April 2, 1865 — 11 a.m.

Dispatches frequently coming in. All going finely. Parke, Wright, and Ord, extending from the Appomattox to Hatcher's Run, have all broken through the enemy's intrenched lines, taking some forts, guns, and prisoners. Sheridan, with his own cavalry, Fifth Corps, and part of the Second, is coming in from the west on the enemy's flank, and Wright is already tearing up the South Side Railroad.

To Mary Todd Lincoln

City Point, Va., April 2, 1865.

Mrs. Lincoln: At 4:30 p.m. to-day General Grant telegraphs that he has Petersburg completely enveloped from river below to river above, and has captured, since he started last Wednesday, about 12,000 prisoners and 50 guns. He suggests that I shall go out and see him in the morning, which I think I will do. Tad and I are both well, and will be glad to see you and your party here at the time you name.

To Ulysses S. Grant

Head Quarters Armies of the United States,

City-Point,

Lieut. General Grant.   April. 2. 8/15 P.M. 1865.

Allow me to tender to you, and all with you, the nations grateful thanks for this additional, and magnificent success. At your kind suggestion, I think I will visit you to-morrow.

To Edwin M. Stanton

Head Quarters Armies of the United States.

Hon. Sec. of War   City-Point,

Washington D.C   April 3. 8/00 A.M. 1865

This morning Gen. Grant reports Petersburg evacuated; and he is confident Richmond also is. He is pushing forward to cut off if possible, the retreating army. I start to him in a few minutes.

To Edwin M. Stanton

Head Quarters Armies of the United States,

Hon. Sec. of War   City-Point,

Washington, D.C.   April 3. 5. P.M. 1865

Yours received. Thanks for your caution; but I have already been to Petersburg, staid with Gen. Grant an hour & a half and returned here. It is certain now that Richmond is in our hands, and I think I will go there to-morrow. I will take care of myself.

To John A. Campbell

As to peace, I have said before, and now repeat, that three things are indispensable.

1. The restoration of the national authority throughout all the States.

2. No receding by the Executive of the United States on the

slavery question, from the position assumed thereon, in the late Annual Message to Congress, and in preceding documents.

3. No cessation of hostilities short of an end of the war, and the disbanding of all force hostile to the government.

That all propositions coming from those now in hostility to the government; and not inconsistent with the foregoing, will be respectfully considered, and passed upon in a spirit of sincere liberality.

I now add that it seems useless for me to be more specific with those who will not say they are ready for the indispensable terms, even on conditions to be named by themselves. If there be any who are ready for those indispensable terms, on any conditions whatever, let them say so, and state their conditions, so that such conditions can be distinctly known, and considered.

It is further added that, the remission of confiscations being within the executive power, if the war be now further persisted in, by those opposing the government, the making of confiscated property at the least to bear the additional cost, will be insisted on; but that confiscations (except in cases of third party intervening interests) will be remitted to the people of any State which shall now promptly, and in good faith, withdraw it's troops and other support, from further resistance to the government.

What is now said as to remission of confiscations has no reference to supposed property in slaves.

April 5, 1865

To Godfrey Weitzel

Head Quarters Armies of the United States,
Major General Weitzel   City-Point,
Richmond, Va.   April 6. 1865

It has been intimated to me that the gentlemen who have acted as the Legislature of Virginia, in support of the rebellion, may now desire to assemble at Richmond, and take measures to withdraw the Virginia troops, and other support from resistance to the General government. If they attempt it, give them permission and protection, until, if at all, they attempt some action hostile to the United States, in which case you will notify them and give them reasonable time to leave; & at the end of which time, arrest any who may remain. Allow Judge Campbell to see this, but do not make it public. Yours &c.

To Ulysses S. Grant

Head Quarters Armies of the United States,
Lieut. Genl. Grant   City-Point,
In the Field.   April. 6. 12. M. 1865

Secretary Seward was thrown from his carriage yesterday and seriously injured. This, with other matters, will take me to Washington soon. I was at Richmond yesterday and the day before, when and where Judge Campbell (who was with Messrs. Hunter and Stephens in February) called on me and made such representations as induced me to put in his hands an informal paper, repeating the propositions in my letter of instructions to Mr. Seward (which you remember) and adding that if the war be now further persisted in by the rebels, confiscated property shall, at the least, bear the additional cost; and that confiscations shall be remitted to the people of any State which will now promptly, and in good faith, withdraw its troops and other support, from resistance to the government. Judge Campbell thought it not impossible that the rebel Legislature of Virginia would do the latter, if permitted; and accordingly, I addressed a private letter to Gen. Weitzel (with permission for Judge Campbell to see it) telling him, Gen. W. that if they attempt this, to permit and protect them, unless they attempt something hostile to the United States, in which case to give them notice and time to leave, and to arrest any remaining after such time.

I do not think it very probable that anything will come of this; but I have thought best to notify you, so that if you should see signs, you may understand them. From your recent despatches it seems that you are pretty effectually withdrawing the Virginia troops from opposition to the government. Nothing I have done, or probably shall do, is to delay, hinder, or interfere with you in your work. Yours truly

To Ulysses S. Grant

Head Quarters Armies of the United States,
City-Point,

Lieut Gen. Grant.   April 7. 11 A.M. 1865

Gen. Sheridan says "If the thing is pressed I think that Lee will surrender." Let the *thing* be pressed.

Response to Serenade, Washington, D.C.

"FELLOW CITIZENS: I am very greatly rejoiced to find that an occasion has occurred so pleasurable that the people cannot restrain themselves. [Cheers.] I suppose that arrangements are being made for some sort of a formal demonstration, this, or perhaps, to-morrow night. [Cries of 'We can't wait,' 'We want it now,' &c.] If there should be such a demonstration, I, of course, will be called upon to respond, and I shall have nothing to say if you dribble it all out of me before. [Laughter and applause.] I see you have a band of music with you. [Voices, 'We have two or three.'] I propose closing up this interview by the band performing a particular tune which I will name. Before this is done, however, I wish to mention one or two little circumstances connected with it. I have always thought 'Dixie' one of the best tunes I have ever heard. Our adversaries over the way attempted to appropriate it, but I insisted yesterday that we fairly captured it. [Applause.] I presented the question to the Attorney General, and he gave it as his legal opinion that it is our lawful prize. [Laughter and applause.] I now request the band to favor me with its performance."

April 10, 1865

Speech on Reconstruction, Washington, D.C.

We meet this evening, not in sorrow, but in gladness of heart. The evacuation of Petersburg and Richmond, and the surrender of the principal insurgent army, give hope of a righteous and speedy peace whose joyous expression can not be restrained. In the midst of this, however, He, from Whom all blessings flow, must not be forgotten. A call for a national thanksgiving is being prepared, and will be duly promulgated. Nor must those whose harder part gives us the cause of rejoicing, be overlooked. Their honors must not be parcelled out with others. I myself, was near the front, and had the high pleasure of transmitting much of the good news to you; but no part of the honor, for plan or execution, is mine. To Gen. Grant, his skilful officers, and brave men, all belongs. The gallant Navy stood ready, but was not in reach to take active part.

By these recent successes the re-inauguration of the national authority—reconstruction—which has had a large share of thought from the first, is pressed much more closely upon our attention. It is fraught with great difficulty. Unlike the case of a war between independent nations, there is no authorized organ for us to treat with. No one man has authority to give up the rebellion for any other man. We simply must begin with, and mould from, disorganized and discordant elements. Nor is it a small additional embarrassment that we, the loyal people, differ among ourselves as to the mode, manner, and means of reconstruction.

As a general rule, I abstain from reading the reports of attacks upon myself, wishing not to be provoked by that to which I can not properly offer an answer. In spite of this precaution, however, it comes to my knowledge that I am much censured for some supposed agency in setting up, and seeking to sustain, the new State Government of Louisiana. In this I have done just so much as, and no more than, the public knows. In the Annual Message of Dec. 1863 and accompanying Proclamation, I presented *a* plan of reconstruction (as the phrase goes) which, I promised, if adopted by any State, should be acceptable to, and sustained by, the Executive government of the nation. I distinctly stated that this was not the only plan which might possibly be acceptable; and I also distinctly protested that the Executive claimed no right to say when, or whether members should be admitted to seats in Congress from such States. This plan was, in advance, submitted to the then Cabinet, and distinctly approved by every member of it. One of them suggested that I should then, and in that connection, apply the Emancipation Proclamation to the theretofore excepted parts of Virginia and Louisiana, that I should drop the suggestion about apprenticeship for freed-people, and that I should omit the protest against my own power, in regard to the admission of members to Congress; but even he approved every part and parcel of the plan which has since been employed or touched by the action of Louisiana. The new constitution of Louisiana, declaring emancipation for the whole State, practically applies the Proclamation to the part previously excepted. It does not adopt apprenticeship for freed-people; and it is silent, as it could not well be otherwise, about the admission of members to Congress. So that, as it applies to Louisiana, every member of the Cabinet fully approved the plan. The Message went to Congress, and I received many commendations of the plan, written and verbal; and not a single objection to it, from any professed emancipationist, came to my knowledge, until after the news reached Washington that the people of Louisiana had begun to move in accordance with it. From about July 1862, I had corresponded with different persons, supposed to be interested, seeking a reconstruction of a State government for Louisiana. When the Message of 1863, with the plan before mentioned, reached New-Orleans, Gen. Banks wrote me that he was confident the people, with his military co-operation, would reconstruct, substantially on that plan. I wrote him, and some of them to try it; they tried it, and the result is known. Such only has been my agency in getting up the Louisiana government. As to sustaining it, my promise is out, as before stated. But, as bad promises are better broken than kept, I shall treat this as a bad promise, and break it, whenever I shall be convinced that keeping it is adverse to the public interest. But I have not yet been so convinced.

I have been shown a letter on this subject, supposed to be

an able one, in which the writer expresses regret that my mind has not seemed to be definitely fixed on the question whether the seceded States, so called, are in the Union or out of it. It would perhaps, add astonishment to his regret, were he to learn that since I have found professed Union men endeavoring to make that question, I have *purposely* forborne any public expression upon it. As appears to me that question has not been, nor yet is, a practically material one, and that any discussion of it, while it thus remains practically immaterial, could have no effect other than the mischievous one of dividing our friends. As yet, whatever it may hereafter become, that question is bad, as the basis of a controversy, and good for nothing at all—a merely pernicious abstraction.

We all agree that the seceded States, so called, are out of their proper practical relation with the Union; and that the sole object of the government, civil and military, in regard to those States is to again get them into that proper practical relation. I believe it is not only possible, but in fact, easier, to do this, without deciding, or even considering, whether these states have even been out of the Union, than with it. Finding themselves safely at home, it would be utterly immaterial whether they had ever been abroad. Let us all join in doing the acts necessary to restoring the proper practical relations between these states and the Union; and each forever after, innocently indulge his own opinion whether, in doing the acts, he brought the States from without, into the Union, or only gave them proper assistance, they never having been out of it.

The amount of constituency, so to speak, on which the new Louisiana government rests, would be more satisfactory to all, if it contained fifty, thirty, or even twenty thousand, instead of only about twelve thousand, as it does. It is also unsatisfactory to some that the elective franchise is not given to the colored man. I would myself prefer that it were now conferred on the very intelligent, and on those who serve our cause as soldiers. Still the question is not whether the Louisiana government, as it stands, is quite all that is desirable. The question is "Will it be wiser to take it as it is, and help to improve it; or to reject, and disperse it?" "Can Louisiana be brought into proper practical relation with the

Union *sooner* by *sustaining*, or by *discarding* her new State Government?"

Some twelve thousand voters in the heretofore slave-state of Louisiana have sworn allegiance to the Union, assumed to be the rightful political power of the State, held elections, organized a State government, adopted a free-state constitution, giving the benefit of public schools equally to black and white, and empowering the Legislature to confer the elective franchise upon the colored man. Their Legislature has already voted to ratify the constitutional amendment recently passed by Congress, abolishing slavery throughout the nation. These twelve thousand persons are thus fully committed to the Union, and to perpetual freedom in the state—committed to the very things, and nearly all the things the nation wants—and they ask the nations recognition, and it's assistance to make good their committal. Now, if we reject, and spurn them, we do our utmost to disorganize and disperse them. We in effect say to the white men "You are worthless, or worse—we will neither help you, nor be helped by you." To the blacks we say "This cup of liberty which these, your old masters, hold to your lips, we will dash from you, and leave you to the chances of gathering the spilled and scattered contents in some vague and undefined when, where, and how." If this course, discouraging and paralyzing both white and black, has any tendency to bring Louisiana into proper practical relations with the Union, I have, so far, been unable to perceive it. If, on the contrary, we recognize, and sustain the new government of Louisiana the converse of all this is made true. We encourage the hearts, and nerve the arms of the twelve thousand to adhere to their work, and argue for it, and proselyte for it, and fight for it, and feed it, and grow it, and ripen it to a complete success. The colored man too, in seeing all united for him, is inspired with vigilance, and energy, and daring, to the same end. Grant that he desires the elective franchise, will he not attain it sooner by saving the already advanced steps toward it, than by running backward over them? Concede that the new government of Louisiana is only to what it should be as the egg is to the fowl, we shall sooner have the fowl by hatching the egg than by smashing it? Again, if we reject Louisiana, we also reject one vote in favor of the proposed amendment to the national constitution. To meet this proposition, it has been argued that no more than three fourths of those States which have not attempted secession are necessary to validly ratify the amendment. I do not commit myself against this, further than to say that such a ratification would be questionable, and sure to be persistently questioned; while a ratification by three fourths of all the States would be unquestioned and unquestionable.

I repeat the question. "Can Louisiana be brought into proper practical relation with the Union *sooner* by *sustaining* or by *discarding* her new State Government?

What has been said of Louisiana will apply generally to other States. And yet so great peculiarities pertain to each state; and such important and sudden changes occur in the same state; and, withal, so new and unprecedented is the whole case, that no exclusive, and inflexible plan can safely be prescribed as to details and colatterals. Such exclusive, and inflexible plan, would surely become a new entanglement. Important principles may, and must, be inflexible.

In the present *"situation"* as the phrase goes, it may be my duty to make some new announcement to the people of the South. I am considering, and shall not fail to act, when satisfied that action will be proper.

April 11, 1865

To Godfrey Weitzel

"*Cypher*"   Office U.S. Military Telegraph,
Major General Weitzel   War Department,
Richmond, Va   Washington, D.C., April 12. 1865

I have just seen Judge Campbell's letter to you of the 7th. He assumes as appears to me that I have called the insurgent Legislature of Virginia together, as the rightful Legislature of the State, to settle all differences with the United States. I have done no such thing. I spoke of them not as a Legislature, but as "the gentlemen who have *acted* as the Legislature of Virginia in support of the rebellion." I did this on purpose to exclude the assumption that I was recognizing them as a *rightful* body. I dealt with them as men having power *de facto* to do a specific thing, towit, "to withdraw the Virginia troops, and other support from resistance to the General Government," for which in the paper handed Judge Campbell I promised a specific equivalent, to wit, a remission to the people of the State, except in certain cases, the confiscation of their property. I meant this and no more. In as much however as Judge Campbell misconstrues this, and is still pressing for an armistice, contrary to the explicit statement of the paper I gave him, and particularly as Gen. Grant has since captured the Virginia troops, so that giving a consideration for their withdrawal is no longer applicable, let my letter to you, and the paper to Judge Campbell both be withdrawn or, countermanded, and he be notified of it. Do not now allow them to assemble; but if any have come, allow them safe-return to their homes.

Concerning Passes to Richmond

No pass is necessary now to authorize any one to go to & return from Petersburg & Richmond. People go & return just as they did before the war.

April 13 or 14, 1865

Chronology

1809   Born February 12, in log cabin on Nolin Creek, three
        miles south of present-day Hodgenville in Hardin (now
        Larue) County, Kentucky, second child (sister is Sarah, b.
        1807) of pioneer farmer and carpenter Thomas Lincoln (b.
        1778) and Nancy Hanks Lincoln (b. circa 1784). Named
        Abraham after paternal grandfather.

1811   Moves with family to 230-acre farm (only about thirty
        acres of which are tilled) on Knob Creek, eleven miles
        northeast of Hodgenville.

1812   Brother Thomas born. He dies in infancy.

1815   Attends school with Sarah for short period in fall. (Nei-
        ther parent can read, father can write only his own name.)

1816   Briefly attends school with sister in fall. Father, who is
        involved in suit over title to his land, moves family across
        Ohio River to southwestern Indiana in December. There
        they settle in backwoods community along Little Pigeon
        Creek in Perry (later Spencer) County. Family lives in
        three-sided shelter for several weeks until log cabin is
        built.

1817   Helps father clear land for planting on 80-acre plot. Fam-
        ily is joined late in the year (or in early 1818) by great-aunt
        Elizabeth Hanks Sparrow, her husband, Thomas Sparrow,
        and 19-year-old cousin Dennis Hanks, who becomes
        Lincoln's close companion.

1818   Sometime after his birthday Lincoln is kicked in the head
        by a horse and is momentarily thought to be dead. Tho-
        mas and Elizabeth Sparrow die of milk sickness in Sep-
        tember. Mother dies of milk sickness on October 5 and is
        buried near Sparrows on knoll a quarter mile from cabin.

1819   On December 2, father marries Sarah Bush Johnston, 31-
        year-old widow with three children (Elizabeth, b. 1807,
        John, b. 1810, and Matilda, b. 1811), during visit to Elizabeth-

town, Kentucky. (Father and stepmother knew each other when Lincolns lived in Hardin County.)

1820   Attends school briefly with sister Sarah.

1822   Attends school for several months.

1824   Helps with plowing and planting and works for neighbors for hire. Attends school in fall and winter. Reads family Bible, and borrows books whenever possible (reading will include Mason Locke Weems's *The Life and Memorable Actions of George Washington*, Daniel Defoe's *Robinson Crusoe*, Aesop's *Fables*, John Bunyan's *Pilgrim's Progress*, William Grimshaw's *History of the United States*, and Thomas Dilworth's *A New Guide to the English Tongue*).

1827   Works as boatman and farmhand at junction of Anderson Creek and the Ohio River, near Troy, Indiana.

1828   Sister Sarah, now married to Aaron Grigsby, dies in childbirth on January 20. In April, Lincoln and Allen Gentry leave Rockport, Indiana, on flatboat trip to New Orleans with cargo of farm produce. While trading in coastal Louisiana sugar-growing regions, they fight off seven black men trying to rob them. Returns home by steamboat. Watches trials at county courthouses.

1830   In March, moves with family to Illinois, where they settle on uncleared land ten miles southwest of Decatur in Macon County. Makes first known political speech, in favor of improving navigation on Sangamon River, at campaign meeting in Decatur.

1831   Builds flatboat with stepbrother John D. Johnston and cousin John Hanks in spring and makes second trip to New Orleans, carrying corn, live hogs, and barreled pork. Returns to Illinois in summer and moves to village of New Salem, twenty miles northwest of Springfield in Sangamon County (family has moved to Coles County, Illinois). Clerks in general store, where he sleeps in the back, helps run mill, and does odd jobs. Accepts challenge to wrestle Jack Armstrong, leader of the "Clary's Grove boys," local group of rowdy young men, and stands his ground when they rush him to prevent Armstrong's defeat. Match is agreed to be a draw, and Lincoln gains respect and friendship of group. Becomes friends with tavernkeeper James Rutledge, his daughter Ann, and schoolmaster Mentor Graham. Learns basic mathematics, reads Shakespeare and Robert Burns, and participates in local debating society.

1832   Borrows and studies Samuel Kirkham's *English Grammar*. Announces candidacy for House of Representatives, lower chamber of Illinois General Assembly, in March. Volunteers for Illinois militia at outbreak of Black Hawk Indian War in early April and is elected company captain. Reenlists as private when his company is mustered out in late May and serves until July 10 in Rock River country of northern Illinois, covering much ground but seeing no action. Loses election on August 6, running eighth in field of thirteen candidates seeking four seats. Becomes partner in New Salem general store with William F. Berry.

1833   Store fails and leaves Lincoln deeply in debt. Works as hired hand and begins to write deeds and mortgage papers for neighbors. Boards with different families, moving every few months. Appointed postmaster of New Salem in May (serves until office is moved to nearby Petersburg in 1836); regularly reads newspapers in the mail. Studies surveying with Mentor Graham's help after being appointed deputy surveyor of Sangamon County.

1834   Makes first known survey in January and first town survey on site of New Boston, Illinois, in September (works as surveyor for three years). Elected as a Whig on August 4 to Illinois House of Representatives, running second in field of thirteen seeking four Sangamon County seats. Begins to study law, reading Blackstone's *Commentaries* and Joseph Chitty's *Precedents in Pleading* and borrowing other lawbooks from attorney John T. Stuart. Takes his seat on December 1 at capital in Vandalia. Rooms with Stuart, who is elected floor leader by Whig minority in House. Meets Stephen A. Douglas, 21-year-old lawyer active in Democratic party politics.

1835   Serves on twelve special committees and helps draft bills and resolutions for other Whigs. Votes with the majority to charter state bank and to build canal linking the Illinois River and Lake Michigan. Death of former store partner William Berry in January increases Lincoln's debt to approximately $1,100, which he repays over several years. Returns to New Salem after legislature adjourns on February 13. Ann Rutledge dies on August 25 from fever at age twenty-two. Attends special legislative session in December, called to speed up work on Illinois and Michigan Canal and other internal improvements. Votes for bill pledging credit of state to payment of canal loan.

1836   Returns to New Salem after legislature adjourns on January 18. Wins reelection on August 1, running first in field of seventeen candidates contesting seven Sangamon County seats in lower chamber. Receives license to practice law on September 9. Begins halfhearted courtship of Mary Owens, 28-year-old Kentucky woman visiting her sister in New Salem. Has episode of severe depression ("hypochondria") soon after returning to Vandalia in early December for new legislative session.

1837   Lincoln and other members of nine-man Whig delegation from Sangamon County (known as the "Long Nine" because they average over six feet in height) lead successful campaign to move state capital from Vandalia to Springfield, a shift that reflects population growth in central and northern counties. Supports ambitious internal improvements program. With fellow Whig representative Dan Stone, enters protest against anti-abolitionist resolutions adopted in their chamber. Legislature adjourns on March 6. Moves to Springfield on April 15, rooming with storeowner Joshua F. Speed, who becomes a close friend. Becomes law partner of John T. Stuart and begins extensive and varied civil and criminal practice. (Lincoln occasionally acts as prosecutor, but appears for the defense in almost all of his criminal cases throughout his career.) At special legislative session in July, votes with majority to continue internal improvements despite national financial panic. Mary Owens rejects his proposal of marriage, and courtship is broken off in August.

1838   Delivers address on "The Perpetuation of Our Political Institutions" to the Springfield Young Men's Lyceum on

January 27. Helps defend Henry Truett in widely pub-
licized murder case, delivering final argument to jury;
Truett is acquitted. In May, debates Douglas, who is
running for Congress against Stuart. Reelected to the legislature, August 6, running first of seven successful candidates in field of seventeen. Nominated for speaker by Whig
caucus when legislature convenes on December 3, but
is defeated by Democrat W.L.D. Ewing. Serves as Whig
floor leader.

1839   Legislature adjourns on March 4. Lincoln makes first extensive trip on Illinois Eighth Judicial Circuit, attending
court sessions held successively in nine counties in central
and eastern Illinois. Chosen presidential elector in October by first Whig state convention. Debates Douglas in
Springfield on issue of national bank. Assumes greater
share of legal partnership when Stuart leaves for Congress
in November. Admitted to practice in United States Circuit Court on December 3. Legislature convenes in special
session, December 9, meeting at Springfield for the first
time. Becomes acquainted with Mary Todd, 21-year-old
daughter of prominent Kentucky Whig banker, sister-in-
law of Illinois Whig legislator Ninian W. Edwards, and
cousin of John T. Stuart.

1840   Votes in minority against repeal of internal improvements
law of 1837, which has caused financial crisis (state defaults
on its debt in July 1841). Legislature adjourns on February
3. Campaigns for Whig presidential candidate, William
Henry Harrison, debating Douglas and other Democratic
speakers. Argues his first case before Illinois Supreme
Court in June (Lincoln will appear before it in over 240
cases). Reelected to the legislature, August 3, polling lowest vote of five candidates elected from Sangamon County.
Becomes engaged to Mary Todd in fall. Legislature meets
in special session on November 23. Lincoln is again defeated by Ewing in voting for speaker. In parliamentary
maneuver to protect failing state bank, Whigs attempt to
block adjournment of special session by preventing quorum. When plan fails on December 5, Lincoln and two
other Whigs jump out of ground-floor window in unsuccessful attempt not to be counted as present; incident
causes widespread derision in the Democratic press.

1841   Breaks engagement with Mary Todd on January 1. Is se-
          verely depressed for weeks and absent from legislature for
          several days. Legislature adjourns, March 1. Dissolves part-
          nership with Stuart, who is often absent on political busi-
          ness, and forms new partnership with Stephen T. Logan,
          prominent Illinois Whig known for methodical legal
          work. Wins appeal before Illinois Supreme Court in case
          of *Bailey* v. *Cromwell*, successfully arguing that unpaid
          promissory note written by his client, David Bailey, for
          purchase of slave was legally void in Illinois due to the
          prohibitions against slavery in the Ordinance of 1787 and
          the state constitution. Visits Speed at his family home
          near Lexington, Kentucky, in August and September. On
          return trip by steamboat, sees twelve slaves chained to-
          gether "like so many fish upon a trot-line."

1842   Delivers address to local temperance society on February
          22. Does not seek reelection to legislature. Resumes court-
          ship of Mary Todd during summer. In September, accepts
          challenge from Democratic state auditor James Shields,
          who is angered by four published pseudonymous letters
          ridiculing him (one was written by Mary Todd and a
          friend, another by Lincoln). Lincoln chooses broadswords
          as weapons, but duel is averted on September 22 when
          Shields accepts Lincoln's explanation that the letters were
          purely political in nature and not intended to impugn
          Shields's personal honor. Marries Mary Todd on Novem-
          ber 4 in parlor of her sister's Springfield mansion, then
          moves with her into room in the Globe Tavern.

1843   Unsuccessfully seeks Whig nomination for Congress, then
          tries to establish arrangement with John J. Hardin and
          Edward D. Baker for each of them to be nominated in
          turn to serve for one term. Son Robert Todd Lincoln born
          August 1. Lincolns move into rented cottage.

1844   Lincolns move in May into house, bought for $1,500, at
          Eighth and Jackson streets in Springfield (their home until
          1861). Campaigns as Whig elector for Henry Clay in the
          presidential election. Visits former Indiana home in fall.
          Partnership with Logan is dissolved in December so that
          Logan can take his son as new partner; Lincoln establishes

his own practice and takes 26-year-old William H. Herndon as junior partner.

1845   Works to assure himself Whig congressional nomination when Hardin refuses to abide by principle of rotation. Income from law practice is approximately $1,500 a year.

1846   Second son, Edward Baker Lincoln, born March 10. Wins congressional nomination at Whig district convention held on May 1. Speaks on May 30 at mass meeting in Springfield that calls for united support of recently declared war against Mexico. Helps prosecute manslaughter charge in June; jury deadlocks and case is never retried. Elected to U.S. House of Representatives on August 3, defeating Democrat Peter Cartwright, a Methodist preacher, by 6,340 to 4,829 votes.

1847   Makes first visit to Chicago in early July to attend convention protesting President James K. Polk's veto of bill for river and harbor improvements. In October, represents slave-owner Robert Matson at habeas corpus hearing in Coles County. Lincoln argues that Bryants, slave family Matson had brought from Kentucky to do seasonal farmwork on his Illinois land, were not state residents and thus were not freed by antislavery provisions of Illinois law. Court rules against Matson and frees Bryants. After visit with wife's family in Lexington, Kentucky, travels with wife and sons to Washington, D.C., and moves into boarding house near the Capitol. Takes seat in the House of Representatives when Thirtieth Congress convenes on December 6. Presents resolutions on December 22 requesting President Polk to inform the House whether the "spot" where hostilities with Mexico began was or was not on Mexican soil.

1848   Serves on Expenditures in the War Department and Post Office and Post Roads committees. Attacks Polk's war policy in speech on floor of the House, January 22 (almost all fighting had ended with the American capture of Mexico City in September 1847, but peace treaty had yet to be signed). Ridiculed as "spotty Lincoln" by Illinois Democratic press. Wife and children leave Washington to stay with her family in Kentucky. Attends national Whig

convention at Philadelphia in early June as supporter of
General Zachary Taylor, who is nominated for president.
Abides by his own rule of rotation and does not seek
second term in Congress. Rejoined by family in late July.
House adjourns on August 14. Campaigns for Taylor in
Maryland and Massachusetts; meets former New York
governor William H. Seward at Whig rally in Boston on
September 22. Visits Niagara Falls before taking steamer
to Chicago. Campaigns in Illinois until election. Returns
to Washington, December 7, for second session of Thirtieth Congress. Supports the principle of the Wilmot
Proviso by voting to prohibit slavery in the territory acquired from Mexico.

1849   Votes to exclude slavery from federal territories and abol·
        ish slave trade in the District of Columbia, but does not
        speak in congressional debates on slavery. Congress ad-
        journs on March 4. Makes only appearance before United
        States Supreme Court, March 7–8, unsuccessfully appeal-
        ing U.S. circuit court ruling concerning application of
        Illinois statute of limitations on nonresidents' suits. Ap-
        plies for patent (later granted) on device for reducing draft
        of steamboats in shallow water. Returns to Springfield on
        March 31. Visits father and stepmother in Coles County in
        late May. Goes to Washington in June in pursuit of posi-
        tion as commissioner of the General Land Office, but fails
        to receive appointment from the new Taylor administra-
        tion. Resumes law practice in Illinois. Declines appoint-
        ment as secretary and then as governor of Oregon
        Territory.

1850   Son Edward dies on February 1 after illness of nearly two
        months. Lincoln returns to Eighth Judicial Circuit (now
        covering fourteen counties), making 400-mile, 12-week
        trip in spring and fall. Becomes a closer friend of David
        Davis, who had practiced law with Lincoln on the circuit
        before becoming its judge in 1848. Delivers eulogy of
        Zachary Taylor at Chicago memorial meeting in July.
        Studies Euclidean geometry. Third son, William Wallace
        (Willie), born December 21.

1851   Learns that father is seriously ill in Coles County. Writes
        to stepbrother John D. Johnston that he cannot visit be-
        cause of wife's health. Father dies on January 17.

1852   Wife joins First Presbyterian Church in Springfield. Lincoln rents a pew and attends at times but never himself becomes a member of any church. Delivers eulogy of Henry Clay at Springfield memorial meeting in July. Serves as Whig elector and makes several speeches in support of Winfield Scott during presidential campaign.

1853   Fourth son, Thomas (Tad), born April 4. In May, Lincoln serves as court-appointed prosecutor in child-rape case and wins conviction (defendant is sentenced to eighteen years in prison). Accepts retainer from Illinois Central Railroad in October in suit to prevent taxation by McLean County, a case crucial to railroad's claim that it could be taxed only by the state government.

1854   Helps argue McLean County case in Illinois Supreme Court, February 28; court orders that it be re-argued. Lincoln's declining interest in politics is revived when Congress passes the Kansas-Nebraska Act on May 22, repealing antislavery restriction in the Missouri Compromise. Completion of direct railroad link increases Lincoln's practice in U.S. district and circuit courts in Chicago. Runs for Illinois House of Representatives to help campaign of Richard Yates, a congressman who opposed the Kansas-Nebraska Act. Speaks against the act at Bloomington, September 26, Springfield, October 4, and Peoria, October 16, appearing before or after Senator Stephen A. Douglas, its principal author. Elected to legislature, but declines seat to become eligible for election to the United States Senate.

1855   Legislature meets to elect United States senator, February 8. Lincoln leads on first ballot, but eventually throws dwindling support to anti-Nebraska Democrat Lyman Trumbull, who is elected on tenth ballot. Goes to Cincinnati in September to appear for defense in *McCormick* v. *Manny*, federal patent infringement suit originally scheduled to be tried in Illinois. Is excluded from case by other defense attorneys, including Edwin Stanton of Pittsburgh, and does not participate in trial, but stays to watch arguments. Lincoln's earnings now total about $5,000 a year.

1856   Re-argues McLean County tax case before Illinois Supreme Court, January 16–17 (court later rules in railroad's favor, but Lincoln is forced to sue railroad for payment of his fee). Attends meeting of anti-Nebraska newspaper editors, held in Decatur on February 22, that calls for convention to organize new free-soil political party. Joins in founding Republican Party of Illinois at convention in Bloomington, May 29, and inspires delegates with address that goes unrecorded (later known as the "Lost Speech"). Receives 110 votes from eleven delegations on first ballot for vice-presidential nomination at the first Republican national convention, held in Philadelphia, June 19. Makes more than fifty speeches throughout Illinois as presidential elector for Republican candidate John C. Frémont.

1857   Helps prosecute murder case in which defendant is acquitted for reasons of insanity. Wins suit against Illinois Central Railroad over his fee in the McLean County tax case on June 23 (receives $4,800 in August as balance of $5,000 billed, his largest legal fee, and continues to represent Illinois Central in important litigation). Delivers major speech against Dred Scott decision in Springfield on June 26. Visits New York City, Niagara Falls, and Canada with wife in late July. In September defends Rock Island Railroad in the *Effie Afton* case, involving steamboat destroyed by fire after striking the first railroad bridge across the Mississippi River. Trial ends when jury deadlocks 9–3 in railroad's favor, a significant setback to riverboat interests in their efforts to block railroad expansion.

1858   In May, wins acquittal for William (Duff) Armstrong, son of New Salem friends Jack and Hannah Armstrong, by using almanac to discredit testimony of key prosecution witness as to height of the moon at time of alleged murder, and by suggesting that deceased had died because of a drunken fall from his horse. Charges no fee for defense. Accepts endorsement on June 16 by the Republican state convention at Springfield as its "first and only choice" for Senate seat held by Douglas and delivers "House-Divided" speech. Attends speech by Douglas in Chicago, July 9, and replies the following day. Begins following Douglas through state, occasionally riding as ordinary passenger on the same train that carried Douglas in his private car. On July 24, invites Douglas to "divide time" on the same platform for remainder of campaign. Douglas declines, but agrees to seven debates, which are held on August 21, 27, September 15, 18, and October 7, 13, 15. Audiences at debates probably number between 10,000 and 15,000, except for about 1,200 at Jonesboro on September 15 and perhaps as many as 20,000 at Galesburg on October 7. Both candidates also deliver scores of speeches throughout state, concentrating on counties of central Illinois. Republicans win a plurality in the election on November 2, but they do not gain control of the legislature because of Democratic holdovers and an unfavorable apportionment of seats. In December, Lincoln assembles newspaper clippings of debates and major campaign speeches in scrapbook.

1859   Legislature reelects Douglas to the Senate on January 5 by vote of 54 to 46. Lincoln begins negotiations in March for publication of debates. Son Robert fails Harvard College entrance exams and enrolls at Phillips Exeter Academy in New Hampshire. From August to October Lincoln makes speeches for Republican candidates in Iowa, Ohio, and Wisconsin. Begins to be mentioned as possible presidential candidate. In fall makes last trip through Eighth Circuit (reduced to five counties in 1857). Speaks in Kansas before its territorial elections in early December.

1860   Delivers address on slavery and the framers of the Constitution to audience of 1,500 at Cooper Union in New York City on February 27. Visits Robert at Exeter and speaks to enthusiastic crowds in Rhode Island, New Hampshire, and Connecticut before returning to Springfield. *Political Debates between Hon. Abraham Lincoln and Hon. Stephen A. Douglas in the Celebrated Campaign of 1858, in Illinois*, printed from Lincoln's scrapbook, published in March by Follett, Foster & Co. in Columbus, Ohio. Republican state convention, meeting at Decatur on May 10, instructs Illinois delegation to vote for Lincoln at national convention. Lincoln remains in Springfield while team of supporters, led by Judge David Davis and Norman B. Judd, chairman of the Illinois Republican state central committee, canvasses delegates at Republican national convention in Chicago. Wins nomination for president on the third ballot, May 18, defeating main rival Senator William H. Seward of New York as well as Senator Simon Cameron of Pennsylvania, Senator Salmon P. Chase of Ohio, and Edward Bates of Missouri. Learns of his victory and of nomination of Senator Hannibal Hamlin of Maine for vice-president at office of *Illinois State Journal*. Studies platform, which opposes the extension of slavery, vaguely endorses a protective tariff policy, and calls for homestead legislation, internal improvements, and a transcontinental railroad. Following established practice, Lincoln does not campaign and makes no formal speeches, but corresponds extensively with Republican leaders. Makes one of his last court appearances on June 20 in a federal patent case. (At conclusion of legal career has net worth of approximately $15,000.) Hires 28-year-old John G. Nicolay and 22-year-old John Hay as personal secretaries. Son Robert is admitted to Harvard College. Follows election returns in Springfield telegraph office, November 6. Defeats Stephen A. Douglas (Northern Democratic), John C. Breckinridge of Kentucky (Southern Democratic), and John Bell of Tennessee (Constitutional Union) to become first Republican president. Receives 180 of the 303 electoral votes while winning plurality of 40 percent of the popular vote. Meets with Republican leaders in Springfield, considers Cabinet appointments, and is beset by office-seekers. South Carolina secedes from the Union on December 20 (Mississippi, Florida, Alabama, Georgia, Louisiana, and Texas follow within two months).

1861   Works on inaugural address. Sees stepmother for the last time at her home in Coles County, January 31– February 1. Leaves Springfield by train on February 11, making brief speeches and appearances in Indiana, Ohio, Pennsylvania, New York, and New Jersey. Warned in Philadelphia that he might be assassinated in Baltimore, travels secretly to Washington on night of February 22–23; trip is ridiculed by opposition press. Finishes selecting Cabinet that includes the other major contenders for the Republican presidential nomination: William H. Seward (secretary of state), Salmon P. Chase (secretary of the treasury), Simon Cameron (secretary of war), and Edward Bates (attorney general), as well as Gideon Welles (secretary of the navy), Montgomery Blair (postmaster general), and Caleb B. Smith (secretary of the interior). Inaugurated on March 4. Decides, after much discussion with Cabinet, to send naval expedition to resupply Fort Sumter in Charleston harbor. Confederates open fire on the fort, April 12, and its garrison surrenders two days later. On April 15, Lincoln calls forth 75,000 militia and summons Congress to meet on July 4 in special session. Meets with Douglas, who supports Lincoln's efforts to preserve the Union and advises calling for 200,000 troops. Virginia secedes on April 17 and is followed within five weeks by North Carolina, Tennessee, and Arkansas, forming eleven-state Confederacy. On April 19, Lincoln proclaims blockade of Southern ports, and on April 27 he authorizes the military to suspend the writ of habeas corpus along the Philadelphia–Washington railroad line. Issues proclamation on May 3 directing expansion of the regular army and navy. Consults with various members of Congress, including Massachusetts senator Charles Sumner, beginning a personal friendship. Suffers first sense of personal loss in the war at the news of the death on May 24 of his young friend Colonel Elmer Ellsworth, shot while removing a Confederate flag from a building in Alexandria. Disregards *Ex parte Merryman* opinion of Chief Justice Roger B. Taney, finding his suspension of habeas corpus unconstitutional (Taney had sought unsuccessfully to enforce a writ issued by himself, not the full Court, which did not hear the case). Has White House draped in mourning after Douglas dies in Illinois on June 3 while rallying support for the Union. Follows progress of battle and Union defeat at Bull Run, July 21, from War Department telegraph office (will receive news and send orders from there for remainder of war). Appoints George B. McClellan commander of the Department (later Army) of the Potomac on July 27. Sees visitors, including Cabinet members, senators, congressmen, military officers, office-seekers, and ordinary citizens, for several hours each weekday. Often takes carriage rides in the afternoon. Writes letters and signs commissions in the evening. Enjoys attending theater, opera, and concerts. Reads Shakespeare, the Bible, and humorous writings of Artemus Ward, Orpheus C. Kerr, and Petroleum V. Nasby. On September 11, revokes General John C. Frémont's proclamation of emancipation in Missouri, bitterly disappointing many antislavery advocates. Saddened by death on October 21 of friend and former Illinois Whig colleague Edward D. Baker in skirmish at Ball's Bluff, Virginia. On October 24, signs order relieving Frémont of

his command. Replaces him with General David Hunter.
On November 1, appoints McClellan commander of the
Union army after Winfield Scott retires. In message to
Congress, December 3, recommends program of emancipation and colonization for slaves confiscated from Confederate owners. After Cabinet meetings on December 25
and 26, agrees to the release of two Confederate envoys
seized from British ship *Trent* in November, resolving
serious Anglo-American crisis.

1862   Reads General Henry Halleck's *Elements of Military Art
and Science*. Meets with congressional Committee on the
Conduct of the War and rejects demand of its chairman,
Ohio Republican senator Benjamin Wade, that McClellan
be dismissed for inaction. On January 13, replaces Simon
Cameron with Democrat Edwin Stanton amid charges of
widespread corruption and incompetence in the War
Department. Nominates Noah Swayne of Ohio to the
Supreme Court. Issues General War Order No. 1 on January 27, calling for a simultaneous Union advance on several
fronts beginning February 22. Is frustrated by McClellan's
unwillingness to take offensive action in Virginia. Recommends promotion of Ulysses S. Grant to major general
after capture of Fort Donelson in Tennessee by Grant's
army on February 16. Son Willie falls ill in early February
(probably with typhoid fever) and dies on February 20.
Wife is overcome with grief and never recovers emotion-
ally. Lincoln relieves McClellan as general-in-chief on
March 11 and assumes direct command of the Union
armies (retains McClellan as commander of the Army of
the Potomac). Appoints Halleck as commander of western
armies. Reluctantly agrees to McClellan's plan for an advance on Richmond by way of the peninsula between the
York and James rivers and is frustrated by its slow
progress. Signs act on April 16 abolishing slavery in the
District of Columbia. Refuses to dismiss Grant, who is
widely blamed for heavy Union losses at battle of Shiloh.
Visits Peninsula, May 5–12, and directs successful Union
attack on Norfolk, Virginia. On May 15, approves legislation establishing the Department of Agriculture, and signs
the Homestead Act on May 20. Visits General Irvin Mc-
Dowell's corps at Fredericksburg, May 22–23. On May 24,
concerned about safety of Washington, cancels planned
movement of McDowell's troops to join McClellan's army

near Richmond and orders that McDowell launch an attack on Thomas (Stonewall) Jackson's command in the
Shenandoah Valley. To escape the heat, moves with family
in early June to cottage at Soldiers' Home on hill four
miles northwest of White House (will live there each summer). On June 19, approves legislation prohibiting slavery
in the territories. Issues order on June 26 that consolidates
Union forces in the Shenandoah Valley and northern Virginia as the Army of Virginia, under General John Pope.
Signs Pacific Railroad Act and bill providing land grants
for agricultural colleges on July 2. Visits Peninsula, July
7–10, conferring with McClellan and his corps commanders in aftermath of the Seven Days' battles. Returns to
Washington and appoints Halleck general-in-chief on July
11 (does not name new overall western commander to replace Halleck). Nominates Iowa Republican Samuel
Miller to Supreme Court. On July 17, signs Second Confiscation Act, authorizing seizure of slaves and other property of persons found by federal courts to be supporting
the rebellion, after Congress appends resolution satisfying
most of his reservations. Reads draft of preliminary Emancipation Proclamation to Cabinet on July 22, but delays
issuing it, apparently agreeing with Seward that it should
follow a Union military victory to avoid being seen as an
act of desperation. Agrees with Halleck's decision to abandon Peninsula campaign and withdraw Army of the Potomac (order is issued on August 3); move is widely
criticized, with campaign's failure attributed to Lincoln's
withholding of troops for defense of Washington. Relieves
Pope after his defeat at the second battle of Bull Run, August 29–30, and places his army under McClellan's command, despite distrust of McClellan in the Cabinet and
Congress. Union victory at Antietam on September 17
ends Lee's invasion of Maryland. Lincoln issues preliminary Emancipation Proclamation on September 22, to take
effect January 1, 1863, in all territory still in rebellion
against the national government. Worried by significant
Democratic gains in fall congressional and state elections.
Nominates his friend David Davis to the Supreme Court.
Removes Don Carlos Buell from command of the Army
of the Ohio, October 23, and replaces him on October 30
with William Rosecrans (command becomes Army of the
Cumberland). Replaces McClellan with Ambrose Burn-

side as commander of the Army of the Potomac on November 5, and confers with Burnside at Aquia Creek, Virginia, on November 27. In annual message to Congress, December 1, recommends constitutional amendment authorizing gradual, compensated emancipation. Extends clemency to 265 of 303 Sioux Indians condemned to death after summer uprising in Minnesota. Army of the Potomac suffers costly defeat at Fredericksburg on December 13. Lincoln holds lengthy meeting on December 19 with Cabinet (excluding Seward) and nine senators from Republican caucus seeking Seward's dismissal and greater Cabinet role in running government. Meeting results in submission of resignation by Chase, Seward's chief Cabinet critic; Lincoln rejects it, along with previously submitted resignation of Seward, thereby resolving crisis. Signs bill on December 31 admitting West Virginia to the Union.

1863   On January 1, issues the Emancipation Proclamation freeing all slaves in Confederate-held territory. Responding to protests, on January 4 revokes Grant's order of December 17, 1862, that expelled all Jews from the Department of Tennessee. John P. Usher succeeds Caleb B. Smith as secretary of the interior. Appoints Joseph Hooker to succeed Burnside on January 25. Approves bill on February 25 creating a national banking system, and signs act on March 3 introducing military conscription. Nominates California judge Stephen J. Field to the Supreme Court. Concerned by allegations that Grant is incompetent and frequently drunk, is reassured by reports of Charles A. Dana, Stanton's special emissary at Grant's headquarters. April 4–10, visits Army of the Potomac at its winter quarters in Falmouth, Virginia, and views Fredericksburg battlefield from Union front line. Battle of Chancellorsville, May 1–4, ends in Union defeat, and Lincoln returns to Falmouth on May 7 to confer with Hooker. Replaces Hooker with George G. Meade, June 28, during Lee's invasion of Pennsylvania. Greatly encouraged by Lee's defeat at Gettysburg on July 3 and by capture of Vicksburg, last major Confederate stronghold on the Mississippi, by Grant's army on July 4. Discusses recruitment and treatment of Negro troops with abolitionist Frederick Douglass at White House on August 10; Douglass is impressed by seriousness with which Lincoln receives him. Encouraged by victories of administration supporters in Ohio and Pennsylvania state elections. With Chattanooga under Confederate siege after the Union defeat at Chickamauga, September 19–20, appoints Grant to command of all operations in the western theater and authorizes him to replace Rosecrans with George H. Thomas as commander of the Army of the Cumberland. Delivers dedicatory address at the Gettysburg Cemetery on November 19 to audience of 15,000–20,000, following two-hour oration by Edward Everett. Ill with varioloid (mild form of smallpox) for three weeks after return to Washington. Issues proclamation of amnesty and reconstruction, a program for restoration of the Union, on December 8. Retains Chase in Cabinet despite Chase's willingness to challenge him for the Republican nomination.

1864   "Pomeroy Circular," a letter produced by radicals supporting Chase's candidacy and distributed to influential Republicans, is published in late February. It embarrasses Chase and rallies support for Lincoln. He receives endorsement for second term from Republican caucus in Ohio, Chase's home state, and in early March Chase withdraws from campaign. On March 12, appoints Grant general-in-chief of the armies, Halleck chief of staff, and William T. Sherman as Grant's successor commanding in the West. Grant makes his headquarters with the Army of the Potomac while retaining Meade as its commander. Responding to a recommendation from Lincoln and Stanton, Congress repeals provision in conscription law that allows payment of $300 in lieu of service. Signed by Lincoln on July 4, the act retains the provision that permits hiring a substitute. Nominated for president June 8 on first ballot by nearly unanimous vote of the National Union Convention, a coalition of Republicans and War Democrats. Convention nominates Democrat Andrew Johnson, military governor of Tennessee, for vice-president and endorses proposed constitutional amendment abolishing slavery. Lincoln accepts Chase's resignation on June 30 and names Republican senator William P. Fessenden of Maine as his successor. Pocket-vetoes the Wade-Davis bill, congressional reconstruction plan he considers too severe, on July 4. Observes fighting on outskirts of Washington from parapet of Fort Stevens during unsuccessful Confederate attack, July 11–12, and comes under fire. Writes private memorandum on August 23, acknowledging that he probably will not be reelected. Feels less pessimistic about his election prospects after capture of Atlanta by Sherman's army on September 2 and General Philip H. Sheridan's decisive victory in the Shenandoah Valley at Cedar Creek on October 19. Appeases Republican radicals by replacing conservative Montgomery Blair as postmaster general with William Dennison on September 23. On Grant's advice, approves Sherman's planned march from Atlanta to the sea. Follows election returns at War Department telegraph office on November 8. Defeats Democratic nominee, General George B. McClellan, winning 55 per cent of popular vote and 212 of 233 electoral votes. Appoints James Speed (brother of friend Joshua F. Speed) as attorney general to replace retiring Edward Bates. Nominates Salmon P. Chase as chief justice of the Supreme Court on December 6.

1865   Uses influence to gain some Democratic support in House of Representatives for resolution proposing submission of Thirteenth Amendment, abolishing slavery, to states for ratification (Senate had approved amendment in April 1864). House passes resolution by three-vote margin on January 31. Meets with Confederate representatives in unsuccessful peace conference at Hampton Roads, Virginia, on February 3. Signs bill on March 3 creating bureau for relief of freedmen and refugees. Inaugurated for second term on March 4. Names Comptroller of the Currency Hugh McCullough as secretary of the treasury when Fessenden returns to Senate. Leaves for City Point, Virginia, on March 23 and confers with Grant, Sherman, and Admiral David D. Porter on military and political situation, March 27–28. Visits Richmond on April 4 after its evacuation by the Confederate army. Returns to Washington on April 9, the day of Lee's surrender to Grant at Appomattox Court House. Makes last public speech on April 11, devoting it mainly to problems of reconstruction. Shot in the head by well-known actor John Wilkes Booth while watching performance of comedy *Our American Cousin* at Ford's Theatre shortly after 10 P.M., April 14. Dies in nearby house without regaining consciousness at 7:22 A.M., April 15. After funeral service in the White House on April 19, casket is viewed by millions as it is carried by special train to Illinois before burial in Oak Ridge Cemetery, outside Springfield, on May 4.

Note on the Texts

This volume presents the texts of 555 letters, speeches, messages, proclamations, orders, memoranda, drafts, and fragments written or delivered by Abraham Lincoln from early January 1859 to shortly before his death in April 1865. Almost all of the texts included here are from volumes three through eight of the Abraham Lincoln Association's *The Collected Works of Abraham Lincoln* (eight volumes and an index, 1953–55), edited by Roy P. Basler, with the assistance of Marion Dolores Pratt and Lloyd A. Dunlap. Eight items are from *The Collected Works of Abraham Lincoln: Supplement 1832–1865* (1974), edited by Roy P. Basler, and one item is taken from the June 15, 1863, *New York Tribune*.

Many of the items in this volume existed only as autograph manuscript during Lincoln's lifetime. His speeches, however, were often printed in newspapers, based on reporters' shorthand transcriptions and notes or set from manuscripts provided by Lincoln, and he proofread and corrected his Cooper Institute address for pamphlet publication. Some official presidential documents were put in print by the government press, or copied out by government scribes.

The first major collection of Lincoln's writings was the *Complete Works of Abraham Lincoln*, edited by John G. Nicolay and John Hay, published first in two volumes in 1894 and later expanded to twelve volumes in 1905. Nicolay and Hay had served as secretaries to Lincoln during his presidency, and they prepared the *Complete Works* with the cooperation of Lincoln's son, Robert Todd Lincoln, who gave them access to a large archive of papers under his control. Their edition continues to be valuable because it is the only source for some items of which the originals have since been lost or destroyed. However, Nicolay and Hay frequently made changes in Lincoln's spelling, diction, punctuation, sentence structure, and paragraphing. Subsequent collections of Lincoln's writings, which were published as new material was found in the decades following the Nicolay and Hay edition, also adopted editorial policies that allowed great freedom with the original documents.

In contrast, Roy P. Basler, as editor of *The Collected Works* (1953–55), and its *Supplement* (1974), restricted the emendation of previously printed pieces to the correction of typographical errors, and he transcribed and printed manuscripts without alterations, except in a few instances: a single period after abbreviations and initials replaces the double period Lincoln often used, and periods are substituted for the dashes Lincoln used to close his sentences. Basler began his editorial work for the Abraham Lincoln Association in 1947, using its large collection of Lincoln materials, as well as the recently opened Robert Todd Lincoln Collection in the Library of Congress, which contained material that previously had been available only to Nicolay and Hay. If an item still existed in manuscript and was not later revised by Lincoln, he used that version, showing variants in printed versions either in brackets or in footnotes. If an item existed in manuscript but was subsequently revised by Lincoln, Basler usually used the revised version, and printed the earlier readings in footnotes. Where no manuscript source was available, the editors of *The Collected Works* chose the best alternative source as their copy, usually the newspaper version that most fully reported Lincoln's words or the printed government document. In a few cases, when the original source for an item could not be located or was no longer available for publication, Basler took the text from a later printed version, most often from the Nicolay-Hay edition or from *The War of the Rebellion: A Compilation of the Official Records of the Union and Confederate Armies* (70 volumes, 1880–1901).

Because *The Collected Works* (1953–55), and its *Supplement* (1974), best preserves Lincoln's own usage, texts from that edition are printed here. The following are the eight items in this volume taken from the *Supplement*: Notes for Speech at Columbus, Ohio, September 16, 1859; Speech at Cincinnati, Ohio, September 17, 1859 (section missing from middle of *Collected Works* version); To Samuel Galloway, December 19, 1859; To Mary Todd Lincoln, March 4, 1860; To Edwin M. Stanton, July 22, 1862; To David Davis, August 27, 1862; Verses on Lee's Invasion of the North, July 19, 1863; To Charles Sumner, May 19, 1864. One item, To Erastus Corning and Others, June 12, 1863, is taken from the June 15, 1863, *New York Tribune*.

In the present volume bracketed conjectural readings, provided by Basler in cases where the original manuscript text was damaged or difficult to read, are accepted without brackets when that reading seems the only possible one; otherwise the missing words are indicated by a bracketed space, i.e., [   ]. The same rule is followed in handling omissions by Lincoln in manuscript; if Lincoln's omission could be filled by any of several words, no conjecture is offered and the sentence is printed as Lincoln wrote it. The present volume omits the editorial *sic* used after repeated letters and words and accepts the indicated corrections. In addition, four of Lincoln's slips of the pen are corrected here even though the words were not emended in brackets or followed by "[*sic*]" in Basler: at 390.33, "brigdge" is changed to "bridge"; at 466.35, "unchanged' " is changed to "unchanged.' "; at 466.35, "Doubless" is changed to "Doubtless"; and at 470.33, "preval" is changed to "prevail."

Where there were apparent errors in the printed text, or in a copy made by someone other than Lincoln, the editors of *The Collected Works* printed the error and bracketed the conjectural correction next to it; for example at 80.18 the editors have "Union [at]." If the conjectured reading is clearly correct, this volume removes the brackets and accepts the editorial emendation. In those cases where bracketed words were inserted by Basler to show variant readings among two or more printed sources, the present volume removes the bracketed word (some of these variants can be found in the notes to this volume). Three errors in the originals not corrected in *The Collected Works* are corrected here: at 74.20, "notwithstanding," is changed to "notwithstanding"; at 202.1, "homoepathist" is changed to "homœopathist"; and at 543.24, "$901,125,674 86" is changed to "$901,125,674.86."

This volume presents the texts of the editions chosen for inclusion here but does not attempt to reproduce features of their typographic design. Some headings have been changed, and Abraham Lincoln's name at the end of letters (which he almost invariably signed "A. Lincoln") has been omitted. The texts are printed without alteration except for the changes previously discussed and for the correction of typographical errors. Spelling, punctuation, and capitalization are often expressive features, and they are not altered, even when inconsistent or irregular. The following is a list of typographical errors corrected, cited by page and line number: 10.13, equality; 29.35, "control" &c"; 42.35, provincial; 106.27, material; 107.31, year in Illinois—; 107.31, New-Salem,; 107.38, I have; 143.20, designate man; 172.4, Baltimore?.; 260.1—2, sailor is is; 276.28, *pro*vided; 350.16, on.]; 350.19, it?]; 366.18, idex; 392.5—6, resignation?; 415.5, our selves; 457.12, civil; 462.3, relieve; 553.40, hertofore; 588.7, intance; 674.6, *sent.* Errors corrected sixth printing: 384 3, in the,

Notes

In the notes that follow, the reference numbers denote page and line of this volume (the line count includes item headings). No note is made for material included in a standard desk-reference book. Correspondents and names mentioned by Lincoln are identified only when they are essential to an understanding of the text. Some persons are identified in greater detail in the notes for the preceding volume, *Speeches and Writings 1832–1858* (New York: The Library of America, 1989). Prefatory and end notes within the text are Lincoln's own. For more detailed notes and references to other studies, see *The Collected Works of Abraham Lincoln*, 8 volumes plus index (New Brunswick: Rutgers University Press, 1953–55), edited by Roy P. Basler, Marion Dolores Pratt, and Lloyd A. Dunlap; *The Collected Works of Abraham Lincoln: Supplement 1832–1865* (Westport, Connecticut: Greenwood Press, 1974), edited by Roy P. Basler; *Lincoln Day by Day: A Chronology*, 3 volumes (Washington, D.C.: Lincoln Sesquicentennial Commission, 1960), edited by Earl Schenck Miers, William E. Baringer, and C. Percy Powell; and Mark E. Neely, Jr., *The Abraham Lincoln Encyclopedia* (New York: McGraw-Hill, 1982).

1.33   brother's speech] Delivered in Congress on January 10, 1859, by Israel Washburn, Jr., a representative from Maine, 1851–61.

2.25   Cuba] At the request of President Buchanan, legislation had been introduced in the Senate appropriating thirty million dollars for use as an advance payment in negotiating the purchase of Cuba from Spain. Republican opposition prevented adoption of the measure before the Senate adjourned in March 1859.

3.1   *Lecture . . . Inventions*] Presented at Illinois College in Jacksonville on February 11, 1859, and repeated in Decatur and Springfield over the next ten days. Lincoln had delivered a different lecture on the same subject in April 1858.

3.27–28   "a pleasing . . . after"] Joseph Addison (1672–1719), *Cato* (1713), V, i.

9.10–11   the present . . . 1434] Lincoln refers to the opening of the African slave trade, which began with the importation of slaves into Portugal.

12.1   *Speech at Chicago*] Although this speech was taken down in shorthand by Robert Hitt, the reporter who recorded the Lincoln-Douglas debates for the Chicago *Press and Tribune*, it was not published until 1893, when it appeared in the *North American Review*. In a prefatory note, Hitt wrote that Lincoln had objected to its publication on the grounds that his criticism of the New York *Tribune* (see p. 15.7–20) would needlessly offend Horace Greeley.

12.2–3   your . . . triumphed]   Chicagoans had that day reelected their Republican mayor.

14.11–13   Haskin . . . Davis]   Congressmen Haskin, John Hickman of Pennsylvania, and John G. Davis of Indiana were anti-Lecompton Democrats who, despite administration efforts to purge them, had won reelection with Republican help.

18.1   *To Henry L. Pierce*]   This letter was widely printed in the Republican press.

19.7–8   One . . . lies"]   Rufus Choate (1799–1859), a leading Massachusetts Whig, wrote of the "glittering and sounding generalities of natural right which make up the Declaration of Independence" in an August 9, 1856, letter to Maine Whigs that endorsed James Buchanan for president. John Pettit (1807–77), a Democratic senator from Indiana, called the Declaration of Independence "a self-evident lie" during the debate over the Kansas-Nebraska bill in 1854. For earlier references by Lincoln to the Pettit statement, see Abraham Lincoln, *Speeches and Writings 1832–1858* (New York: The Library of America, 1989), pp. 339.10–24 and 795.9–12; and for Lincoln's assertion that the attack on the Declaration of Independence began with John C. Calhoun and other Southerners, see pp. 269.18–270.6 and 795.2–8 in that volume.

20.30   Ossawatan]   The Kansas Republican convention was held in Ossawatomie.

21.26   *To Theodore Canisius*]   This letter was printed in a number of newspapers, including the *Illinois Staats-Anzeiger*, a German-language paper published by Canisius and subsidized by Lincoln.

23.19   *ex vi termini*]   From the force of the term.

26.23   *Samuel Galloway*]   Galloway (1811–72), a Columbus, Ohio, attorney, had served in Congress, 1855–57.

26.32   Judge Swan]   Joseph R. Swan (1802–84), member of the Ohio supreme court, who had recently delivered a decision upholding the constitutionality of the fugitive-slave laws.

28.34–35   division . . . authority]   A reference to Stephen A. Douglas's article "The Dividing Line Between Federal and Local Authority: Popular Sovereignty in the Territories," published in the September 1859 issue of *Harper's Magazine*.

29.17   *D. P. S.*]   Douglas Popular Sovereignty.

29.20   *Copy right essay*]   See note 28.34–35.

32.29   Upon . . . occasion]   In the fourth debate, held at Charleston, Illinois, on September 18, 1858.

41.33–34   "I tremble . . . just!"]   Cf. *Notes on the State of Virginia* (1785), Query XVIII, "Manners."

55.1   recently . . . Douglas']   Probably a letter from Douglas to John L. Peyton of Virginia, written on August 2 and published in the Chicago *Times* on August 16, 1859, that opposed on constitutional grounds the reopening of the African slave trade. In a letter of June 22, 1859, to J. B. Dorr, editor of the Dubuque, Iowa, *Express and Herald*, Douglas had listed the revival of the slave trade as one of several "new issues" that he was unwilling to have included in the "creed of the party."

70.6–7   a letter . . . Iowa]   See note 55.1.

74.12–13   Seward . . . conflict"]   Seward used the phrase in a speech delivered in Rochester, New York, on October 25, 1858.

74.36–37   made . . . paper]   The Washington *States*.

83.32–86.19   At least . . . discussion.]   This portion of the speech, though recorded at the time, was omitted from the contemporary newspaper report and published for the first time in *Lives and Speeches of Abraham Lincoln and Hannibal Hamlin* (1860), a campaign biography by William Dean Howells.

87.35   loaves and fishes"]   A colloquial expression for the emoluments of office. Cf. John 6:1–14, 24–27.

88.37–38   he who . . . scattereth]   Cf. Matthew 12:30; Luke 11:23.

90.25   Pope . . . aim,"]   *An Essay on Man* (1734), Epistle IV, line 1.

102.7   *William Kellogg*]   Kellogg (1814–72) was a Republican congressman from Illinois, 1857–63.

102.35–36   Lecompton & Slave . . . man]   Congressman Thomas S. Bocock of Virginia, whom Democrats were supporting in a fierce contest for Speaker of the House of Representatives against Republican John Sherman of Ohio. On February 1, 1860, and on the forty-fourth ballot, the House elected William Pennington of New Jersey, a Whig recently turned Republican.

103.11   justice to Mr. Judd]   Lincoln was defending Norman B. Judd, the Republican state chairman and national committeeman, against attacks originating in the Chicago *Democrat*, owned and edited by Judd's political rival, John Wentworth. Over a period of many months in 1859, Wentworth had accused Judd of helping to cheat Lincoln out of the senatorship in 1855, mismanaging the 1858 campaign, wasting party funds, and using his position to promote Lyman Trumbull for the presidency and his own candidacy for governor. The *Democrat* also linked Judd with a major financial scandal that tarnished the reputation of former governor Joel A. Matteson. Judd brought suit for libel against Wentworth on December 1 and wrote to Lincoln the same day demanding vindication. In responding to Judd's letter on December 9, Lincoln said: "It has a tone of blame towards myself which I think is not quite just; but I will not stand upon that, but will consider a day or two, and put something in the best shape I can . . ." Lincoln went on to assure Judd that he did not believe the charges laid against him and did not consider Trumbull a rival. "You know I am pledged," he wrote, "to not enter a struggle with him for the seat in the Senate now occupied by him; and yet I would rather have a full term in the Senate than in the Presidency." Judd was meanwhile arranging for Dole, Hubbard, and Brown to draft a letter of inquiry which Judd himself mailed to Lincoln on December 12. Lincoln sent his response, not to the addressees, but to Judd, who found it satisfactory but waited six weeks before publishing it. In late December Lincoln was drawn further into the quarrel when Wentworth tried to retain him as counsel. The publication of the Dole, Hubbard, and Brown letter angered Wentworth's supporters and others opposed to Judd's candidacy for governor (see Lincoln to Judd, February 9, 1860, p. 109 in this volume). Convinced that he should try to mediate the feud, Lincoln wrote to Wentworth suggesting that he visit Springfield on February 8, 1860, at which time Judd would also be there for a meeting of the Republican state central committee. Wentworth replied on February 7 that he was sick and could not travel at the moment, but would be willing to go to Springfield at a later time. Mistakenly believing that Lincoln wanted him to sit in on a meeting of the central committee, he expressed doubt about the propriety of doing so. He also gave Lincoln some advice about strategy at the Republican national convention: "Look out for *prominence*. When it is ascertained that no one of the prominent candidates can be nominated, then *ought* to be your time." Lincoln responded on February 9 by proposing terms of a settlement with Judd. This letter, now owned by the Chicago Historical Society, is printed here for the first time (the closing and signature have been cut off the original):

Hon: John Wentworth   Springfield, Feb. 9. 1860
Dear Sir:

Yours of the 7th was not received till this morning— You seem to mistake, somewhat, the object of my last letter to you— I wished you here for no object but to try to settle the difficulty between you & Judd, which I thought there would be a better chance of doing if I could have you both near me at the same time. I selected the meeting of the Committee because that would bring Judd here at any rate, and would furnish an *outside* reason for your being here; and not because I wished, or expected you to interfere with the business of the Committee in any way— I repeat, I am anxious to have that difficulty settled, so that both you and he can pull square in the cause and not be expending your strength in fighting oneanother— In your paper of December 10th you said what ought to almost, if not quite satisfy Judd, if it were said distinctly from everything else, and placed upon the record— I propose the following: You write, sign and place on the files of the court the following—

"I have made no reflections upon Mr. Judd, morally, socially, pecuniarily, professionally, and in no other way, save" politically; and if I have used language capable of different construction, I have not intended it, and now retract it—

Upon which, Judd to continue the suit till after the Presidential election, at which time I to dismiss the suit, if, in my judgment, both you and he have, in the mean time, in good faith, let oneanother alone— I mean you are to let him alone, both in and out of your paper; and that he is to let you alone both in and out of the Press & Tribune— Let the papers, as such contend with oneanother on measures of policy as much as they like; but John Wentworth and N. B. Judd, to be absolutely let alone in both of them—

Write me what you think of it— I think both you and he ought to do it—

I have not time now to say more about a nomination on the National ticket, than that I thank you for your kind suggestions and expressions; and that I will try to write you a letter more fully about it soon.

Wentworth balked at the terms, wanting immediate withdrawal of the suit. On March 6, he won the Chicago mayoral election with Judd lending reluctant support, and nothing more was heard of the lawsuit. Judd failed in his bid for the gubernatorial nomination, which went to Richard Yates.

105.33   six . . . speeches] Lincoln's "House Divided" speech, given at Springfield on June 16, 1858; Douglas's and Lincoln's speeches at Chicago, delivered on July 9 and 10 respectively; Douglas's speech at Bloomington on July 16; and the speeches Douglas and Lincoln gave in Springfield on July 17.

106.20   *To Jesse W. Fell*] Fell (1808–87), a lawyer and land speculator, was secretary of the Illinois Republican state central committee. He requested the sketch on behalf of the West Chester, Pennsylvania, *Chester County Times*, which used it in preparing an article published on February 11, 1860, that was later reprinted in other Republican papers.

108.16   *James W. Sheahan*] Editor of the Chicago *Times*, a pro-Douglas paper.

111.1   *Address at Cooper Institute*] The manuscript of the speech is not known to be extant, but Lincoln supervised preparation of the pamphlet edition from which this text is taken. Extensive historical footnotes, prepared for the pamphlet by Charles C. Nott and Cephas Brainerd, are omitted here.

124.2–4   Southampton . . . Ferry] On August 22–24, 1831, insurgent slaves led by Nat Turner killed approximately sixty white men, women, and children in Southampton County, Virginia. Over a hundred blacks were indiscriminately killed during the suppression of the revolt. In addition, Turner and twenty others were executed. Fifteen people were killed during John

Brown's raid on Harpers Ferry, October 16–18, 1859, and Brown and four of his men had been hanged by the time of Lincoln's speech.

124.33–38   "It is . . . up."] From the *Autobiography*, written in 1821 but not published until after his death.

125.23   Helper's Book] *The Impending Crisis of the South: How to Meet It* (1857), by Hinton R. Helper of North Carolina. Helper attacked slavery as being harmful to the economic and social well-being of nonslaveholding Southern whites. The publication in the North of an abridged version, and its endorsement by sixty-eight Republican congressmen, had been an issue in the recent contest for Speaker of the House (see note 102.35–36).

130.28   the boys] Robert Todd Lincoln and a classmate at Phillips Exeter Academy.

130.31–32   Pemberton Mill tragedy] The collapse of the mill building on January 10 had killed eighty-eight workers and injured almost three hundred others.

146.2   white list] A list of Democratic (rather than "Black Republican") firms that would presumably be exempt from the Southern boycott of New England manufactures.

150.33–34   such as . . . did] Cf. the corresponding passage in the Cooper Institute speech, p. 130.15–17 in this volume.

154.14–15   Charleston hangs fire] Lincoln refers to the Democratic national convention then in session at Charleston, South Carolina. Hopelessly split between Northern supporters and Southern opponents of Douglas, it adjourned on May 3 without having nominated a presidential candidate.

157.9–10   without . . . delay] The text printed is from the *Illinois State Journal*. According to the New York *Tribune*, Lincoln said "without unnecessary or unreasonable delay."

158.37   collection more] This may be a misreading of "collective noun" in Lincoln's original letter, which has not been found.

160.1   *Autobiography . . . Campaign*] Lincoln prepared this sketch at the request of John L. Scripps of the Chicago *Press and Tribune*, who used it in writing his short campaign biography, *Life of Abraham Lincoln*, published in July 1860.

164.2   "rail . . . Decatur] On May 9, 1860, Hanks helped carry two rails supposedly split by Lincoln into the Republican state convention at Decatur. This demonstration, which was arranged by attorney Richard J. Oglesby, was the beginning of the "Rail Splitter" theme in the 1860 campaign.

165.19–20   The protest . . . it)] The protest is printed on page 18 of Abraham Lincoln, *Speeches and Writings 1832–1858*.

167.24–26   Galena . . . speech] Lincoln spoke at Galena on July 23, 1856, and his speech was reported in the Galena *Daily Advertiser* three days later. According to this account, which was prefaced by the reporter's admission that he was "re-producing from memory," Lincoln argued that Southerners, if they believed that prohibition of slavery in the territories was unconstitutional, should seek a judicial remedy and accept the decision rendered, rather than break up the Union. The newspaper quotes Lincoln as saying: "I grant you that an unconstitutional act is not a law; but I do not ask, and will not take your construction of the Constitution. The Supreme Court of the United States is the tribunal to decide such questions, and we will submit to its decisions; and if you do also, there will be an end of the matter. Will you? If not, who are the disunionists, you or we?"

168.9   American party] The party organized in the 1850s to oppose Catholic and immigrant influence in American public life. It was also known as the Know-Nothing party.

168.24   Gov. Reeder] Andrew H. Reeder (1807–64) served as territorial governor of Kansas, 1854–55, before being dismissed by President Franklin Pierce for supporting the free-soil settlers there.

169.6   Cousin Annie's] Dickson's wife, Annie Parker Dickson, was a cousin of Mary Todd Lincoln.

170.6   *J. Mason Haight*] A journalist and member of a temperance society in Madison, Wisconsin.

170.23–24   Follett . . . Life] *Lives and Speeches of Abraham Lincoln and Hannibal Hamlin*, by 23-year-old William Dean Howells, at the time a writer for the *Ohio State Journal*.

170.31–32   Mr. Howard] James Q. Howard, a young law student who had visited Springfield to gather information for the biography.

171.30–31   Logan and Baker] David Logan, son of Lincoln's former law partner, Stephen T. Logan, was an unsuccessful candidate for Congress in Oregon. Edward D. Baker, a friend of Lincoln's who had been a leading Illinois Whig before moving to California and then to Oregon, was elected to the U.S. Senate.

172.4–5   Baltimore . . . Breckenridge] The Democratic national convention reconvened in Baltimore June 18–23 and again split along sectional lines. The Northern Democrats nominated Douglas for president, while the Southern Democrats, having withdrawn to another hall, chose John C. Breckinridge as their candidate.

173.8   Richardson] William A. Richardson (1811–75), an Illinois Democrat, served in Congress, 1847–56, and in the Senate, 1863–65.

174.27   your Oregon election] Francis (1796–1872) published the *San-*

gamo Journal (later the *Illinois State Journal*), Springfield's Whig newspaper, from 1831 to 1856. He moved to the new state of Oregon in 1859.

176.19   John M. Botts]   Botts (1802–69), a Virginia Unionist, was a Whig congressman, 1839–43 and 1847–49. He opposed secession in 1861, and was imprisoned by the Confederate military for eight weeks in 1862.

176.29   *George G. Fogg*]   Fogg (1813–81), a New Hampshire lawyer and newspaper editor, was secretary of the Republican national committee. Lincoln appointed him minister to Switzerland in 1861.

177.11   respectable gentleman]   Samuel Haycraft. See Lincoln's letter to him, June 4, 1860, pp. 167–68 in this volume.

177.31–32   Please try . . . used.]   On August 23 Fogg wrote Lincoln that James Gordon Bennett, the owner and editor of the *Herald*, refused to print the correction unless it was attributed to Lincoln, or to Fogg, or was dated at Springfield. Fogg did not agree to these conditions, a decision Lincoln endorsed in a letter to him on August 29. By that time Lincoln had written twice to Samuel Haycraft, denying that he had felt threatened by Haycraft, or by any other Kentuckian.

178.6–7   *supposed* . . . Brougham]   George M. Dallas, the American minister to Great Britain, had not replied to the antislavery criticism of the United States made at an international statistical congress by Brougham, a former lord chancellor long active in the fight against the slave trade. Fisher had sent Lincoln a newspaper clipping in which his brother, Sidney G. Fisher, set forth his idea of how Dallas might have replied. Lincoln did not finish this letter, having apparently decided not to send it.

178.26   Mr. McC——]   Alexander K. McClure, chairman of the Republican state committee in Pennsylvania, sided with Andrew G. Curtin in the latter's feud with Simon Cameron. At the Republican national convention, McClure had played a leading role in swinging the state's vote from Cameron to Lincoln.

180.12   Your Uncle]   John T. Hanks was the son of Sarah Elizabeth Johnston Hanks, Lincoln's stepsister. He was also related on his father's side to Lincoln's mother, Nancy Hanks.

180.23   *Daniel P. Gardner*]   Gardner sold bars of his soap as the price of admission to his humorous lectures. His claim to have been a professor at Brown University is not supported by the institution's records.

181.3   Louisville . . . Sep. 29. 1860]   Douglas spoke in Louisville on this date, making points similar to those attributed to him here by Lincoln.

182.8   *Grace Bedell*]   This eleven-year-old Westfield, New York, girl had written to Lincoln on October 15: "I have got 4 brother's and part of them will vote for you any way and if you will let your whiskers grow I will try and get the rest of them to vote for you   you would look a great deal better for your face is so thin. All the ladies like whiskers and they would tease their husband's to vote for you and then you would be President."

182.30–31   "If . . . dead."] Luke 16:31.

184.2   Astor House] A New York hotel.

184.5   *George D. Prentice*] Prentice (1802–70) was editor of the Louisville *Journal*. In 1861 he opposed secession in Kentucky.

185.8   *Confidential*] This endorsement appears on the back of the letter. How long Lincoln held the letter before mailing it is not known, but Prentice did not reply until January 24, 1861.

185.11   *Truman Smith*] Smith (1791–1884), a Whig congressman from Connecticut, 1839–43 and 1845–49, had urged Lincoln to issue a statement calculated to allay public anxiety.

186.1   *Nathaniel P. Paschall*] Editor of the *Missouri Republican* in St. Louis, a Democratic paper.

186.28   *Passage . . . Speech*] In delivering his speech on November 20 at Springfield, Trumbull used the first paragraph of this passage, but not the second.

188.8   (The Times)] The New York *Times*, which Raymond had co-founded in 1851.

188.26–27   "They . . . them."] Cf. Matthew 12:39, 16:4; Mark 8:12; Luke 11:29.

189.25   Gov. S.] William H. Seward.

190.23   *John A. Gilmer*] Gilmer (1805–68) was an American congressman from North Carolina, 1857–61. An opponent of secession in 1860–61, he later served in the Confederate Congress, 1864–65.

192.20–21   Eli Thayer's] Thayer (1819–99) founded the Massachusetts (later, the New England) Emigrant Aid Society in 1854 to send free-soil settlers to Kansas. As a Republican congressman, 1857–61, he advocated the colonization of antislavery settlers as the solution to the slavery question in the territories.

193.12   Scott] Robert Eden Scott (1808–62) was a Virginia Unionist who nevertheless served in the Confederate Congress, 1861–62.

193.20   Smedes] William C. Smedes of Vicksburg, Mississippi, had written to Raymond denouncing Lincoln, especially for a speech he had allegedly made in Cincinnati when some free blacks presented a pitcher to Salmon P. Chase.

195.29   Gen. C.] Simon Cameron.

196.1   Mr. Bryant]   William Cullen Bryant, poet and editor of the New
York *Evening Post*.

198.3   New-Mexico]   The immediate admission of New Mexico, with the
understanding that it would enter as a slave state, was one of the compromise
measures being considered in Congress in response to the secession crisis.

198.9   a certain gentleman]   Benjamin F. Camp, a member of the New
York legislature.

199.1   *Farewell Address*]   This autograph version is partly in Lincoln's
handwriting and partly in that of his secretary, John G. Nicolay. The following variant version, which appeared the next day in the *Illinois State Journal*,
may be closer to what Lincoln actually said:

Friends,
   No one who has never been placed in a like position, can understand my
feelings at this hour, nor the oppressive sadness I feel at this parting. For
more than a quarter of a century I have lived among you, and during all
that time I have received nothing but kindness at your hands. Here I have
lived from my youth until now I am an old man. Here the most sacred ties
of earth were assumed; here all my children were born; and here one of
them lies buried. To you, dear friends, I owe all that I have, all that I am.
All the strange, chequered past seems to crowd now upon my mind. To-day
I leave you; I go to assume a task more difficult than that which devolved
upon General Washington. Unless the great God who assisted him, shall be
with and aid me, I must fail. But if the same omniscient mind, and
Almighty arm that directed and protected him, shall guide and support me,
I shall not fail, I shall succeed. Let us all pray that the God of our fathers
may not forsake us now. To him I commend you all—permit me to ask
that with equal security and faith, you all will invoke His wisdom and
guidance for me. With these few words I must leave you—for how long I
know not. Friends, one and all, I must now bid you an affectionate
farewell.

200.1–2   "The gates . . . them."]   Cf. Matthew 16:18.

201.11   * * * * *]   These asterisks appear in the Indianapolis *Daily Sentinel* text, which is printed here. They probably represent a passage not clearly
heard by the reporter in the cheering.

203.1   *Speech to Germans*]   This text appeared in the Cincinnati *Daily Commercial* on February 13. The Cincinnati *Daily Gazette* printed a variant version
the same day.

212.12   useless . . . now]   The text printed here is from the Philadelphia
Inquirer. According to the New York *Tribune* report, at this point Lincoln
added: "If I do speak, then it is useless for me to do so now."

212.20   long . . . consult]   According to the New York *Tribune* and the

New York *World*, Lincoln said: "long enough to consult your merchants and manufacturers."

212.31–33   May . . . mouth]   Cf. Psalm 137:5–6.

213.35   assassinated . . . spot]   Lincoln had been told the night before of a plot to kill him on his way through Baltimore.

218.31–33   The power . . . government]   In the first draft, written in Springfield in January 1861, this passage read: "All the power at my disposal will be used to reclaim the public property and places which have fallen; to hold, occupy and possess these, and all other property and places belonging to the government . . ." Lincoln followed the advice of Orville H. Browning in revising this passage for the final version.

224.5–11   I am . . . nature.]   This final paragraph was proposed and drafted by Seward as follows: "I close. We are not we must not be aliens or enemies but ~~countrm~~ fellow countrymen and brethren. Although passion has strained our bonds of affection too hardly they must not ~~be broken they will not~~, I am sure they will not be broken. The mystic chords which proceeding from ~~every ba~~ so many battle fields and ~~patriot~~ so many patriot graves ~~bind~~ pass through all the hearts and ~~hearths~~ all the hearths in this broad continent of ours will yet ~~harmon~~ again harmonize in their ancient music when ~~touched as they surely~~ breathed upon ~~again~~ by the ~~better angel~~ guardian angel of the nation."

224.22–23   anything . . . 1858]   Colfax was one of those Republican leaders who had been disposed to form an alliance with Douglas in opposition to the Lecompton constitution.

224.25   Mr. Smith]   Caleb B. Smith, whom Lincoln had appointed to be secretary of the interior.

225.12   your opinion endorsed]   Scott had written: "I now see no alternative but a surrender."

225.28   *To William H. Seward*]   This letter was sent to each member of the Cabinet. Seward, Cameron, Gideon Welles, Edward Bates, and Smith responded negatively. Montgomery Blair and Chase returned affirmative answers, but Chase's was qualified by the dubious assumption that such action would not lead to hostilities.

226.4   Cousin Lizzie]   Mary Todd Lincoln's cousin, Elizabeth Todd Grimsley.

226.6   William Jayne]   Brother of Trumbull's wife, Julia Jayne Trumbull.

227.8   *To William H. Seward*]   It appears that this letter was never sent and that Lincoln instead responded orally to Seward's memorandum. In addition to recommending the evacuation of Fort Sumter, Seward called for an aggressive foreign policy, perhaps carried even to the point of asking Congress for a declaration of war against Spain and France.

227.29   St. Domingo]   The Dominican Republic was being re-annexed by Spain.

228.13   *To Robert Anderson*]   Though signed by Cameron, this letter was drafted by Lincoln, who also added the endorsement.

228.17   Capt. Fox]   Gustavus V. Fox (1821–83), assistant secretary of the navy, 1861–65.

229.4   *To Robert S. Chew*]   This letter was drafted and endorsed by Lincoln.

232.1–2   *Proclamation . . . Congress*]   On May 3, 1861, Lincoln issued another proclamation in which he called for 42,034 army volunteers, ordered that the regular army be increased by 22,714, and ordered that 18,000 men be enlisted in the naval service.

234.25   punishment of piracy]   The Lincoln administration soon retreated from this threat to treat the officers and crews of Confederate vessels as pirates.

235.7   *Hicks . . . Brown*]   Hicks (1798–1865) was elected governor of Maryland as an American in 1857. He served in the Senate as a Republican, 1862–65. Brown was elected mayor of Baltimore as an independent in 1859. In September 1861 he was arrested by the military and imprisoned without trial until November 1862.

237.8   *To Winfield Scott*]   This is the only version of this order known to exist in manuscript, signed by Lincoln, but it is probably not the one actually sent to Scott. Another version, which broadened the scope of the order by omitting the words "via Perryville, Annapolis City, and Annapolis Junction," was provided to Congress, at its request, on July 13, 1861, and later was published in *The War of the Rebellion: A Compilation of the Official Records of the Union and Confederate Armies*. This broader version, in slightly different form, was included by Nicolay and Hay in their *Complete Works*. Significantly, Hay wrote in his diary on April 28, 1861: "Yesterday the President sent an order to General Scott authorizing and directing him to suspend the writ of habeas corpus on all necessary occasions along the lines of military occupation leading to this city from Philadelphia, &c." The text of the order as it appears in the *Official Records* is as follows:

The COMMANDING GENERAL ARMY OF THE UNITED STATES:
    You are engaged in repressing an insurrection against the laws of the United States. If at any point on or in the vicinity of any military line which is now or which shall be used between the city of Philadelphia and the city of Washington you find resistance which renders it necessary to suspend the writ of habeas corpus for the public safety, you personally or through the

officer in command at the point where resistance occurs are authorized to suspend that writ.

237.16–17   suspend . . . Corpus]   Later in 1861, Lincoln extended his authorization as follows: July 2, along the military line to New York City; October 14, along the military line to Bangor, Maine; December 2, within the state of Missouri.

237.31   war vessel]   The *Powhatan*, which, through the agency of Seward, was detached from the Fort Sumter expedition and sent to Fort Pickens in Florida.

239.20   *Francis P. Blair, Jr.*]   Blair (1821–75) was a Missouri congressman and brother of Postmaster General Montgomery Blair. He joined the Union army as a colonel in 1862 and eventually served as a corps commander under William T. Sherman.

239.26   Gen. Harney]   Brigadier General William S. Harney (1800–89), commander of the Department of the West and a Tennessean, was suspected of having pro-Confederate sympathies. He was relieved of duty on May 29 and given no other command for the remainder of the war.

240.18–19   an old friend]   Robert Irwin, a Springfield banker who handled many of Lincoln's financial affairs.

240.24   Mr. ——]   Parke Godwin (1816–1904), who was associated with William Cullen Bryant in publishing the New York *Evening Post*.

242.17   Elmer E. Ellsworth]   Ellsworth (1837–61) had read law in Lincoln's office. One of the war's first military heroes, he was killed on May 24, 1861, after hauling down a Confederate flag in Alexandria, Virginia.

243.13   Col. Meigs]   Montgomery C. Meigs (1816–92), who did serve as quartermaster general throughout the war.

244.26   *Ninian W. Edwards*]   Mary Todd Lincoln's brother-in-law; he received an appointment as a commissary at the rank of captain.

262.1   *To Simon B. Buckner*]   Governor Beriah Magoffin had sent Buckner to seek presidential approval of Kentucky's proclaimed policy of "neutrality" in the war between North and South.

266.20–21   proclamation . . . 30th]   Frémont, commander in Missouri, proclaimed that armed persons captured within Union lines would be court-martialed and, if found guilty, shot. He also ordered that the property of enemies of the Union be confiscated and their slaves emancipated.

266.33–34   conform . . . Congress]   The Confiscation Act of 1861 provided only for the forfeiture of slaves employed as soldiers or military laborers against the United States government.

268.6   *Orville H. Browning*]   Browning (1806–81), a long-time friend of

Lincoln's, was appointed to succeed Stephen A. Douglas in the Senate after Douglas's death on June 3, 1861. He served until 1863.

269.17   Gen. Anderson]   Robert Anderson (1805–71), commander of the Fort Sumter garrison, now commanding Union forces in his native Kentucky.

270.9   Hurlbut]   General Stephen A. Hurlbut (1815–82), an Illinoisan serving under Frémont in Missouri, was accused of habitual drunkenness. He did not resign and served through the war.

272.15   inclosure . . . Fremont]   The order relieving Frémont of his command and replacing him with Hunter.

272.26   *To David Hunter*]   The first two paragraphs of this letter were drafted in the War Department and revised by Lincoln, who then added the remainder of the letter.

274.10–11   a battle . . . value]   On November 7 Union forces under Ulysses S. Grant had captured a Confederate camp at Belmont, Missouri, before withdrawing in the face of numerically superior Confederate reinforcements.

276.1   *Drafts of Bill*]   The measure was never formally introduced in the Delaware legislature.

291.37   *pro tanto*]   To that extent.

298.22   *To David Hunter*]   According to Hunter's endorsement on the envelope, Lincoln held this letter for a month and then sent it by private messenger with directions to hand it to the general only when he was "in good humor."

298.29–30   the time . . . Leavenworth]   Hunter had been appointed military commander in Kansas on November 20.

299.25–26   "Act . . . lies."]   Alexander Pope, *An Essay on Man* (1734), Epistle IV, line 193.

299.36   Columbus]   Kentucky town on the Mississippi, fortified by the Confederates.

300.29   My despatch]   Lincoln had telegraphed Buell on January 4, asking him if arms had been sent to Union supporters in eastern Tennessee. Buell replied on January 5 that he could only send arms under the protection of troops, and that he preferred to move on Nashville instead.

303.16–17   I will . . . brigadier-general]   Lincoln changed his mind and instead appointed Koerner, a former lieutenant-governor of Illinois, minister to Spain in June 1862.

304.35   the Ocoquan]   Occoquan Creek is joined by Bull Run and flows into the Potomac southwest of Washington.

305.34–36   respite . . . A.D. 1862]   Gordon was hanged on February 21, the only slavetrader ever executed under federal law.

306.23   Clarksburg]   Clarksville.

307.3   Joint Resolution]   Congress passed the resolution on April 10.

310.4–5   specimen . . . handiwork]   A buggy whip presented by the delegation, which included Nathaniel Hawthorne.

310.19   *James A. McDougall*]   McDougall (1817–67) was a Democratic senator from California, 1861–67. He continued to oppose Lincoln's plan, questioning its constitutionality.

311.32   A domestic affliction]   The death of eleven-year-old William Wallace Lincoln on February 20.

315.4   Pope's splendid achievements]   Yates, governor of Illinois, and Butler, the state treasurer, wanted General John Pope, an Illinoisan, to be rewarded for having commanded the troops that captured Island No. 10 in the Mississippi on April 17.

316.20   femes-covert]   Married women.

316.22   supplemental act]   Congress passed the recommended legislation.

316.28   Parrott guns]   Rifled cannon.

320.5–6   McDowell . . . land]   Lincoln, fearing for the safety of Washington, refused to let McDowell's corps proceed by the water route to reinforce McClellan on the York Peninsula. Instead, McDowell was ordered by Stanton on May 17 to move overland toward a junction with McClellan's army, while holding himself "in such position as to cover the capital of the nation against a sudden dash of any large body of the rebel forces."

321.4   Shields']   James Shields, who had nearly fought a duel with Lincoln in 1842 over a series of letters satirizing his actions as state auditor of Illinois.

328.31   to all points]   Lincoln wrote and then deleted these additional words: "and last I must be the Judge as to the *duty*, of the government in this respect."

330.16   the same route]   Through the Shenandoah Valley of Virginia.

331.7   two late battles]   The two-day battle of Fair Oaks (also known as Seven Pines), May 31–June 1.

331.9–10   Gen. Wool's . . . Gen. Dix]   John E. Wool (1789–1869) had commanded the troops occupying Norfolk and Portsmouth until June 1, when these forces were placed under McClellan. Wool, a veteran of the War of 1812 and a major general in the regular army, replaced John A. Dix (1798–1879) as commander of the Middle Department, headquartered in Baltimore. Dix, a former Democratic senator and secretary of the treasury, was ordered to serve under McClellan.

332.20   Blecker]   Louis Blenker (1812–63), German-born general.

333.24   see Gen. SCOTT]   Lincoln had traveled to West Point for consultation with Scott about the disposition of forces in the Virginia theater. Returning late at night, he found a small crowd gathered to greet him in the
Jersey City station.

334.1   *To George B. McClellan*]   In a telegram to Stanton on June 25,
McClellan complained of having to face "overwhelming numbers" and spoke
of a possible "disaster" for which he would accept no responsibility.

334.14   *To George B. McClellan*]   After the battle of Gaines Mill on June
27, McClellan sent another bitter dispatch to the War Department absolving
himself of all blame and lodging it with the administration. "I have lost this
battle because my force was too small," he declared.

338.1   *To Union Governors*]   Although written primarily to New York's
Governor Edwin D. Morgan, this letter was telegraphed to the other governors as well.

339.10   two despatches]   McClellan reported completion of his withdrawal to a base on the James River, said that his troops were in excellent
spirit, and promised that if Washington were threatened he would move the
army "at whatever hazard" to divert the enemy.

343.22   *To Reverdy Johnson*]   Johnson had been appointed by the Department of State to investigate complaints made by foreign consuls about the
military occupation of New Orleans.

347.3   Mr. W]   Thurlow Weed.

348.1   *Agénor-Etienne de Gasparin*]   Gasparin (1810–76) was a French politician and political writer who moved to Switzerland after the February 1848
revolution.

348.35   volume and letter]   With an earlier letter dated May 19, 1862, Gasparin had sent Lincoln a copy of his recently published book, *L'Amérique
devant l'Europe*. Lincoln also received a copy of the American edition, *America
before Europe*, from its translator.

352.12–13   decided . . . service]   The gun was never adopted by the army.

357.32   *To Horace Greeley*]   Greeley's open letter, headed "The Prayer of
Twenty Millions," contained an enumerated list of complaints against Lin-
coln's policy with regard to slavery and urged stronger enforcement of the
Second Confiscation Act.

359.20   *To Jeremiah T. Boyle*]   Boyle, military governor of Kentucky, complained when some of his troops were transferred to Cincinnati by General
Horatio G. Wright, commander of the Department of the Ohio.

361.1   *Reply to . . . Emancipation Memorial*]   The text is from the report of
the two-man delegation that presented the memorial to Lincoln. It was published in the Chicago *Tribune* on September 23.

364.39   Paul's . . . work]   Cf. 2 Thessalonians 3:10.

367.16   despatches of to-day]   McClellan had sent an exaggerated report of his success in engagements at Crampton's Gap and South Mountain, Maryland, preliminaries of the battle of Antietam.

367.21   paroled prisoners]   Union soldiers taken prisoner by Confederate forces and paroled on condition that they remain in Union camps as noncombatants until exchanged for Confederate soldiers held or paroled by the Union. The governor of Minnesota had asked that these soldiers be sent to his state to fight the Sioux uprising there.

368.1   *Preliminary . . . Proclamation*]   Lincoln had presented a draft emancipation proclamation to the Cabinet on July 22, 1862, but had then decided to delay issuing it, apparently agreeing with Seward that it should follow a Union military victory to avoid being seen as an act of desperation. The first paragraph of the draft, warning those in rebellion against the government to cease, on pain of suffering the forfeitures and seizures called for by the recently passed Second Confiscation Act, was issued as a proclamation on July 25. The remainder of the draft read as follows:

And I hereby make known that it is my purpose, upon the next meeting of congress, to again recommend the adoption of a practical measure for tendering pecuniary aid to the free choice or rejection, of any and all States which may then be recognizing and practically sustaining the authority of the United States, and which may then have voluntarily adopted, or thereafter may voluntarily adopt, gradual abolishment of slavery within such State or States—that the object is to practically restore, thenceforward to be maintained, the constitutional relation between the general government, and each, and all the states, wherein that relation is now suspended, or disturbed; and that, for this object, the war, as it has been, will be, prossecuted. And, as a fit and necessary military measure for effecting this object, I, as Commander-in-Chief of the Army and Navy of the United States, do order and declare that on the first day of January in the year of Our Lord one thousand, eight hundred and sixtythree, all persons held as slaves within any state or states, wherein the constitutional authority of the United States shall not then be practically recognized, submitted to, and maintained, shall then, thenceforward, and forever, be free.

372.24–26   On the . . . fought.]   The battles of Crampton's Gap and South Mountain, on September 14, and of Antietam, fought near Sharpsburg on September 17.

376.6   *Thomas H. Clay*]   A son of Henry Clay, soon to be appointed minister to Nicaragua.

379.35   fatiegued horses]   McClellan replied on October 25 that his cavalry had engaged in extensive picketing and scouting, and had also pursued Stuart's cavalry over 200 miles. He referred to its "laborious service" on the

Peninsula and concluded: "If any instance can be found where overworked cavalry has performed more labor than mine since the battle of Antietam, I am not conscious of it."

380.7 Yours of yesterday] On October 26 Lincoln responded to McClellan's defense of his cavalry's performance. He wrote that after Antietam, "Stuart's cavalry outmarched ours, having certainly done more marked service on the Peninsula, and everywhere since." McClellan replied the same day and partially attributed Stuart's recent success in outdistancing his Union pursuers to the theft of 1,000 horses in Pennsylvania. He also suggested that Lincoln had been misinformed.

380.21–22 Indians . . . death] The Indians had been sentenced by a military commission for their part in the Sioux uprising of August 1862.

381.1 lost the elections] The Democrats had won the governorship in New York and New Jersey, gained legislative majorities in Illinois and Indiana, and reduced the Republican majority in the House of Representatives to twenty-five seats.

383.30 *George Robertson*] Robertson (1790–1874) was a Kentucky Unionist. This letter was apparently never sent, but see Lincoln to Robertson, November 26, 1862, pp. 389–90 in this volume.

384.2 Patrick Henry] According to an 1817 biography by William Wirt, Henry made this speech while defending a former army commissary who, during the Revolution, had seized two steers from a suspected loyalist in order to feed some American troops.

384.9 *George F. Shepley*] Shepley (1819–78) was military governor of Louisiana, 1862–64.

385.28 your expedition] To Louisiana, where Banks was replacing Benjamin F. Butler as departmental commander.

389.13–15 Baker . . . Mansfield] Lincoln names one colonel and seven generals killed or mortally wounded in battle.

390.3–4 pay . . . sum] Robertson did not accept Lincoln's offer but instead continued a suit against Colonel William L. Utley, obtaining a judgment nine years later in the amount of $908.06. Utley was subsequently reimbursed by act of Congress.

391.16–18 Note . . . time] Lincoln apparently added this note after a conference with Halleck and Burnside on November 29.

403.12–13 "One . . . forever."] Ecclesiastes 1:4.

420.4–5 death . . . Father] Lieutenant Colonel William McCullough, well known to Lincoln as the former clerk of the county court in Bloomington, Illinois, was killed on December 5.

420.29   place you seek]   Military governor of the District of Columbia.

426.16–17   Withdrawn . . . Jan. 1. 1862]   Lincoln's note, which he misdated. Halleck responded to the letter by offering his resignation.

426.23   Dr. McPheters]   Military authorities in Missouri had ordered Samuel B. McPheeters, pastor of a Presbyterian church in St. Louis, to leave the state because of his "sympathy with the rebellion."

427.27   retreat of enemy]   After the battle of Stones River, December 31, 1862, to January 2, 1863.

431.29–30   address and resolutions]   The address said in part: "We honor your free States, as a singular, happy abode for the working millions. . . . One thing alone has, in the past, lessened our sympathy with your country and our confidence in it; we mean the ascendency of politicians who not merely maintained negro slavery, but desired to extend and root it more firmly. Since we have discerned, however, that the victory of the free north, in the war which has so sorely distressed us as well as afflicted you, will strike off the fetters of the slave, you have attracted our warm and earnest sympathy."

433.15   To John A. McClernand]   A response to McClernand's savage attack upon Halleck for favoring Grant in a dispute over command responsibilities in the West.

434.36–435.1   Schurz . . . Stahl]   Carl Schurz had been made a corps commander ahead of Julius Stahel, who, according to Sigel, had deserved the appointment on the basis of seniority. Sigel proposed that, in the interest of harmony, a new cavalry corps be organized, with Stahel in command.

435.8   To Ambrose E. Burnside]   On February 14, Burnside responded with the following reminder: "General Humphreys is the general that behaved so gallantly at Fredericksburg, and when I spoke to you of him you said he ought to be rewarded by promotion to rank of major-general." There was much further delay, however, and Humphreys did not receive his promotion until May 12, 1864.

435.29   increased Cavalry command]   Stahel was made commander of a cavalry division on March 2.

436.23–26   While . . . March 27, 1863.]   This is Lincoln's endorsement on a copy of the letter sent to Stanton.

436.27   To Mrs. L. H. Phipps]   Lincoln apparently did not send this letter. See the letter to Stanton of the same date.

440.8   Commutation of Sentence]   A court-martial had convicted Pleasants, a Maryland citizen, of feeding and harboring the enemy.

441.1   Speech to Indian Chiefs]   The delegation included chiefs from the Cheyenne, Kiowa, Arapaho, Comanche, Apache, and Caddo tribes.

444.18   Gen. S.]   General George Stoneman, whose cavalry movement across the Rappahannock was a preliminary phase of Hooker's spring campaign against Lee. Stoneman was supposed to have crossed the river on April 14, but heavy rains made it unfordable until April 29.

444.29   *Resolution on Slavery*]   This resolution, suggested for adoption by public meetings in England, was sent by Charles Sumner to John Bright, a Liberal member of Parliament and prominent British advocate of the Union cause.

445.7   *Memorandum on Patronage*]   Endorsement on a letter complaining that secessionists were better treated than loyal Republicans in St. Louis, especially with respect to printing contracts. The *Missouri Democrat* was a Republican paper.

445.22   *Commutation of Sentence*]   Sergeant Chase had been convicted of attacking his superior officer.

447.15   recent movement . . . ended]   Hooker's well-planned turning movement, aimed at dislodging Lee from Fredericksburg, ended in defeat at the battle of Chancellorsville, May 1–4.

448.27   compelled . . . case]   Lincoln appointed John M. Schofield to replace Samuel R. Curtis as commander of the Department of Missouri. See Lincoln to Schofield, May 27, 1863, p. 450 in this volume.

448.28   *Isaac N. Arnold*]   Arnold (1815–85) was a Republican congressman from Illinois, 1861–65.

451.10   *To William T. Otto*]   Lincoln's endorsement on an appeal from George F. Kelly, the agent for certain Californians who complained about a land-title decision rendered by a federal district court in their state. Otto, as acting secretary of the interior, made the formal reply to Kelly, following the line of reasoning that Lincoln had laid out.

451.26   Chicago Times]   On June 1, General Ambrose E. Burnside issued an order suppressing the *Times* for "the repeated expression of disloyal and incendiary sentiments." The order was revoked on June 4.

452.19   *Draft . . . Letter*]   The version published in the *Chronicle* of June 7 over the signature "Illinoisan" contains revisions probably not made by Lincoln.

454.9   *To Erastus Corning*]   The letter as sent to Corning has not been found. There is an autograph draft in the Library of Congress, but the version presented here, which appeared in the New York *Tribune* on June 15, 1863, is probably closer to Lincoln's final text.

461.21–27   He on whose . . . Jackson.]   Burnside ordered Vallandigham's arrest, and federal district court judge Humphrey H. Leavitt, appointed by Jackson in 1834, refused to discharge Vallandigham on a writ of habeas corpus.

467.10   Mr. V.] Clement L. Vallandigham.

468.11–13   original . . . modification] Vallandigham was sentenced by a military commission to imprisonment for the duration of the war, but Lincoln decided to banish him to the Confederacy instead.

472.20–21   Gen. Schenck . . . order] Milroy insisted, apparently with some justice, that he never received explicit orders to withdraw from Winchester. He was eventually exonerated by a board of inquiry.

473.1   *To Alexander K. McClure*] This was Lincoln's response to a telegram urging that McClellan be called to a command for the defense of Pennsylvania against Lee's invading army.

473.16   McClellan] Parker had telegraphed: "The people of New Jersey want McClellan at the head of the Army of the Potomac."

473.20   *To Samuel P. Lee*] This draft of a telegram was not sent; it was replaced by the briefer message immediately following it, which Lincoln may or may not have written.

474.20   crossing . . . river] The Confederates were retreating across the Potomac after the battle of Gettysburg, July 1–3.

475.30   Another President] James Monroe.

477.19   justify an arrest] Congressman Blow, a Republican, had protested the arrest of William McKee, editor of the *Missouri Democrat*, for publishing Lincoln's letter of May 27 to General Schofield (p. 450 in this volume). See Lincoln to Schofield, July 13, p. 478 in this volume.

478.11   arrest . . . editor] See note 477.19.

478.17   *To George G. Meade*] Lincoln never sent this letter.

478.28   Couch . . . Smith] General Darius N. Couch (1822–97) was commander of the Department of the Susquehanna and in charge of Pennsylvania militia levies. William F. ("Baldy") Smith (1824–1903) was commander of a division stationed at Carlisle, Pennsylvania.

480.7   fight . . . shot] Private Michael Delany of a Colorado cavalry unit had been sentenced to death for desertion.

481.1   *To Oliver O. Howard*] Howard, a corps commander at Gettysburg, wrote to Lincoln defending Meade's leadership in the campaign. He was probably responding to an article critical of Meade that appeared in the New York *Tribune* on July 18.

481.27   Gen. Thomas] Lorenzo Thomas (1804–75), former adjutant general.

482.3   cross letter] Denouncing Lincoln's letter of May 27 to Schofield,

Governor Gamble said that its language was "grossly offensive" and its publication "a most wanton and unmerited insult."

483.8–10   Gen. Hooker . . . corps]   Meade agreed, but Hooker was soon sent to the West, where he served under George H. Thomas and William T. Sherman.

486.8   Dr. Wright]   On July 11, 1863, Dr. David M. Wright shot and killed Anson L. Sanborn, a white lieutenant marching through Norfolk at the head of his company of the First United States Colored Volunteers. He was tried, convicted, and sentenced to death by a military commission. See Lincoln to Gray, September 10 (pp. 502–3); Lincoln's approval of the sentence, October 7 (p. 527); and Lincoln to Foster, October 15 and 17, 1863 (pp. 528–29, all in this volume).

486.20   events in Mexico]   French troops had occupied Mexico City in June and overthrown President Benito Juárez.

489.24   Mrs. Cuthbert]   Mary Ann Cuthbert, seamstress and stewardess at the White House.

489.34   Old Mr. Wickliffe]   Charles A. Wickliffe (1788–1869) served in Congress as a Democrat, 1823–33, and as a Union Whig, 1861–63. He had run for governor as a Peace Democrat.

490.1–2   Mr. Menzies]   John W. Menzies (1819–97) was a Unionist congressman, 1861–63.

490.16   Gen. Thomas]   Lorenzo Thomas.

490.26   Mr. Dana]   Charles A. Dana, Stanton's personal representative at Grant's headquarters.

492.14   Yates . . . Dubois]   Richard Yates (1815–73), Ozias M. Hatch (1814–93), and Jesse K. Dubois (1811–76), all Republicans, were, respectively, the governor, secretary of state, and state auditor of Illinois.

493.2   "cloud of witnesses"]   Hebrews 12:1.

493.9   your book]   *Notes and Comments upon Certain Plays and Actors of Shakespeare, with Criticism and Correspondence* (1863).

493.20–21   "O, my . . . to be."]   *Hamlet*, III, iii, 36–72; III, i, 55–89.

493.26   *To James G. Blunt*]   Blunt (1826–81) commanded troops in Kansas, Arkansas, and Indian Territory (Oklahoma). He wrote to Lincoln on July 31, denouncing Thomas Carney, the governor of Kansas, among others.

495.1–2   counties . . . Northampton]   See also Lincoln to Stanton, September 1, 1863, p. 500, and Lincoln to Joseph Segar, September 5, 1863, pp. 501–2 in this volume.

495.14   *To James C. Conkling*]   With this letter Lincoln sent a personal note to his old friend saying: "I can not leave here now. Herewith is a letter instead. You are one of the best public readers. I have but one suggestion. Read it very slowly."

497.30–498.3   I know . . . faith.]   This passage was added to the original letter by means of a telegram sent five days later.

499.22   very flagrant cases]   The convicted men were substitute conscripts who enlisted and then deserted after receiving their bounties. They were executed.

500.4   hard earned victory]   The battle of Stones River, December 31, 1862, to January 2, 1863.

501.32   *To Joseph Segar*]   Segar (1804–80), a Virginia Unionist, served in Congress, 1862–63.

502.1   Major Hayner]   Henry Z. Hayner was the staff officer sent to the Eastern Shore of Virginia to administer the oath of allegiance and collect the punitive tax levied for destruction of a lighthouse.

504.5   Gov. Harris]   Isham G. Harris (1818–97) was governor of Tennessee, 1857–63. After the Union army occupied most of the state in 1862, he became a staff officer with the Confederate headquarters in the West. He was a Democratic senator from Tennessee, 1877–97.

504.21   *Opinion . . . Draft*]   Although phrased in the form of a public letter, this document was never issued by Lincoln.

509.35–36   Quarter-Master-General]   An erroneous report that Montgomery C. Meigs had been removed led Dubois and Hatch to recommend General Robert Allen as his successor. Lincoln's sarcasm pained his two old friends, and he hastened to make amends. See his letter of September 22, 1863, p. 514 in this volume.

512.17   *Draft of Order*]   This order was revised by the military and issued to provost marshals on September 17.

514.30–31   the late battle]   Chickamauga, September 19–20.

515.13   *To Ambrose E. Burnside*]   This letter was not sent.

518.18   removing the inhabitants]   After Confederate guerillas under William C. Quantrill murdered over 150 people at Lawrence, Kansas, on August 21, General Thomas Ewing expelled the inhabitants of four Missouri counties bordering on Kansas in an effort to suppress further guerilla raiding.

521.34–35   I intend . . . suggest]   Rosecrans had suggested offering "a general amnesty to all officers and soldiers in the Rebellion."

522.1   *Charles D. Drake*]   Head of a delegation of Missouri radical Republicans that presented a long "address" to Lincoln and conferred with him for several hours on September 30.

525.21   Grierson, John Morgan]   Colonel Benjamin A. Grierson led Union cavalry on a 600-mile raid through Mississippi in April 1863. General John Hunt Morgan led Confederate cavalry on raids in Tennessee, Kentucky, and Ohio.

528.4   John Murphy]   The records indicate that Murphy remained in the service but deserted again the following year.

529.10   *four* corps]   See Lincoln to Rosecrans, September 28, 1863, p. 516 in this volume.

529.21   case is settled]   Wright was hanged on October 23, 1863.

530.18   *To James M. Cutts, Jr.*]   A court-martial sentenced Cutts, the brother of Mrs. Stephen A. Douglas, to dismissal from the service for conduct unbecoming an officer; one of the charges was that he had peeked into the hotel room of a lady while she was undressing. Lincoln remitted the sentence, substituting a reprimand. According to John Hay's diary, the president remarked that Cutts "should be elevated to the peerage for it with the title of Count Peeper." The second half of this double pun was no doubt a reference to the Swedish minister in Washington, Edward Count Piper.

530.29–31   "Beware . . . thee,"]   *Hamlet*, I, iii, 65–67.

532.7   the promise made]   That Hackett would perform in Washington in December.

532.10   My note to you]   Lincoln's letter of August 17, 1863, which Hackett had circulated in a broadside printing.

533.22–28   Mr. Durant . . . Mr. Flanders]   Thomas J. Durant and Benjamin F. Flanders, leading Louisiana Unionists.

536.1   *Address at Gettysburg*]   This is Lincoln's final text, prepared in the spring of 1864 for facsimile reproduction in *Autograph Leaves of Our Country's Authors*, a book published by the Baltimore Sanitary Fair. The Associated Press report, based upon shorthand notes, may be closer to what he actually said at Gettysburg, but a comparison with other newspaper accounts, and with Lincoln's autograph drafts, indicates that it probably contains several errors, among which are "our power" instead of "our poor power" and "re-finished work" instead of "unfinished work." The Associated Press version is as follows:

Four score and seven years ago our fathers brought forth upon this continent a new Nation, conceived in Liberty, and dedicated to the proposition that all men are created equal. [Applause.] Now we are engaged in a great civil war, testing whether that Nation or any Nation so conceived and so dedicated can long endure. We are met on a great battle-field of that war. We are met to dedicate a portion of it as the final resting-place of those who here gave their lives that that nation might live. It is altogether fitting and proper that we should do this. But in a larger sense we cannot dedicate, we cannot consecrate, we cannot hallow this ground. The brave men living and dead who struggled here have consecrated it far above our power to add or detract. [Applause.] The world will little note nor long remember what we say here, but it can never forget what they did here. [Applause.] It is for us, the living, rather to be dedicated here to the refinished work that they have thus far so nobly carried on. [Applause.] It is rather for us to be here dedicated to the great task remaining before us, that from these honored dead we take increased devotion to that cause for which they here gave the last full measure of devotion; that we here highly resolve that the dead shall not have died in vain [applause]; that the nation shall, under God, have a new birth of freedom; and that Governments of the people, by the people, and for the people, shall not perish from the earth. [Long-continued applause.]

537.6   elections this autumn]   The Republicans won a legislative majority in New York and retained the governorships of Ohio and Pennsylvania. In the Ohio election, Clement L. Vallandigham, the Democratic gubernatorial candidate who had conducted his campaign from exile in Canada, was defeated by over 100,000 votes.

537.17–18   a short address]   Everett gave a two-hour oration at Gettysburg before Lincoln spoke.

549.10–11   remodelling . . . Indian system]   Bills to do so were introduced in 1864, but they did not become law.

549.37–553.36   When Congress . . . way.]   These eleven paragraphs of the incomplete preliminary draft are in Lincoln's hand, indicating that he himself composed the message from this point on, whereas the preceding parts were probably written by various members of the Cabinet, with the likely exception of the opening paragraph.

551.24   issue a proclamation]   See the proclamation of amnesty and reconstruction, pp. 555–58 in this volume.

558.10   *Amnesty*]   Emily T. Helm (1836–1930), Mary Todd Lincoln's half sister and the widow of a Confederate general, had arrived in Washington with the aid of a presidential pass and was on her way to the Todd family home in Kentucky. In his diary entry for December 14, Orville H. Browning wrote: "The President told me his sister in law, Mrs Helm was in the house, but he did not wish it known. She wished an order for the protection of some Cotton she had at Jackson, Mississippi. He thought she ought to have it, but he was afraid he would be censured if he did so." See the documents of the same date and also Lincoln to Stephen G. Burbridge, August 8, 1864, p. 616 in this volume.

560.26   Henry F. Luckett]   Convicted of smuggling percussion caps to the enemy, Luckett, according to some of his friends, was "insane." Lincoln pardoned him on March 30, 1864.

560.33   Gen. Schofield . . . relieved]   William S. Rosecrans replaced

Schofield as commander in Missouri on January 30, 1864. Schofield held field commands under Sherman and George H. Thomas for the remainder of the war.

564.32   *Bayard Taylor*]   Taylor had recently returned from service as secretary of the legation in St. Petersburg.

565.1   *Henry Andrews*]   Andrews, a private in an Ohio regiment, had been sentenced to death for desertion.

566.4   your city]   Pittsburgh.

566.11   Mr. Hay]   Lincoln's secretary, John Hay, whose mission to Florida was unsuccessful.

566.29–30   artical . . . Policy"]   The author was James Russell Lowell.

567.3   theory . . . States]   Lowell had written: " . . . while he was still enforcing the Fugitive Slave Law, under some theory that Secession, however it might absolve States from their obligations, could not escheat them of their claims under the Constitution . . ."

567.16   thereof;]   The space that follows this word appears in Lincoln's autograph original.

568.26   *To Alpheus Lewis*]   The text printed here is from an autograph draft. The letter given to Lewis has not been found.

571.8   class of cases]   Louisianans who, having taken an oath to vote in the 1862 congressional election, were now resisting taking another one.

571.18–19   colored colony . . . Vache]   With money provided by Congress, 453 black colonists had been settled on Vache, an island off the coast of Haiti, in the spring of 1863. This experiment in colonization was a failure from the beginning, and the 368 survivors all chose to return on the transport.

573.31–32   What . . . done]   The order was modified to exempt Missouri.

575.31   *To Benjamin F. Loan*]   Loan (1819–81) was a Unionist congressman from Missouri, 1863–69. This letter was drafted by Lincoln, presumably for Stanton to sign, but whether or not it was actually sent is not known.

576.13   Gov. Pierpoint]   Francis Harrison Pierpoint (also spelled "Pierpont") was governor of the "restored" state of Virginia, functioning in those areas held by Union forces.

576.23   Mr. Pomeroy's letter]   The "Pomeroy Circular," named after Senator Samuel C. Pomeroy of Kansas, called for the presidential nomination of Chase in place of Lincoln. In a letter written on February 22, Chase had disavowed knowledge of the document before its publication.

577.4–5   no assault . . . countenance]   Francis P. Blair, Jr., had attacked

Chase in a speech in Congress on February 27. Blair charged that corruption and political favoritism were widespread in the Treasury Department, particularly among the agents who granted permits to trade in cotton.

577.23   *John A. J. Creswell*]   Creswell (1828–91) was a Republican congressman from Maryland, 1863–65, and a senator, 1865–67.

578.25   *To George D. Ramsay*]   General Ramsay was chief of ordnance for the U.S. Army. The Absterdam projectile was a type of artillery ammunition.

579.9   the elective franchise]   The Louisiana convention adopted a state constitution limiting the suffrage to whites, but empowering the legislature to enfranchise Negroes if it saw fit.

580.13–14   emancipation in Maryland]   A new state constitution was drafted by a convention in April and approved by Maryland voters on October 13, 1864. It prohibited slavery.

580.24   all that . . . life]   Job 2:4.

581.28   *Remainder of Draft*]   Lincoln did not send this part of his letter of March 18 to Stanton.

583.20   case of Smithson]   William T. Smithson had been imprisoned for selling Confederate securities.

583.29   The letter]   Lincoln to Schurz, March 13, 1864, p. 579 in this volume.

584.4   *Benjamin B. French*]   Commissioner of public buildings.

584.22–23   a slip . . . Herald]   A letter in the New York *Herald* of March 12, signed "Historicus," criticized Meade's performance at Gettysburg. Meade suspected that the author was one of his corps commanders in that battle, General Daniel E. Sickles.

585.6   Bramlette . . . Dixon]   Thomas E. Bramlette (1817–75), a Union Democrat, was governor of Kentucky, 1863–67. Archibald Dixon (1802–76) was a Whig senator from Kentucky, 1852–55.

587.29   *Draft . . . Fair*]   This is probably an abandoned portion of the address that follows.

592.19   good news . . . army]   After a drawn battle in the Wilderness, May 5–7, Grant, instead of retreating, pushed onward to Spotsylvania.

593.14   you and Lane]   Pomeroy and Senator James H. Lane were leaders of rival Republican factions in Kansas. Unlike Pomeroy, who wanted Chase to be president, Lane supported the reelection of Lincoln.

593.18   *Thomas Carney*]   Carney (1824–88), a Republican, was governor of Kansas, 1863–65.

594.8   *To Edwin M. Stanton*]   It appears that this letter was never delivered to Stanton.

595.15 placed in law] Legislation to this effect was passed by Congress and signed by Lincoln on July 4, 1864.

595.19 *To Isaac N. Arnold*] A revised version of this letter, dated May 27, was drafted by Congressman Arnold and presumably approved by Lincoln. It appeared in the Chicago *Tribune* on July 15, 1864.

597.2–3 "In . . . bread,"] Genesis 3:19.

597.11–12 "As ye . . . them"] Cf. Matthew 7:12; Luke 6:31.

597.18–19 "Judge . . . judged."] Cf. Matthew 7:1; Luke 6:37.

600.1 *Speech . . . Fair*] This text, from the Philadelphia *Press* of June 17, 1864, is at best a close approximation of what Lincoln said. Reporters found it difficult to take notes, and there are numerous verbal variations in other newspaper reports of the speech.

600.11 "heavens . . . black."] Cf. *1 Henry VI*, I, i, 1.

600.30 passes to and fro,] After these words, according to the Philadelphia *Inquirer*, Lincoln added: "from city to city."

600.34 as much . . . him] After these words, according to the *Inquirer*, Lincoln added: "in the continual reminders he sees in the newspapers, that while he is absent he is yet remembered by the loved ones at home."

601.11 not the end.] After these words, according to the *Inquirer*, Lincoln added: "We accepted this war; we did not begin it. But . . ."

602.9–10 what pay . . . color] In his reply of July 14, Bates declared: "I give it to you unhesitatingly as my opinion that the same pay, bounty, and clothing are allowed by law to the persons of color referred to in your communication . . . as are . . . authorized and provided for and allowed to other soldiers in the volunteer services of the United States."

604.1 *John L. Scripps*] Scripps, now serving as the Chicago postmaster, was a candidate for the congressional seat held by Isaac N. Arnold. Neither man received the nomination, which went to John Wentworth. The text printed here is from Arnold's *The History of Abraham Lincoln and the Overthrow of Slavery* (1866). It appears that Arnold, as a matter of delicacy or prudence, decided to publish the letter with blanks in place of Scripps's name and his own.

604.13 *certain* other nomination] Lincoln was referring to his own renomination for the presidency by the National Union party convention at Baltimore on June 8.

605.4 Congress passed a Bill] The Wade-Davis bill, passed on July 2, which Lincoln pocket-vetoed. The bill provided that the process of reconstruction should begin with the election of a state constitutional convention, to be held only after fifty percent of the state's white male citizens had taken an oath of allegiance to the United States. It also required that the new state constitution include a provision abolishing slavery.

607.7 the present emergency] The raid of Jubal Early, which reached the outskirts of Washington on July 11.

607.30 Post-Master-General] Early's troops had burned Montgomery Blair's house in Silver Spring, Maryland.

608.10 *To Horace Greeley*] A telegram. Greeley had written that two agents of the Confederate government empowered to negotiate for peace were in Canada near Niagara Falls and desired to confer with Lincoln or his appointed spokesmen.

608.18 *To Horace Greeley*] This letter was carried to Greeley by John Hay.

613.5 + . . . +] These symbols appear in Lincoln's original manuscript.

613.22 *Abram Wakeman*] New York City postmaster.

613.36–614.1 he who . . . Gilmore] Jefferson Davis, in a discussion of peace terms with unofficial Northern negotiators James F. Jaquess and James R. Gilmore, had declared that the South was fighting for independence and would settle for nothing less.

614.6–7 whoever . . . remembered] The final clause was a bid for the support of James Gordon Bennett, owner of the New York *Herald*, to whom Wakeman read the letter.

614.8 *To James C. Welling*] This letter, though signed by Hay, was drafted by Lincoln.

614.12 Mr. Gibson's . . . resignation] Charles Gibson resigned as solicitor for the Court of Claims on the ground that radical elements had gained control of the party in power. He instructed Welling, the court's assistant clerk, to have his letter of resignation published.

614.28 *To Edwin M. Stanton*] Endorsement on a communication pointing out that the pay for women working in the U.S. arsenal at Philadelphia had been reduced since 1861, even though the cost of living had sharply increased.

615.22 *To John McMahon*] Drafted by Lincoln, but sent out over the signature of John G. Nicolay. McMahon had telegraphed the following sentiment to Lincoln on August 5: "Equal Rights & Justice to all white men in the United States forever. White men is in class number one & black men is in class number two & must be governed by white men forever."

616.27 *To Benjamin F. Butler*] This unfinished letter was not sent at the time, but Lincoln enclosed a copy of it in a letter to Butler written December 21, 1864.

618.18   the correspondence]   Between Lincoln and Greeley about the latter's meeting with Confederate agents at Niagara Falls.

620.6   where you are]   The Army of the Potomac was laying siege to Petersburg.

620.9   *To Charles D. Robinson*]   It appears that this letter to Robinson, a Wisconsin editor and War Democrat, was never sent.

623.18–19   There may . . . system.]   This text is taken from the New York *Times*. In the New York *Tribune* version, this sentence reads: "There may be some inequalities in the practical working of our system."

624.25–26   *Memorandum . . . Re-election*]   According to the diary of John Hay, at a Cabinet meeting on November 11, 1864, Lincoln took the paper from his desk and said: "Gentlemen, do you remember last summer when I asked you all to sign your names to the back of a paper of which I did not show you the inside? This is it."

625.1   *To Henry J. Raymond*]   This letter, drafted in response to a letter from Raymond of August 22, was not acted upon. Raymond had suggested offering Davis peace, on the sole condition that the Union be restored, in the expectation that Davis's probable rejection of the offer would unite the North behind the administration. At a meeting on August 25, Lincoln, Seward, Stanton, and Secretary of the Treasury William P. Fessenden convinced Raymond that his proposal was unwise.

628.23   *Memorandum . . . Lamon*]   Drafted by Lincoln for possible rebuttal to a story circulated in some newspapers that, as a visitor to the Antietam battlefield at a time when it was still being cleared of bodies, he had called upon Lamon to sing a comic song. The memorandum was not released for publication.

630.4   Sheridan]   In early August, after Early's raid had threatened Washington, 33-year-old Philip H. Sheridan was given command of a newly organized army with orders to destroy Confederate power in the Shenandoah Valley. See Lincoln to Grant, August 3, 1864, p. 615 in this volume.

630.9   *Draft . . . Schermerhorn*]   Lincoln did not finish this draft, deciding instead to send the letter that immediately follows it.

630.20   the Star . . . West]   On January 9, 1861, Confederate batteries in Charleston harbor opened fire on the *Star of the West*, a merchant steamer chartered by the U.S. Army to carry supplies and reinforcements to Fort Sumter. The ship suffered minor damage and returned to New York without casualties.

632.4   *To William T. Sherman*]   Governor Oliver P. Morton and other

Indiana Republicans wrote Stanton on September 12, asking that the draft be suspended until after the state elections, and that soldiers be furloughed home to vote. Sherman, however, warned Stanton on September 17 that any suspension of the draft would cause the army to vote against Lincoln.

632.23   *To Montgomery Blair*]   Removal of the conservative Blair was a concession to radical Republicans generally and a gesture of conciliation to the splinter group that had supported Frémont for the presidency until his withdrawal from the contest on September 22.

643.13   arrests an editor]   Thomas P. May, editor of the New Orleans *Times*, had been arrested for a description of the convention that depicted many of its members as being drunk.

644.5   you may do]   Wolf was not executed.

644.8   *To Mrs. Lydia Bixby*]   The text is that published in the Boston *Transcript* on November 25, 1864. Neither the letter itself nor any handwritten draft or copy is known to be extant. The assertion that John Hay composed the letter is disbelieved by most scholars.

644.13   five sons . . . died]   Lincoln was misinformed. Only two of Mrs. Bixby's sons were killed in battle; one was honorably discharged, one deserted, and one either deserted or died in a Confederate prison.

644.25   *John Phillips*]   A 104-year-old citizen of Sturbridge, Massachusetts, who had voted for Lincoln's reelection.

645.1   Psalmist's limit]   Seventy to eighty years. Cf. Psalm 90:10.

649.37–38   Canadian . . . depredations]   A band of Confederate raiders attacked St. Albans, Vermont, on October 19, 1864, and robbed its banks.

657.6   The war continues.]   Autograph fragments in existence indicate that the message from this point on was Lincoln's own composition.

663.1   *Reply . . . Woman*]   Lincoln read this account to Noah Brooks, a reporter for the Sacramento *Daily Union*, saying, "Here is one speech of mine which has never been printed, and I think it is worth printing." The paragraph appeared in the Washington *Chronicle* on December 7, 1864.

663.20–21   have anything]   Probably a reporting or typographical error. It seems more likely that Lincoln said "haven't anything" or "have nothing."

663.26   where he . . . at]   Sherman had begun his march from Atlanta to Savannah on November 15.

665.17–18   capture of Savannah]   Sherman's army captured the city on December 21.

665.24–25   work of Gen. Thomas]   George H. Thomas's smashing defeat of John B. Hood at Nashville, December 15–16.

667.19–21   My son . . . ends.]   Robert Todd Lincoln was appointed a captain and served for four months on Grant's staff.

668.31   beautiful gift]   A vase of dried leaves, gathered from the Gettysburg battlefields.

672.6   *To William Lloyd Garrison*]   This letter, although signed by Lincoln, was drafted by John Hay.

672.12   "Waiting . . . Hour"]   "Watch Meeting, Waiting for the Hour, Dec. 31st. 1862," an oil painting by William T. Carlton (1816–88) depicting a group of black men, women, and children waiting for the Emancipation Proclamation to take effect.

673.4   certain States]   The eleven states of the Confederacy.

685.8   *To Ulysses S. Grant*]   Lincoln drafted the text of this telegram.

687.5   let us . . . judged]   Cf. Matthew 7:1; Luke 6:37.

687.7–9   "Woe . . . cometh!"]   Matthew 18:7.

687.24–25   "the judgments . . . altogether"]   Psalm 19:9.

689.4   Every . . . compliment.]   Actually, Weed's letter of March 4 complimented Lincoln only on the notification speech of March 1 (see pp. 684–85 in this volume) and said nothing about the Inaugural Address.

691.16–17   Benjamin . . . Smith]   Boston merchants convicted of fraud in carrying out a government contract.

696.9   an occasion]   Lee's surrender to Grant at Appomattox on April 9.

698.7   One of them]   Salmon P. Chase.

Index

reconstruction, 556–57
and slavery, 113, 114
See also Vicksburg.
Mississippi, Department of the, 383
Mississippi River, 335, 383, 549
opening of, 486, 490, 498, 550
Missouri
in Civil War, 269, 273, 293, 335, 657
elections, 518, 522, 526, 633, 657, 659
and emancipation, 465, 485, 550–51
factions and quarrels, 448, 450, 522–27, 684
jurisdiction of troops in, 391–92
loyalty to Union, 293–94
military government in, 517–19, 522–27 *passim*, 561, 667
and slavery, 80
See also St. Louis; Springfield.
Missouri, Department of the, 262, 450, 453, 522–27, 560–61
Missouri Compromise (1820) and repeal, 34, 38, 45–46, 71–72, 103, 108, 115, 134, 138, 167, 452
Missouri Democrat (St. Louis), 481–82
Missouri Republican (St. Louis), 186
Mitchell, James, 353
Mobile, Ala., 490
Monarchs, 19, 295
Monocacy River, 607
Monroe, James, 143
Montana, 654–55
Montgomery, William, 15
Montgomery, Ala., 325
Morel, Pierre L., 462
Morgan, Edwin D., 326, 536
letters to, 240–41, 338
Morgan, George D., 326
Morgan, Gen. George W., 453
Morgan, Gen. John H., 525, 587
Morocco, 396, 541
Morris, Gouverneur, 117
Morris, James R., 466
Morris, Robert, 113
Morristown, Tenn., 515
Morton, Mary E., 667–68
Morton, Oliver P., 320
letters to, 199–200, 270–71
Mountain Department, 332
Mount Jackson, Va., 330

Munfordville, Ky., 303
Murfreesboro (Tenn.), battle of, 498. *See also* Stones River, battle of.
Murphy, Isaac: letter to, 591
Murphy, John, 527–28

Napoleon I, 434
Nashville, Tenn., 299, 300, 306
National Union Convention: A.L.'s replies to (9 June 1864), 597–98, 602–3
Naturalization of citizens, 21, 540
Naval Academy (U.S.), Annapolis, Md., 546
Naval operations
(1861), 226, 280, 325–26
(1862), 306, 309
(1863), 544–46
(1864), 653
blockade. *See* Blockade, naval.
in Gulf of Mexico, 304
See also Coastal defenses; Rivers: defense of, and offensive maneuvers.
Navy, 246, 284, 497, 653–54, 697
buildup of, 325–26, 544–45, 653
cost of, 399, 543, 653
organization of, 284
resignation of officers, 246, 259–60
training of personnel, 546
Navy appointments, 240–41
Navy recruitment, 252, 546
and army recruitment, 545, 610
number of seamen, 546, 653
Negro equality, 29, 32–33, 353
Negroes
as "brutes," 57, 58, 66, 68, 139–40
Douglas on, 67, 68, 137, 139
delegation of, A.L.'s address on colonization to (14 Aug. 1862), 353–57
education for, 486, 567, 700
forced into military, 672
free. *See* Free Negroes.
as hired labor, 144, 343, 412, 425, 568–69, 572, 574, 698
marriage with whites, 33
women, 33

Cataloging Information

Lincoln, Abraham, 1809–1865.
  Speeches and Writings: 1859–1865:
  Speeches, Letters, and Miscellaneous Writings;
  Presidential Messages and Proclamations.
  Edited by Don E. Fehrenbacher

  (The Library of America ; 46)
  Includes index.
  1. United States—Politics and government—1857–1861.
2. United States—Politics and government—Civil War,
1861–1865. 3. Republican Party (U.S. : 1854–   )—
History—19th century. I. Title. II. Series.
E457.92 1989b   973.6'8   89-45349
ISBN 0–940450–63–1   (alk. paper)

For a list of titles in The Library of America, write:
The Library of America
14 East 60th Street
New York, New York 10022

THE LIBRARY OF AMERICA SERIES

The Library of America fosters appreciation and pride in America's literary heritage by publishing, and keeping permanently in print, authoritative editions of America's best and most significant writing. An independent nonprofit organization, it was founded in 1979 with seed money from the National Endowment for the Humanities and the Ford Foundation.

This book is set in 10 point Linotron Galliard,
a face designed for photocomposition by Matthew Carter
and based on the sixteenth-century face Granjon. The paper
is acid-free lightweight opaque and meets the requirements
for permanence of the American National Standards Institute.
The binding material is Brillianta, a woven rayon cloth made
by Van Heek-Scholco Textielfabrieken, Holland. Com-
position by The Clarinda Company. Printing by
Malloy Incorporated. Binding by Dekker Book-
binding. Designed by Bruce Campbell.